URANTIA

the great cult mystery

URANTIA

the great cult mystery

MARTIN GARDNER

WITH A NEW POSTSCRIPT BY THE AUTHOR

Prometheus Books

59 John Glenn Drive
Amherst, New York 14228–2119

Published 2008 by Prometheus Books

Inquiries should be addressed to
Prometheus Books
59 John Glenn Drive
Amherst, New York 14228–2119
VOICE: 716–691–0133, ext. 210
FAX: 716–691–0137
WWW.PROMETHEUSBOOKS.COM

12 11 10 09 08   5 4 3 2 1

Library of Congress Cataloging-in-Publication Data

Gardner, Martin, 1914–
    Urantia : the great cult mystery / by Martin Gardner.
        p. cm.
    Originally published: Amherst, N.Y. : Prometheus Books, 1995.
    Includes index.
    ISBN 978–1–59102–622–8 (pbk.)
    1. Urantia book—Controversial literature. 2. Urantia Foundation—Controversial literature. I. Title.

BP605.U75G37 2008
299—dc22

                                                            2008018398

Printed in the United States of America on acid-free paper

In religion, what damned error, but some sober brow will bless it, and approve it with a text, hiding the grossness with fair ornament.

Shakespeare, *Merchant of Venice*, Act 3, Scene 2

There is no purpose here to shake the faithful, for I am completely free of the messianic itch, and do not like converts. Let those who believe, and enjoy it, heave this book into the dustbin.

H. L. Mencken, *Treatise on the Gods*

Contents

1. *The Urantia Book*   9

2. Dr. William Sadler   35

3. Dr. John Kellogg   51

4. Ellen White's Plagiarisms   75

5. *The Living Temple*   83

6. Wilfred Custer Kellogg   97

7. The Revelation Begins   113

8. Harold Sherman and Harry Loose   135

9. *OAHSPE*   161

10. Science in *The Urantia Book*, Part I   179

11. Science in *The Urantia Book*, Part II   203

12. Adventist Influence on *The Urantia Book*   227

13. Sadler and Sister White   257

14. Did Sadler Contribute to the Papers? Part 1   277

15. Did Sadler Contribute to the Papers? Part II   303

16. Plagiarisms in *The Urantia Book*   327

17. Bitter Schisms   365

18. Joe Pope and the New Teachers   377

19. The Great Rebellion   403

Appendices

    A. Books by William Sadler Sr.   417

    B. Books by Harold Sherman   421

    C. Sherman's Letter to Sadler   425

    D. The Story of Joseph of Arimathaea   427

    E. Unusual Words and Phrases That Sadler
        and *The Urantia Book* Have in Common   431

    F. Acknowledgments   445

Postscript   447

Name Index   461

1

The Urantia Book

In the last half of the nineteenth century, when Spiritualism was rampant, thousands of what were called "direct-voice" trance mediums flourished around the civilized world, especially in England and the United States. The most famous such medium was Mrs. Leona Piper of Boston, who convinced no less a famous psychologist and philosopher than William James that she had paranormal powers. Like most direct-voice mediums, Mrs. Piper would fall into a deep sleep during which her vocal chords would be taken over by spirits of the dead who spoke in voices markedly different from her own. Until a decade ago such mediums were hard to find in the United States. Now they are all over the map, especially in Pacific coast states. Skeptics have described them as mediocre ventriloquists who speak in funny voices, but you can see their lips move.

Today's fashionable phrase for such phenomena is "trance channeling." These new mediums, of whom J. Zebra Knight was the first to achieve fame and fortune (thanks to the hype of Shirley MacLaine), do not channel dead relatives. Instead, they channel higher entities who either once lived on earth, sometimes thousands of years ago, or who live on distant planets or in higher-dimensional spaces. Most of these channelers are charlatans, out to gouge money from gullible New Agers. There is, however, little doubt that occasionally certain persons (often someone who as a child suffered a severe head injury) have the ability to go into trances during which alternate personalities seem to speak through their lips or to write by seizing their hand. Mrs. Piper was capable of having three spirits simultaneously control her, one speaking through her mouth, one writing with her left hand, and a third writing with her right hand. Invariably such mediums profess to recall nothing that goes on while they are asleep or in trance.

Many religions have Bibles said to have been channeled by higher intelligences. Joseph Smith claimed to be the channel through whom the angel Moroni gave humanity the *Book of Mormon*. Mohammed claimed to be the instrument through whom Gabriel wrote the Koran. The Reverend Sun Moon was divinely inspired to produce the Bible of his Unification Church. Mary Baker Eddy believed that every line in *Science and Health* was inspired by God.

During the decades when Spiritualism was at its peak, hundreds of dreary volumes were said to have been channeled by departed spirits. In recent decades, especially in the United States, a rapidly growing number of books profess to be dictated, not by souls of the dead, but by higher intelligences. Examples include the Seth books of Jane Roberts, the Ramtha books of J. Z. Knight, and the currently popular *Course in Miracles* (1976), said to have been dictated by none other than Jesus himself. We will ignore these books because none has become, at least not yet, the "Bible" of any organized cult.

Until 1955 the largest sacred work of a religious movement said to be written by nonhumans was *Oahspe*, subtitled *A Kosmon Bible in the Words of Jehovih and His Angel Embassadors*. The author of this strange tome—it is almost a thousand pages—was John Ballou Newbrough, a New York City dentist. He stoutly maintained that angels manipulated his fingers while he typed. The book was written in 1881, privately published in 1882, followed by a much altered edition in 1891. It inspired a cult called Faithism. Members established Shalam, a colony in New Mexico, which issued a journal called *The Faithist Messenger*. An advertisement by Owl Press, which until 1992 sold an edition of *Oahspe*, describes the book this way:

> A history of the higher and lower heavens and of the Earth for the past 24,000 years, also a brief history of the preceding 55,000 years. An explanation of all the world's religions; the cosmogony of the universe; the creation of the planets, of man; new commandments applicable to the present day; the unseen worlds. Written in 1881, *Oahspe*'s science is today being confirmed by space satellites, new archaeological discoveries and many other sources. Perhaps the most remarkable and important book in the world today!

Oahspe revealed for the first time a fantastic cosmology of inhabited worlds ruled by an elaborate hierarchy of bizarrely named gods who occupy levels between Jehovih, the Ultimate God, and ourselves. Faithists believed they were divinely chosen to replace Christianity with a new revelation that would ultimately lead to establishing God's kingdom on earth. For a good summary of this Bible's complex cosmology, mythology, and eschatology, see "Oahspe" in *Hasting's Encyclopedia of Religion and Ethics*. Here is how the article opens:

> The Book of Oahspe, though little known, possesses considerable interest for students of the pathology of religion; and from this point of view it is, perhaps, of greater value even than the Book of Mormon . . . its author had evidently read fairly widely, the result being an indigested—and indigestible—farrago of superficial Orientalism, Gnosticism, baseless history, fantastic cosmology, Freemasonry, spiritualism, and fads of every sort, combined with hatred of Christianity.

We will discuss *Oahspe* at greater length in chapter 9.

Oahspe's record of being the largest "Bible" ever said to be dictated word for word by higher intelligences was shattered by the publication in 1955 of *The Urantia Book*. Urantia, the book's name for Earth, is pronounced you-ran´-sha. The *UB*, as I shall from now on abbreviate the book's title, is a mammoth tome of 2,097 pages and weighing 4.3 pounds.

This Bible is now in its eleventh printing. In 1993 translations appeared in Spain and Finland. An earlier French translation is being revised, and work is proceeding on Dutch and Russian editions, with plans for translations into Korean, German, Swedish, Hungarian, and Italian. The Urantia Foundation in Chicago, which publishes the English edition, hopes to market soon an audio and an electronic version.

No author's name is on the *UB*'s blue cloth cover or on its title page. The contents consist of 196 "Papers," as the chapters are called, each allegedly written by a celestial being. These "Revelators" have such names as Divine Counselor, Perfector of Wisdom, Mighty Messenger, Chief of Archangels, Brilliant Evening Star, Melchizedek, and One Without Name and Number. The Papers are divided into four parts: 1. The Central and Superuniverses, 2. The Local Universe, 3. The History of Urantia, and 4. The Life and Teachings of Jesus.

The story of how this Bible came into existence, and the curious role played by Seventh-day Adventism, has never been fully told until now. However, before disclosing all the wild historical facts, I will try to summarize some of the *UB*'s main doctrines. This obviously is impossible to do adequately, but what follows should at least convey something of the book's astonishing claims.

The *UB*'s cosmology outrivals in fantasy the cosmology of any science-fiction work known to me. At the center of the Master Universe—the entire creation, the universe of universes—is the enormous Isle of Paradise, the largest body in the entire Master Universe. It is elliptical in shape, motionless, flat, and completely outside our space and time. It is not made of matter, but of a substance called "absolutum," which is neither dead nor alive, and which exists nowhere else.

Paradise is the dwelling place of the great I AM, the ultimate, eternal, infinite God. His triune nature of Father, Son, and Spirit is symbolized by the Urantian copyrighted trademark of three azure blue concentric circles on a white background. This is said in the *UB* (606) to be the emblem of the Creator Son Michael, incarnated in the flesh on Urantia as Jesus. It was on his banner 200,000 years ago when he waged war against Lucifer. The three circles also graced the breastplate of Machiventa Melchizedek (*UB* 1143), another of God's many Sons. He was "bestowed" on Urantia, in human flesh, 1,973 years before the birth of Jesus. Lucifer's emblem was a solid black circle in the center of a red one (*UB* 606). There are two lower trinities called the Ultimate Trinity and the Absolute Trinity, making a trinity of trinities.

Surrounding Paradise are three elliptical orbits each containing seven worlds. Around these twenty-one worlds are seven elliptical rings, each containing a billion, perfect, timeless worlds, no two alike. Altogether they constitute the Universe of Havona. Havona and Paradise had no beginning; they have always existed. Outside Havona are two more elliptical rings of what are called "dark gravity bodies." They keep the interior universes in a state of perfect balance.

There is much more! Beyond the gravity bodies revolve seven superuniverses. They are imperfect, still evolving, in an unfinished state. When their evolution is completed, each will contain 100,000 local universes, each with about ten million inhabited planets. We are in the seventh of these superuniverses.

Urantia's locale in this awesome scheme is given in the *UB* on page 182. Our earth is number 606 of a planetary group called Satania. Satania contains 619 inhabited worlds and 200 more that are evolving toward becoming inhabitable. The headquarters of Satania is a world called Jerusem.

Although the *UB* is highly imaginative in its cosmology, the opposite is true in its descriptions of the "mortals" who live on inhabited planets. All mortals are erect animals who walk on two feet. They belong to six different races: the primary races (red, yellow, and blue) and the secondary (orange, green, and indigo). Each race consists of male and female sexes, with sex equality prevailing on all advanced worlds. "Family life is fairly uniform on all types of planets" (*UB* 564). There are none of science fiction's "bug-eyed" intelligent monsters. All mortals are humanoids.

Heights of mortals vary from ten feet on low-gravity planets to thirty inches on more massive worlds (*UB* 562). Planets with little or no air are inhabited by people who do not breathe. We are told that "millions upon millions of meteorites" strike Urantia's atmosphere at a rate of "almost 200 miles per second," but friction of the air causes them to burn out before they can damage our cities. On low or no atmosphere planets, the non-breathers construct "electrical installations. . . . to consume or shunt off" the meteors. Nonbreathers neither eat food nor drink water, and in almost all respects differ enormously from breathing mortals.

"You would be more than interested," says Melchizedek of the Jerusem School of Planetary Administration (*UB* 564), "in the planetary conduct of this type of mortal because such a race of beings inhabits a sphere in close proximity to Urantia."

Satania belongs to a "constellation" of one hundred systems known as Norlatiadek, with headquarters on a world called Edentia. ("Constellation" is a term used in the *UB* to mean a system of stars.) Norlatiadek in turn is number 70 in the universe of Nebadon. Nebadon consists of one hundred constellations, and has a capital called Salvington.

Nebadon is number 84 in the minor sector of Ensa. Ensa consists of one-hundred local universes, with a capitol called Uminor the Third. Ensa is third in the major section of Splandon. Splandon has one hundred minor sectors with its headquarters on Umajor the Fifth. Splandon in turn is the fifth major sector of Orvonton, a superuniverse that is the seventh sector of the grand universe.

The grand universe registry number of Urantia is 5,342,482,337,666 (*UB* 182). All this information is in a paper written by a Universal Censor on Uversa, who ought to know.

Could it be that the thirteen digits in Urantia's registry number conceal some sort of message? I asked my old friend Dr. Irving Joshua Matrix,* the world's most famous numerologist, for his opinion of this mysterious number. A few days later he faxed the following analysis of the number from his current residence in Singapore.

Satan, Dr. Matrix reminded me, likes to take things backward. So let's reverse the number and partition it like so:

---

*See my *Magic Numbers of Dr. Matrix* (Prometheus Books, 1985), and chapter 21, "The Return of Dr. Matrix," in *Penrose Tiles to Trapdoor Ciphers* (W. H. Freeman, 1989).

14   URANTIA: THE GREAT CULT MYSTERY

666-73-328-42435

The first three digits are, of course, the number assigned to the Beast, an incarnation of Satan, described in the Bible's last book. The next two digits, 7 and 3, add to 10, the number of letters in "Revelation." The three digits in the next set, 3, 2, and 8, add to 13, a chapter in Revelation. The last set of five digits, 4,2,4,3,5, add to 18, the number of a verse. Now Revelation 13:18 is the very verse in which 666 is assigned to the Beast! Does this not suggest, Dr. Matrix asked, that Urantia was numbered when Caligastia was still ruling it? (We will come to Caligastia in a moment.) I was surprised to learn that Dr. Matrix has been studying the *UB* ever since its publication in 1955.

The first two digits of Urantia's number, 5 and 3, Dr. Matrix also pointed out, are closely tied to 666. The fraction 5/3, expressed as an endlessly repeating decimal fraction, is 1.66666. . . . The Urantia movement's headquarters have always been at 533 Diversey Parkway, Chicago. Is it coincidental, Dr. Matrix asked, that 53, the first two digits of this address, are also the first two digits of 5342482337666? Is it a coincidence that 606, Urantia's Satania number, has long been the number of Chicago's postal zone?

Eighteen billion "conciliatory commissions" operate in Orvonton, with 9,666 [666 again!] billion "universal conciliators" and 138 billion "servitals." Surrounding Uversa, Orvonton's capital, are 490 "study worlds" where "seconaphim" instruct ascending mortals who are on their way to Paradise.

The capitals of Uversa and Jerusem are what the *UB* calls "architectural worlds." These are colossal spheres which did not evolve but were specially constructed by celestial artisans. All architectural worlds, and their surrounding architectural satellites, "increase in material size, morontia beauty, and spirit glory from Jerusem to the central Isle" (*UB* 174). They are the abodes of mortal creatures as they ascend toward the Isle of Paradise. When we die, our soul goes into a deep slumber to awake on the first of the seven "mansion worlds" that surround Jerusem. They are what our New Testament calls "heaven." Recall how St. Paul was once transported to the third heaven? (II Corinthians 12:2).*

---

*The ancient Hebrews distinguished three heavens: the earth's atmosphere, the starry firmament, and the abode of God, so Paul was probably not referring to the third of seven heavens. However, the Hebrew Cabalists as well as the Koran describe seven heavens. Each is on a higher spiritual plane and of greater grandeur than the preceding one, with God and the archangels occupying the seventh. Hence the expression "in seventh heaven" as a way of saying one is in a state of extreme bliss. Muslims believe that Mohammed was taken by the archangel Gabriel to the seventh heaven where he encountered Allah, surrounded by his angels.

Each architectural sphere has its sun, although the sphere is not heated by the sun. The heat is produced by currents of morontia energy. On each architectural world there are one hundred forms of morontia energy, and twice as many chemical elements as on Urantia and other evolving worlds.

When we awake on the first mansion world, we have left behind on earth, to decay, our former body of flesh and blood. We are then given a new and improved body, made of morontia, with a brain in which all our memories at the time of death are intact. Because our sleeping soul was unaware of time, it will seem to us that we are resurrected instantly after we die. When we have completed residence on the other six mansion worlds, we are translated from the seventh heaven to Jerusem.

Jerusem, the headquarters of Satania, is one hundred times the size of Urantia. The *UB* (519ff.) tells a great deal about this remarkable Oz-like planet:

1. Its "mile" is equal to seven Urantia miles. Its standard unit of weight, the "gradant," is almost exactly ten ounces. Jerusem weights and measures are based on a decimal system.
2. A Jerusem day is equal to three Urantia days, minus 1 hour, 4 minutes, and 15 seconds. One hundred days make a year. Jerusem time is regularly broadcast by the "master chronoldeks."
3. Because Jerusem's sun is far away, there are no days, nights, or seasons on Jerusem. Power transformers, from one hundred thousand centers, project morontia energy into the air to maintain a "full-light" temperature of 70 degrees Fahrenheit. There are periods of "light recession" in which the heat is lowered to 50 degrees. Light during these periods has the intensity of a full earth moon on a clear night. The light comes from no one place, emanating in all directions to diffuse over the entire sky.
4. There are no earthquakes, no storms or blizzards, and no rainfall, though there are dewfalls.
5. There are no towering mountain ranges. The highest mountain is Mount Seraph, with an elevation of 15,000 feet.
6. There are no oceans or "raging rivers," but there are thousands upon thousands of small lakes. The "grandeur" of Jerusem scenery "is quite beyond the powers of human imagination."
7. Jerusem's atmosphere is similar to ours, with the addition "of a gas adapted to the respiration of the morontia order of life."
8. Material and "early morontia" beings travel on the backs of birds

that fly at one hundred miles an hour. (We will meet these transport birds again in chapter 11.) There also are mechanical systems that carry beings at 200 to 500 miles per hour. Spirit personalities on Jerusem can go much faster by using spiritual energy.

9. There are seraphim on Jerusem called seraphic transports whose task it is to transport personalities from world to world. How they do it remains a mystery. At Jerusem they are constantly arriving from other worlds on a "crystal field" or "sea of glass." There a student visitor can "ascend the pearly observatory and view the immense relief map of the entire headquarters planet."

10. Jerusem constantly sends out and receives audio broadcasts. The word "television" is not used, though there is a suggestion that the broadcasts are made visible. I quote from page 522:

This Jerusem broadcast-receiving station is encircled by an enormous amphitheater, constructed of scintillating materials largely unknown on Urantia and seating over five billion beings—material and morontia—besides accommodating innumerable spirit personalities. It is the favorite diversion for all Jerusem to spend their leisure at the broadcast station, there to learn of the welfare and state of the universe. And this is the only planetary activity which is not slowed down during the recession of light.

At this broadcast-receiving amphitheater the Salvington messages are coming in continuously. Near by, the Edentia word of the Most High Constellation Fathers is received at least once a day. Periodically the regular and special broadcasts of Uversa are relayed through Salvington, and when Paradise messages are in reception, the entire population is assembled around the sea of glass, and the Uversa friends add the reflectivity phenomena to the technique of the Paradise broadcast so that everything heard becomes visible. And it is in this manner that continual foretastes of advancing beauty and grandeur are afforded the mortal survivors as they journey inward on the eternal adventure.

11. The most remarkable animals on Jerusem are the "landscape gardeners" responsible for the planet's agriculture. They are called "spornagia." They did not evolve but were fabricated by Life Carriers. We are told that they combine the traits of "a faithful horse and an obedient dog." Their intelligence is higher than a chimpanzee's. They have no "survival souls," but in some far off future may develop them.

12. Many of the buildings on Jerusem are made of crystal gems. "All the architectural worlds abound in crystals and the so-called pre-

cious metals." Jeweled cities are common in the religious mythology of many cultures, including the Judaeo-Christian traditions; one also cannot help thinking of the Emerald City of Oz!

If you wish to know more about Jerusem before you arrive there after you die, including Jerusem's ethics and politics, consult the *UB*'s Paper 46. It is devoted entirely to describing this "wonderful world" which we are told is typical of architectural spheres.

After our long sojourn on Jerusem we are prepared to go on to the architectural world of Edentia, headquarters of the Norlatiadek constellation. It has seventy satellites on which ascenders are further trained. There are two kinds of plants on Edentia. Those made of matter are green. Those made of morontia energy have a violet or orchid tinge. When eaten, the morontia plants leave no residue to be excreted. Also on Edentia are thousands of animal species. They are gentle, friendly, and noncarnivorous— nothing like the "gross species" on Urantia. "There is nothing in all Edentia to make any living being afraid." (*UB* 492).

After leaving Edentia we proceed to Salvington, the capital of Nebadon. It is surrounded by ten clusters of forty-nine spheres. Before reaching Salvington, where we become "first-stage spirits," we will have had 570 morontia bodies at 570 stages of our progress (*UB* 542).

Our next abode is Uminor the Third, headquarters of Ensa, then on to Umajor the Fifth, headquarters of Splandon. Uminor the Third has only seven surrounding spheres. Umajor the Fifth has seventy, for "advanced intellectual training." The last stop in our superumverse is Uversa. After Uversa we go on to Havona, and after Havona, to our final residence in Paradise.

Uversa, the headquarters of Orvonton, your superuniverse, is immediately surrounded by the seven higher universities of advanced spiritual training for ascending will creatures. Each of these seven clusters of wonder spheres consists of seventy specialized worlds containing thousands upon thousands of replete institutions and organizations devoted to universe training and spirit culture wherein the pilgrims of time are re-educated and re-examined preparatory to their long flight to Havona. The arriving pilgrims of time are always received on these associated worlds, but the departing graduates are always dispatched for Havona direct from the shores of Uversa.

Uversa is the spiritual and administrative headquarters for approximately one trillion inhabited or inhabitable worlds. The glory, grandeur, and perfection of the Orvonton capital surpass any of the wonders of the time-space creations.

If all of the projected local universes and their component parts were established, there would be slightly less than five hundred billion architectural worlds in the seven superuniverses. (*UB* 175.)

This still is not all! Outside the seven superuniverses are elliptical rings of primordial matter in which millions of new galaxies are being formed. The inner and third rings revolve counterclockwise (to one looking down on paradise). The second and fourth rings go the other way. As a result of all the motions of structures in the Master Universe, our earth participates in seven different revolutions.

Guardian angels and Thought Adjusters help us along the way to Paradise. The pilgrimage will not be monotonous as we move from world to world. There will be endless adventures and surprises until we finally awake, from the last Big Sleep, to find ourselves on Paradise. There will be no more death sleeps. We will live forever. It will not be the Nirvana of Eastern religions in which our personalities are absorbed in the ultimate God. We will retain our individual memories and character. Some of us will even be assigned duties on evolving universes.

The *UB* bristles with neologisms and bizarre proper names. A small sample includes such terms as mind-gravity circuit, absonity, reflectivity, trinitization, eventuation, finaliters, agondonters, Lanonandeks, midwayers, Grandfanda, everywhereness, ultimate quartan integration, and hundreds more.

The authors of what Urantians call "The Papers" of the *UB* have a curious compulsion to divide things into sevens. The Thought Adjusters, for instance, come in seven flavors: virgin, advanced, supreme, vanished, liberated, fused, and personalized. Three is another number that occurs often in the *UB*, as well as ten, the sum of seven and three. Scores of numbers in the *UB* are powers or multiples of seven and ten, or products of seven and other numbers. We are told (*UB* 479) that seven is characteristic of the spiritual worlds, and ten is basic to material worlds, though the two numbers are often applied to both worlds. The number of stars in our local universe, for example, is 1,013,572, which is a multiple of seven. Our sun has the number of 1,013,628, another multiple of seven.

The frequency of seven in the *UB* correlates with its frequency in the Bible (consult any comprehensive Bible concordance). In the *UB* (page 184) we are told that seven is fundamental in the organization and administration of the grand universe because the Infinite Spirit, in its three-fold form of Father, Son, and Spirit has exactly seven subsets known as the Seven Master Spirits: Father, Son, Spirit, Father and Son, Father and Spirit, Son and Spirit, and Father, Son, and Spirit.

Although most of the *UB* is written in clear, easily understood prose, one occasionally comes upon a murky passage such as this:

> The triodity of actuality continues to function directly in the post-Havona epochs; Paradise gravity grasps the basic units of material existence, the spirit gravity of the Eternal Son operates directly upon the fundamental values of spirit existence, and the mind gravity of the Conjoint Actor unerringly clutches all vital meanings of intellectual existence. (*UB* 1265.)

The quotation is from Paper 115, on "The Supreme Being," which we are told was "Sponsored by a Mighty Messenger temporarily sojourning on Urantia." Note that it is "sponsored" by, not "written by." The paper concludes:

> By the process of summating evolutionary experience the Supreme connects the finite with the absonite, even as the mind of the Conjoint Actor integrates the divine spirituality of the personal Son with the immutable energies of the Paradise pattern, and as the presence of the Universal Absolute unifies Deity activation with the Unqualified reactivity. And this unity must be a revelation of the undetected working of the original unity of the First Father-Cause and Source-Pattern of all things and all beings.

Urantians seldom mention it, but if you remove the "t," Urantia becomes Urania, the name of one of the nine muses of Greek mythology. A daughter of Zeus, Urania was the muse of astronomy, usually depicted with one arm on the round earth, her other hand pointing upward. Frequently she wears a crown of stars. Urania was also taken by the Greeks to be a personification of the love that unites the earth with the universe, making her name even more appropriate for the Urantian revelation.

Below I AM are billions of lesser gods, so many in fact that the *UB*'s polytheism puts Greek and Hindu mythology to shame. One god is a finite deity now evolving toward becoming the supreme god of all the evolving universes. It would take many pages just to list the generic names of all these higher intelligences. There are the Truth Revealers, the Mystery Monitors, the Universal Censors, the Divine Counselors, the Perfectors of Wisdom, the Ancients of Days, and a hundred others.

Technical Advisors include Supernaphim, Seconaphim, Tertiaphim, Omniaphim, Seraphim, Cherubim, and Sanobim. The Master Physical Controllers (some are machines) are the Power Directors, Mechanical Controllers, Energy Transformers, Energy Transmitters, Primary Associators, Secondary Associators, Frandalanks, and Chronoldeks. On Urantia's Advisory Council are Onagar, Mansant, Onamonalonton, Orlandof, Porshunta, Singlangton, Fantad, Orvonon, Adam, Eve, Enoch, Moses, Elijah, Machiventa Melchizedek, John the Baptist, and 1-2-3 the First.

The frandalanks, stationed on all inhabited worlds and so numerous that their total number is beyond human comprehension, are "living machines." They perform "stupendous calculations," involving all forms of "force-energy," with great accuracy. In today's vocabulary, they are intelligent, living computers. A subset of the frandalanks, concerned with time calculations, are called chronoldeks (*UB* 328–29). On Jerusem, the time of day is "broadcast by the master chronoldeks" (*UB* 519).

Some notion of the staggering complexity of gods and their classifications into sevenfold orders can be gained by glancing through Papers 18 through 30 of the *UB*. Below the Paradise Trinities are seven Supreme Trinity Personalities: The Trinitized Secrets of Supremacy, Eternals of Days, Ancients of Days, Perfections of Days, Recents of Days, Unions of Days, and Faithfuls of Days.

The seven Co-ordinate Trinity Origin Beings are: Trinity Teacher Sons, Perfectors of Wisdom, Divine Counselors, Universal Censors, Inspired Trinity Spirits, Havona Natives, and Paradise Citizens. The seven Descending Sons of God are: Creator Sons or Michaels, Magisterial Sons or Avonals, Trinity Teacher Sons or Daynals, Melchizedek Sons, Vorondadek Sons, Lanonandek Sons, and Life Carriers. The Trinity Embraced Sons, also in seven orders, are: Mighty Messengers, Those High in Authority, Those Without Name and Number, Trinitized Custodians, Trinitized Ambassadors, Celestial Guardians, and High Son Assistants.

It is true that in the *UB*'s mythology there is one supreme, undivided, absolute deity, the great I AM, who is above all the other gods. But this does not turn the mythology into a theism. Hinduism is universally regarded as polytheistic, yet above the trinity of Brahma, Vishnu, and Shiva is Brahman, the eternal absolute, ultimate deity, so transcendent that nothing can be said about Brahman except "not this, not that."

I spare readers the lists of the seven Solitary Messengers (Paper 23), the seven divisions of the Higher Personalities of the Infinite Spirit (Paper 24), or the seven orders of the Messenger Hosts of Space (Paper 25). These only scratch the surface of the *UB*'s dazzling hierarchy of divinities. Paper 30 attempts to summarize some of these gods and their classifications, but warns readers that the lists and classifications are only partial:

> The personalities and other-than-personal entities now functioning on Paradise and in the grand universe constitute a well-nigh limitless number of living beings. Even the number of major orders and types would stagger the human imagination, let alone the countless subtypes and variations. It is, however, desirable to present something of two basic classifications of living beings—a suggestion of the Paradise classification and an abbreviation of the Uversa Personality Register.
>
> It is not possible to formulate comprehensive and entirely consistent classifications of the personalities of the grand universe because *all* of the groups are not revealed. It would require numerous additional papers to cover the further revelation required to systematically classify all groups. Such conceptual expansion would hardly be desirable as it would deprive the thinking mortals of the next thousand years of that stimulus to creative speculation which these partially revealed concepts supply. It is best that man not have an overrevelation; it stifles imagination. (*UB* 330.)

Among the higher early inhabitants of Urantia, the most bizarre are the secondary midwayers. Here is how they came about. Adamson, the eldest son of Adam, lived 396 years, during which he and his wife Ratta begat 67 children. Every fourth child, to the vast astonishment of their parents, turned out to be invisible! "Never in the world's history," the *UB* tells us, "had such a thing occurred. Ratta was greatly perturbed. . . ." These invisibles were mated with one another to produce the secondary midwayers, using a "combined technique of sex and nonsex liaison." (See the *UB* 861–65.)

The secondary midwayers were "electrically energized," whatever that means. Of the 1,974 of these strange creatures, 873 fell into sin and caused lots of mischief. They are now in prison somewhere. The loyal secondary midwayers still exist on earth "just outside the range of mortal vision." They are able at will to reveal themselves to mortals, and to perform "unperceived" good deeds to help the human race.

Lucifer, one of three system sovereigns who rebelled, is now the deposed sovereign of Satania, named after Satan, his first lieutenant. Under Satan are lesser rebels such as Caligastia and Beelzebub. Caligastia is a name that suggests the Emperor Caligula (mentioned in the *UB*, page 1915), but is probably derived from the word "caligation," and its adjective form "caliginous," meaning dim and dark. These fallen celestials are confined to Satania, although they can still work mischief on Urantia. Some of them have repented. Those who never repent will eventually be annihilated.

Urantia's first human beings were not Adam and Eve. They were black-eyed twins called Andon and Fonta, whose parents were beasts. They were born 993,419 years prior to 1934 (*UB* 707). The Garden of Eden was not established until almost a million years later. Adam and Eve were dematerialized on higher worlds and materialized on Urantia 37,848 years before 1934 (*UB* 828) to "uplift" the human race. Each was more than eight feet tall, with blue eyes, and bodies that shimmered with light. They were vegetarians. Their offspring began what the *UB* calls the "violet race" even though its members had fair skin and blue eyes.

Adam and Eve had the power to communicate with each other by ESP, and to see angels and midwayers, even to see the fallen Caligastia. Their descendants had similar psi powers, although they diminished with each new generation and are now lost. Although the pair "defaulted" by disobeying higher authorities, there was no "fall of man." It is unthinkable, says the *UB*, that a loving God would allow all humans to suffer for the sins of two remote ancestors.

> There has been no "fall of man." The history of the human race is one of progressive evolution, and the Adamic bestowal left the world peoples greatly improved over their previous biologic condition. The more superior stocks of Urantia now contain inheritance factors derived from as many as four separate sources: Andonite, Sangik, Nodite, and Adamic.
>
> Adam should not be regarded as the cause of a curse on the human race. While he did fail in carrying forward the divine plan, while he did transgress his covenant with Deity, while he and his mate were most certainly degraded in creature status, notwithstanding all this, their contribution to the human race did much to advance civilization on Urantia. (*UB* 846.)

There was no tree of the knowledge of good and evil in the Garden of Eden—this is just a Biblical metaphor—but there *was* a Tree of Life. It grew from a plant in the architectural world of Edentia, and was later transported to Urantia. Adam and Eve have been "repersonalized" and now live on Edentia with two-thirds of their repersonalized children. Adam once wanted to communicate with Urantians, but higher authorities would not allow it. Like the Koran and the Book of Mormon, the *UB* retells Old Testament tales with hundreds of corrections and embellishments.

Our bodies and minds are created at birth, but our souls do not develop until about the age of six. Surviving our death is our personal "thought adjuster"—a fragment of God assigned to dwell within us. After our first resurrection, we start a long series of journeys from world to world, universe to universe, traveling always inward through the Master Universe until we eventually reach Paradise.

All the world's great religions assume the existence of beings as superior to us as we are to the beasts that perish. Today this notion of a "great chain of being," with endless gradations in which we occupy a middle ground (though much closer to plants and animals than to the Gods), is most commonly encountered in science fiction. There angels and gods are replaced by sentient beings on other planets, or in higher spacetimes. The *UB*'s elaborate polytheism is unique in that most of its higher beings are not outside our spacetime but living on spheres within the universe.*

Instead of surviving our first death in a region beyond our spacetime, as in the great religions, we proceed from world to world in a series of reincarnations not unlike the reincarnations of Eastern faiths in which our successive new bodies are on Earth. Of course when we finally reach the *UB*'s Paradise we are in a region beyond our spacetime, in seven dimensions, but Paradise is a long, long way off.

The *UB* goes into great detail about the early geological history of the earth (we will come to this again in chapter 10), and about the evolutionary development of various races. The races are identified by colors. Again, one thinks of L. Frank Baum's Oz where the Winkies live in a yellow region, the Munchkins in blue, the Quadlings in red, and the Gillikins in purple. The dominant color of the Emerald City is, of course, green.

Here is how the Urantian races came about. Five hundred thousand years ago the Sangkik family, one of the Badonan tribes of northern India, suddenly produced nineteen children whose skins turned various colors

---

*John Locke, in his *Essay Concerning Human Understanding*, gave a succinct defense of a hierarchy of gods, semi-gods, and angels, on a continuum between God and humanity:

When we consider the infinite power and wisdom of the Maker, we have reason to think that it is suitable to the magnificent harmony of the Universe, and the great design and infinite goodness of the Architect, that the species of creatures should also, by gentle degrees, ascend upward from us toward his infinite perfection, as we see they gradually descend from us downwards.

I quote this passage from the section on angels, in Mortimer Adler's *Syntopicon of Great Books of the Western World*, vol. 1 (*Encyclopaedia Britannica*, 1952). This section anticipates what Adler has to say in what I consider his funniest book, *The Angels and Us* (1982). The *Syntopicon* has an extensive bibliography of references on angelology. We will have more to say about angels in chapter 12.

when exposed to sunlight. Five of the children turned red, two orange, four yellow, two green, four blue, and two indigo. These colors became permanent when they grew older, and their offspring had the same color as their parents.

The three primary-colored races (red, yellow, and blue) were the most intelligent. The secondary-colored races (orange, green, and purple) were less intelligent (*UB* 584). The reds had the highest intelligence. They crossed over the Pacific, along the Bering islands, to America where they became our native Indians. Their greatest spiritual leader was a man named Onamonalonton.

The yellows, slightly inferior to the reds, became our present Orientals. Their great spiritual leader was Singlangton.

The blues had a great spiritual leader named Orlandof. After a slight mixing with yellows and reds, they became the ancestors of the present white race. (It figures: a spectral mixing of the three primary colors makes white.)

The inferior orange race had a leader named Porshunta. It ceased to exist about a hundred thousand years ago after being wiped out in a prolonged battle with the greens.

The inferior greens, whose greatest leader was Fantad, also eventually died out, being absorbed by other races.

The indigo race was the least advanced of the six. Its members migrated to Africa to become the Negro race. Their top spiritual leader was Orvonon, not to be confused with Orvonton.

That the *UB* regards the black race as the most inferior of all races is something the small number of blacks in the Urantia movement find embarrassing and hard to rationalize. It coincides with the racist views of Dr. William S. Sadler, the leader of the Urantia movement whom we will meet in the next chapter. Although genetically below other races, the *UB* (725) assures us that "notwithstanding their backwardness, these indigo peoples have exactly the same standing before the celestial powers as any other earthly race." That is exactly what southerners in the United States, including their ministers, used to say about the African American slaves. Although obviously inferior to whites, and destined by God to slavery, nevertheless God loves them as much as he does their white masters!

Mongrelization of the races, says the *UB*, produced the present inhabitants of Mexico, Central America, and South America, as well as the people of India. The brown races of India derived from a mixture of the reds and yellows.

I have given only a thumbnail sketch of the history of races set forth in such bewildering detail in the *UB*. All sorts of subgroups are involved, such as the Adamites, Adamsonites, Andites, Nodites, and many others.

The last third of the *UB*, almost eight hundred pages, is devoted to a colorful history of the incarnation and life of Jesus. Critics of the Urantia movement have been so cynical as to suggest that this long Jesus section was added at the last hour to the earlier papers in order to recruit Christians who otherwise would be repelled by a book so clearly non-Christian. Many devout Urantians have told me, personally and in letters, of the enormous spiritual benefit and comfort they derived from the Jesus papers. It is true that beside these papers the four gospels of the Bible offer only a pallid account of Jesus' life and teachings.

I can see how the *UB*'s Jesus papers would appeal to some liberal Christians, and to persons who are into various New Age doctrines, but how they could interest any conservative Protestant or Catholic is difficult to fathom. The doctrines of the *UB* are a weird mix of recorded teachings of Jesus with views that are offensive to conservative Christians. Because there was no Fall of Man, there was no need for an atonement in the form of a blood sacrifice. The following passage from the *UB* (60) is particularly disturbing to conservative Christians:

> The barbarous idea of appeasing an angry God, or propitiating an of-fended Lord, of winning the favor of Deity through sacrifices and pen-ance and even by the shedding of blood, represents a religion wholly puerile and primitive, a philosophy unworthy of an enlightened age of sci-ence and truth. Such beliefs are utterly repulsive to the celestial beings and the divine rulers who serve and reign in the universes. It is an affront to God to believe, hold, or teach that innocent blood must be shed in order to win his favor or to divert the fictitious divine wrath. . . .
>
> What a travesty upon the infinite character of God! this teaching that his fatherly heart in all its austere coldness and hardness was so untouched by the misfortunes and sorrows of his creatures that his tender mercies were not forthcoming until he saw his blameless Son bleeding and dying upon the cross of Calvary!

So declares the Divine Counselor of Uversa in the *UB*'s fourth paper.

At the same time that the *UB* offends orthodox Christians—it pleads for readers not to believe *in* Jesus but to believe *with* Jesus—it equally offends non-Christians by defending the Incarnation and many of the New Testament's greatest miracles.

Let's start with the miracle of the Virgin Birth. The *UB* considers this a legend without foundation. Jesus was born of normal parents on August 21, 7 BCE Although he had a father and mother, he was the incarnation of Michael of Nebadon, number 611,121 among the more than 700,000 Creator Sons of the Eternal Son, who in turn are part of the Ultimate Trinity. (The number 611,121 is 3 times 7 times the prime number 29,101.) Michael was the actual creator of our entire universe, a view the *UB* shares with Seventh-day Adventists and Jehovah's Witnesses. Coming to Urantia was his seventh, most recent incarnation as one of God's lesser creatures.

Jesus' real father, Joseph, we are told died of injuries after a derrick fell on him during work. This left Jesus as head of the family and its chief wage earner. At 19 he was a handsome, virile youth to whom young women were strongly attracted. Rebecca, the beautiful daughter of a wealthy merchant, fell in love with him and even proposed marriage. Her father's money, she said, would take care of his family. Jesus politely explained that he could never marry anyone because of the mission before him, but he thanked her for her "admiration," and added, "It shall cheer and comfort me all the days of my life."

Rebecca never lost her admiration. She was present when Jesus made his triumphal entry into Jerusalem and was among the women who stood by the cross when he died.

You will be intrigued to learn that Jesus wrote the Lord's Prayer when he was a mere 15, and that he took the title "Son of Man" from the apocryphal Book of Enoch which he admired and carefully studied. I doubt if you know that Peter's wife was named Perpetua and that she headed a "woman's corp" of fifty. After Peter was crucified in Rome, her body was fed to wild beasts in the city's arena. And did you know that when Jesus was 28 and 29 he toured Rome, Greece, and nearby regions in the company of two natives of India, Gonod and Ganid? Did you know that he studied books on religion and philosophy at the great library in Alexandria?

Contrary to all evidence, the Jesus of the *UB* is as knowledgeable about Greek philosophy, mathematics, art, and science as Aristotle. We are told (*UB* 1476) that when Jesus visited a university in Athens he "thoroughly discussed the teachings of Plato." After this discussion he said "in terms of modern thought":

> Scientists may some day measure the energy, or force manifestations, of gravitation, light, and electricity, but these same scientists can never (scientifically) tell you what these universe phenomena *are*. Science deals with physical-energy activities; religion deals with eternal values. True

philosophy grows out of the wisdom which does its best to correlate these quantitative and qualitative observations. There always exists the danger that the purely physical scientist may become afflicted with mathematical pride and statistical egotism, not to mention spiritual blindness.

Logic is valid in the material world, and mathematics is reliable when limited in its application to physical things; but neither is to be regarded as wholly dependable or infallible when applied to life problems. Life embraces phenomena which are not wholly material. Arithmetic says that, if one man could shear a sheep in ten minutes, ten men could shear it in one minute. That is sound mathematics, but it is not true, for the ten men could not so do it; they would get in one another's way so badly that the work would be greatly delayed.

Mathematics asserts that, if one person stands for a certain unit of intellectual and moral value, ten persons would stand for ten times this value. But in dealing with human personality it would be nearer the truth to say that such a personality association is a sum equal to the square of the number of personalities concerned in the equation rather than the simple arithmetical sum. A social group of human beings in co-ordinated working harmony stands for a force far greater than the simple sum of its parts.

The Greeks who heard those words were understandably amazed. Said a philosopher: "At last my eyes have beheld a Jew who thinks something besides racial superiority and talks something besides religion."

If you know only the gospel accounts of Jesus, you'll be astounded to learn that Jesus had a "baby sister" named Ruth, and that Jesus' "business manager" was David, a brother of the former fishermen apostles James and John. Ruth was among the women present at the crucifixion. She and David fell in love and married. Urantian Helena Sprague has even written a novel about this non-biblical romance which Urantians take to be historical truth because it is in the *UB*. The novel, privately published in 1986, is distributed by the David Project Committee, Schenectady, New York.

Jewish readers of the *UB* will not be pleased to learn (*UB* 1736) that Jesus "greatly enjoyed the keen sense of humor" of the gentiles, and "greatly regretted that his people—the Jews—were so lacking in humor." He once said to Thomas: "My people take themselves too seriously; they are just about devoid of an appreciation of humor. The burdensome religion of the Pharisees could never have had origin among a people with a sense of humor."

Jesus' skill at carpentry was legendary. As a young man he spent a year in the shop of his friend John Zebedee building boats. "He created a new style of boat and established entirely new methods of boat building" (*UB* 1419).

Thousands of such details about Jesus are in the *UB* and nowhere else. I'll bet you are unaware that as a boy Jesus studied mathematics and acquired a "keen sense of numbers, distances, and proportions" (*UB* 1364). He was also interested in flowers and plants and the stars (*UB* 1360). Jesus took lessons on the harp and became a skillful harpist at age eleven (*UB* 1364). He "greatly enjoyed entertaining both family and friends with his extraordinary interpretations and able improvisations."

Among the many miracles attributed to Jesus in the gospels, the *UB* accepts some, denies others. There was, for instance, no miraculous draught of fishes. "Jesus was a close student of nature; he was an experienced fisherman and knew the habits of the fish in the Sea of Galilee. On this occasion he merely directed these men to the place where the fish were usually to be found at this time of day" (*UB* 1629).

A man who seemed demon possessed was merely "a victim of ordinary epilepsy" (*UB* 1631). Demon possession, we are assured, was always rare, and never occurred on earth again after the day of Pentecost. However, later that same day, Jesus did miraculously cure the same man of epilepsy. On another occasion, after Jesus healed the mind of a lunatic, a dog chased a herd of swine into the sea, giving rise to the legend that devils had left the man to enter the pigs.

Although the New Testament speaks of several resurrections of the dead, only one, the resurrection of Lazarus, was a genuine miracle. The others were not dead, but merely sleeping. The story of Lazarus is given in detail in the *UB*'s Paper 168. It was not the power of Jesus, however, that revived him. Lazarus' corpse had been truly decomposing for four days. So great was Jesus' sorrow over the death of his friend that a group of celestial beings under the leadership of Gabriel, the Bright and Morning Star who is chief executive of the Universe of Nebadon, decided to revive Lazarus. It took the higher powers twelve seconds of earth time to do the trick. As soon as Lazarus walked out of the tomb, Jesus' Personalized Adjuster commanded the former Adjuster of Lazarus to reenter the man's mind and soul.

Gabriel then "dismissed the extra groups of the assembled heavenly host while he made record of the first instance on Urantia, and the last, where a mortal creature had been resurrected in the likeness of the physical body of death" (*UB* 1846). Lazarus recalled nothing of the four days he was dead because "Time is nonexistent to those who sleep the sleep of death." As we shall learn, soul sleeping is basic Seventh-day Adventist doctrine.

Have you ever wondered what happened to the revivified Lazarus? The *UB* will enlighten you. Finding himself under severe persecution by the

Sanhedrin, he fled to Philadelphia (a town in Perea) where he eventually became treasurer of the local congregation of Christians. He died at age 67 of the same illness that killed him when he was young.

The most amazing case of miraculous healing occurred in Capernaum. No less than "683 men, women, and children [683 is a prime number] were made whole, were perfectly healed of all their physical diseases and other material disorders. Such a scene was never witnessed on earth before that day, nor since . . . it was indeed a thrilling spectacle" (*UB* 1633). However, again it was not Jesus who worked this stupendous miracle. The healings were accomplished by "a vast retinue of seraphim, physical con rollers, Life Carriers, and midwayers." They always attended Jesus, and on this occasion were instructed by God himself to carry out the healings (*UB* 1632). "What a *Creator Son* desires and his Father *wills* IS" (*UB* 1633).

Did Jesus turn water into wine at the wedding feast? He did not. Once more, this was done by higher powers. They "abrogated" time, made the wine, then exchanged the water for wine in what seemed to be an instantaneous magic feat to those present. "No law of nature was modified, abrogated, or even transcended," the *UB* explains on page 1530. On the other hand, surprisingly, we are told (*UB* 1702) that multiplying the loaves and fishes was the only "natural miracle" that Jesus performed himself. He did it by "conscious preplanning." It, too, involved the "abrogation" of time, but was a "genuine supernatural ministration."

The *UB*'s approach to the so-called miracles of Jesus is more closely related to science fiction than to Christian theology. Although Jesus did indeed seem to perform miracles in the sense of violating natural laws, the *UB* makes clear (1516-1523) that Jesus deliberately decided never to violate the laws of nature. The laws only appeared to be violated because the gods accelerated time sufficiently to allow them to apply natural laws with great rapidity. In this way they caused events to occur that would seem miraculous to onlookers.

Jesus had the power (*UB* 1521) to step off a temple pinnacle and walk on air, but he chose not to display such powers. He never, for example, walked on water (*UB* 1519). In such ways the *UB* endorses the reality of certain "miracles" in the New Testament, explaining them as cases of time "abrogation" by the gods. Other miracles, such as water walking, are dismissed as legends. We are told that Jesus did not want to be known as a worker of wonders. However, by permitting celestials to change water to wine, and to multiply loaves and fishes, the effect on those present was just as awesome as if he had used his own powers to violate natural laws.

After Jesus' death, his body remained in the tomb until the gods caused it instantly to disintegrate, then rolled away the stone from the entrance to an empty sepulchre. It was not a resurrected material body of Jesus that later appeared to so many, but his reconstituted spiritual body.

The gospels tell how Jesus promised to send, after his death, the Comforter or Holy Spirit, and the book of Acts describes the arrival of this aspect of the Trinity on the day of Pentecost. The *UB* calls this the Spirit of Truth, which it distinguishes from the Holy Spirit. Its bestowal at Pentecost is described on page 2060. Two pages later we learn of the seven adjutant mind-spirits through which it operates inside our hearts. When we are baptized by the Spirit of Truth, we are enabled to expand our spiritual knowledge, gain greater spiritual power, and better restate the Jesus revelation to new generations. It is typical of the *UB* that the Spirit of Truth is given (2061) male pronouns.

Exactly who was Jesus? In the *UB*'s complex mythology he was one of more than 700,000 Creator Sons, or "Michael Sons" who are given the responsibility of creating and governing local universes. Each Creator Son is a unique personality, the "only-begotten Son" of a pair of gods who dwell in Paradise. When a Creator Son is "personalized," he is given a "Mother Spirit" to assist him.

Each Creator Son, by his own free will, goes through seven "self-bestowals" in which he suddenly appears on one of the planets in his local universe. The final bestowal is an incarnation as one of his own mortal creatures. As the *UB* (239) puts it:

> Avonal bestowals are always in the likeness of mortal flesh, but the seven bestowals of a Creator Son involve his appearing on seven creature levels of being and pertain to the revelation of the seven primary expressions of the will and nature of Deity. Without exception, all Creator Sons pass through this seven times giving of themselves to their created children before they assume settled and supreme jurisdiction over the universes of their own creation.

The seven bestowals of the Creator Son of our universe of Nebadon are described in the *UB*'s Paper 119. Each bestowal came about 150 million years after the previous one, covering a period of almost a billion years in all. Michael's seven bestowals were:

1. As a Melchizedek Son on Salvington
2. As a Lanonandek Son on Palonia, in System 11, of Nebadon's Constellation 37, where he deposed the evil ruler Lutentia

3. As a Material Son on planet 217 of System 87, in Constellation 61, to depose a Planetary Prince who had "defaulted"
4. As a seraphim (angel) teacher on 22 different worlds
5. As Eventod, a "spirit mortal," on Uversa, the headquarters of Orvonton
6. As a "morontia mortal" on the headquarters planet of Constellation 37
7. As Jesus, the "babe of the realm," on Urantia

Note that 11, 37, and 61 are primes, that 217 is a product of primes 3 and 31, and 87 the product of primes 3 and 29.

How such bestowals were accomplished are mysteries which even the authors of the *UB* papers admit they do not understand. This is especially true of the mystery of Michael's incarnation as Jesus. The *UB* (1137) says:

Joshua ben Joseph, the Jewish baby, was conceived and was born into the world just as all other babies before and since *except* that this particular baby was the incarnation of Michael of Nebadon, a divine Son of Paradise and the creator of all this local universe of things and beings. And this mystery of the incarnation of Deity within the human form of Jesus, otherwise of natural origin on the world, will forever remain unsolved. Even in eternity you will never know the technique and method of the incarnation of the Creator in the form and likeness of his creatures. That is the secret of Sonarington, and such mysteries are the exclusive possession of those divine Sons who have passed through the bestowal experience.

When on the cross Jesus cried, "It is finished," he meant that his seventh and final bestowal was complete. Henceforth he would be the sovereign ruler of all Nebadon. Like other Creator Sons of other local universes, when he is absent from Nebadon his duties are taken over by Gabriel, a chief executive known as the Bright and Morning Star. He is also aided by his Mother Spirit, and by advice from his older brother Immanuel, also called a Union of Days.

The Jesus section, like the rest of *The Urantia Book*, is strongly fideistic. Its central theme is that the highest religion known on Urantia was preached by Jesus, who was Michael of Nebadon, as part of God's plan for the spiritual progress of humanity. The message of Jesus was corrupted by Paul and other early disciples, but has now been rediscovered and given in the Papers of the *UB*. There is, however, no way to prove by reason that this revelation is authentic; indeed, there is no way to prove that there is an Ultimate God. Our Thought Adjuster, the fragment of God within us, urges us to believe, but it is only by a turning of our free will, by a leap of faith, that we can accept the reality of God and the truth of the new revelation.

The *UB* puts its fideism succinctly on page 24:

> The existence of God can never be proved by scientific experiment or by the pure reason of logical deduction. God can be realized only in the realms of human experience; nevertheless, the true concept of the reality of God is reasonable to logic, plausible to philosophy, essential to religion, and indispensable to any hope of personality survival.

I happen to believe in the above assertions, as any reader will know who has read my "confessional," *The Whys of a Philosophical Scrivener.* Of course there is nothing new in this point of view. The passage could have been written by Charles Peirce, William James, or Miguel de Unamuno. It is a capsule summary of the heart of Kant's theology.

The pervasive fideism of the *UB* seems to be contradicted by what we are told on page 665 of the *UB*:

> The Urantia midwayers have assembled over fifty thousand facts of physics and chemistry which they deem to be incompatible with the laws of accidental chance, and which they contend unmistakably demonstrate the presence of intelligent purpose in the material creation. And all of this takes no account of their catalogue of more than one hundred thousand findings outside the domain of physics and chemistry which they maintain prove the presence of mind in the planning, creation, and maintenance of the material cosmos.

I'm not sure how a Urantian can best explain this seeming conflict between fideism and the claim that there are thousands of scientific facts which "prove" the existence of a creator God. Maybe such arguments from design, which go back to the ancient Greeks, constitute "proof" only for the superior minds of celestial beings.

Urantians look upon the *UB* with an awe and reverence far greater than they look upon the Bible with its hundreds of crude historical errors. Here, for example, are two lyrical passages from an article by Patije Mills in *Sonshine Messenger* (Fall 1992), a periodical she edits from her home in Sarasota, Florida:

The Urantia Book has turned my living experience inside out and upside down as I attempt to practice what I know from reading this mind-stretching book! There is a peace which passes mere understanding that permeates my attitude and my consciousness when confronted with the unexpected challenges of an ordinary life among the unpredictable mortals in my life experience—which I find as a result of this book.

"Help me, Father, to express you as I share this unmatched, unsurpassed, inspirational, mind-expanding, harmony producing, emotionally balanced, historical report and complex guide—*The Urantia Book!*" It is more than a textbook! It is more than an inspiration! It is more than a revelation! It is my LIGHT *to* LIFE as I finish my experiences in the Time and Space of this mortal life on Urantia. "Thank you, Father, for the astounding discovery and influence of the great life lessons in this book which is to correct our religious history and plant the seeds with which to enable mankind to begin to comprehend and grow into our destiny of Light and Life."

Compared to such major cults as Mormonism, Christian Science, Jehovah's Witnesses, and other large Christian sects, the Urantia movement is small. There are some 200 Urantian "study groups," almost all in the United States, which meet regularly to socialize and discuss the *UB*. Out of these study groups have grown more than twenty "societies," many of which publish their own newsletter and other documents.

A society consists of ten or more believers. Until recently it had to be chartered by the Urantian headquarters in Chicago, at 533 Diversey Parkway. The first society was formed in Chicago in 1956, the second in Los Angeles the following year. In chapter 19 we will learn of the great rebellion which resulted in the societies parting company with the Urantia Foundation.

Because there is no Urantian church with an initiation ritual it is difficult even to guess the number of Urantian believers here and abroad. Defining a believer is difficult because many who attend a study group are affiliated with mainstream Christian churches and attend more out of curiosity and partial belief than with full-fledged faith. I have no idea whether the number in study groups is currently increasing, diminishing, or staying about the same. Members keep moving in and out of the study groups, and the groups themselves are constantly forming and dissolving. I would estimate the number of Urantians firmly convinced that the *UB* was written by supermortals to be no more than a few thousand.

No one can read through the *UB*, or even just parts of it, without wondering how such an incredibly detailed mix of science, ethics, politics, and polytheology ever got set down in one monstrous blue-covered volume. The story involves many people who lived in Chicago during the first half of the twentieth century, but the two most responsible for the *UB* were two ex-Seventh-day Adventists, Dr. William Samuel Sadler (1875–1969), a famous Chicago psychiatrist, and his brother-in-law Wilfred Custer Kellogg (1876–1956), a painfully shy, self-effacing, neurotic businessman. They are the subjects of chapters 2 and 6.

2

Dr. William Sadler

Willilliam Samuel Sadler was born June 14, 1875, in Spencer, Indiana, the son of Samuel Cavins Sadler and Sarah Isabelle Wilson. He was the oldest of three children. We learn from a passage in his book *The Truth About Spiritualism* (page 170) that his two younger siblings were twin sisters, "one living and one dead." I do not know the name of the sister who died. Sadler's obituary in the *Chicago Tribune* (April 27, 1969) listed Mary Sadler, a sister in Seattle, as one of his survivors. I do not know if she married or had children.

According to a biographical sketch in a Chicago Urantian periodical called *Pervaded Space* (Spring 1979), Sadler's father taught music in various Indiana towns and ran several general stores. Young William had no formal education because his mother had a fear of his catching a disease in public schools. Will's father is said to have had no interest in religion, but his mother secretly joined a Christian church. After one of their twin daughters died, both parents became converts to Seventh-day Adventism. The father spent the rest of his life as a Bible salesman.

William grew up in Wabash, Indiana, but left town at age 14 to live in Battle Creek, Michigan. For a while he worked as a bellboy and also in the kitchen of the famed Battle Creek Sanitarium run by Dr. John Harvey Kellogg. Kellogg was then the country's most prominent Seventhday Adventist. Sadler enrolled in the Adventist's Battle Creek College, of which Dr. Kellogg was then chairman of the board.

We know from a long letter Sadler wrote in 1906 to Ellen G. White, the inspired leader of the Adventist faith (the letter is reprinted in chapter 13), that Sadler became an Adventist at age 11 and was baptized into the church several years later when he was 13. William Covert, he says, was the minister who baptized him. Young Sadler was a devout Adventist while attending Battle Creek College, during which time he and Dr. Kellogg became intimate friends.

After graduating in 1894, Sadler was hired by Dr. Kellogg as salesman for a line of health foods promoted by his Sanitarium. The doctor's brother, as we shall learn in the next chapter, was William Keith Kellogg, founder of the Kellogg Cornflake Company. When Dr. John Kellogg opened his Life Boat Mission, on Chicago's decaying "skid row" section of South State Street, he decided to put Sadler in charge, but only after Sadler attended the fundamentalist Moody Bible Institute, on Chicago's north side, where he was trained in evangelistic techniques.

Dr. Kellogg also operated half a dozen other organizations in Chicago, including a home for unwed mothers. It found foster parents for their unwanted babies and tried to persuade those who were prostitutes to give up their trade. While running the Life Boat Mission, Sadler founded and for four years edited its *Life Boat Magazine*, a periodical modeled after the Salvation Army's *War Cry*. It was hawked on Chicago streets, and said to have reached a circulation of 200,000. Sadler's evangelistic fervor is reflected in what I believe was his first published book, *Self-Winning Texts, or Bible Helps For Personal Work*, issued in Chicago in 1909 by the Central Bible Supply Company.

In 1897, in Paris, Illinois, Sadler married John Kellogg's niece, Lena Celestia Kellogg (1875–1939). They had met in 1893 when she was a student nurse. Born in Abscota, Michigan, Lena was the daughter of John Kellogg's half-brother Smith Moses Kellogg. All three brothers were raised in the Seventh-day Adventist faith and lived in Battle Creek where Sister White also then lived. For many years, as we shall consider in chapter 13, Sadler was a loyal friend and great admirer of Sister White.

From 1901 until 1903 Sadler and Lena lived in the San Francisco area where they attended Cooper Medical College. The college later became part of Stanford University. I have seen letters written by Sadler to Ellen White's son in 1902 on stationery of the San Francisco Medical Missionary and Benevolent Society, 995 McAllister Street. Sadler is listed as president. Other 1902 letters to Elder William White are on the stationery of the church's California Conference, 301 San Pablo Avenue, Oakland, California. Sadler is listed as superintendent of young people's work.

It was in 1901, in San Francisco, that Sadler was ordained an elder— Adventists call their ministers elders. By 1904 the Sadlers were back in Battle Creek attending the church's American Medical Missionary College.

Sadler obtained his medical degree from this college in 1906. In 1907 he took postgraduate work at the University of Chicago's medical school, then called the Rush Medical College.

I do not know when or under what circumstances the Sadlers abandoned their Adventist faith. It is clear, however, that about 1906 both Sadler and Dr. Kellogg became deeply disturbed by flaws in Mrs. White's "Testimonies," which she insisted were divinely inspired, and by evidence that hundreds of passages in Mrs. White's books were copied from earlier works without giving credit to the real authors. Dr. Kellogg's excommunication from the Church will be covered in chapter 5 and Sadler's similar disenchantment in chapter 13.

In 1906 Sadler left Battle Creek to found the Chicago Institute of Physiologic Therapeutics, housed in a medical building at 100 North State Street. The building's number was later changed to 32 North State, and the institute's name changed to the Chicago Therapeutic Institute. It was there that Sadler established a private practice specializing in surgery. His wife, an M.D., assisted him in many operations, as did her sister Anna B. Kellogg, a registered nurse.

From 1906 to 1913 Sadler and his wife lived in the Chicago suburb of La Grange. It was during this period that he decided to abandon surgery for psychiatry. "After taking out ten gall bladers," he is quoted as saying in the *Pervaded Space* article cited previously, "there wasn't much charm left. But minds are all different." In 1910 Sadler and Lena went abroad to study psychiatry at clinics in Leeds, England, and in Vienna where for a year they attended lectures by Sigmund Freud and Alfred Adler. About 1921 Sadler moved his institute from State Street to 533 Diversey Parkway, on Chicago's near-north side. Until his death in 1969 he was the institute's head and chief psychiatrist. For 27 years he taught pastoral psychiatry at Chicago's McCormick Theological Seminary, a Presbyterian school now located near the University of Chicago.

In 1920 the Sadlers and their twelve-year-old son Bill lived in an apartment building at 2748 Pine Grove, Chicago. Living in the same building were Wilfred Kellogg, his wife Anna (Lena's sister), and their six-year-old daughter Emma Ruth. By 1922 the Sadlers had moved to 533 Diversey Parkway. I do not know whether the Kelloggs also went to 533 for a short time before they found an apartment nearby.

The La Grange, Illinois, City Directory for 1906-1907 lists Sadler and Lena as living at 38 Calender. Residing at the same address are Smith Moses Kellogg, Lena's father, and his other daughter Anna Bell. In 1908 and 1909, Smith Moses left this address, but the other three remained. Sadler and Lena are listed as physicians with offices at 100 N. State Street, Chicago, and with a La Grange residence at 56 Sixth Street. Sadler, Lena, and Lena's sister Anna are also listed as living at 56 Sixth. Anna is identified as a trained nurse. Her father has moved to 46 S. Fifth, in La Grange.

In 1912 a small ad in the *La Grange Citizen* says that Sadler and his wife are practicing medicine at 32 N. State, in Chicago, specializing in "women's and children's diseases." Their home residence continues to be in La Grange at 56 Sixth. In 1913 the Sadlers are still at this address, but now Anna is identified as Mrs. Wilfred C. Kellogg. As we shall learn in chapter 6, she and Wilfred were married in La Grange in 1912. Curiously, the La Grange *City Directory* for this year makes no mention of Wilfred. By 1914 the Sadlers and Anna have vanished from the directory, having taken up residence in Chicago. I do not know how to square all this with records of the Sadlers' trip abroad in 1910. 1 assume they maintained their La Grange residence while overseas.

From 1909 until his death in 1969 Sadler was a prolific author of books, most of them written for the general public. In Appendix A I will list more than forty of his books, many written with his wife, and many going through several editions, sometimes considerably enlarged and with a title change. Sadler never achieved high status among his peers, but his popular books on physical and mental health made him one of the nation's best known psychiatrists. His 400-page *Mind at Mischief* (1929) was a best seller. Eight of his books each exceed 400 pages. His magnum opus, *Theory and Practice of Psychiatry* (1936) has 1,231 pages and actually weighs a pound more than the *UB*. *Modern Psychiatry* (1945), a book of 896 pages, went through many reprintings. In addition to his books, Sadler also wrote scores of articles for such mass-circulation periodicals as *American Magazine* and *The Ladies' Home Journal*.

A man of enormous energy, Sadler also found time to lecture widely on the Chautauqua circuit. A doctor's thesis about his oratorical skill was written by G. Vonne Meussling for Bowling Green (Ohio) University in 1970. It is titled *William S. Sadler: Chautauqua's Medical Orator*. Although it contains a biographical chapter on Sadler, and a flawed bibliography of his books and articles, nowhere in the dissertation is any discussion of his Adventist past or a single word about his connection with the Urantia movement.

I am told that Ms. Meussling is a Urantian and that the Urantia Foundation forbade her to speak of Sadler's connection with the *UB*. In any case, this failure to mention Sadler's altered religious convictions strikes me as analogous to writing a book about Gilbert Chesterton without mentioning his conversion to Roman Catholicism, or a book about Billy Graham that concealed the fact that he is a Baptist preacher.

In spite of its enormous blanks, Meussling's thesis gives a good picture of Sadler as a spell-binding speaker. He is described as a rotund little man with a keen sense of humor, snow-white hair, thick gold-rimmed spectacles, heavy jowls (one student likened his appearance to Alfred Hitchcock), and a man who usually wore baggy gray suits, white shirts, and out-of-style neckties. Many of his students spoke of how his extroverted, outgoing platform manner sharply contrasted with efforts to keep a cold distance from them. So far no one has written an adequate biography of this complex and curious man. One has to rely mainly on Ms. Meussling's thesis, a short entry in *Who's Who in America*, and a longer one in vol. 54 of *The National Cyclopedia of American Biography*.

Lena Sadler, who obtained her medical degree from the Adventist's American Medical Missionary College in the same 1906 graduating class as her husband, became almost as well known to the public as Dr. Sadler. Until her death in 1939 she was assistant director of Sadler's institute, and, like her husband, affiliated with numerous Chicago hospitals and organizations. Both Sadlers were Republicans and members of Chicago's conservative Fourth Presbyterian Church, where Lena's funeral was held.

Starting in 1907 and continuing for more than a decade Sadler and his wife Lena were enormously popular lecturers on the Chautauqua circuit. Sadler had many topics, drawn mainly from his books, on physical and mental health. They stressed hydrotherapy and the drugless remedies favored by the Adventist Church and by his former employer Dr. John Kellogg. One of Sadler's lectures, "Men and Morals," was for men only. Lena also had a variety of lecture topics, including "Child Purity" for women only. She would be assisted on the platform by her sister Anna Kellogg, who also lectured on "Household Nursing." Occasionally Sadler's son Bill, then a little boy, would assist in health demonstrations.

It was during the Sadlers' first Chautauqua engagement that they met Sarah Mildred Willmer, an actress who specialized in reciting poems, plays, and giving prose readings. Sarah and Lena become great friends. Two of Sarah's most popular recitations were "The Sign of the Cross" and "The Woman of Samaria," the latter featuring a day in the life of Jesus. In 1912 Sarah married Edward Van Bond in a double ceremony in Sadler's La Grange home. The other couple was Anna and her cousin Wilfred Kellogg.

Mrs. Bond had joined the Sadlers in 1911 to form a company called

"The Sadlers and Miss Willmer." The four members were always booked as a team for two- or three-day engagements. A typical day would begin with a morning lecture by Anna, followed by a Medical Round Table conducted by Sadler and Lena. In the early afternoon Miss Wilhner would give a dramatic recital, then Lena would lecture. Sadler concluded the day with an evening lecture. The sequence varied from day to day, with a special program for Sundays. The meetings would be held in auditoriums or under a tent, with Sadler's books on display for sale. The company got rave reviews in local papers, where the four were often described as "a whole Chautauqua in themselves—except for music." Even music by a local orchestra would sometimes be provided as a morning prelude to the day's events.

The Sadlers had two sons. Willis, the first born, died in infancy. The second, William Samuel Sadler Jr., died at age 56 in Chicago on November 22, 1963. It was the day President John Kennedy was assassinated.

Bill II and his wife Leone Gill had three children. William Sadler III died in 1955 when he was 19. Patricia Helen is now married to Manfred K. Mundelius who owns an insurance agency in Danville, California. In 1990 Mrs. Mundelius became a trustee of the Urantia Foundation. The third child, Charles, became a professor of history at Western Illinois University, in Macomb, Illinois. He died of cancer in 1985. At one time he considered writing a history of the Urantia movement, but the project never got started. His widow Judith (Jody) works for the university's Special Education Department. As was Charles, she is a true believer in the Urantia revelation.

Leone worked for 20 years at 533 Diversey where her main job was handling UB orders, assisted by her sister Helen Gill (later Mrs. Carlson). Leone, a heavy smoker, died of lung cancer in Chicago in 1976. Helen still lives at 533.

It has been difficult to obtain facts about the life of Bill Sadler Jr. It is said that as a young man he suddenly disappeared and it was months before his parents learned from him that he had joined the Marines. Apparently he had two separate hitches in this service. Back from duty, he became a dedicated Urantian who played a major role in the preparation of the UB papers. For a brief period in 1928 he was enrolled in the College of the University of Chicago, but did not graduate. He and Leone were married in 1935.

I do not know when or why Bill and Leone divorced. I am told that this precipitated a serious fallout with his father who was furious with Bill for abandoning Leone. In turn, Bill became angry with his father for what he considered a betrayal of trust—using funds from UB sales to pay off the mortgage on his headquarters at 533 Diversey. Bill also objected to the Foundation's "slow growth" policy, arguing that the Urantian movement should be strongly promoted as an organized religion destined to sweep the world. Several people who knew Bill told me that at this time be was drinking heavily and spending most of his waking hours talking about *UB* doctrines. Bert Salyer, of Oklahoma City, now a disenchanted Urantian, described Bill to me as a chain smoker and an alcoholic.

An old-timer in the Urantian movement, who asked that his name not be mentioned, told me about his friendship with Bill and how much he admired him. He described Bill as having an unusually large head, short neck, and stocky build. He said Bill knew almost all of the *UB* by heart, could talk on almost any topic, and play the piano. Bill, my informant declared, was the most intelligent person he ever knew.

After his divorce, Bill married Urantian Florine Seres, a woman less than half his age. It was she who arranged for the publication of his two posthumous books: *A Study of the Master Universe* (1968) and a larger work, *Appendices To a Study of the Master Universe* (1975). The first book is "Dedicated to Tabamantia for reasons the author believes to be good and sufficient."

Who is Tabamantia? According to the *UB* (579) he is an agondonter of finaliter status, the chief of universe directors (565), and the "sovereign supervisor of all life-experiment planets in the universe of Nebadon" (1189). He inspected Urantia and reported it suitable for the arrival of Adam and Eve about a hundred years later (821–822). Apparently Bill II and Tabamantia were in close touch with each other.

Both of Bill's books were printed by the Second Society Foundation, a breakaway firm listed in the current Chicago phone directory as headquartered at 333 North Michigan. Bill was an energetic, popular lecturer on *UB* dogmas. One of his long talks, *Simplification of the Foreword from the Urantia Book*, was published in 1977 as a 51-page paperback by Oklahoma City's Asoka Foundation.

I found Bill's second wife, Florine, listed in the Chicago telephone book as "Florine S. Sadler, consultant, 333 North Michigan." Before he died Bill was president of Sadler and Associates, at that address, a management consulting firm he had founded in 1947. Florine was the younger sister of Urantian John J. Seres, also in the Chicago phone book as a "consultant" at 333 North Michigan. This is also the address of the Second Society Foundation which still sells Bill's two posthumous books. After Bill's death, Florine married a Mr. Hemmings of Chicago, whose first name

I do not know. They have since divorced. Florine responded to a letter by saying she would not answer any questions and that I should not try to contact her again.

Bill III's death on December 26, 1955, at age 19, occurred under mysterious circumstances still far from clear. He was at that time a third-year student at the University of Chicago. The *Chicago Tribune* (December 28, 1955) reported the opening of an inquest into the cause of death. At about 4:20, after a Christmas dinner at 533 Diversey with his mother and Dr. Sadler, his grandfather, young Bill fell into a coma while drinking a cup of coffee. Sadler tried vainly to revive him before calling an ambulance. He was later criticized for negligence in waiting such a long time.

Because an autopsy failed to reveal the cause of death, a chemical analysis was ordered by coroner Walter McCarron. The next day the *Tribune* reported that a second inquest was scheduled for February 14 to complete the chemical analysis and to allow a further police investigation. Bill Jr. testified at the first inquest that in 1953 his son had lost all sight in his left eye and vision in the other eye had deteriorated. Medical examination had failed to disclose the cause of this, but his son's condition had since improved. The *Tribune* added that Bill III had collapsed while answering a phone call. He died the following day at Columbus Hospital without recovering consciousness.

According to the *Tribune*, the hospital's first diagnosis suggested a brain tumor. Tests showed a concentration of sugar in Bill's system indicative of diabetes. Dr. Sadler is quoted as saying that his grandson's coma did not resemble one induced by barbiturates.

Sadler told the *Tribune* that Bill had been perturbed because his fianceé Sharon Russakov, 17, had decided to go to the University of Illinois, in Champaign, rather than to the University of Chicago. Miss Russakov is quoted as saying Bill had been in "excellent spirits" the night before when he escorted her home from a Christmas Eve party at the Sadlers.

On December 30 the *Tribune* reported that Sharon denied she was Bill's fianceé. She was merely a friend who had been introduced to Bill by his younger sister at a school party. Rumors of suicide persisted.

The second inquest was delayed until May. I am indebted to Urantian Buddy Roogow for finally locating the coroner's report. A complete autopsy was performed at Dr. Sadler's request. Surprisingly, no trace of a brain tumor was found. There were minor traces of barbiturates, but at such a late date it was impossible to determine the cause of death.

Alcohol had been consumed at the party the night before in the Sadler home. Bill had a prescription for sleeping pills, of which he was a heavy user. It was conjectured that a combination of alcohol with barbiturates may have done him in. He could have accidently overdosed before retiring at his grandfather's house.

About 4 P.M., after Christmas dinner, Bill received a phone call from a woman named Joan. He answered the phone holding a cup of coffee and collapsed after picking up the receiver. He did not recover consciousness before he died 24 hours later at the hospital. It came out that he had suffered blackouts on previous occasions. Dr. Sadler, who was recovering from a recent heart attack, went upstairs to bed, assuming his grandson would sleep off the coma. Not until four hours later, when Bill was still unconscious, did he call an ambulance. The trace of barbiturates in Bill's body gave rise to the rumor of suicide, though there was no evidence that an overdose of sleeping pills had been intentional. I do not yet know if reports of the final inquest were published in any Chicago paper.

Later in 1956 Bill II married Florine Seres. In a document I have seen, a Forum member named Elsie Baumgartner claimed that Florine had earlier been Bill III's fianceé, and that she was 19 at the time. I have not been able to verify either claim. Several old-timers tell me that Florine was in her early twenties. Bill II was then in his late forties.

Bill II lived seven more years. A stroke deprived him of speech. While being trained to recover the ability to talk he was hospitalized for cirrhosis of the liver. In 1963 he again went to a hospital, this time for embolisms in both legs. A few months later a heart attack ended his life. Bill and Florine were then living at 900 North Lake Shore Drive. He died in Wesley Memorial Hospital anticipating his awakening on the first mansion world.

Dr. Sadler and Lena adopted a daughter, Emma Louise Christensen, known to everyone as Christy. Tall and thin, with a happy disposition and a bright smile, Christy became the doctor's most trustworthy aide. As we shall learn, she played a crucial role in the creation of the *UB* Papers. She was twice president of the Urantia Foundation, and the only person, aside from Dr. Sadler, to receive what the Foundation called the Brotherhood's Van Award for service to the cause.

Christy was born January 29, 1890, near Mud Creek, in Gem Township, Brown County, South Dakota. She was the sixth of eight children of Nels Christensen and Rosalia Thora Nana Bald. I have been unable to determine her religious background, if any. After two years in the University of Minnesota's Extension School, in St. Paul, she became office manager for the Bureau of the Comptroller of Currency, in their Minneapolis office. In 1922 she was moved to Chicago as office manager of the National Bank Examiner's Office of the Seventh Reserve District. She held this position for 28 years until she retired about 1950.

Christy never married. She died in Chicago on May 2, 1982, at age 92. A Memorial Service at Chicago's Union League Club, on May 22, was conducted by Meredith Sprunger and Vern Grimsley, both of whom we shall meet again in chapter 18. In his address, Grimsley told the following anecdote:

> My personal very favorite memory of all my years of knowing Christy is the simple memory of our friendship. And the most touching thing that I remember from all my years of knowing and loving Christy was something that happened just this last January, when we were invited back to Chicago to celebrate her 92nd birthday. We all spent several days at 533 Diversey, but it is one very special moment which is forever emblazoned in my memory.
>
> Christy and I had been talking for several hours on the third floor of 533, and I was leaving to go buy something at the grocery store . . . I got in the elevator, closed the big door of it, then closed the metal gate and was just reaching over to touch the button to take me down to the first floor, when suddenly I heard a pounding on the big outer door of the elevator. I looked, and through that little square glass window in the elevator door, I saw Christy's face with her nose practically pressed against the glass, and she was pounding away on the elevator door with one fist and her cane that she held in the other hand.
>
> My instant reaction was to think "My heavens, there must be something wrong; maybe she's having heart pains." I quickly slid the metal gate aside and opened the door and said, "What is it, Christy, are you all right?" She said, "Yes, but I just wanted another hug before you leave." And she gave me one, and I gave her one, and that was one of the most precious moments, and precious memories, of my entire life, because my greatest memory of Christy is the memory of twenty years of her warm and loving friendship. And I can't wait to see her once again and give, and get, another good hug from Christy.

According to Reverend Sprunger, a Urantian since the mid-1950s and a friend of Sadler's, Mrs. Sadler had a dream in which she was informed by a celestial that a young lady would come to their attention and should be hired as an assistant. This occurred in 1923 when Christy was recuperating in a hospital after a taxicab accident. She would have then been 33 years old.

A different story was told to me by a Urantian friend of Bill Sadler Jr.

He said that Christy was in her late twenties when she fell on an icy sidewalk and broke her leg, or maybe some other bone. The Sadlers took her in, gave her medical attention, and later adopted her. In any case, when she died she was the last member of what was called the Contact Commission—those who were in closest contact with the man used by the supermortals as the "instrument" through whom the *UB* papers were originally transmitted, and who were the most responsible for the *UB*'s editing and publication.

It is not easy to know just what portions of Adventist doctrine Sadler retained after leaving the Church. That he kept his belief in Christianity as the best and truest of all world religions there is not the slightest doubt. In *Worry and Nervousness* (1914), in a chapter on "The Faith and Prayer Cure," he stressed the value of prayer as a therapeutic agent. "It is," he wrote, "the avenue by which the diseased mind is eliminated and the Divine Mind brought in to replace it." Although effective in any religious context, it is most effective, he writes, when combined with Christian faith:

> We are forced to recognize the therapeutic value of prayer, no matter with what system of belief or religion it may be associated; but we have spoken of prayer in this text with the thought of its being a part of practical Christianity. The author regards prayer as the master mind cure, and Christianity as the highest and truest form of psychotherapy. There can be no question that the Christian religion, when properly understood and truly experienced, possesses power both to prevent and cure numerous mental maladies, moral difficulties, and physical disorders. It must be evident to the reader that fear and doubt are disease-producing, while faith and hope are health-giving; and in the author's opinion, the highest possibilities of faith and the greatest power of hope are expressed in the Christian religion. The teachings of Christ are the greatest known destroyers of doubt and despair.
>
> No one can appreciate so fully as a doctor the amazingly large percentage of human diseases and sufferings which are directly traceable to immorality, dissipation, and ignorance—to unwholesome thinking and unclean living. The sincere acceptance of the principles and teachings of Christ with respect to the life of mental peace and joy, the life of unselfish thought and clean living, would at once remove more than one-half the difficulties, diseases, and sorrows of the human race. In other words, more than one-half of the present afflictions of mankind could be prevented by the tremendous prophylactic power of the Christian religion.
>
> Christianity applied to our modern civilization—understandingly applied, not merely believed or accepted—would so purify, uplift, and

vitalize us that the human race would immediately stand out as a new order of beings, possessing superior mental power and increased physical force. Irrespective of the future rewards of the Christian religion, laying aside all discussion of future life, it would pay any man or woman to live the Christ-life just for the mental and physical rewards which it affords here in this present world. Some day the world may awake to the point where it will recognize that the teachings of Christ are potent and powerful in the work of preventing and curing disease. Some day our wonderful boasted scientific developments, as regards mental and moral improvement, may indeed catch up with the teachings of the Christian religion.

Faith, Sadler goes on to say, is much more than mere belief:

To believe a thing is merely to accept it by our reason; to realize that no facts or logical consideration of any kind exist which can prevail against it. Faith implies such acceptance even in the face of considerations of fact or of logic; their reality may be recognized, but they are consistently ignored when they appear in relation to the object of our faith. Faith calls for a complete and unconstitutional surrender of one's whole body, soul, and spirit, to the idea or thing which is believed in. Faith, of necessity, must further include the idea of obedience to that which it accepts.

Belief only requires the cooperation of the intellectual powers, and an impartial distribution of the affections, over the whole field of those mental processes by the activity of which belief is attained. Faith demands the consecration of the whole mind, the concentration of the affections upon a given idea or upon a preconceived object. Faith demands and implies a thorough control of the emotions; the cooperation of the spiritual forces on the one hand, and the physical forces on the other. The highest known development of faith is to be found in the faith of Christianity, which represents the most all-inclusive, the most powerful and transcendent mental action, moral exercise, and spiritual force known to man. The "Faith of Jesus" is a supernatural power—divine attribute, and must not be confused with our discussions of faith in the psychologic sense.

The religions of modern times have been in imminent danger of becoming weak and effeminate. The world today needs more of the militant but wisely directed spirit of the early Christian religion. We must come to exercise more faith and manifest more determination in the pursuit of the higher and nobler aims of life. Faith is a tremendous motive power and when it once dominates the soul, it is able to harness the mind and control the body; it is able to combat disease and relieve suffering; yes, it is able to vanquish sorrow and establish peace.

Similar sentiments are expressed in many of Sadler's later books. Here is another typical passage from *Mental Mischief and Emotional Conflicts*, written in 1947 when Sadler was working hard on the Urantia revelation:

> Belief only requires the co-operation of the intellectual powers and an impartial distribution of the affections over the whole field of those mental processes by the activity of which belief is attained. *Faith demands the consecration of the whole mind*, the concentration of the affections upon a given idea or upon a preconceived object. *Faith demands and implies a thorough control of the emotions*—the co-operation of both the spiritual and the psychical forces. Its highest known development is to be found in the life and teachings of Jesus, which represent the most all-inclusive, the most powerful, and the most transcendent mental action, moral exercise, and spiritual force known to man. The "Faith of Jesus" is a mighty force—a Divine-human power—and must not be confused with the faith we discuss in a purely psychologic or theologic sense.
>
> The religions of modern times have been in imminent danger of becoming weak and effeminate. Today the world needs more of the militant but wisely directed spirit of the Carpenter's Son. We must exercise more faith and manifest more determination in the pursuit of the higher and nobler aims of life. Faith is a tremendous motive power, and when it once dominates the soul, it is able to harness the mind and control the body, to combat disease and relieve suffering; yes, it is able to vanquish sorrow and establish peace.

In a much earlier book, *The Physiology of Faith and Fear* (1912), Sadler was even more explicit in recognizing supernatural elements in Christian faith:

> The reader's attention is again called to the fact that the author is here considering the purely psychologic side of religion. We again disclaim any intention of discussing the spiritual and miraculous elements concerned in theological belief. While he recognizes the fact that any and all religions, when sincerely accepted and devoutly believed, are able profoundly to influence both mind and body; and while, as far as the body is concerned, it apparently makes no difference what brand of religion is accepted—certain physiological effects being the same, modified only by the intensity of the patient's faith—nevertheless, the author would by no means lead the reader to think that he regards the Christian religion as just one among equally good religions of the past and the present. In his personal belief he recognizes the sublime power of the true Christian religion

not only to accomplish all the desirable physiological and psychological effects herein noted, but, in addition, to bring about a host of other and marvellous spiritual manifestations and mighty moral transformations; and so, while he continues to note the fact that all forms of religious belief exert a salutary effect upon certain bodily functions, the reader is cautioned not to form the conclusion that the author would in the least detract from the belief in Christianity as the supreme and genuine religion—as a supernatural influence designed to uplift humanity in a sense entirely different from and additional to, all the various psychic and physical benefits herein noted, and which apparently result from the nominal acceptance of any form of religious belief.

While he desires to make it plain to the reader that any sort of religious belief favorably influences the psychic state and the physical functions, he desires to make it equally emphatic and plain that the author, in his own belief, recognizes in the teachings of Jesus Christ something entirely above, and different from, the other great religions of the world. The author sincerely believes that there is a distinct and definite supernatural element in the Christian religion; but since such supernatural element does not lend itself to scientific investigation and laboratory inquiry, and since this work is devoted to the study of the psychology and physiology of faith and fear, it is entirely out of place further to discuss the matter in this connection. This paragraph has been added merely to prevent any Christian reader from gaining the impression that the author does not recognize Christianity as the supreme religious belief—as a spiritual energy and a supernatural force. Paul's statement is still true, that "The world by wisdom knew not God."

Although Sadler may have later drastically modified and abandoned many aspects of his youthful beliefs, he never wavered in his conviction that Jesus was the greatest of all spiritual teachers, a view which permeates the *UB*, especially in its long Jesus section. In later years, like his friend John Kellogg, he greatly broadened his faith to accept the theory of evolution, the antiquity of the earth, and the still older age of the universe we know. If we can assume that he shared the doctrines of the *UB*, he came to reject many of the Bible's miracles, such as the Virgin Birth and the bodily resurrection of Jesus. More significantly, he abandoned the doctrine of the blood Atonement. Although he lost his faith in Sister White as an inspired prophetess, and no longer believed that Christians should return to a Saturday Sabbath, he retained (as we shall see in later chapters), many Adventist doctrines.

I do not know to what degree Sadler's early friendship with Dr. Kellogg cooled in later years. A few quotations from Kellogg appear in

Sadler's early books. In *Worry and Nervousness*, for example, there is a long excerpt from one of Kellogg's writings in which he speaks of city life as more conducive to neurotic behavior than country living. The book has a picture of a patient sitting in one of Kellogg's light baths (see the next chapter), and he follows Kellogg in stressing the great virtues of water cures and electrical therapy. One topic on which Sadler and Kellogg were in strong disagreement was over the evils of masturbation. As we shall learn in chapter *3*, Kellogg believed that what he called "self-abuse" was physically damaging to both children and adults. In many of Sadler's books, notably *Piloting Modern Youth, Mental Mischief, Living a Sane Sex Life*, and *The Theory and Practice of Psychiatry*, Sadler maintained that masturbation's only harm resulted from worry over its supposed baleful effects.

In his early books Sadler accepted most of the health views of Sister White and Dr. Kellogg, occasionally adding dubious opinions of his own. Figure 5 reproduces an amusing picture opposite page 126 of *The Physiology of Faith and Fear* (1912). It depicts an experiment Sadler says was first performed at an Eastern university, and which he personally repeated and confirmed. When the subject worked on an arithmetical problem, the rush of blood to his head tipped the plank down on the head side. When he concentrated on his feet, blood rushed to his feet and tipped the plank the other way!

On page 423 of the same book Sadler has a whimsical list of two kinds of tunes. On the left are tunes he found "uplifting" to his patients. On the right are tunes he found "depressing."

MUSIC WHICH IS GENERALLY STRENGTHENING AND STIMULATING	MUSIC WHICH IS GENERALLY WEAKENING AND DEPRESSING
Dixie.	Ben Bolt.
America.	Old Black Joe.
My Maryland.	Old Cabin Home.
Rock of Ages.	My Jesus, I Love Thee.
Yankee-Doodle.	Home, Sweet Home.
The Old Oaken Bucket.	John Brown's Body.
The Old Folks at Home.	My Jesus, I Love Thee.
My Old Kentucky Home.	Jesus, Saviour, Pilot Me.

Jesus, Lover of My Soul.	I would not Live Alway.
Nearer, My God, to Thee.	We are Tenting To-night.
Listen to the Mocking-Bird.	The Star Spangled Banner.
Onward, Christian Soldiers.	Depths of Mercy can Ever Be.
Blest be the Tie that Binds.	Do They Think of Me at Home?
All Hail the Power of Jesus' Name.	Jesus, I My Cross have Taken.
The Mighty Fortress of Our God.	Behold, a Stranger at the Door.

Sadler was still active when, as he approached 94, he died in Chicago on April 26, 1969. A few years before, he had lost a diseased eye and was wearing a glass one. His obituary in the *Chicago Tribune* credited him with having predicted as early as 1917 that human organ transplants would someday become common. In lieu of flowers, mourners were asked to make a donation to the Urantia Foundation.

3

Dr. John Kellogg

U ntil his church expelled him in 1907, John Harvey Kellogg (1852–1943) was America's best known Seventh-day Adventist. As we have seen, he was Sadler's friend, benefactor, and first employer. Both Sadler and Wilfred Kellogg married nieces of Dr. Kellogg who were sisters. Many of John Kellogg's heretical views worked their way into the *UB*.

Dr. Kellogg was born in 1852 in Tyrone Township, Livingston County, Michigan. His father, John Preston Kellogg, was first a Baptist, later a Congregational Church elder, and finally a convert to Seventh-day Adventism. A vigorous opponent of medical drugs and a strong booster of "natural" remedies, John Preston was an early supporter of the health views of Ellen White and her husband James. During abolitionist days John Preston operated on his farm an "underground railroad station" for runaway slaves. He owned a broom factory which he later moved to Battle Creek, then Adventist headquarters. As boys, both John and his younger brother William Keith worked for the factory. They were among their father's 16 children.

After almost no formal education (in those days many Adventists saw little value in educating children because of their belief that the Second Coming was close at hand), John was studying to be a teacher at Michigan State Normal College (later Eastern Michigan University) when the Church urged him to switch to medicine. Under the leadership of Mrs. White and her husband, the Adventists placed enormous emphasis on natural healing. They recommended a diet free of meat, like the supposed diet of Adam and Eve. Alcohol and tobacco were taboo, as well as tea, coffee, and strong spices. Sister White wrote book after book on diet and health, stressing the importance of rest, exercise, sunshine, fresh air, clean clothing, and of

51

course prayer. "Poisonous drugs" were to be avoided except for such natural remedies as herbs and roots.

At that time hydropathy, commonly called the "water cure," had become a fashionable craze throughout Europe and America. More than two hundred water-cure spas flourished in the United States alone, mostly in New England, along with a flood of books and periodicals promoting the craze. This, too, became part of Adventist health measures. Sister White was so enthusiastic about the healing powers of water that for many years she personally gave water cures to ailing church members.*

John had been working as a typesetter in the church's Review and Herald printing plant, in Battle Creek, when he decided on a career in medicine. His first move in this direction was inconsequential. At that time one of the nation's top advocates of water cure was Dr. Russell Thatcher Trail, author of the *The Hydropathic Encyclopedia* (1852). He edited *The Water-Cure Journal* and ran a worthless little medical school called The Hygieo-Therapeutic College, in Florence Heights, New Jersey. Lorenzo Fowler, a famous phrenologist, was on the faculty. Later, the Fowler brothers took over the publication of *The Water-Cure Journal*. Sister White at first regarded phrenology as the work of Satan, but later decided it was a genuine science, especially after convincing readings were made of her two sons' head bumps. Her early writings contain many favorable references to phrenology. In *A Solemn Appeal*, for example, she frequently speaks of "amativeness," a term used only by phrenologists.

John attended Trail's shabby college for five months before realizing that he was learning nothing. His half-brother Merritt Gardner Kellogg (their father had twice married) also attended Trail's college along with Mrs. White's two sons. Merritt, too, became an Adventist doctor, though as far as I know his only medical degree was from the Trail school. After his first wife, ten years his senior, died, he married an Australian Irish woman

---

*The danger of relying solely on nature cures or other forms of alternative medicine is that one can die as a result. The great popularity of water cures led to many such tragedies. I willcite only one. John Roebling, the engineer who designed the Brooklyn Bridge, had a foot amputated after an accident that occurred while surveying the bridge's piers. His faith in hydrotherapy was so strong that he refused medical treatment and promptly died of preventable tetanus. (I am indebted to correspondent Charles Hruska for calling this to my attention.) Details are given in David McCullough's book *The Great Bridge* (1983).

Richard Metcalfe's *Rise and Progress of Hydrotherapy* (1906) is a detailed history of the water-cure craze. For a scrupulously documented account of Adventist health practices and thecommanding role of Sister White, see Ronald Numbers' excellent book *Prophetess of Health: A Study of Ellen G. White* (1976). On the history of hydropathy in the United States, see *The Great American Water-Cure Craze*, by Harry Weiss and Howard Kemble (1967), and *Wash and Be Healed*, by Susan Caylett (1987).

of 21–42 years his junior! He remained a loyal Adventist until his death in California in 1921.

Eager for more reputable medical instruction and encouraged by the Whites, John enrolled in the College of Medicine at the University of Michigan. From there he transferred to the Bellevue Hospital Medical School, in Manhattan, where he finally obtained a legitimate degree in 1875.

The Adventists had earlier founded the Western Health Reform Institute, in Battle Creek. In 1876 John, then 24, was made director. The following year he changed the institute's name to the Battle Creek Sanitarium, coining "sanitarium" by altering the spelling of "sanitorium." For 67 years, until his death in 1943, he remained the sanitarium's head and chief surgeon. In 1931 he founded a similar sanitarium in Miami, Florida, where he liked to spend winters. The U.S. Army acquired the Miami Sanitarium in 1943.

The Battle Creek Sanitarium, popularly called "The San," became the country's most famous health resort. One could fill pages with just the names of famous persons who were treated there. They included such business men as the Rockefellers, Fords, and Du Ponts; J. C. Penney, Montgomery Ward, S. S. Kresge, Harry Sinclair, and hundreds of others. European royalty came frequently to the San. George Bernard Shaw, Thomas Edison, and President William Taft were among the doctor's strongest boosters. Dr. Kellogg (from now on "Dr. Kellogg" will refer only to John Harvey, not to his half-brother Merritt) became much better known than Sister White.

Dr. Kellogg was 45 when in 1887 he married one of his employees, Ella E. Eaton. She had graduated at Alfred University, then a Seventh-day Baptist College in New York. Although the marriage ceremony was Seventh-day Adventist, Ella remained a lifelong Seventh-day Baptist. For reasons unknown, the Kelloggs were unable to have children, but they reared no fewer than 42 orphans or otherwise disadvantaged youngsters, of whom fewer than a dozen were legally adopted. The burden of caring for them rested mainly on Ellen. She died in 1920 at age 67. Of several biographies of Dr. Kellogg, the best and most trustworthy is *John Harvey Kellogg, M.D.*, by Richard W. Schwarz, an Adventist historian. I will make no effort even to summarize the bewildering variety of schools and other organizations Dr. Kellogg founded and ran during his long career. The most important was The American Medical Missionary College, in Chicago. In 1910 it merged with the University of Illinois Medical School.

Dr. Kellogg became a world famous surgeon. He made frequent trips abroad to study the latest techniques, and is said to have performed more than 22,000 operations. About a third of them were on charity patients. It is always difficult for laymen to rate a surgeon's knowledge and skill. For all I know, the doctor was an excellent surgeon. Apart from this, however, it is impossible not to recognize him as an amusing, colorful crank. He accepted totally the natural health views of Sister White. Like Mrs. White he supported prohibition. He wrote an entire book, *Tobaccoism* (1923) on the evils of smoking. He was, of course, right about tobacco and even cited lung cancer as one of its awful effects. When offered a cigar, he liked to accept it solemnly, light it, then plunge it into a glass of water.

A stricter vegetarian than most of his church brethren, Dr. Kellogg never ate meat, not even eggs. He was particularly down on pickles and oysters.

> If the oyster lover would take a look with a microscope at the juice of the oysters which he swallows with so much complacency he would hesitate before risking the slimy morsel down his throat. The oyster is a scavenger; he dines on germs. His body is covered and filled with bacteria of various sorts, and the slimy juice in which he is immersed is simply alive with wriggling germs of various descriptions. (*The New Dietetics*, p. 390.)

> Pickles are unwholesome not only because of their utter indigestibility, but because the acetic acid (vinegar) with which they are saturated is a gastric poison, arresting at once the action of the saliva and giving rise to gastric catarrh and sclerosis of the liver. (*The New Dietetics*, p. 471.)

Kellogg also considered ice cream bad for the health. In *The Miracle of Life* (538) he called it an "unnatural preparation" that chills the stomach, suspends digestion, and "gives rise to fermentation and decomposition" of food already eaten.

Dr. Kellogg did not drink tea, coffee, colas, or cocoa, or use condiments. In a 1907 interview he boasted of not having used salt for thirty-five years, and that his meals consisted entirely of bread, potatoes, and fresh fruits. Rhubarb and spinach were no good because of their oxalic acid. He believed, with Sister White, in having only two meals a day.

For several years the doctor opposed milk and cheese, though he later accepted raw milk, preferring it to pasteurized. He was enthusiastic about yogurt, for dubious reasons we will come to in a moment. Candy and sweet desserts were also to be avoided. For dessert he liked to crush a banana and pour lemon juice over it. While a student at Bellevue he lived on apples and Graham crackers, with an occasional bowl of oatmeal and a potato which he baked in his room's fireplace. The doctor's dietary views are given at length in several books, notably *The Itinerary of a Breakfast* (1918), *The Natural Diet of Man* (1923), and *The New Dietetics* (1921).

How can one remove brown spots from the face? Kellogg answered like this on page 546 of *The Miracle of Life:* "The bowels must be regulated by a proper dietary, exercise, and simple hydrotherapeutic measures, and the general health must be improved. Cold bathing, the cool sitz bath (75° F. for fifteen minutes daily before breakfast), and the wet girdle are excellent measures."

A firm believer in water cures, Dr. Kellogg wrote a massive, two-volume work, *Rational Hydrotherapy* (1900), extolling the great healing powers of cold, hot, and tepid water for hundreds of ailments. *Uses of Water* (1876) was an earlier and more popularly written book on the same topic.

Although Dr. Kellogg constantly warns his readers against extravagant water-cure claims of "quacks," he goes on to make wildly extravagant claims himself. Of the "wet-sheet pack" (a wet sheet wrapped around the body), he writes in *Uses of Water:*

> The applications of the pack in treating disease are very numerous. In almost all acute diseases accompanied by general febrile disturbance, and in nearly all chronic diseases, it is a most helpful remedy if rightly managed. It is an admirable remedy for nervousness, skin diseases, and irritations of the mucous membrane. The warm pack is a remedy worth more in the treatment of children' diseases than all the drugs in the materia medica, as many physicians have proved.

He has this to say about the sitz bath—bathing in a sitting position with water above the hips:

> The sitz bath is useful for chronic congestions of the abdominal and pelvic viscera, diarrhea, piles, dysentery, constipation, uterine diseases, and genital and urinary disorders. In treating female diseases it is an indispensable remedy. It is very valuable in various nervous affections, especially those which immediately involve the brain.

Bathing the feet, we are informed, is useful in the "treatment of headaches, neuralgia, toothache, catarrh, congestion of the abdominal and pelvic organs, colds, and cold feet." It is good to know that warm water helps cold feet! A wet towel wrapped around the waist "is a very efficient remedy for constipation, chronic diarrhea, and most other intestinal disorders. It is equally valuable in dyspepsia, torpid liver, enlarged spleen, and uterine derangements."

The head bath—resting the back of the head in shallow cool water—is a "promptly efficacious remedy" for "hysteria, epilepsy, apoplexy, sunstroke, acute mania, delirium tremens, and cerebral congestions from any cause." I spare readers the doctor's comments on nose, ear, and eye baths.

The remedial effects of electricity, Dr. Kellogg states in *Uses of Water*, are increased when combined with water because water is such a good conductor of electric current. A metal plate is applied to part of the body, say the feet, and joined to one pole of a galvanic battery. The other pole has a wire going to a sponge which is then applied to the ailing part of the body while the patient sits in water. "This bath is applicable to a very large variety of conditions," Dr. Kellogg writes. "Electricity is generally acknowledged to be a powerful remedial agent; but its use requires costly apparatus." Because electric baths are much abused by "quacks and charlatans," it should "not be employed by unskilled persons."

Dr. Kellogg's *Rational Hydrotherapy* is one of the great classics of medical quackery. It must be seen to be believed. My copy is the third revised edition (1906) in a single volume three inches thick, 1,217 pages, and weighing five pounds. It has 278 illustrations, some in full color. Every disease known to man is covered, with specific instructions for the best kind of water cure. In his preface Kellogg says he began his study of water cures in 1883, making hundreds of experiments with the aid of numerous instruments, some of which he invented.

> Water, applied externally or internally, and at such temperatures as may be required, is an agent which more fully than almost any other co-operates with the healing powers of the body in resisting the onset and development of pathogenic processes. There is no other remedy by which the movements of the blood and the blood supply, both general and local, and in fact every form of vital activity, may be so readily controlled as by hydriatic applications.

Kellogg defines a "douche" as a single or multiple stream of water aimed at some part of the body. More than 30 different kinds of douches are discussed and their effect on various diseases and ailments. "Cold friction" is Kellogg's term for combining cold water applications with vigorous rubbing. He believed that the soles of the feet were connected by nerves to the bowels, genitals, and brain. "A short, very cold douche to the feet," he wrote in a passage typical of a hundred others, "combined with strong pressure (25 to 35 lbs.), dilates the vesicles of the uterus, and is hence useful in amenorrhea." Because immersing the hands in cold water contracts vessels in the brain and nose, it is useful in combating "cerebral hyperemia." And on and on and on for a thousand pages of unbelievable balderdash.

Dr. Kellogg also firmly believed in the curative power of electric lights. One of his many profitable inventions was the "electric light bath cabinet" in which one stood or sat, nude of course, to be bathed on all sides by light from strong bulbs. Kellogg introduced the machine at Chicago's 1893 World's Fair, but for some reason it became more popular in Europe than here. He invented an electric-light chair for illuminating the spine and an electric-light foot bath. He may also have been the inventor of the electric blanket. At any rate, he was among the first to make and sell them.

Among the doctor's dozens of other inventions, many of which he patented, was a mechanical horse for indoor exercise, a vibrating chair, a table on which one lay that tilted back and forth eight times per minute, and a ribbed cylinder that rotated rapidly for massaging parts of the body. His most whimsical invention was a large canvas tube. It ran from an open window to a small tent over a person's head so that on winter nights a sleeper could breathe fresh air without the room getting too cold.

Dr. Kellogg was even more prolific an author than his friend Sadler. He wrote more than fifty books, both popular and technical, and hundreds of articles for mass-circulation magazines and medical journals. Moreover, he edited numerous periodicals. The most important was an Adventist journal called originally *The Health Reformer*, edited by Sister White's husband. When Dr. Kellogg took it over he changed the name to *Good Health Magazine*. For 65 years he edited it with the help of his wife and others. Ella also found time, apart from raising 42 foster children, to write several health books of her own. Other periodicals edited by Dr. Kellogg included *The American Health Temperance Quarterly* and two technical journals, *Bacteriological World* and *The Bulletin of the Battle Creek Sanitarium*.

Like Sadler, Dr. Kellogg was small (five feet, four inches) and often called "the little doctor" by associates. He was a man of tireless energy and irrepressible optimism. In his elder years he enjoyed golf. It is said that after teeing off he would race after the ball while it was still airborne. Among his hobbies was playing the piano and violin. He could read several languages and write in a shorthand that he invented.

I have space for only a few more of Dr. Kellogg's controversial opinions. He opposed soft beds. During one summer he slept on a hard floor thinking it would correct a tendency to round shoulders. He opposed aspirin on the grounds that pain was God's warning to stop the bad habits causing the pain. He opposed vaccinations, refusing to be vaccinated for smallpox even though Sister White did not refuse. He recommended a cold bath every morning and daily change of underwear. Once a week, he believed, one should drink a glass of water every hour during the day to flush out poisons.

The doctor's most unfortunate foray into fringe medicine was his enthusiasm for colon hygiene. Elie Metchnikoff, a Russian chemist, started this fad by claiming that "autointoxication" was a debilitating illness caused by toxic wastes in the lower intestine. The view was taken up in France by Charles Bouchard, a physician. In England, Sir Arbuthnot Lane began the practice of curing patients of supposed autointoxication by removing parts of the colon, a practice that peaked in America and abroad about 1915. Dr. Kellogg wrote two books about the craze: *Colon Hygiene* (1912) and *Autointoxication* (1918). One of the most shameful periods of his life was when he tried to cure autointoxication by removing large sections of lower colons, a practice that raises serious doubts about the doctor's wisdom as a surgeon.

Long after the colon mania faded, the doctor continued to blame a toxic colon for numerous diseases, senility, pimples, colds, and even tooth decay! He regarded constipation as one of the most common causes of autointoxication, "the most destructive blockade that has ever opposed human progress." The faster the body's wastes passed through the body, the better. Having just one bowel movement a day produces "constipation of a pronounced degree."

> Train the bowels to move three times a day. After breakfast, after dinner or luncheon and before retiring are the times when residues are ready for dismissal. If an extra movement occurs before breakfast, so much the better.

To facilitate these bowel movements, one must have a proper meatless diet, with plenty of roughage, adequate exercise, and a dose of paraffin oil to lubricate the intestines. Moreover, instead of sitting upright on a high commode, one should always assume a squat position. Kellogg assured his readers that if all these practices were followed, there would be no foul odors in the bathroom! The doctor's fondness for yogurt rested on his belief that it introduced benign bacteria into the colon where they combated toxic bacteria.

Dr. Kellogg's popularly written book *The Itinerary of a Breakfast* (1918) ostensibly follows the course of a breakfast from mouth to anus, but actually is another treatise on the evils of autointoxication. It is, he writes in his preface, "the most universal of all maladies, and the source of autointoxication is the colon with its seething mass of putrefying food residues." A primary purpose of the book, he continues, is to combat the myth that one bowel movement a day is sufficient. "Food residues and wastes should be evacuated at least three times a day, or after every meal." Most people are like "poor house-broken dogs." They "pay for this sinister education an infinite price, not only in misery and inefficiency, but in deadly disease and shortened life."

The whole civilized portion of the human race is house-broken. The mother or nurse of every infant begins the work of training the child to control its bowels, which means to thwart the automatic process by which the wastes are normally dismissed from the body, and by the time the child is two years old it is well house-broken and hence constipated. In this respect the infant house dog learns faster than the human infant.

A house-broken colon is a damaged colon. The natural automatic process of discarding the body wastes demands a prompt response to the "call" for evacuation. As soon as the pelvic colon, the discharging gate, is filled and lifted ready for action, a desire for evacuation is experienced. When the fecal matters begin to pass into the rectum the desire becomes so pronounced that it must be firmly resisted to avoid immediate evacuation. After a time the desire disappears, but the fecal wastes remain in the rectum. The "call" is now lost. It may return later when the rectum is still more distended by the advance into it from the pelvic colon of additional waste matters. This "call" may be resisted also, and so the rectum may become distended to the extreme limit and will no longer give notice of the entrance of feces even when it has been artificially emptied. In other words, the "call" is permanently lost, the rectum is paralyzed.

Thousands of sufferers from constipation never have a desire for evacuation except when a laxative drug has been taken.

When the call is lost, no warning is given of the condition of the colon and accumulation of waste matters may occur to an astonishing extent. Once or twice a week, perhaps, a dose of salts or of some other cathartic is taken for a sort of housecleaning and the rest of the time, filthy, putrefying wastes fill and distend the colon and cause injuries which in many instances can never be repaired.

Semi-civilized people and savages have a keen appreciation of the importance of prompt attention to the automatic demands of the body. A medical missionary who had spent many years in Arabia told the writer that a common objection offered by the tribal Arab to living in Aden was the necessity for looking up a suitable place for evacuation in compliance with the law.

A new and sensitive colon conscience must be developed among civilized people if the world is to be saved from the soul- and body- and even race-destroying effects of universal constipation and world wide autointoxication.

The universally prevalent idea that one bowel movement daily is sufficient is proof of the universal prevalence of constipation. One bowel movement means constipation of a pronounced degree. X-ray examination after an opaque meal shows that persons whose bowels move once a day are constantly carrying in their colons the putrefying residues of five to ten meals or even a larger number. The colon is never empty even after a movement, and toxemia is present and often shown in the coated tongue, foul breath, headache, depression, and other indications usually present.

One bowel movement a day is very marked constipation. (pp. 91–93)

Failure to move the bowels three times a day was seen by Dr. Kellogg as a primary cause of colon cancer. As for stomach cancer, he suspected (*The New Dietetics*, page 908) that it was caused by the fact that wives pour their husband's coffee first, hence the poor man drinks it at too high a temperature.

Even eye ailments can result from improper bowel-moving habits. I quote from *The New Dietetics* (pages 925–26):

A young woman of eighteen years found her sight failing. Examination by an eye specialist showed that the young woman's eye accommodation was so much impaired that she needed glasses such as are usually worn by a person of fifty years. By a change of regimen and improvement of bowel action, as recommended in this work, the abnormality in a few weeks disappeared and her eyes were young again.

A college professor of fifty years, wearing glasses adapted to a presbyopic person of his age, after following for a few months the regimen recommended in these pages found his eyes improved to such a degree that he had the same range of accommodation as a normal person of thirty-five years. . . .

In view of the above facts, it is evident that the eye is very sensitive to conditions which may result from errors in diet, particularly intestinal toxemia. In both acute and chronic eye affections, thorough attention should be given to elimination of food residues by the aid of a laxative diet and the diet should be strictly antitoxic. The intestinal flora should be changed by an efficient application of the fruit regimen with lactose or lactodextrin and this should be from time to time repeated whenever the stools show any trace of putridity.

In an article on "The Cause of Colds," in his *Good Health Magazine* (January 1913), Kellogg listed autointoxication as the most common cause, with overeating (especially flesh foods) as the next major cause. Meats swarm with harmful bacteria, he warned, "capable of producing endless mischief when they take possession of the intestine." Elsewhere he put it more colorfully: "Each juicy morsel of meat is fairly alive and swarming with the identical micro-organisms found in a dead rat in a closet or the putrefying carcass of a cow and in barnyard filth." (I found this quote in the chapter on "Muscular Vegetarianism," in James Whorton's excellent book *Crusaders For Fitness: The History of American Health Reformers*, Princeton University Press, 1982.) Other causes of colds include artificial heat, fatigue, alcohol, tobacco, tea, coffee, heavy clothing, and rubber rain-coats which "tend to hold the perspiration upon the body, and thus, re-ducing the vigor of the skin, pave the way for colds."

What is the best way for a person susceptible to colds to avoid them? Kellogg answered this way in *The Miracle of Life* (page 553): "Take a cold bath every morning, followed by vigorous rubbing and exercise out of doors for half an hour."

In his *The New Dietetics* (pages 413–16) Kellogg lists almost every ail-ment known to man as partially caused by meat eating and relieved by shifting to a fleshless diet. The list includes kidney diseases, arthritis, cir-rhosis of the liver, gallstones, cancer, prostatitis, tuberculosis, asthma, appendicitis, skin disorders, migraine, epilepsy, and many others.

Kellogg was so horrified by the eating of pig meat that he wrote a booklet about it titled *Pork: Or the Dangers of Pork Eating Exposed* (Good Health Publishing Company, 1897). The doctor's rhetoric is so marvelous that I must quote two passages:

Look at that object in a filthy mud-hole by the roadside. At first, you dis-tinguish nothing but a pile of black, slimy mud. The dirty mass moves! You think of a reptile, a turtle, some uncouth monster, reveling in his Sty-gian filth. A grunt! The mystery is solved. The sound betrays a hog. You avert your face and hasten by, sickened with disgust. Stop, friend, admire your savory ham, your souse, your tripe, your toothsome sausage in its native element. A dainty beast, isn't he!

Gaze over into that sty, our pork-eating friend. Have you done so before? and would you prefer to be excused? Quite likely; but we will show you a dozen things you did not observe before. See the contented brute quietly reposing in the augmented filth of his own ordure! He seems to feel quite at home, doesn't he? Look a little sharper, and scrutinize his skin. Is it smooth and healthy? Not exactly so. So obscured is it by tetter, and scurf, and mange, that you almost expect to see the rotten mass drop off as the grunting creature rubs it against any projecting corner which may furnish him a convenient scratching-place.

Do you imagine that the repulsiveness of this loathsome creature is only on the outside? that within everything is pure and wholesome? Vain delusion! Sickening, disgusting, as is the exterior, it is, in comparison with what it covers, a fair cloak, hiding a mass of disease and rottenness which grows more superlatively filthy as we penetrate deeper and deeper beneath the skin.

I spare sensitive readers Kellogg's description of the tapeworm, which he finds common in pork, or his claims that pork eating causes consumption, scrofula, leprosy, and other terrible diseases.

What did Sadler think of all this nonsense? In his early books on health, especially in *Worry and Nervousness* (1914), he looked favorably on Dr. Kellogg's extreme views. He defended autointoxication, hydrotherapy, light baths, electrical stimulation, and warned against the evils of alcohol, tobacco, and meat. "Tea and coffee come next in the list of popularly used poisons."

In many of his early books Sadler urged his readers to abandon the tobacco habit "at once." (Discontinuing tea and coffee can be spread over a month's time.) Here are his suggestions for giving up smoking, from *Worry and Nervousness* (p. 411):

Some patients are able to give up their tobacco without a struggle, even when the habit is of years standing, while others succeed only after a severe fight or after repeated attempts. We are never able to estimate the hold which tobacco has upon a given patient, and we are not, therefore, in position to estimate the effort which will be required to gain one's freedom from this drug habit. I have found the so-called silver nitrate treatment of the cigarette habit valuable—it at least possesses a psychological value—in that it represents something definite being done for the "cure" of the patient. Other aids in breaking up the nicotine habit are the use of Turkish or Russian baths, the wet sheet pack, and the electric light bath. Electricity, preferably in the form of galvanism to the spine, fomentations to the spine, leg baths with cold applications to the head, fomentations or arc light over the stomach and liver, warm baths and cold salt rubs, are all effective measures in relieving the nervousness from which so many patients suffer immediately after giving up tobacco. Graduated cold baths may also be given daily in connection with these eliminative procedures.

In his later years Sadler became more skeptical of the eccentric medical opinions of Sister White and Dr. Kellogg. There is no reference to tea, coffee, alcohol, or tobacco in Sadler's 1943 book *Mastery of Worry and Nervousness*. He himself backslid with respect to tobacco. I do not know if he began eating meat, or took occasional drinks of tea, coffee, or booze, but he did acquire the smoking habit. Richard Schwarz, the Adventist historian who wrote the biography of Dr. Kellogg cited earlier, told me that when he interviewed Sadler the doctor made an unsuccessful effort to hide the fact that he had become a heavy pipe smoker. Lena, Leone, and others at 533 Diversey were cigarette puffers. Christy liked to smoke cigarettes in a long holder. Visitors to Sadler's headquarters often complained of finding the rooms thick with smoke.

Here is a sensible passage on autointoxication from Sadler's *Modern Psychiatry* (1945):

In so-called *endogenous* toxins, or chemical poisons, we are dealing with our old friend "autointoxication." During the opening years of this century, particularly in France, many physicians were devoted to this idea of self-poisoning. Even today many American physicians believe that nervous exhaustion is largely caused by this so-called autointoxication. My observations do not confirm this contention. In my opinion the cases are very rare where a neurosis or psychosis is brought about by this supposed absorption of deleterious toxins from the alimentary tract. I am well aware that many hypochondriacs and other victims of nervous depression, together with numerous insane sufferers, have bad breaths, and that stubborn constipation is sometimes associated with these disorders; but I look upon this delayed intestinal elimination as the result of the lowered nerve tone, the emotional and psychologic depression which is such a prominent feature of these disorders, rather than as the cause of all these mental and nervous troubles.

Practically all the arguments formerly brought forward to prove autointoxication to be a clinical entity and a cause of mental and nervous disorders, have been largely disproved. We have about reached the place where we must look upon autointoxication as a medical bugaboo, on the one hand, and as an alibi of chronic neurasthenics, on the other.

Although Dr. Kellogg occasionally changed an opinion, he always held every new view with the same assurance that he had for the old one. For many years he advocated "Fletcherizing," a practice of masticating all food to a liquid form before swallowing. This crazy view was put forth by Horace Fletcher, one of the great food crackpots of all time. Dr. Kellogg finally decided that Fletcherizing reduced the stomach's needed roughage and thus led to autointoxication.

In his 1921 book *The New Dietetics* (this work of more than a thousand pages is one of the great crank diet books of all time), Dr. Kellogg devotes a chapter to mastication. Fletcher was not the first to discover its value, Kellogg writes. He himself discovered it "more than fifty years ago as a result of an elementary study of physiology." Even before that, it had been recommended in a "great work" titled *Digestion* by an eighteenth-century Italian named Spallanzani.

Unfortunately, Kellogg tells us, Fletcher carried mastication to absurd extremes. He recommended that food even in liquid form, such as soups and purees, should be thoroughly masticated before swallowing. Moreover, he believed in limiting one's diet to soft, easily masticated foods. Here is the stirring conclusion of Kellogg's mastication chapter:

> One result of the use of soft foods which required little chewing was rapid decay of his teeth. On his various visits to Battle Creek, he was constantly in the hands of a dentist, who told the writer more than once that he was astonished at the bad condition in which he found Mr. Fletcher's teeth, and at the rapidity with which they were undergoing decay.
>
> But another and a still more serious result of the soft diet, wholly free from indigestible elements, was a most obstinate constipation. Mr. Fletcher told me on several occasions that his bowels moved only once or twice a week.
>
> After a time he came to look upon this chronic constipation as a great advantage, and as proof of the virtue of extra mastication. He argued that thorough chewing secured such perfect digestion and such complete absorption and utilization of the food that there was left no residue for germs to act upon, and so was a sort of sterilizing process. As proof of this, he offered the fact that the small hard stools which he dismissed from his colon at intervals of several days were almost odorless.*
>
> Mr. Fletcher overlooked the important facts that the bile and mucus of the intestine are highly putrescible materials and that the odorless character of dry fecal masses is the result of the nearly complete absorption of skatol and indol during their long retention in the colon. This was proven

---

* Perhaps Dr. Kellogg should have operated on Fletcher's nose.

to be true in his own case. A mild laxative gave rise to a stool which greatly astonished him by its loathsomeness.

Mr. Fletcher was so carried away with this idea that for some time, at least, he made quite a hobby of it, and it came to be generally understood that infrequency of bowel movements was a regular part of the Fletcher regime, or "Fletcherism," as he preferred to call it.

There is reason to believe that at last Mr. Fletcher saw his error and endeavored to correct it, at least so far as his own habits were concerned. But, unfortunately, it was too late. The mischief had been done. His vital stamina and resistance to disease had been exhausted by many years' struggle against colon poisons, and he died of chronic bronchitis, doubtless due to the toxemia from which he had long suffered.

Mr. fletcher's experience inculcates the lesson that there is no simple panacea for the ravages of time. Long life cannot be made sure by any simple formula. Thoroughgoing obedience to all the laws of "biologic living" is the price which must be paid. "For whosoever shall keep the whole law, and yet offend in one point, he is guilty of all," says Holy Writ.

Although the little doctor, unlike many naturopaths and other fringe medical groups, fully accepted the germ theory of disease, then slowly gaining acceptance, he was, as Schwarz says in his biography of Kellogg, "not altogether clear as to the way in which bacteria spread from place to place."

"Don't kill the fly," he said on one occasion. "Let him live. He is one of our best friends. He is a sanitary sheriff with a commission from the Creator to arrest and devour these agents of disease and death when they get into our dwellings." Within three years, however, the doctor changed his mind, and recognized that the common housefly was a major carrier of disease. He saw it as an evidence of filth which needed to be eliminated. (p. 226)

Dr. Kellogg was thin in his youth, with dark hair and black beard. In later years, when he became a trifle plump and his hair turned white, he sported a neatly trimmed white mustache and white Van Dyke beard that made him look like Buffalo Bill. After the turn of the century he dressed entirely in white—white suit, overcoats, shirts, socks, hats, shoes, and even white-rimmed spectacles. He owned a white cockatoo which he liked to display on a shoulder. The little doctor was firmly convinced that white clothing was best for one's health.* He even performed some plant experiments to prove it. Was it possible, I sometimes fancy, that white unconsciously symbolized the doctor's former love and admiration for Sister White? Needless to add, his white attire also was a startling attention getter that he surely enjoyed.

Outside Adventist circles, Dr. Kellogg is best remembered today as the father of breakfast cereals. He began producing them from rice, corn, and wheat in his Sanitas Food Company. Later it became the Battle Creek Food Company. The firm also sold various kinds of bread, drugless "natural" laxatives, and "vegetable meats" made from nuts and legumes.

Dr. Kellogg's younger brother, William Keith (1860–1951), was manager and accountant of the Battle Creek Food Company from 1880 until 1906 when the two brothers had a bitter falling out. Will broke away to form his own company, the Kellogg Toasted Corn Flake Company. For a while Wilfred Kellogg, Sadler's brother-in-law, was its business manager. Dr. Kellogg carefully avoided putting sugar into his cornflakes. To his great dismay, brother Will added sugar to make his manufactured flakes more tasty.

Dr. Kellogg claimed that the idea for flaked cereals came to him in a dream shortly after a lady patient in the San broke her false teeth on a hard piece of zwieback. This impressed the doctor of the need for a breakfast food easier to chew. The little doctor also claimed he was the first to make peanut butter. As the story goes, an assistant accidentally smashed a peanut and found that the pulp tasted good. The doctor was said to have given the man fifty dollars for his discovery. (This may be a myth. In *The New Dietetics* Kellogg credits himself with the idea of mashing peanuts to make the butter.)

In 1913, after the courts invalidated Dr. Kellogg's patents for flaked cereals, some forty rival companies were flourishing in Battle Creek. Most were short-lived. The one that lasted longest was founded in 1895 by

---

*Dr. Kellogg defended white clothing as early as 1904 in a section headed "White Garments Preferable to Colored," in his book *The Miracle of Life*. Here is a portion of what he had to say:

On the whole, white garments offer advantages over those of any other color, for the reason that they transmit a considerable amount of light. Contact of light with the skin is necessary for its health. Exposure of the skin to the direct rays of the sun is also advantageous and promotive of skin cleanliness, as by this means many disease-producing germs which accumulate upon the skin may be destroyed, even though they may have escaped removal by the bath.

The exhortation of the prophet, "Come ye, and let us walk in the light of the Lord" (Isa. 2:5), has a physical as well as a spiritual application. Light is energizing and vitalizing to a marvelous degree. The body of one who clothes himself in white garments is continually bathed in light during the hours of daylight. It is the universal custom of the peasantry in Mexico and other hot countries to clothe themselves in white garments at all seasons, a custom which might with advantage be adopted in all civilized countries.

Charles Williams Post, who had once been a patient in the San. He began making grape nuts (which contained neither grapes nor nuts), Postum (named after himself), and a brand of corn flakes he first called Elijah's Manna. Later it became Post Toasties, a cereal so popular that his company became Will Kellogg's chief rival.

Post was even more eccentric than Dr. Kellogg. He consulted mediums. In the panhandle of Texas he established Post City (now called only Post) where he tried vainly to make rain by exploding large charges of dynamite. He got the idea from a widespread superstition that it usually rains after violent war battles. In 1914, aged 59 and in ill health, he shot himself to death. General Foods took over his company in 1929.

There were intense legal battles between Dr. Kellogg and his brother over the use of the name Kellogg. In 1917 the doctor lost a suit to prevent Will from using the name. In 1930 Will established the W. K. Kellogg Foundation, a philanthropic organization with billion-dollar assets that still flourishes in Battle Creek. Dr. Sadler was one of its honorary trustees. Will was a genius at effective advertising. In 1915 he toured the United States in a specially built car 37 feet long. The estrangement of the two brothers never healed.

Like Sadler, Dr. Kellogg was an ardent supporter of eugenics. In 1906 he founded an organization that later took the name Race Betterment Foundation. Sir Francis Galton, who started the modern eugenics movement, was opposed to the notion that traits acquired by a species could be transmitted to progeny. Dr. Kellogg, who in his later years accepted evolution, believed that acquired traits were transmitted to children. Good health, obtained by what he liked to call "biologic living," was hereditary. The goals of the Race Betterment Foundation were "to call attention to the dangers which threaten the race; for research and discovery of causes of race deterioration, and to initiate activities to promote radical reforms in habits of living."

The Race Betterment Foundation sponsored several conferences at which prominent educators and scientists spoke. Although the conferences were widely publicized, the foundation expired soon after Dr. Kellogg's death. As we shall see, Dr. Sadler's books on eugenics were greatly indebted to Dr. Kellogg's views.

Although not a great orator, Dr. Kellogg, like Sadler, was a popular lecturer on the Chautauqua circuit, and to hundreds of other groups. Politically he was, again like Sadler, a Republican. He supported Herbert Hoover for president, and in 1936 supported Alf Landon.

In personality, the little doctor was a mixture of kindness, arrogance, egotism, and biblical piety. It was said that if a medical conference of several days failed to show him proper respect, he would leave after the first day. He disliked delegating authority, was jealous of colleagues, and authoritarian toward employees. He had a sharp, sarcastic tongue, and a tendency to dominate conversations by speaking rapidly and doing most of the talking. He surrounded himself with yes-men, and was impatient with anyone who disagreed with him. I have been unable to learn the extent to which he and Sadler remained friends. I suspect that each man envied the other's reputation.

Among the doctor's books, the most elaborate was *The Home Handbook of Domestic Hygiene* and *Rational Medicine* (1880). Lavishly illustrated, it ran to more than 1,600 pages and went through endless revised editions. Will Durant wrote that the doctor's *New Dietetics* (1921) was among the one hundred best books ever published! The doctor's most important theological work, *The Soul and the Resurrection* (1879), still in print, continues to be one of the best defenses ever written of the Adventist doctrine of soul-sleep until the day of Resurrection. Of all the doctor's many books, however, the most widely read was *Plain Facts For Old and Young*, published by the Adventists in 1877 when the doctor was 24. He claimed to have written it in two weeks. The book remained in print for forty years, going through endless revisions and enlargements. My 1884 edition is 512 pages.

Before the Flood, Kellogg tells us in this book, human corruption had become so great that only eight persons were fit to survive in Noah's Ark. That "lustful generation with their filthy deeds" were expunged from the earth, but humanity soon fell again into vice. Of all vices, the two worst are illicit sex and masturbation. More than a third of *Plain Facts*, almost 200 pages, are devoted to what Dr. Kellogg likes to call "the solitary vice." He considers this a sin even greater than fornication, an evil with "no parallel except in sodomy." Here is a typical passage:

> The sin of self-pollution is one of the vilest, the basest, and the most degrading that a human being can commit. It is worse than beastly. Those who commit it place themselves far below the meanest brute that breathes. The most loathsome reptile, rolling in the slush and slime of its stagnant pool, would not demean itself thus. It is true that monkeys sometimes have the habit, but only when they have been taught it by vile men or boys. A boy who is thus guilty ought to be ashamed to look into the eyes of an honest dog. Such a boy naturally shuns the company of those

who are pure and innocent. He cannot look with assurance into his mother's face. It is difficult for any one to catch his eye, even for a few seconds. He feels his guilt and acts it out, thus making it known to every one. Let such a boy think how he must appear in the eyes of the Almighty. Let him only think of the angels, pure, innocent, and holy, who are eyewitnesses of his shameful practices. Is not the thought appalling? Would he dare commit such a sin in the presence of his father, his mother, or his sisters? No, indeed. How, then, will he dare to defile himself in the presence of Him from whose all-seeing eye nothing is hid?

One can understand Dr. Kellogg's antipathy toward self-abuse, which reflected the opinion of many writers of the time, but it is not easy to comprehend how a man with a medical degree from Bellevue could crank out such rubbish about the causes, symptoms, and baleful health effects of the practice. Among the many causes, he cites evil associates, corruption in the schools, wicked nurses, constipation, piles, irritable bladder, too warm a covering at night, lying on one's stomach or back, poor heredity, evil thoughts, tobacco, booze, candy, and spices. "Tea and coffee," he declares, "have led thousands to perdition in this way."

Here are some signs that give parents clues about the practice of self-abuse by their children: lassitude, sudden disposition changes, early symptoms of tuberculosis, stunted growth, insomnia, fickleness, love of solitude, round shoulders, stooped posture, weak back, bashfulness, boldness, mock piety, mental confusion, shuffling gait, pain in the joints, paleness, acne, fingernail biting, lackluster eyes, fondness for salt, voracious appetite, heart palpitations, bed wetting, and obscene speech. The use of tobacco, we are told, "is good presumptive evidence that a boy is also addicted to a practice more filthy."

Some of the results of masturbation, according to the doctor, are enlarged prostate, urinary diseases, piles, prolapse of the rectum, deformity of the penis, atrophied testicles, too frequent wet dreams, impotence, consumption, indigestion, epilepsy, poor vision and hearing, and of course insanity. Females who masturbate incline toward cancer of the womb, atrophied breasts, sterility, and most of the effects cited above.

On masturbation as a cause of insanity, here is what the pious doctor wrote:

"Religious insanity," so-called, may justly be attributed to this cause in a great proportion of cases. The individual is conscience-smitten in view of his horrid sins, and a view of his terrible condition—ruined for both worlds, he fears—goads him to despair, and his weakened intellect fails; reason is dethroned, and he becomes a hopeless lunatic. His friends, knowing nothing of a real cause of his mysterious confessions of terrible sin, think him over-conscientious, and lay the blame of his insanity upon religion, when it is solely the result of his vicious habits, of which they are ignorant.

In other cases, the victim falls into a profound melancholy from which nothing can divert him. He never laughs, does not even smile. He becomes more and more reserved and taciturn, and perhaps ends the scene by committing suicide. This crime is not at all uncommon with those who have gone the whole length of the road of evil. They find their manhood gone, the vice in which they have so long delighted is no longer possible, and, in desperation, they put an end to the miserable life which nature might lengthen out a few months if not thus violently superseded.

If the practice is continued uninterruptedly from boyhood to manhood, imbecility and idiocy are the results. Demented individuals are met in no small numbers inside of hospitals and asylums, and outside as well, who owe to this vice their awful condition. Plenty of half-witted men whom one meets in the every-day walks of life have destroyed the better half of their understanding by this wretched practice. . . .

Reader, have you ever seen an idiot? If you have, the hideous picture will never be dissipated from your memory. The vacant stare, the drooping, drooling mouth, the unsteady gait, the sensual look, the emptiness of mind,—all these you will well remember. Did you ever stop to think how idiots are made? It is by this very vice that the ranks of these poor daft mortals are being recruited every day. Every visitor to an insane asylum sees scores of them; ruined in mind and body, only the semblance of a human being, bereft of sense, lower than a beast in many respects, a human being hopelessly lost to himself and to the world!—oh, most terrible thought!—yet once pure, intelligent, active, perhaps the hope of a fond mother, the pride of a doting father, and possibly possessed of natural ability to become greatly distinguished in some of the many noble and useful walks of life; now sunk below the brute through the degrading, destroying influence of a lustful gratification.

Boys, are you guilty of this terrible sin? Have you even once in this way yielded to the tempter's voice? Stop, consider, think of the awful results, repent, confess to God, reform. Another step in that direction and you may be lost, soul and body. You cannot dally with the tempter. You must escape now or never. Don't delay.

How should parents cure children of this terrible vice? Dr. Kellogg suggests bandaging the sex organ, covering it with a cage, or tying the child's hands to a bedpost. As for adults, "If a lewd thought enters the mind, dispel it at once." One should sleep always on the side, and "if supper as been taken, the right side is preferable." A knotted towel attached to the back will prevent back sleeping. Bed pillows should be hard, covers thin. "The floor, with a single folded blanket beneath the sleeper, is better than a soft bed." Daily baths are indispensible. Bathing the genitals in old water before retiring is another big help.

The little doctor was convinced that meat, tobacco, and alcohol contribute to the impulse to masturbate. "Wine, beer, tea, and coffee should be taken under no circumstances. The influence of coffee in stimulating the genital organs is notorious." Chocolate, too, must be avoided. "It is recommended" only by those who "suppose it to be harmless, being ignorant of the fact that it contains a poison practically identical with that of tea and coffee."

Electricity applied to the penis or vagina is also effective. "Probably no single agent will accomplish more than this remedy when skillfully applied. It needs to be carefully used and cannot be trusted in the hands of those not acquainted with the physical properties of the remedy and scientific methods of applying it."

Dr. Kellogg did not overlook prayer:

We cannot forbear to add a word further respecting the worth of religion in aiding these sufferers. If there is any living creature who needs the help of true religion, of faith in God, in Christ, and in the efficacy of prayer, it is one of these. If there is any poor mortal who can not afford to be deprived of the aid of a sympathizing Saviour, it is one who has enervated his will, degraded his soul, and depraved his body by the vile habit of self-abuse. A compassionate Redeemer will succor even these defiled ones, if they truly "hunger and thirst" after purity, and if they set about the work of reforming themselves in good earnest, and with right motives.

The little doctor's views on self-abuse were echoed by Sister White. Her first health book was *An Appeal to Mothers: The Great Cause of the Physical, Mental, and Moral Ruin of Many of the Children of Our Time* (Battle Creek: Steam Press, 1874). It is a paperback booklet of 63 pages, the first 30 devoted to Sister White's poorly written, rambling, repetitious tract on the horrors of masturbation.

Although Mrs. White recognizes that not all youths engage in this "secret vice," an astonishing number do. She sees it as a major cause of headaches, colds, dizziness, nervousness, pain in the limbs, back, shoulders, and sides, loss of appetite, insomnia, tiredness, a complexion either too sallow or too flushed, absent-mindedness, sadness, unwillingness to work, disobedience toward parents, diseases of the liver and kidneys, dropsy, consumption, and cancer. Satan, of course, is behind it all.

Wrong kinds of food can contribute to the vice. "Our food should be prepared free from spices. Mince pies, cakes, preserves, and highly-seasoned meats, with gravies, create a feverish condition in the system, and induce the animal passions."

Ellen White recalls that when she was injured at age nine, and her health "ruined," she considered it a great calamity. But now she sees it as a blessing. Why? Because her bad health kept her from society and "preserved me in blissful ignorance of the secret vices of the young."

Here is a memorable description of one of her visions:

> Everywhere I looked, I saw imbecility, dwarfed forms, crippled limbs, misshapen heads, and deformity of every description. Sins and crimes, and the violation of nature's laws, were shown me as the causes of this accumulation of human woe and suffering. I saw such degradation and vile practices, such defiance of God, and I heard such words of blasphemy, that my soul sickened. From what was shown me, a large share of the youth now living are worthless. Corrupt habits are wasting their energies, and bringing upon them loathsome and complicated diseases.

In another vision she was shown the cause of a brother Adventist's terrible condition:

> A Mr. ——— professed to be a devoted follower of Christ. He was in very feeble health. Our feelings of sympathy were called out in his behalf. He could not hold his head steady. His eyes had a glassy appearance, his hands trembled, and when he walked, his knees shook; he staggered like a drunken man, and often seemed ready to fall. He was obliged to fix his eyes upon an object in the distance before him, and then make for that object. He would thus gain force enough to reach the place he desired.
>
> His case was shown me in vision. I saw that he was deceived in regard to himself, that he was not in favor with God. He had practiced self-abuse until he was a mere wreck of humanity.

The man has since died, Sister White adds, a self-murderer destined for annihilation. "The purity of heaven will never be marred with his society." It would be better, she writes, that such people had never been born.

The last half of the booklet consists of quotes from other writers who issued similar warnings against masturbation. The editors preface this section with a note saying that Mrs. White is not a "copyist," and that "she has read nothing from the authors here quoted, and had read no other works on this subject, previous to putting into our hands what she has written."

It is now universally agreed in the medical and psychiatric professions that masturbation is neither physically nor mentally harmful, but the extreme views of Sister White and Brother Kellogg reflected the prevailing opinions of many respectable physicians of the late 1800s. It would require several pages just to list influential nineteenth-century books containing rhetoric on the topic almost as inflamatory as Kellogg's.

Dr. Sadler, whose medical training came much later than Kellogg's and who was less inclined to crank opinions, never bought this nonsense. Many of his books speak of the physical harmlessness of masturbation. Here is a typical passage from *Modern Psychiatry*:

> In almost forty years of the practice of medicine I have yet to see a single bona fide case where masturbation has been definitely and unquestionably responsible for ill health of any sort—*except* in those hundreds upon hundreds of cases where worry over its supposed physical harmfulness or moral sinfullness had led to such long-continued and serious anxiety as directly to produce so-called sexual neurasthenia. In brief, the *worry* over the *practice* and not the physical result has been responsible for the nervous manifestations I have observed. True, excessive masturbation often accompanies marked neurasthenic states, but this is the result of the neurasthenia, not its cause.
>
> Many of the books of twenty-five to fifty years ago on the evil effects of autoeroticism, particularly those written by clergymen, grew out of observations made in the institutions for the feebleminded which were then just coming into existence. The abnormal boys and girls, the village nitwits, who had been gathered up and segregated in these institutions, afforded opportunity for observation of autoerotic practices on a large scale. When clergymen and other well-meaning members of boards of directors and social-uplift advisory committees visited these institutions, they discovered the majority of the inmates indulging in these practices right out in public, "playing with themselves," enjoying secret vice, or self-pollution as it was termed. Quite naturally these unscientific people associated masturbation and feeblemindedness as cause and effect. They failed to realize that these boys and girls were masturbating no more generally than normal-minded youths, but the latter hid themselves away to do this, whereas these subnormal children did not hesitate to indulge in it in public.

Even yet the idea still persists in the minds of a very considerable part of the population that autoeroticism is in some way harmful to the health. The time has come in the discussion of this problem frankly to recognize that *masturbation is not directly harmful to the physical health*, certainly not as it is ordinarily practiced; and as far as my personal experience goes I have yet to see a case where definite physical results can be attributed to it if the individual is free from all idea that it is harmful and from all fear that it is morally wrong.

In the seven pages devoted to masturbation in his 1948 book *Adolescence Problems*, Sadler has the following paragraph:

It is not morally wrong. When we get right down to the bare facts, masturbation cannot be regarded as unethical or morally wrong. In the light of our present religious standards, it is not a violation of any commandment. It is not a sin.

One can imagine how shocked both Dr. Kellogg and Sister White would have been by those remarks had they been alive to read them. Did Sadler intend to be witty when he spoke of getting "right down to the bare facts"?

4

Ellen White's Plagiarisms

Until about the turn of the century both Dr. Kellogg and Dr. Sadler had unbounded faith in Sister White as a divinely inspired prophetess whose visions and dreams, and whose books and "testimonies" (documents addressed to the brethren) came directly from God. After 1900 both "little doctors" began to have serious doubts.

As early as 1907, Dr. Charles E. Stewart, a physician at the Battle Creek Sanitarium, or one of his friends, published an 89-page booklet containing unarguable proof that Mrs. White had a compulsion to copy material, with trivial word changes, from books by others. There was never an indication that the words were not her own. Stewart listed so many parallel passages from Mrs. White's *Sketches from the Life of Paul*, and a much earlier book about Paul, that the church was forced to take White's book off the market. They did not reprint it until 1974 when a facsimile reproduction was allowed. Dr. Stewart also listed parallel passages from Mrs. White's masterpiece, *The Great Controversy Between Christ and Satan*, and books by others. It is now known that at least 50 percent of this work consists of stolen passages, with no hint in the first edition that the writing was not Mrs. White's own.

An eight-hour interview with Dr. Kellogg in 1907, 34 days before he was excommunicated, reveals that he was fully aware of Sister White's compulsive literary thievery. In her early books on health she had shamelessly copied from a book titled *Philosophy of Health*, by Larkin B. Coles. In his biography of Mrs. White, Ronald Numbers reports finding Coles's book in the Adventist library, at Loma Linda University, with marginal shorthand notes by Dr. Kellogg indicating passages Mrs. White had stolen.

Dudley Marvin Canright (1840–1919), an Adventist elder who left the church to become a Baptist minister, briefly called attention to Mrs. White's plagiarisms in an 1887 article. This was expanded to three para-

graphs in his 1889 book *Seventh-day Adventism Renounced* and enlarged to
a chapter in his *Life of Mrs. White: Her False Claims Refuted* (1919).
Church leaders did everything they could to blacken Canright's reputation
and to keep his revelations from the rank and file.

Not until 1982, when excommunicated elder Walter T. Rea published
The White Lie, did evidence of Mrs. White's plagiarisms reach a wide audience.* Rea's tireless research uncovered many further instances of White
piracies that had not been known before. In 1907 her White lies were black
secrets known only to top church officials. What most angered Kellogg and
Sadler, and other Adventist leaders such as Alonzo T. Jones, was that Mrs.
White never had the courage to admit her plagiarizing.

Here is how Dr. Kellogg talked candidly about the scandal in his 1907
interview:

> I am willing to tell you a little history, something that might be infor-
> mation to you. When the "Great Controversy" came out and the chapters
> of the history of the Waldenses, my attention was called to it by somebody
> right away; I could not help but know about it, because there was the little
> book, Wiley's "History of the Waldeneses," right there on the "Review
> and Herald" book counter, and here was the "Great Controversy" coming
> out with extracts from it that were scarcely disguised, some of them.
> There was a disguise because words were changed; it would not have
> been so proper to use quotation marks because words were changed in the
> paragraph so they were not exact quotations, but at the same time were
> borrowed, and your explanation that it was simply an oversight won't
> hold, Brother Amadon, because it would not have been proper to put it in
> quotation marks when there were so many words and phrases changed;
> they were not quotations; they were borrowed. They were plagiarisms and
> not quotations. There is a difference between plagiarism and quotation.
>   Plagiarism is when you use a thing almost word for word, but not
> quite, but just enough different so it is not proper to call it a quotation. There
> is not a single one of those things that could have quotation marks about
> them. If you should put it in quotation marks, it would be telling an untruth,
> because you would be representing this thing as being word for word from
> the author when it is not word for word from the author at all. So your
> exception would not hold good on that thing. Now, I saw this thing there;

---

*The White Lie, by Walter T. Rea, was published by himself in 1982. It can be obtained by
writing to M & R Publications, Box 2056, Turlock, California 95381. On the turmoil produced by
Rea's explosive book—more than 100 Church ministers resigned or were forced to do so—see "Seventh-Day Adventists Face Change and Dissent," by Kenneth A. Briggs, in *The New York Times*
(November 6, 1982); and "The Church of Liberal Borrowings: Plagiarism and Fraud Charges Rock
the Seventh-day Adventists," in *Time* (August 2, 1982).

my attention was called to it by somebody, and I sent for W. C. White right off, and I said, "I won't stand for this, Will White. Now, I am standing right here, standing by your mother, by her writings, and I expect to, but if anybody comes to me with this thing, I shall tell them straight out what I think about it, that it is an unwarrantable use of other people's writing; that you have no right to do it, and that I am ashamed of it and I am sorry for it."

He said, "Don't you think that when mother sees things, runs across things that agree with what she has seen in vision, that it is all right for her to adopt it?' I said, "No, not without giving credit for it. It may be all right for her to quote it and make use of it, but she ought to put quotation marks on and tell where she got it, and should say this is in harmony with what she had 'seen.'" She had no right to incorporate it with what she had "seen" and make it appear that she had seen it first of all. The preface says this book has been written by special illumination, that she has gotten new light by special inspiration; so people read things here, read those paragraphs, and they say, "Here, I saw that in Wiley's book." And I said to Will, "That will condemn your book, detract from the book and the character of it, and it never will do; it is wrong" I said, "I simply won't stand for it, and I want you to know that I won't and that this thing ought to stop." Now, then, they went on and sold that whole edition, at least 1500 copies of that thing that they had on hand, and they went on and sold that thing off with that thing there.

They went right on selling it, but they changed the preface in the next edition so as to give a little bit of loophole to crawl out of, giving a little bit of a hint in it, in a very mild and rather in a hidden way that the author had also profited by information obtained from various sources as well as from Divine inspiration. That is my recollection. I remember I saw the correction and I didn't like it. I said, "That is only a crawl out; that is simply something put in so that the ordinary reader won't discover it at all, but will see the larger statements there of special inspiration; so they will be fooled by that thing." Then there came out other books. Your explanation did not help the case at all about other books. Where is "Great Controversy" and other books, even "Desire of Ages" and "How To Live"? I don't think you ever knew about "How To Live"—with reference to things that were borrowed from Cole's (book).*

---

*The interview with Dr. Kellogg was conducted in his home on October 7, 1907, by church elders George Washington Amadon and A. C. Bordeau. Unknown to them the doctor had the entire conversation recorded in shorthand by two stenographers who were concealed behind a screen! Thirty-four days later the church disfellowshipped the doctor.

The full text of the interview was not published until 1986 by the Omega Historical Research Society of Tempe, Arizona. It is a paperback of 110 pages titled *The Kellogg File 1907 Closed. Reopened 1986.* A shorter version of the interview appeared in *Spectrum* (April and June 1990). *Spectrum is* a periodical representing the Adventist Church's liberal faction.

The ability of Adventists, both in the past and now, to justify Sister White's plagiarisms is almost beyond belief. Was it not possible, some argued, that when angels knew of passages in published books that expressed the truth, they allowed Mrs. White to make use of them? Dr. David Kress, an Adventist colleague of Dr. Kellogg in Battle Creek, is quoted by Kellogg in his 1907 interview as saying: "I have discovered a book here that reads just like [Mrs. White's] *How to Live*—such a wonderful thing that the Lord should put this into two minds at different times, but the curious thing about it is that this book was written *before How to Live* was written." Kellogg replied that he owned Coles's book, that Sister White had read it, and simply copied from it.

Francis B. Nichol, in *Ellen G. White and Her Critics* (1951), devotes three chapters to defending Sister White against the plagiarism charges. I read those chapters with growing astonishment over Nichol's convoluted and absurd justifications. He quotes parallel passages from a book by Canright proving that Canright himself had copied from an earlier work. But if a thief testifies in court about the thievery of another thief does that somehow make the other thief's thievery morally right? Many of Nichol's devious arguments bear a striking resemblance to justifications put forth by Urantians for the scientific mistakes in the *UB* and for passages that repeat passages in earlier books, often word for word. (We will discuss *UB* plagiarisms in chapter 16.)

Few rank and file Adventists, even today, know that Mrs. White's education never went beyond the equivalent of third grade. Her unedited writing was crude beyond belief. She did not know how to spell, punctuate, or organize sentences and paragraphs. Her knowledge of grammar was close to zero. At first it was her husband who corrected her mistakes, but he too was poorly educated, and it soon became essential to hire competent literary assistants to turn her chaotic handwritten material into polished prose. How many such assistants worked for her is not known, but the number is much greater than anyone suspected until recently. Walter Rea in *The White Lie* (p. 199) lists seventeen names. Most of them kept quiet about Mrs. White's plagiarisms, in which of course they willingly participated.

It has been suggested that it was Mrs. White's editors who copied passages by other writers without telling Mrs. White. If this were the case, obviously there is no way to defend her books as divinely inspired. However, the notion that it was her literary assistants who did all the pilfering simply is not true. There is now overwhelming evidence that Mrs. White firmly believed, throughout her long life, that whenever she came upon a passage in a book that expressed accurately what the Holy Spirit told her was true, she was free to copy the passage without adding a footnote to indicate its source.

Mrs. White's son Willie, in a letter to a friend, described the copying process this way:

> In the early days of her work, Mother was promised wisdom in the selection from the writings of others, that would enable her to select the gems of truth from the rubbish of error. We have all seen this fulfilled, and yet when she told me of this, she admonished me not to tell it to others.

Mrs. White's purloined material seldom appeared as exact word for word quotes, as Dr. Kellogg pointed out, but always with slight changes. Did Sister White make these alterations to conceal her sources? It seems more likely that the changes were made for that purpose by her literary editors. They would alter a word here and there, transpose sentences, and rearrange paragraphs if the stolen material was lengthy. In this way, as Kellogg once put it in a letter, they could "hide the piracy."

Although most of Mrs. White's editors seemed undistressed by the practice, some were deeply disturbed. Several who refused to keep quiet about piracy, including Ellen White's own niece Mary Clough, were fired. Although Mrs. White was fully aware of the plagiarisms—after all, it was she who copied the material—she believed it would severely damage the influence of her writings if the sources she used became widely known. Occasionally one of her hundreds of source books would contain an outright historical error. The error would appear on one of Mrs. White's pages. Knowledge of such errors, she rightly perceived, would cast strong doubt on her constant claims that everything she wrote had been guided by angels or the Holy Spirit.

The assistant who became most troubled by Sister White's massive piracies was Fanny (often written Fannie) Bolton. Born Frances Eugenia Bolton in Chicago, 1859, she was the attractive dark-haired daughter of a Methodist minister. Miss Bolton converted to Seventh-day Adventism in 1885, when she was 26. Two years later Mrs. White hired her to edit her sermons. At that time Sister White's chief editor was Miss Marian Davis. Fanny's task was to assist her. Marian carefully explained to Fanny that Mrs. White was a poor writer, and their job was to shape her crude scribblings into readable English. When Fanny first learned that she was working on material that Sister White had copied in longhand almost word for word from other writers, she was profoundly shaken. Moreover, there was never any credit given in Sister White's books for the labors of her literary helpers.

Fanny's efforts to persuade Mrs. White to indicate her sources, and to acknowledge her debt to her editors, fell on deaf ears. Miss Bolton was fired in 1890, after three years of service. From then on, Sister White was torn between having a valuable, competent editor and one who could damage her reputation by talking about the extent of her plagiarizing. There also seems to have been a curious love-hate aspect to their personal relationship.

Fanny, on the other hand, was equally torn between her love and admiration for Mrs. White, whom she believed to be the inspired leader of the remnant church, and her revulsion over Mrs. White's stubborn refusal to acknowledge copying. Besides, it was not easy to find work elsewhere, and Mrs. White paid well. Fanny sent Sister White a letter of apology. When Mrs. White sailed for Australia, she took Fanny along.

But Fanny was still unhappy over the deceptions in which she once more was collaborating. In his splendid biography of Ellen White, Ronald Numbers reports what Fanny said to Dr. Kellogg's half-brother Merritt when he visited her in Australia:

> "Dr. Kellogg I am in great distress of mind. I come to you for advice for I do not know what to do. I have told Elder [George B.] Starr what I am going to tell you, but he gives me no satisfactory advice. You know," said Fanny, "that I am writing all the time for Sister White. Most of what I write is published in the *Review and Herald* as having come from the pen of Sister White, and is sent out as having been written by Sister White under inspiration of God. I want to tell you that I am greatly distressed over this matter for I feel that I am acting a deceptive part. The people are being deceived about the inspiration of what I write. I feel that it is a great wrong that anything which I write should go out as under Sister White's name, as an article specially inspired of God. What I write should go out over my own signature, then credit would be given where credit belongs." I gave Miss Boulton [sic] the best advice I could, and then soon after asked Sister White to explain the situation to me. I told her just what Fanny had told me. Mrs. White asked me if Fanny told me what I had repeated to her, and my affirming that she did she said, "Elder Starr says she came to him with the same thing." Now said Sister White, with some warmth, "Fanny Boulton shall never write another line for me. She can hurt me as no other person can."

A few days after blabbing to Merritt, Fanny was fired again. Mrs. White had a vision in which Jesus himself, seated on a gold chariot drawn by silver horses, repeated three times, "Fanny Bolton is your adversary!"

In letters to friends, Sister White was harsh in her attacks on Fanny's character. She intimated that Fanny was under the control of Satan and his demons. She likened Fanny to Judas. Incredibly, in 1884 Miss Bolton, stung with remorse and probably in dire need of money, again sent Mrs. White a letter affirming her love for her and the church, and apologizing for her behavior. Mrs. White wrote back that she was "deeply touched." She accepted Fanny's "confession," adding "I have and do forgive you."

Fanny was rehired! "She [Fanny] has remarkable talent," Mrs. White's son Willie wrote to his brother Edson, "and handles mother's matter very intelligently and rapidly, turning off more than twice as much work in a given time as any other editor mother has ever employed." Fanny and Ellen needed one another.

A new difficulty now arose. Fanny fell in love with a married man who had been hired to help with her typing. Mrs. White's opinion of the man couldn't have been lower. Soon she was writing again to friends about Fanny's character flaws. "I never expect to give her another chance to seek to betray me and turn traitor," she wrote to Marian Davis. In 1895 Fanny was fired once more.

Later that same year, incredible as it may seem, Mrs. White had a vision in which the Holy Spirit told her to take Fanny back again! Miss Bolton had worked for Sister White on and off for seven years, but now she had no desire to return. In America she continued to talk about the piracies. "I will cut off the influence of your tongue in every way I can," Mrs. White wrote to her in 1897.

As far as I have been able to determine, all Fanny was doing was telling the truth. In spite of Mrs. White's rage, in 1901 Fanny apologized again, this time even more abjectly:

> I thank God that He has kept Sister White from following my supposed superior wisdom and righteousness, and has kept her from acknowledging editors or authors; but has given to the people the unadulterated expression of God's mind. Had she done as I wished her to do, the gift would have been degraded to a common authorship, its importance lost, its authority undermined, and its blessing lost to the world.

As a loyal Adventist Fanny had finally concluded, or pretended to conclude, that not only was Mrs. White justified in massive plagiarizing, but she was also to be praised for keeping this thievery hidden from her readers! As we shall see in chapter 16, Urantians are now saying exactly the same thing about the recent discovery of widespread plagiarisms in the *UB*.

In 1911, at age 52, Fanny spent 13 months in a mental hospital in Kalamazoo, Michigan. She was later readmitted for three months, and still later spent time in a Florida mental hospital. She died in Battle Creek in 1926, ill and almost penniless, having been supported for several years by an Adventist man who wanted to marry her, but whose identity remains unknown.

My source for these sad details is "Fannie's Folly," the first of an eye-opening two-part essay by Alice Elizabeth Gregg, in *Adventist Currents* (October 1983). The second part, "Marian the Bookmaker," appeared in the journal's February 1984 issue. It concerns the career of Fanny's older associate Marian Davis.

Marian did less talking about the plagiarisms than Fanny, but she was equally troubled by them, perhaps more so because she tried so hard to suppress her anger. Born 1847 in North Berwick, Maine, her parents were devout Adventists who had settled in Battle Creek. Marian's first job was proofreading for the Church's Review and Herald publishing company. Her youngest sister, Ella, married William K. Kellogg, owner of the Kellogg Cornflake Company and brother of Dr. John Kellogg. For twenty-five years she labored faithfully as Mrs. White's chief literary assistant.

Dudley Canright, in his biography of Ellen White, reports that one day Marian was heard sobbing in her room. Asked what bothered her, she replied, "I wish I could die! I wish I could die!" When her visitor asked why, her answer was, "This terrible plagiarism."

It was Marian who turned Mrs. White's chaotic writing on the life of Christ into the beautifully written *Desire of Ages*. Adventists still talk about the beauty of Sister White's books, unaware that the lovely passages came from other writers and assistants whose names and books are nowhere mentioned. Only in a late printing of *The Great Controversy* did church officials add footnotes to indicate principal sources. Church officials are still doing all they can to conceal from their flock the enormous extent to which Mrs. White's books were copied from others.

Always frail, Marian slowly wasted away. When she died of anemia in 1904, she weighed the same as her age, 57 years and 57 pounds. "Could it have been," Alice Gregg asks, "that starvation was the only way out of a situation she could no longer tolerate?"*

The controversy over Mrs. White's piracies will never subside, Gregg concludes her two-part essay, until the Adventist church can "acknowledge that Ellen was wrong to copy without giving credit to the sources used."

---

*In the fourth volume of Arthur L. White's six-volume biography of his grandmother, *Ellen G. White: The Australian Years*, chapter 32 is devoted to Marian Davis. It details the close collaboration of Mrs. White and Davis on *The Desire of Ages*. Chapter 20 covers the on-again, off-again relationship between Mrs. White and Fanny Bolton.

5

The Living Temple

Until 1900 Dr. Kellogg and Sister White were on the best of terms. As a young man he lived in her house where he was treated like another son by Mrs. White and her husband, James. As late as 1889 he wrote to her, "I have loved and respected you as my own mother." A year later he wrote a preface to *Christian Temperance and Bible Hygiene*, by Sister White and others, in which he said that Mrs. White's health views bore "unmistakable evidence of divine insight and direction." In sanitarium meetings the little doctor often read from Sister White's books with tears streaming down his cheeks.

Mrs. White in turn loved and admired the doctor. In a *General Conference Bulletin* (1901, p. 203) she wrote that Dr. Kellogg "took up the most difficult cases, where, if the knife had slipped one hair's breadth, it would have cost a life. God stood by his side and an angel's hand was upon his hand, guiding it through operations." This statement did not sit well with the doctor. He feared it might cause patients to expect miracles.

In a 1901 testimony in which Mrs. White described one of her visions, she wrote:

> Well, while I was praying and was sending up my petition there was, as on other times, I saw a light circling right around the room, and a fragrance like the fragrance of flowers, and the beautiful scent of flowers, and then the voice seemed to speak gently, and said, that I was to accept the invitation of my servant John Kellogg, and to make his house my home. Then the word was "I have appointed him as my physician. You can be an encouragement to him."

When Mrs. White entered a trance state and experienced visual and auditory delusions, she usually saw the room flooded with a soft light, sometimes colored pink or blue. There would be the fragrance of roses or violets, or some other flower. No one else ever observed the light or smelled the flowers. A trance could last for hours, during which she would speak nonstop about what she saw and heard.

Let me digress a moment to describe how Ellen White, in her teens, began to display her visions. In 1839 William Miller (1782–1849), an uneducated New York Baptist farmer, after diligent study of biblical prophecies concluded that Christ would return to Earth sometime between March 21, 1843, and March 21, 1844. Later he extended the date to October 1844. His charismatic preaching won an enthusiastic following among New England fundamentalists.

When 1844 passed, with no sign of Jesus, farmer Miller was honest enough to admit he had been mistaken, and to retire from the revival scene. Most Millerites, sad and disenchanted, returned to mainline churches, but a small group of more dedicated believers discovered a marvelous way to explain what came to be called the Great Disappointment.

What actually happened in 1844? That was the year, they said, when Jesus "entered the Sanctuary" of Heaven to close the door of salvation. Miller was right about the date, but wrong about the event. In other words, the destiny of every person had been settled; no more conversions were possible before the Second Coming. Later there would be great controversy over what became known as the "Shut Door" doctrine. It would have had a certain plausibility if Jesus had returned in a year or so, as the post-disappointment Millerites believed, but as years and decades went by, with no end in sight of history as we know it, the Shut Door view became too grim to maintain.

James White, a Millerite elder, and his friend Ellen Harmon of Portland, Maine, then 18 or 19, were two Adventists who for a few years defended the Shut Door. The pair, after being persuaded by Millerite Joseph Bates that God intended his remnant church to worship on Saturday instead of Sunday, became the leaders of Seventh-day Adventism. It was the largest of several warring factions of Millerites who continued after 1844 to preach the soon Second Coming. For more details on all this, consult Richard Schwarz's history of his church, *Light Bearers to the Remnant* (1979).

The Millerites, both before and after 1844, liked to hold meetings around New England during which they gave vent to an emotionalism that rivaled Pentecostal congregations. They engaged in shouting, loud and simultaneous praying, and vigorous hymn singing. To demonstrate humility, they practiced foot washing—washing one another's feet as Jesus had washed the feet of his disciples—and crawling on the floor while sometimes barking like a dog. They would give one another what they called a "holy kiss," and indulge in uninhibited "holy laughter."* Occasionally someone "slain by the Lord" would faint and fall to the floor. Still believing that Jesus would arrive any month now, farmers let their crops decay and stopped milking cows. Store owners closed down their small businesses. For a short time Elder White predicted the Second Coming on or before October 22, 1845.

In February 1845, during a Maine snowstorm, wild meetings were held in Atkinson, near Bangor, at the home of Millerite James Ayer Jr. The group's leader, Elder Israel Dammon, a former sea captain from Exeter, was arrested for disturbing the peace. Lurid accounts of his arrest and trial appeared in a local newspaper. These accounts, along with commentary, were published in the unauthorized periodical *Adventist Currents* (April 1988), along with many photographs and illustrations.

Both Ellen Harmon and James White were present throughout this

---

*Few Pentecostals today are aware that "holy laughter" was once a common practice in their earlier days. Amazingly, the practice had a revival in 1993. According to "Laughing for the Lord," an article by Richard Ostling in *Time* (August 15, 1994), the revival began in meetings conducted by Rodney Howard-Browne of Louisville, Kentucky, then spread to charismatic churches in Canada and England. *Time* describes an outbreak of holy laughter at Holy Trinity, a London evangelical Anglican church:

> Oblivious to the hot, airless sanctuary, the youthful throng buzzes with an anticipation more common at a rock concert or rugby match. After the usual Scripture readings, prayers and singing, the chairs are cleared away. Curate Nicky Gumbel prays that the Holy Spirit will come upon the congregation. Soon a woman begins laughing. Others gradually join her with hearty belly laughs. A young worshipper falls to the floor, hands twitching. Another falls, then another and another. Within half an hour there are bodies everywhere as supplicants sob, shake, roar like lions and. strangest of all, laugh uncontrollably.

Ray Waddle, in the *Nashville Tennessean*, late August 1994, reports that holy laughter—also known as "joyful laughter" and "Holy Ghost joy" has broken out in the Restoration Fellowship Church in Hendersonville, Tennessee. "In the middle of a recent sermon, dozens of people let rip giggles, guffaws and belly laughs. A few were on the floor, doubled over in hilarity."

Holy laughter is spreading like wildfire through Pentecostal churches around the world. It has erupted in San Francisco's Vineyard Church, in a Vineyard Church in Toronto, and in many other Pentecostal congregations. Richard Roberts, son of Oral, has preached on how holy laughter has changed his ministry and revived students at his father's university in Tulsa. Pat Robertson endorsed holy laughter on his "700 Club"TV show of October 28, 1994. Jimmy Swaggart increasingly guffaws during his Bible pounding sermons.

At least two books on the new wave have appeared: *Holy Laughter* by Charles and Frances Hunter, and *Fresh Annointing* by Mona Johnian. Howard-Browne, called the Holy Ghost Bartender, is on the cover of *Charisma* (August 1994) to accompany an article titled "Praise the Lord and Pass the New Wine." The same issue advertises a video, "The Laugh That Was Heard 'Round the World."

meeting. Ellen is described as lying on the floor for hours, eyes wide open, shouting about what she saw in vision, occasionally pointing to someone present and revealing facts about that person. Ellen preached the Shut Door. She warned everyone present that he or she would go straight to hell if not rebaptized by immersion.

Also supine on the floor during this meeting, shouting her own visions, was Dorinda Baker, described by the press as a "sickly" woman of 23 or 24. You won't read about her in Schwarz's history. I sometimes wonder what happened to her. Ellen and James were married in 1846 by a Portland Justice of the Peace. The rest is history.

Newspaper accounts of the trial of Elder Dammon leave not the slightest doubt that young Ellen participated wholeheartedly in what Adventists like to call the "fanaticism" of the early Millerites. Fifteen years later, in *Spiritual Gifts* (vol. 2, pp. 40–42), Mrs. White gave her own version of the meeting and Dammon's arrest. In many points it contradicts what the newspaper said happened. She later insisted she had fought against the emotionalism of the early Adventists and even denied she had ever defended the Shut Door doctrine.

Both Dr. Kellogg and Dr. Sadler became convinced that Mrs. White's visions were a form of partial epilepsy caused by a severe injury to her temporal lobes when she was a child.* The injury put her into a semicoma for weeks.

Here is a copy of a letter Dr. Kellogg wrote on March 3, 1933, to a Mrs. E. B. Tower of Glendale, California:

> I have your letter of February 18 in which you speak of some tests being applied by me to Mrs. White while in vision. There is no truth whatever in this statement to which you refer. I never saw Mrs. White while she was in a state of vision. It is my belief that her condition while in vision was that of catalepsy. This is a nervous state allied to hysteria in which sublime visions are usually experienced. The muscles are set in such a way that ordinary tests fail to show any evidence of respiration, but the application of more delicate tests show that there are slight breathing movements sufficient to maintain life. Patients sometimes remain in this condition for several hours.

In addition to Dr. Kellogg's growing annoyance with Sister White for not acknowledging the extent of her plagiarisms, other events slowly

---

*See "Visions or Partial-Complex Seizures?" by Dr. Delbert H. Hodder in *Evangelica*'s special issue "Ellen G. White Reconsidered," vol. 2, no. 5 (November 1981): 30–37.

widened the rift. The doctor was shocked to discover that for many years Mrs. White not only ate meat, but what to him was even worse, she ate oysters.* She and her sons, during a period of some 25 years, were fond of chicken as well as eggs, butter, fish, and cheese. Not until 1894 did she revert to strict vegetarianism. Moreover, Dr. Kellogg never got over his horror produced by the extent to which Church leaders and elders had become "flesh eaters."

In 1900 Mrs. White became angry at Dr. Kellogg for not sending money for the Church's work in Australia where she had taken up temporary residence. In a testimony she accused him of stealing funds from the San and squandering it on new buildings in Chicago. She had seen these new buildings in a dream, she wrote, and they were designed to "harbor the unworthy poor" and to promote Dr. Kellogg's fame. (As Dr. Sadler and others had predicted, after her menopause Mrs. White's trance visions ceased, the angels communicating with her only in dreams.)

Dr. Kellogg at once wrote to say that Sister White's dream was false because no new buildings had been constructed. Mrs. White did not believe him. Rather than keeping up the argument, the doctor revealed in his 1907 interview, he decided to set a trap for Sister White. He sent no more letters denying the charge, certain that Mrs. White would take his silence for guilt. She fell for the bait and continued to send him letters hammering on him for wasting money on the new buildings. When Sister White returned from Australia and visited Chicago, she was amazed to discover that the buildings did not exist. How did she wiggle out of this obvious error? There had been *talk* about the building of new structures in Chicago. What the angel intended was to prevent the new buildings from going up. Dr. Kellogg was not pacified by this explanation.

In another vision Mrs. White saw "tongues of fire" descending on the San in Battle Creek. Sure enough, a mysterious fire destroyed the San's two main buildings on February 18, 1902. In 1905 Sister White made public for the first time a testimony she had recorded in her diary three years earlier. It strongly censored Dr. Kellogg for rebuilding the San. The Lord had told

---

*In Mrs. White's letter to her daughter-in-law, written in 1882, are these words: "Mary, if you can get me a box of herrings, fresh ones, please do so. The last ones that Willie got are bitter and old . . . if you can get a few cans of good oysters, get them."

In an 1873 letter Mrs. White described a vacation trip during which she and her family dined on wild duck. As Douglas Hackleman pointed out in his article "Ellen White's Habit" (*Free Inquiry*, Fall 1984) Mrs. White had written two years earlier: "Those who digress occasionally to gratify the taste in eating a fattened turkey or other flesh meats, pervert their appetites. . . . The lack of stability in regard to the principles of health reform is a true index of their character and their spiritual strength."

her that he should have built many small sanitariums in rural areas, far from cities.

So furious was Mrs. White over what she saw as the doctor's rising ambitions that she predicted he would, like Nebuchadnezzar, "be humbled and driven out to eat grass like an ox."

Referring to this unkind remark, Merritt said to John, "You will not miss the savory roasts and juicy joints at that time, as will many of the Seventh-day Adventist preachers when they have to eat grass like an ox, as many of them still, or starve, when the fallacies of their teachings is revealed, as it will be in God's own good time."

Another major source of growing friction between Dr. Kellogg and Mrs. White and her son Will was the publication in 1903 of Kellogg's 568-page book *The Living Temple*. The book stressed the immanence of God in all living things. "There is present in the tree a power which creates and maintains it," the doctor wrote, "a tree-maker in the tree, a flower-maker in the flower." To Mrs. White this sounded suspiciously like pantheism, putting God within nature rather than above and outside it. Dr. Kellogg repeatedly denied it was pantheism. It was, he maintained, no more than a recognition of a transcendent God's presence in all things, no different from what Sister White herself had said in a chapter on "God and Nature" in her book *Education*.

Here is how that chapter opens:

Upon all created things is seen the impress of the Deity. Nature testifies of God. The susceptible mind, brought in contact with the miracle and mystery of the universe, can not but recognize the working of infinite power. Not by its own inherent energy does the earth produce its bounties, and year by year continue its motion around the sun. An unseen hand guides the planets in their circuit of the heavens. A mysterious life pervades all nature,—a life that sustains the unnumbered worlds throughout immensity; that lives in the insect atom which floats in the summer breeze; that wings the flight of the swallow, and feeds the young ravens which cry; that brings the bud to blossom, and the flower to fruit.

The same power that upholds nature, is working also in man. The same great laws that guide alike the star and the atom, control human life. The laws that govern the heart's action, regulating the flow of the current of life to the body, are the laws of the mighty Intelligence that has the jurisdiction of the soul.

Dr. Kellogg tried vainly to pacify Mrs. White and the Church theologians by slicing out offending pages and pasting in new ones. Five thousand copies of the first edition had been printed, of which about 2,000 had been sold. The remaining 3,000, with the tipped-in pages, were then released. The first edition is now rare enough, but tipped-in editions are even harder to find. Later Dr. Kellogg completely rewrote the book as *The Miracle of Life*.

Reading *The Living Temple* today it is hard to find in it anything that would disturb a Protestant fundamentalist. I suspect it was not so much this book that distressed Ellen White as his growing criticism of her testimonies and his increasing attacks on what he considered the dishonesty of her husband and her son Will. In his seven-hour interview with two church leaders in 1907, Dr. Kellogg's attacks on James and Will are harsh indeed.

A lavishly illustrated book, *The Living Temple* is devoted primarily to the physiology of the human body, its text liberally sprinkled with biblical quotations. All of Kellogg's familiar health rules are here. One should abstain from alcohol, tea, coffee, spices, and of course flesh food. Not only does meat cause "autointoxication" of the colon as well as all sorts of other ills and diseases, but it is also morally wrong:

A lady artist once remarked to a friend, "How can you eat a thing that looks out of eyes?" The gentleman declared that from that moment whenever he sat down to a table where mutton was served, he saw a pair of gentle sheep's eyes peering at him, and was unable to touch his meat. Eyes imply a mind, an intelligence, something that has feeling and capacity for enjoyment, and that looks out upon the world, forms its opinions, its likes, its dislikes, enjoys, suffers, loves, *hates*,—experiences in which *all* creatures belonging to the animal kingdom are one. So there is, in a certain sense, not only a universal brotherhood of man,—although few recognize even this fact,—but there is likewise a greater brotherhood, which includes not only man, civilized man, savage man, Christian man, heathen man,—all men,—but likewise man's humble relatives of the animal world, into whose nostrils as well as into man's God breathed the breath of life.

Man rears his cattle, his sheep, and his poultry much like household pets. His children make his lambs their playmates. Side by side his oxen toil with him in the field. In return for kindness, they give affection. What confidence they repose in him! how faithfully they serve! With winter's frost an evil day arrives,—a day of massacre, of perfidy, of bloodshed and butchery. With knife and ax he turns upon his trusted friends, the sheep that kissed his hand, the ox that plowed his field. The air is filled with shrieks and moans, with cries of terror and despair; the soil is wet with warm blood, and strewn with corpses.

Of all flesh foods, the "oyster is the most objectionable." Fresh eggs are harmless, but milk and its products such as butter and cheese are abominations:

> Milk and its products are unquestionably the most filthy articles which come upon our tables. Milk generally contains the dung of animals in such quantities that straining is necessary before it can be even tolerated, and after ordinary straining the last drops from the pitcher are always found to contain a very disgusting quantity of stable cleanings.

One should eat only two meals a day, with no drinking of water during mealtime. A cold bath is desirable every morning, and a warm bath at night. White clothing is best because it lets light through to the body but screens out harmful radiation. Readers are advised to sleep on a hard mattress, with no pillow or at least a thin one. All forms of hydrotherapy (water cures) are described and recommended.

The best way to reduce, says the doctor, is to eat only one kind of food. Monotony does the trick. "He will soon get so tired of this that he will be very careful not to eat too much."

Persons who live and eat right, we are informed, will never break wind. Passing gas is "caused by unnatural fermentation and putrefaction in the colon through retention of the fecal matter." The bowels should be emptied two or three times a week by a "copious enema."

Throughout the volume Kellogg stresses the indwelling of God in all things, and especially within the bodies of men and women. Did not St. Paul tell us (1 Corinthians 6:19) that our bodies are temples of the Holy Spirit?

> Suppose now we have a boot before us,—not an ordinary boot, but a living boot, and as we look at it, we see little boots crowding out at the seams, pushing out at the toes, dropping off at the heels, and leaping out at the top,—scores, hundreds, thousands of boots, a swarm of boots continually issuing from our living boot,—would we not be compelled to say, "There is a shoemaker in the boot"? So there is present in the tree a power which creates and maintains it, a tree-maker in the tree, a flower-maker in the flower,—a divine architect who understands every law of proportion, an infinite artist who possesses a limitless power of expression in color and form; there is, in all the world about us, an infinite, divine, though invisible Presence, to which the unenlightened may be blind, but which is ever declaring itself by its ceaseless, beneficent activity. "The heavens declare the glory of God; and the firmament showeth his handiwork."

God's immanence in all things is certainly something no fundamentalist, least of all an Adventist, would deny. Moreover, Kellogg repeatedly stresses his belief in a definite, personal God, with a mind analogous to our own, but infinitely greater. However, there are occasional passages in which the transcendence of God seems denied. "God is the explanation of nature—not a God outside of nature, but in nature, manifesting himself through and in all the objects, movements, and phenomena of the universe" (p. 28). ". . . a great Designer, a personal being, working not above nature, but in nature, of whom nature is the expression" (p. 451). "God is not behind nature nor above nature: he is in nature—nature is the visible expression of his power" (p. 40).

These are the passages which so disturbed Ellen White. It is hard to know exactly what Kellogg meant when he said God is not above nature. My guess is that he meant no more than that God is not absent from nature. That he recognized the transcendence of God, beyond space and time, seems clear from such passages as the following (p. 33):

> Discussions respecting the form of God are utterly unprofitable, and serve only to belittle our conceptions of him who is above all things, and hence not to be compared in form or size or glory or majesty with anything which man has ever seen or which it is within his power to conceive. In the presence of questions like these, we have only to acknowledge our foolishness and incapacity, and bow our heads with awe and reverence in the presence of a Personality, an Intelligent Being to the existence of which all nature bears definite and positive testimony, but which is as far beyond our comprehension as are the bounds of space and time.

As I have said, the offending pages were removed from unsold copies of the book's first edition, and other pages substituted. When the entire book was rewritten and published by Dr. Kellogg in 1904 as the 575-page *The Miracle of Life*, there was no trace of pantheism.

Of special interest to Urantians are pages 460–74 of *The Living Temple* on which Kellogg defends the Adventist (and Urantian) doctrines of soul sleep and the reconstitution of one's body. In 1878 Kellogg had written (as I mentioned earlier) an entire book about this, *The Soul and the Resurrection*, but his views, he tells us, have since matured. A dozen pages in *The Living Temple* are a splendid summary of his earlier book. Our personal identity is not preserved by the material substance of our body because that substance is continually being renewed as new molecules replace old ones. Our identity is preserved by the continuity of what Aristotle called the body's "form"—the entire, incredibly complex *pattern* of our brain's molecules.

When we die, we are totally unconscious because we have no functioning brain. On resurrection day God gives to our pattern a new and glorified body. It is this pattern that constitutes our "soul." Because God dwells within us, it is easy for him to recall the pattern. After our resurrection we are not "a new thing" because our identity has been retained in God's infinite mind. We will experience no passage of time between death and resurrection, while our "soul" sleeps, because we have no brain to measure a time lapse. We will seem to awake instantly, in what Paul called the "twinkling of an eye," with all our memories intact.

> The plan of the temple is its soul; not the external form, nor merely the internal arrangement, but the entire temple scheme, including the minutest details of bodily form and structure. Every brain cell, every nerve fiber, every string of the living harp, every tone which it produces, a complete description of the human instrument and every particle of its work in human acts and words and thoughts,—all these are recorded; where?—In the universal mind, in the memory of Him who said, "Before I formed thee I knew thee." Jer. 1:5. Said David, "In thy book all my members were written, which in continuance were fashioned, when as yet there was none of them." Ps. 139:16. The same power that formed David in accordance with a plan which existed before he did, carrying forward this same plan represented in David's character, his personality, remembered in the mind of God even from before his birth, can reform him in the future world, and so secure to him a future life. David recognized the existence of such a record before his birth, and the Bible in many places recognizes the existence of such a record of all human lives. Jer. 1:5; Isa. 4:3; Rev. 20:12.
>
> God's presence in the temple gives him the minutest information possible respecting every detail of its history; not an outward act nor an innermost thought can escape his notice. Although a man may die, although his very thoughts may perish, his personality, his character, survives. Without a human brain there can be, of course, no human thinking, no human willing, no human joy or sorrow. With the death of the body the man ceases to be: the spirit of life, the vital power which animates the dust of which his body is composed, and makes him a living soul, returns to God who gave it. The human will surrenders its authority and control. God no longer serves. Man goes to his "long home," the dust; the divine spirit which dwelt in the temple, the creative power which formed him, which cared for him during life, which shared all his sorrows, his griefs, his struggles, bore his burdens, which "knoweth his

frame" in its minutest detail, survives the wreck of the body. And thus while man's body smolders in the dust, his individuality, his "life," his soul (not his human consciousness), is safely lodged in the great heart of God, awaiting that critical moment to which the ages have looked forward when a purified universe will permit of the rehabilitation of the souls of those who have loved righteousness and truth, and are hence suited to an endless life "in tune with the Infinite." Such will enter upon a state of endless spiritual human existence through the building for each of a body suited to its character, and capable of reaching the high ideals and responding to the highest purposes to which the soul in its previous state of existence may have aspired, but which, through weakness of the flesh it could but imperfectly attain.

All this is, of course, sound Adventist and Urantian doctrine. I am convinced that neither Wilfred Kellogg nor Dr. Sadler, or their respective wives, ever abandoned it. I believe that is how it found its way into *The Urantia Book.*

Mrs. White and other church leaders were more understandably distressed by rumors that Dr. Kellogg was beginning to have doubts about many basic Adventist doctrines. The rumors were true. Here is how Richard Schwarz, in his biography of Kellogg, summarizes the doctor's heresies:

By the 1920's considerable evidence had accumulated that Dr. Kellogg had seriously modified some of the religious beliefs in which his parents had reared him. For several years he had been sponsoring "quiet" Sabbath recreational activities for sanitarium guests. He also began with increasing frequency to cite evolutionary theories in support of his system of biologic living. Old Adventist associates reported that the doctor no longer professed belief in certain parts of the Bible, such as the stories of Jonah and Job; denied the virgin birth and divinity of Jesus and the need for an atonement; constantly joked about the personal appearance of God; and expressed the view that it was possible for human beings to work out their own salvation through a program of eugenics and biologic living.

It is my belief that both Wilfred Kellogg and Dr. Sadler shared Dr. Kellogg's heresies, and that many of these views entered the *UB.* The book denies such doctrines as the Virgin Birth of Jesus, and his blood atonement for the sins of mankind. It denies the historicity of many Old Testament myths and many New Testament miracle tales. On pages 26–28 the *UB* speaks of God's "indwelling" in all his creatures. On pages 26 and 1609 our bodies are called "temples of God," echoing the title of Kellogg's book. Most significant of all, the *UB* accepts evolution as God's method of creation.

Adventists today are divided over creationism, but in those days they were all "young earthers," convinced that the entire universe is only about 10,000 years old and that fossils are relics of life that perished in the Great Flood of Noah. Their "geologist" (he had no formal training in the science), George McCready Price, would soon be turning out book after book defending a young earth and the flood theory of fossils.

I do not know just when Dr. Kellogg abandoned the young-earth view. In a January 1913 issue of his *Good Health Magazine* (which I chanced to pick up at an antiques show), Dr. Kellogg devotes three pages to a recent discovery of fossil men who lived at least 100,000 years ago. He cites favorably the opinions of a London scientist that "modern man is not descended from Neanderthal men, as many suppose," but from another inferior human species closely related to the chimpanzee and gibbon." The article leaves no doubt that the doctor had discarded the flood theory of fossils.

It is also worth mentioning that Dr. Kellogg's stress on eugenics for improving the human race did not sit well with those who were convinced the world was about to end! Dr. Sadler shared Kellogg's passion for eugenics. This too is strongly reflected (as we shall see in chapter 14) in the *UB*.

If by 1907 Dr. Kellogg had departed this far from his Church, as I believe he had, it seems to me that the Church had ample grounds for his disfellowship. If a person ceases to accept the essential dogmas of a faith, I think he or she should leave that faith. I have never been able to understand how a Catholic theologian such as Hans Küng, who has abandoned all distinctively Catholic doctrines, would want to remain a Catholic. I have never ceased to be amazed that Paul Tillich, who believed neither in a personal God nor an afterlife, would choose to keep calling himself a Protestant. I cannot understand the mind of persons who call themselves Mormons, but have no interest in *The Book of Mormon*, or call themselves Christian Scientists but have no interest in the writings of Mary Baker Eddy.

In his 1907 interview Kellogg made clear that he would not voluntarily leave the Church, even though he predicted its downfall if its leaders continued to behave as they had in the past. On the other hand, he said he would not object to expulsion. "If the Adventist Church is not good enough for me, there isn't any other church that is." True to his word, he never adopted another religion. Nor did he ever abandon his deep faith in God and Jesus, or in the Adventist doctrine of soul-sleep until the body is reconstituted on Resurrection morning.

According to an article in the *Battle Creek Journal* (November 11, 1907), six other Adventists were disfellowshipped along with Dr. Kellogg. They were Elder George C. Tenney, D. Duffy, N. Winebrener, Deo Paul, Arthur Abegg, and a Mr. Moore whose initials the paper did not know. The excommunications took place at the SDA Tabernacle, in a meeting behind locked doors. Elder R. S. Owen and Moses Eastman Kellogg (we will meet him in the next chapter) were forcibly denied entrance.

A few years before he died, Dr. Kellogg was still riding his bicycle— white of course—and jogging daily. As his death approached, he suffered from impaired hearing and eyesight, and from palsy. After dying of pneumonia in 1943, he was buried in Battle Creek's Oak Hill Cemetery alongside his wife. Three ministers delivered eulogies at his funeral: an Adventist elder, a Congregational Church pastor, and a Seventh-day Baptist who was then the San's chaplain. Brother Will was too ill to attend. Their full sister Clara Butler also could not be there. She had been struck by a car and was recuperating in the San.

The San reached its apex of opulence in 1931 when a 16-story tower was added. During the great depression it went into receivership and was taken over by the federal government in 1942 to serve as an army hospital. Today, at 74 North Washington, it is the headquarters of numerous federal agencies.

When Dr. Kellogg died in 1943, tributes by former patients poured in from all over the world. Let writer Will Durant have this chapter's final word:

> The passing of our beloved scientist and saint leaves us bereaved but not offended. Death is forgivable when it comes after a life completely lived and nobly spent. He was one of the wisest and kindliest men we have ever known. Our deepest sympathy goes to those who were nearest to him, and who will feel his absence every hour of the day for many years. May the work which he carried on in the great tradition of Pythagoras be carried forward by his able and devoted aides for the enlightenment and happiness of mankind.

6

Wilfred Custer Kellogg

The other star player in the history of the Urantia movement—the man who in his sleep I am convinced was the conduit through whom the supermortals first communicated their revelations to Sadler—was Wilfred Custer Kellogg, Sadler's brother-in-law.

Wilfred was born October 3, 1876, in Berkshire, Vermont. At about age 20 his mother took him to Battle Creek after the death of his father. A 1910 Battle Creek census lists Wilfred as a bookkeeper living with his mother. Although without any formal education beyond the sixth grade, he became business manager of W. K. Kellogg's Toasted Corn Flake Company. This is not so surprising when you consider that Will Kellogg, the company's founder and president, also had no college training. Wilfred resigned from the company in 1910. After his marriage in 1912 he sold his holdings in the company and joined Sadler in Chicago.

Wifred's father, Charles Leonidis Sobeski Kellogg (1847–1896) was a circuit-riding minister of the Seventh-day Adventist's New England Conference. After his death from pneumonia at age 48, in Norwich, Connecticut, his body was reinterred in Battle Creek. As a youth he had been a private during the Civil War, serving in Company D, first regiment of the Vermont Volunteer Heavy Artillery.

Charles's father, Edward Kellogg (1802–1891), was also an Adventist elder. Wilfred's uncle (a son of his father's brother Ray Stanley Kellogg), was Moses Eastman Kellogg, a prominent Adventist editor and writer in Battle Creek. His book *The Supremacy of Peter* (Review and Herald, 1897) vigorously attacked the Roman Catholic claim that Peter was the first pope. (Adventists of the time, many even today, believed the Catholic Church to be the Antichrist.) Moses Eastman Kellogg was a good friend of Sister

White's eldest son James Edson. In his book *The Coming of Jesus* (1900), James thanks Moses for his contributions.

Moses also collaborated with John Kolvoord on a 119-page book titled *The Vision of the Evening and Morning, a Study of the Prophecy of Daniel VIII*. The book attacked the early church dogma known as the "Shut Door" which maintained that in 1844 the door to salvation was closed for everyone except living Adventists (see chapter 4). The book was published in 1907, the same year that Dr. John Kellogg was excommunicated. Wilfred's nephew Ray Stanley Jr. recalls that his father told him that all the related Kelloggs, then living in Battle Creek, were dropped from the church along with Dr. Kellogg.

The "dropping" was not excommunication. Milton Raymond Hook, in *Flames Over Battle Creek* (1977), a biography of George Washington Amadon, tells the story in his final chapter. He says that in 1907 about twenty-five of the "Battle Creek rebels" asked that their names be dropped from Adventist membership rolls. The names include Dr. Kellogg's brother William Keith, Wilfred Kellogg, and his uncle Moses Eastman Kellogg. I would not be surprised if Dr. Sadler was also among those dropped.

Wilfred was the oldest of five children. His brother Ray Stanley Kellogg, 18 years younger, was a dentist in the Battle Creek area for half a century. His two sons, Ray Stanley Jr. and John Phillips, are both living, though regretably neither had any personal contacts with Wilfred. They knew of his close connection with the Urantia cult, and either Wilfred or Sadler sent their father a copy of the *UB*, but they did not know that Wilfred was the initial channeler. Wilfred died in Chicago on August 31, 1956, less than a year after the *UB* was published. Ray Stanley Jr. accompanied his father to Wilfred's funeral in Chicago. He tells me it was a Urantian service and that his father was angry because Dr. Sadler did not attend.

It was probably in Battle Creek that Wilfred met John Kellogg's niece, Anna Bell Kellogg (1877–1960), the sister of Sadler's wife, Lena. An Illinois law prohibited the marriage of first cousins. To make their marriage legal, the couple were first married in Kenosha, Wisconsin (a state that did not forbid cousin marriages), on the morning of Wednesday, August 28, 1912. The ceremony took place at the office of Judge George W. Taylor. On the evening of the same day they were married a second time in La Grange, a Chicago suburb. Notices the following day, in Battle Creek's *Daily Moon* and the *Battle Creek Enquirer*, place the wedding at the home of the Sadlers, in La Grange. It was an elaborate double wedding performed by ex-Adventist George C. Tenney, then chaplain of the Battle Creek Sanitarium. The other betrothed couple was Edward Van Bond, of Dallas, and Sarah Willmer, of La Grange.

According to the *Enquirer*, Sarah and Anna were old friends, both having lived with the Sadlers "during recent years." Wilfred and Anna are said to be planning to return to Battle Creek to live at 61 Oak Lawn. Wilfred is called one of Battle Creek's "most promising young business men, and everyone will be deeply interested in his marriage with one of Illinois' fairest daughters." Wilfred is identified as secretary of the Battle Creek Sanitarium Company, as well as secretary-treasurer of the Battle Creek Optical Company.

A 1911 notice in the Ross Coller Collection of Battle Creek's Willard Library says that Wilfred is completing a new house on Ann Avenue, in Battle Creek. He is said to be associated with Dr. Kellogg's *Good Health* magazine, and with the Battle Creek Optical Company. It adds that he also is "in charge of the electrical equipment at the San."

Anna and Wilfred were first cousins by way of Wilfred's mother, Emma Kellogg. Emma was the daughter of John Preston Kellogg by his second wife, and John Preston was the father of Smith Moses Kellogg and Dr. John Kellogg. Thus Wilfred and Anna had John Preston Kellogg as their common grandfather. Wilfred's mother and father were also cousins, though four or five generations removed. Both were descended from Nathaniel Kellogg, of Amherst, Maine, whose father, Joseph Kellogg, had emigrated to the U.S. from England in the mid-seventeenth century.

It is amusing to find in the *UB* (933) the statement: "The transition from the mother-family to the father-family explains the otherwise meaningless prohibitions of some types of cousin marriages."

In his earlier books Sadler defended the view that cousin marriages caused no harm provided both members of the couple are from "good stock." For example, in *The Truth About Heredity* (1927) we find these sentences:

Cousin marriages. The existing legislation on the statute books of the various states of this country, restricting cousin marriages, must be regarded on the whole as being unscientific and more or less unjustified.

It would seem that the laws regulating consanguineous marriage—cousin marriages in particular—would better be based on the pedigree of the individuals concerned and not on the mere fact of relationship. Biologists are of the opinion that marriage of cousins and other near relatives, of strong and efficient stock, would perhaps help the race, whereas all are agreed that cousins possessing hereditary defects should be prevented from entering into the marriage relation.

Legislation restricting cousin marriages is wholly unscientific. Only defective relatives should be denied marriage. Biologists incline to the opinion that cousin marriages in sound and normal stock would benefit the race.

East and Jones concluded that consanguineous marriages were not hurtful to the race, unless the stock already carried inheritable defects.

Similar remarks were even earlier expressed in Sadler's *Race Decadence* (1922). In their 1931 book *Piloting Modern Youth*, Sadler and his wife devote four pages to cousin marriages. They stress the dangers of first-cousin marriages when the parental stock is poor, but "if the heredity is good, the stock is improved." Sadler recalls a case that surely is a carefully disguised account of Wilfred and Anna. He speaks of two first cousins who wanted to marry. Sadler says he did not oppose the marriage, because "I have learned from experience that, when folks make up their minds to get married, you can do little or nothing about it. Even when they pray about it, I have discovered that God always answers yes."

Although Sadler made no attempt to "break up the match," he warned the couple about the possibility that their children might be adversely affected, and "advised them to have no offspring." They consulted another physician, "and took his contrary advice." A daughter was born. After the first few days she began to have convulsions and show signs of great nervousness. Fortunately, the parents used great wisdom, aided by Sadler's advice, in rearing the girl who at the time of Sadler's account was eleven and "robust, healthy, well nourished, and well controlled." Sadler does not name the parents, but he calls the daughter Mary.

Wilfred and Anna had only one child, Emma Ruth, who was born almost totally deaf. She later learned to speak and lip read. I do not know when she was born or the date of her marriage. Anna outlived her husband by four years, dying in Chicago on February 24, 1960, at age 82.

According to notes made by Martha Sherman (we will meet her in the next two chapters), Ruth died in February 1944. Martha drove through the rain to a memorial for her in Chicago on February 25. Ruth and her husband Jerry Picard (he died in 1991) lived on the outskirts of San Diego in a small apartment where they did not even have a telephone. Ruth developed a cold which rapidly turned into pneumonia followed by an attack of measles. A baby was born during this turmoil "but Jerry was inexperienced

in how to care for it and the baby died. Ruth passed on Thursday night."
There has been much speculation among Urantians that Ruth's hearing
abnormality, and other genetic defects that may have caused her early
death, were related to her parents being first cousins.*

I strongly suspect that Sadler, in his dramatic account of a first-cousin
marriage, changed the name of the child from Ruth to Mary, and her hereditary defect from deafness to an unspecified nervous condition. In recalling
his experiences with first-cousin marriages, one would expect him to write
about the case closest to him, but to alter the facts to preserve the identities
of Wilfred and Anna, and their eleven-year-old daughter.

After Sadler established his institute in a three-floor brick mansion at
533 Diversey Parkway, on Chicago's near-north side (it is still the Urantia
Foundation's headquarters), Wilfred and Anna found an apartment at 2754
Hampden Court, a few blocks away. The building has since been replaced
by a high-rise condominium. Wilfred was made the institute's business
manager, a post he held until his death in 1956.

I have found only two references to Wilfred in Sadler's books, although
I have not seen all of his books and there may be other such references. At
the close of the preface to *The Theory and Practice of Psychiatry* (1936),
Sadler thanks his "faithful secretary, Miss Norma Lucas," for her help on the
manuscript and "my wife and professional associate, Dr. Lena K. Sadler."
He adds: "My long-time associate, Wilfred C. Kellogg, afforded invaluable
assistance in going over the manuscript and in the preparation of the index."
And at the end of the preface to Sadler's *Prescription for Permanent Peace*
(1944) he writes: "My long-time associate, Wilfred C. Kellogg, contributed
many valuable suggestions in the preparation of this manuscript."

Throughout his life Wilfred was plagued by ill health and a shyness
that almost amounted to a fear of others. Thanks to Buddy Roogow I have
a copy of a 1906 letter from Wilfred to his employer, W. K. Kellogg, in
which he complained of "bad days" and said that his doctor, a Dr. Read, had
advised him to stop working for a few months of "quiet and rest" either out
of town or in the Battle Creek Sanitarium where he could receive treat-
ments. He does not specify the nature of his illness, but according to letters
from Harry Loose to Harold Sherman, as we shall learn in chapter 8, Wilfred suffered from chronic stomach ulcers.

In Sadler's *The Physiology of Faith and Fear* (1912) we find the following remarkable passage.

---

*In *Racial Decadence* (p. 330) Sadler claims that 4.5 percent of deafness is the result of parents being cousins.

In the cataleptic state consciousness is diffused—seems to be pushed far out toward the periphery. It is at a dead level of intensity. The mental life is largely in the dim marginal state. The physiological processes of the body are slowed down; in fact, they come to assume conditions very much like those which prevail in the hibernating animal. The body may become stiff and extraordinarily rigid. It is in this condition that the great trance mediums of history and of the present time usually are found when they receive their wonderful revelations and visions.

It is not uncommon for persons in a cataleptic trance to imagine themselves taking trips to other worlds. In fact, the wonderful accounts of their experiences, which they write out after these cataleptic attacks are over, are so unique and marvellous as to serve as the basis for founding new sects, cults, and religions. Many strange and unique religious movements have thus been founded and built up. It is an interesting study in psychology to note that these trance mediums always see visions in harmony with their own theological beliefs. For instance, a medium who believed in the natural immortality of the soul, was always led around on her celestial travels by some of her dead and departed friends. One day she changed her religious views—became a soul sleeper, and ever after that, when having trances, she was piloted about from world to world on her numerous heavenly trips by the angels; no dead or departed friends ever made their appearance in any of her visions after this change in her belief.

Nearly all these victims of trances and nervous catalepsy, sooner or later come to believe themselves to be messengers of God and prophets of Heaven; and no doubt most of them are sincere in this belief. Not understanding the physiology and psychology of their afflictions, they sincerely come to look upon their peculiar mental experiences as something supernatural, while their followers blindly believe anything they teach because of the supposed divine character of these so-called revelations.

Sadler liked to repeat passages, almost word for word, over and over again in later books. The paragraphs quoted above, for example, reappear with only trivial modifications in *The Truth About Spiritualism* (1923), *Modern Psychiatry* (1945), and *Menial Mischief and Emotional Conflicts* (1947). The 1912 book, from which I quoted, was surely written in 1911 before Sadler discovered that his brother-in-law was a trance channeler. In later books, where he discusses trance channeling, he inserts suggestions that there may be channelers who are actually in contact with a higher reality.

Mental Mischief contains a paragraph that skeptics of the *UB* would apply directly to Wilfred:

From time to time some self-styled "prophet" attempts to convince other people of the authenticity of the things he sees and hears in his own mind. If such odd geniuses are reasonably sane and otherwise conventional, they sometimes create large followings, build up cults, and establish churches. On the other hand, if they see a little too far or hear a little too much, they very shortly find themselves within the walls of an insane asylum. That is what happens when this "feeling of reality" is allowed to take such possession of the mind that one fails to distinguish between the creatures of consciousness and those of material existence.

However, this paragraph is soon followed by:

The great majority of these victims of trances and nervous catalepsy, undoubtedly many of them sincerely, believe themselves to be messengers and prophets of God. And this is not strange, since they know nothing about the physiology and psychology underlying their experiences. Neither is it hard to understand why their followers blindly believe anything they teach them.

In my many years of observation of many different *trance mediums* who have had these peculiar dreams and visions, I have found more than four-fifths of them to be women. Both the nervous and the endocrine systems of women appear to lend themselves more readily to these phenomena than do those of men. Certainly, the spiritual forces of the universe do not visit the female of the species more frequently than the male because she is a more highly spiritualized creature. It is probable that the posterior pituitary body and other endocrine or chemical factors which subject the nervous system of the female to periodic upheavals, both psychologic and physiologic, are responsible. I have never seen a case where these phenomena continued after the menopause.

I am not questioning the validity of true prophets, either ancient or modern; I am not even raising that question here. Although I willingly grant that such divinely taught persons may have lived or may even now live, I believe that most of those who have made these claims to supernatural experiences were either frauds or self-deceived persons, who, unacquainted with things psychical, actually believed their spells, visions, or visitations to be of divine origin.

Among those persons who have seizures or experiences of this sort whom I have been able to study, there have been but few in whom I could not discover certain psychic, chemical, and physical influences which accounted to my complete satisfaction for their extraordinary behavior.

Here are Sadler's early opinions about automatic writing and speaking. The paragraphs quoted below, from *The Physiology of Faith and Fear* (1912), also reappear with trivial changes in later books:

> As close of kin to trances and so-called visions should be mentioned the practices of automatic writing and speaking. The study of multiple personality has shed much light on the psychology of automatic writing. When practising it the patient may appear to be in his usual state; in fact, he may be conversing with some one in a perfectly normal and natural manner, when, if a pencil is placed in his hand, he will begin to write continuously, writing long essays which are carefully composed, logically arranged, and sometimes extraordinarily fine in rhetorical expression; and all this is accomplished while the central consciousness is entirely ignorant and unconscious of everything that is going on.
>
> This automatic writing is in no essential different from the experiences of crystal-gazing, shell-hearing, and hypnosis. In automatic writing the activities of the marginal consciousness are projected outward along the motor line of writing. In this case the subconscious activities are not sensory; the primary cause rests neither in auditory nor visual sensation, as in shell-hearing and crystal vision, but in sensations of touch and movement—they are entirely motor. The central consciousness does not become aware of what is going on in the marginal consciousness until it sees the thoughts expressed by means of the words automatically written. It will be apparent that to the central consciousness these messages would indeed appear as coming from another world; and so many a psychically unbalanced person, who has been exercised by automatic writing has been led in this way verily to suppose that these written messages were from the dead, or from the spirits inhabitating other planets.
>
> The phenomenon of automatic speaking occurs in the same way. It is another case of a motor expression of psychic projection. This time the subject is concerned with spoken words, instead of written words.

In 1929, in *The Mind at Mischief: Tricks and Deceptions of the Subconscious and How to Cope with Them*, Sadler explicitly disclosed his encounter, eighteen years before, with what he came to believe was a trance channeler in genuine contact with higher beings. Chapter 17, on "Dissociation and Double Personality," opens by saying that multiple personality is one of the most interesting of modern discoveries. In the book's later section on spiritism, Sadler discusses the relation of this malady to mediums. His experience, he tells us, is that 75 percent of all mediums are conscious frauds, but the other 25 percent are honest, self-deceived victims of secondary personalities. He adds that he has encountered "only one or two cases" in which phenomena similar to that of trance mediums may have a "spiritual or supernatural" basis. The phrase "one or two" indicates that Sadler had not yet made up his mind about Mrs. White. A footnote refers readers to the book's appendix.

Sadler's next chapter, on automatic writing, also is about its close relation to multiple personality disorders. A patient's hand will seem to be grasped by an invisible entity, perhaps a dead relative or an angel, and begin to write. This often produces "long essays which are carefully composed, logically arranged, and sometimes extraordinarily fine in rhetorical expression, and all this is accomplished while the central consciousness is ignorant of everything that is going on." Sadler is here repeating what he said in 1912.

Although like direct-voice mediums, automatic writers may be either charlatans or honest, or a strange mixture of both, "it may be altogether possible that some of them are manifestations of genuine activity on the part of actual spiritual forces, but that is not a point for further discussion in this connection." Again, a footnote says "See Appendix." The chapter ends: "The reader is referred to the Appendix for brief notice of a very unusual case of supposedly automatic writing associated with other psychic phenomena which came under my observation many years ago."

The appendix is so essential to our story that I quote it in full:

In discussions of fraudulent mediums or self-deceived psychics, the reader of this book has several times encountered the statement that there were certain exceptions to the general indictments there made, and was referred to this appendix. It now becomes my duty to explain what I had in mind when those footnotes were inserted.

In the interests of scientific accuracy on the one hand, and of strict fairness on the other, it becomes necessary to explain that there are one or two exceptions to the general statement that all cases of psychic phenomena which have come under my observation have turned out to be those of auto-psychism. It is true that practically all the physical phenomena have proved to be fraudulent, while the psychic phenomena are almost invariably explainable by the laws of psychic projection, transference, reality shifting, etc. But many years ago I did meet one trance medium, a woman now deceased, whose visions, revelations, etc., were not tainted with spiritualism. As far as my knowledge extends, at no time did she claim to be under the influence of spirit guides or controls, or to communicate messages from the spirits of departed human beings. Her work was largely of a religious nature and consisted of elevated sayings and religious admonitions. I never had the privilege of making a thoroughgoing psychic analysis of this case, and am not in a position to express myself as to the extent to which her revelations originated in the subconscious realms of her own mind. I make mention of the case merely to record the fact that I have met one instance of psychic phenomena apparently of the trance order that was not in any way associated with spiritualism.

The other exception has to do with a rather peculiar case of psychic phenomena, one which I find myself unable to classify, and which I would like very much to narrate more fully; I cannot do so here, however, because of a promise which I feel under obligation to keep sacredly. In other words, I have promised not to publish this case during the lifetime of the individual. I hope sometime to secure a modification of that promise and to be able to report this case more fully because of its interesting features. I was brought in contact with it, in the summer of 1911, and I have had it under my observation more or less ever since, having been present at probably 250 of the night sessions, many of which have been attended by a stenographer who made voluminous notes.

A thorough study of this case has convinced me that it is not one of ordinary trance. While the sleep seems to be quite of a natural order, it is very profound, and so far we have never been able to awaken the subject when in this state; but the body is never rigid, and the heart action is never modified, tho respiration is sometimes markedly interfered with. This man is utterly unconscious, wholly oblivious to what takes place, and, unless told about it subsequently, never knows that he has been used as a sort of clearing house for the coming and going of alleged extra-planetary personalities. In fact, he is more or less indifferent to the whole proceeding, and shows a surprising lack of interest in these affairs as they occur from time to time.

In no way are these night visitations like the séances associated with spiritualism. At no time during the period of eighteen years' observation has there been a communication from any source that claimed to be the spirit of a deceased human being. The communications which have been written, or which we have had the opportunity to hear spoken, are made by a vast order of alleged beings who claim to come from other planets to visit this world, to stop here as student visitors for study and observation when they are en route from one universe to another or from one planet to another. These communications further arise in alleged spiritual beings who purport to have been assigned to this planet for duties of various sorts.

Eighteen years of study and careful investigation have failed to reveal the psychic origin of these messages. I find myself at the present time just where I was when I started. Psychoanalysis, hypnotism, intensive comparison, fail to show that the written or spoken messages of this individual have origin in his own mind. Much of the material secured through this subject is quite contrary to his habits of thought, to the way in which he has been taught and to his entire philosophy. In fact, of much that we have secured, we have failed to find anything of its nature in existence. Its philosophic content is quite new, and we are unable to find where very much of it has ever found human expression.

Much as I would like to report details of this case, I am not in a position to do so at present. I can only say that I have found in these years of observation that all the information imparted through this source has proved to be consistent within itself. While there is considerable difference in the quality of the communications, this seems to be reasonably explained by a difference in state of development and order of the personalities making the communications. Its philosophy is consistent. It is essentially Christian and is, on the whole, entirely harmonious with the known scientific facts and truths of this age. In fact, the case is so unusual and extraordinary that it establishes itself immediately, as far as my experience goes, in a class by itself, one which has thus far resisted all my efforts to prove it to be of auto-psychic origin. Our investigations are being continued and, as I have intimated, I hope some time in the near future to secure permission for the more complete reporting of the phenomena connected with this interesting case.

Sadler's first case, the woman with visions and dreams untainted by spiritualism, was of course Mrs. White. Although Sadler had by now become convinced that her revelations were at least partly invalid, he never lost his admiration and fondness for her. When Richard Schwarz visited an aging Sadler—Schwarz was then researching his biography of John Kellogg—he was surprised to find ex-Adventist Sadler still speaking of Sister White with great respect. The second person mentioned in the appendix, who spoke and wrote while in trance, was in my opinion Wilfred Kellogg. He never gave Sadler permission to disclose his identity.

Sadler had acquired from his Adventist background a firm belief in "soul sleeping" until resurrection day, a belief that rendered any communication with the dead absolutely impossible. Whenever Sadler encountered a medium claiming to channel a departed soul, he knew at once that the channeling was invalid and could best be explained as outright fraud or by the medium dredging up false communications from his or her unconscious. However, he was quick to add (*The Mind at Mischief*, p. 352):

Again I must record that I have come in contact with a few individuals of psychic peculiarity, who were the channel of communication for numerous messages that were not of a trivial nature but in no instance did these messages lay claim to have had their origin with deceased human beings. They always claim an origin separate and apart from the realm of departed spirits.

Note that Sadler uses the word "channel" to describe the parts played by Ellen White and Wilfred Kellogg in communicating nontrivial messages from on high. Similar remarks are in Sadler's *The Truth About Spiritualism* (1923). This book is one of the strongest attacks ever written about fraudulent mediums and their methods. In the book's preface Sadler says he intends to publish the following year a much larger work titled *Spiritualism,* but it never appeared. I do not know whether Sadler completed or even started its manuscript.

It is worth noting that although Sadler says he never personally encountered examples of physical phenomena (rising tables, ectoplasm, voices from floating trumpets, luminous ghosts, and so on) that he could not explain as outright legerdemain, he is unwilling to rule out the possibility that some mediums may have been assisted by demons. Here is what he says about this on pages 207–208:

Of course I cannot be scientifically certain that evil ghosts and vagabond spirits, or some other agency of His Satanic Majesty, may not be at the bottom of certain rare cases of psychic phenomena brought forward under the guise of spiritism. I say, I cannot, as a scientist, settle this question. It may be true that in some cases the devils are in league with the mediums, and cunningly assist them in perpetrating some of the psychic phenomena which they bring forward in the name of spiritualism. But while I admit the possibility of some sort of connection between spiritualism and demonism, I desire emphatically to record that I have not personally investigated the case of any medium, or other psychic, professing to be a channel of communication between the living and the dead, where I have been in the least inclined to resort to this hypothesis in order to account for the phenomena observed.

In his 1912 book, *The Physiology of Faith and Fear*, Sadler was even more explicit in stating his belief that evil spirits are responsible for the nonfraudulent phenomena produced by spiritualist mediums:

The readers of this book are no doubt familiar with the Biblical standard by which these phenomena are measured. According thereto, they are disreputable, owing to their source in and connection with evil spirits. Consequently, we have the scriptural denunciation of the practice of seeking information from the dead and the exhortation to make our appeal to the Living God.

The author of this book is personally inclined to accept the Biblical diagnosis, and urges again, as he repeatedly does in this volume, that his readers adopt the attitude of faith in their own better selves and in the Supreme Being. This, he believes, is the key which, together with a rational use of material means, will unlock the mysteries of the present and the future. From his personal experiences with spiritualistic mediums, he thinks that we have in them themselves about the strongest imaginable empirical evidence pointing to the existence of those spiritual powers which are by nature liars and deceivers. We feel confident that the phenomena of spiritualism will never be settled by so-called scientific investigation and laboratory experimentation. (p. 467)

Two years later, in *Worry and Nervousness* (p. 288) Sadler again expresses his belief in demonology:

I do not for a moment undertake to say that I am personally able to explain all the phenomena connected with spiritualistic mediums and their séances. Personally, I am a believer in supernatural influences; but I am not at all persuaded that all supernatural agencies are good in their influence, and from what I know of spirit mediums and spiritualism (if it should prove in the end to be supernatural in origin), I think I have already made up my mind as to what sort or manner of spirit is connected with these manifestations. I look upon spiritualism as a problem largely outside of the pale of scientific investigation, although many phases of the phenomena are subject to both physiological and psychological study.

Throughout his book on spiritualism, as well as in later writings about mediums, Sadler is extremely careful to distinguish between mediums and seers. By mediums he means persons who claim to be in communication with the dead. By seers he means persons who do not channel the dead, but may be in genuine contact with a transcendent spiritual reality. Among the seers of modern times, although he does not name them, he surely had in mind (as in the famous appendix of *The Mind at Mischief*) Ellen White and Wilfred Kellogg. By 1923 Sadler had broken with Adventism and had become disenchanted with Mrs. White, but he was still not certain she was a total charlatan or even self-deceived. Hence his cautious phrasing of "one

or two cases" of authentic supernatural phenomena. He was sure Wilfred was genuine. He was not so sure about Sister White.
Here are some relevant passages:

> So far as my personal experience goes, I have never detected anything in the line of mediumship, thus far, which would call for a resort to a spiritual hypothesis for explanation. I have met, in my practice, peculiar psychic cases, some of which I have not been able fully to understand in the light of physiologic and psychologic laws, but as before stated, none of these have been mediums, and in no case did they claim to communicate with the dead. (p. 136)
>   It is my opinion that about seventy-five per cent of our commonplace spiritistic manifestations are frauds—conscious, deliberate, commercial frauds, and that about twenty-five per cent belong to the order which we are describing at this time, and include the possible cases of actual spiritual or supernatural phenomena, which I, it will be observed, all the way along, accept as possible, though I have never personally come in contact with but one or two cases that could lay even remote claim to falling into this last named group. (pp. 143–44)

> Again, I would distinctly disclaim all intention of discussing or commenting upon the genuine Seers of either ancient or modern times. The prophets of the Almighty are not under discussion in this thesis. If there be those who had visions in the olden time, who were the voice of "One crying in the wilderness;" and if there be those who have visions in modern times (and I have met a few of this sort who were very difficult to understand and adequately explain on purely psychologic grounds) I say, if there be those who have seen a vision in our day and generation, it is farthest from our purpose either to judge or stigmatize them. But again, I hasten to record the fact that those few cases of psychic phenomena coming under my observation, which might possibly be of supernatural origin, had nothing whatever in common with spiritualism. In fact, I may say that they were more or less actively anti-spiritualistic, and therefore their presentation or study does not concern us in this work. (p. 209)

It is interesting to note that in his appendix to *The Mind at Mischief* Sadler tells us that the unnamed channeler remained indifferent to the content of what came through him while asleep. This curious indifference is underscored in the *UB* (1208–1209):

> The Adjuster of the human being through whom this communication is being made enjoys such a wide scope of activity chiefly because of this

human's almost complete indifference to any outward manifestations of the Adjuster's inner presence; it is indeed fortunate that he remains consciously quite unconcerned about the entire procedure. He holds one of the highly experienced Adjusters of his day and generation, and yet his passive reaction to, and inactive concern toward the phenomena associated with the presence in his mind of this versatile Adjuster is pronounced by the guardian of destiny to be a rare and fortuitous reaction. And all this constitutes a favorable co-ordination of influences, favorable both to the Adjuster in the higher sphere of action and to the human partner from the standpoints of health, efficiency, and tranquillity.

I have been unable to determine the extent to which Wilfred and his wife actually believed that the material coming through a sleeping Wilfred was genuine. In spite of Wilfred's indifference, they must have believed because both of them participated actively in the Urantia movement.

In 1911 the Sadlers were living in La Grange, a Chicago suburb, as we have noted, waiting for an apartment in Chicago to become available. In 1912 Wilfred and his wife Anna occupied rooms in the same building. The only account in print of Sadler's discovery that his brother-in-law was a trance channeler is given in a paperback by Harold Sherman. This will be the main content of the next chapter.

7

The Revelation Begins

The only detailed account in print of how the Urantia papers were first channeled is chapter 5, "Pipeline to God," in *How to Know What to Believe*, a Fawcett paperback by Harold Sherman that was published in 1976. Sherman (1898–1987) was a prolific writer of sports fiction until his later years when he became a well known author of self-help books and books about the paranormal. Although admired for his psychic abilities and his research on ESP, Sherman never wanted to be called a psychic. He had a lifelong fascination with the potentialities of the human mind, and a consuming urge to prove to others that thoughts could be transferred from one person to another. In the next chapter we shall have much to say about his colorful career and his ill-fated involvement for five years in the Urantia movement.

It was in 1941 that Sherman and his wife, Martha, joined what was called the Forum, a group of Chicagoans who met on Sundays to discuss the Urantia Papers while their content was being channeled at night by the sleeping Wilfred.

Although at first intrigued and sympathetic, the Shermans soon became suspicious of how the channeled material was being rewritten and expanded by Sadler. Sherman tried to persuade Sadler to incorporate into the *UB* some information about psychic research and communication with the dead—to be checked and authorized by the sleeper (see Appendix C). It was a futile effort because Sadler, still loyal to many Adventist doctrines, firmly believed that no communication with the departed is permitted by God. Hostility between Sadler and the Shermans intensified until both Harold and Martha were rudely expelled from the Forum. Sadler accused Sherman of starting a rebellion against the new revelation, acting under the influence of the wicked Caligastia. Our next chapter will cover all this in more detail.

In Sherman's account of this acrimonious conflict, the word Urantia is never used. The *UB* is called *The New Revelation Book*. Sadler is thinly disguised as Dr. Henry P. Norton. Wilfred and his wife are Alfred and Lucy Buxton. Eight pages are devoted to a report, within quotation marks, of what Sadler told Sherman about the *UB*'s mysterious origin.

The exact date on which Wilfred's channeling first came to Sadler's attention remains to this day obscure. Sherman quotes Sadler as saying it began "about 35 years ago." Sadler made this remark in 1942, so subtracting 35 gives a date of 1906 or 1907. This is flatly contradicted by Sadler in his appendix to *The Mind at Mischief* where he explicitly says the channeling started in the summer of 1911. Sherman himself contradicts the "35 years ago" on page 69 of his chapter about the *UB*'s origin. "Thus began a strange and dramatic human saga," he writes, "which started in 1911 and continued for almost half a century."

The 1911 date given by Sadler could not have been a deliberate error because twice he speaks of having observed the subject for 18 years. The *Mind at Mischief* was published in 1929, and Sadler's preface is dated August 1929. Subtracting 18 years yields 1911. Sadler says he has made a sacred promise not to write about this case during the lifetime of the subject, though he hopes someday he can secure a modification of that promise and be allowed to report fully on the case. The modification was never given.

I am convinced that 1911 was an unintended error, and that Sadler meant the summer of 1912. According to Sherman, the channeler was married when the messages began to come through. As we have seen, Wilfred was married in La Grange in August 1912, at a time when he and Anna were living in an apartment below the Sadlers. It was in Sadler's house that the marriage had taken place.

Sherman reports Sadler as saying that at the time the revelations began he and his wife were living in a "furnished apartment." City Directories for La Grange, Illinois, show that in 1911 and 1912 the Sadlers lived at 56 Sixth Avenue in a house owned by Sadler that served as both their office and residence. However, the Sadlers rented rooms to others. The 1910 directory lists at that address, in addition to the Sadlers, Anna Kellogg and Frances Givens, both described as "trained nurses," and Sarah M. Willmer, a "reader" (we met her in chapter 2). The 1911 directory lists the same residents except Givens is no longer among them.

The 1913 directory puts at 56 Sixth Avenue the Sadlers, Mrs. Wilfred

Kellogg, and Mrs. Edward Van Bond, reader. Mrs. Van Bond was the former Sarah Mildred Willmer. She married Edward in 1912, as we learned earlier, in a double wedding, the other couple being Wilfred and Anna. The absence of Wilfred and Edward from the 1913 list was either an oversight or the two new husbands were temporarily at other addresses. The Sadlers and Kelloggs moved to Chicago in 1914 where they lived within a few blocks of each other.

That the 1911 date was a mistake is strongly supported by Carolyn Kendall, a Forum member who recalled in 1993 that she had heard that the 1911 date was an error, but that the publisher of Sadler's book never got around to correcting it. Kendall thinks the correct date was 1906. I believe it was 1912. It is easy to understand how Sadler could have been off by one year, but by five? Remember that in 1929 twice he speaks of 18 years as having passed since he first observed the sleeping conduit.

Late one evening, Sadler told Sherman, a woman living directly below them rapped on their door to say something very strange was happening to her husband. Sadler and his wife (Sherman calls her Dr. Ruth) slipped on their bathrobes and followed the lady downstairs. In her bedroom a "medium-sized man, approaching middle age" was in a deep sleep. Occasionally he would hold his breath for long periods. Sadler was astonished to find the man's pulse normal, and that he could not arouse him by jabbing him with pins. His body frequently "gave several jumps and starts." The sleeper awoke an hour later, feeling fine. Sadler examined him next day and found him in good health. Although he had witnessed many persons who went into trances, Sadler told the Shermans, they had mostly been "emotionally unstable" women. "Here was a hard-boiled business man, member of the board of trade and stock exchange, who didn't believe in any of this nonsense and who had no recollection of what happened during these strange unwakeable sleep states."

A few weeks later the man, whose name Sadler never revealed to Sherman, had another spell, including periods of nonbreathing. The spells continued until the Sadlers moved into their new apartment in Chicago, and the man and his wife took rooms in the same block. One night, during one of the man's seizures, Lena Sadler tried asking him a question. The sleeper replied in a voice not his own. "It was that of what we afterward learned to be a *student visitor* on an observation trip here from a far distant planet! This being apparently conversed with us through this sleeping subject and expressed ideas and philosophies which struck us as entirely new."

Sadler could find no evidence that the spoken words were coming from the man's unconscious. The sleeper never recalled anything said during his trances, nor could he recall anything under hypnosis. More celestial visitors started to come through the man's lips as Sadler and his wife began conversing with them, asking questions that "always brought the most stimulating and unexpected answers."

Sadler said he "worked out"—I assume he meant that he wrote down—and memorized 52 questions to ask the higher beings. One night, when a "particularly electrifying personality" seemed to be coming through from a distant planet, Sadler asked if he could prove who he was. The being stunned Sadler by saying "I have just received permission to answer 46 of the 52 questions you have been holding in your mind." The entity then proceeded to answer all 46 even though, as Sadler was convinced, the sleeper had no way of knowing the questions existed.

For ten years the Sadlers conversed with the celestial intelligences channelled vocally by the sleeper. Their adopted daughter Christy later was present to take notes in shorthand. According to Harry Loose, whom we shall meet in the next chapter, Christy was hired by Sadler because of her shorthand skill, then later made a member of the family.

In 1923 the Sadlers began to invite 20 or 30 friends over for Sunday afternoon teas to discuss religious topics. At about the fourth meeting Sadler began telling the group, which came to be called the Forum, about the sleeping subject and his startling revelations. Sadler asked the Forum members to come back next Sunday with questions for the higher intelligences. They arrived with more than 4,000! The Sadlers spent many days sorting and classifying them.

Nothing happened for a few weeks, then early one morning the man's wife called on the phone to come quickly. The Sadlers dressed "like voluntary firemen" and rushed downstairs. During the night the man had written a manuscript of 472 pages that answered all the questions asked by Forum members! It was in the man's handwriting, but he had no knowledge of having written it. Sadler estimated it would take a person eight hours of writing at top speed to produce such a document, yet the "subject matter was so profound and yet so intelligently set down that I knew it was beyond human capacity to achieve." The next day Sadler tested the man's right arm for fatigue, but found the arm normal.

The handwritten manuscript was typed by Christy (Sherman calls her Cynthia Frederick or Cindy) and read to an "awestruck and speechless" Forum. This led to more questions. More answers were channeled through the sleeper either verbally, or in writing, or both. Sadler said to Sherman:

We found there seemed to be an organized group of high intelligences on "the other side," prepared to present to us the whole astounding story of the universe, leading from God, the Universal Father, down to the origin of the human creature, man, and his ultimate glorious destiny beyond the reaches of time and space.

This continued for perhaps seven or eight years when what we considered the first edition of the papers was finished. At that time, the Forum received its first direct message, and its members were advised that now, since their knowledge had been expanded, they should be able to ask more intelligent questions and that if they would do so, as they commenced a rereading of each paper, these intelligences would completely revise the entire, tremendous manuscript.

After each message was obtained from the sleeper, Christy would type out her shorthand notes and the typescript would be read aloud to the Forum, usually by Dr. Sadler, but sometimes by his son Bill Jr. Forumites were never permitted to see Christy's shorthand notes, or anything written by the sleeper, or Christy's typescripts until after the material had been revised and retyped on the basis of feedback from the Forum.

The best description of the process by which the papers were revised is in a lengthy sworn deposition made on June 29, 1994, in Chicago, by Helen Carlson. The deposition was given in connection with a sensational court trial which we will cover in our final chapter. Helen's husband died in 1932. In 1935 her sister, the first wife of Bill Jr. brought her into the Forum. She has been permitted to live at 533 Diversey from 1935 until the present.

The Sunday afternoon Forum meetings, Helen said, were held at 533 in a room that contained about fifty folding chairs. The seats were usually filled, and at times the Forumites overflowed into an adjacent room that is now Helen's living room. After the doctor or Bill read a paper, Forumites wrote questions on slips of paper that were placed in a basket or a fishbowl on a table at one side of the room. Bill would collect the slips, then later screen the questions by eliminating duplicates, and arranging the relevant ones on a page or two to present to the midwayers. Helen described the midwayers as invisible entities living on Urantia and halfway "between the spiritual and the human."

Helen was secretive about how the questions were presented to these "unseen friends." They were, she said, "put in a certain spot" where the midwayers would take them. Asked where the spot was, she replied: "I don't know the answer to that. I tried to find out sometimes, but I wasn't successful." It was, she added, information kept secret by persons who had taken oaths not to reveal it. Asked who told her about such oaths, she said: "I know the answer to that but I am not permitted to disclose it."

A week or so after the questions were collected by Bill, answers would be read to the Forum in a revised paper or a new paper. Helen recalled that Paper No. 1 was first expanded to two papers, then later to five. On one occasion Forumites wanted to know what a paper meant by "personality." Soon a paper appeared giving a direct answer. This constant revising of the papers, on the basis of Forum feedback, continued (Helen insisted twice) until at least 1949.

Where were the papers kept? Not in a safe, Helen disclosed, but in a "chest of drawers on the third floor." No Forumite was allowed to take a paper from the building. They were permitted to read papers on the premises provided they took no notes. Later, when advanced students known as "the Seventy" began to meet on Wednesday evenings, they were allowed to keep notes in three-ring spiral binders. These notebooks were kept in a bookcase from which they could be removed at will, though they were not allowed to take them from the building until after the *UB* was printed in 1955.

In 1991 Mark Kulieke, of Green Bay, Wisconsin, published a 16-page document titled *Birth of a Revelation: The Story of the Urantia Papers*. He revised and expanded it to 24 pages for a second edition in 1992. It was further enlarged to 37 pages for a third printing later that year, and in 1994 a fourth edition had 43 pages. It was published by his newly formed Morning Star Foundation. In a preface to this edition Kulieke says that several thousand copies of earlier editions were sold to twenty nations. Next to Sherman's account, this is the most valuable history of the *UB* written to date.

Kulieke's credentials as a *UB* historian are high. His father, Warren H. Kulieke, followed Bill Sadler Jr. as the Urantia Brotherhood's second president. Warren's brother Alvin also served as president. Mark Kulieke's sisters and his former wife, Barbara Newsom (they were later divorced), are devout Urantians.

For more than four years Mark worked full-time at 533 Diversey as an assistant to Christy. A past president of the First Urantian Society of Chicago, he holds a bachelor's degree in history, and a master's in library science.

The only persons with direct knowledge of the revelation process, Mark Kulieke writes, were the members of a group that became known as the Contact Commission. Kulieke believes there were at least six members:

Dr. Sadler and his wife, Lena; Wilfred Kellogg and his wife, Anna; Bill Sadler Jr.; and Christy. There could have been others. Kulieke suggests that Dr. Meyer Solomon, who wrote one of the two introductions to *The Mind at Mischief*, may have been a member. I was surprised by this suggestion because Solomon was a lifelong atheist and there is no reason to believe he accepted the Urantian revelation. A more likely person was Robert H. Galt, a psychologist at Northwestern University who wrote the other introduction to Sadler's book. There is evidence that he was allowed to witness the sleeper's channeling.

The Commission was formed, Kulieke says, in response to an order from revelator Machiventa Melchizedek on February 11, 1924, to plan for the production of the *UB*. Kulieke believes the revelations began in Battle Creek in 1906, "converged" in La Grange, and culminated in Chicago. Why Chicago? "Probably Chicago was selected for a large variety of reasons much as Palestine was selected for the scene of Jesus' life and teachings."

Dear old Chicago, the sooty Windy City where I lived for so many years before World War II. Who would have suspected that the Gods would have chosen Chicago for what the *UB* calls the Fifth Epochal Revelation? There have been many revelations to humanity (*UB* 1007), but only five were great enough to be called epochal. The first was the teaching of members of Caligastia's staff before he rebelled. These teachings continued for 300,000 years, but were gradually lost. The American Indians held on to them longest.

The second epochal revelation, about 38,000 years ago, was through Adam. The third came through Melchizedek of Salem who taught the goodness of God and that "faith was the act by which man earned God's favor." This was about 1920 BCE. The fourth epochal revelation was through Jesus, the incarnated Michael of Nebadon. The fifth was the appearance of the Urantia Papers. In the fourth revelation, Urantians like to say, the Word was made flesh. In the fifth, the Word was made book.

Kulieke believes that members of the Contact Commission were given "inner impulses" from the supermortals that were "something akin to so-called channeling." Kulieke dropped this phrase in the second edition of his booklet, replacing it with "rendering the invisible visible."

Urantians strongly dislike the word channeling as a description of how revelations came through the sleeping contactee because the word is so commonly applied to the hundreds of New Agers now said to be "channels" for spiritual beings. However, Wilfred obviously served as a "channel" for such communications. It is often said that he differed from trance channelers in that messages came through him while he slept, but many famous mediums, Boston's Mrs. Piper for instance, channeled after falling into deep slumber.

"Someone," Kulieke continues, "other than the human subject who was also a member of the contact group received inner impulses of words and meanings of which he was conscious and which he then wrote down, but which would not be heard or noticed by others. This seems to be how some instructions came. It would not surprise me if all members of the Contact Commission had this capability." The "someone" clearly was Sadler.

Kulieke also believes that there was "direct audio contact between members of the Contact Commission and the superhuman revelators" and that "materialization, dematerialization, and editing of physical papers by superhumans" also took place.

Genuine visions of the invisible world occurred. "The Contact Commission was enabled to see seraphic transports. They witnessed a seraphic train pass over Lake Michigan. Urantia was simply a junction point for this seraphic train which had emptied a doomed planet of salvable personalities and was heading for a new world to deposit their human cargo." This is one of the craziest of Urantia myths that Kulieke takes seriously.

Sadler was allowed other clairvoyant visions. He was "enabled to see the mansion world life prior to his death. It would appear that reflectivity was also employed to enable him to see certain events on Earth in distant locations." Reflectivity is a word used in the *UB* for instant communication of information. (See the section on "Universe Reflectivity," p. 105.)

In brief, Kulieke is persuaded that Sadler and others on the Contact Commission were divinely inspired, or "indited" as the *UB* prefers to say, to contribute to what he calls a "pervasive, complex, multidimensional, and evolutionary" process that culminated in the *UB*.

This contention that Sadler acquired psychic powers from the celestials is supported by Harold Sherman in *How to Know What to Believe:*

> The doctor surprised them by stating that he knew what they were coming to see him about, that he had been *"taken out of his physical body the night before and transported to the Deane home in his spirit form,"* where he *"saw and listened to everything that was said in the invisible."*

The Deane in this quotation is called Ben Deane by Sherman. His real name was Dent Karle. As Sherman correctly recalls, "Ben Deane, disillusioned and threatened with blindness, committed suicide by shooting himself."

Mark Kuliekes ex-wife Barbara worked for two weeks with Christy in

1976 on a history of the *UB*. Three years later Christy announced that the material for the history had been lost or stolen. This prompted Mark and Barbara to prepare a slide-history, with voice-over, almost an hour long, which was shown at several Urantian gatherings. I have not seen it, and it now seems to be in limbo. If notes for Christy's planned history still exist and can be recovered, it would be an invaluable find. No one knew the details about Wilfred's trance channeling better then Christy.

I must add that Kulieke does not buy the view, now accepted by so many older Urantians, that Wilfred was the sleeper. He believes that Sadler's 1911 date is five years off, that the channeling began in 1906 in Battle Creek, and that this counts heavily against identifying Wilfred as the channeler. In line with Sadler's pronouncements, Kulieke is convinced that the channeler's identity will never be revealed.

Only two known documents support the 1906 date. We have mentioned one—Sadler's supposed statement to Sherman in 1942 that the revelations began "about 35 years ago." As we shall learn in the next chapter, Sherman's friend Harry Loose gave this figure of 35 years in a 1941 letter to Sherman. I believe this was the sole basis for Sherman attributing that date to Sadler.

Kulieke's main source for the 1906 date was Forum member Carolyn Kendall, a loyal Urantian now living in Wheeling, Illinois. Like Kulieke she takes the 1906 date as proof that Wilfred could not have been the sleeper because in 1906 Wilfred was still single. At a Urantia conference in Montreal, in August 1993, Mrs. Kendall said that if she learns on the first mansion world that Wilfred was the contactee, she will "faint dead away."

At this point let me make clear that I am not absolutely certain Wilfred did the initial channeling, but the evidence seems to me so overwhelming that in this book I assume it is true. I have good reasons to believe that some early officials of the Urantia Foundation, as well as many old-timers in the movement, know that Wilfred was the contactee, but are loyal to Sadler in maintaining vows of silence on this question. If definitive evidence ever turns up that the sleeper was someone else, I will not faint dead away, but I shall be astounded.

In an interview with Polly Friedman, in a Urantian periodical *The Conjoint Reader* (Summer 1993), Mrs. Kendall says that in 1951, when she was almost 19, Sadler told her how the revelation began. The story, she adds, was "essentially the same as in Sherman's book." Mrs. Kendall refers to the "35 years ago" in Sherman's account, and correctly states that this would take the date of the first channeling back to 1906. "Supposedly," she adds, "the printer made an error and they decided to leave it."

Note that Mrs. Kendall does not explicitly say that Sadler gave her the 1906 date. I believe she is relying entirely on Sherman's reference to "35 years ago" which he found in one of Harry Loose's letters. It is hard to believe that Sadler would have mistakenly added five years to 1906 when he wrote the appendix to his 1929 book. Although I do not believe Sadler told Mrs. Kendall the revelation began in 1906, I think she correctly recalls the discovery, after *The Mind at Mischief* was off the press, that 1911 was a mistake. It was the summer of 1912, not the summer of 1911. It would have been easy for Sadler to have missed the date by one year. Because the difference was so small, Sadler allowed it to go uncorrected in later printings of his book.

Another possibility deserves mention. Wilfred may have started to have his nightly seizures as early as 1906, but not until 1912, after he and his wife were living in an apartment below the Sadler's in La Grange, did Wilfred's new wife and the Sadlers become aware of his channeling. Loose may have confused the year the seizures began with the year it came to Sadler's attention.

I should add that many Urantians are unhappy with Kulieke's booklet. In the Spring/Summer 1992 issue of *Sojourn*, a periodical published by disgruntled Urantians in Boulder, Colorado, Larry Muffins reviews the document unfavorably. Kulieke is castigated for mixing fact with myth, and never telling his readers which is which. "I do not believe it is wise," writes Muffins, "of Mark to propagate information that cannot be verified and that panders to the pathetic human weakness to seek to be special, unique and of particular value to celestial beings."

Members of the commission, Kulieke tells us in his pamphlet, had "direct audio contact with the revelators."

> The procedure was as follows: They were to read a paper each Sunday afternoon. It was ordinarily read to them by one of the Contact Commission, usually Dr. Sadler. They were to write down any questions that came to mind and hand them in each week. Mr. Kellogg was generally responsible for collecting them. Answers to their questions were then considered by the superhuman revelators. The answers were incorporated into a subsequent paper or an editing of the original paper. In this way, one paper about God eventually mushroomed into five papers about God—the first five in the book. Other parts likewise expanded as the superhumans monitored the human reaction to their material.

Mrs. Harold Sherman, who for five years attended Forum meetings with her husband, told me that Wilfred was the only person in the group who never made a comment or asked a question.

Kulieke continues:

This process initially took approximately five years and then consisted of 57 papers. But the process does not stop there. The book was advanced another generation in human understanding between 1929 and 1935. After years of reading papers, the first draft of Parts I–III, the Forum was told approximately: "With your increased understanding derived from reading and study of the material, you can now ask more intelligent questions. We are going to go through the book again." And so the book was edited and expanded week by week and year by year as the Forum members learned and grew.

It had been reported by several Forumites that some revelatory material was recalled—either because it was just too incomprehensible to the human mind or because it was deemed best not to reveal the information to the future readership. Very little explanation was given beyond the fact that it was their decision to withdraw the paper. Other papers were edited after being read to the Forum. For instance, one of the papers stated that the apostle Nathaniel had a good sense of humor for a Jew. At this comment the members of the Forum chuckled. The next time they got this paper from the safe, they discovered the phrase "for a Jew" was deleted. Human reaction to the material was obviously monitored closely. At least one Forumite believed that several of the most difficult papers would not have been included in *The Urantia Book* without the questions formulated by William S. Sadler Jr. *The Urantia Book* bears the birthmark of the collective mind of the people who composed the Forum during the birth phase.

Dr. Sadler said in one paper that about 150 people participated in this creative process. In another, he mentions 300 people while citing the total Forum membership as 486. The original charter membership numbered 30. Then as now, there was a mix of people including the very committed, the indifferent, and even a few with negative reactions to the whole business. They came from diverse backgrounds. In the march of human events over the years, some dropped out, some moved out of town, some moved on to the mansion worlds.

By 1934 and 1935, the process was essentially complete for the first three parts of the book. A third and final creative round was undertaken between 1935 and 1942 to clarify concepts and remove ambiguities. This apparently resulted in only minor editing by the superhuman revelators.

About 1935, the Forum received the Jesus papers from the midwayers who had waited for approval from Uversa before undertaking the story. The final round of clarification and editing between 1935 and 1942 seems to have included Part IV. Part IV is undated. No one has said why. I believe it is because Parts I to III contain cosmology that will become dated and eventually need revision. Part IV on the other hand contains "historic facts and religious truths" which should "stand on the records of the ages to come." (1109) Its date need not be fixed.

The process of intimate cooperation between revelators and the Contact Commission, with input from several hundred Forum members, finally produced what Sadler considered a publishable work. On page 354 of the *UB* we are told that the 31 papers that constitute the book's Part I were "formulated and put into English" in 1934. On page 648 we are told that the 25 papers that make up Part II were "indited" and put into English in 1934. On page 1319 we are told that the 63 papers of Part III "were authorized by a Nebadon commission of twelve acting under the direction of Mantutia Melchizedek. We indited these narratives and put them in the English language, by a technique authorized by our superiors, in the year CE 1935 of Urantia time."

In 1939 a group called "The Seventy," because it originally consisted of 70 members, was formed and charged with preparing the *UB*'s final text, and arranging for its printing by the Donnelley Press of Chicago. The Seventy was a closely knit group which met on Wednesday nights in addition to Sunday meetings with other Forum members. They worked in extreme secrecy, in a state of great exultation and anticipation. "There was considerable dialog," Kulieke tells us, "and input from seraphim and midwayers." He recalls the day his father, in great excitement and pride, brought home copies of the first printed volumes. It is no coincidence, he reminds us, that Jesus (as we learn in Luke 10:1) appointed 70 disciples to spread out over the land to proclaim the good news of the gospel.

It was decided that the *UB* would not be published until the long Jesus section had been completed. Its papers would give a full account of the life of Jesus, correcting hundreds of errors in the four gospels and supplying thousands of details about the life and teachings of Jesus never before revealed. The higher beings wanted the final book to be published, in Sadler's words as spoken to Sherman, "without any human personalities tobe identified . . . and no author ascribed to it."

"There are only a few of us still living, " Sadler ended his remarks, "who were in touch with this phenomenon in the beginning, and when we die, the knowledge of it will die with us. Then the book will exist as a great spiritual mystery, and no human will know the manner in which it came about."

As we have said, the Forum originally consisted of no more than 30 members. This number slowly increased, and of course there was constant movement of members in and out of the group. Before a person could join the Forum he or she would be personally interviewed by Sadler and sworn to secrecy about all that was going on. From time to time documents channeled by Wilfred and typed by Christy, or written by others, were destroyed. More were shredded after Sadler's death in 1969. Before her final illness in 1982, Christy ordered the destruction of all remaining original documents. This of course makes it impossible for anyone today to determine the extent to which channeled material was revised, cut or supplemented by Sadler or by other members of the Contact Commission or Forum.

On at least two other occasions Sadler wrote cryptically about the *UB*'s origin. In 1941 he lectured on "The Evolution of the Soul" to the Plymouth Congregational Church, of Lansing, Michigan. (This was reprinted in 1990 as a pamphlet by the Jesusonian Foundation, a Urantia firm in Boulder.) The lecture is a stirring defense of Urantia doctrines, especially the dogma, so essential to Seventh-day Adventists, that a person consists of three parts: body, mind, and a "spirit" that is a fragment of God.

After a mortal's first resurrection, at which he or she is reconstituted with all earthly memories restored, Sadler said, the person begins a long adventure during which his or her mind and spirit gradually fuse to create an immortal soul. The soul continues to evolve in reconstituted bodies on other planets, in higher and higher realms, until it finally achieves perfection in Paradise. "And so does man pass from the dependence of cosmic childhood to that supernal height of universe citizenship wherein he actually begins to take part in the fascinating drama of eternity as it majestically unfolds the eternal purpose of the Gods."

Note Sadler's capitalized plural, "the Gods." The term "Gods" appears more than a hundred times in the *UB*. Here is one such passage from page 364:

There is a great and glorious purpose in the march of the universes through space. All of your mortal struggling is not in vain. We are all part of an immense plan, a gigantic enterprise, and it is the vastness of the undertaking that renders it impossible to see very much of it at any one time and during any one life. We are all a part of an eternal project which the Gods are supervising and outworking. The whole marvelous and universal mechanism moves on majestically through space to the music of the meter of the infinite thought and the eternal purpose of the First Great Source and Center.

"Many of the concepts embraced within this presentation of my theory," Sadler said in his 1941 lecture, "are not original with me, but I have deemed it best not to encumber this discussion with numerous quotations, citations, and acknowledgements." A footnote adds: "In the case of some of my 'borrowed' concepts which are unpublished I desired to give credit to the original sources. While permission to make use of this material was granted, the request to accord acknowledgement was denied."

In 1958 Sadler produced a 26-page manuscript titled *Consideration of Some Criticisms of the Urantia Book*. In it he replied to eighteen common objections. Was the *UB* a fraud or hoax? Sadler points out that he and his wife had extensive experience exposing fake mediums and "psychic humbugs." Had they detected a glimmer of such fraud about the *UB* they would have at once abandoned it. No Urantian has profited financially from the *UB*, he insists. Aside from professional proofreading, no one received "one cent" from the book's sales. On the contrary, over $100,000 was spent on its editing and printing.

The *UB* contains more than a million words, Sadler adds, yet no one has found in it a single contradiction. This may have been true in 1958, but over subsequent years a number of changes have been made in the *UB*'s text. Most of the changes are trivial corrections of spellings and punctuation, but there have been a few that eliminate contradictions. For example, on page 1317 of the *UB*'s first printing we are told that the three wise men "visited the newborn child in the manger." On page 1351 we learn that at the time of this visit Jesus and his parents had moved to a room at the inn. When this contradiction was noticed, the words "in the manger" were removed from the next printing. On page 1943 is a mention of the twelve apostles at the close of the Last Supper. Actually, as both the *UB* and the New Testament make clear, only eleven were then present because Judas had hurriedly left to go out into the night. In later printings "the twelve" was replaced by "the apostles."

Another apparent contradiction (although Urantian fundamentalists, like their Christian counterparts, have ingenious ways of explaining away such things) is between statements in the *UB* about Father Melchizedek and Gabriel. Father Melchizedek is Gabriel's "first executive associate." On page 385 we are told "Gabriel and Father Melchizedek are never away from Salvington at the same time, for in Gabriel's absence the Father Melchizedek functions as the chief executive of Nebadon." On page 1753, however, we learn that both Gabriel and Father Melchizedek were present during the Transfiguration of Jesus on the mountaintop when his face shone, as the *UB* puts it, "with the luminosity of a heavenly light." The Bible tells us that Moses and Elijah were present on this occasion, but the *UB* informs us that this was not the case. "Peter erroneously conjectured that the beings with Jesus were Moses and Elijah; in reality, they were Gabriel and the Father Melchizedek. The physical controllers had arranged for the apostles to witness this scene because of Jesus' request."

Why was the identity of the *UB*'s channeler never disclosed? Sadler's answer: "We do not want future generations to be concerned with the adoration of a Saint Peter or Saint Paul, a Luther, Calvin, or Wesley. We want no individual to be exalted by the Urantia Papers. The book should stand on its own nature and work."

Keeping important information secret is not new, Sadler continues. He quotes several New Testament passages in which Jesus asks his followers "to tell no one" of certain facts, including the fact that he is the Christ. As for the Bible itself, we do not know the real authors of its books. We don't have to know who composed a symphony to enjoy it. In military organizations higher officers often have information that is unwise to give to an army's rank and file. Even after we attain Paradise, Sadler assures us, there will be secrets we will never understand about the seven sacred worlds that revolve around it.

As for how the Urantia papers were transmitted, Sadler declares, there are aspects which neither he nor anyone else fully understands. "If you knew all we know, you would still be ignorant of much concerning the phenomena of factualizing these documents. No living person fully understands just how the Urantia Papers got translated into the English manuscript which was authorized for publication."

In reply to Criticism 10, which calls the book a product of automatic speaking and writing, Sadler says: "While we are not at liberty to tell you even the little we know about the technique of the production of the Urantia Papers, we are not forbidden to tell you how we did not get these documents." The book, he insists, is not the product of automatic writing, talking, hearing, seeing, thinking, remembering, acting, personalization, or any combination of these or other psychic states.

It is important to understand what Sadler means by "automatic." He means that the *UB* did not come from the channeler's unconscious. A skeptic, of course, believes it was exactly that—that Wilfred, like Mrs. Piper and Mrs. White, was a trance channeler who spoke and wrote what emerged from his subconscious. Sadler, convinced of the divine origin of the papers, could honestly deny they were the product of any kind of "automatic" (that is, subconscious) behavior.

Although Sadler was careful never to identify the channeler, Sherman and his wife were able to learn the man's identity. Sherman's notes about this have been sealed in a carton and placed in the archives of the Torreyson Library, at the University of Central Arkansas, at Conway. The carton is not to be opened until the year 2000. It contains detailed records of the Shermans' experiences with Sadler and the Forum from 1942 to 1947, experiences that led to their expulsion from the Forum and accusations that they were under Caligastia's control. That the sleeping subject was Wilfred has since been confirmed by Mrs. Sherman as well as by other former Urantians still living.

The Urantia Foundation, which owns the copyright on the *UB*, has remained faithful to Sadler's command that the identity of the channeler should never be revealed. A 1978 pamphlet currently obtainable from the Foundation is titled *The Urantia Book: The Question of Origin*. Here is how it justifies the Foundation's refusal to name the channeler:

Who the human being was whose versatile Thought Adjuster aided in bringing the fifth epochal revelation to our world will never be known because the revelators asked the few people who knew to take a pledge of secrecy. They did not want any human beings to be mystically associated with *The Urantia Book*. It is amazing that the authors of the Urantia Papers tell us as much as they do. Upon reflection, you will recognize the persistent questions about the unrevealed "details" concerning the origin of the book as a psychological parallel to the reoccurring demand put to Jesus, "Show us a sign."

Now let us turn to the human side of the story which may be interesting, but has no spiritual significance. In preparation for presenting the papers of the fifth epochal revelation and placing them in the custody of a responsible group of human beings, the revelators made contact with a small group of people in Chicago. The leaders of this group were asked by the revelators not only to refrain from revealing the identity of the individual associated with the presentation of the papers, but also not to discuss details related to the arrival of the papers. We will, therefore, never know just where or how the papers were received. Even these early leaders were puzzled; no human being knows just how this materialization was executed. The reason given for this request of secrecy is the revelators are determined that future generations shall have *The Urantia Book* wholly free from mortal connections.

The Foundation's efforts to conceal the identity of the sleeping conduit have been so strenuous as to lead its members into outright deception. This is the only good explanation I can think of for Christy's repeated denials that the famous appendix to Sadler's *Mind at Mischief* (reproduced in chapter 6) had any reference to either Mrs. White or to the *UB*'s sleeping conduit. Several of her letters survive in which she made such denials. I have one before me as I type. It was sent on March 31, 1978, on Foundation stationery, to David Biggs, of Flint, Michigan. "Poppy" was the name Christy called her father. The letter reads in full:

Dear David:

In response to your letter of March 25 enclosing pages from Dr. Sadler's "The Mind At Mischief", which I'm returning to you, as I have copies of all of Poppy's books in a special bookcase, I am well familiar with this one.

Others have written me similar letters as you have. "The Mind At Mischief" was written some years before *The URANTIA Book* and at that time Dr. Sadler says he had been studying this case for 18 years. I had never connected this with *The URANTIA Book*, nor did I ever hear any discussion that it had any connection therewith. Therefore, I can give you no information as to whether your assumption is correct or not.

When I asked Mark Kulieke about this letter, he explained it by saying that in her declining years Christy became so fearful she might let slip some clue as to the channeler's identity that she went to extreme lengths to avoid commenting on anything relating to the man.

How did Sherman first learn that Wilfred was the sleeping conduit for the fifth epochal revelation? Sherman discloses this in a remarkable letter dated January 18, 1971, written to his friends Robert and Ruth Burton. This married couple were devout Urantians who together with Bert M. Salyer Jr. had been among the founders of the Urantian study group in Oklahoma City. We will meet Mr. Burton again in chapter 17 as a defendant in a lawsuit brought against him by the Urantia Foundation.

Here is the relevant passage from Sherman's letter. The ellipses are all in the original.

I spent a most interesting 3 hours with Bert Salyer in Tulsa, who came over from Oklahoma City to see me, following my lecture on How To Create Your Future, for the Tulsa Town Hall Forum. He insists that both the doctor and Bill took him in confidence and told him that Kellogg was the "sensitive" through whom the papers came . . . that they had him move in with them . . . and assist in editing the manuscript as it came through, etc. It was a well kept secret . . . but this explains much . . . the story we had was that a young stockbroker, whose mind was free of prejudicial religious concepts, etc., was the "receiver."

I recall, when we had our difficulties with the doctor, how frightened Kellogg was of us . . . he may have felt we would have sensed his identity and would have revealed it . . . We did wonder a bit but that was all . . . what the Kelloggs' role was in this project. Salyer said the doctor told him it was Mrs. Sadler who finally convinced him that the papers Kellogg was writing were coming from a higher source and should be taken seriously . . .

Kellogg himself didn't know what to make of them [the papers] . . . and as they continued to come through, the system was worked out for handling them. This explains our own discovery that Sadler was revising and creating some of the sections. Even Bedell discovered that the papers had borrowed from a book on economics written by [Stuart] Chase, and was told, "wherever humans had created something of value, the authors of the Urantia Papers had used it." Remember????

There are many mysteries which remain to be solved.

In fairness to those elderly Urantians who cannot believe that Wilfred was the sleeper, I should mention a claim by Melvin (Bud) Kagan, a devout, long-time Urantian now living in Honolulu. In a deposition made in 1992, for a court case we will cover in our last chapter, Kagan said that his good friend Bill Sadler Jr. once told him that the sleeper "was not a Kellogg." Kagan is convinced that the identity of the sleeper will never become known and that no human contributed a single word to the *UB*.

On November 23, 1993, I had a two-hour phone conversation with Bert Salyer, a widower with three adult children, all four living in Oklahoma City. He became a Urantian in 1957, he said, when he first discovered the *UB*. At that time he was preaching in a New Thought church he had founded. He took about twenty members of his congregation out of the church to establish the city's First Urantia Society. For 15 years he was a dedicated Urantian, even privately publishing a book titled *We Believe*.

After 15 years he became convinced that the *UB* was a fraud, "as phony as a three-dollar bill." Salyer spoke briefly about his many business ventures—half ownership of a cotton gin, president of The Salyer Oil Company, inventor of a perpetual motion machine based on a modified steam engine. At one time or other he has been associated with masonry, theosophy, a California cult called The Lemurians, Silva Mind Control, and various New Thought churches. He once ran a clinic where he practiced hypnotherapy. He called his present religion Universalism and told me he talks constantly with his dead wife and with two celestials known as Gus and

Charley. He urged me to read Barbara G. Walker's *The Woman's Encyclopedia of Myths and Secrets*, which he called "the greatest book of the twentieth century."

Salyer could not recall meeting Harold Sherman. He denied any knowledge of who the *UB*'s contactee was.

I should add that Clyde Bedell (Sherman calls him Floyd Winters) wrote a 27-page typescript blasting Sherman's account of the Urantia Movement. Titled "A Response To a Thinly Disguised Attack on *The Urantia Book*," it is an abridgement of a talk Bedell gave to the First Urantia Society of Oklahoma, September 3, 1976. Although the *UB*, especially in its Jesus section, teaches that one should love one's enemies and be kind to them, many Urantians explode with unbelievable animosity whenever they encounter someone who dares question their beliefs.

Clyde Bedell was the advertising manager of a Chicago firm called Butler Brothers when in September 1924 he joined the Forum and remained a loyal Urantian until his death in 1985. He brought his secretary Marian Rowley into the Forum. She, too, became a lifelong, active Urantian. Bedell edited the *UB*'s massive *Concordex*, an indispensable reference for *UB* scholars. We will have more to say about him in chapter 10.

Here are some samples of Bedell's rhetoric:

Sherman's chapter is called "an appalling mass of fiction fleshed over a fragile skeleton of misshapen fact." It is filled with "fabrications," "misstatements," and is utterly "contemptible."

Bedell correctly describes Sherman as a believer in paranormal phenomena. Once he found he could not "get control of the papers," he stayed in the Forum for years to learn as much as he could so he could later discredit the movement. All Forum members except Sherman remained "dedicated, devout believers in the Mighty Christian Revelation that was unfolding before them." Why did Sherman alone disbelieve? Because he lacked the "spiritual fortitude to give up his stake in spiritualism" and other financially profitable occult beliefs.

Bedell accuses Sherman of failing to tell anyone of his secret intent to attack the *UB*. Without knowing it, the Forum "embraced as one of themselves a snooper disguised as a normal forthright member." Sherman's "machinations, his provocations of the doctor . . . his questioning of the good faith of the doctor," were all part of his devilish plan.

Sherman wrote that he and Martha attended Forum meetings for five years. Bedell says he talked to five old-timer Forumites who could not recall the Shermans being there. But they were. Martha and her daughter

Marcia assure me that after the blow-up Harold and Martha went to Forum meetings regularly for five years, but they sat in a back row, did not participate in discussions, and left after the readings of each paper. Many Forum members would have been unaware of their silent presence.

Sherman told of an occasion when he was seized by "two husky brothers," as well as threatened by Sadler's husky son. Bedell calls this a "bold outright fiction." It was only he, Bedell, who "walked to the front of the room, grasped the Author's [Sherman's] left arm firmly with both my hands . . . and exerting the necessary pressure, I ushered him back to his seat. . . . No one other person touched the Author."

If we can trust Sherman's memory, Christy (called Cindy in his account) was sympathetic to his desire to have the UB include material about psychic phenomena.

> One night we invited Cindy to our apartment as a dinner guest. During the evening we quite naturally discussed *The New Revelation Book*. I pointed out to her that when it would be published, people would wonder why no mention was made of telepathy or other psychic phenomena as a preparation for the existence of such powers in higher realms. Then came the "shocker." Cindy said she agreed with my contention, and since Sir Hubert Wilkins and I, as a result of our thought transference tests, had perhaps as much knowledge as anyone, why didn't we write a chapter explaining them. The doctor could submit our paper for consideration of the "higher ups," and if they okayed it, it could be inserted in *The New Revelation Book*.

In a letter to Harry Loose (November 9, 1942) Sherman had this fuller account of his conversation with Christy:

> Harry, a statement made to me by Christy was shocking, a long while ago—it seems long, last June. She was having dinner with us and I was remarking that the Book of Urantia dealt so authoritatively with supernatural phenomena of a high order, why wasn't there something in the book explaining many so-called "psychic happenings" which millions of people have experienced. (I know that the Doctor has a closed mind on this subject and have come to feel that he had influenced, by his attitude, all data of this nature from coming through.) Christy agreed that it would be good for a chapter on this subject to be in the book and then she said: "Harold, you know a great deal about these things. Why don't you write up a statement as to how you think they can be explained and we can submit it and see if the Angels of Progress will okay it for the book?"

What could she have meant by this? Has the Doctor dared to write up his ideas of different subjects and submitted them for an okay? Have some discrepancies crept into this amazing document through the Doctor's attempted interjection of his own ideas into this spiritual revelation? If so, he should be eventually banished, someone else placed in touch with the "instrument" as a contact commissioner, and any false writings replaced by the true ones and any material which should have been in the book brought through to the end that the Book of Urantia finally exists as intended.

This question of Christy's disturbed me no end for a while, though I was positive these Urantia Papers were not the product of the Doctor's mind. But why should she ever have made such a proposal to me if something was not right over there? I hope many of these points eventually clear up. Christy could tell plenty were the way ever opened.

Christy's astonishing response, Sherman adds in his book, was proof that "humanly written insertions had been put in the [UB] manuscript." Bedell ridicules this suggestion. He maintains that Christy was not being serious. She was simply doing her best to "get rid of the Author's [Sherman's] suggestion without argument," knowing the UB's "sacred inviolability."

Sherman reports Sadler telling him that he (Sadler) was once teleported to someone's home "in his spirit form." This account of an astral projection, says Bedell, is a "deliberate fabrication" arising from Sherman's "hatred" of Sadler.

Sherman speaks of an almost word-for-word similarity of a passage in the UB and one in Eery Reves's book A Democratic Manifesto (1942). Bedell reminds us that the revelators admitted (UB 1343) that they would not hesitate to use "information from human sources." This does not invalidate the fact that "every word of the Urantia Papers, even in the use of 'the highest existing human concepts,' was placed in the Urantia Papers by the Revelators. None was inserted by any human being whatsoever. I would stake my life on this." To suggest otherwise is "sheer—perhaps malicious—fabrication."

Sherman says that Sadler was feared by many Forum members. Bedell calls this "calumny" on a "kind and much-loved man." The charge comes from an "abusive," "spiteful," and "abysmally ignorant" scribbler who not only was a "worthless researcher," but also a "careless writer" who dished out "unsavory pottage." Sherman says he heard Forum members refer to Sadler as "the little Pope." Bedell denies that anyone ever said this. "Dr.

Sadler was a great man—a giant—vouchsafed perhaps the greatest trust and responsibility on this planet in many hundreds of years. The unseen Revelators chose well."

Bedell is particularly incensed by Sherman's assertion that Sadler's grandson, the son of his son Bill, killed himself because of "unhappy home conditions." On the contrary, says Bedell, the young man had a brain tumor and faced certain death. "*If* he committed suicide, which [Sherman] does not *know* was the case, he chose not to wait."

As we learned in chapter 2, the final inquest on Bill III's death failed to disclose a trace of a brain tumor. It was not possible to determine the cause of death because the inquest was held too many months after Bill's death, but traces of barbiturates were found in the boy, giving rise to the possibility of suicide.

Bedell is astounded that all Sherman can say in praise of the *UB* is that he found some material in it that was "thought provoking."

> Dear God! How the majestic Celestial Revelatory Commission and the Angels of Progress and of the Churches must rejoice on high! This spiritually shallow psychic finds that their fabulous Revelation that is to make vast changes on this earth contains *some material* he finds *thought provoking!*

In spite of Sherman's "trashy" attack on the *UB*, Bedell says that he and other Urantians will forgive him. "His attempt to discredit the *Urantia Book* is like an angry child with a popgun trying to stop the greatest ship on earth from carrying the gift of eternal life to a needy civilization on another shore . . . I pity the Author."

It is not Sherman's account that is filled with errors and lies, but Bedell's. As we shall see in the next chapter, at no time did Sherman wish to discredit the Urantia Papers or to take over the movement. When he and Martha were expelled from the Forum they still believed Wilfred's channeling to be coming from celestials. Sherman's chief concern was to make Forum members aware of how Sadler was altering and enlarging what he, Sherman, then believed to be a genuine new revelation from on high.

Why have I quoted so extensively from Bedell's angry speech? Because its abusive language conveys so starkly the obsessive devotion of Urantians to Dr. Sadler, and their convictions, so impossible to alter, that every sentence in the *UB* came directly from the supermortals, untainted by human hands.

8

Harold Sherman and
Harry Loose

I n August 1992 my wife and I drove to the Ozark region of Northern
Arkansas where we had the pleasure of spending several hours with
Martha Sherman, Harold Sherman's widow, her daugher Marcia, and
David Lynch, Marcia's husband. Mrs. Sherman is a small, beautiful
woman, now in her nineties. Her mind is as sharp as ever, although some
memories, as she likes to put it, have "flown out the window."

Harold Sherman's detailed diary, along with letters and notes about his
five years as a believing member of the Urantia Forum, are sealed in a
carton stored in the archives of the Torreytown Library, at the University of
Central Arkansas, in Conway. As I said earlier, the box is not to be opened
until the year 2000. However, Mrs. Sherman has generously allowed
Marcia to visit the library and copy for me scores of letters that her husband
exchanged with a mysterious, shadowy Chicago policeman and psychic
named Harry Jacob Loose.

It was Harry Loose who persuaded the Shermans to make a thorough
investigation of the Urantia papers, then in Dr. Sadler's custody, but not yet
published as a book. In *How to Know What to Believe* Sherman precedes
his chapter on the Urantia movement, "Pipeline to God," with a chapter
titled "The Wisdom of Harry J. Loose." What follows is taken mainly from
this chapter, from the letters Loose and Sherman wrote to each other, and
from a document titled "How it Began" which Martha Sherman dictated to
Marcia shortly before our visit.

Sherman first met Harry Loose in 1921, less than a year after his marriage. The Shermans were then living in Marion, Indiana, where young

Harold had his first writing job as a reporter for the *Marion Chronicle*. When Loose lectured in Marion, on the Redpath Chautauqua Circuit, Harold was asked to cover the talk. Loose had been a policeman and detective in Chicago. He later worked as a plainclothesman assisgned to Jane Addams's famed Hull House. In 1920 the Boston firm of Christopher Publishing printed his 206-page book, *The Shamus*, described on the title page as "a true tale of thiefdom and an exposé of the real system of crime, by Detective Harry J. Loose of the Chicago Police Department." Before he retired to California in 1934, he headed the police staff at the Chicago *Daily News*.

How did Loose become acquainted with Dr. Sadler? It is possible that he consulted Sadler as a patient. In *The Mind at Mischief* (pp. 137–38) Sadler writes:

There came to me a few years ago an ex-police officer, a big strapping fellow, who would go down a dark alley any night and shoot it out with half a dozen burglars, but who, as a result of a long emotional strain, experienced a partial nervous breakdown. He was several months recovering, but when he did get well there was one of his many fears that lingered on, behaving after the fashion of a residual fear. He simply would not go anywhere alone. He would find some excuse for getting out of any errand that required him to go anywhere by himself. He had to do considerable traveling for a year or two, and so he hired an old chum to go along with him. Finally he was cured, but it required more effort to conquer this one phobia than all his other fears, and he wasn't cured by reasoning, talking, explanation, or rationalization, as he was of his other fears. This one he had to go right out and defy; he had actually to go through all the misery, and suffer all the physical manifestations, of the fear which accompanied his going any place alone.

The paragraph is repeated, in the same words, in *Mental Mischief* (p. 142) and *Theory and Practice of Psychiatry* (p. 465).

If the policeman described by Sadler was indeed Loose, his traveling companion, as we shall see in a moment, was a Chicago police officer named William Gray. Letters to Sherman from other Urantians speak of Loose becoming depressed over his daughter's romance with a man he thought unsuitable for her. He is said to have contemplated suicide. This could have contributed to what Sadler calls the policeman's "long emotional strain" that led to a "partial nervous breakdown." Letters indicate that a Reverend Williams of Chicago taught Loose how to speak at Chautauqua meetings, and arranged for him to do so. Martha and Marcia tell me that Loose was indeed a "big strapping fellow." According to letters from Williams, Loose was never a member of the Contact Commission and had no knowledge of who the human instrument was, though he attended early meetings of the Forum.

I have a copy of a letter (dated February 15, 1917), written by Sadler to the president of the International Lyceum Bureau, in Chicago. It reads in full:

> I have just heard that Mr. H. J. Loose has consented to go on the lecture platform under your direction, and I have just been looking over the circular announcement of his lectures. Not always are the great things advertised in Lyceum circulars actually true, but in this case I happen to know that Mr. Loose has achieved the very things which his circular claims; and furthermore, I know Detective Loose to be a man of splendid ideals, lofty principles, and high moral character.
>
> I congratulate you on securing Mr. Loose. He will make good. He will do good. He knows whereof he speaks. He is an unusual character to find on the Police force of any city, and will prove a revelation to most communities who may be fortunate to hear him.

I also own, thanks to research by friend Leo Elliott, copies of many letters between Loose and those in charge of booking him as a Redpath lecturer. At that time Loose lived at 4218 North Monticello Avenue, Chicago. He complains constantly of suffering from injuries received as a policeman, of his need for money, and of his terrible loneliness on lecture tours.

Loose typically lectured seven times a week, his topic always on the causes, prevention, and nature of crime. He believed the chief cause was "getting away from God and the church." During lectures he would display a collection of guns, knives, and other weapons used by Chicago's underworld. He called for censorship of motion pictures that glorified crime and violence. A newspaper in Holden, Missouri, described his lecture as "the most stunning, sledge hammer, solar plexus wallops . . . ever handed to a Holden audience."

A publisher's press release on Loose's book *The Shamus* has these two paragraphs about some of his exploits:

> In cooperation with the U.S. Department of Justice, Mr. Loose made the investigation, arrest and prosecution of Samuel J. Rosenthal, "The Fake Bankruptcy King," recently sentenced to Fort Leavenworth. In cooperation with the U.S. Postoffice Inspectors, he made the investigation, arrest

and prosecution of Dr. Ottoman Zar Adusht Hanisch of Sun Cult fame. He collected and produced the evidence for the Chicago Council Crime Committee that proved to them the existence of the "System" in crime; that it was just as highly organized as any legitimate business; that the receivers of stolen property are the centre of the web of thievery and that 95 per cent of organized crime could be traced to them.

Mr. Loose assisted in the compilation of the report of the Vice Commission of Chicago, and has handled every known class of criminal from the "pickpocket trust" to the so-called $1,000,000.00 Burglar Trust.

Dr. Otoman Zar-Adusht Ha'nish was the name taken by Leipzig-born Otto Hanish (1844–1936) when he became the guru of a U.S. sun cult called Maz-Daz-Nan. I do not know anything about this cult or details of Ha'nish's Chicago arrest. William C. Hartmann's *Who's Who in Occultism, New Thought, Psychism, and Spiritualism* (1927) refers to two articles about the cult by Louis Adamic, in the *Haldeman-Julius Monthly* (June and July 1926), and gives a Los Angeles address for "Dr." Ha'nish.

Hanish was a naturopath who authored many books in German, French, and English. His *Health and Breath Culture According to Mazdaznan* was published in Chicago in 1902 by his Sun-Worshipper Company which later became the Mazdaznan Press, in Los Angeles. His other books include *How to Fast Scientifically* (1912), *Mazdaznan Dietetics and Cookery Book* (1914), *Omar Khayyam* (a biography, 1924), and *Yehoshua Nazir* (1917), a life of Jesus.

Loose liked to emphasize that he knew every street and alley in "wicked Chicago." His lectures went into details about prostitution, pickpocketing, shoplifting, lock picking, safe cracking, con games, drug addition, rigged prize fights and horse races, card cheating, and so on.

Born in Springfield, Illinois, in 1880, Loose was appointed to the State Police in 1901. After serving more than four years, he left to join the Pinkerton detective agency for a year or two, then became a Chicago police officer in 1906. He was a detective at Hull House for six years. Loose made hundreds of arrests, some of notorious criminals.

Unable to combat what he called the "awful loneliness" of his lecture tours, Loose arranged to be accompanied by William Gray, a policeman friend who would assist him on the platform in full police regalia. This did not improve Loose's behavior. A 1920 letter from a Chautauqua official calls him a "fine fellow, but with a peculiar disposition." Loose is accused of abruptly breaking off a tour ten days before it was supposed to end without making adequate arrangement for a replacement "except his sister who did not fit the bill at all." In a letter that same year, from Loose to "Uncle Crotty," he said he knew Sadler "years ago" when the doctor was on the Municipal Court Bench. Antagonism toward Sadler was beginning to surface. Loose complains to his uncle that Sadler had given a talk which followed one of his own too closely to be accidental:

> A man must be in great need, be kind of short on brains himself and not be bothered with an oversupply of conscience to deliberately "lift" another man's effort and make off with it like this.
> Imitation is the sincerest flattery but, from the outline given in the clipping, Sadler can hardly be called "imitating" in this. A shorter, uglier, name would be more appropriate and probably describe his efforts more truthfully.

Two years later Loose speaks in a letter of his "hard fight" getting back to normal after a breakdown. A letter that same year from one Redpath official to another complains that Loose "did us a lot of damage. . . . We just lost a $2,000.00 contract at Marshalltown [Iowa] and one of the reasons given was of Loose's conduct there."

Another 1922 letter by a Redpath official accuses Loose of paying a cab driver only fifty cents, then submitting an expense account bill of five dollars. The cab driver complained to Redpath, seeking $3.50 for his service. A group in Richland, Iowa, demanded a rebate because Loose refused to answer questions after a lecture, as he had promised, as well as exhibit his collections of crime "curiosities." Redpath accused him of disloyalty to the bureau and to the communities where he lectured. This seems to have ended his lecturing career. He returned to the Chicago police force where he remained until he retired in 1934 and moved to California.

Loose's lecture in Marion was his usual one on crime in Chicago. After the lecture, Harold felt strangely impelled to call on Loose for a personal interview. He checked the Marion Hotel, unsure that Loose was staying there. He was. As he tells it in *How to Make ESP Work for You* (1964), he did not give the hotel clerk his name. When he entered the hotel room he found Loose propped up in bed in his underwear, having undressed to escape the intense July heat.

Sherman was startled to hear Loose call out, "Come in, Sherman, and sit down. You're late. I've been expecting you for half an hour!"

As Mrs. Sherman recalls, Loose told her husband that the real purpose of his lecture tour was to locate young persons of high intelligence and spiritual potential and enlist them for a special mission. He did not specify the nature of the mission.

Loose said he had the ability (today it is called PK or psychokinesis) to translocate objects. "See that handkerchief on the dresser? I don't have to get out of bed to get it." According to Martha's account, the handkerchief "was suddenly in Mr. Loose's hands."

Loose showed an intimate knowledge of Harold's life, and ended the interview by what Martha calls "demonstrating telepathy" with his wife in Chicago. About two weeks later a handwritten letter from Loose arrived, dated July 27, 1921. The letter told Sherman that he was destined for a "mission of tremendous good and importance." After giving advice about diet, exercise, and sleep, Loose added, "if all goes well, writing on paper won't be necessary for communication." They would communicate by telepathy. "Your plane," he assured Sherman, "is far above mine—plane is some degree higher than mine—wish I could say more."

In the third chapter of *How to Know What to Believe* Sherman calls this first meeting with Loose "three of the most remarkable and inspiring hours I have ever experienced on this planet."

> There was nothing in what he said on the platform to indicate that Mr. Loose possessed any unusual psychic powers, but when I felt strongly impelled to call at his hotel that evening and seek a personal interview with him, he astounded me by calling me by name and stating that he had known he was to meet me at this time for the past three weeks! He then explained that a highly spiritual woman, ninety-six years of age, who resided near Boston, had given him the equivalent of a college education while he slept at night; and that she was attracting young people to him on this lecture trip who had a potential for psychic development, who needed encouragement. He said she could "tune in" on the minds of such people as she mentally surveyed the towns he was to be in—and transmit to the ones she wanted him to meet the impulse to seek him out. According to Harry, he had been waiting in his room for me to appear!

At midnight Harry asked to be excused while he spent a half hour communicating by ESP with "Mother Loose," his wife. He said he would receive her thoughts for the first fifteen minutes, then send his for the last fifteen minutes.

> Harry had been stretched on his bed in his BVDs when I came in, this hot July night, and had drawn up a chair, on which I was now seated, beside the bed, as though expecting company. I sat watching him, fascinated, as he lay on his back, commencing to draw deep breaths, eyes closed. Occasionally, during the first fifteen minutes, he would raise up and make

some notes on a pad that he had placed on the bedside table. After a time
he pushed the pad away and remained unmoving. Finally, almost exactly
at twelve-thirty, he opened his eyes, smiled at me, and said, "I have been
permitted to let you see this little telepathic practice of mine. You and
your Martha should be able to do this in time—if you continue to work at
it." (We have never become this accomplished, but we have accurately
sensed each other's thoughts for years.)

Curiously, after strong hints of a special mission for Sherman, communication between the two men ceased and two decades passed before
they were in touch again. Sherman and Martha moved to New York City in
1924 to a fifth-floor walkup overlooking the Hudson. Sherman began his
writing career with hundreds of sports and adventure stories for boys and
girls that appeared in periodicals such as *Boy's Life*, *American Boy*, *Target*,
Top Notch, and *Ropeco*. In addition to his own name, he used the by-lines
of Thomas Baldwin and Edward Morrow. These tales were collected into
some three dozen books.

For a while Sherman conducted a radio show called "Your Key to Happiness." His 1935 book with the same title became a best-seller. Two science-fiction novels ran in *Amazing Stories* magazine before they became
books titled *The Green Man* and *The Green Man Returns*. It was these
novels that introduced the phrase "little green men from Mars" into the literature of UFOlogy.

Sherman became deeply interested in all aspects of parapsychology
and the paranormal, and in later years became convinced that he himself
possessed psi powers. He wrote more than twenty-five books about ESP,
PK, precognition, poltergeists, animal ESP, dowsing, ouija boards, UFOs,
and so on. One of his books tells how to tape-record voices from the dead.
He made a trip to the Philippines with his friend Henry Belk, son of the
founder of the Belk department store chain, to investigate the psychic surgeons—self-styled "surgeons" who pretend to remove diseased tissues
from a patient's body without cutting the skin.

Both Sherman and Belk took the psychic surgeons seriously. It is now
well known that these men are charlatans who perform their seemingly
miraculous feats with the aid of what magicians call a thumb tip. This invisible device carries fake human tissues and blood to the spot where the "surgeons" appear to remove bloody tissue from a person's belly. Sherman's
book *Wonder Healers of the Philippines*, a hardcover of 339 pages, was
published in 1967 by the California firm of DeVorss and Company. The
book's jacket has the subtitle, *Is Psychic Surgery True?* Sherman grants that

fraud is often involved, but he and Belk were convinced that some of the surgery was genuinely paranormal. In any case, they thought it worthy of scientific investigation.

One of Sherman's books was enthusiastically endorsed by his friend Norman Vincent Peale, the nation's top "feel good" preacher on the power of positive thinking. Sherman's advertisements for the book quote the following extract from one of Peale's letters:

> Dear Harold: "The Dead Are Alive" is a masterpiece and could be the greatest of all your great books. I hope it will be widely read. I find it very thoughtful indeed.

Harold Morrow Sherman was born in 1898 in Traverse City, Michigan. His mother was Methodist, his father was Catholic-born. As we learned in chapter 2, a youthful Sadler had worked as a bellhop at Dr. John Kellogg's Sanitarium in Battle Creek, Michigan. By a remarkable coincidence, young Sherman, in 1914 (he was then 16) also worked at the "San" as a bellhop and elevator boy. Unlike Sadler, Sherman never became a Seventh-day Adventist; indeed, he never affiliated with any religious church or organization.

In 1918 Sherman dropped out of the University of Michigan to serve briefly in the First World War. In 1920, while working for Henry Ford, in Detroit, he married Martha Frances Bain, a young woman from his home town. She was then a student nurse at Grace Hospital in Detroit. They had attended the same public schools in Traverse City from the sixth grade through high school, though their personal paths had seldom crossed. He and Martha had two children, Mary Alcinda and Marcia Anne.

When Sherman died in 1987—or as Martha prefers to say, "when he left this dimension"—he had been running for more than two decades the ESP Research Association Foundation, in Little Rock, Arkansas. The Foundation sold his many books, issued a lively newsletter, and sponsored lectures, seminars, and workshops around the country.

Sherman and the Australian Arctic and Antarctic explorer Sir Hubert Wilkins became good friends. In 1937 and 1938, when Sherman was in New York and Wilkins was three thousand miles away at the North Pole, the two men conducted long-distance telepathy experiments under the supervision of Dr. Gardner Murphy, a respected parapsychologist then at Columbia University. Wilkins was the sender, Sherman the receiver. They claimed 70 percent accuracy. Sherman first wrote about these tests in *Cosmopolitan* magazine (March 1939), then provided a more detailed account in *Thoughts Through Space* (1942). A 1971 paperback reprint has an enthusiastic foreword by Edgar Mitchell, the former astronaut who has become an energetic promoter of psi phenomena through his Institute of Noetics.

In 1973 Sherman and Scientologist and psychic Ingo Swann collaborated on an effort to make out-of-body trips to Jupiter before Pioneer 10 flew by the planet to take pictures. Each wrote down what he saw, then Harold Puthoff and Russell Targ, paraphysicists then at Stanford Research International, supervised the experiment. Their report has not to my knowledge been published. Sherman and Swann later collaborated on two similar remote-viewing probes, of Mercury in 1974, and of Mars in 1976. The results of those two probes also remain unpublished.

In July 1941 Sherman was asked by Warner Brothers to come to Hollywood to work on the movie script of *The Adventures of Mark Twain*, a script based on a play Sherman had written. On the drive from New York to Hollywood, accompanied by his wife and two daughters, Sherman stopped off in Chicago to meet Sadler. They had been given a letter of introduction to Sadler from Mrs. Josephine Davis, a cousin who lived in Marion.

In the Urantia chapter of *How to Know What to Believe* Sherman alters Mrs. Davis's name to Susan Saunders, adding that in the early 1920s she and her husband "had engaged in psychic research with us." A cordial Sadler spoke glowingly about the Urantia Papers, regretting that the Shermans did not have time to stay and read them. It was such a casual meeting that the Shermans soon forgot about it and later could not even recall Sadler's name.

For two decades Sherman had tried without success to locate Harry Loose. He finally succeeded through the help of a friend. Loose was then retired and living in a house at 123 North Elizabeth Avenue, in Monterey Park, a suburb about eight miles east of the center of Los Angeles. Sherman's letter to Loose (January 31, 1941) was the first communication between them since they had met twenty years earlier in Marion. Loose's reply (February 5) contains his first mention to Sherman of the *UB*. This remarkable letter is printed in full in Sherman's *How to Know What to Believe*. I reproduce it below:

Greetings!

May I thank you for you letter. I was not given to expect it until later in the month.

    With a good wife and two beautiful and dutiful daughters, you are very fortunate. Mary and Marcia. Both are Biblical. Marcia is a derivative of Martha. I am pleased with your writing success. I congratulate you. You have been helped—as you helped yourself.

I live on a very modest income, in an old brown house in a small and humble suburb of Los Angeles. I drive downtown in twelve minutes. My lot is large but I am a sad farmer. My time is not occupied physically.

Intelligences with whom I am in contact have accomplished much in service to this atom of a world. I serve in a very humble capacity. My mission has not been completed. I have progressed but had hoped for release and much greater progress before this. Much has been done in regard to the crisis looming for this nation, but the forces in opposition are of tremendous psychic power. An untaught, untrained mind could not comprehend. [We were within a few months of the surprise Japanese attack on Pearl Harbor and the outbreak of the Second World War.]

Long distance telepathy—or short distance—is much in use and operates perfectly. It has been in operation for thousands of years amongst certain groupings in all periods. Its method is very simple when once understood. Time or space is nothing. There is nothing else REAL but MIND. "It is the Spirit that quickeneth, the flesh profiteth nothing."

I do not know your present development. I have to be careful. I do not want to talk over your head and be misunderstood.

Remember to watch for a tremendous book which will be published in about two years. It has been now thirty-five years in the building. It is not mine but I had something to do with it. You will recognize it when it appears. It will clarify so very much that is already in our present day Bible. It is a true spiritual revelation to this age written by intelligences who have never been earthbound and who have to do with the governing of this tiny earth in this very limited part of the universe. Please believe every astonishing word. It is the TRUTH . . . I KNOW.

I talked with you on the night of July 21st, 1921, in my room in the old Marion Hotel. I knew so little myself then. Life is all an individual proposition—whether there will be growth or not. No one can grow for you. This applies hereafter just as much as here. You will not be satisfied to sit on a damp cloud and play on a four-string harp forever. You would get very tired of it after the first few hundred years. You will find that you will be kept very busy instead of cloud-sitting.

With every good thought to surround and support you and yours—Sincerely, Harry J. Loose.

Loose was then in his sixties, with a severe heart condition. Now that he and the Shermans were living close to one another, the two families became good friends. There were many back-and-forth Sunday visits at

Loose's home in Monterey Park and at the Hollywood apartment the Shermans had rented.

It was during this period that Loose introduced the Shermans to the Fifth Epochal Revelation. Loose knew Sadler in the early years of the Forum, and had played some sort of role in the formation of the Papers. He never revealed to the Shermans just what role this was. He believed that he himself was in direct contact with the celestial revelators. They had told him, he said, to initiate Harold and Martha into the wonders of the new revelation.

As Sherman relates in his chapter on Loose, his friend claimed the power to make out-of-body astral visits during which his spirit form would appear completely real to others. He said that he and Father John Carlos, a Catholic priest in South America, occasionally visited one another by astral projection. Sherman quotes Loose as saying:

> I'd like to have you meet my friend, the Catholic priest, someday. Maybe he will visit while you are here. We generally meet in our little local park where we can sit and watch the children. He can only stay ten hours because of his church duties. He comes home to dinner with me at noon time, but he cannot eat anything. Air and water are necessary to him, however. He will be perfectly visible to you, and I know that you would enjoy talking to him. I would like to have you see him particularly when he starts for home. No, I am not a Catholic.

On Thanksgiving Day, 1941, Sherman claims that Loose's astral body actually called on him at the Canterbury Apartments, 1746 North Cherokee Avenue, Hollywood. Unfortunately, he and Martha were out motoring, but Loose was seen by the desk clerk and a woman attendant. In chapter 4, "A Verified Case of Projection of the Psyche," in *You Live After Death* (1940), Sherman prints a letter from William A. Cousins, the desk clerk. I am writing to you," he began, "as you suggested, a detailed account of my experience with what I now consider the most thrilling happening of my life."

Cousins recalls that on Thanksgiving afternoon a man had approached the desk. He had a rugged complexion, and was wearing the clothes of a workingman—cap, brown sweater, corduroy pants, and a dark blue shirt. Without asking if the Shermans were in, he gave the clerk the following brief message: "Tell Mr. Sherman Mr. Loose was here—I will see him Sunday." The man made a face after each word that suggested to the clerk he was having difficulty keeping false teeth in place. He seemed out of breath. The clerk recalled the time as "about 2:30."

The Shermans were back at about three o'clock. Sherman told the clerk he was sorry to have missed his friend, but would telephone him right away. A half-hour later Sherman came down to the lobby with incredible news. He had spoken to Loose at his home, some fifteen miles away, only to learn that Loose had not left the house. He had been home all day celebrating a Thanksgiving family reunion dinner!

Sherman visited Loose next Sunday. When he told him the desk clerk's story, Loose became extremely agitated and surprised. He proposed a visit to talk to the clerk and verify the account he gave Sherman. Here is how Cousins tells it in his letter:

> He came in the side door of the apartment house, wearing the same clothes he had been wearing Thanksgiving day, except for a lighter shirt. I stood up and said, "Good morning, Mr. Loose," and he asked for Mr. Sherman. I said I didn't think Mr. Sherman was in, and at that time, Mr. Sherman stepped up behind Mr. Loose, when he found I had recognized him.
>
> I became a little excited and said, "This is the gentleman who called on you Thanksgiving Day." They both laughed and Mr. Sherman introduced Mr. Loose to me, who explained that the darker blue shirt he had worn on Thanksgiving Day was now in the wash.
>
> Mr. Loose then asked me to explain what had happened on Thanksgiving Day, and I repeated to him what I have related above.

Sherman's more detailed account of Loose's astral visit is the chapter devoted to it in *You Live After Death*. He quotes Loose as saying:

> Harold, I think the time has come when I must tell you a few things about myself that I was afraid you would not understand and believe. For some years now I have had the ability to leave my body and consciously to appear in spirit form at distant places on visits to certain individuals. During the time I am absent from my physical body, it remains in a deep sleep state and is cared for by Mother Loose. If I am gone in the daytime and should neighbors drop in, she simply explains, having closed off the bedroom, that Harry is sleeping and can't be disturbed. To try to arouse me during those periods would be a great nervous shock. I may tell you that one of the friends I meet in this manner is a John Carlos, a highly developed Catholic priest who lives in South America. At times he visits me in the same manner. I myself am not Catholic as you know, and this spiritual development has nothing to do with any creed.
>
> Do you remember, Harold, . . . how I have liked to walk you down to the little park near here and to sit on a certain bench with you under the

pepper tree where we could see the children playing innocently about and the majestic mountains in the distance? . . .

It's the place . . . where I go to meet John Carlos when he calls on me. We communicate telepathically and when he has something of spiritual importance he wants to discuss, either he or I go to the other. There is much I cannot tell you because spiritual growth and understanding is a matter of development. But if you had been in the park with me and were permitted to share this experience, you would suddenly see another man standing near the bench or seated besides me. To the casual observer, we would look just like two ordinary old men, inconspicuously dressed— such old men as you often see whiling away their time on park benches throughout the country.

These meetings between John Carlos and myself were always pre-arranged. Each was expecting the other when he arrived and each was entirely conscious of the visitation, able to return to his physical body and, upon regaining normal consciousness, retain a memory of the experience. But what has greatly concerned me, in the evidence you present of my visitation to the Canterbury, is the fact that I have no recollection whatsoever of such a projection.

Sherman reprints a letter (dated December 20, 1941) written by Loose's daughter, Mrs. Raymond A. Burkhart, and also signed by her husband, by Loose's wife, Emily, and by Miss Dorothy Hesse, Emily's sister. The letter reports that after finishing Thanksgiving dinner at 12:30, Emily and her sister began their customary after-dinner nap at 1:30. The Burkharts and their small son, John, then left. Mr. Loose was in a chair in the sitting room, reading a book and wearing his old pants, a blue shirt, and a gray and black figured tie.

Emily and Dorothy finished their nap, as they recall, about 2:30. They found Mr. Loose still in the sitting room, wearing slippers and reading. He had not, they said, left the house all day. He therefore could not possibly have been at the Canterbury Apartments that afternoon.

What is one to make of this? As a hard-nosed skeptic of astral projection I can think of only one good possibility. Mrs. Burkhart said she and her husband left about 1:40. As she put it in her letter, this ended her and her husband's knowledge of her father's whereabouts later that day. Emily recalls that she and her sister awoke from their nap about 2:30. Thus from 1:40 to 2:30, a period of at least 50 minutes, no one really knew the whereabouts of Mr. Loose.

A current map of Los Angeles and its suburbs shows the locations of Sherman's apartment and Loose's house to be twenty inches apart, almost on the same horizontal line. The map is based on .68 of a mile to an inch, making the direct distance 13.6 miles. I estimate a car's odometer distance to be about 15 miles.

I have no idea what the map looked like in 1941, or what freeways were then in existence. If Loose drove the distance at 60 miles per hour, or a mile a minute, he would have had time to drive to Sherman's apartment, rush into the lobby (the clerk recalled him as out of breath), hurriedly leave a message, drive home, and be back in his chair before his wife awoke, with twenty minutes to spare. Surely the roads would have been less congested in 1941 than today, and we must remember that this was on a Thanksgiving Sunday when traffic would be minimal.

Counting against this conjecture is the fact that Emily recalls waking at "about 2:30," and the clerk recalls Loose leaving the apartment building at "about 2:30." "About" is a fuzzy word. Both Emily and the clerk could have been slightly off in their recollections, as well as eager to support the claim of an astral visit. If Emily awoke at, say, 2:45, and Loose left Sherman's abode at 2:15, this would have allowed Loose a full 30 minutes to make the 15-mile drive. Recall that in Loose's letter to Sherman, printed here on page 143, Loose says, "I drove downtown in twelve minutes."

It is clear from Loose's correspondence that he was extremely proud of his psi powers. Such individuals are not averse at times to using fakery to persuade others. One thinks of how Uri Geller convinced his friend and biographer, Andrija Puharich, that he had teleported himself from downtown Manhattan to the back porch of Puharich's home in Ossining, many miles north. As Puharich tells it in his book *Uri*, there was even a large hole in the screen of his porch through which Geller claimed to have plummeted.

Sadler, in his investigations of mediums, was fully aware that mediums and psychics, even true believers in psi phenomena, frequently resort to fraud to bolster their ego. Here is a passage from *Mental Mischief and Emotional Conflicts* (p. 269) that I believe applies to Loose's claim of astral projection, though of course there is no way at this late date to prove it:

> To separate the sincere automatic writers from those who are, at least to some extent, consciously fraudulent is no small task. These psychic freaks and so-called "sensitives" almost inherently exaggerate their gifts and, childlike, magnify their performances. Every medium seems to try to outdo other "psychics," so that they are always subject to the *urge to perpetrate fraud*.

Sherman's accounts of Loose's astral visit are given at length in *How to Make ESP Work for You* and *You Live After Death*. A briefer account can be found in the chapter on Loose in *How to Know What to Believe*. Sherman repeatedly said he considered this event one of the "most authentic cases of astral visitation in the history of psychic phenomena."

We now return to Loose and the Urantia Papers. The Shermans were so fascinated by their friend's high praise of this new revelation that they moved to Chicago in May 1942 for the express purpose of studying the Papers. Their oldest daughter, Mary, took a job as switchboard operator at Hull House. (Sherman, by the way, was then considering writing a movie about the life of Jane Addams.) The younger daughter, Marcia, spent the summer with cousins in Michigan.

Harold and Martha took up residence at the Cambridge Apartments, directly across the street from Sadler's headquarters at 533 Diversey. On their earlier visit to Chicago the Shermans had been admitted to the Forum after signing the pledge demanded by Sadler that they would not reveal to outsiders any information about the Papers. For five years, from May 1942 to May 1947, they attended the Sunday Forum meetings. In 1943 Mary and her husband, Bernard J. Kobiella, were also admitted to the Forum after signing the pledge. They attended only a few sessions because Mr. Kobiella, a Catholic, could not accept *UB* doctrines.

"We were never told," Mrs. Sherman writes in her report to me, "what part Harry Loose actually played in the assembling and development of the Urantia material, although Bill Sadler Jr. once remarked that there was a mystery about a Harry Loose and the early days of the material." The Shermans respected Loose's request never to mention his name to Sadler or to other members of the forum. Sadler, in turn, never spoke of his relationship with Loose.

The most striking aspect of Loose's letters is his vast dismay over how Sadler was handling the Papers. In Loose's opinion it was Lena who kept the doctor on an even keel. After she died, Loose writes, "something snapped" in Sadler's brain. He became extremely authoritarian, more vain than ever before, quick to anger, and brooking not the slightest criticism or deviation from his orders. His ego, always strong, became monumental. In one letter Loose writes: "The truth is that Sadler is mentally unsound. A paranoiac with a religeo-power complex—feverishly grasping for greater jurisdiction over the mentalities of the many. . . . O that Dr. Lena had lived. How different developments would have been today! Sadler has the usual evidence of long latent, and of these later years, aroused, *mental* sadism, which is just as definite, and fully recognized a condition as physical sadism."

More important to our story, Sadler became convinced he was in direct contact with the celestial beings, authorized by them to edit the papers, to take out sections, and to add fresh material. After Lena's death, according to Loose, Sadler claimed that a midwayer acted as her proxy in decisions made by the Contact Commission! Loose is certain that Sadler lied about this. Wilfred Kellogg is described by Loose as a nervous man who suffered from severe stomach ulcers (understandable!), and who shared with Christy a strong dislike of how Sadler was mutilating the revelations.

In letters to Loose dated October 22 and November 2, 1942, Sherman tells an incredible story. A Forum member named Mrs. Rachel Gusler, of Oak Park, visited the Shermans. She was visibly disturbed. Sadler had told her that Ruth Kellogg had told him that Sherman had asked her to steal the plates of the unpublished *UB*! Sherman said he would then copyright the book in his own name, publish it, and sell movie rights! This was an outright lie. "We knew the doctor must have said some dastardly things about us," Sherman wrote, "but we could not believe he would dare go this far."

Loose replied on October 25:

> The story about Ruth does not ring true to me. I do not doubt but that Sadler told it though. I cannot conceive of Ruth saying what is credited to her by Sadler. I can far more readily believe an entire untruth by Dr. S or "much made from little" by him. It will take more evidence than just Sadler's word to make me fully believe what he has said of Ruth.

The Shermans found Ruth as friendly toward them as she was unfriendly toward Bill Jr. Anna Kellogg likewise was always friendly, though her husband Wilfred "runs every time he sees me coming as though he is afraid to face me," Sherman wrote to Loose. A Mr. Steinbeck, president of "The Seventy," was also on Sherman's side. In a letter to Loose (September 28, 1942), Sherman reports that Mrs. Steinbeck told him: "Most of the Forum members are *for* you, but we can't do much about it right now. . . . I regret to have to say this, but Dr. Sadler is NOT a spiritual person." Some Forum members told Sherman that if they couldn't believe everything Sadler said, they might have to doubt the authenticity of the Papers.

Christy, Sherman wrote to Loose, is "terribly afraid," "a soul in absolute bondage" to Sadler. Bill Jr. is described as "burning up with hate" toward him and Martha.

Sherman was convinced that after Lena died Sadler became paranoid, his mind "perverse and deranged." Both he and his son Bill, Sherman wrote, "will lie and frame anybody and [do] anything to accomplish their purposes." In a letter of September 10, 1942. Sherman wrote: "I do not hold any malice toward him [Sadler]—I am not forgetting his great service—but it is pitiful to see how he has fallen."

In the same letter Sherman writes that when a meeting of disgruntled Urantians had been held at the home of Dent Karle, Sadler told Forum members that higher beings had enabled him to be present out of body at the Karles' home where he saw and heard everything. As we learned in the previous chapter, Sherman repeats this story in his book's account of the Urantia movement. Elsie Baumgartner, in the Forum at the time, told Martha Sherman that this was a lie. Urantian Albert H. Dyson, Elsie said, was there and had informed Sadler of everything that had transpired.

It is essential to understand that Sherman's main reason for disenchantment with Sadler was that the doctor no longer behaved as "custodian" of the Papers. Believing himself in direct contact with midwayers, he felt "indited" to add whatever he liked to the Papers, and to discard whatever he liked.

In letters to Loose on September 7, 10, and 28, and October 2, 22, 1942, Sherman reports another example of Sadler's willingness to lie to strengthen his claim that the Shermans were under the influence of Caligastia and other fallen celestials. He told Forum members that before the Shermans had arrived in Chicago, a midwayer identified only as "DEF" warned him against an unnamed married couple who would be allowed into the Forum where they would cause endless trouble. The warning had come, Sadler said, during a "personal visit by the midwayer, when everyone else had to leave the room." Sadler said he had taken notes on the warning, but had told no one, not even Christy, about it until now.

This was another "deliberate lie." The Shermans soon learned from Forum members that Sadler had repeatedly mentioned the warning message to them. Although the midwayer supplied no names, Sadler said the warning obviously applied to the Shermans.

Martha exploded. "Doctor, there is not a word of truth in this. . . . It definitely does not apply to us and I do not see how you could possibly interpret it as applying to us." But Sadler's charge was effective. From then on, most Forum members avoided the Shermans as if they were lepers. As Harold put it in a letter to Loose (September 7, 1942), the doctor expected him to "crawl on my belly, with my ears pinned back," and to appear at the next Forum meeting "thoroughly squelched, a sinner forevermore and an ally of Lucifer."

A curious sentence follows. Sherman writes that "no condemnation of the Forum's actions has come from the Angels of Progress and Sonsovocton, who have the book of Urantia in charge." Sherman refers to Sonsovocton in other letters. Can any old-timer in the movement tell who in heaven's name this celestial being is? The name appears nowhere in the *UB*.

Loose was particularly disturbed by Sadler's discarding of material, coming through the contactee, about a strange class of beings on Urantia called the "hybrids." It seems that ascended personalities from older and more advanced planets had been sent to earth to be "enfleshed" as small intelligent primates. Their mission was to aid primitive humans who had evolved on the now submerged continent of Lemuria. I am taking most of this information from Sherman's chapter on Loose where you will find several pages about the hybrids. Here are some paragraphs:

> They were here to teach and lead and help upward these beginning humans. BUT THEY DID NOT COME TO MATE WITH THEM. They were instructed not to have progeny with them and thus cross the already full spiritual with the undeveloped flesh. However, through accident and mistake and a misunderstanding of orders, this very thing DID happen, and before it could be stopped and corrected, there were many thousands of these small creatures born that were in a position which had never before arisen.
>
> These hybrid offspring were actually partially in two worlds. There was born in them a sensitivity and a vague awareness of things beyond the merely physical. The normal evolutionary progression which nature had decreed for those of their kind who had not become admixed with these higher beings was denied to them. They were destined to remain in an in-between dimensional state until the physical evolutionary side of their progression could match their spiritual endowment. In other words, their soul or identity was caught in a state of evolutionary suspension.
>
> This unfortunate condition has existed among their descendents for centuries, and they are only now beginning to be released, at death, to the Second Dimension, where they are at last free to continue their normal spiritual progression.
>
> These hybrids exist in all races. They are often tormented by deep yearnings and wonderments about life and are plagued with feelings that they may have lived before. These feelings are understandable since they carry within them the influence of the Second Dimensional beings who were their ancestors.

This explains, to a great degree, the false and mistaken concept of reincarnation. These hybrids, because of their greater sensitivity, are able to recall, at times, fleeting memories and visions of past-life experiences, which they have wrongly interpreted as having happened to them, but which experiences really belonged to one or more ancestors in their direct ancestral line.

You will find no mention of hybrids in the *UB*, nor any reference to Lemuria, sometimes called Mu. It is a mythical lost continent believed to be now below the waters of the Pacific and beloved by numerous occult writers. Why was this part of the revelation omitted from the *UB*? Urantians will say that for some unknown reason the revelators asked Sadler to leave it out. A simpler explanation is that Sadler realized it was too absurd to be believed even by Urantian fundamentalists.

In one of his letters to Loose, Sherman reveals that a paper contained a passage lifted word for word from a book by Stuart Chase which Sadler had found of great interest. Devout and gullible Urantians—Loose calls them Charlie McCarthys because they were dummies easily manipulated by Sadler—expressed amazement (Sherman writes) over the fact that the celestials could put identical sentences into both a *UB* Paper and into the mind of Chase!

In one letter Loose comments on Sadler's interest in attractive young women. "Normally an age is reached where sex rightly loses its call. But there are those instances with the elderly where this rule does not always obtain." Loose speaks of Sadler's fondness for embracing and kissing the young women in his flock. "And if the truth were known there are other such kisses and embraces under other subterfuges in the privacy of the office with the closed door—other 'feeling' and 'squeezes.'" When Sherman's good friend Henry Belk visited me a few years ago, he told me that Sherman told him that on one occasion Sadler had made a romantic pass at Martha. When I asked Martha about this, her guarded comment was "Mr. Belk spoke out of turn."

After Sherman became disenchanted with Sadler, and tried to convince Forum members that the "little Pope" was mishandling the revelations, Loose was totally on Sherman's side. Seventy-six percent of the Forum members, Loose wrote, are tired of Sadler's dictatorial and possessive attitude toward the Papers, and his constant lying about them.

Loose speaks of the sinister influence on Sadler of what he calls one of the original contact commissioners, G. Willard Hales, a wealthy man who lived in Oak Park, Illinois, where his home was a frequent site for Urantian picnics. He refers also to Hales's wife, Carrie, who had been one of Sadler's patients, and to her intense dislike of Bill Sadler Jr. (Hales's son, William, and his wife, Mary Lou, became active Urantians, and their son, John, became president of the Urantia Brotherhood in 1979.) According to Loose, Willard Hales was a member of the original contact commission which he claims numbered 17 at the outset. Sherman is repeatedly warned to avoid all the Hales. In his chapter on the Urantia movement, Sherman may have had the Hales in mind when he refers to "the financier Raymond Stafford, with his wife, his son Ray, Junior, and wife Marjory."*

One wonders how Loose, in California, knew so much about the later goings on in Chicago. Mrs. Sherman tells me that he had contacts with seven persons in the Forum. His letters urge Sherman to keep in touch with "the seven." They are not named in Loose's letters, though there are references to "Number 1" and "Number 4."

Contrary to what Mark Kulieke writes in his history of the Urantia movement, at no time did Sherman consider trying to unseat Sadler and take over the cult's leadership. As a true believer in the Revelation, his sole motive was to bring into the open the way Sadler was manipulating the Papers.

As we have seen, Sherman also tried to persuade Sadler to let the contactee request information from the supermortals about the validity of ESP and other paranormal powers. Sherman's acceptance of psychic phenomena was shared by the late Brendan O'Regan, who died of cancer in 1992, at age 47. For a dozen years O'Regan worked for the Noetic Institute, an organization that promotes all forms of psi and was responsible for funding Stanford Research Institute's notorious authentication of Uri Geller's psi powers. I mention O'Regan because I was astonished to learn that he spoke at the Second Scientific Symposium, sponsored by the Oklahoma City Urantians in 1991. O'Regan defended the ability of Geller to bend spoons with his mind, as well as the ESP powers of Scientologist Ingo Swann to view distant scenes. Had Sadler been alive, he would have been as annoyed as Sherman would have been pleased by allowing O'Regan to speak.

Sherman was convinced that mediums can communicate with the dead. As we have seen, Sadler retained his Adventist belief, so strongly urged by Sister White, that no communication with the dead is possible and that all of Spiritualism is the work of Satan. Apparently Sherman was unaware of

---

*George Willard Hales was president of the Northwestern Malt and Grain Company, in Chicago, since 1910. A Congregationalist and Republican, he was director of the Chicago Theological Seminary since 1941, a member of the Board of Trade and a life member of the Chicago Art Institute. For more details see *Who's Who in Chicago and Illinols* (Eighth edition, 1945).

Sadler's Adventist background, or he would have realized the impossibility of altering Sadler's mind on this matter.

Stung by Sadler's charges that he was trying to take control of the Urantia movement, Sherman wrote the following statement of his motives, signed and notarized on September 10, 1942:

> To Whom It May Concern:
>
> I, the undersigned, do hereby declare that my sole and only interest with respect to the BOOK OF URANTIA is strictly spiritual.
>
> I have not in the past nor do I now or ever desire, nor will I accept any moneys which might be forthcoming through any efforts of mine in connection with its publication.
>
> By the same token, I seek no identification and glorification of my name in connection with said publication. The use of my name I will not permit, since I believe that this TRUE REVELATION must stand alone, unembarrassed and unencumbered by any human affiliation.
>
> I do now take this occasion to declare and solemnly promise, under oath, once and for all, that no circumstances which can arise in the future can or will compel me to seek mercenary gain for any services rendered with respect to the publication of the BOOK OF URANTIA.
>
> Whatever I possess that I can give in time and services in this work of the Kingdom is gladly offered to my Creator, to the Angels of Progress and to Sonsovocton for the privilege of this service is beyond price.
>
> Signed by me this tenth day of September, 1942.

A few days later (September 14) Sherman sent Sadler a long letter in which he did his best to make clear he had no intention of challenging Sadler's authority. "It is not my nature to be a 'trouble-maker' or a 'dissenter,' as my entire life record will show. My one deep interest is in everything that will lead to the best presentation of this TRUE REVELATION to the world." The letter ends:

> I cannot conceive of any humans receiving spiritually decreed punishment for such an honest act. I will face my God any time, and have faced Him, through prayer, during these past days, and have called upon the Angels of Progress to examine my mind and heart and know that I have been sincere and well-intentioned in everything I have done.

In one letter Loose writes that both Wilfred and his wife were "much troubled in mind" by Sadler's efforts to "play God" with the Papers. Both

Wilfred and Anna, Loose says, were sympathetic to Sherman's so-called rebellion. The two Kelloggs, he adds, are "superior" to the Sadlers, but unable to cross the doctor because of their financial dependence on him. Christy, too, Loose maintains, sided with Sherman in his battle with Sadler, but could not express this openly out of fear. "Her very soul is sick," Loose writes. "What a story she could tell! But she is filled with FEAR—deadly, horrible, shaking fear."

Loose died on November 21, 1943, still a firm believer in the genuineness of the original Urantia Papers and without revealing to the Shermans what role he had played in their reception. His letters constantly urged Sherman to "fight, fight, fight!" and to rely at all times on the support and spiritual wisdom of his wife. Loose was very fond of Martha, always referring to her as "small Martha." He repeatedly advised Sherman to keep careful records of everything that happened and all that he learned. This Sherman did. In his letters he calls these notes his "Diary." The notes were dictated every day to Martha. He hoped eventually, with Loose's strong encouragement, to edit the diary into a book that would reveal for the first time the true history of the Papers, how they were edited and distorted by Sadler, and to identify the contactee.

Sherman had no desire to discount or undermine the Fifth Epochal Revelation, but to authenticate it. At this period of his life the *UB* was, in his own words, "indescribably wonderful," "unassailable," and "the greatest piece of news that could ever be presented to humans at any time, anywhere, in the history of the world." Those words were written, of course, before he and Martha were viciously attacked by Sadler and excommunicated from the movement.

The bitter conflict between Sadler and Sherman reached a climax at a Forum meeting on September 13, 1942. Sherman has a brief account of this in his book *How to Know What to Believe*, but a fuller account is given in a long letter he wrote to Harry Loose on September 13. I give here the relevant passages:

> Sadler appeared before the Forum body himself and welcomed us as his guests, which was my cue that he was taking no chances . . . the implication being that no one should speak out of turn if he is a guest.
> I waited until he got ready to dismiss the Forum members for the first hour intermission when I arose and said: "Dr. Sadler, at the start of this new epoch . . . may I speak to the members of the Forum?"
> He immediately bristled and said: "No, not at this time."
> I stepped out into the aisle from my chair and proceeded up front to

stand beside him, saying, "I'm sorry, doctor, but there are some things I *must* say to the Forum."

He said: "Sit down! And I'll tell you when you can talk to the Forum. You are a guest in my home. You have no right to speak."

I said, "I am a member of the Forum, doctor, and Mrs. Sherman and I are here as outcasts. We have been accused and we have a right to be heard."

Dr. Sadler repeated: "Sit down. You are not going to speak now."

I said, "Doctor, are you afraid of the truth?"

He said, "I repeat, you are my guest. Take your seat. There is going to be no argument here."

I stood my ground and by this time other Forum members, as anticipated, were jumping up. Clyde Bedell, who had been a hold-out before, but who capitulated along with the rest, grabbed my arm and said, "Harold, you are harming yourself by this stand. The doctor is right in asking you to take your seat. We are all guests here. You wouldn't come into my home and do this, would you?"

I said, "Clyde, this is different. This is the only place a man may speak of these things and we stand accused. . . . We have a right to defend ourselves."

Dr. Sadler said, "If Sherman wants to speak and will take his seat, I'll tell him when he can."

I said, "May I speak later today, doctor? I want to speak today."

He said, "No, you will not speak today."

I said, "Will you be there when I speak?"

And he said, "I refuse to answer that."

Hales was now at my elbow, grabbing my coat lapels and telling me what a good fellow he had always thought I was, how he'd read lots of "stuff" I'd written, and how I was hurting my cause taking a stand like this—losing respect of all the Forum members.

He kept on talking in this vein, asking me why I wouldn't listen to Clyde Bedell. Then Dent Karle, another "friend" . . . tried to intercede, and still I refused to take my seat. Meanwhile Martha was being high-pressured where she sat by women begging her to ask me to come and sit down . . . but Martha sat unmoved.

And now Russell Bucklin joined the group around me, with the Kulieke boys, two strapping young men, excitedly asking the doctor if they should throw me out. The doctor didn't quite go for this suggestion although he would have liked to give the "go ahead." Bill Sadler began to edge down the aisle toward the group surrounding me. . . .

I still stood my ground with questions coming from the floor, "Doctor, do you want us to adjourn?" Some members, men and women, were crying. Others were defiant. I think many felt sheepish that they had lacked the courage to take a stand and had left us to face things down. . . .

I finally agreed to take my seat and managed to get in this comment to the Forum members that we had respect for them and loved them all . . . which statement the doctor tried to prevent . . . but it got across. At the intermission, many gathered around to shake our hands and express friendship.

I feel absolutely free in my own conscience and do not see how I could have acted differently under the circumstances, although I know the doctor feels he has won a great victory, and Bill was laughing hysterically at the proceedings, which indicates how unstable he is and would be as a leader. The doctor was visibly shaken when I did not immediately take my seat and held the floor for at least fifteen minutes or more. He poured out the syrup thick after the intermission. . . .

Clyde Bedell got hold of me afterward and said, "Harold, I had a fine opinion of you until today . . . but if you let your ego run away with you after this and do not take a more humble position . . . and stop being impatient . . . your usefulness to the Forum will be entirely impaired. I think the next two weeks are going to decide your fate. I have had to eat humble pie because I get impatient and want to see different things done myself."

I said, "Clyde, you are not in the same position as Martha and myself or your viewpoint might be different. . . . We have been singled out for special punishment and held with an indictment over our heads because the doctor has not made his peace with us. What about his own ego and stubborn pride? Are we always to bow to it . . . is he always right?"

You should know by this time, Harry, that I am not moved by fear . . . I felt your presence today . . . and I felt a Great Presence . . . I want to be so sure that I am in the right. I hope I have not failed today, I repeat, in the eyes of those [the celestials] who are watching. The doctor puts on such a disarming front, he is such an actor, that he wins ready sympathy. . . .

I feel good tonight after the ordeal and thank you for your letter. No court action unless a very last resort. Love to you both.

Harold hoped to write a book that would give for the first time a true account of the Urantia movement. On January 15, 1967, two years before Sadler died, Sherman sent Sadler the following remarkable letter. Martha Sherman has kindly allowed me to reprint it.

Your days have to be numbered at your age. You have little time left to make it possible for the true story to be told about the origin and history of the Urantia book.

I have just completed research on native faith and spirit healers in the

Philippines and my book: "WONDER" HEALERS OF THE PHILIP-
PINES has just been published.

I am now considering the writing of a new book detailing the "inside
story" of the Urantia development, from the early beginning, as much as
can be known, to the present—based upon voluminous notes, observations, information from many and some surprising sources—dealing
with personalities involved and actions that have been taken.

I feel it is time that the TRUTH about Urantia should be given the
public. If you really believe in the "Urantia Revelation," you can make a
valued contribution to such a book.

Here are some of the points that need to be clarified:

1. Specific knowledge about the "sleeping subject"—Your first contacts . . . how the book itself developed, with you, as the apparent
   "appointed" custodian.
2. The formation of the Forum; its financing of the project; the reading
   of the papers, the supposed observation of Higher Beings and their
   "correction" of the papers, based upon the reaction of the listeners.
3. The reported appearance (materialization) of these papers after
   they had been corrected, in typewritten form.
4. The statement that the papers were considered to be completed in
   1934—and yet the writing of the Jesus papers took place at a later
   date?
5. Proof that the Jesus papers were dictated through the "sleeping
   subject" and not written by you and adapted to the Urantia philosophy, with your knowledge of comparative religions.
6. The reason why all original manuscripts purportedly written by
   the "sleeping subject" were not preserved in a vault, and witnessed and annotated by observers at the time, as evidence, so that
   proof could be presented that the book, as originally written, had
   not been altered.
7. Explanation of how much editorial license has been taken with the
   original manuscript, by what authorization, and how much has
   been interpolated, so that the reader can know what is true and
   what is false with respect to its contents.
8. Explanation as to why powers of ex-communication were exercised by you if the conduct or attitude of any of the Forum members did not meet with your approval. Proof that such authority to
   threaten Forum members or to punish them was given you by
   these Higher Beings, purportedly in charge of the Urantia Project.

These are just a few of the mysterious phases of the Urantia development which need to be cleared up before the public-at-large can be

expected to accept some of the remarkable contents as anything but glorified Science Fiction.

You, if you really believe, fundamentally, in the Urantia revelation, owe a great debt before you leave this earth, as the ONE person who can reveal the WHOLE TRUTH. Personally, were I in your position and actually believed, I could not face an entrance into the Next Dimension with certain unrevealed facts on my heart and soul. I would not want to have to answer for some of the things that have been said and done in the name of TRUTH.

Christy, as one of the surviving commissioners, who holds as well a great responsibility in the name of TRUTH, can be of great help to you in this regard.

This is the time for the TRUTH to be made known, and if I undertake the writing of such a book on URANTIA, I will speak the TRUTH as frankly as I have set it forth in my exploration of the Psychic Surgery in the Philippines, without fear or favor.

Enough time has now elapsed for a perspective to be drawn on the URANTIA BOOK—and its contents.

How much is TRUE?

How much is FALSE?

The book has not sold widely in its present form. It needs a development to vitalize it—to point out its significant factors—to separate the human side from the metaphysical, in its creation.

Do you have the courage and integrity to make these disclosures?

If not, the book will always remain a great Question Mark—and the vast amount of work gone into its creation will be lost to mankind.

Sincerely
Harold Sherman

There is no evidence that Sadler replied.

9

OAHSPE

*O**AHSPE A Kosmon Bible in the Words of Jehovih and His Angel Embassadors*, was mentioned briefly in chapter 1. There are so many interesting similarities between the Faithist cult and the Urantia movement that I decided a chapter on *Oahspe* would not be out of place. Although Faithists like to capitalize all the letters of *Oahspe*, I will capitalize only its initial.

When I wrote the first chapter I was under the impression that the Faithists had long ago expired. Not so! The cult has never ceased to exist, though in recent decades its members have been scattered here and there in steadily diminishing small groups. From time to time a remnant will publish a short-lived periodical. As I write, a colony in Utah, The Universal Faithists of Kosmon, issues a newsletter called *Kosmon Voice*. Now in its sixteenth year, it contains 24 pages of inspirational articles, news reports of conferences, poetry, cartoons, and photographs. There are six issues annually. Its photos show most of the faithful as quite elderly. From the publisher, POB 154, Riverton, Utah 84065, you can also obtain a variety of books and pamphlets including a 254-page Faithist hymnal, and a *Dictionary of Words and Terms Used in Oahspe*.

A Faithist group sprang up in London in 1904. Their periodical, *Kosmon Unity*, now issued twice a year, I am told, is the longest running Faithist journal. It is published in London by Kosmon Press. In the United States, other leading Faithist periodicals are *The Faithist Journal*, printed in Hualapai, Arizona, and *Four Winds Village News*, a quarterly issued by the Essene Faithist Church and Missionary Society, Route I, Box 2120, Tiger, Georgia 30576. The society runs a commune called Four Winds Village, founded in 1969 by Virginia Howard, whose grandmother was an

Ojibwa Indian. *Radiance*, another Faithist magazine, is a bimonthly issued by The Eloists, POB 83, Henniker, New Hampshire 03242.

Copies of *Oahspe* were until recently obtainable from the Owl Press, POB 81, Rosholt, Wisconsin 54473.* The first half of the book, annotated by Walter Wiers in two large paperbound volumes, was also distributed by Owl Press. Like Urantians, Faithists insist that no one is qualified to reject their Bible who has not carefully read and pondered its every sentence. This I have not been able to do (the book is almost a thousand pages), but I have read enough to see that it is vastly inferior to the *UB* both in ideas and style of writing. Sadler was a well educated, talented writer and editor. The author of *Oahspe*, John Newbrough, was a mediocre writer. A few striking similarities between the *UB* and *Oahspe* deserve discussion, but first a brief account of how this mammoth Bible came about.

John Ballou Newbrough (1828–1891), named after John Ballou, a famous Universalist preacher, was born in a log cabin in Springfield, Ohio. His father was a Scot, his mother a Swiss. The mother was a devout spiritualist, and young John grew up sharing his mother's faith. He is said to have graduated at a Cincinnati medical college. I am not sure which one. Perhaps it was the city's Eclectic Medical College whose faculty stressed natural remedies in opposition to mainline medicine.

In 1849 young Newbrough joined the gold rush to California where for several years he mined successfully. He became a strong champion of the civil rights of California's cruelly exploited Chinese laborers. Together with his friend John Turnbull, from Scotland, he prospected in the gold fields of Australia.

In 1859 Newbrough married Turnbull's sister Rachel. They settled at 128 W. 43rd Street, in Manhattan, where for 23 years Newbrough practiced dentistry. Always generous, much of his work for the poor was done free. Two boys and one girl came from this marriage. One boy died in infancy, the other is said to have graduated from Columbia University as a civil engineer. The marriage degenerated, and in 1886 Newbrough sued for and won a divorce. A year later he married divorcee Frances Van deWater Sweet.

---

*In July 1992 I sent Owl Press a check for $29.20 for their edition of *Oahspe*. The check was cashed. More than two years went by, but no copy arrived. Letters to Owl Press were unanswered and they were unreachable by phone. I finally obtained a copy of the Palmer edition through a rare book store. Owl Press never refunded my check.

I am told Owl Press is bankrupt. There are rumors that La Toya Jackson, sister of Michael, has volunteered to fund a reprinting of *Oahspe*, but I have been unable to verify this. La Toya is currently sponsoring a psychic phone-answering service called the Zodiac Group, headquartered in Boca Raton, Florida. The cost is $3.99 per minute.

Newbrough was six feet, four inches, tall and handsome, with a massive body and large hazel eyes. A great admirer of Battle Creek's Dr. Kellogg, he was a lifelong vegetarian and teetotaler. Following the doctor, he ate only one or two meals a day, avoided milk and eggs, and eventually abandoned all root vegetables because they grew without benefit of sunlight. This spare diet was said to have reduced his weight from 270 to 160 pounds.

Newbrough traveled widely in Europe and the Orient, lecturing to spiritualist groups while wearing brightly colored Oriental robes. His fame as a medium and automatic writer spread. Legends grew up around him. He was said to be able to paint pictures in total darkness, using both hands. It was claimed that he could close his eyes and read any book in any library. Without effort he could lift weights of a ton or more. His astral body was able to visit any spot on earth. For two years he was active as a medium in "The Domain," a small spiritualist colony in Jamestown, New York.

One night at 4 A.M., as Newbrough himself tells it, he felt a hand on his shoulder and heard a voice urging him to wake. In his bedroom, flooded by a mysterious soft light, he saw the forms of beautiful, wingless angels. The voice told him he was destined for a special mission. He was to continue to abstain from flesh foods and to live a pure life, helping as many unfortunates as he could.

Ten years went by before he was awakened again by the mysterious light. The voice commanded him to buy a typewriter. Angels, it said, would control his fingers while he typed. These automatic typewriting sessions began on the pre-dawn morning of January 1, 1881, and lasted until December 15 of the same year. Every morning before sunrise Newbrough pounded his Sholes typewriter, unaware, he insisted, of what he typed. All this, by the way, is from an account Newbrough gave in a long letter (dated January 21, 1883) that was published in *The Banner of Light*, Boston's leading spiritualist journal.

Many years before he began automatic typewriting, Newbrough had acquired the ability to write automatically in longhand. While sitting in spiritualist séances, "my hands could not lie on the table without flying into these 'tantrums.' Often they would write messages, left or right, forward or backward, nor could I control them any other way than by withdrawing them from the table."

After ten years of pure living, and bathing twice a day, "a new condition of control came upon my hands." The control was through typing. The power descended upon him every morning before sunrise as he sat alone in his tiny apartment. One morning he glanced out the window and saw a long line of light that rested on his hands and "extended heavenward like a telegraph wire toward the sky. Over my head were three pairs of hands, fully materialized. Behind me stood another angel with her hands on my shoulders. . . . My looking did not disturb the scene; my hands kept right on printing, printing."

Was Newbrough lying? Did he actually experience these hallucinations? We shall probably never know.

For fifty weeks, Newbrough goes on in his letter, the angels controlled his typing for thirty minutes every morning before daylight. Suddenly the controls stopped. He was told by the angels to read for the first time what he had written, and to publish it as a book titled *Oahspe*. Newbrough printed the book himself in Boston, in 1882, on a press bought with money from seven anonymous associates. No author's name was on the title page. A revised edition was issued in 1891, and reprinted in London in 1910. The book was illustrated with pencil sketches drawn by the angels who controlled his hands. "A few of the drawings," he wrote, "such as Saturn, the Egyptian ceremonies, etc., I was told to copy from other books."

In 1960 Ray Palmer, a science-fiction writer and editor, published an offset copy of *Oahspe*'s first edition. From the 1891 edition Palmer reproduced twelve oil paintings by Newbrough of various *Oahspe* prophets, and photographs Newbrough had taken of ten cult children. In a second edition (1970) Palmer added "The Book of Discipline," also from *Oahspe*'s 1891 edition. Two years later in a third printing Palmer supplied a 70-page index.

Palmer's final edition (1972) is called the "green *Oahspe*" because of its all-green hardcover. Although half the number of pages as the *UB*, its paper is heavier, making both books the same thickness. The green *Oahspe* weighs four ounces more than the *UB*. Palmer clearly intended his *Oahspe* to imitate the *UB* in appearance. The two books have covers of almost exactly the same size, one all blue, the other all green. The only printing on the blue *UB* is its title in gold letters on the front cover and spine. The only printing on the green *Oahspe* is its title in gold on the front cover and spine.

Palmer is best known for being fired by the publisher of *Amazing Stories*, which Palmer edited, for hoaxing readers into believing that evil creatures called Deros live under the earth's surface. As founder and editor of *Fate*, he was the first magazine publisher to promote the flying saucer craze, arguing that UFOs come from inside a hollow earth through a huge hole at the North Pole. See "Who Was Ray Palmer?" a chapter in my *New Age* (1991).

Like the *UB*, *Oahspe* teaches that there is one ultimate God who oversees a vast bureaucracy of lesser deities. This God has many names: I AM, Ormazda, Eloih, Creator, Most High, and Jehovih-Om. Jehovih is the Creator's masculine and positive aspect. Om is God's negative, feminine side. Like Christian Scientists and today's feminist theologians, Faithists like to think of the great I AM as Mother-Father, Him and Her. Jehovih is the term they most often use for the ultimate Creator. As in the *UB*, a lower God is assigned to each inhabited planet. Such gods are known as Emuts. The god assigned to earth occupies a heavenly city called Hored. It is "situated over and above the mountains of Aotan in Ughoqui, to the eastward of Ul." It is hard to believe, but proper names in *Oahspe* are far more numerous and even uglier than those in the *UB*.

Oahspe speaks of thousands of millions of gods, though unlike the millions in the *UB*, half are female. Closest to Jehovih are his countless Sons. Below the Sons are still lesser gods, and below the gods are billions of archangels, angels, and Lords. The Sons have such names as Sethantes, Ah'shong, Aph, Sue, Apollo, Thor, Osiris, I'hua Mazda, Yima, Lika, Uz, and Fragapatti. The goddesses have such names as Cpenta-Armij, Pathema, Harrwaiti, Dews, Cura, Yenne, Wettemaiti, and D'zoata.

As in the *UB*, and in many world religions, humans pop into existence at birth, with no previous lives, but after death they ascend from heaven to heaven in an endless series of adventures as they move toward perfection. Three days after death the souls of most mortals are carried by guardian angels, called ashars, to the lowest heaven where their souls are reborn in a "birth blanket." Angels who receive the souls are called asaphs.

> And the ashars shall make a record of every mortal, of the grade of his wisdom and good works; and when a mortal dieth, and his spirit is delivered to the asaphs, the record shall be delivered with him; and the asaph, receiving, shall deliver such spirit, with the record into such place in these heavens as is adapted to his grade, where he shall be put to labor and to school, according to the place of the resurrections which I created.
>
> As ye shall thus become organic in heaven, with rulers, and teachers, and physicians; and with capitals, and cities, and provinces; and with hospitals, and nurseries, and schools, and factories, even so shall ye ultimately inspire man on the earth to the same things.
>
> And mortals that are raised up to dominion over mortals shall be called kings and emperors. As My Gods and My Lords are called My sons, so shall kings and emperors be called sons of God, through him shall they be raised up to their places, and given dominion unto My glory.

The heaven to which we go after death is in a higher dimension and therefore invisible. It occupies a region called Atmospheria because it lies within the atmosphere of the earth's vortex. All heavenly bodies—suns, planets, moons—arose from and are sustained by rotating vortices of space-time.

Beyond Atmospheria are heavens of still higher dimensions in a vast region called Etheria. The food there is called heine, the drink haoma. One smells a potent perfume called homa. Etheria's dominant color is golden yellow. Everything in Etheria is made of ethe, a solvent of corpor. Corpor is the matter of our corporeal world and our corporeal bodies. The unseen world is called Es in contrast to the visible world of Corpor. Inhabitants of Es are Es'eans. Those of Corpor are Corporeans. As in the *UB*, no two heavenly worlds are alike—"Every one differing from another, and with a glory matchless each in its own way." The heaven called Haraiti, and six others, were founded by Fragapatti.

As in the *UB*, there is no eternal hell. Those unprepared to enter the first heaven are imprisoned until they can be "weaned from evil." There is no final annihilation of the unredeemable.

As in the *UB*, angels move rapidly about in nonmaterial Etherean spirit ships. The ships have such names as:

Arrow, Firre, Abattos, Adavasit, Airavagna, Airiata, Avalanza, Beyan-float, Ballast Flags, Cowpon, Ese'lene, Koa'loo, Oniy'yah, Otevan, Ometer, Obegia, Piedmazar, Port-au-gon, Seraphin, Yista.

One ship, Koa'loo, is almost as large as the earth. Some are propelled by musical vibrations, others by the vibrations of colors. Many Faithists today believe, like some Urantians, that these spaceships are responsible for the UFO sightings of recent decades.

Like the *UB*, *Oahspe* retells many of the tales in the Christian Bible, including the disobedience of Adam and Eve in eating the fruit of a forbidden tree. *Oahspe*'s account of Noah's flood reflects the submergence of Whaga, a vast continent in the Pacific that later was called Pan. *Oahspe* is a word in the forgotten language of Pan. The "O" means earth, "ah" means air, and "spe" means spirit. The word is pronounced to imitate the sound of wind as it passes through trees, over oceans, and through mountains. The inhabitants of Pan were destroyed by Jehovih because of their wicked ways.

When Pan sank, the waters of the Pacific swallowed up the rich valleys of Mai, the wide plains of Og, the great capital of Penj, the temples of Khu,

Bart, Gam, and Saing. Today's Zha'Pan (Japan) is a fragment of Pan that survived the sinking. After the submergence of Pan, human culture spread from Zha'Pan to Jaffeth (China). In *Oahspe* Asia is called Jud, Africa is Vohu, Europe is Dis, and America is Thouri.

Biblical personalities in *Oahspe*, much more so than in the *UB*, are given strange names. Satan is Anra'mainyus, Jesus is Joshu, Judas is Zoodas, Adam is A'su, Abel is I'hin, Cain is Druk. Curiously, Eve remains Eve. A'su was made by the Creator out of se'mu. The A'suans, descendants of A'su, disobeyed Jehovih by eating the fruit of the Tree, and were punished for it.

The admirable I'hins (descendants of Abel) were white and yellow, small and slender. The giant Druks (descendants of Cain) were brown and black, tall and stout—an evil race of murderers. Cohabitation between Druks and I'hins produced a hybrid race called I'huans. Cohabitation between Asu'ans and Druks, later between I'huans and Druks, produced the Yaks, or "ground people." They had long arms, curved backs, walked on all fours like apes, and were incapable of speech or of surviving death. The I'hins castrated them and made them slaves. The I'huans were copper colored and became the ancestors of the Ong'wee, or American Indians.

Moses and the Old Testament prophets, we are told, were early Faithists. They were called Eseans (Essenes). Joshu (Jesus) descended from this line. He was stoned to death at age 36 by Jews who worshiped heathen gods. Forty years later a phony deity named Looeamong called himself Christ. His warrior tribes became the early Christians. The Christians, says *Oahspe*, are "warriors to this day."

Rather than reading all of *Oahspe*, which I find too boring to keep my eyes open, I let the plot summary in the *Encyclopedia of Religion and Ethics* finish the story:

Looeamong, with the other Triunes, Ennochissa and Kabalactes, endeavoured to overthrow Jehovih, assuming the names of Brahma, Budha, and Kriste to combat Ka'yu (Confucius), Sakaya (Buddha), and Joshu. But Looeamong failed to keep his word to his chief angel warrior, Thoth, or Gabriel, who rebelled in consequence, and raised up Muhammad. Muhammadanism is to perish first, then Brahmanism, then Buddhism, and finally Christianity. During the period treated by the Book of Es (c. 1448–c. 1848) there is an abrogation of revelations, ceremonies, etc., and liberty of thought begins to prevail. Melkazad is divinely sent to inspire a migration to Guatama, and he raises up Columbo to discover it to broaden the sphere of Jehovih's kingdom and to aid in overthrowing the Triunes and Thoth. Then Looeamong inspires his followers (Roman Catholics) to punish heresy, thus giving rise to Protestantism, which also is inspired by evil spirits.

The Pilgrim Fathers were inspired by the God, but corrupted by Looeamong; the Quakers were Faithists at heart. Thomas Paine was inspired by Jehovih, the other chief men 'raised up by God, to establish the foundation of Jehovih's kingdom with mortals,' being Jefferson, Adams, Franklin, Carroll, Hancock, and Washington. During the decay of Looeamong's kingdom petty Drujan Gods set up little principalities, such as Methodists, Presbyterians, and Baptists, while Pirad founded the Mormons, Lowgannus the Shakers, and Sayawan the Swedenborgians.

For *Oahspe*'s high praise of Thomas Paine's attack on Christian doctrines, at the same time defending theism and a hope for immortality, see chapter 13 of the *Book of Es*. Chapter 20 of the same book tells how angels came to Lincoln in dreams and inspired him to free the slaves.

Aside from the fact that *Oahspe* and the *UB* each profess to contain papers written by celestial beings who channeled their words through a human conduit, there are many other ways in which *Oahspe* foreshadowed the *UB* revelation.

Both books outline an elaborate, fantastic cosmology with little support from modern astronomy. *Oahspe* cosmology is on the whole more primitive than that of the *UB*, but we should remember that the *UB* was written half a century later and could therefore reflect new astronomical discoveries. There is, however, one aspect of *Oahspe* cosmology that rises above the cosmology of the *UB*. I refer to its theory about the origin of our solar system.

As we shall learn later, the *UB* defends the Chamberlin-Moulton hypothesis, popular at the time the Papers were written, but since totally discarded by astronomers in favor of the theory that stars and planets condensed from rotating nebulas. This is precisely the view taken by *Oahspe*! It speaks of stars, planets, and moons as condensing from huge vortices, or swirls in the "etherian firmament." Our Sun is at the center of a mammoth vortex. Its planets and moons are the centers of smaller vortices. By stretching things a bit, one could take this to be prophetic of general relativity in which massive objects like stars and planets bend space-time into what could be called surrounding vortices that generate gravity. In *Oahspe*, the energy created by each vortex is called vortex-ya. Ionized molecules, shaped like magnetized needles, align themselves with the lines of vortex'ya. Here is Jehovih's description of how he created the universe:

By the power of rotation, swift driving forth in the extreme parts, condense I the atmospherean worlds that float in the firmament; and these become My corporeal worlds. In the midst of the vortices made I them, and by the power of the vortices I turn them on their axes, and carry them in the orbits I allotted to them. Wider than to the moons of a planet have I created the vortices, and they carry the moons also.

Around about some of My corporeal worlds have I given nebulous belts and rings, that man might comprehend the rotation of My vortexan worlds.

For each and every corporeal world created I a vortex first, and by its rotation and by the places in the firmament whither it traveleth, caused I the vortex to conceive the corporeal world.

A great vortex created I for the sun, and, within this vortex and subject to it, made I the vortices of many of the corporeal worlds. The sun vortex I caused to rotate, and I gave it power to carry other vortices within it. According to their density and position are they thus carried forth around about the sun.

Jehovih adds that our solar system travels an orbit so huge that it takes 4,700,000 years to complete one revolution. Astronomers today estimate that the solar system completes its orbit around the center of the Milky Way galaxy in about 200,000,000 years. However, in Newbrough's day, 4,700,000 was not such a bad guess.

When Ray Palmer's *Mystic Magazine* (February 1955) reprinted excerpts from *Oahspe*, in an article headed "The Most Amazing Book in the World," an unidentified writer (probably Palmer) supplied footnotes. Here are his comments on *Oahspe*'s anticipations of present-day cosmology:

The book is intensely interesting in the light of present-day science, whose discoveries were not known in 1880 when the book was written, yet agree wholly with the precepts given in the book. . . .

Most recently accepted theory of the creation of the solar system and the planets is the "whirlpool" or "vortex" formation of matter which eventually becomes suns and planets by condensation of the primal matter of space. In 1880 this concept was unheard of, yet is given in great detail in OAHSPE.

Both Faithists and Urantians have a logo. As we have learned, the Urantian registered trademark is three concentric blue circles. The unregistered Faithist symbol, depicted on *Oahspe*'s title page and in its "Book of

Jehovih," is a circle divided by a cross into four quarters with an oak leaf in the center.

Both books outline an ideal government for earthlings. In the *UB* it is a democracy with socialist aspects. In *Oahspe* it is closer to anarchism—a loose federation of autonomous groups that cooperate out of love for one another.

Urantians repeatedly insist that it is not important to know who the *UB*'s sleeping conduit was or just how the Papers were edited and put together. The *UB*, they maintain, must be judged solely on its intrinsic merit. In Newbrough's letter, from which I quoted earlier, he expresses the same sentiment:

> If a book have merit, what matters it who wrote it? And if it have no merit, then certainly it does not matter whence it came. The time has been when the name of an author clothed his product with some sort of authority. I rejoice that that day is past, that man-worship is at an end and that all books, including bibles, are perused not as authorities but as pastimes to lead us nearer and nearer to the Everlasting Light. But I rejoice most of all because our Heavenly Father provided us a government that protects us in publishing our highest conceptions.

An anonymous editor, in a preface to *Oahspe*'s first edition, put it this way:

> If a book were to fall down from the sky with Jehovih's signature to it, man would not accept the book on that account. Why, then, should anything be said about how this book was written? It blows nobody's horn; it makes no leader. It is not a destroyer of old systems or religions. It reveals a new one, adapted to this age.

Like the *UB*, *Oahspe* clearly states that it is not to be taken as containing absolute truth. The following passage appears in *Oahspe*'s first paper: "Not infallible is this book, OAHSPE; but to teach mortals how to attain to hear the Creator's voice and to see His heavens, in full consciousness, whilst still living on the earth; and to know of a truth the place and condition awaiting them after death."

Unlike the *UB*, *Oahspe* is written in the style of the King James Bible, with lots of "ye's," "thee's," "beholds," and other Biblical words and phrases. Like the Bible it is divided into books, in turn divided into chapters, in turn divided into numbered verses. All three sacred works—Bible, *UB*, and

Oahspe—consist of documents supposedly written by authors who are identified. Above all, *Oahspe* resembles the *UB* in containing thousands of strange proper names for persons and places, and neologisms never used before or since. Here is a typical example from chapter 2 of the "Book of Aph":

> 4. Hear Me, O ye Chieftains, of Or and of Oot, and in the plains of Gibrathatova. Proclaim My word to thy hosts of swift messengers of Wauk'awauk and Beliathon and Dor, and they shall speed it abroad in the a'ji'an mounds of Mentabraw and Kax of Gowh.
> 5. Hear My voice, O ye Goddesses of Ho'etaivi and of Vaivi'y-oni'rom in the etherean arcs of Fas and Leigge, and Omaza. Proclaim My decrees of the red star and her heavens in the crash of her rebellious sides, for I will harvest in the forests of Seth and Raim
> 6. Hear My voice, O ye H'monkensoughts, of millions of years' standing, and managers of corporeal worlds! I have proclaimed the uz and hiss of the red star in her pride and glory. Send word abroad in the highway of Plumf'goe to the great high Gods, Miantaf in the etherean vortices of Bain, and to Rome and to Nesh'outoza and Du'ji.

In *The First Book of God*, proper names reach lengths comparable to the thunderclap words in Joyce's *Finnegans Wake:*

> Chiawassaibakanalszhoo was the son of Tenehamgameralhuchsukzhais-tomaipowwassaa, who was son of Thusaiganganenosatamakka, who built the great east canal, the Oseowagallaxacola, in the rich valley of Tiedas-wonoghassie, and through the land of Seganeogalgalyaluciahomanhom-hom [most likely Louisiana and Mississippi—ED.], where dwelt the large men and women, the Ongewahapackaka-ganganecolabazkoaxax.

Like Urantians, Faithists delight in claiming that all sorts of scientific truths in their sacred book, unknown at the time, have been confirmed by recent discoveries. An Owl Press advertisement for *Oahspe* declares that the book's science "is today being confirmed by space-satellites and new archeological discoveries of ancient races, dead cities and civilizations."

Harold Sherman and his wife Martha, who for five years were loyal members of the Forum, were fully aware of ways in which *Oahspe* resembled the *UB*. In *How to Know What to Believe*, Sherman reports that he and Martha were once "deeply drawn to the remarkable book, OAHSPE." He closes chapter 10 with the following *Oahspe* verses:

THEN answered Jehovih to the songs of praise that rose up from His hundreds of thousands of millions, to the sum of His mighty creations.

2. Peace, My beloved! And great joy! I have heard your voice of praise! I answer you with millions of new creations! Farther than the farthest, boundless! Thousands of millions of years are the works of My hand! I go not about turning water into wine, like a magician, or professing to raise the dead!

3. But yet I raise the dead, the souls of the dead, into worlds shining, brilliant, full of loveliness! I take them not backward to toil and sorrow; but upward, onward, to heavens of delight, that perish not, forever.

4. Mine is the Tree of Life, forever growing and rich in blossoms and sweet perfumes. The dead are Mine, the spirits of the dead My young blossoms full of promise, speaking soul-words for the glory of My heavens.

5. Whom I quickened into life are Mine, and I watch over them Fatherly and in great wisdom. Nor suffer I them to go out of being forever. And I provide My heavenly places broad, boundless, so that the soul of man can never reach the boundary thereof.

6. Though they stray away for a season, yet have I provided them to return to Me in the end. And I make them a banquet, and provide unto them a feast, a home of love, with music and dancing even on the threshold of wisdom.

7. Weep not for the dead, O My beloved! I have places of delight for the righteous, full of rejoicing and wonderful! And the soul of the dead entereth therein, as one that emerges from a veil, to shout with great joy for the provisions I created, plentiful and brilliant.

8. Heaven after heaven have I created as a new surprise of great happiness to My Sons and Daughters, in the way of My resurrection. Rejoice and be merry in holiness! Open your eyes, My beloved, and behold the works of My hands which I provide to be yours forever!

Walter Wiers, in a Prologue to the first volume of his annotated reprinting of parts of *Oahspe*, describes the book this way:

Even a brief examination of *Oahspe* will convince the reader that it is something special—that it is not just another book by another man looking up and writing about God. On the contrary, it reads like a book from another world. The point of view manifested in its pages is always that of someone above the earth and above man in the hierarchy of the universe looking downward and back to man, calling to him to improve himself and his society so that he may the sooner rise up and enjoy the greater splendors of the higher worlds. If only for this, its tranquilizing view of our affairs from a great height, its sanity-restoring perspective, *Oahspe* is well worth reading. But essentially, *Oahspe* is a new revelation, a veritable revelation, more reasonable, more consistent, and more complete than any other so far. This is, while not claiming infallibility, *Oahspe* purports to be new help from above, new light from the All Highest on mankind's most enduring questions, including some of the grave ones of this era.

In order that we may intelligently direct our lives toward trustworthy goals and eliminate much wearisome, self-cancelling toil and error, and in order that collectively we may stay on the road to the stars, we are given in *Oahspe* vital, indispensable information we could not otherwise get for ourselves in time to do us much good. We are given information about causes and origins, about things, personages, and events, about right and wrong, about space, gravity, and extraterrestrial organizations, and above all, about the continued life of the human spirit and what this really means.

Who give us this information? It is our present conviction that *Oahspe* consists of authentic and official disclosures made for our orientation and guidance by organized space-dwelling entities above us in the hierarchy of life forms. These space-dwelling entities of *Oahspe* claim to be, and indeed may very well be, members of a cosmic society older than the earth.

Replace the word *Oahspe* in the above quotation with *The Urantia Book*, and the sentences could have been written by a dedicated Urantian.

I was surprised to hear from my old friend Dr. Matrix, the eminent numerologist, that he had once made a detailed study of the numerological significance of names and numbers in *Oahspe*, but his monograph on this was never published. I begged him *not* to send me a copy! I owe it to my readers, however, to mention one remarkable discovery that Dr. Matrix included in his faxed letter. Faithists often refer to Jehovih as the great I AM. If you shift each letter of "I AM" forward one step in the alphabet you arrive at JBN, the initials of John Ballou Newbrough!

Oahspe divides all living humans into two classes. Those who accept the new revelation are the Faithists. Outsiders who are not Faithists are called Uzians. All Urantians are, of course, hopeless Uzians.

Uzian reviewers of *Oahspe* were merciless in their criticisms, although they marveled that any one man could single-handedly produce such a monumental work. Urantians are similarly awed by the *UB*, claiming that no one person, not even Sadler, could possibly have written anything so imposing. If *Oahspe* is a true revelation, said the critics, it has to be the greatest book ever written, even more important to mankind than the Bible.

If not true, it is either the work of a psychotic, or a monstrous hoax. Similar remarks have been made about the *UB*.

Soon after *Oahspe* was published, plans for a colony of Faithists began to jell. A small commune was set up in Woodside, New Jersey, later moving to Pearl River, New York. It did not last long.

Enter Andrew M. Howland, a wealthy Quaker and businessman from Massachusetts. He was Faithism's most notable convert, and almost as mad as Newbrough. The two became great friends.

A book in *Oahspe* titled "The Book of Shalam" recommended the establishment of a colony to take care of unwanted orphans. In the mid 1880s, under the direction of angels, Newbrough and Howland founded the Children's Land of Shalam, near the village of Dona Ana in southern New Mexico, on the east banks of the Rio Grande. When the colony failed, Howland and other backers lost more than a million dollars.

The first settlers in Shalam came mainly from the Pearl River colony—only about 20 at first, but the ranks soon swelled to 50. These historical details, as well as those to come, are based entirely on two works: *The Land of "Shalam,"* by Mrs. K. D. Stoes, and *Inside the Shalam Colony*, by Elnora W. Wiley.

Mrs. Stoes's history first appeared in *The New Mexico Historical Review* (vol. 33, no. 1 and 2, January and April 1958.) It was reprinted as a 68-page booklet currently obtainable from The Universal Brotherhood of Faithists, in Tiger, Georgia. Ms. Wiley's longer work, a 166-page paperback, was published in 1991 by the Los Alamos, New Mexico, Document Shop. It is available from the Universal Faithists of Kosmon, Post Office Box 654, McCook, Nebraska 69001.

I have no idea how accurate either of these histories are. Ms. Wiley was formerly the Registrar of New Mexico State University. Her account, told almost in the form of a novel, is based on what was told to her by Justine Newbrough, John Newbrough's daughter, when she was 83. Justine defends her father as an honest, decent man, totally sincere in his strange beliefs although he and his closest followers were, she admits, lacking common sense. The book contains photographs of Newbrough, his tombstone, and many of the Shalam buildings.

For five years, Mrs. Stoes writes, people came to Shalam and left. They included "adventurers, religious fanatics of dubious faiths, habitual new creeders, and a few mentally deficient." Accommodations were available for a hundred. Money flowed in from Eastern philanthropists, most of whom knew nothing about Newbrough or the weird doctrines of *Oahspe*. Unwanted foundlings from large cities were taken in. There were no racial bars. The orphans were white, black, brown, and yellow—babies the world did not want. They were given such Oahaspian names as Pathocides, Astraf, Thouri, Hiatisi, Hayah, Thalo, Ninya, Havalro, Hiayata, Des, Fiatsi, Vohnu, Whaga, and Ashtaroth. No records of parents were kept. In later years, many of the children, grown to adults, would desperately try to learn who their parents were.

With the help of cheap Mexican labor, buildings were erected. Howland became known as Father Tae, and the first building to go up was designated the Temple of Tae. Here is how Mrs. Stoes described the Temple:

> The TEMPLE OF TAE was one storied, circular, and conical, a miniature blue firmament, glistening with silver stars. On the altar lay an open copy of *Oahspe*. Copper bells of exquisite tone fed the imagination. Wall lockers with weird vestment and astonishing masks. Manifestations of uncanny ceremonials were a part of symbolical ritual of the First Church of Tae. Here Dr. Newbrough, Faithist High Priest, vested in strange robes, suave, polished, learned and convincing, presented the precepts of *Oahspe*, and revealed its oracles.
>
> Under the panoply of silver stars this modern prophet foretold World War One, the failure of prohibition, the passing of present-day orthodox religion, and the extension of the southern boundary of the United States to the Isthmus of Panama. He predicted the disappearance of tariffs and in time national boundaries, civil wars in Mexico, the eventual banishment of military forces, the effacement of poverty, and the supremacy of science.

Mrs. Newbrough was known to all as "Mama." Everyone in the colony followed Dr. Kellogg's recommendations of a strict vegetarian diet and no more than two meals a day. By the late 1880s the colony held about 25 Faithists and some 50 children.

Great emphasis was placed on the properties of colors. Yellow was the most sacred. Blue was a cold color that could cure baldness and induce sleep. Gastritis was relieved by water from blue bottles after they had been radiated with sunlight. Pictures of the great prophets mentioned in *Oahspe* were painted by Newbrough on the walls of a building called the Faturnum. He is said to have painted them with both hands at once. Angels constantly gave him advice on how to manage his colony.

In 1891, at the age of 63, Newbrough died of pneumonia along with many other Faithists in an influenza epidemic that swept the region. Howland was in Boston at the time, seeing to the printing of a revised second edition of *Oahspe*. Newbrough died before it left the press. A lifelong Mason, his body eventually found rest in a Masonic cemetery in Las Cruces.

On his tombstone, under the Faithist logo of cross and leaf, are these words: "Unto Thee, Jehovih-Creator, be praise and thanks for brother John B. Newbrough, June 5,1828–April 23, 1891, through whose hands OAHSPE, the new Bible, was transcribed for the World."

Howland, now the colony's patriarch, with his large gray beard, blue eyes, long hair, white trousers, and sandaled feet, took over Shalam's management. In 1893 he married Newbrough's widow. For a few years the colony prospered. Howland established a chicken farm. Eight windmills pumped to the buildings water from the Rio Grande. There was a machine shop, a general store, stables, stock pens, and a bee aviary to provide honey. Efforts were made to build Levitica, a town of 20 small houses. Residents were brought in from Kansas City and elsewhere. They began to quarrel. Some fancied that the colony permitted free love. Disgusted, Howland packed them off to where they came from.

Like so many other small religious colonies with bizarre doctrines, Shalam slowly disintegrated. Funds dwindled. Storms and floods destroyed property. By 1901 the commune was bankrupt. About 25 children were placed in foster homes or sent to orphanages in Denver and Dallas. Booker T. Washington adopted a bright little black boy called Thail. The Howlands blamed the failure of Shalam on evil angels. Had they been Urantians, they would have pinned it on Caligastia. For a couple of years in California the couple tried to preserve their faith. They and a few followers settled in El Paso where Howland died in 1917, age 83. Five years later his wife followed him upward through the stars.

In 1918 the American poet Ella Wheeler Wilcox published an autobiography titled *The World and I*. Mrs. Wilcox is now forgotten by both critics and the public, but she was then at the height of her fame. In addition to writing poetry, novels, and essays, she was a leader of what was then called New Thought, a precursor of today's New Age. Ella was the Shirley MacLaine of her day—theosophist, spiritualist, and true believer in all things psychic and occult. After her husband died in 1916, she began a desperate search around the nation for spiritual solace and for genuine communications from her husband's spirit. Eventually she established contact with him by way of a Ouija board, but before this her search took her to California where she visited the remnants of the Oahspian cult. She found them to be "a strange and earnest handful of men and women, following altruistic ideals, but leaving me sadder than before I visited them. They seemed to have eliminated from life on earth all idea of beauty."

Urantians believe that the Fifth Epochal Revelation began when supermortals made contact with humanity through a sleeping contactee, eventually producing the Papers of the *UB* that were published in 1955. Faithists date the new revelation, the beginning of what they call the Kosmon era, from March 31, 1848. Why this year? Two reasons. It was the year that California was settled, marking the time that Guatama (North America) was "inhabited from east to west . . . with men of wisdom and learning" (Book of Es 2:25,26). More importantly, it was the day when angels made their most significant direct contact with humans through the spirit rappings of the Fox sisters at Hydesviile, New York. This "opened the door in Jehovih's name, to be not closed again forever, forever!" (*Book of the Daughter of Jehovih* 19:18).

Although the rappings began in mid-March, 1848, it was not until the night of March 31 that they became unusually intense. The Fox sisters later confessed that they produced the raps by cracking toe joints, but spiritualists refused to believe them. Here is how Sir Arthur Conan Doyle described the occasion in the first volume (pages 62–63) of his *History of Spiritualism* (1926):

> Upon the night of March 31 there was a very loud and continued outbreak of inexplicable sounds. It was on this night that one of the great points of psychic evolution was reached. . . . Search all the palaces and chancelleries of 1848, and where will you find a chamber which has made its place in history as secure as this little bedroom of a shack.

Urantians celebrate August 21, the day they believe Jesus was born. The Faithists, obeying commands in *Oahspe*, celebrate March 31 as their holy day.

Both Faithists and Urantians look upon their revelation as the start of a religious awakening that will transform human history. Here is a passage from *Kosmon Voice* (vol. 16, January/February 1993, page 6) that could be written by any Urantian with the word changes indicated inside brackets:

> It is the dawn of the Kosmon [fifth epochal] Era. Faithism [Urantianism] glimmers like the first faint flicker of a flame in a dark jungle that it will presently consume.
>
> Faithism [Urantianism] today seems to others, and indeed often seems to us, a pitifully inadequate force for the task of world regeneration which lies before us. But in that task, we, as Faithists [Urantians], are but the advance-guard of an approaching army which is the focus of cosmic and transcendant forces.
>
> Working within the slow warp and woof of time, these forces may

clearly be discerned by those who will examine the affairs of mankind. We have potent and resistless allies guiding us, and nowhere is it more evident than in the events and accomplishments of the lives of people who are reshaping the affairs of our planet.

The Shermans were not the only Urantians impressed by *Oahspe*. Dan Massey, writing on the Internet in 1994, recalls a group in Australia during the 1960s and 70s that combined a belief in both the *UB* and *Oahspe*! It was led by a man named Fred Robinson who traveled about the continent wearing a robe with the three blue circles stenciled on the front. The Foundation persuaded him to change the group's name from Urantia Brotherhood to Universal Brotherhood, to discard the robe, and to play down *Oahspe*. After Robinson died, according to Massey, the group became "less Urantian and more Oahspish." He does not know what finally happened to the followers. Massey also recalls a man from Kansas City known as "Willy the *Oahspe* mugger" who attended Urantian conferences and tried to persuade Urantians that *Oahspe* was a more imporant revelation than the *UB*.

There is a fundamental difference between the two revelations, with their massive Bibles. *Oahspe* emerged from the spiritualist mania that began with the Fox sisters' toe snapping. Its pages bristle with spiritualist beliefs. The *UB* emerged from the Seventh-day Adventist movement which denied all possibility of converse with the dead and regarded all the phenomena of spiritualism as the work of Satan.

The *UB* obviously is a much more intelligent work, far better written than *Oahspe*, with fewer neologisms and less crazy science. After all, the *UB* papers were written more than 50 years after the books of *Oahspe* and had the advantage of a skillful editor, well acquainted with the science of his day. It would be interesting to know if Sadler or Wilfred Kellogg ever read *Oahspe*. If so, what did they think of it? I would guess that if Sadler had encountered *Oahspe* in his early years he would have agreed with Ellen White and his church that the Faithist Bible, like all books channeled by spiritualist mediums, was either a deliberate fraud or the work of Satan and his demons.

Many Urantians believe that Newbrough was under Caligastia's influence when he channeled *Oahspe*. Last year a prominent Adventist historian told a friend of mine that Satan unquestionably was the true author of *The Urantia Book*. Only a Protestant or Muslim fundamentalist could believe that the two Bibles have in common a demonic authorship, but there is one thing they do have in common that nobody can deny. Each makes an excellent doorstop.

10

Science in *The Urantia Book,*
Part I

Over the decades a large Urantian literature has been published as hardcover books, paperback books, and pamphlets. Of the hardcover "companions" to the *UB*, the most impressive is the *Concordex of the Urantia Book*. It was compiled by Clyde Orvis Bedell (1898–1985), published by his Santa Barbara, California, Estate in 1971, and is now in a third edition. A monumental 507-page labor of love, it lists alphabetically, with brief definitions and *UB* page references, all the *UB*'s major terms and personalities, both human and celestial.

Bedell was a Chicago advertising executive. He worked for Butler Brothers from 1924 to 1932, was advertising manager of Marshall Field from 1936 to 1939, and later sales promotion manager of the Fair department store. He and his wife Florence Evans, formerly his secretary at Butler Brothers, attended Forum meetings from 1924 until their deaths as dedicated Urantians. In his chapter on the Urantia movement (see chapter 7 of this book), Harold Sherman calls him Floyd Winters.

Bedell wrote many books and pamphlets. The books include *Let's Talk Retailing* (1946), *Seven Keys to Retail Profits* (1931), and *Your Advertising, Is It a Profit-Making Force or the Usual Money Wasting, Opportunity-Wasting Farce?* (1953). His most important book, *How to Write Advertising That Sells* (McGraw-Hill, 1940), has gone through many reprintings and is still on sale today. Pamphlets by Bedell include *Chef's Perpetual Menu-Planner* (1951), and *Grist, Grit, and Gristle* (1932).

Urantia Foundation leaders were not pleased when Bedell took it upon himself to write, print, and sell his *Concordex* rather than issue it through the Foundation. Bedell remained bitter about the Foundation's attitude toward him until he died in Boulder, Colorado, having moved there from Santa Barbara.

In a 16-page "Unofficial White Paper" (my copy is undated) Bedell vigorously lambasted the Foundation for its strange reluctance to produce an index which the Foundation had announced on page lxvi of the *UB*'s first three editions. "An exhaustive index," the Foundation wrote, "to *The Urantia Book* is published in a separate volume." This suggests that as early as 1955 an index had actually been prepared.

According to living Forum members, work on the index was done without pay by the elderly ladies at 533 Diversey, often referred to as the "nuns." From 1955 until now the Foundation has maintained it was working on just such an index and would issue it soon. It never did, even though for many years it solicited money for it. Angered over these delays, Bedell decided to do the index himself "as a labor of love. Not to make a profit. Not to make a living. If 533 will not accept it for what it is and what I created it for, my entire views for distribution may have to change." He continues:

> There has never been one word of *recognition* of the CONCORDEX from 533, aside from a request I deed it over to the FOUNDATION—which in a way is an endorsement.
>
> But NEVER, NEVER, NEVER, has anyone sat down with me and said: "Clyde, we recognize the great value of the CONCORDEX and the extraordinary service it rendered THE URANTIA BOOK and its readers, and how valuable it can be in interesting new readers in the BOOK. We know that almost every Society and Study Group uses the Concordex a great deal, and that almost all speakers use it in preparing talks. We believe there must be ways we could use the CONCORDEX to help sell more URANTIA BOOKS, and you have probably thought about this. Let's talk about it."

The second most valuable reference work about the *UB* is *The Paramony*, compiled and privately published in 1986 by Duane L. Faw. It consists of 15,000 cross references that link *UB* passages to verses in the Bible. We shall have more to say about Faw in chapter 17.

Sadler's son Bill Jr. was extremely active and influential in the Urantian Movement by giving lectures and holding study groups. After his death in 1963 the Second Society Foundation published his 150-page *Study of the Master Universe* (1968) and his 372-page *Appendix to a Study of the*

Master Universe (1975). The former book is dedicated to Tabamantia, a celestial entity in charge of periodically inspecting Urantia and other planets on which life is evolving.

Bill was the Urantia Brotherhood's first president. A talk he gave to young people, *Simplification of the Foreword From the Urantia Book*, was published as a pamphlet in 1977 by the Asoka Foundation of Oklahoma City. Urantians consider this and all the other books mentioned above as "secondary." Although not divinely inspired they are of major importance to *UB* students.

A *Resource Guide*, available from the Fifth Epochal Fellowship, 529 Wrightwood Avenue, Chicago, Illinois 60614, lists many secondary works currently on sale. They include reproductions of paintings of *UB* cosmology, pamphlets, news letters issued by numerous study groups, and books of Urantian poetry. *It Is Finished* contains 45 sonnets by David Glass, a Urantian living in Fort Worth, Texas.

Why have I become so intrigued by the *UB* and its growing secondary literature? One reason is that I have always been interested in the history of Seventh-day Adventism ever since as a young boy, for a period of about a year, I considered myself an Adventist. It was mainly the result of reading uncritically the crank geological books by the Adventist creationist George McCready Price and a book by Adventist Carlyle B. Haynes titled *Our Times and Their Meaning*. When I learned about Adventist influence on the Urantia Movement it piqued my interest.

I also was challenged by the mystery of who was the *UB*'s sleeping conduit to higher powers. Most of all, however, as a science journalist I was fascinated by the enormous amount of science in the *UB*. It is absolutely unique in this respect among all literature said to be channeled by higher intelligences through a person either asleep or in trance. *UB* science is a strange mix of knowledge widely accepted by mainline scientists during the years the *UB* was crafted, and wild speculation about truths either unknown to science or contradicted by recent science.

Since the *UB* was published in 1955 there has been a steadily proliferating literature about its scientific content. In 1961 Sadler himself, with the help of Alvin L. Kulieke, published two volumes of paperbound typescripts titled *Science in the Urantia Book*. Both books, however, consist almost entirely of mere summaries of what the *UB* has to say on scientific topics.

Three symposiums on science in the *UB* have been held. The first, in Nashville, May 1988, is covered by a special issue of the *Journal of the*

Urantia Brotherhood. The second symposium was held in Oklahoma City, May 1991. Both audio and video tapes of the 1991 lectures are available. A two-volume collection of thirteen of the 1991 talks was published by the Fellowship Forum in 1993. At this second symposium Michael B. Wisenbaker distributed his privately printed booklet *Cosmic Design.* It covers *UB* science with special emphasis on modern cosmology and quantum mechanics.

The third science symposium took place in Oklahoma City in July 1994. At the time I write, its tapes have not been available, or their contents printed. However, some Internet postings by Philip Calabrese, Byron Belitsos, and Dan Massey commented on some of the papers. Massey's address on "Time and Space" gave an interpretation of *UB* passages that he finds consistent with special relativity. They also explain how midwayers and seraphim can exceed the velocity of light, and why the universe has seven dimensions. From a "secular point of view," Massey adds in a surprisingly perceptive remark, his lecture was "the epitome of crankiness."

Our next chapter will cover the *UB*'s absurd theory that inside every electron are "huddled" exactly one hundred particles called "ultimatons." Michael Pitzel, who considers himself an astrologer, has patented a way of folding a piece of paper to form a kind of "magician's hat" he calls a "trimobius." Pitzel described this structure and claimed that it modeled an ultimaton! He says the idea for the trimobius struck him while he was taking a course in topology. The trimobius emerged when he tried to construct a closed one-sided surface called a Klein bottle. At first the conference leaders tried to prevent Pitzel from speaking, but they finally allowed him a spot after he complained he was being unjustly censored because his theory of the ultimaton differed from a rival theory defended at the symposium by Calabrese.

Michael Wisenbaker gave a paper arguing that the big bang never happened, and that the *UB*'s denial of the bang will eventually be proved correct. A female professor from nearby Oklahoma University lectured on the Faust myth, a topic totally unrelated to the *UB.* I wonder who asked her to speak and why. Matthew Block (we will come to his sensational discoveries in chapter 16) read a passage from a geology textbook of the 1920s, which he said was the source for the *UB*'s paragraph (page 662) on lava flow.

As we all know, in both Catholic and Protestant Christianity, as well as in Judaism, a rift has developed between so-called fundamentalists, who refuse to see any historical or scientific blunders in Scripture, and moderates or liberals who concede mistakes but maintain that they do not diminish the great spiritual truths in the sacred writings. A similar split exists among Moslems with respect to the Koran. It also exists among such sects as the Mormons, with respect to *The Book of Mormon*, and even among Seventh-day Adventists with respect to the "inspired" writings of their prophetess Ellen White.

In recent years Urantians are starting to bifurcate into similar camps. The division is sharpest in reference to the *UB*'s science. Liberal Urantians freely admit that the *UB* contains serious scientific errors. Urantian fundamentalists, like their Jewish, Christian, and Moslem counterparts, are tireless in their efforts to show that their Bible's science not only is error free, but in many cases far ahead of its time.

As more information surfaces, the fundamentalists are rapidly losing ground. Most of the science in the *UB* obviously reflects opinions that prevailed from the time the revelation began until 1955 when the *UB* was published. In many cases modern research has shown much of this science to be wrong. As we shall see, the revelators themselves stated that *UB* science was based on current scientific opinion, to be revised in future decades. In view of such caveats, it is not easy to understand why Urantian fundamentalists are so quick to defend every scientific statement in the *UB* which critics contend is outdated.

None of the great scientific discoveries of the last half of this century is in the *UB*. It contains, for example, no hint of big-bang cosmology. Recent evidence that the universe is much lumpier than previously supposed has produced difficulties in explaining how galaxies could have formed in light of the smoothness of the microwave "glow" left over from the primeval fireball. A few maverick astronomers have put forth alternate cosmic models, the most impressive being a plasma model by the Swedish physicist and Nobel winner Hannes Alfvén. An American plasma physicist, Eric J. Lerner, even wrote a book about Alfvén's model titled *The Big Bang Never Happened* (1991). The media gave Lerner's book a great deal of publicity without making clear that the overwhelming majority of astronomers consider it a crank work. Recent evidence of large-scale structures in the universe does not falsify big-bang cosmology; it merely calls for more work on how galaxies form and on the nature of the yet unfound "dark matter" required to sculpt them.

It is understandable that Urantian fundamentalists would eagerly seize on recent doubts about the big bang to support the *UB*'s denial of big-bang cosmology. Their hopes were dashed in 1992 when new observations of the microwave radiation showed fluctuations and patterns that strongly support the bang. As one astrophysicist exclaimed, "The big bang is alive and well, very well!" Of course all science is corrigible, and big-bang theory may indeed some day be discarded for a better model.

Also missing from the *UB* is any hint that the atom would be split in 1942, more than a decade before the *UB* was published. Why was this news not added to the *UB*? Because its papers dealing with atomic structure had been finalized by 1934, and it would not have seemed right to rewrite them in the light of the latest scientific discoveries. It would, however, be absolutely necessary to add to the papers the proviso that the *UB*'s science would not go beyond scientific opinion at the time the papers were written, and that Urantians should expect UB science soon to be contravened by new developments.

None of the great and still continuing scientific discoveries in particle physics since 1955 is in the *UB*. The papers say nothing about the computer revolution. Much is said about rapid methods of communication on worlds far more advanced than Urantia in their technology, but nothing is said about television. The papers are silent about the helical structure of the DNA molecule, the discovery of which sparked an explosive new era in genetics, a field in which Sadler considered himself an expert.

How do Urantians, both liberal and fundamentalist, justify the failure of the *UB* even to hint at these stupendous scientific breakthroughs? They call attention to a statement in the *UB* (1109) by Melchizedek of Nebadon. The revelators, he says, are forbidden to disclose scientific truths before they have been "earned" by Urantian scientists. Here are portions of Melchizedek's cautionary remarks:

> Any cosmology presented as a part of revealed religion is destined to be outgrown in a very short time. . . . We are not at liberty to anticipate the scientific discoveries of a thousand years . . . within a few short years many of our statements regarding the physical sciences will stand in need of revision in consequence of additional scientific developments and new discoveries. These new developments we even now foresee, but we are forbidden to include such humanly undiscovered facts in the revelatory records. . . . The cosmology of these revelations is *not inspired*. It is limited by our permission for the co-ordination and sorting of present-day knowledge. While divine or spiritual insight is a gift, *human wisdom must evolve*.

These statements by Melchizedek not only justify the *UB*'s silence about great discoveries, they also justify scientific errors in the *UB*.

Because the revelators cannot reveal unearned science, they are forbidden to correct errors that are to be discovered after the *UB* is published. In spite of the *UB*'s clear statement that its science will soon be found inadequate, Urantian fundamentalists never tire in their efforts to deny that the *UB* contains scientific mistakes. Moreover, they continue to search for evidence, contrary to Melchizedek's plain warning, of spots in the *UB* where unearned science is anticipated.

In 1991 the Brotherhood of Man Library, POB 1355, Mason City, Iowa 50401, published a 35-page booklet titled *The Science Content of the Urantia Book*. Four devout Urantians collaborated on this work: Richard Bain, Ken Glasziou, Matt Neibaur, and Frank Wright. Because I lack space to consider all the claims in this fantastic document, I will touch only on its highlights. I will show that the four authors are deceiving themselves in precisely the same way that creationists deceive themselves by taking the Genesis account of creation to be historically accurate, or the way that ardent disciples of Immanuel Velikovsky deceive themselves in seeking justifications for every error in Velikovsky's crazy cosmology. In the past century, true believers in the *Oahspe* Bible made the same strenuous efforts to justify all the science in that mass of channeled balderdash. Of course in any large work like *Oahspe*, as in the many books of Velikovsky, there are sure to be a few lucky hits among the hundreds of misses.

In what follows I will deny an assumption made by the four Urantian authors. They assume that nothing in the original *UB* Papers was altered after 1934. I do not believe this. The evidence is strong that the Papers were continually edited and revised by Sadler and possibly other Forum members, and that he himself wrote some of them under the conviction that he had been divinely "indited" to do so. The *UB* was set by linotype. Helen Carlson, in a sworn 1994 deposition, said that the Papers were not set in type until the "late forties or early fifties." Even after the linotype slugs were locked into frames and plates made for the 1955 printing, it would have been easy to unlock frames, make changes, and cast new plates.

Helen Carlson, sister of Bill Sadler Jr.'s first wife, worked most of her life at 533 and still lives there. If anyone knows the history of the papers it is Helen. In the deposition she made in 1994 for a court case we shall come to in our last chapter, she described the revelation process as follows. Sadler would read a single paper to the Forum, then questions from those present would be written on slips of paper and collected either in a basket or what was called a fishbowl. Bill would screen the questions to avoid duplications, and they would be taken to the midwayers. How they were given to the midwayers Helen said she did not know.

After the midwayers had responded to the queries, the paper would be revised accordingly. How long did this procedure last? For at least "ten years after 1939," Helen answered. She refused to call the *UB* a "divine revelation"—a revelation, yes, though not a divine one. "I don't think you can call even the Bible divine," she added.

The same dubious assumption that no changes occurred in the papers after 1934 is made by Irwin Ginsburgh and Geoffrey Taylor in their address "Scientific Predictions of the Urantia Book," given at the 1991 Scientific Symposium II, in Oklahoma City. They cited several "predictions" of scientific facts not known before 1934, but well known many years before the *UB* was printed in 1955.

For example, they point out that the *UB* (260) gives the velocity of light as 186,280 miles per second. In 1931, they say, the estimate was 186,270, but by 1949 measurements had raised it to the present figure of 186,282, just two miles above the *UB*'s figure. This is a bit misleading because numerous measurements were made of light's velocity prior to 1935. In 1882, Michelson's result was 186,284. The writer of Paper 23 may have come across this figure in old encyclopedias or astronomy books, and rounded it down four miles. Or did the *UB* author find the 186,282 figure in a 1949 or later reference and round it down two miles?

It seems likely that material revised or written entirely by Sadler and perhaps others (I will consider this again in chapters 14 and 15) was "authenticated" by checking it with the revelators through the sleeping Wilfred. This would justify Sadler in denying that he "wrote" any part of the *UB*. In his mind it would be the revelators who did the writing by putting the ideas in his head, then authenticating them through Wilfred.

Let's begin by considering how the *UB* (Papers 57 through 65) explains the origin of our solar system. Each paper purports to be written by a Life Carrier, some still residing (though invisible) on Urantia. Astronomers today date the age of the universe as about 15 billion years, give or take 5 billion. The entire universe, it is believed, started with a primeval explosion which the British astronomer Fred Hoyle derisively called a "big bang." At that time Hoyle was defending a steady-state cosmology. It has since been abandoned, mainly because of the discovery of a microwave "glow" left over from the fireball.

The *UB* denies any big bang. Our galaxy, it says, came into existence 875 billion years ago following a mandate by the Ancients of Days. First the higher powers created a enormous nebula called Andronover. Its number is 876,926. Andronover evolved into a two-arm spiral similar to the Andromeda galaxy. As it contracted, it spun faster and faster, finally breaking up into 1,013,628 suns (*UB* 655). Our sun is number 1,013,572. (The revelators delight in giving these precise giant numbers, which of course nobody can verify.) Only a million suns in our galaxy? Astronomers count billions.

Our solar system, called Monmatia in the *UB*, came into existence 4,500,000,000 years ago (this figure agrees with current estimates) as a result of the near approach of Angona, a stellar system with a giant dark star at its center. The big star pulled from our sun two filaments which condensed into twelve planets. (As mentioned earlier, we know of only nine; the *UB* predicts two more, not yet detected, beyond the orbit of Pluto.) Slowly, over billions of years our planets and their moons steadily enlarged by an accretion of meteorites until they reached their present size about a billion years ago.

This theory of how our solar system evolved was the most popular such conjecture during the twenties and thirties when the *UB* papers were being written. It was called the "planetesimal hypothesis" or the "Chamberlin-Moulton hypothesis" after the two University of Chicago professors who first proposed it in 1900. They were geologist Thomas Chamberlin and astronomer Forest Ray Moulton. You'll find the theory covered in detail in Moulton's *Astronomy* (1931), a widely used textbook of the time. (It was the one I used in 1936 when I took Astronomy 101 at the University of Chicago.) Chamberlin gives a good account of the theory in many papers, and in a popular anthology edited by Moulton, *The World and Man As Science Sees Them* (1937).

In England, Sir James Jeans, then the world's most famous astronomer, accepted the theory as early as 1916. The "tidal theory," as he liked to call it, is defended at length in his popular book *The Universe Around Us* (1929), a book that I suspect (for reasons I will come to later) Sadler carefully read.

On page 320 Jeans writes:

As we know how the stars are scattered in space, we can estimate fairly closely how often two stars will approach within this distance of one another. The calculation shows that even after a star has lived its life of millions of millions of years, the chance is still about a hundred thousand to one against it being a sun surrounded by planets.

Sir Arthur Stanley Eddington, another famous British astronomer, also defended the tidal theory in his 1927 book *The Nature of the Physical World* (176ff.). Like Chamberlin, Moulton, and Jeans he stressed the extreme rarity of two suns coming close enough to give birth to planets. The probability, he writes, is like the probability that two tennis balls, among twenty moving randomly inside a sphere as large as the earth, will approach within a few yards of each other.* He estimates that not one in a hundred million stars could have undergone a close enough approach to another star to draw out filaments that would later condense to form planets.

The *UB* gives a concise account of the Chamberlin-Moulton theory, including a statement about the enormous unlikelihood of such a close encounter of two massive bodies. Alas, major flaws in this theory were soon discovered, and by 1940 it was dead. If this death was known to Sadler, as it must have been, why did he not remove it from the *UB*? The obvious answer is that the Paper in which it is described had become so well known to Forum members that they would have been greatly disturbed if Sadler had excised it. Besides, there was no need to do this. Does not the *UB* explicitly deny the accuracy of its cosmology, and say that much of it will be out of date in a few years?

I find this a hollow excuse for a false theory to have so prominent a place in a book supposedly dictated by higher beings. Surely many Urantians, although they may not admit it, must be troubled by the fact that superior intelligences, knowing the tidal theory to be false, would give it so much space in the *UB*. It adds nothing whatever to the book's spiritual content.

The *UB* does not call the massive body that approached our sun a star. It is called a "dark giant of space." It had "tremendous gravity pull." In spite of the *UB*'s warning about unearned science, Urantian fundamentalists like to call this, as well as other references in the *UB* to "dark bodies," an anticipation of "black holes."

The suggestion that these dark bodies are black holes is extremely far-fetched. Long before black holes became fashionable, astronomers knew that massive stars could collapse to form white dwarfs, small stars that are extremely dense with enormous gravity fields. On a white dwarf a match folder would weigh several tons. Astronomers conjectured that white dwarfs can cool to form black dwarfs which radiate no light. No black dwarfs have so far been observed (it is not easy to see such stars!), but the existence of

---

*I suspect that Eddington's tennis-ball analogy was the source of the *UB*'s statement (458) about the density of the suns in Nebadon: "They have just as much comparative elbow room in space as one dozen oranges would have if they were circulating about throughout the interior of Urantia, and were the planet a hollow globe."

black dwarfs was widely defended. Because the *UB* says nothing about the singularities of time and space inside a black hole, it seems plausible that the *UB*'s dark bodies are simply stars producing no light.

The *UB* (173) explicitly identifies "the dark islands of space" as "dead suns and other large aggregations of matter devoid of light and heat." It correctly describes these black stars as having an unbelievable density that can be calculated by their effect on nearby luminous suns. It may well turn out that such stars are more plentiful than supposed, and may contribute to the mysterious "dark matter" that today's cosmologists are searching for.

If big-bang theory is correct, as almost all astronomers believe, he universe is 10 to 20 billion years old. The *UB* gives the age of our universe as more than 1,000,000,000,000 years. This was not a far-out estimate at the time. Writing before big-bang theory became standard, Jeans (in his book cited earlier) estimates the age of the universe as 200,000,000,000,000 years, with stars forming about 5,000,000,000,000 years ago. The *UB* (469) speaks of matter arising from the "space potency" of the "Unqualified Absolute." I suspect that whoever wrote that line had read the following sentence (page 316) in Jeans's book: "If we want a concrete picture of such a creation [of matter], we may think of the finger of God agitating the ether."

The *UB* (656 and 658) unequivocally states that our solar system has two undiscovered planets beyond the orbits of Neptune and Pluto. At the time the Urantia papers were written, the existence of a tenth planet, called Planet X, was suspected by some astronomers. The latest evidence, based on extremely accurate measurements of the orbits of Uranus and Neptune, show no discrepancies that indicate an object beyond Pluto large enough to be called a planet. There may, however, be hundreds of tiny objects, the size of asteroids, moving around the sun in the conjectured Kuiper belt of comets. See the paper on this by Dr. E. Myles Standish, an astrophysicist at the Jet Propulsion Laboratory, in *The Astronomical Journal* (May 1993), and "Planet X is Dead," by Robert Naeye, in *Discover* (September 1993).

If future space probes drive the final nail into the coffin of Planet X, will loyal Urantians shrug and say that the *UB*'s claim of two planets was another joke by fun-loving celestials? You can be sure they will not be in the least dismayed. Indeed, I can think of no fact, scientific, historical, or otherwise that would cause them to doubt the divine origin of their treasured Bible.

It is now known that the sun's radiant energy is produced by a thermonuclear reaction in which hydrogen is converted into a variety of helium. No electrons or protons are destroyed by this process. When the

Urantia papers were written, however, it was widely believed that the sun's radiant energy came from the annihilation of atoms and protons. As Sir James Jeans says in *The Universe Around Us*, the sun's energy "originates out of the annihilation of electrons and protons. The sun is destroying its substance in order that we may live." This notion that matter is being totally converted to energy by the sun is the view taken in the *UB*. The main source of the energy, the *UB* asserts (on page 463) is the "annihilation of atoms and, eventually, of electrons."

On the same page the *UB* gives the sun a surface temperature of 6,000 degrees, and an internal temperature of 35,000,000 degrees, adding that both figures are based on our Fahrenheit scale. I suspect that these temperatures were picked up from books by Jeans and other astronomers of the time. Unfortunately, whoever copied down the figures made a whopping mistake. The sun's interior temperature is indeed based on the Fahrenheit scale, but its surface temperature of 6,000 is based on the Kelvin scale in which the units are the same as on the centigrade or Celsius scale, but zero is taken as -273 degrees, or absolute zero. Jeans, on page 241 of *The Universe Around Us* (1929) gives 6,000 for the sun's surface temperature, using the Kelvin scale. On the Fahrenheit scale it is about 10,000. It is hard to comprehend how a superhuman intelligence could make such an elementary blunder, but easy to understand how a human, reading Jeans hastily, would be unaware that Jeans gave temperatures in the Kelvin or absolute scale.

The *UB* swarms with scientific assertions obviously impossible to verify or refute. This is especially true of parts of the book's cosmology. According to the *UB* our entire known universe is a tiny portion of a much vaster realm of being in which flourish a raft of other universes, totally beyond the reach of any conceivable telescope. One must take the existence of these superuniverses entirely on Urantian faith.

The same can be said of many "scientific" statements about angels and higher beings. How, for example, could science ever verify that seraphim can travel 555,000 to 559,000 miles per second, or more than three times the speed of light (*UB* 433); or that Thought Adjusters can go from Divinington, one of the sacred spheres of Paradise, to Urantia in 117 hours, 42 minutes, and 7 seconds? (*UB* 1186)

The great speed with which angels travel has been much discussed by theologians, and praised by poets. Here is the first stanza of a forgettable jingle on angels by the nineteenth-century Scottish poet Marion Paul Aird:

> Like an arrow through the air,
> Or the fountain flow of light,
> Ministering angels fair
> Cleave the deep of night:
> Quick as thought's electric glow,
> Down into earth's chambers dark,
> Fire-wheels running to and fro,
> Like the eye of God, they dart;
> Watching o'er the earth's green bound,
> Searching all in cities round.

The angels that appear scores of times in the Bible are not described as having wings except in the cases of seraphim and cherubim. In Isaiah's vision of God on his throne (Isaiah 6:2) we are told that above the throne "stood the seraphim: each one had six wings; with twain he covered his face, and with twain he covered his feet, and with twain he did fly." In the tenth chapter of Ezekiel the cherubim are pictured as flying with wings. In I Kings 6 we learn that Solomon's Temple contained huge olive wood figures of cherubim with outstretched wings.

In the Old Testament's apocryphal books of Enoch and Elijah angels are described with six wings. The antecedents of the Judaic-Christian angels were the great angels of Zoroasterianism who traveled by flapping enormous wings. Even Ahura Mazda, the supreme God and creator, was depicted as winged.

Although wings are not mentioned, Revelation 8:13 describes an angel as "flying through the midst of heaven," and 14:6 speaks of "another angel flying in the midst of heaven." One assumes they used wings.

Large white wings began to appear on angels in Christian art during the Middle Ages and Renaissance, and it has been traditional to show them with wings ever since. In Doré's illustrations for Milton's *Paradise Lost*, and for Date's *Divine Comedy*, all good angels have white wings. Satan and his cohorts all have dark, batlike wings. The bat wings also adorn fallen angels in William Blake's paintings. In Adventist literature the angels, good and bad, appear in illustrations with large feathered wings. Mrs. White repeatedly described the angels she saw in visions and in dreams as winged. In one of her earliest visions she herself was given wings and allowed to visit an unfallen planet with seven moons.

The *Inferno*'s final canto portrays a giant Satan with three faces, one red, one black, one yellow. Below each face are "two mighty wings, at size befitting such a bird: sea-sails I never saw so broad. No plumes had they; but were in form and texture like a bat's: and he was flapping them, so that three winds went forth from him." The winds keep frozen the ice of hell's final circle—ice in which Satan is confined up to his chest. Milton's Satan was a clever, handsome devil. Dante's Satan is a hideous, hairy idiot.

In the second canto of the *Purgatorio*, Dante describes an angel as flying with "eternal plumes," like a "bird divine." In Canto 8 of the same book, two angels have green wings, green serving throughout Purgatory as a symbol of hope for redemption. In Paradise, hope is no longer an emotion, so the wings of angels become gold in color. Canto 31 of the *Paradiso* pictures angels as having "faces all of living flame, and wings of gold, and the rest so white that never snow reacheth such a limit."

Hermas, a Roman apostolic Father, taught that each person has two guardian angels, one good, one evil, a view taken up by only a few later Fathers. The book of Daniel has a guardian angel for each nation, with Michael assigned to Israel. From time to time cults arose in which angels were worshipped. Many churches were dedicated to individual angels, especially Michael.

Angelolatry is still prevalent, and not just among Urantians. A cult is flourishing in Germany and Austria among devout Roman Catholics. Based on a special revelation of one Gabriella Bitterlich, the members engage in elaborate rituals dedicated to the veneration of angels.

In the Middle Ages almost all theologians agreed that a single guardian angel is assigned to every Christian, though there was no agreement on whether they are also assigned to sinners. Protestant theologians were similarly divided. All agreed that evil angels are unable to influence the saved unless their free will allows it.

The Scholastics wrote voluminously about angels, their number, nature, and habits. Such speculation reached awesome heights in the writings of Thomas Aquinas. With nary a trace of humor, the Angelic Doctor seriously considered such profound riddles as whether angels are capable of defecating and breaking wind—questions on which the *UB* is mercifully silent. For an excellent history of angelology, both Christian and otherwise, see the papers on "Demons and Spirits" in James Hastings' *Encyclopedia of Religion and Ethics*.

A basic reference on angelology is Gustav Davidson's *A Dictionary of Angels* (Free Press, 1967, reissued in paper covers in 1971). Malcolm

Godwin's *Angels: An Endangered Species* (Simon and Schuster, 1990) is rich in color plates but the text is marred by New Age notions and is not too accurate. For example, Godwin says on page 11, "in the Old Testament there is no reference to the fallen angels at all. There is nothing to suggest that Satan was evil." How about Isaiah 14 which speaks of Satan's pride in wanting to be like God, and includes that marvelous line: "How art thou fallen from heaven, O Lucifer, son of the morning!"

How did the myth ever arise that angels travel by flapping wings? The *UB* has a clever explanation. We are told (*UB* 438) that a few minutes before death persons sometimes get a dim glimpse of an attending angel just prior to being transported. They see what seem to be double sets of wings. These are not wings. They are "energy insulators—friction shields" required because of the seraphim's great speed as they transport an unconscious person's soul to another world. When these energy shields are wide open, the sleeper is "skillfully deposited" by seraphic assistants, "directly on top of the transport angel." The shields are then carefully closed and adjusted.

As the transport angel prepares to "swing into the energy currents of the universe circuits," a "strange metamorphosis" occurs. The angel becomes pointed at both front and back, enshrouded in a "queer light of amber hue." After the chief of transport inspects everything to make sure the angel is properly "enseraphimed," the angel becomes an "almost transparent, vibrating, torpedo-shaped outline of glistening luminosity." The transport dispatcher summons a thousand "auxiliary batteries of living energy," then reaches out to touch the near point of the "seraphic carriage." It "shoots forward with lightninglike speed, leaving a trail of celestial luminosity" in the planet's atmosphere—a trail that lasts for ten minutes.

Philip Calabrese, a Urantian mathematician living in San Diego, has worried for years about a seeming contradiction in the *UB*. We are told (*UB* 260) that seraphim travel about three times faster than light.* On page 569 we learn that when we die our sleeping soul is transported from Urantia to

---

*Seraphim speed is slow compared to the speed of the Solitary Messengers, described in Paper 23 by the Divine Counselor from Uversa. He tells us that 7,960 trillion Solitary Messengers operate in Orvonton alone, and that this is one seventh of their total number. To render their seven different kinds of service they travel at 841,621,642,000 miles per second. Even this incredible speed is nothing compared to that of the Gravity Messengers from Divinington (*UB* 346–47). They transcend space and time by going from *A* to *B* instantaneously!

Thomas Aquinas defended the belief that angels, like tunneling electrons in today's quantum theory, can travel instantly from one place to another without occupying any spots in between. If relativity theory is correct, no object or information can exceed the velocity of light without going backward in time and creating all sorts of logical contradictions.

the first mansion world, which orbits Jerusem, in just three days! Now Alpha Centauri, the star (aside from our sun) nearest earth, is more than four light years away. A seraphim, going at triple light's speed, would need more than a year to get to our nearest star, let alone to Jerusem which is much more distant!

Urantians have long been troubled by this seeming contradiction. Troy Bishop wrote about it in "Seraphic Velocity," an article in the Fall/Winter 1982–83 issue of *Ascender*. Merritt Horn followed it with "Seraphic Velocities," in another Urantian periodical titled *Planetary Prints* (January 1984).

Calabrese addressed this puzzle in a speech "On Seraphic Velocities and Resurrection on the Third Day," delivered at the first Urantian Scientific Symposium, held in Nashville, Tennessee, May 13–15, 1988. He pointed out that according to the *UB* (261) a "solitary messenger" can travel 841,621,642,000 miles per second, which is almost a million times faster than light. However, the *UB* clearly says that it is the transport seraphim, not the solitary messengers, who take souls of the dead to Jerusem.

Calabrese summarized several bizarre ways Urantians have struggled to account for the "third day" on which souls are "repersonalized." He discards them all in favor of taking "day" to be an indefinite period of time. Here is his final conclusion:

> So my answer to the anomaly is that it really takes at least 11 years and more likely 20, 50 or more years to resurrect "on the third period" without significant delay. Circumstances must be ripe. Many people who died in years past must be asleep in transit right now. Twenty years is less than a half hour in a Paradise day!

In 1991, when Calabrese spoke at the second Urantian Scientific Symposium in Oklahoma City, he revealed a change of mind. He opened his talk on Urantian particle theory and the topology of space by recanting his former solution. Nowhere, he said, does the *UB* assert that when a seraphim carries a mortal soul from Urantia to the first mansion world does she travel under her own power. Calabrese now thinks she is moved more rapidly by some technique that Urantian science does not yet understand.

It is impossible not to recall that medieval theologians were said to have debated the question of how many angels can stand on the point of a pin!

∿⤬∿

Six hundred million years ago, according to the *UB*, a scouting party from Jerusem made a survey of Urantia, planet 606, and reported it was favorable for a life experiment. The Life Carriers had to wait until our oceans were salty enough to support the protoplasm they fabricated on the planet and dropped into its seas at three different places. This occurred, we are told, 550,000,000 years ago. The process of evolution then began. As I will consider again in chapter 15, the process was not Darwinian in the sense that life evolved by a gradual accumulation of tiny variations. Although such small changes could introduce variations within a species, each species arose by an abrupt large-scale mutation.

Urantians like to see this as an anticipation of the modern theory of punctuated equilibrium, often called a "jump theory" of evolution, proposed by Stephen Jay Gould and his friends. This, however, betrays a complete misunderstanding of jump theory. The jumps are a set of small genetic mutations that occur over thousands of years. They are called jumps not because they are sudden, but because they occur closer together in time than the long periods of slow evolution in classical Darwinian theory. Darwin thought the gaps in the fossil record were due to the rarity of conditions for fossilization. Gould believes the gaps are too large to be explained entirely in this way. In chapter 15 we will see how the *UB*'s flawed theory of evolution by "sudden" large mutations was taken from Sadler's 1927 book *The Truth About Heredity*.

The most important mutation, of course, was the sudden appearance, about a million years ago according to the *UB*, of the first humans, the twins Andon and Fonta. As mentioned before, their father and mother were primate beasts. Both parents were killed, we are told, by hostile gibbons. The twins ran off to the north to start the Andonite race by bearing nineteen children. Black eyed and swarthy skinned, the Andonites were the first to make fire by igniting a dried, abandoned bird's nest with sparks produced by banging flints. Sontad, their first born, married one of his sisters. At age 42, Andon and Fonta were killed by an earthquake (*UB* 713). Another set of twins that appeared at the same time, from another sudden mutation, were mentally and physically inferior to Andon and Fonta. It was from this subhuman pair that today's simian species evolved (*UB* 706).

The view that species arose by sudden mutations, rather than tiny changes spread over thousands of years, is more than a century old. One of the first biologists to defend it was St. George Mivart, a student of Thomas

Huxley. His *Genesis of Species* was published in 1871, its title playing on the title of Darwin's *Origin of Species*. Darwin took Mivart seriously enough to devote many pages to him in later editions of *The Origin of Species*. Mivart was a Roman Catholic who did his best to persuade his church to embrace evolution. For this he was excommunicated and denied a Christian burial. (You'll find an account of this shameful episode in my 1992 book On *the Wild Side*.)

The notion that God guided the process of evolution by causing abrupt changes, especially by infusing an immortal soul into the first humans after their bodies had evolved far enough, has been popular among liberal Christians who accept evolution but struggle to harmonize it with Genesis. The *UB* takes a similar approach. Although sudden mutations occur by natural laws, the entire process had been carefully planned, and was and is being guided by the Gods. Liberal Christians tend to hold similar views, with God substituted for Urantian polytheism.

The conjecture that a single mutation can be large enough to produce a new species is now totally discredited. However, the *UB*'s history of life forms, as they evolved through various geological ages from the Proterozoic to the Cenozoic, follows closely the standard textbooks of historical geology available in the 1920s and 1930s. It would be interesting to check some of these books to see if the *UB*'s account mimics any of them closely in phrasing and technical details.

The four authors of *The Science Content of the Urantia Book* freely admit that the *UB*'s astronomy is in spots hopelessly flawed. For example, the *UB* (170) says that the Andromeda galaxy is a million light years from the earth. This was an accepted estimate in the 1920s, but modern instruments have doubled the distance.*

Mercury is described in the *UB* (657) as always keeping its same side toward the sun. This too was the established view until it was discovered that Mercury rotates fast enough to present all sides to the sun. (The notion that Mercury has a twilight belt between its dark and sunlit sides, so pop-

---

*Recent evidence from the Hubble telescope suggests that the Hubble constant (the rate of the universe's expansion) may be larger than suspected. If so, it reduces both the size and age of the universe, and restores to Andromeda a distance of about one million light years from the earth. (See "Candles of the Night," in *Astronomy*, September 1994.) This is highly controversial, and in any case has no relevance to the *UB*'s accuracy because the *UB* merely reflected the opinion of astronomers in the 1930s.

ular in science fiction, had to be abandoned.) The *UB* also errs in saying that, like Mercury, the moon does not rotate on its axis. To keep the same face always toward a central body, a revolving body has to rotate once on its axle for each revolution. The *UB*'s mistake is a common one, to be expected from a human writer who was not an astronomer, though not to be expected from a higher intelligence.

It is amusing to note that *Oahspe*, in spite of its preposterous cosmology, does not make this mistake about the moon's rotation. In the *Book of Cosmogony and Prophecy*, chapter 5, verse 16, the angels write: "Now the moon hath, as to the earth's face, no axial revolution. But it must be remembered the moon can not go around the earth without making an actual axial revolution."

How do the four authors of the booklet on *UB* science justify the *UB*'s science errors? It is hard to believe, but they have a truly marvelous rationalization. The revelators, they argue, deliberately put mistakes in the *UB* as "time bombs"—assertions designed to later explode. Why? To convince Urantians not to fall into the habit of venerating the *UB*, turning it into a fetish of inerrancy in the way fundamentalists make a fetish of the Bible or the Koran!

This notion that science mistakes in the *UB* are "time bombs" planted there to curb excessive veneration of the *UB* comes from Dick Bain, one of the four coauthors. Bain is a large, friendly, electrical engineer living in Hickory, North Carolina, who publishes a semiannual newsletter called *Cosmic Reflection*. Before converting to Urantianism he had been active in Unity, a cult that spun off from Christian Science. Today he attends a Unitarian Church. He visited me in August 1993, arriving in a car with a large bumper sticker that said URANTIA. (Today he has the word on his license plate.) In spite of the few trivial "time bomb" errors he allows in the *UB*, my impression was that the *UB* is for him very much a fetish. He had quick justifications for every major scientific error in the *UB* that I called to his attention.

If the idea of "time bombs" is extended to cover all mistakes in the *UB*, obviously there is no way any amount of bad science in the Papers can damage the sacred tome in the eyes of true believers. Urantians thus have it both ways. If errors of science and history are found in the *UB*—well, the revelators, in their great wisdom, put them there on purpose! On the other hand, wherever one can find a seeming anticipation of later science, then those anticipations are proof that the *UB* had a divine origin! Just as astonishing is that, in spite of Melchizedek's warning that the *UB* contains no unearned knowledge, defenders of the *UB* continue searching for the very anticipations of science the revelators said they were forbidden to disclose! Consider the way in which the four authors strive to convince readers that the *UB* (663) exhibited foreknowledge by defending the theory of continental drift long before it became part of mainstream geology. They are aware, of course, that the theory had been proposed earlier than the *UB*'s fifth epochal revelation, so they can argue that the *UB is* not giving out "unearned" science. It had been earned by Alfred Wegener. However, they maintain, Wegener's theory had been strongly rejected by geologists at the time the *UB* papers were written. Therefore, they argue, the *UB* was genuinely prophetic in accepting the theory.

Unfortunately, the four authors did not trouble to check on the history of Wegener's guess. In the early 1920s, when the first Urantia Book papers were coming through Wilfred and being edited by Sadler and the Forum, continental drift was a controversial but widely respected theory. Alfred Lothar Wegener (1880–1930) first proposed continental drift in a 1912 paper, the year Wilfred's channeling probably began.

In 1915 Wegener published *The Origins of Continents and Oceans.* This 94-page book went through three revised and expanded German editions and was translated into French and English. *Nature* favorably reviewed the book in 1922. Its theory was supported by many top geologists around the world, especially in Holland. Wladimir Köppen, a distinguished German astronomer, was an early convert. Harvard geologist Reginald Daly, South African geologist Alexander du Toit, and Arthur Holmes, of Edinburgh, were among other enthusiastic allies. Du Toit even wrote a book titled *Our Wandering Continents* (1937, revised 1957), that is dedicated to Wegener. As Michael Friedlander says in the chapter on continental drift in his *At the Fringes of Science* (1994), Wegener's theory "remained in a state of suspended credibility until after World War II."

Wegener "earned" the theory by being the first to give a reasonable though faulty explanation of continental drift. The close fit of the two continents had, of course, been noticed much earlier. The German scientist Alexander von Humbolt, the French scientist Antonio Sider-Pelligrini, and the English scientist Osmond Fisher had suggested that the two continents were once joined, but in the absence of a good theory and strong confirming evidence, they were not taken seriously. In 1930 Wegener died on an expedition which he led into Greenland. Companions buried him there in the snow. For good histories of Wegener's theory, see *Continental Drift* (1983), by U. B. Marvin, and *Continents in Collision* (1983), by Russell Miller.

A 1926 symposium on the theory was held in my home town of Tulsa. Its papers (most of them opposing Wegener) were later published as a book, with a long introduction supporting the theory, and a closing essay opposing it. Sir James Jeans, in his popular book *Through Space and Time* (1934), calls Wegener's theory "more interesting" than an older theory of continental alteration, "although it [Wegener's theory] has not yet gained acceptance from scientists."

Wegener maintained for various reasons—mainly the remarkable fit of Africa's west coast to South America's east coast, and the similarity of fossils on both sides of the Atlantic—that 200 million years ago the two continents were joined as a single land mass. He called it Pangaea (all-earth). It later broke up and parts floated away like glaciers, on a foundation of liquid basalt, at a rate of about twelve meters a year.

Wegener's conjecture was one that would have appealed to both Wilfred and Sadler. Opposition to the theory, especially in the United States, did not start to build until the mid-twenties. It culminated in the early fifties, too recent to have influenced the Urantia papers. It was in the late fifties that evidence supporting plate tectonics provided for the first time a plausible mechanism for the drift, and opinions favoring the theory were revived.

Today's theories about continental drift depart in many ways from both Wegener and the *UB*. Plates of the earth's crust do not drift on liquid basalt. They are pushed apart by molten rock that wells up from great depths to solidify and shove the plates. "Seafloor spreading" it is called, a hypothesis proposed by Robert Dietz in 1961. The movement of continents is much slower than Wegener supposed.

The four Urantian authors also make much of two ancient supernova explosions. A red giant in the center of the Crab nebula exploded in 1054. The *UB* (464) says that this explosion came from a "mother star" in the nebula's center. The authors contend that this was not known until after 1955.

The facts are otherwise. The search for the mother star began long before 1955. In the 1960s Rudolf Minkowski found what he believed to be the mother star because of a remarkable absence of absorption lines in the star's spectra. In 1969 came the discovery that this star is a pulsar. It even pulsed in visible light, but so rapidly (thirty times a second) that it seemed to burn with a steady glow. It is now thought to be a neutron star whose gravitational collapse produced the supernova. Had its pulsing been mentioned in the *UB*, or if the *UB* had anything at all to say about pulsars, that would have been something for Urantians to crow about. The mere belief that a mother sphere was inside the Crab nebula, although yet to be identified, was old stuff at the time the Urantia papers were being written.

The other supernova mentioned in the *UB* is one that Tycho Brahe observed in 1572. The four authors are impressed by the fact that it was not identified as an explosion of two stars until 1952, when the explosion's remnants were discovered. Of course 1952 is earlier than 1955, which would have given Sadler a chance to put that in the *UB* (458). But even if this was in the papers earlier it would not be surprising.

For many years before 1952 astronomers favored the theory that the 1572 supernova was of Type 1, which they suspected results from a white dwarf pulling into itself a normal star. This causes the dwarf's mass to swell until it triggers a rapid gravitational collapse. Type 2 results from a much larger single star collapsing when it consumes all its nuclear fuel and turns into a neutron star or a black hole. Because the supernova of 1572 was Type 1, the belief that it resulted from the merging of two stars was the opinion of most astronomers long before 1952 when the remnants of the nova's explosion were first observed.

Astronomers distinguished between the two types of supernovas in the late 1930s, and in 1941 Walter Baade proved what had earlier been suspected, that Tycho's supernova was Type 1, and therefore probably the product of an exploding white dwarf in close proximity to another star. The belief that a binary star was involved in the 1572 supernova was the favored view of astronomers well before the *UB* was published. As early as 1911, in the article "Star" in the eleventh edition of the *Encyclopaedia Britannica* (vol. 25, page 786), two explanations of novas are given: the sudden explosion of a single star (then the favored theory), or the collision of "two stars or between a star and a swarm of meteoric or nebulous matter."

One of the *UB*'s most successful predictions about future science is on pages 378–79:

> The four points of the compass are universal and inherent in the life of Nebadon. All living creatures possess bodily units which are sensitive and responsive to these directional currents. These creature creations are duplicated on down through the universe to the individual planets and, in conjunction with the magnetic forces of the worlds, so activate the hosts

of microscopic bodies in the animal organism that these direction cells ever point north and south. Thus is the sense of orientation forever fixed in the living beings of the universe. This sense is not wholly wanting as a conscious possession by mankind. These bodies were first observed on Urantia about the time of this narration.

As early as 1855 the Russian biologist E. von Middendorf conjectured in a paper that migrating birds are able to sense the earth's magnetic field. Since then the theory has continued to be controversial, although evidence is now extremely strong that birds do indeed have a magnetic sense.

Note that the *UB* says magnetic "bodies" were first found in Urantia life forms "about the time of this narration." This implies that evidence for such bodies had been claimed by someone prior to 1955 when the *UB* was printed.

Sure enough, in 1947 *Life* (September 22, pages 105–108) ran an article titled "How Homing Pigeons Find Their Way." It described research with army pigeons conducted by H. L. Yeagley, a physics professor at Penn State. Yeagley attached tiny magnets to the wings of a group of pigeons, and identical nonmagnetic pieces of metal to the wings of a control group. Birds with the magnets got lost. The others found their way home. *Life* even included a drawing showing the possible location of the magnetic "bodies" in pigeons. My guess is that Sadler or someone in the Forum read this article, and it became the basis for the paragraph quoted.

In 1979 particles of magnetite (iron oxide), sensitive to magnetic fields, were found in the heads of pigeons between their brain and skull. Today it is widely believed that pigeons use the earth's magnetism, among a variety of other navigational cues (including "compasses" provided by positions of the sun and stars), when they find their way at night or on foggy days. Just how their brains use the magnetite remains a profound mystery.

In the late 1970s conclusive evidence showed that certain bacteria sense the earth's magnetism. In the 1980s magnetite was found not only in bacteria but also in mollusks, butterflies, dolphins, and in the abdomens of bees. There is now good evidence of a magnetic sense in paramecia, flat-worms, fruit flies, beetles, termites, worms, snails, salamanders, salmon,tuna, sharks, skates, rays, newts, and even sea turtles. (See "How Turtles Navigate," by Kenneth Lohman, in *Scientjflc American*, January 1992.)

The *UB* states that humans also have a magnetic sense. Robin Baker, a British zoologist, claims he has found such evidence. In *The Mystery of*

Migration (Viking 1981, pages 241–42) he reports on his experiments with blindfolded students. They were taken to an unknown area, and with eyes still covered asked to point toward home. Baker claims that a statistically significant number succeeded, although they were unable to explain how. When they wore helmets with electric coils inside to produce magnetic fields, they were confused and scored at chance levels.

Baker has defended this experiment in numerous technical papers beginning with "Goal Orientation by Blindfolded Humans After Long-distance Displacement: Possible Involvement of a Magnetic Sense," *Science* (vol. 210, 1980, pages 555–57). His popularly written article, "We May Have an Inner Compass That Points Us Toward Home," appeared in *Psychology Today* (vol. 14, 1980, pages 60–73). His book *Navigation and the Sixth Sense* was published in England in 1981. Baker's recent paper on the topic, "Human Navigation: Sun, Star, and Magnetic Orientation by Naive Subjects," can be found in *Orientation and Navigation: Birds, Humans, and Other Animals*, edited by London's Royal Institute of Navigation, 1993. I do not know how well Baker's claims have been received by other zoologists and psychologists.

No one can deny that the *UB* scored a lucky hit in extending the magnetic sense from pigeons to other forms of life, though whether it applies to "all living creatures" including humans remains to be seen. If in the future conclusive evidence shows that humans have such a sense, it would of course be another case of the *UB* violating its own proviso of not revealing scientific facts unknown at the time the papers were materializing.

11

Science in *The Urantia Book,*
Part II

The *UB* states (657) that our moon is slowly moving away from the earth. Only recently has it been shown that the movement is about 1.5 inches per year. The four authors of the booklet on *UB* science tell us that astronomers previously thought the moon was moving toward the earth. Is this not, they ask, another example of scientific knowledge known only to the supermortals at the time the Papers were written?

The authors failed to do their homework. Modern astronomers have for decades known that the moon is moving away from Urantia. Sir James Jeans, in *The Universe Around Us* (cited in the previous chapter as a likely source for certain aspects of *UB* cosmology), explains why the effects of tides would cause the moon to recede. This had been explained much earlier by the British astronomer George Darwin. Eventually, some 50,000 million years from now, Jeans thinks the situation will be reversed. The earth and moon will start drifting closer together.

Here is how Jeans puts it on pages 214–15:

> In the same way, tidal friction has in all probability been mainly responsible for the present configuration of the earth-moon system, driving the moon away to its present distance from the earth and causing it always to turn the same face towards us. Tidal friction must of course still be in operation. The moon is responsible for the greater part of the tides raised in the oceans of the earth; these, exerting a pull on the solid earth underneath, slow down its speed of rotation, with the result that the day is continually lengthening, and will continue to do so until the earth and moon

are rotating and revolving in complete unison. When, if ever, that time arrives, the earth will continually turn the same face to the moon, so that the inhabitants of one of the hemispheres of the earth will never see the moon at all, while the other side will be lighted by it every night. By this time the length of the day and the month will be identical, each being equal to about 47 of our present days. Jeffreys has calculated that this state of things is likely to be attained after about 50,000 million years.

After this, tidal friction will no longer operate in the sense of driving the moon further away from the earth. The joint effect of solar and lunar tides will be to slow down the earth's rotation still further, the moon at the same time gradually lessening its distance from the earth. When it has finally, after unthinkable ages, been dragged down to within about 12,000 miles of the earth, the tides raised by the earth in the solid body of the moon will shatter the latter into fragments, which will form a system of tiny satellites revolving around the Earth in the same way as the particles of Saturn's rings revolve around Saturn, or as the asteroids revolve around the sun.

Compare the above paragraphs carefully with the following passage from the *UB* (657–58):

When the tidal frictions of the moon and the earth become equalized, the earth will always turn the same hemisphere toward the moon, and the day and month will be analogous—in length about forty-seven days. When such stability of orbits is attained, tidal frictions will go into reverse action, no longer driving the moon farther away from the earth but gradually drawing the satellite toward the planet. And then, in that far-distant future when the moon approaches to within about eleven thousand miles of the earth, the gravity action of the latter will cause the moon to disrupt, and this tidal-gravity explosion will shatter the moon into small particles, which may assembly about the world as rings of matter resembling those of Saturn or may be gradually drawn into the earth as meteors.

Which conjecture is the more plausible? That celestials read Jeans' book and summarized his account of the moon's future, or that Sadler (or some other human) did the reading and summarizing? This is exactly the same kind of partial copying from other books that was practiced by Ellen White. Note the minor change of Jeans' 12,000 miles to 11,000 miles. I believe Jeans goes on to say, in his next paragraph, that the history of the earth-moon system suggests an age of the earth and moon of about 4 billion years. Since the solar system had to start forming earlier, it brings the age of the solar system close to the 4.5 billion years given in the *UB* (655).

There are conflicting theories about the origin of the asteroids that zip around the sun in orbits between Jupiter and Mars. The *UB* (657–58) defends the theory that they resulted from the breakup of a planet which came within what astronomers call the Roche limit of Jupiter's strong gravity, rather than rock fragments prevented by Jupiter's gravity from forming a planet. The rings of Saturn are similarly explained as a breakup of one of Saturn's moons that spiraled within Saturn's Roche limit.

I believe that these *UB* pages were also based on Jeans' *The Universe Around Us*. If you check its pages 233 through 237 you will see that the phrasing is too similar to that of the *UB* to be coincidental. Jeans writes that the breakup of a body occurs "when the radius of its orbit" falls "to 2.45 times the radius of the large body." The *UB* (658) says the breakup occurs "when the radius of its orbit becomes less than two and one-half times the radius of the larger body." The breakup of our moon, the *UB* tells us (page 658), will produce "rings of matter resembling those of Saturn." Jeans predicts that the moon's breakup will leave the earth "surrounded by rings like Saturn."

The *UB* (561) speaks of the earth's atmosphere as midway in density between that of Mars and Venus. Why the four authors consider this highly prophetic beats me. Telescopic observation of the two planets long ago showed Venus totally covered with dense clouds, and Mars to have an atmosphere too thin even to be visible. True, no one before 1955 had previously measured the density of the two atmospheres. Had the *UB* provided such data, in particular evidence that Venus's atmosphere was enormously denser than had previously been suspected, it would have been worth mentioning. Merely to declare that Venus's atmosphere is denser than the earth's was a good bet a century ago.

UB authors like to give large and precise numbers for facts that cannot be confirmed, such as the speed angels can travel or the number of inhabited worlds, but when it comes to unearned data likely to be obtained in the near future, such as the density of Venus's atmosphere, the papers are silent.

To say there are two yet unobserved planets beyond the orbit of Pluto is safe enough because it is difficult to prove conclusively that no such planets exist. Their existence is, of course, unfound knowledge. Why, then, would the celestials refrain from revealing the sizes and distance from the sun of these two planets? To skeptics, it indicates that the human authors of the papers were simply guessing about the two planets, but careful not to provide data that could be falsified if these planets were ever found. Urantians, of course, can argue that giving such data would be positive proof that the Papers came from supermortals, and that would tend to turn the *UB* into a "fetish."

The *UB* says (464) that carbon plays a role in the nuclear reaction by which stars turn hydrogen into helium, thereby releasing enormous amounts of energy. There is nothing surprising about this being in the *UB* (as the four authors seem to think) because Hans Bethe—the authors themselves tell us this—announced in 1938 that carbon plays a catalytic role in the sun's nuclear reactions. The authors are assuming, of course, that the Urantia papers were finalized in 1934 and never revised thereafter.

Nor is it surprising that the *UB* (473) speaks of a low degree of heat pervading our universe. That space cannot be absolutely zero was obvious long before the *UB* was published because too many atoms are floating around out there, a large proportion of them produced by nova explosions. Indeed, all the heavy metals, including calcium (*UB* 461–62), were then known to come from the stars. The only discovery after 1955 was how high this heat was. That was when radiation left over from the big bang was detected—a bang which (as we have seen) the *UB* does not recognize. If the *UB* had given the temperature of this microwave radiation, it would have indeed been startling. Merely to assert that space is not absolute zero was to state something obvious.

Equally vacuous is the *UB*'s assertion (463) that the sun emits X-rays. Such rays from the sun were detected in the late thirties, and accurately measured in 1949, six years before the *UB* was published. In *The Universe Around Us* (chapter 5) Jeans has many pages on X-ray radiation from all stars. "A star is in effect nothing but a huge X-ray apparatus . . . the rate at which they are generating X-rays is merely the rate at which they are radiating energy away into space."

As I explained in the previous chapter, the notion that massive stars can be black has long been recognized. Astronomers called them dark bodies, and so does the *UB* in several places. The four authors do their best to see these remarks as anticipations of black holes. For example, the *UB* (655) describes the Angona star system as containing "a dark giant of space, solid, highly charged, and possessing tremendous gravity pull." The four authors comment: "This description aligns with most recent concepts regarding black holes." As I said earlier, it is much more likely that whoever wrote about a dark body in Angona was simply thinking of a massive burned-out star.

When I first read the booklet about science in the *UB*, the section that most surprised me had to do with the exact dates of a famous conjunction of Saturn and Jupiter. It occurred in 7 BCE in the constellation of Pisces (the Fish). The *UB* (1352) says that these conjunctions gave the appearance of a single star which in turn gave rise to the legend of the Star of Bethlehem, as recounted only in the gospel of Matthew. It was this "star" that seemed to guide the three Wise Men to the spot where Jesus was born.

Kepler apparently was the first to suggest a conjunction theory. Unfortunately, the two planets were never close enough to appear as a single star. (A much closer conjunction of the same two planets occurred in 66 BCE.) Moreover, the three conjunctions were spread over a few days, whereas it took the Magi several weeks to complete their journey. Kepler finally decided that the star must have been a new one, specially created by God to guide the Magi. This had been the opinion of Saint Augustine, as well as most Christian theologians of later centuries.

The main objection to the notion that the star was a conjunction of planets is the fact that such a "star" would rise and set like the sun, moon, stars, and planets, whereas the Bible clearly describes it as lingering in the sky and moving steadily in the direction of Bethlehem. Seventh-day Adventists follow the more sensible approach taken by Mrs. White. "It was not a fixed star or a planet," she writes in chapter 6 of her life of Jesus. "It was a distant company of shining angels."

The conjunction conjecture was popular among some German scholars of the nineteenth century, notably the astronomer Christian Ludwig Ideler (who died in 1846), and Karl Georg Wieleler (who died in 1843) in his treatise of Biblical chronology.

A rival contender for the Star of Bethlehem is a conjunction of Jupiter and Venus that occurred on June 17, 2 BCE. This is close to the traditional year for the birth of Jesus, but ruled out by the *UB*'s unsupported birthdate of August 21, 7 BCE. The two planets were much closer together (their disks may even have overlapped) than the Jupiter-Saturn conjunction defended in the *UB*. See "Star of Bethlehem," by James DeYoung and James Hilton, in *Sky and Telescope* (April 1973), pp. 357–58; and Roger Sinnott, "Computing the Star of Bethlehem," *Sky and Telescope* (December 1986), pp. 632–35.

Another contender for the star is a supernova explosion that occurred in the spring of 5 BCE in the constellation of Capricorn. This possibility was defended in a paper by British astronomer David H. Clark in *The Quarterly Journal of the Astronomical Society* (December 1977).

The three conjuctions of Saturn and Jupiter in 7 BCE were caused by the looping of their orbits as seen from the earth. The four authors of the paper on science in the *UB* tell us that in the early sixties the dates of these triple conjunctions were calculated as May 27, October 6, and December 5. The *UB*, however, gives the dates as May 29, September 29, and December 5. Not until 1976, the authors reveal, 21 years after the *UB*'s publication, was a more careful check made by a computer program at California's Jet Propulsion Laboratory.

The program found the dates to be May 29, September 30, and December 5—dates that differ from those in the *UB* only by one day in September. These corrected dates were not published until 1986. How, the authors ask, could the *UB* have been this accurate on the dates unless it was written by celestials?

Here again, the four authors were careless in their research. When the *UB* was published, all astronomers believed the dates to be May 29, October 1, and December 5. Kepler had tried to calculate those dates but was considerably off. In 1856 the British astronomer Charles Pritchard made a careful calculation and produced the dates just cited. They are given in William Smith's *Dictionary of the Bible*, second edition, vol. 1, London 1893. They are also reported in a book Sadler may have seen, *The Life of Our Lord Upon the Earth Considered in its Historical. Chronological and Geographical Relations* (Scribner's, 1891, revised 1906, pp. 7–10), by Samuel J. Andrews.

In 1949, six years before the *UB* was published, the noted American astronomer Roy K. Marshall wrote a booklet titled *The Star of Bethlehem,* published by the Morehead Planetarium at the University of North Carolina, Chapel Hill. It went through many reprintings, and was widely sold at planetariums around the nation, including the Adler Planetarium in Chicago which peddled the booklet during its annual Christmas show on the star. Marshall gives the conjunction dates as Pritchard had calculated them except that the last date is said to be December 4 instead of December 5. Several pages in the booklet deal with New Testament chronology, giving the probable date of Jesus' birth as the spring of BCE 6 or 7 (the *UB*'s date is August 21, 7 B.C.), and the dates of the last supper, crucifixion, and resurrection as (respectively) Thursday, April 6, CE 20; Friday, April 7, and Sunday, April 9. These are the same as the dates cited by Andrews (p. 649) as well as by the *UB*.

Marshall points out, as did Pritchard, that at no time during the three conjunctions were Jupiter and Saturn closer than two diameters of the moon as seen in the sky. To quote Pritchard: "Even with . . . the strange postulate of someone with weak eyes, the planets could not have appeared as one star, for they never approached each other within double the apparent diameter of the moon" (Andrews, p. 8). "Only an abysmally weak pair of eyes could have ever merged them," was how Marshall put it. This has always counted strongly against the guess that the Saturn-Jupiter triple conjunction was the basis for the Bethlehem Star legend. It also counts strongly against the credibility of the *UB*.

The Christmas Star (1987) by astronomer John Mosley, a booklet published by the Griffith Observatory, in Los Angeles, has a chapter title "What Was the Star?" Among the various conjunction theories, he opts for the June 17, 2 BCE date when Venus passed so close to Jupiter that the two planets would be seen as a single star. The booklet has a bibliography of 22 earlier references on the star. The *UB* says that Jesus was born at noon, August 21, 7 BCE Mosley provides strong evidence that Jesus could not have been born earlier than 4 B.C., and was probably born in 3 or 2 BCE.

Most New Testament scholars today, and I agree with them, regard the Star of Bethelem as no more than a colorful myth concocted by early Christians, probably to link the birth of Jesus to a prophecy in Numbers 24:17: "I shall see him [God], but not now. I shall behold him, but not nigh: there shall come a star out of Jacob, and a Sceptre shall rise out of Israel."

Let me add that I take a dim view of trying to explain the great miracle stories of the Bible by searching for natural causes—a technique that Immanuel Velikovsky carried to ridiculous lengths. Better to accept the clearly intended meaning of the myths as God-created phenomena. With respect to the star, better to exclaim with the old Christmas hymn:

> O star of wonder, star of night,
> Star with royal beauty bright,
> Westward leading, still proceeding,
> Guide us to thy perfect light.

On page 988 of the *UB* we are told that a Shawnee Indian shaman named Tenskwatawa predicted a solar eclipse in 1808. The date is wrong because there was no such eclipse in 1808. A total eclipse did occur on June 16, 1806, with the path of totality cutting across New England. Near totality was visible in northern U.S. cities. Another total eclipse of the sun took place on November 29, 1807, but was visible only in Africa.

Tenskwatawa, popularly called "The Prophet," was a twin brother, blind in one eye, of the famous Shawnee Indian chief Tecumseh. The Prophet, who claimed to have psychic powers, and to be an earthly agent of the Great Spirit, learned of the coming eclipse because astronomers had come to the Ohio area to take photographs, and the eclipse was widely heralded. Just before it occurred, Tenskwatawa gathered his ignorant and superstitious followers in Greenville, Ohio, and pretended to use his psi powers to blot out the sun. Naturally, he then used the same magic to bring the sun back again. His Indian audience was duly awed. You can read about this in Benjamin Drake's *The Life of Tecumseh and of His Brother the Prophet* (1841). Drake gives the correct year for the eclipse, so either Melchizedek of Nebadon was careless in his research, or someone on the contact commission made a copying error.

Dick Bain, in the Summer/Fall, 1994, issue of his periodical *Cosmic Reflections*, calls attention to a careless error on pages 460–61 of the *UB*. In a section on solar radiation the authors refer to sunbeams as "highly heated and agitated electrons." Solar radiation consists of photons, not electrons. As Bain points out, the sun does emit particles that include electrons, but its radiation consists entirely of photons, and it is photons in the infrared portion of the light spectrum that generate the sun's heat. "It is odd," Bain comments, "that the authors did not use the term 'photon' since the papers were received in the mid 30's, and the word 'photon' was first used about 1926." He wonders if the mistake was purposeful—another of the *UB*'s "time bombs."

Although this is not in the *UB* science booklet, one of its authors, Matt Neibaur, in a letter, called my attention to a spot in the *UB* (170) that speaks of multiple concentric rings surrounding a central sun. Astronomers know these as planetary nebulae or ring nebulae. Neibaur was under the impression that all known ring nebulae had only one ring. He sent me a recent article from *Sky and Telescope* that showed a picture of a nebula with three rings. Did not the *UB* anticipate this new discovery? No, because such nebulae with two or three rings, although rare, were well known decades before the *UB* was published. The rings, by the way, are caused by spherical shells of glowing gas. They appear as rings in our telescopes because luminosity is greater on the rims of the spheres than in their centers.

The *UB*, as mentioned earlier, gives the age of the earth as 4.5 billion years. The four authors take this as anticipating recent estimates that give the same age. I have not yet found this specific figure in early astronomy books, although an estimate of 4 billion was quite common. I have earlier mentioned that Jeans gives this figure, based on changes in the moon's orbit. The same figure can be found in the fourteenth edition (1929) of the *Encyclopaedia Britannica*. George Gamow, in *Biography of the Earth*

(1941), gives the earth's age as about 5 billion, as indicated by radiation measurments of old rocks. I wouldn't be surprised to find a 4.5 billion estimate in pre-1955 astronomy texts, and will be grateful if any reader can locate an instance. Or it could be that a human author of the *UB*, encountering estimates of 4 and 5 billion, compromised on 4.5.

Incidentally, the *UB*'s dating of the various geological ages in earth's history closely follows the dating given in standard textbooks of the time. Modern methods of dating rocks have considerably modified these dates. Urantian fundamentalists are fond of emphasizing the uncertainty of modern dating techniques, and of hoping that the dates in the *UB* will someday be vindicated. Why they hope this beats me, because the *UB* clearly states that its science will quickly be modified and that the supermortals were not permitted to give unearned knowledge.

The Life Carrier of Nebadon, assigned to Urantia, in his description of the Cambrian period (Paper 59, page 674), made a glaring mistake. He makes crustaceans such as shrimps, crabs, and lobsters contemporaneous with the trilobites in the Cambrian period, when actually those crustaceans appeared on Urantia much later in the Triassic. A few Urantians have tried to justify this howler by saying that it was a typing or printing error. The Life Carrier, they suggest, originally wrote "ancestors of shrimps, crabs, lobsters." It seems far more likely that the author of the paper did some careless copying from a book on historical geology.

We now turn from the vast universe to the incredibly small. Many pages in the *UB* are devoted to a theory of particles that is sheer fantasy. If some day it turned out to be correct, or even partly correct, it would be a monumental instance of the kind of unearned science which the revelators said they were forbidden to include.*

At the heart of the *UB*'s particle theory, as well as at the heart of all matter, is a single ultimate particle called the "ultimaton" (pronounced I assume, with the accent on "tim"). Atomism, the view that matter is composed of invisible particles, of course goes back to Democritus. However,

---

*When I asked Dick Bain about this he floored me with the following rationalization. Should it turn out that the ultimaton theory is false, then the authors of the *UB* will not have provided unearned knowledge and therefore not have violated their mandate! The ultimaton would be what Bain has called a "time bomb" deliberately put in the *UB* to prevent readers from taking it as a fetish. If the electron is someday found to be made of, say, twelve smaller particles, he says, then this time bomb will detonate!

the "atoms" of the ancient Greek atomists varied in sizes and shapes. The same is true of Newton's particles. Leibniz, Newton's great German rival, was the first major thinker to posit a single, ultimate particle, although the notion had earlier been suggested by Bruno and others. Leibniz's particles, which he called monads, were nonmaterial metaphysical units without size, shape, position, or movement.

In the early eighteenth century the Italian philosopher G. B. Vico based matter on pointlike particles, and similar views were later put forth by many others. (For an excellent history, see Lancelot Whyte's *Essay on Atomism*, a 1971 book.) It was not until 1758, however, that the Swiss Jesuit scientist R. J. Boscovitch developed a detailed, formal theory of ultimate particles, all identical. (I devote a section to Boscovitch's ingenious and influential theory in my *New Ambidextrous Universe*.) Other scientists after Boscovitch constructed clever theories along similar lines. When Sadler wrote in his 1958 reply to critics that he had never heard of the concept of an ultimaton until he encountered it in the Urantia papers, he obviously had not bothered to check on the history of atomism.

At the moment, matter seems to be made of two kinds of ultimate particles, quarks and leptons, with six different kinds of each, not counting their antiparticle forms. Both quarks and leptons are pointlike, with no known interior structure. It is certainly possible that some time in the future physicists may discover a more fundamental particle that forms leptons and quarks, though there is now no sign of empirical data to support such a conjecture. Had the revelators been content merely to introduce the concept of a new particle, unknown to our physicists, they would have been on safe ground, and may even have anticipated some unearned physics. Unfortunately, they develop in detail a theory of ultimatons that no particle physicist can see as anything but absurd.

The *UB*'s preposterous claim is that every electron (the electron is a lepton) consists of exactly 100 ultimatons. They do not orbit the electron's center, the way electrons orbit the nucleus of an atom. Instead, they "huddle" together inside the electron, each rotating on an axis that can point in any direction. The nucleus of each ultimaton resides in the timeless, spaceless Isle of Paradise where it is subject to the "circular Paradise gravity-pull." If you need to know more details about this mad theory, consult pages 474–79 of the *UB*.

According to the four authors, one of the *UB*'s seeming hits is its claim (*UB* 479) that a particle called the mesotron serves as a carrier force between neutrons and protons inside an atom's nucleus, binding them together. To me this is strong evidence that Sadler tinkered with the *UB*'s papers after 1934 and before 1955. The reference to the mesotron is hardly surprising. It was in 1935 that Japanese physicist Hidekai Yukawa conjectured that just such a particle exists. Because it had to have a mass between that of a proton and electron, he called it a "meson," meaning "middle." Some physicists preferred to call it a mesotron. Two years later, in 1937, the meson was finally observed. Its mass was estimated as 200 times that of the electron. This was close to the *UB*'s estimate of 180.

A prophetic hit? Not at all. Later measurements made the mesotron 250 times more massive than an electron. It is one of a variety of mesons, and is now called the plus pion or pi-meson. The particle consists of a quark joined to an antiquark. The *UB* could rightly call it an "undiscovered force" when the paper about it was first written, but at that time all physicists were expecting it soon to be observed. Any reader of popular science books and magazines would have known about it. Again, the four authors treat the *UB*'s reference to it as prophetic only because they believe that nothing was added to the papers after 1934.

That the *UB* speaks of uncharged particles shot out from atoms in beta-decay (*UB* 479) is another instance of something well known before 1955. As early as 1930 Wolfgang Pauli proposed just such a particle. Enrico Fermi named it a neutrino, or little one. All physicists expected that neutrinos would soon be detected, as indeed they were in 1953.

In describing the atom's interior (*UB* 477), the revelators draw upon Niels Bohr's early pre-1920 model of the atom in which electrons are taken not as waves but as little spheres revolving around the nucleus in a manner similar to planets going around a sun:

> Within the atom the electrons revolve about the central proton with about the same comparative room the planets have as they revolve about the sun in the space of the solar system. There is the same relative distance, in comparison with actual size, between the atomic nucleus and the inner electronic circuit as exists between the inner planet, Mercury, and your sun.

This planetary model of the atom had been proposed by Bohr at about the time Wilfred began channeling, but after the rise of quantum mechanics in the twenties it soon became obsolete. Why did Sadler not remove it from the *UB*? Because Forum members had already found it in the papers, and he could not risk taking it out. Note that in the above passage the nucleus is called a "central proton." Only the hydrogen nucleus is a proton. All larger atoms have nuclei consisting of more than one proton, and are usually a mixture of protons and neutrons.

The supermortals state categorically (*UB* 477–78) that 100 is the maximum number of electrons that can orbit the nucleus of an atom. Why 100? Because "the local universes are of decimal construction"! It is impossible, the *UB* says, for the number of electrons in an atom to exceed 100. If a 101st electron is added, the element instantly disintegrates.

Now 100 was a good guess in the 1950s because fermium, which has exactly 100 electrons, was discovered in 1953. Unfortunately, in 1955, the year the *UB* was printed, mendelevium, with 101 electrons, was found. It has a half-life of three hours, hardly instantaneous.

Since then chemists have created elements with 102 through 111 electrons. (The last two were created in Germany in 1994.) "In all of Orvonton," says the *UB* (478), "it has never been possible naturally to assemble over one hundred orbital electrons in one atomic system." Surely the celestials knew better than to make such a false statement, basing it on the numerological significance of a multiple of ten.

It won't do to say that the elements with atomic numbers above 100 are all extremely short-lived, and therefore not true elements, because some elements below 100 have shorter lives than some of those above 100. Dick Bain considers this another of the "time bombs" deliberately placed in the *UB* to prevent fundamentalists from taking the book as a fetish.

The *UB*'s anthropology is as uninspired as its physical science. I have already described (in chapter 1) its bizarre history of races. Here I will take up a point about fossil humans only because it is cited in the booklet on *UB* science as another instance of prophetic insight. The four authors make hay out of the fact that although the *UB* mentions a number of fossil humans (Papers 61–63), there is no mention of Piltdown man. Because Piltdown man is now known to be a fraud, is this not proof that the revelators knew something scientists did not know until recently?

Let's consider the facts. Immediately after the 1912 announcement of finding a skull fragment and a jawbone that became known as the remains of a Piltdown man, scientists began to question whether the two parts belong together. In 1913 William Gregory, at the American Museum of Natural History wrote: "It has been suspected for some time that geologically they are not old at all; that they may represent a deliberate hoax, a

Negro or Australian skull and a broken ape jaw, artificially fossilized and planted in the gravel bed to fool the scientist." Similar complaints were voiced at the same time by anatomist David Waterson, zoologist Gerrit Miller, and many others. Seventh-day Adventist George McCready Price, in his massive textbook *The New Geology* (1923) poked fun at the Piltdown fragments.

At the time the Urantia Papers were being written, almost every geologist and anthropologist considered Piltdown man a fake. This was finally proved in 1951 when several scientists found that the skull fragment had been artificially aged and the teeth of an orangutan jaw had been filed down to make them look more human. One of the scientists, J. S. Weiner, wrote an entire book about it, *The Piltdown Forgery* (1955). The fraud was disclosed in *Time*, November 30, 1953, in an article Sadler could hardly have missed. From 1951 on, the only question was who perpetrated the hoax, a question not yet answered though there are several good suspects. There is no mystery about why Piltdown man isn't in the *UB* as a genuine fossil.

One portion of the booklet by the four Urantians is unquestionably correct. Matt Neibaur, using a computer program to check on more than one hundred dates in the Jesus papers to see if their days of the week were accurate, found that all of them were. Only a few had been checked at the time the booklet was written, but since then Neibaur has checked them all without finding an error. What does this prove? It proves only that someone, of whom Sadler and Wilfred are the prime suspects, was careful to check all these dates to make sure the weekdays were correct.

One does not need a computer program to do this. Formulas for calculating days of the week have long been known. You'll find one in the *Encyclopaedia Britannica*'s famous eleventh edition under "Calendar." Indeed, it is easy to make such calculations rapidly in one's head, as I explain in a chaper on "Tricks of Lightning Calculators" in my book *Mathematical Carnival*. It would have been simple, though tedious, for Sadler or Wilfred or someone else to make sure that all week days were correctly assigned to events in the life of Jesus. Sadler may have supplied the month dates, believing himself indited to do so by Midwayers, or they could have come from Wilfred's unconscious, with days of the week added later to the Papers. Wilfred, remember, was a trained accountant who would have found such date checking an enjoyable enterprise.

Dr. Ken T. Glasziou, of Maleny, Australia, published in 1989 a booklet titled *Science and Religion: The New Age Beyond 2000 CE* He acknowledges that "some of the science (in the *UB*) is recognizable as virtually direct quotation from documents of that era, which means that some authors of the papers obeyed their mandate strictly to the letter." By "mandate" he means that they were forbidden to provide unearned knowledge, but were free to use whatever science was available at the time, however faulty. On the other hand, Glasziou goes on, the revelators were permitted to provide some genuinely prophetic material.

Glasziou is particularly impressed by Neibaur's finding the correct weekday for Jesus' crucifixion:

> If facts such as have just been cited are insufficient to convince potential readers of the URANTIA Book to give serious consideration to its authenticity, let me add some extra material that was discovered by Dr. Neibaur, one of my sceintifically minded friends, during his early exploration of this book. In relating the story of the life of Jesus, the Book names both the day of the week and the actual date on which many events occurred. For example, it states that the date of Jesus' crucifixion was Friday, April 7, CE 30.
>
> Dr. Neibaur pondered on how, in 1955, one could know that April 7 was a Friday for a day occurring almost 2000 years ago. Such a task would have been a near impossibility in 1955 when computers and computer programs that could perform such a task were unavailable.

Actually, the weekday for the crucifixion on April 7 was calculated a century before the *UB* was published. Here is a passage from Roy Marshall's booklet on the Star of Bethlehem cited earlier as a work Sadler may have read:

> Victorius discovered that, if we multiply the 28-year period of the Sundays by the 19-year cycle of the Moon's phases discovered by the Greek engineer Meton, about 433 B.C., we get 532 years as the period after which the Easter dates will repeat themselves. Again, this requires careful use, to make sure that the leap-years will not interfere, but it is a good figure and, in the sixth century, when Victorius lived, it was even better. According to this Victorian Cycle, if we know and tabulate all the dates of Easter in their proper order for 532 years, we can write them all down in the same order for the next 532 years.
>
> Before we leave the subject of Easter, it may be noted here that the dates of the Last Supper, the Crucifixion and the Resurrection have been established with considerable certainty, because the day of the Last Supper was Thursday evening, the eve of the Passover. It is only in the year 30 A.D., of all possible years, that the Passover opened at sundown on Thursday; this has been known for about two centuries, at least. The

date of the Last Supper was April 6; the Crucifixion occurred on April 7, the Resurrection on April 9, in the year 30 CE As will be evident in what follows, it is by no means as easy as this to date the birth of Jesus.

In 1928 D. R. Fotheringham published his landmark *The Date of Easter*. Basing his arguments on astronomical tables and old Babylonian calendars he concluded that Jesus died on April 7, CE 30. This may have been the *UB*'s source.

The same date had been conjectured much earlier. Peloubet's *Bible Dictionary* (1925), on pages 780 and 782, also gives the date as April 7, CE 30. My parents' huge, leather-bound, brass-clasped family Bible contains a *Bible Dictionary*, by Albert Bigelow Rawson, copyrighted 1872. On page 21, in its entry on "Chronology," it gives April 7, CE 30 as the day Jesus died. Samuel J. Andrews, in his *The Life of Our Lord* (1891, revised 1906), has a long section (pages 35–51) headed "Date of the Lord's Death." He gives excellent reasons for making it Friday, April 7, CE 30, as well as a learned historical summary of conjectures going back to the Church Fathers. Irenaeus is quoted as saying that "diversities of opinion are infinite," and "we cannot be ignorant of how greatly all the fathers differ among themselves."

As for the date of Jesus' birth, evidence is totally lacking, and many different years and days of the month have been proposed. Andrews argues (pages 1–17) for an unspecified day in December, 5 BCE If there is a precedent in Christian literature for the *UB*'s date of August 21, 7 B.C., I have not yet come across it.

Another example of a clear error in *UB* science is its assertion on page 397 that the number of chromosomes in a human cell—they are called "units of pattern control" or "trait determiners"—is 48. In 1923 a false count of chromosomes yielded the 48 number and it was accepted as correct until 1956. Indeed, Sadler himself, in *The Truth About Heredity* (page 76) writes: "it has been calculated, in the case of the human species, if the number of chromosomes be set down as 48, that after a division there would be 24 pairs of maternal and paternal chromosomes." A footnote reads: "Painter recently found in fresh sex glands from both a white man and a negro that each of the germ cells carried 48 chromosomes."*

---

*The University of Chicago zoologist Horatio Hackett Newman, in his classic *Evolution, Genetics, and Eugenics* (1921), gives the number of human chromosomes as 48. The figure remains in his book's seventh printing (1947). The book may have heavily influenced Sadler, who cites it in the bibliography of *The Truth About Heredity*, not only for its support of eugenics, but also for its favorable commentary on Hugo de Vries's theory of evolution. We will consider de Vries's theory, accepted by the *UB*, in chapter 15.

Unfortunately, in 1956, a year too late to give Sadler a chance to correct, the number was positively established as 46. Both males and females contain in each cell the same 22 pairs of non-sex chromosomes, known as "autosomes." Females have a 23rd pair of XX sex chromosomes. Males have a 23rd pair of XY sex chromosomes. Each person, therefore, has 23 pairs of chromosomes, or 46 individual ones.

During mitosis, each germ cell divides twice, the first time duplicating all the chromosomes, but the second time only half of the chromosomes go to each cell. In other words, an unfertilized human egg contains only 23 chromosomes, and a sperm also contains only 23. When sperm and egg fuse, the egg acquires 23 chromosomes from each parent, giving it the full number of 46. If the egg gets an X chromosome from the sperm, the child will be a girl. If it gets a Y chromosome, the child will be a boy. It is the father, therefore, who determines an embryo's sex.

In a lecture at the first Urantian Science Symposium (Nashville, 1988), Kermit Anderson tried manfully to make the *UB*'s 48 number seem correct after all. Genetic information, he reminded his listeners, is now known to be carried as a code along a double-stranded DNA molecule, one inside each chromosome. There are 22 nonsex chromosomes, and two sex chromosomes X and Y, making 24 different chromosomes in all. Because each molecule is a double strand, we multiply 24 by 2 to get 48 different "trait determiners." (It is true, as Anderson points out, that the *UB* does not use here the term chromosome.) Of course no single human cell contains all 48 of these "trait determiners," but in Anderson's convoluted logic the number of such units is 48. I can only be amazed at the lengths to which Urantian fundamentalists can go in trying to find unearned science in the *UB*!

Which is the simpler explanation? That the *UB* has the number 48 because at the time its papers were written this was the accepted number of human chromosomes in each cell, or that the revelators reasoned like Anderson, anticipating a future discovery of double-stranded DNA molecules?

Today's anthropologists are rapidly accepting the view that ritual cannibalism, as opposed to cannibalism for survival and other reasons, never existed. See *The Man-Eating Myth* (1979) by William Arens, an anthropologist at SUNY, in Stony Brook, New York. Arens argues convincingly that belief in such rituals rests entirely on hearsay statements by missionaries, or by naive anthropologists reporting what was told to them by neighboring enemy tribes about practices they never witnessed.

UB authors were of course unaware of this recent research. A section of

Paper 89 describes cannibalism as universal among primitive societies. We are told that in Queensland the first child is still often killed and devoured, and that cannibalism is practiced today by many African tribes, though none is specified. In some tribes aged parents are said to beg their children to eat them. On page 770 we learn of a tribe that "not long since" ate every fifth child born! All this is nonsense, though I have no doubt that such wild claims can be found in books readily accessible to *UB* authors. One of the most unreliable articles ever written about cannibalism is the 16-page contribution to Hastings' *Encyclopedia of Religion and Ethics*. The author, John Arnott MacCulloch, was an Anglican priest who bought every horrible myth he could find in the vast pseudoscientific literature on cannibalism.

Let me close this rambling chapter with what I regard as the most outlandish claim ever put forth in a book that pretends to give accurate information about the earth's early history—information coming straight from higher intelligences who were presumed to know more than any Urantian geologist, archeologist, or historian.

We are told in the *UB* that when animals were first domesticated, carrier pigeons were trained to carry messages back and forth. This is plausible enough, but then we are informed that the largest of such pigeons were trained as "passenger birds" to carry humans here and there. These giant birds are called "fandors," a name that at once suggests "condors."

Allow me to digress a moment to call attention to the curious way in which terms in the *UB* turn into English words by only slight (or no) alterations of letters:

Absolutum — absolute
Edentia — Eden
Gravita — gravity
Jerusem — Jerusalem
Ascendington — ascending
Salvington — salvation
Divinington — divinity
Majeston — majestic
Ultimaton — ultimate
Abandonters — abandoners
Servitals — servants

Andronover — Andromeda
Conciliators — conciliators
Inceptors — inceptors
Realizers — realizers
Consummators — consummators
Transcendentalers — transcendentalers
Havona — Havana, heaven
Caligastia — caliginous
U Major — Ursa Major
U Minor — Ursa Minor
Grandfanda — grandfather

And scores of other terms.

Did the revelators enjoy this kind of punning? Was it Wilfred's unconscious mind modifying familiar words? Did Sadler playfully invent the
terminology?

An interesting example of this sort of word play is what the *UB* (1139)
calls "mota logic." It is a logic beyond our understanding, but which higher
beings use to prove theorems we are unable to prove. Logicians have long
used the term "meta logic" for a logic in which theorems on a lower level
of a formal system can be validated or proved false. Are such proofs final?
No, because there is an infinite hierarchy of meta logics, each containing
statements provable only by jumping to the next higher level. Psychologists
have a similar term, "meta-analysis," for the analysis of data obtained from
many independent sources.

Why was it necessary to change meta to mota? Was it an error made by
Christy when she wrote down something Wilfred said, or an error made in
something Wilfred wrote or that Christy later typed? Or did Sadler, having
read about meta logic, alter the spelling to suggest that the Gods know of a
logic far superior to any that can be formalized on Urantia? Is the fact that
"mota" backward is "atom" an accident or another amusing bit of intended
word play?

Correspondent Mark Ross called my attention to what is probably just
a coincidence. In the *UB*, "morontia" is a term for a substance unknown on
Urantia. It is more spiritual than matter, but less spiritual than the pure spirit
of Paradise. Moroni is the name of a powerful angel in the *The Book of
Mormon*. A person I know has suggested that morontia is an appropriate
neologism because only a moron can take the existence of such a substance
seriously.

Now back to fandors and condors. Condors are among the largest of all flying birds. They have a wing-span of ten feet and fly fifty miles an hour. The California black-feathered condor is now almost extinct. According to the *UB* (746), fandors became extinct 30,000 years ago. Why no fandor fossils have been found is a mystery.

Fandors are mentioned six times in the *UB* (521, 590, 694, 746, 831, and 832.) On page 694 we learn how these huge birds evolved: "A large ostrichlike land bird developed to a height of ten feet and laid an egg nine by thirteen inches. These were the ancestors of the later passenger birds that were so highly intelligent, and that onetime transported human beings through the air."

When Adam and Eve first inspected the Garden of Eden (*UB* 832), they were carried through the air by fandors. Because Adam and Eve were at least eight feet tall (*UB* 580), they must together have weighed more than 400 pounds. However, as one Urantian fundamentalist has suggested, maybe each rode on a separate fandor.

Here is a memorable passage (*UB* 590) about these giant birds:

> The early races also make extensive use of the larger flying animals. These enormous birds are able to carry one or two average-sized men for a nonstop flight of over five hundred miles. On some planets these birds are of great service since they possess a high order of intelligence often being able to speak many words of the languages of the realm. These birds are most intelligent, very obedient, and unbelievably affectionate. Such passenger birds have been long extinct on Urantia, but your early ancestors enjoyed their services.

Did Wilfred's unconscious mind, or Sadler's conscious mind, put fandors in the *UB* as a joke? Is there a devout Urantian, of sound mind and a knowledge of historical geology, who actually believes that the above paragraph was dictated (as we learn on page 600) by a "Mighty Messenger attached to the staff of Gabriel"?

The answer is yes. At a weekend science symposium in Oklahoma City, in 1991, an aeronautical engineer named Paul Herrick gave a fascinating semitechnical lecture on fandors. Herrick obviously knows a great deal about the structure of airplanes and the mechanics of bird flight. We are told in the *UB* that a fandor could fly 100 miles per hour and carry a person for 500 miles. Assuming that this giant bird could take off vertically, Herrick estimated from the *UB*'s accounts that it must have weighed 900 pounds, have a wing-span of 55 to 75 feet, and a wing area of 500 square feet. Its horse power, Herrick guessed could not have been more than 35, considerably less than the power needed by a helicopter. Fandors were probably carnivores, he said, because plants would not have supplied sufficient energy. A woman in the audience wanted to know how a person riding on a fandor could have withstood a 100-mile-per-hour wind. Herrick had a good answer. Maybe they rested their head on the bird's neck.

No fossils of fandors have been found, though Herrick said he hoped they would be some day. Fossils of large winged dinosaurs have been unearthed, one with a wing-span of 36 feet. However, as Herrick pointed out, dinosaurs are not birds (though they later evolved into birds), and the *UB* unequivocally calls the fandor a bird. Herrick showed slides of pictures found by archeologists which show huge birds carrying a person, and he cited ancient myths about persons riding on birds.

When I first listened to a tape of Herrick's talk, I thought he was speaking with tongue in cheek. But no, the engineer was deadly serious. Like the Bible's sea monster that swallowed Jonah and later disgorged him alive, the *UB*'s fandors have become a litmus test for distinguishing a liberal Urantian from a fundamentalist. The fundamentalists are sure that the fandors once existed, and that Adam and Eve rode on their backs. The liberals wonder why the revelators put these bizarre birds in the *UB*. Urantians do not have to believe they existed in order to be good Urantians, any more than Seventh-day Adventists have to believe Mrs. White's early visions in which she saw the saved and the little children in heaven as having actual wings that enabled them to fly about like birds. A Urantian fundamentalist, however, must believe in fandors, just as Christian and Jewish fundamentalists must believe in a sea monster capable of swallowing Jonah, or that Lot's wife turned into a pillar of salt.

When I asked Dick Bain what he thought of fandors I expected him to say they belonged to the "time bombs" which he believes were planted in the *UB* to prevent Urantians from taking the Papers too seriously. He surprised me by saying that the absence of fossil evidence that fandors existed could be explained by the fact that bird bones are hollow and easily disintegrate. Reverend Meredith Sprunger answered the same question in a letter by saying that although he had serious doubts about these passenger birds, he kept an open mind in case such skeletons would be discovered. He reminded me that there are traditions of passenger birds, and that a story about such a bird was in one of his grade-school readers. He did not respond to my pointing out that if fossils of fandors are ever found, it would be another example of the *UB* providing startling unearned science.

Sprunger is a liberal Urantian who is also a retired minister in the United Church of Christ. He expressed the liberal/fundamentalist split well in a 1992 editorial that appeared in his *Spiritual Fellowship Journal*. Over the years, he writes, research "has revealed that virtually all of the scientific material found in the *UB* was the accepted scientific knowledge of the period in which the book was written, was held by some scientists of that time, or was about to be discovered or recognized." Sprunger continues:

> Scholarly evaluation shows that *Urantia Book* fundamentalism is just as untenable as Biblical fundamentalism. In the same way that higher criticism established sound foundations for Biblical studies, so must critical scholarship prepare the way for creative study of *The Urantia Book*. Thus freed from any illusions about its literal infallibility, we are delivered from defensive, fundamentalistic attitudes and open to evaluate its spiritual insights, cosmology, theology, and its view of human origins, development, and destiny. In this capacity its potentials are without parallel on the human scene.

There is strong support for Sprunger's liberal way of viewing the *UB* in the *UB* itself. In Paper 88, on "Fetishes, Charms, and Magic," we are told that believing everything in a sacred book is a form of fetishism:

> Concerning the accumulated fetish writings which various religionists hold as *sacred books*, it is not only believed that what is in the book is true, but also that every truth is contained in the book. If one of these sacred books happens to speak of the earth as being flat, then, for long generations, otherwise sane men and women will refuse to accept positive evidence that the planet is round.

Urantian Denver Pearson is an excellent specimen of an "otherwise sane" man who refuses to accept scientific evidence that contradicts anything in the *UB*. In *The Journal of the Fellowship* (Spring 1993) his article on "The Scientific Integrity of the Urantia Book" grants that here and there in the *UB* are statements that contradict currently held science. However, science is not infallible, and when it comes to a choice between today's science and the *UB*, such as on the question of the big bang, he will unhesitatingly choose the *UB*. Why? Because he cannot believe that the supermortals would knowingly put false information in their Papers!

Pearson says he has never come across a Urantian who regards the *UB* as a fetish. He seems totally blind to the fact that he himself takes the book to be a fetish. The following paragraph from his article could not be a better expression of the mind set of a fundamentalist:

> If there are verifiable flaws to be found in the revelation, then, in my opinion, they must be due to recording errors, printing errors or some aspect involving the production of the book itself.

Rivaling the fandors in ridiculous fantasy is the notion that on every inhabited planet, including the earth, there is a "universe energy pole" (*UB* 438). This is the locale where invisible seraphim arrive and depart to transport properly "enseraphimed" dead personalities from Urantia to Jerusem. It is also the spot where "planetary space reports" are received at noon, although the departure time of the seraphim is usually at midnight (*UB* 439).

In Appendix B to the second edition (1992) of *Birth of a Revelation*, Mark Kuleike speculates on the location of Urantia's energy pole:

> It is known that this spiritual energy pole is ordinarily identical with the headquarters of the spiritual government of a planet and thus Urantia's would have been located at Dalamatia in the days of the Planetary Prince. What happened at the outbreak of rebellion is not known though this pole may have been at Van's headquarters until the days of Adam and Eve and then in the garden location. It is well known among Forumites that the Contact Commission was told the current location of the spiritual energy pole. It is located in the Mariposa Grove of giant sequoias in Yosemite National Park which is located in east central California. This is not only where seraphim arrive and depart Urantia, but also the location of the archangel headquarters. Indeed, due to the rebellion, broadcasts are only received by courtesy of the archangel divisional headquarters. Of course, this is also the location of the headquarters of the current spiritual planetary government of Urantia. Other than the scenic beauty of the place, you will notice nothing unusual there.

The strongest indictment of the *UB*'s science was made by Sadler himself, though he was attacking the "spirits" of spiritualism, not the *UB*'s celestials. Here is how he put it in *The Truth About Spiritualism* (167):

> If the spirits are so wise, why have they never whispered the principles of some new and great invention to the mediums? Why is it that our mechanical inventions all originate in the brains of our natural-born geniuses, or are worked out in the persistent sweat of such men as Thomas A. Edison?

What a time and labor saving it would be if the secrets of the wire-less-telegraph, or the principles of an internal combustion gas engine, could be secured at a spiritualistic seance. Why is it that these discarnate spirits and spirit beings of invisible space, if they are so interested in human kind, do not whisper to the mediums the cure for cancer, the remedy for infantile paralysis, or the most successful method of treating pneumonia?

Why did the celestials, like spirits who chat through mediums, refuse to put into the *UB* some statements about science that would prove they possessed a knowledge greater than known to Urantian scientists in 1955? Why did they merely reflect the science of the day, or deface it with absurd statements about fandors and ultimatons—assertions as wild as the "science" in *Oahspe*? We are told that they were forbidden to include "unearned" science. It is a hollow excuse. I believe that Sadler himself inserted this "out" in the *UB* when he realized how feeble and faulty some of its science would quickly become.

12

Adventist Influence on *The Urantia Book*

Only three views are viable about the *UB*'s origin.

1. Wilfred Kellogg was a charlatan. Like other phony direct-voice mediums and automatic writers, his ego derived enormous and secret satisfaction from counterfeiting trances during which he pretended to channel material he had consciously concocted over a long period of reading and thinking.
2. Wilfred actually was chosen by supermortals to transmit a new revelation to humanity.
3. Wilfred belonged to a small class of sincere, honest persons who, for causes not well understood, experience spells of deep trances during which they channel information fabricated by secondary personalities who are part of their unconscious. It would be interesting to know if Wilfred ever experienced, like Ellen White and Mrs. Piper, a severe head injury when a child.

As Sadler himself pointed out in *Mind at Mischief*, honest trance channelers occasionally have a streak of deception in their character which causes them to lie at times to boost their reputations as genuine seers. For example, Wilfred may have seen Sadler's list of the 52 questions he later answered in trance by genuine automatic writing, but refrained from telling Sadler he had earlier observed the list. It is not uncommon in the history of psychic phenomena for persons who sincerely believe they possess paranormal powers to stoop occasionally to subtle flimflam.

I hold to the third alternative. Wilfred's symptoms were classic. Like Mrs. Piper, his pulse remained normal throughout a trance state, yet his breathing was highly irregular. Adventists may recall that Mrs. White, while in trance, was thought to have stopped breathing entirely. On several occasions someone actually held his hand over her mouth, pinching her nostrils for many minutes without disturbing her. Like almost all automatic writers, Wilfred's trance writing was said to be rapid; each written sheet would be pushed off on the floor.

The *UB*'s doctrines are a strange blend of Seventh-day Adventist opinions and Adventist heresies, just what one would expect from the subconscious mind of a man who had abandoned his earlier Adventist beliefs. The Adventist doctrines in the *UB* are also precisely those fundamental beliefs that an ex-Adventist would find hard to discard, beliefs that would be favorably received by three other ex-Adventist relatives on the Contact Commission, the two Sadlers and Wilfred's wife. It is said that Lena Sadler was the first to be convinced that Wilfred's channeling was genuine. Sadler took much longer to make up his mind. We do not know at what time Wilfred and Anna became similarly persuaded, if indeed they ever did.

The two most basic Adventist beliefs in the *UB*—beliefs that distinguish Seventh-day Adventism from mainline Christianity—are the doctrines of soul sleeping until the body is reconstituted by a resurrection, and the denial of hell. We learn from the *UB*'s Paper 47 that after death you are totally unconscious until you awake in a gigantic Resurrection Hall with your memory restored. You start your new life exactly where it left off to begin a long journey spiritually upward and spatially inward, first through the seven mansion worlds, until eventually you acquire an immortal soul.

The *UB* speaks of myriads of inhabited worlds. On none has a Fall comparable to the Christian Fall occurred—namely a curse that renders all inhabitants of a planet, in all future generations, destined for eternal punishment unless they are "redeemed" by the blood sacrifice of a God. Mrs. White's universe also teems with inhabited worlds, though only on Earth is the great controversy between Christ (Michael) and Satan taking place.

In both the *UB* and Sister White's books, intelligences on other worlds—Mrs. White likes to call them "unfallen worlds"—are constantly watching earth's history with intense interest. Even specific events, such as Abraham's near sacrifice of his son Isaac (symbolic of God sacrificing his own Son), are monitored by our unseen friends. Here is how Mrs. White puts it in *Patriarchs and Prophets:*

The sacrifice required of Abraham was not alone for his own good, nor solely for the benefit of succeeding generations; but it was also for the instruction of the sinless intelligences of heaven and of other worlds. The field of the controversy between Christ and Satan,—the field on which the plan of redemption is wrought out,—is the lesson book of the universe. Because Abraham had shown a lack of faith in God's promises, Satan had accused him before the angels and before God of having faded to comply with the conditions of the covenant, and as unworthy of its blessings. God desired to prove the loyalty of His servant before all heaven, to demonstrate that nothing less than perfect obedience can be accepted, and to open more fully before them the plan of salvation.

Heavenly beings were witnesses of the scene as the faith of Abraham and the submission of Isaac were tested. The trial was far more severe than that which had been brought upon Adam. Compliance with the prohibition laid upon our first parents involved no suffering; but the command to Abraham demanded the most agonizing sacrifice. All heaven beheld with wonder and admiration Abraham's unfaltering obedience. All heaven applauded his fidelity. Satan's accusations were shown to be false. God declared to His servant, "Now I know that thou fearest God [notwithstanding Satan's charges], seeing thou hast not withheld thy son, thine only son, from Me." God's covenant, confirmed to Abraham by an oath before the intelligences of other worlds, testified that obedience will be rewarded.

Sadler and Wilfred, perhaps other former Adventists, may well have carried into the *UB* memories of Sister White's vast cosmology in which billions of inhabited planets circle around "God's Throne." Change the word Throne to Paradise, Satan to Caligastia, and the two versions of Urantian history are not as far apart as one might suppose. Caligastia, the Bible's Satan, still roams the earth, invisible to our eyes, causing as much suffering as he can. Eventually, like Lucifer and the other rebel angels, the *UB* tells us, he will finally be annihilated "as though he had not been." Michael's great struggle with Caligastia—what the title of Mrs. White's most famous book calls *The Great Controversy Between Christ and Satan*—will finally end, as it will end on all the other "fallen worlds" mentioned in the *UB*.

The belief, common to many religions, that after death each soul ascends through a series of heavens, moving inward toward Paradise, is absolutely basic to Urantian theology. This, too, was Ellen White's view. On the closing pages of *The Great Controversy* she speaks of souls who "wing their tireless flights to worlds afar," and of how God's throne is at the center of the universe, with all the "stars and suns and systems" revolving around it:

> Every faculty will be developed, every capacity increased. The acquirement of knowledge will not weary the mind or exhaust the energies. There the grandest enterprises may be carried forward, the loftiest aspirations reached, the highest ambitions realized; and still there will arise new heights to surmount, new wonders to admire, new truths to comprehend, fresh objects to call forth the powers of mind and soul and body.
>
> All the treasures of the universe will be open to the study of God's redeemed. Unfettered by mortality, they wing their tireless flight to worlds afar—worlds that thrilled with sorrow at the spectacle of human woe and rang with songs of gladness at the tidings of a ransomed soul. With unutterable delight the children of earth enter into the joy and the wisdom of unfallen beings. They share the treasures of knowledge and understanding gained through ages upon ages in contemplation of God's handiwork. With undimmed vision they gaze upon the glory of creation— suns and stars and systems, all in their appointed order circling the throne of Deity. Upon all things, from the least to the greatest, the Creator's name is written, and in all are the riches of His power displayed.
>
> And the years of eternity, as they roll, will bring richer and still more glorious revelations of God and of Christ. As knowledge is progressive, so will love, reverence, and happiness increase.

The last chapter of Mrs. White's book *Education* is titled "The School of the Hereafter." In it she stresses, in sentences similar to those above, the saved person's endless increase in knowledge after departing from the earth. The following paragraphs could have come straight out of the *UB*:

> There every power will be developed, every capability increased. The grandest enterprises will be carried forward, the loftiest aspirations will be reached, the highest ambitions realized. And still there will arise new heights to surmount, new wonders to admire, new truths to comprehend, fresh objects to call forth the powers of body and mind and soul.
>
> All the treasures of the universe will be open to the study of God's children. With unutterable delight we shall enter into the joy and the wisdom of unfallen beings. We shall share the treasures gained through ages upon ages spent in contemplation of God's handiwork. And the years of eternity, as they roll, will continue to bring more glorious revelations. "Exceeding abundant above all that we ask or think" will be, forever and forever, the impartation of the gifts of God.
>
> "His servants shall serve Him." The life on earth is the beginning of

the life in heaven; education on earth is an initiation into the principles of heaven; the life-work here is a training for the life-work there. What we now are, in character and holy service, is the sure foreshadowing of what we shall be.

In the *UB*, the abode of the ultimate God is the Isle of Paradise, at the center of everything, with all the galaxies and star systems revolving around it. Mrs. White also puts God's throne at the center of the cosmos, with the rest of the universe whirling around it. In one of her early visions she located God's throne as somewhere beyond the great Nebula in Orion. Here are her words:

December 16, 1848, the Lord gave me a view of the shaking of the powers of the heavens. I saw that when the Lord said "heaven," in giving the signs recorded by Matthew, Mark, and Luke, He meant heaven, and when He said "earth" He meant earth. The powers of heaven are the sun, moon, and stars. They rule in the heavens. The powers of earth are those that rule on the earth. The powers of heaven will be shaken at the voice of God. Then the sun, moon, and stars will be moved out of their places. They will not pass away, but be shaken by the voice of God.

Dark, heavy clouds came up, and clashed against each other. The atmosphere parted and rolled back; then we could look up through the open space in Orion, whence came the voice of God. The holy city will come down through that open space. I saw that the powers of earth are now being shaken, and that events come in order. War, and rumors of war, sword, famine, and pestilence are first to shake the powers of earth, then the voice of God will shake the sun, moon, and stars, and this earth also. I saw that the shaking of the powers in Europe is not, as some teach, the shaking of the powers of heaven, but it is the shaking of the angry nations.

Adventist Lucas Reed, in *Astronomy and the Bible* (1919) took Sister White's vision with utmost seriousness:

We believe, then, that without question, beyond or through this inapproachable light of Orion lie, somewhere, heaven and the throne of God. Mrs. White, without astronomical knowledge, told something about Orion that no astronomer of that time had yet measured up to. Now, without knowing a thing about her statement, and probably not caring to know, they tell us facts which bear out her statement about an "open space in Orion."

I would have thought that by now this bizarre view had been discarded by most Adventists, but apparently it has not. George Vandeman, who until his recent retirement had a weekly telecast called "It Is Written," is a leading Adventist spokesman. In 1970 he published a booklet titled *Look! No Doomsday*, in which a chapter is headed "Rescue from Orion." In 1989 I visited Robert Gentry, a devout Seventh-day Adventist who loudly promotes in his published writings a "young earth" view of creationism. Gentry is convinced, as were almost all Adventists until recently when "old earth" views began creeping into Adventist colleges, that God created our Milky Way Galaxy about 6,000 years ago. He outlined for me a cosmology in which the entire universe revolves around God's dwelling place, located a few million light years beyond the constellation of Orion.

Not everyone will obtain immortality. Those who persist in iniquity and rebellion against God will eventually be annihilated. Here is how the *UB* puts it on page 37:

> The greatest punishment (in reality an inevitable consequence) for wrongdoing and deliberate rebellion against the government of God is loss of existence as an individual subject of that government. The final result of wholehearted sin is annihilation. In the last analysis, such sin-identified individuals have destroyed themselves by becoming wholly unreal through their embrace of iniquity. The factual disappearance of such a creature is, however, always delayed until the ordained order of justice current in that universe has been fully complied with.
>
> Cessation of existence is usually decreed at the dispensational or epochal adjudication of the realm or realms. On a world such as Urantia it comes at the end of a planetary dispensation. Cessation of existence can be decreed at such times by co-ordinate action of all tribunals of jurisdiction, extending from the planetary council up through the courts of the Creator Son to the judgment tribunals of the Ancients of Days. The mandate of dissolution originates in the higher courts of the superuniverse following an unbroken confirmation of the indictment originating on the sphere of the wrongdoer's residence; and then, when sentence of extinction has been confirmed on high, the execution is by the direct act of those judges residential on, and operating from, the headquarters of the superuniverse.
>
> When this sentence is finally confirmed, the sin-identified being instantly becomes as though he had not been. There is no resurrection from such a fate; it is everlasting and eternal. The living energy factors of identity are resolved by the transformations of time and the metamorphoses of space into the cosmic potentials whence they once emerged. As for the personality of the iniquitous one, it is deprived of a continuing life vehicle by the creature's failure to make those choices and final decisions which would have assured eternal life. When the continued embrace of sin by

the associated mind culminates in complete self-identification with iniquity, then upon the cessation of life, upon cosmic dissolution, such an isolated personality is absorbed into the oversoul of creation, becoming a part of the evolving experience of the Supreme Being. Never again does it appear as a personality; its identity becomes as though it had never been. In the case of an Adjuster-indwelt personality, the experiential spirit values survive in the reality of the continuing Adjuster.

What about the fates of Lucifer, Satan, and other rebel angels? Michael offered them a second chance to repent. Thousands did. Along with unrepentant angels, they are now confined to Jerusem where they await a final verdict. Those who are truly repentant will be saved (*UB* 619). Lucifer, who led the rebellion, is now a prisoner on satellite number one of the Jerusem transition spheres (*UB* 611). Satan is also a prisoner in Jerusem.

Caligastia, once Urantia's Planetary Prince, and his "disgusting" assistant Daligastia, each refused Michael's offer of mercy. "Caligastia . . . is still free on Urantia to prosecute his nefarious designs, but he has absolutely no power to enter the minds of men, neither can he draw near to their souls to tempt or corrupt them unless they really desire to be cursed with his wicked presence."

In *The Great Controversy* (chapter 30) Mrs. White said it this way: "No man without his own consent can be overcome by Satan. The tempter has no power to control the will or to force the soul to sin." Like all Planetary Princes, Caligastia is invisible to ascending mortals.

The rebellion has ended on Jerusem. It ends on the fallen worlds as fast as divine Sons arrive. We believe that all rebels who will ever accept mercy have done so. We await the flashing broadcast that will deprive these traitors of personality existence. We anticipate the verdict of Uversa will be announced by the executionary broadcast which will effect the annihilation of these interned rebels. Then will you look for their places, but they shall not be found. "And they who know you among the worlds will be astonished at you; you have been a terror, but never shall you be any more." And thus shall all of these unworthy traitors "become as though they had not been." All await the Uversa decree. (*UB* 611.)

The doctrine of annihilation of the wicked, including the Bible's Satan, is at the heart of Seventh-day Adventist eschatology. It is another doctrine Sadler never abandoned. "When this sentence is finally confirmed, the sin-identified being instantly becomes as though he had not been. There is no resurrection from such a fate; it is everlasting and eternal" (*UB* 37). However, there can be long periods of what the *UB* (615–20) calls a "mercy time lag" before such a drastic termination of a person's life is ordered. Many Christian sects other than Seventh-day Adventism have, over the centuries, defended the doctrine of annihilation as being more merciful than everlasting torment. Two examples that flourish today in the United States are Jehovah's Witnesses and the deceased Herbert Armstrong's World Wide Church of God.

Mrs. White was eloquent in her attacks on the doctrine of hell and eternal punishment. "How repugnant to every emotion of love and mercy, and even to our sense of justice," she wrote in chapter 31 of *The Great Controversy*, "is the doctrine that the wicked dead are tormented with fire and brimstone in an eternally burning hell; that for the sins of a brief earthly life they are to suffer for as long as God shall live."

The annihilation doctrine is intimately interlocked with Adventist denial that we possess intrinsically immortal souls. This is called the doctrine of "conditional immortality." Immortality is not innate. It is a gift of God. Death is a state of temporary unconsciousness, or "soul sleep," until the day of resurrection when, by the grace of God, we put on immortality. At death our body returns to dust, but our "spirit" returns to God until the time it is reunited, in the twinkling of an eye (as Paul put it) with a new body and mind.

Adventists believe that individuals of past ages will soul sleep for many thousands of years until their bodies are reconstituted on resurrection day. They will not, of course, be aware of any passing of time. The *UB* teaches (page 341) that many who die without having reached the needed levels of "intelligence mastery and endowment of spirituality" will not go directly to a mansion world:

> Such surviving souls must rest in unconscious sleep until the judgment day of a new epoch, a new dispensation, the coming of a Son of God to call the rolls of the age and adjudicate the realm, and this is the general practice throughout all Nebadon. It was said of Christ Michael that, when he ascended on high at the conclusion of his work on earth, "He led a great multitude of captives." And these captives were the sleeping survivors from the days of Adam to the day of the Master's resurrection on Urantia.
>
> The passing of time is of no moment to sleeping mortals; they are wholly unconscious and oblivious to the length of their rest. On reassembly of personality at the end of an age, those who have slept five thousand years will react no differently than those who have rested five

days. Aside from this time delay these survivors pass on through the ascension regime identically with those who avoid the longer or shorter sleep of death.

Note that the resurrection of these sleepers occurs on a judgment day that coincides with the arrival of a Son of God. If I read the above paragraphs correctly, they say that many soul sleepers on Urantia before the first arrival of Christ Michael were revived when he ascended into heaven, and those who endure a lengthy soul sleep since then will be reawakened at the time of Christ's Second Coming.

Readers interested in the history of the doctrine of conditional immortality will find it covered at great length in *The Conditionalist Faith of Our Fathers*, an impressive two-volume work by Adventist scholar LeRoy Edwin Froom (Review and Herald, 1965). Dr. John Kellogg's much earlier treatise, *The Soul and the Resurrection* (Review and Herald, 1879), has been reprinted in paper covers by Leaves of Autumn Books, Box 440, Payson, Arizona 85541.

Because Adventists believe that the dead are totally unconscious until their resurrection, it follows that there is no way they can communicate with us through mediums. Mrs. White wrote extensively about the rise of spiritualism, which she believed to be the work of Satan. Hundreds of Adventist books and pamphlets have contained similar warnings. Although Sadler left the Adventist faith, this was another aspect of its teaching he never abandoned. His *Truth About Spiritualism* (1923) is one of the best attacks ever written on mediums, with exposures of their methods. In its preface Sadler said he intended to follow it in 1924 with a much larger work, *Spiritualism*, but this never materialized. Does a manuscript exist? If so, perhaps it contains the names of actual psychics investigated by Sadler, some of them his patients, but whose names are carefully omitted from *The Truth About Spiritualism*.

Ten years later in his book on spiritualism, Sadler again says (207–208) that although he has never encountered psychic phenomena he could not explain by cheating or natural causes, he cannot rule out the possibility of demons at work:

Of course I cannot be scientifically certain that evil ghosts and vagabond spirits, or some other agency of His Satanic Majesty, may not be at the bottom of certain rare cases of psychic phenomena brought forward under the guise of spiritism. I say, I cannot, as a scientist, settle this question. It may be true that in some cases the devils are in league with the mediums and cunningly assist them in perpetrating some of the psychic phenomena which they bring forward in the name of spiritualism.

In this same book, as in both earlier and later books, Sadler considered telepathy, and concluded it had not been scientifically established. In *The Physiology of Faith and Fear* (1912), in a chapter on "Psychic Fads and Fakes," he attacks the notion that laws of nature allow one person's mind to communicate directly with another. He is inclined to think that cases taken to be telepathic are really caused by a Universal Mind that simultaneously sends the same message to two individuals. In *Theory and Practice of Psychiatry* (1936) he continues to defend this view:

> After all is said and done, of all the theories so far advanced to account for the undoubted ability of certain minds thus to communicate, I am more inclined to accept either the hypothesis of the cosmic mind or that of spiritual projection. With the passing of years I am more and more convinced of the fact of the phenomena which are commonly spoken of as telepathy. I have had some personal experiences that would be difficult to account for on the theory of pure coincidence or mathematical chance. Not being a mechanist, I suppose it is easy for me, at least temporarily, to seek for a satisfactory explanation of these experiences in the hypothesis of the cosmic mind—spiritual attunement.

We know from other sources that Sadler is here referring to psychic experiences connected with the writing of the *UB*. He is now open, he adds, to the possibility that telepathy is genuine. He speaks favorably of the work of parapsychologist Joseph Banks Rhine, and says he intends to follow it with great interest, always maintaining toward it a scientific attitude.

Adventists teach that we each possess, in addition to our mind and body, a "spirit" that is an indwelling portion of God. This doctrine is reflected in the *UB*'s central notion of a Thought Adjuster. A Thought Adjuster is a nonpersonalized "fragment of God," also called the Mystery Monitor or the Indwelling Presence. A Thought Adjuster enters every child as soon as he or she reaches the age at which moral decisions can be made. Today this occurs (*UB* 1187) when a child reaches the age of five years, ten months, and four days. The *UB* likes to give specific figures; it correctly adds that this is on the 2,134th day of a child's terrestrial life.

As in Adventist doctrine, the Thought Adjuster provides continuity between a person's death and resurrection. When we die, our Thought Adjuster "proceeds to the bosom of the Father" (*UB* 431). Our former body of flesh and blood remains on earth, but the instant we awake on the first Mansion World, we receive a new body made of morontia, a substance midway between matter and pure spirit. The Thought Adjuster leaves the bosom of the Father to reunite with our new body and mind.

There are many kinds of Thought Adjusters in the universe of universes. On page 1178 of the *UB* we are given one of the many ways they can be classified. They fall into seven types: Virgin Adjusters, Advanced Adjusters, Supreme Adjusters, Vanished Adjusters, Liberated Adjusters, Fused Adjusters, and Personalized Adjusters. The Fused Adjusters become permanently linked to persons as they advance upward from world to world on their way to Paradise. If someone rejects endless life, choosing instead to be annihilated, his or her Thought Adjuster can become "personalized"—that is, acquire a personality—provided this is recommended by the Ancients of Days.

As noted above, Thought Adjusters are also called Mystery Monitors. In *The Truth About Heredity* (1927, page 101), Sadler speaks of "the spiritual destiny of the Divine Monitor which so many believe lives alongside and with the human intellect in its earthly tabernacle." Did Sadler's "so many" refer to the small group of Urantians then studying the *UB* papers, or did he mean the Adventists? The *UB*'s Mystery Monitor is what Adventists know as the indwelling "spirit," a fragment of God that is part of a person's personality. When a person dies, the spirit returns to the bosom of God (Eccl. 12:7) until it is reunited with that person's reconstituted body on resurrection day.

The New Testament passage that most strongly seems to contradict the doctrine of soul sleep is the remark Jesus made to the good thief on the cross. "Verily I say unto thee, Today shalt thou be with me in paradise" (Luke 23:43). Adventists contend that in the King James translation just quoted a comma has been misplaced. What Jesus actually said was "I say unto thee today, thou shalt be with me in paradise." One could fill a book with quotations of passages from Adventist literature that stress this misplaced comma. I content myself with only one, a footnote in *Seventh-Day Adventists Believe* (Review and Herald, 1988).

> The solution to the understanding of the text involves its punctuation. The early manuscripts of the Bible did not have any commas or spaces between the words. Insertion of punctuation and word divisions can make considerable difference in the meaning of the text. Bible translators use their best judgment in placing punctuation marks, but their work is certainly not inspired.

If the translators, who did such excellent work in general, had placed the comma in Luke 23:43 *after* "today" instead of *before* it, this passage would not contradict the teaching of the rest of the Bible on death. Christ's words would then be properly understood to mean: "Assuredly, I say to you today [this day, when I am dying as a criminal], you will be with Me in Paradise."

Here is how Mrs. White's life of Jesus, *The Desire of Ages*, phrases Jesus' remark to the good thief:

Quickly the answer came. Soft and melodious the tone, full of love, compassion, and power the words: Verily I say unto thee today, Thou shalt be with Me in Paradise.

The comma is similarly shifted in the *UB* (2009): "Verily, verily, I say to you today, you shall sometime be with me in Paradise."

In the first edition of Mrs. White's life of Jesus, either she or her editors put it this way in a footnote:

NOTE 4. PAGE 751.—It is well known that the punctuation of the Bible is not the work of the inspired writers. Indeed, punctuation is but a modern art, the comma in its present form having been invented in 1490 by a printer of Venice. We are therefore at liberty to change the punctuation of Scripture as the sense may require. In Luke 23:43, place the comma after "to-day," and give the direct instead of the inverted form of the verb, and the text reads, "Verily I say unto thee to-day, Thou shalt be with Me in Paradise." There is now no lack of harmony between this text and Christ's later statement, that He had not yet ascended to His Father.

For a more extensive, more passionate defense of the shifted comma, see chapter 15, "Christ's Majestic Answer to the Penitent's Plea," in volume 1 of *The Conditionalist Faith of Our Fathers* (1966), by Adventist historian LeRoy Edwin Froom.

According to Norman T. Bums, in his excellent *Christian Mortalism from Tyndale to Milton* (Harvard University Press, 1972), arguments of soul sleepers for moving the comma go back at least to the early seventeenth century. Thomas Edwards, in *Gangraena* (London, 1646), mentions it as an argument well known at the time, and Richard Overton, a Baptist, defends it in *Man Wholly Mortal* (London, 1655). Overton reasons, as does Froom, that Jesus and the good thief could not possibly have been in Paradise that day because both of them died later.

Jehovah's Witnesses, who share with Adventists the belief that the dead remain unconscious until Resurrection day, are similarly obliged to shift the comma. In their *New World Translation* of the Bible, Luke 23:43 reads: "And he said to him: 'Truly I tell you today, you will be with me in Paradise.'"

There is something to be said for the comma shift. St. Paul clearly taught that the dead have no consciousness until they are given new bodies at a future date, so shifting the comma does harmonize Jesus' remark with many New Testament teachings about life after death. But there are equally strong reasons for not shifting it. The phrase "Verily I say unto you" is a translation of the Greek *amen soi lego*. This occurs 74 times in the Gospels as an introductory phrase, always followed by a comma. It would be highly unusual if only once out of 74 usages it was not a phrase introducing a statement.

An even more compelling argument against the comma shift is that the thief had just said, "Lord, remember me when thou comest into thy kingdom." Now the coming of the kingdom was believed to be at a future date when Jesus returned to earth. It would be appropriate, therefore, for Jesus to say, in effect, you don't have to wait until then. Today you will be with me in Paradise. What would be the reason for saying "I tell you today" since obviously he is speaking today? Paradise, by the way, was the place where many Jews of Jesus' time believed souls of good people would go, awaiting a future resurrection.

The early Christians and Church Fathers all took the comma to be where it is placed in the King James Bible. This is evident from the twentieth chapter (verses 5–14) of the apocryphal *Gospel of Nicodemus*, earlier called the *Acts of Pontius Pilate*. The verses describe the arrival of the good thief in Paradise:

5. And while the holy Enoch and Elias were relating this, behold there came another man in a miserable figure carrying the sign of the cross upon his shoulders.
6. And when all the saints saw him, they said to him, Who art thou? For thy countenance is like a thief's; and why dost thou carry a cross upon thy shoulders?
7. To which he answering, said, Ye say right, for I was a thief, who committed all sorts of wickedness upon earth.
8. And the Jews crucified me with Jesus: and I observed the surprising things which happened in the creation at the crucifixion of the Lord Jesus.

9. And I believed him to be the Creator of all things, and the Almighty King; and I prayed to him, saying, Lord, remember me, when thou comest into thy kingdom.

10. He presently regarded my supplication, and said to me, Verily I say unto thee, this day thou shalt be with me in Paradise.

11. And he gave me this sign of the cross saying, Carry this, and go to Paradise; and if the angel who is the guard of Paradise will not admit thee, shew him the sign of the cross, and say unto him: Jesus Christ who is now crucified, hath sent me hither to thee.

12. When I did this, and told the angel who is the guard of Paradise all these things, and he heard them, he presently opened the gates, introduced me, and placed me on the right-hand in Paradise.

13. Saying, Stay here a little time, till Adam, the father of all mankind, shall enter in, with all his sons, who are the holy and righteous servants of Jesus Christ, who was crucified.

14. When they heard all this account from the thief, all the patriarchs said with one voice, Blessed be thou, O Almighty God, the Father of everlasting goodness, and the Father of mercies, who hast shewn such favour to those who were sinners against him, and hast brought them to the mercy of Paradise, and hast placed them amidst thy large and spiritual provisions, in a spiritual and holy life. Amen.

Apocryphal and medieval literature has assigned various names to the penitent thief: Desmas, Dysmas, Demas, Matha, and Vicimus. The unrepent thief was called Gesmas, Destas, Sesmas, Joca, and Justinus. Longfellow, in *The Golden Legend*, calls the good thief Titus and the bad thief Dumachus. He imagines the two thieves attacking Mary and Joseph when they were fleeing to Egypt. When Dumachus wanted a payment for their release, Titus, who had compassion on the holy family, paid the ransom out of his own pocket. The child Jesus then prophesied:

> When thirty years shall have gone by,
> I at Jerusalem shall die,
> By Jewish hands exalted high
> On the accursed tree,
> Then on my right and my left side,
> These thieves shall both be crucified,
> And Titus thenceforth shall abide
> In paradise with me.

A medieval Greek manuscript called *The Story of Joseph of Arimathaea* purports to be a first-hand account of the crucifixion. The author is described in the gospels as a wealthy man who was a secret follower of Jesus. After the crucifixion, Joseph asked Pilate for permission to bury Christ's body. Pilate consented, and the burial was carried out by Joseph and Nicodemus. Because this apocryphal work gives such a graphic account of the deaths of the two thieves, I have given it in full as Appendix D.

Incidently, the New Testament does not mention that the good thief had been led into sin by evil companions. This is another of Sister White's additions to the gospels. She writes in chapter 78 of her life of Christ: "he [the good thief] had been led astray by evil associations." The *UB* (2009) says: "This young man, the penitent brigand, had been led into a life of violence and wrongdoing by those who extolled such a career of robbery."

The *UB* is laced with similar details about the life and times of Jesus which echo details supplied by Mrs. White. John 8 tells the story of the adulteress who was about to be stoned for her sins. While the accusers stood there, we learn that Jesus wrote something in the sand, but the gospel does not say *what* he wrote. Mrs. White, in chapter 50 of *The Desire of Ages*, reveals that he wrote "guilty secrets" of the accusers. The *UB* (1793) does not disclose exactly what words Jesus wrote, but implies that they were guilty secrets because he wrote "for the benefit of her would-be accusers; and when they read his words, they, too, went away, one by one."

The Bible is also silent on what happened later to the adulteress. According to Sister White, "the penitent woman became one of His most steadfast followers." According to the *UB* (1793), "this woman, Hildana [only the *UB* gives her name] forsook her wicked husband and joined herself to the disciples of the kingdom."

Mrs. White opens her account of Jesus at the Pool of Bethesda by writing, "At certain seasons the waters of this pool were agitated, and it was commonly believed that this was the result of supernatural power, and that whoever first after the troubling of the pool stepped into the waters, would be healed of whatever disease he had."

Now for a similar statement in the *UB* (1649): "This periodic disturbance of the warm waters was believed by many to be due to supernatural influences, and it was a popular belief that the first person who entered the water after such a disturbance would be healed of whatever infirmity he had."

Both sentences derive from John 5:4, but the rephrasings by Sister White and the *UB* seem too much alike to be coincidental.

Nowhere does the New Testament disclose how Pilate died. According to Mrs. White (chapter 77): "stung by his own remorse and wounded pride, and long after the crucifixion, he ended his own life." According to the *UB* (1989), Pilate "never fully recovered from the regretful condemnation of having consented to the crucifixion of Jesus. Finding no favor in the eyes of the new emperor, he retired to the province of Lausanne, where he subsequently committed suicide."

There are apocryphal accounts of Pilate's suicide. An appendix to the *Acts of Pilate* describes Pilate as killing himself with a knife. Caesar then had a millstone tied around Pilate's neck and the body thrown into the Tiber. (See *The Apocryphal New Testament*, translated by Montague Rhodes James, Oxford, 1924, page 158.)

Here is still another of many places in the *UB*'s Jesus section where assertions of fact are made that are not in the Bible but are in Sister White's *The Desire of Ages*. Both Matthew and Mark tell how Herod, at his birthday party, was so pleased with Salome's dancing that he offered to give her anything she desired. She asked for the head of John the Baptist, a request Herod sorrowfully granted. Mrs. White discloses (chapter 22) that "the king was dazed with wine" although this is not mentioned by either Matthew or Mark. In the *UB* (1508) we learn that "Herod did all this while well under the influence of his many wines."

There is not a line in the gospels to suggest that the young Jesus made any special effort to study nature. In chapter 1 we referred to passages in the *UB* about how the boy Jesus studied the stars and plants. "Much of his spare time—when his mother did not require his help about the house—was spent studying the flowers and plants by day and the stars by night" (*UB* 1360).

Watching steam escape from a boiling pot "caused the lad to think a great deal about the physical world and its constitution; and yet the personality embodied in this growing youth was all the while the actual creator and organizer of all these things throughout a far-flung universe" (*UB* 1367).

At age 12, the *UB* tells us (1371), Jesus "continued to make progress at school and was indefatigable in his study of nature, while increasingly he prosecuted his study of the methods whereby men make a living."

I suspect that Sadler, perhaps aided by his wife and others, wrote the *UB*'s life of Jesus. I suggest that in detailing Jesus' youthful studies of nature Sadler drew on memories of what Mrs. White had written in chapter 7 of *The Desire of Ages:*

> And spread out before Him was the great library of God's created works.
> He who had made all things studied the lessons which His own hand had

written in earth and sea and sky. Apart from the unholy ways of the world, He gathered stores of scientific knowledge from nature. He studied the life of plants and animals, and the life of man. From His earliest years He was possessed of one purpose; He lived to bless others. For this He found resources in nature; new ideas of ways and means flashed into His mind as He studied plant life and animal life.

I have not read all of Sister White's voluminous writings, but I chanced upon a passage in her *Patriarchs and Prophets* that has another striking parallel with statements in the *UB*. We are told (*UB* 828) that Adam and Eve were a little more than eight feet tall and that their bodies "gave forth a shimmer of light" (*UB* 834):

> The bodies of Adam and Eve gave forth a shimmer of light, but they always wore clothing in conformity with the custom of their associates. Though wearing very little during the day, at eventide they donned night wraps. The origin of the traditional halo encircling the heads of supposed pious and holy men dates back to the days of Adam and Eve. Since the light emanations of their bodies were so largely obscured by clothing, only the radiating glow from their heads was discernible. The descendants of Adamson always thus portrayed their concept of individuals believed to be extraordinary in spiritual development.

Adam and Eve were Material Sons and Daughters of God. We are told (*UB* 580) that such persons "vary in height from eight to ten feet, and their bodies glow with the brilliance of radiant light of a violet hue. While material blood circulates through their material bodies, they are also surcharged with divine energy and saturated with celestial light."

Here is the relevant passage from *Patriarchs and Prophets* (chapter 3):

> As man came forth from the hand of his Creator, he was of lofty stature and perfect symmetry. His countenance bore the ruddy tint of health, and glowed with the light of life and joy. Adam's height was much greater than that of men who now inhabit the earth. Eve was somewhat less in stature; yet her form was noble and full of beauty. The sinless pair wore no artificial garments; they were clothed with a covering of light and glory, such as the angels wear. So long as they lived in obedience to God, this robe of light continued to enshroud them.

Urantians who are so enormously impressed by the beautiful writing of the *UB*'s Jesus papers should (but probably won't) read Mrs. White's *The*

Desire of Ages. It is just as beautifully written, just as scholarly, just as detailed, and even longer than the *UB*'s Jesus section. If Urantians would read *The Desire of Ages* with an open mind, they should be equally awed, especially in view of the fact that Sister White's education never went beyond the equivalent of third grade. *The Desire of Ages* had a strong influence on Dr. Sadler. Adventists speak of it with the same reverence that Urantians speak of the *UB*'s Jesus section. "I have read many biographies of Jesus," writes Adventist John Robertson in his book *The White Truth* (1981), "but none of these volumes has ever brought me to my knees in love to Christ like the book *The Desire of Ages.*"

Although Mrs. White frequently added dialog and events not in the Bible, she adhered much more closely to gospel accounts than does the *UB*. Believing the Bible to be divinely inspired and infallible in every verse, she could not say anything (as the *UB* often does) that would contradict the Bible. However, as one who believed herself in direct contact with angels and the Holy Spirit, she felt empowered to embroider her narrative, as we have seen, with occasional snippets of information not in the New Testament.* It would be an interesting project for someone with the time and patience to go carefully, line by line, through the two lives of Jesus and list every detail not in the gospels but which the two lives have in common. Such similarities are, of course, just what one would expect if the author or authors of the *UB*'s Jesus papers were former Adventists who knew Sister White's writings by heart.

Many other curious doctrines of Seventh-day Adventism are in the *UB*. Both Adventists and Urantians are convinced that the Bible's archangel Michael and Jesus are one and the same, and that it was through Michael that God created the heavens and the earth (*UB* 24). In Hebrew "Michael" means "one who is like God."

The Jesus-Michael identity is stressed in early Adventist literature and in books as late as Carlyle B. Haynes's influential *Our Times and Their Meaning* (1929). Here is how Haynes puts it in describing the rebellion of Satan:

Finally the open break came.

"There was war in heaven: Michael and His angels fought against the

---

*Mrs. White's earlier writings about Jesus disclose many events not in the gospels, but which were left out of *The Desire of Ages* so as not to offend readers unaware that Mrs. White was able to obtain in visions previously unknown information. For example, in *Spiritual Gifts* (vol. 1), she writes that after someone spat on Christ's face during his trial. "he meekly raised his hand and wiped it off."

dragon; and the dragon fought and his angels, and prevailed not; neither was their place found any more in heaven." Rev. 12:7, 8.

The name "Michael" is one of the names of Christ. This will be made plain by a reference to Jude 9, where Michael is called the archangel, in connection with I Thess. 4:16, where the "Lord himself" is said to be the archangel, whose voice will wake the dead; and John 5:25, where it is said that it is the voice of Christ that raises the dead.

One of the best references on Adventist angelology is *Past, Present, and Future*, by Mrs. White's eldest son, James Edson White (1909, revised 1914). Eight chapters are devoted to "Angels, Good and Evil." On page 67 White gives the church's reasons for identifying Christ and Michael. "Hence Michael is no other than Christ, the archangel, who is 'Captain of the host of the Lord.'"

Adventists got the Jesus-Michael identity from William Miller, whose failed prophecies about the Second Coming led to the formation of the Seventh-day Adventist church. According to the Church's *Encyclopedia*, "Most Adventists have held that Michael is Christ."*

The Michael-Christ identity is an ancient Christian heresy. The most peculiar and longest lasting group to defend it was the mid-tenth-century Bulgarian sect known as the Bogomils. In their weird Manichean mythology God had two sons, Satan and his younger brother Michael. After Satan was kicked out of heaven, he created a new heaven and the earth, and became the Jehovah of the Old Testament. He did his best to fabricate human beings but was unable to do so without God's help in infusing souls into their lifeless bodies.

It was Satan who tempted Adam and Eve and caused the fall of humankind. To oppose Satan's evil plans, God sent Michael to earth, by way of the virgin Mary's womb, to be born as Jesus. The crucifixion was Satan's doing, but Jesus will eventually triumph as prophesied in the Apocalypse. The Bogomils flourished until well into the fourteenth century. For more about their history and beliefs, see the eleventh edition of *The Encyclopaedia Britannica*, Hastings' *Encyclopaedia of Religion and Ethics*, and Dmitri Oblensky, *The Bogomils* (Cambridge, 1948).

In the New Testament's short book of Jude (verse 9) we are told that

---

*Ellen White defended the identity of Christ and Michael. In chapter 10 of *The Desire of Ages*, where she mentions Michael on page 99, she puts "Christ" in brackets after his name. In *Spiritual Gifts* (vol. 4A) and in the first volume of *The Spirit of Prophecy*, where she describes Michael as resurrecting the body of Moses and taking him to heaven, she calls him "Michael, or Christ."

Michael and Satan once disputed over who was to possess the body of Moses. We learn in Revelation (12:7–9) how Michael will finally dispose of Satan. The archangel is traditionally depicted in art as holding an unsheathed sword and standing by a slain Satan in the form of a dragon.

Two Roman Catholic festivals honor Michael: Michaelmas, or the Feast of Michael and All Angels (September 29), and the Apparition of St. Michael (May 8). Most of the churches dedicated to Michael were built on sites where apparitions of the archangel are said to have occurred. In England it has long been a tradition to eat a goose on Michaelmas day. As an old couplet has it:

> September when by custom (right divine)
> Geese are ordained to bleed at Michael's shrine.

For many other quaint customs and traditions that cluster around Michaelmas and the archangel, see the section on Michael in William Walsh's *Curiosities of Popular Customs* (1898). I should add that Michael was the angel who spoke directly to Joan of Arc. In Longfellow's Golden Legend, Michael is the angel of the planet Mercury. No pope has denied the reality of angels. In 1986 the present Pope John Paul III gave five lectures on angels. In 1950 Pope Pius XII made Michael the patron angel of policemen.

In the Muslim faith Michael is the powerful archangel who through his assistants, the cherubim, controls all of nature. His wings are green, but only Allah knows how many he has. From his million eyes fall tears for the sins of Muslims, and from each tear Allah creates another cherubim.

Michael and Gabriel, the most renowned of all angels in both Christian and Islamic literature and art, are the only two unfallen angels whose names are in the Bible. We are told in the *UB* that Gabriel, also known as the Bright and Morning Star, was the offspring of Michael and the Mother Spirit. He is the chief executive of the Universe of Nebadon.

It is Gabriel who dictated the Koran to Mohammed. The Koran describes him as having 140 pairs of wings. In Longfellow's *Golden Legend* he is the angel of the Moon. In the gospel, it is Gabriel who announces the birth of Jesus to Mary in a scene painted hundreds of times by Renaissance artists.

The *UB* (1345–47) accepts the New Testament accounts of Gabriel appearing both to Mary and to Elizabeth. The time he visited Elizabeth, to tell her she would become the mother of John the Baptist, is given as late June, 8 BCE The *UB* denies the Virgin Birth—Joseph is the actual father of

Jesus—but retells the story of Gabriel bringing the "glad tidings" to Mary. This, we are told, was in mid-November, 8 BCE.

> Gabriel's announcement to Mary was made the day following the conception of Jesus and was the only event of supernatural occurrence connected with her entire experience of carrying and bearing the child of promise. (*UB* 1347)

We have here one of the many instances in the *UB* where a traditional Christian miracle, the Virgin Birth, is denied to the great offense of conservative Christians, whereas other supernatural events, such as the visits of Gabriel to Elizabeth and Mary, are affirmed, to the equally great annoyance of non-Christians.

I have visited New Harmony, Indiana, where I saw the huge print in stone of a bare foot said to have been left by Gabriel after he talked to George Rapp. Rapp was the founder of the Rappite adventist colony in New Harmony. Members of the sect expected the Second Coming of Christ so soon that they were forbidden to have children. As a result, the colony quickly evaporated. Rapp is said to have exclaimed on his deathbed that were he not certain God expected him to live to see Jesus return, he might think his last hour had come.

In Seventh-day Adventist theology Michael (Jesus) is an eternal part of the Godhead. Jehovah's Witnesses also identify Christ with Michael, but with a major difference. Like the ancient Anans and today's Urantians, they believe Michael was a created being, not an eternal part of the Godhead. Billions of years ago, say the Witnesses, God created Michael as the first angel. Billions of years later, it was through Michael that God made the universe. As a sacrifice for humanity's sins, God placed Michael inside Mary's womb as Jesus, a genuine human being who died, not on a cross, but a "torture stake"—a single pole without a crossbar. There was no resurrection of Jesus' body. After disposing of Christ's body (see *UB* 2024), Jehovah reconstituted the spirit of Jesus as Michael, the archangel he was previously.

The first chapter of Paul's Epistle to the Hebrews surely makes clear that Jesus was never an angel. This may explain why the Jesus-Michael identity has been so rare in past Christian heresies. Today's Adventists no longer stress this identity, and many have even abandoned it. Paul's Epistle is no obstacle to Urantians because their Jesus-Michael was never an angel. He was the Son of the Eternal Son of the Paradise Trinity.

Herbert Armstrong, the egotistical bumpkin who founded the Worldwide Church of God, adopted many Seventh-day Adventist doctrines, including soul sleep, annihilation of the wicked, and the Saturday Sabbath, though not the Michael-Jesus identity. In Armstrong's crazy theology Michael is merely the archangel whose task it was to protect the twelve tribes of Israel, and today's true church of God, namely the church founded by Armstrong.

On the other hand, Armstrong claimed that Melchizedek (see Genesis 14, Hebrews 5–7, and Psalm 110) and Jesus are "one and the same person" (Armstrong, *Mystery of the Ages*, Chapter 1). This quaint belief also goes back to early Christian centuries. Epiphanius, the fourth century Bishop of Salamis, wrote a book called the *Panarion* in which he attacked eighty varieties of heresies. One was the belief that Melchizedek was Jesus, another the belief that Melchizedek was a deity *superior* to Jesus. The latter belief was central to a third-century heretical cult called the Melchizedek-ians or Melchizedians. That Melchizedek was an incarnation of Jesus was the opinion of Marcus Eremita, known as Mark the Hermit, who flourished around 400 A.D., and was an Abbot at Ancyro. Saint Ambrose, a fourth-century Bishop of Milan, argued that Melchizedek was an incarnation of the Holy Ghost. Some Jewish Bible commentators identified Melchizedek with the yet to come Jewish messiah.

In the *UB* "Melchizedek" is a generic name for a class of Sons of God. Michael's first "bestowal" (incarnation) was a billion years ago on the world of Salvington as a Melchizedek (*UB* 1310). The Old Testament's Melchizedek, according to the *UB*, was Machiventa Melchizedek, a bestowal of one of God's Sons, though not the Son Michael.

Melchizedek has always been a hazy, mysterious figure to biblical commentators, mainly because of strange statements about him in the New Testament's book of Hebrews. He plays such a prominent role in the *UB*'s history of Urantia that an entire paper (Paper 93) is devoted to him. His "bestowal" on Urantia occurred in Salem (an ancient name for Jerusalem) 1,973 years before the birth of Christ. As Hebrews 7:3 describes it: "Without father, without mother, without descent having neither beginning of days, nor end of life, but made like unto the Son of God."

As the *UB* tells it, he materialized on Urantia in a body specially constructed for him by the Gods, but lacking the genetic equipment necessary for producing offspring. The body vanished when he was 94. Abraham was his pupil. The three concentric circles was his insignia.

The Old Testament has little to say about Melchizedek, but there is much about him in the apocryphal *Second Book of Enoch*. When his mother Sothonim died, Melchizedek emerged from her body as a three-year-old child. "Behold, the badge of priesthood was on his chest, and it was glorious in appearance." Did the badge consist of three concentric circles? According to Enoch, there was a second Melchizedek who became the king of Salem. To preserve him from the flood of Noah, God ordered Michael to place him in Eden for safekeeping. Some late Jewish sources identify Michael with the first Melchizedek. A translation of the *Second Book of Enoch* can be found in *The Old Testament Pseudepigrapha*, edited by James H. Charlesworth, volume 1 (Doubleday, 1983).

The story of Melchizedek, king of Salem, is told in the *Book of Mormon* (Alma 13:14–19). The Melchizedek Priesthood is the highest order of Mormon priests—the channels through whom God sends continued revelations. John the Baptist, in the guise of an angel, conferred the priesthood on Joseph Smith and one of his associates in 1829. Since then the Melchizedek priests have ruled the church with iron authority. The order is not open to Mormon women.*

Melchizedek's Thought Adjuster later became the Thought Adjuster of Jesus—the only Thought Adjuster ever to occupy two minds on Urantia (*UB* 1016, 1200, 1357, 1511). Jesus was five when the Thought Adjuster entered his mind on February 11, 2 BCE While Jesus was being baptized by John, the Thought Adjuster left him to return a few moments later as an exalted Personalized Adjuster.

Known as the Planetary Prince of Urantia, less than a thousand years ago Melchizedek was Urantia's "resident governor general," living here invisibly for a hundred years. Paper 56 was co-written by him. Like Jesus, he will someday return to earth in visible form. As the *UB* says (1251) this momentous event, like the Second Coming of Christ, may occur "any day or hour."

Paper 93 concludes ungrammatically (nothing can be "most unique"):

This is the story of Machiventa Melchizedek, one of the most unique of all characters ever to become connected with the history of Urantia and a personality who may be destined to play an important role in the future experience of your irregular and unusual world.

---

*A cult called The Ancient and Mystical Order of Melchizedek is said to have arisen in New York in 1694. According to *Who's Who in Occultism, New Thought, Psychism and Spiritualism*, edited by William C. Hartmann (Occult Press, 1927) this long defunct group had as its first objective: "To form a nucleus of the Universal Brotherhood of Humanity, without distinction of race, creed, sex, caste, or color." Its second objective was: "To encourage the study of comparative religion, philosophy and science, psychology and divinity." Its third goal: "To investigate the unexplained laws of nature and the powers latent in man." Can any reader tell me more about this obscure order?

That guardian angels watch over each of us is another Adventist doctrine also prominent in the *UB*. The Chief of Seraphim, assigned to Urantia., opens Paper 114 as follows:

> The Most Highs rule in the kingdoms of men through many celestial forces and agencies but chiefly through the ministry of seraphim.
>
> At noon today the roll call of planetary angels, guardians, and others on Urantia was 501,234,619 pairs of seraphim. There were assigned to my command two hundred seraphic hosts—597,196,800 pairs of seraphim, or 1,194,393,600 individual angels. The registry, however, shows 1,002,469,238 individuals; it follows therefore that 191,924,362 angels were absent from this world on transport, messenger, and death duty. (On Urantia there are about the same number of cherubim as seraphim, and they are similarly organized.)

I have called attention to the *UB*'s passion for giving huge, precise numbers like those above. It is worth reminding readers again that Wilfred, the sleeping conduit, began his career in Battle Creek as a bookkeeper, and for decades was business manager of Sadler's institution. Accountants are not mathematicians, but their professional success obviously depends on the accuracy with which they record and manipulate large numbers.

In both Urantian and Adventist theology, guardian angels cannot interfere with decisions of your own free will. Only on rare occasions do they interact with the natural causes and effects of history. For details, consult pages 1243–49 of the *UB*. In cases of extreme emergencies the seraphim can and do intervene in mortal affairs by performing "unusual exploits," usually when ordered to do so by their superiors, but sometimes acting on their own. As the *UB* puts it: "In most instances the circumstances of the material realm proceed unaltered by seraphic action, although occasions have arisen, involving jeopardy to vital links in the chain of human evolution, in which seraphic guardians have acted, and properly, on their own initiative" (*UB* 1246).

Adventists, in accord with Thomas Aquinas and almost all Catholic and Protestant theologians of past ages, believe that only one guardian angel is assigned to each believer. The *UB* goes one better by assigning a pair of angels, not just to Christians but to every human being. You are usually unaware of their presence or of the ways in which they guide your footsteps "into paths of new and progressive experiences."

Guardian angels and Thought Adjusters do not communicate, although your angelic pair and your Adjuster are "strangely correlated" to work together in "perfect harmony and exquisite accord." Because seraphim lack physical bodies they cannot shed physical tears, but they have "spiritual emotions" akin to ours. In a figurative sense they "weep because of your willful ignorance and stubbornness." They are not directly concerned with your prayers, but your impulse to pray is often the result of their influence.

After you die it is your guardian angels who preserve all the records that constitute your identity while you soul-sleep until your resurrection. If you have been too wicked to deserve resurrection, you may eventually cease to exist. When the roll is called up yonder, your Adjuster will identify you and your guardian seraphim will "repersonalize" you with a new body made of morontia. For the first time you will see your guardian angels. They will remain with you throughout your long adventures inward from world to world. "And they will be in waiting on the shores of Paradise when their mortal associates awaken from the last transit sleep of time into the new experiences of eternity." (*UB* 1248). Your two angel companions will then fuse to form a "two-in-oneness" and become Paradise Deities.

Here is how Mrs. White, in the final chapter of *Education*, describes our contacts with angels after our resurrection in heaven:

> Every redeemed one will understand the ministry of angels in his own life. The angel who was his guardian from his earliest moment; the angel who watched his steps, and covered his head in the day of peril; the angel who was with him in the valley of the shadow of death, who marked his resting-place, who was the first to greet him in the resurrection-morning,—what will it be to hold converse with him, and to learn the history of divine interposition in the individual life, of heavenly co-operation in every work for humanity!
>
> All the perplexities of life's experience will then be made plain. Where to us have appeared only confusion and disappointment, broken purposes and thwarted plans, will be seen a grand, overruling, victorious purpose, a divine harmony.

In the year I write (1994), angels are almost as "in" as they were in the Middle Ages and Renaissance when angel worship was a widespread heresy. More than thirty books about angels have been published in recent years including one by Billy Graham, and a more academic treatise by Episcopalian philosopher Mortimer Adler. Somehow Adler managed to write *The Angels and Us* (1982) without revealing whether he does or doesn't believe angels actually exist!

Time's cover (December 27, 1993) depicts a youthful angel with glorious white wings. It illustrates an eight-page essay inside, by Nancy Gibbs, titled "Angels Among Us." The cover states: "69% of Americans believe they [angels] exist.* What in heaven is going on?" Like Adler, Ms. Gibbs sits on the fence with respect to whether angels are real or mythical.

Guardian angels are all over today's movie and television screens, including endless reruns of *It's a Wonderful Life*, Jimmy Stewart's most famous film next to *Destry Rides Again*. The late Michael Landon—note his first name—played a guardian angel in a long-running TV series *Highway to Heaven*. In a current Broadway play, *Angels in America*, a man with AIDS is aided by an angel. Sales of angel goods—pins, statues, and so on—are booming. There is a store in my hometown, Tulsa, called Angels and Things that specializes in angel figures. Three-fourths of American teenagers, a recent Gallup poll showed, believe in both good and demonic angels.

In 1994 *Angelic Healing: Working with Angels to Heal Your Life*, by Eileen Elias Freeman, who had previously written *Touched by Angels*, was published by Warner Brothers. The book was an alternate selection of The Literary Guild (for shame!) and the Doubleday Book Club, both owned by Time Warner. "Stunning real-life stories of people who have been healed through the intervention of angels," said the half-page ad in *The New York Times Book Review* (November 13).

In 1995 a bimonthly magazine titled *Angels on Earth* was launched, edited by Fulton Oursler Jr. son of the well-known American author. Charter subscribers received a free wall calendar featuring masterpieces of angelic art. A brochure announcing the magazine carried a message signed by Oursler that begins:

Dear Friend,

Have you ever felt the reassuring touch of an angel's wing as you raced through the trials of everyday life? Or has an angel ever stepped in and saved you from almost certain calamity?

More people are coming to the realization that their lives have indeed been touched by angels. These ministering spirits provide strength and support, comfort and care, often when we're most in need. And now, from the editors of *Guideposts* magazine comes *Angels On Earth*—an inspiring collection of first-hand accounts of ordinary people whose lives have been extraordinarily touched by God's heavenly messengers.

---

*The 69 percent figure comes from a *Time* telephone poll in 1993 of 500 adult Americans. Forty-six percent of the believers also believe they have a guardian angel. Fifty-five percent think angels are higher beings created by God; 15 percent assume they are souls of the deceased. Thirty-two percent said they had felt "an angelic presence" in their life. Only 7 percent did not believe angels existed. Forty-nine percent believed in fallen angels as against 45 percent who did not.

Both Adventists and Urantians see the Catholic Church as a great per-verter of the teachings of Jesus, adding all sorts of strange doctrines not in the Bible. Until recently, Adventists believed the Catholic Church to be the Antichrist of Biblical prophecy. Both Adventists and the *UB* deny that Jesus intended Peter to be the first pope. As we have learned, Wilfred's uncle wrote an entire book about this.

Adventists are vegetarians, and also down on the use of tobacco and alcohol. Adam and Eve, Sister White reminds us, are described in Genesis as strict vegetarians before they disobeyed God and their descendants began eating meat. The *UB* (851) tells us: "Adam and Eve and th ir first generation of children did not use the flesh of animals as food."

Why did God permit Satan and his cohorts to rebel? Because, Adven-tists have always maintained with St. Augustine, God gave his created beings the power of free will, and this necessarily includes the ability to sin. God allowed the conflict so that after the rebel angels are finally anni-hilated, everyone in the universe will understand the awful consequences of sin. When the great conflict between Christ and Satan is over, the uni-verse will be washed clean of evil forever. This, too, is reflected in many places in the *UB*, although on page 618 we are told that "on Uversa we teach forty-eight reasons for permitting evil to run the full course of its own moral bankruptcy and spiritual extinction." The Mighty Messenger who wrote this paper adds that there are just as many reasons he does *not* know, and that some of the reasons he does know he is "not permitted to narrate."

The *UB*'s emphasis on the mystery of evil is good Seventh-day Adven-tist doctrine. Witness the following remarks by Mrs. White in chapter 29, "On the Origin of Evil," in *The Great Controversy Between Christ and Satan*: "It is impossible to explain the origin of sin so as to give a reason for its existence. . . . Sin is an intruder for whose presence no reason can be given. It is mysterious, unaccountable." Mrs. White means, of course, unaccountable from our limited, finite perspective.

As one would expect from the unconscious or conscious minds of dis-enchanted Adventists, the *UB* is in conflict with many fundamental Ad-ventist dogmas. The Second Coming, for example, which Adventists still believe is just around the corner, the *UB* moves to a distant and unknown date. However, as we shall learn in a later chapter, many Urantians involved in what is called The Teaching Mission are now predicting an imminent return of Michael.

There is no claim in the *UB* that a Saturday Sabbath is still binding on today's Christians. On the other hand, the strong emphasis throughout the *UB* on the number seven may be related to Wilfred's unconscious memories of his Adventist past. It is probably coincidental, but amusing to observe, that there are seven letters in *Wilfred* and *Kellogg*, not to mention *Urantia, Nebadon, Michael, Gabriel, Lucifer*, and scores of other *UB* names.

Although Will Kellogg, like his brother John, lost his Adventist faith, he never abandoned his fascination with the number seven. In hotels he always took a room on the seventh floor. His car license plates had to end in seven. "I was my father's seventh son," he liked to say, "born on the seventh day of the week [the Adventist's Sabbath] and the seventh day of the month. My father was a seventh child also, and the name 'Kellogg' has seven letters." He would surely have been intrigued by the omnipresence of seven in the *UB*.

Urantians maintain that their doctrines are "Christian" in the sense that they accept what they believe to be the true teachings of Jesus as contained in the *UB*'s Jesus papers. No conservative Christian could agree, especially in light of the *UB*'s rejection of the Atonement. It is easy to understand why the *UB* has been so bitterly attacked by Protestant fundamentalists in their many recent books on American cults.* Urantians naturally do not like their religion to be called a "cult" any more than Adventists, Mormons, and Christian Scientists like to be called members of a cult. Their objections seem groundless in view of the fact that the Brilliant Evening Star of Nebadon (*UB* 965–66) calls early Christianity a cult, and urges Urantians to replace it with a "new cult" destined to be the "true religion" of the future.

Members of a cult always dislike having their cult called a cult. Webster's *New Collegiate Dictionary* provides several definitions of the word. Almost all its definitions apply to the Urantia Movement, but especially the following: "a religion regarded as unorthodox or spurious. . . . A great devotion to a person, idea, or thing [in the Urantia cult the "thing" is of course the *UB*] . . . a small circle of persons united by devotion or allegiance to an artistic or intellectual movement." Of course Urantianism differs from many of today's cults in lacking a living charismatic leader, and in the low intensity of its proselytizing.

Another major respect in which the *UB* departs from Adventism is its

---

*See for example the sections on Urantianism in Bob Larson's *Larson's New Book of Cults* (updated edition, 1989), Tex Marrs's *Marrs' Book of New Age Cults and Religions* (1949), and other similar books currently on sale in Christian bookstores.

acceptance of an ancient earth and the evolution of all life. Such views are common, of course, among liberal Christians and even among a small but growing minority of Adventists. We will discuss the *UB*'s version of evolution in chapter 15.

Let me close with what may be just an amusing coincidence. On the other hand, it could be an instance of how the name of a person, very familiar to Wilfred because that person played a key role in Dr. Kellogg's disfellowship from the Church, may have turned up in material that emerged from Wilfred's unconscious mind.

In the *UB*'s Paper 67 we meet a character named Amadon. The great Lucifer rebellion of the Christian Bible is described in this paper as taking place on Urantia some 150,000 years before Adam and Eve appeared on the scene. For 300,000 years Urantia had been ruled by Caligastia, a servant of Lucifer. When Caligastia made himself an absolute dictator, he was opposed by Van the Steadfast, chairman of the Supreme Council of Co-ordination.

Throughout the first seven years of Caligastia's rebellion, Van was supported by his loyal assistant Amadon. Amadon was not as intelligent as the superhuman Van, but he was unwavering in his devotion to God and to the Son Michael (Jesus). Eventually Caligastia was deposed. He has, however, been allowed to remain on Urantia where he is invisible to our eyes but continues to do all he can to oppose Michael's plans. It was Caligastia who tempted Adam and Eve. He is the "Devil" of the Bible—the evil protagonist of Michael in Mrs. White's *The Great Controversy Between Christ and Satan*.

The Amadonites were a "noble band" who supported Amadon. Their descendants, along with the rival Nodites, flourished on Urantia until the establishment of Eden. Sustained by the Tree of Life, Amadon continued to serve Van for more than 150,000 years. The Nodites, by the way, settled in the land of Nod (*UB* 758). This clears up the Old Testament mystery of where Cain got his wife. According to Genesis 4:16, he found her in the land of Nod, just east of Eden.

Now for what may or may not be a curious coincidence. George Washington Amadon (1832–1913) was a prominent Battle Creek Adventist editor and publishing executive, no doubt descended from the noble Amadonites. It was he who interviewed Dr. Kellogg about his heretical opinions, and who played a crucial role in the doctor's expulsion from the faith in 1907, just thirty-four days after the fatal questioning. It was then that Wilfred Kellogg and Dr. Sadler both quietly walked out of the church to which their parents had been so dedicated, a church they themselves had once believed to be the only organization preaching the true gospel to a wicked world soon to be destroyed by Michael's return to the earth he had once created.

Fig. 1. A young Dr. William S. Sadler Sr.

Fig. 2. An elderly Dr. Sadler

Fig. 3. Dr. Lena Sadler (Fig. 1–3 taken from "The Evolution of the Soul," a 1941 lecture by William S. Sadler, now published by the Jesusonian Foundation [1990])

Fig. 4. A young Christy (Emma Christensen), the Sadlers' adopted daughter

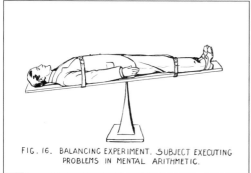

FIG. 16. BALANCING EXPERIMENT. SUBJECT EXECUTING PROBLEMS IN MENTAL ARITHMETIC.

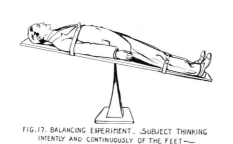

FIG. 17. BALANCING EXPERIMENT. SUBJECT THINKING INTENTLY AND CONTINUOUSLY OF THE FEET

Fig. 5. A German "balancing experiment," which Dr. Sadler claimed he replicated (from William Sadler, *The Physiology of Faith and Fear* [1912], p. 127)

Fig. 6. Dr. John Harvey Kellogg (from David and Elizabeth Armstrong, *The Great American Medicine Show* [New York: Prentice Hall, 1991] Courtesy of the Battle Creek Adventist Hospital)

Fig. 7. Ellen White

Fig. 8. Harold M. Sherman

Fig. 9. Martha Sherman

Fig. 10. Harry J. Loose

Fig. 11. Vern Bennom Grimsley

Fig. 12. Kristen Maaherra (from *Urantian Sojourn* [Spring–Summer 1992])

13

Sadler and Sister White

I n 1901, when Sadler was 26, he wrote six pages of a tract published by the Adventist's Pacific Press, in Oakland, California. Titled *Some One Cares For Your Soul*, it is an impassioned plea to sinners, swarming with biblical quotations. The following typical paragraph will give you an idea of how firmly Sadler was then committed to evangelical Christianity:

> Yes, God loves you, no matter what your condition is. He gave His Son, Jesus, to die for you, *just as you are*; so if you will only believe in Jesus, you can come to Him right now, just as you are. Jesus, the Saviour of sinners, will receive you with outstretched and loving arms. Will you not come?

As late as 1906, when Sadler and his wife were living at 38 Calendar Avenue, La Grange, Illinois, and Sadler was still closely associated with Dr. Kellogg and his Battle Creek Sanitarium, both Sadlers were loyal Adventists. We know this from a remarkable 14-page letter, typed single spaced, that Sadler sent to Mrs. Ellen G. White on April 26, 1906.

As this letter reveals, Sadler retained his strong belief that Sister White was a prophetess whose writings and "testimonies" (writings or speeches directed to officials and church members) were inspired by the Holy Spirit and therefore free from error. Like his good friend Dr. Kellogg, who in 1907 would be expelled from the Church, Sadler was starting to have doubts about Sister White's integrity. Rumors of these doubts reached Mrs. White. On March 30, 1906, she sent the following letter to the doubters associated with Dr. Kellogg:

> Recently in the visions of the night I stood in the large company of people. There were present Dr. Kellogg, Elders Jones, Tenny, and Taylor,

Dr. Paulson, Elder Sadler, Judge Arthur and many of their associates. I was directed by the Lord to request them and any others who have perplexities and grievous things in their minds regarding the testimonies that I have borne, to specify what their objections and criticisms are. The Lord will help me to answer these objections, and to make plain that which seems to be intricate.

Let those who are troubled now place upon paper a statement of the difficulties that perplex their minds, and let us see if we cannot throw some light upon the matter that will relieve their perplexities. . . . Let it all be written out, and submitted to those who desire to remove the perplexities.

I ask that the leaders in the medical work at Battle Creek, and those who have been associated with them in gathering together criticisms and objections to the testimonies that I have borne, shall open to me the things that they have been opening to others. They should certainly do this, if they are loyal to the directions God has given.

Obedient to Ellen White's request, which she said God had directed her to make, several of the Battle Creek men who were having doubts did indeed write to her with specific questions. Dr. Charles E. Stewart, one of the physicians at the San, drew up a list of "perplexities" which he sent to Sister White. Sadler was among those who sent similar letters. His lengthy letter was an impassioned, agonized plea to Mrs. White to clear up their misgivings. Here is Sadler's letter printed in full, exactly as he typed it:

> 38 Calendar Avenue
> La Grange, Ill.
> 26th April 1906

Mrs. E. G. White,
Sanitarium, California

Dear Sister White:
A few days ago I saw a communication from you in which my name was mentioned, and in which you invited those who had difficulties regarding the Testimonies to write direct to you.

There are many things that have come up recently that perplex me; many things which I find myself unable to explain to those who are perplexed; so while I do not have doubts concerning the "Testimonies", I do have many difficulties.

I have not written to you concerning this matter before, for the reason that I held to the position that if the Lord had spoken, it was not proper for me to question and criticize even though I might be wholly unable to understand or comprehend the message. But since you have asked for those who have difficulties, to present them direct to you, and inasmuch as my name was mentioned directly, I now feel at liberty to write you fully respecting my difficulties.

In order to correctly state my present attitude, it will be necessary for me to go back ten or twelve years, to the time when I had just finished a systematic study of your writings, having made a large index of all your published works, including your articles which appeared in the *Review*, *Signs*, and other papers, from back in the fifties. The study of your writings did wonders for me; my soul was ablaze with their value and power, and I conducted frequent public studies at the Sanitarium, at camp-meetings, and before the churches concerning the subject.

It was while conducting such a series of studies with the South Side Church in Chicago, taking the position that all your writings were from the same divine source, in harmony with what you state in Volume 5, page 67:

> You might say that this communication was only a letter. Yes, it was a letter, but prompted by the Spirit of God, to bring before your mind things that had been shown me. In these letters which I write, in the testimonies which I bear, I am presenting to you that which the Lord has presented to me. I do not write one article in the paper expressing merely my own ideas. They are what God has opened before me in vision, the precious rays of light shining from the throne.

and was earnestly presenting these matters to the church at that time, that an older minister questioned the soundness of my position, but I read the passage above quoted, and took my stand firmly on that. So for years I have been holding that all communications from you were "Testimonies." Was I right? Or, as it is claimed, are some "letters", and only refer to and deal with that which is Testimony?

A short time after this, your letter to Dr. Kellogg concerning the buildings in Chicago, came, and of course it troubled me; but I took this position,—I know that the Testimonies come from a source that is higher than human; therefore, although I have now encountered a thing that I cannot explain—a thing which I do not understand,—a matter which even appears to me to be without foundation, I will hold unswervingly to my position.

Later, I heard from you the explanation of this matter, which, so far as I was concerned, satisfied me, but left my mind in this trouble, which I now ask you to help me to understand,—Since the Lord showed you those buildings in Chicago, and since you supposed they *had been erected*, and it afterwards developed that they had not, and that the representation was made merely to prevent their being, may this not be applied to other representations that have been made to you? That is, that the Lord gives you these views of things that are not, but which are likely to occur, for the express purpose of preventing their occurrence, as in the case of the Chicago buildings above referred to?

Accordingly, I find myself in a quandary, when I seek to understand certain things that you have recently written. I am often at a loss to know how to choose between the following two positions:

(1) Am I to acknowledge the conditions or accusations which are stated in the Testimony as true, and as conditions which really exist at *the present time*, even though after prayerful search and careful inquiry I am still unable to recognize that these things do exist? Or,

(2) Is this another instance like the Chicago buildings, in which you presented a thing that does not really exist, but which the Lord is seeking to forestall?

With these two positions before me, concerning some matters, I do not know how to choose, and therefore have held the entire matter in abeyance, in my mind, watching and praying for light.

For instance, I recently read a communication from you to Dr. Paulson and his wife. From reading this, I would suppose that at the present time, Dr. Paulson was completely under Dr. Kellogg's influence; yet, having been associated with him very closely for years, especially since my return from California, I have not seen this, in fact, it had appeared to me that Dr. Kellogg exercised less influence over Dr. Paulson in recent years than over any other of his former colleagues and present associates. I could write at great length to show how in many important matters, Dr. Paulson has during the past two and a half years, stood stiffly by his convictions of right, and been unyielding to the end in various matters respecting Dr. Kellogg.

These matters I have not given serious attention to until recently, for I had settled it in my mind that I *believed the Testimonies*; I had a personal experience in and with them; and, so far as I knew my heart, I had settled it that I believed them so well that I did not think anyone could unsettle my faith in them. But during the last few months such a denominational issue has been made out of your writings, and I have been so sorely pressed for a statement of my position, that I saw it was necessary for me to go to the bottom of these difficulties, and, if possible, reach some definite position.

You must know, therefore, my joy when having reached this conclusion, I received this letter from you inviting me to come direct to you with my difficulties. I know your invitation is extended in good spirit, and

I believe you will receive this letter as the questions of one who is honest, although perplexed.

Another matter which I find is perplexing many, is your words to Dr. Kellogg at the General Conference five years ago in which you stated that you had probably written too strongly to Dr. Kellogg. If you wrote *too strongly* concerning any matter which the Lord presented to you, might you not also write too weakly? Again, it is asked, if you wrote too strongly then, how are we to know that you are not writing too strongly now? The part of your talk referred to, is as follows:

> I thank God that Dr. Kellogg has not sunk into despondency and infidelity. I have been afraid of it, and I have written some very straight things to him; and it may be, Dr. Kellogg—if he is here,— that I have written too strong, for I felt as though I must get hold of you, and hold you by the power of all the might I had. But I have seen the work, I have seen the work that has been carried on, and how can anybody see it and not see that God is at work? That is a mystery to me; I cannot understand it; I cannot explain it.

Are all of the things specified in your writings actually in existence, or are some things prophecies of the dangers that are ahead, and which we are to avoid?

I can't afford to be wrong, whichever way this is: I *must be right*, and I expect the Lord to help me into the light on all these matters, although they seem very perplexing now, and they seem more perplexing as I continue to investigate. I turned a deaf ear to these things for years, but now, since our attitude on the Testimonies is becoming a test throughout the denomination, I realize that I must go to the bottom of all these things, and know just where I stand on all these points.

Some four years ago, when my wife and I were having one of those pleasant and profitable occasions in your upper chamber at St. Helena, you stated to us that you were "not a prophet," but simply "little Ellen White, a messenger with a message." On returning to San Francisco, my wife and I had considerable prayer and discussion concerning this. I had always supposed you were a prophet, but I could not maintain that you were after hearing from your own lips that you were not. However I resolved to say nothing about this to anyone. My wife, however, did tell someone about your statement, and in some way it was told by Sr. Ruef that Sr. Sadler had made this statement; so, upon returning to Battle Creek, the first thing that was handed us upon alighting from the carriage at the Sanitarium, was a letter from Bro. W. C. White, criticizing Mrs. Sadler for having made this statement, and stating that such an idea would greatly hinder your work; and that if it really had been stated, it would be necessary for him to issue a denial.

This greatly perplexed my wife. She knew she had heard you say it, and she did not see any reason why it should be denied; but her perplexity was relieved at the time you stated in public, in the tabernacle at Battle Creek, that you were not a prophet, and it was subsequently published in the *Review*; but, in the same *Review*, there was an article by the editor directly contradicting your statement, and proving that you were a prophet.

Now, Sr. White, what am I to believe? Until I get more light from you, I shall take *your word*. I have confidence that you know more about your gift than anybody else in the world. My personal contact with you and your work at St. Helena and in California, satisfied me, not only of the gift which God has given you, but of your sincerity and earnest faithfulness; and I have therefore purposed in my heart that no man nor any set of men, shall explain to me what you meant when you said you were not a prophet. I will take an explanation from no one but you.

Another matter: that is, Willie's influence over the Testimonies. I came into this truth about 20 years ago, and just before I was baptized by Elder Wm. Covert, (about 18 years ago) I thoroughly made up my mind concerning the Testimonies. In short, I accepted them; but from that day to this, especially the last ten years, and more especially since your return to this country from Australia, I have been hearing it constantly, from leaders, ministers, from those sometimes high in Conference authority, that Willie influenced you in the production of your Testimonies; or, as they would often designate it, the "letters" you sent out.

This talk made little or no impression on me. I resolutely refused to believe it, year after year. I have been given a copy of the communication written by you under date of July 19th 1905, addressed to Brethren I. H. Evans and J. S. Washburn, and I have since then not known what to do or say concerning this matter. I refer to the following quotation:

> After seeing this representation, I awoke, and I fully expected that the matter would take place as it had been presented to me. When Elder Haskell was telling me of the perplexity that they were in to carry forward the Southern work, I said, "Have faith in God; you will carry from this meeting the five thousand dollars needed for the purchase of the church."
>
> I wrote a few lines to Elder Daniels suggesting this be done, *but Willie did not see that the matter* could be carried through thus, because Elder Daniels and others were at that time very much discouraged in regard to the condition of things in Battle Creek. So I told him that he need not deliver the note. But I could not rest. I was disturbed, and could not find peace of mind.

Please won't you help me to understand this? It is the most serious of all the difficulties I have encountered in my experience concerning the Testimonies; and I have it frequently presented to me, and I don't know what to say in answer.

Until recently, I had but little difficulty in answering all the objections I ever met against the Testimonies, but I am now encountering things which I am not fully able to meet.

When I returned to Battle Creek from California, I brought with me a large number of your recent communications, to read to the family there. In the course of my reading I read a statement reprimanding the managers of the Battle Creek Sanitarium for making their workers sign contracts. Then I was immediately confronted with a communication from you stating that the Managers should place workers under contract. In this case, I refer to the communication found in the General Conference Bulletin (1893) pages 162, 163, which says:

Before persons are admitted to our Missionary Training Schools, let there be a written agreement that after receiving their education they will give themselves to the work for a specified time. This is the only way our missions can be made what they should be.

Now, what could I do to explain this? I did say that this might be an instance similar to that in the scriptures where Christ told His disciples at one time, to take no purse nor provision, and in another He told them to take scrip and a cover of raiment. I said, "Maybe the conditions have changed, therefore the instruction changes." What is your explanation of this?

I would like to see from your pen a statement of what you mean in your writings along the line of God in Nature, etc. I refer to the following passages, and others:

Know ye not that ye are the temple of God, and that the Spirit of God dwelleth in you? If any man defile the temple of God, him shall God destroy for the temple of God is holy, which temple ye are. No man can of himself cast out the devil throng that have taken possession of the heart. Only Christ can cleanse the *soul temple*.
—*Desire of Ages.* 161.

They have taken a rigid course, and lived so very plain that their health has suffered, disease has strengthened in the system, and the *temple of God* has been weakened.
—*Testimonies*, Vol. 1. p. 205.

I know many honest souls who are in confusion respecting these passages, in view of your recent writings.

Another thing I want help on, is with reference to the use of the Testimonies.

(1) Do you approve of sending personal testimonies which the Lord has given for men, broadcast to other people?

(2) Is it not the Bible rule that when we have any criticism of a brother, it should be presented to him, then afterwards to two or three, and then, if he reject it, to the church? That is why I am now writing direct to you. Does the Lord follow a different rule from this with regard to the Testimonies?

For instance, the letter to which this is an answer, although it has my name in it, I have not received personally. It was shown me by one who did receive it, but whose name is not mentioned in it at all; and I have in mind many instances of this kind. It does not seem right to me that personal Testimonies should be multiplied and scattered broadcast unless they have been rejected by the individual to whom they were given, and further that they were of general interest to the church. Am I right in this?

Again, is it right for me to use a Testimony given to Bro. A. in my efforts to get Bro. A. to do the thing I think is referred to in the Testimony which the Lord sent him? Are the Testimonies for men to use upon the souls of their fellowmen; or are they messages from God for the Holy Spirit to send home to the human heart with convicting power? I had supposed the Lord intended the latter to be the case; and it has been a great trial to me to see the public and private use that has been made of your writings during this present difficulty between the General Conference and the Medical Missionary Work.

Another matter that has bothered me since it happended, although it did not at the time, is that during the Conference at Berrien Springs, when Prof. Prescott was preaching against Pantheism, you sent for Dr. Paulson and me one morning, to come and see you; and during our conversation you presented to us many things that had been shown to you during the night, and gave us to carry away a copy of a letter addressed to Bro. Prescott, forbidding them to make these public attacks, etc.

We read this, and supposed the matter would stop, but that evening and the following, things continued as they were and when the matter developed further, it appeared that you had given the Testimony to Willie to give to Bro. Prescott, but that he had failed to do so, as he publicly stated before the Conference, thinking that the purpose of the Lord would be better served by his with-holding it, and allowing matters to proceed as they were. I have never been able to fully see through this. Do you give the directions as to when, how, in what order, and to whom, your writings shall be sent, or is it left for others to decide?

Near the close of this meeting at Berrien Springs, I was talking with Bro. J. E. White, concerning the unpleasantness that had arisen there, and he spoke very positively against his brother Willie and his relation to you, and how Willie was seeking to manage things in his way, and make them come his way, by his influence over you. When I asked him what this all meant, he answered that it meant one of three things—either

(1) That you would be removed from the midst of this confusion, so that your gift could not be used to further the purposes of your son Willie and others; or,

(2) That the gift would be taken from you, because men were perverting it; or,

(3) That is would be necessary for him to expose his brother, and others who were doing those things.

He further told me that it was almost impossible for him to see you alone, in California, when he went to see you; that Willie denied him the privilege of a private interview with his own mother.

I have since learned, Sister White, that this was told to many others besides myself, and can you wonder at the trouble and confusion that is abroad in the land, when your own son takes such a view of the matter?

I don't know what to make of such as this, but since you asked me to come direct to you with all that is bothersome, I could not be a Christian man and could not pray with my eyes upturned to heaven, unless I told you the whole story. I am writing in this letter all that bothers me personally, and in addtion, these other things that I am constantly meeting, and don't know how to explain.

Are the letters you write to the leaders in our work, in answer to letters they write, Testimonies? Must I receive everything you write, as from the Lord—just as it is, word for word—or are there communications you send out which are your personal letters,—personal communications from Sr. White? In view of all that has happended and is happening before my eyes, I am becoming unsettled with reference to this, and I ask for word *direct from you* that will clear up this confusion, and state the exact facts and truth.

In this connection, I will explain why I have never written to you or consulted you on any matter, even when so near you in California. I have wanted to, scores, yes hundreds of times, but years ago I took the position—and I know you will be free to tell me whether I am right or wrong—that men had no business tampering with God's messenger. I observed that when David went to Nathan seeking information concerning building the temple, he was told to build a temple. He knew Nathan was a prophet; he had confidence in the messages he gave. But immediately after, Nathan was instructed by the word of the Lord to forbid David's building the temple. From this, I concluded that God's messengers were for God to use, and not man; they were not to be used as *Intelligence Bureaus*, *Courts of Appeal*, or anything of that kind; therefore, I had no right to go to you for information. If it were human information and counsel I sought, I had better be on my knees seeking counsel from God; and if it were divine counsel I wanted, I reasoned that I would get it any way, without going to you for it; for when the Lord had shown you aught for me, you would write it out, and send it to me, without my writing to you. That is why, altho I have so highly appreciated your counsel and advice, which you often gave me in California, and which I can never forget,—I say, this is why, though often perplexed, I did not *write* to you for advice. I have often written to Bro. W. C. White, asking him if he knew anything that had been shown you along a certain line, and if he knew you had any light along that line, to send it to me; and occasionally he has sent me manuscripts and copies of your writings, in answer to such requests.

For one, Sr. White, I would like to see an earnest effort to get this matter straightened out among us. I know many who will stand up in public and say they believe the Testimonies, and try to drive other people into believing them as they do; yet I know, from personal conversation with some of these men, *they do not believe these Testimonies*. Some who are now talking so loudly for the Testimonies, are the very ones who first told me, in past years, that Willie influenced you, etc., and I see these people eating meat, and engaging in other things that are certainly contrary to the light you have so plainly given in the Testimonies. What am I to think?

Moreover, I have frequently been advised to "lay low", and be quiet; to say to the people "These things are all right" and smooth them over, but Sr. White, I can't do that. I have got to meet God before the judgment bar. I want to be right. I want to get out of this confusion into the clear daylight, and then stand like a man in defense of that which I know to be right; but I can't possess a double personality in this matter as it seems to me many are doing. I have kept still for many years, for *I believe the Testimonies*; and the only reason I am making a diligent effort to get to the bottom of these things, and get to the bottom *now, is that I am pressed on all sides to define my attitude concerning the Testimonies, and these difficulties that have arisen.*

Another question—I would like to know from you, as a minister, what use I am to make of the Testimonies as a test of fellowship? Is it right for me to baptize and receive people into the Church, who have not positively accepted the Testimonies? I refer, not to those who have rejected the Testimonies, but those who have not yet felt able to take their stand, yet are otherwise in harmony with the Third Angel's Message. What is my duty in this respect?

It has been reported to me—in fact was told me by a brother before I left San Francisco,—that you sent certain manuscripts to the Pacific Press, to be published, and after they were set up, in type, you recalled and materially changed them, so as to give them an entirely different meaning, and then they were published. Is this so? I didn't believe it when it was told me. The brother who told me said he could prove it, but I told him I was not looking for that kind of evidence. I have heard this many times since, and would like to know if this is so.

I have no inclination to go into these things, but in the fierce contention that is raging over these matters, it is necessary for me to go to the bottom of these things, in order to tell my brethren where I stand, that they may know whether they will choose to fellowship me or not.

I will not be a hypocrite. I will never say to my brethren that I believe *all* these things, unless I do; and I cannot conscientiously nor consistently say I do believe them *all*, till I have gone to the very bottom of every feature of our present misunderstandings.

This is a matter which circumstances have forced upon me and although it is exceedingly unpleasant, and though I would have much preferred to have gone about my work, and let the Lord work these things out in His own good time; yet I could not do this, in view of the situation in which I find myself, and more especially after you yourself personally addressed me, and straightly directed that all these difficulties should be sent direct to you. I am now fully and honestly complying with that request, and hope to get the desired and much needed light.

Another matter: What shall be my attitude toward those who hesitate in accepting a Testimony, or apparently reject the Testimonies? Shall I leave them alone with God and their Bibles, or shall I publicly denounce them, and make war upon them? Or shall I give them a little time in which to be led of God and be convicted by His Holy Spirit?

Another matter—the one that is most confusing of all to me, is your recent writings concerning the Battle Creek Sanitarium. I cannot possibly arrive at a conclusion as to just what you mean with reference to the helpers at Battle Creek, etc. From what the Lord has shown you, is it right for any Seventh-day Adventist to labor in the Sanitarium? Is the institution to be turned over to the world? What attitude should I take toward the situation that I find it in to-day? I fully understand that young and inexperienced workers are not to go there, and I fully agree with it; but does that mean *experienced* workers are not to go? I am perplexed to know what really is your present attitude toward the Sanitarium with reference to these matters.

Is it true that your Testimonies of recent date are any more of the Lord than older ones? Does a late Testimony abrogate all former communications touching the same theme?

Another thing: with reference to the American Medical Missionary College. The impression is going throughout our ranks that it would be better for students to go to outside medical schools than to this School. Now, Sr. White, I don't believe this. I am willing to be convinced, if I am wrong; but I have been in two outside medical schools, and cannot conscientiously advise any of our young people to go to these outside schools; and I have in my possession a communication from you, written 10 or 12 years ago, in which you forbid Dr. Kellogg and others to advise our students to go to Ann Arbor or other worldly medical schools. How am I to understand this former communication in which you forbid students to go to outside medical schools, and later ones which are interpreted as forbidding our people to go to the American Medical Missionary College? Where would you advise me to recommend Seventh-day Adventist young men and women to go to obtain a medical education? In view of what I have seen and heard in worldly medical colleges, I certainly could not conscientiously advise my sister to attend such schools, as long as our medical college is in existence. Now please help me to know what I am to do in this situation. This is just how it looks to me—I am ready to be set right if I am wrong.

Several years ago you sent a Testimony to the Conference concerning the Mt. Vernon Sanitarium, in which you stated that the Conference should not engage in establishing and conducting Sanitariums, yet now I observe that our entire denominational policy is that none but Conference committees and Conference organizations should own and conduct sanitariums; Is it wrong for earnest and well-meaning individuals to engage in private medical missionary work? Can I not be a part of the work of this Message along medical lines unless my work is owned and immediately supervised by the Conference? In view of the Mt. Vernon communication, I took my position on the subject: now, on what grounds am I to change?

Concerning the use of the word "denominational", I think there is great misunderstanding on the part of some as to exactly what you mean by this word. You have recently said concerning our medical work that it should be "denominational"; yet I have before me a communication addressed to "Dr. Kellogg and all who are connected with him in the Sanitarium Board and Council", dated Jan. Il, 1899, in which you speak of the medical missionary work as being "undenominational." If some knew just what you mean by the word, and in what sense it was used, I think it would clear up considerable confusion. The passage referred to, reads:

Our brethren in America who are engaged in medical missionary work can, by appealing to the outside people, obtain help, because theirs is not a denominational work.

Concerning Reform Dress and the change of instruction concernin-gits length, you wrote in the *REVIEW* and *HERALD* that the apparent dis-crepancy was due to the fact that the objects were presented to you, and you were left to describe them in your own language. Is your position today any different from that which you took then and which is stated in the article above referred to?

The article I refer to, is an answer to a question asked you, and appeared in the *Advent Review & Sabbath Herald*, October 8, 1867, and is as follows:

Does not the practice of the sisters in wearing their dresses 9 inches from the floor, contradict the Testimonies No. 11, which says that they should reach somewhat below the top of the lady's gaiter boot? Does it not also contradict Testimony number ten, which says that they should clear the filth of the street an inch or two without being raised by the hand?

Answer- The proper distance from the bottom of the dress to the floor was not given me in inches. Neither was I shown the ladies' gaiter boot; but three companies of females passed before me with their dresses as follows with respect to length: The first were of fashionable length, burdening the limbs, impeding the step, and sweeping the street and gathering its filth; the evil results of which I have fully stated. This class, who were slaves to fashion, appeared feeble and languid.

The dress of the second class which passed before me was in many respects as it should be. The limbs were well clad. They were free from the burdens which the tyrant, fashion, had imposed upon the first class, but had gone to that extreme in the short dress as to disgust and prejudice good people, and destroy in a measure their own influence. This is the style of the 'American Costume", taught and worn by many at "Our Home", Dansville, New York. It does not reach to the knee, I need not say that this style of dress was shown to me to be too short.

A third class passed before me with a cheerful countenance, and free and elastic step. Their dress was the length that I described as proper, modest, and healthful. It cleared the filth of the street and sidewalk *a few inches under all circumstances*, such as ascending and descending steps, etc.

As I have before said, the length was not given me in inches, and I was not shown a lady's boot, and here I would state that altho I am as dependent upon the Spirit of the Lord in writing my views as I am in receiving them, yet the words that I employ in describing what I have seen are my own, unless they be those spoken to me by the angel, which I always enclose in marks of quotation. As I wrote upon the subject of dress, the view of those three companies revived in my mind as plain as when I was viewing them in vision, but I was left to describe the length of the proper dress in my own language as best I could, which I have done by stating that the bottom of the dress should reach near the top of the lady's boot, which would be necessary in order to clear the filth of the street under the circumstances before named.

I put on the dress, in length as near as I had seen and described as I could judge. My sisters in Northern Michigan also adopted it, and when the subject of inches came up, in order to secure uniformity as to length everywhere, a rule was brought, and it was found that the length of our dresses ranged from eight to ten inches from the floor. Some of these were a little longer than the sample shown me, while others were a little shorter.

Numerous letters came to me from all parts of the field, inquiring the length of the dress shown me. Having seen the rule applied to the distance from the floor of the several dresses, and having become fully satisfied that nine inches comes the nearest to the sample shown me, I have given this number of inches in number 12, as the proper length of the dress in which uniformity is very desirable.

If it is said that a lady's boot is not nine inches high, I would say that I wear a boot eight inches high, and when I have walked before my sisters with it uncovered, as those properly dressed walked before me in the vision, they could not see the top of my boot.

In your writings you have stated that all the twelve disciples were present at the Last Supper; but in "Christ our Savior" it is stated that but eleven were present; Judas being absent. A number of years ago, I was told that your son made this change in the manuscript. Is this so? Does anyone have authority to in any way change your writings? To what extent and in just what way, are the Testimonies edited after they leave your pen, before they are crystallized into type?*

Now, Sister White, this is all I have to write. Of course there are scores of rumors in the air at this time, but I am not concerned with rumors. My wife and I are concerned, either personally or in the case of

---

*Curiously, as we noted in chapter 6, a similar confusion over "twelve" versus "eleven" occurred in the *UB* on page 1943. In the first edition, Jesus is said to address the twelve apostles at a time when Judas had clearly left. In later editions the word "twelve" was properly excised. Who had the authority to change twelve to eleven in one of Sister Whie's writings? Sadler wanted to know. Who had the authority to make a similar change in the *UB*?

very dear friends, with all I have written in this letter. The questions I have raised are those which must be speedily settled in our own minds. The situation we find ourselves in, demands it. Our souls desire it. But we cannot settle them until we know we are settling them rightly.

I stood unmoved for years in the face of many of these objections, but now the whole matter has taken such a peculiar turn that we find ourselves sorely perplexed, and are so persistently questioned concerning these matters, and in view of your invitation to write direct to you, if we had difficulties, I feel it is now my duty as a Christian and as a minister, to send to you the things which I have noted in this letter, and await from you that which the Lord may direct you to offer as a means of answering, explaining, denying, or otherwise making clear these things; and I shall forever appreciate anything you may do in this direction, and promise to give it careful and prayerful attention.

We have been made sad to learn of the terrible and disastrous earthquake in San Francisco; and just to think, we ourselves lived there but two short years ago! I see many evidences of the approaching end in the earth, not the least of which is the confusion that has come into our own ranks, and the unsettled condition in which I see many minds. I pray the Lord will guide His own people and bring them once more into unity.

It has saddened our hearts to see these difficulties and perplexities descend upon you in your declining years, and we would not add the least thing to your burdens if we could possibly help it, and would not lay these perplexities before you at this time, but for the reasons that you have requested it; that we must have them settled; and that we know of no other way in which they may be explained, and finally disposed of.

Mrs. Sadler joins with me in wishing you much of the sustaining strength and blessed ministry of our Master's good Spirit, and I remain

Most faithfully,
Your brother in the Work,
W. S. Sadler

Note that Sadler does not mention Sister White's plagiarisms. In view of Dr. Kellogg's interview, reported in chapter 4, it is unthinkable that Sadler would not know about them. Was it because he did not want to offend Mrs. White more than necessary, or was it because he did not find her stealing as objectionable as Dr. Kellogg did? As we shall learn in chapter 16, the *UB* swarms with plagiarisms identical in character with those of Ellen White.

Mrs. White never answered any of the "perplexities" of Sadler and his Battle Creek friends. On June 3, 1906, she issued the following statement:

For many months I have been troubled as I have seen that some of our brethren whom God has used in his cause are now perplexed over the scientific theology which has come in to lead men away from a true faith in God. Sabbath night, a week ago, after I had been prayerfully studying over these things, I had a vision, in which I was speaking before a large company, where many questions were asked concerning my work and writings.

I was directed by a messenger from heaven not to take the burden of picking up and answering all the sayings and doubts that are being put into many minds. "Stand as the messenger of God anywhere, in any place." I was bidden, and bear the testimony I shall give you. Be free. Bear the testimonies that the Lord has for you to bear in reproof, in rebuke, in the work of encouraging and lifting up the soul; 'teaching them to observe all things whatsoever I have commanded you: and, lo, I am with you always, even unto the end of the world.'

I quote from chapter 24 of Francis D. Nichol's *Ellen G. White and Her Critics* (1951). Nichol struggles valiantly to show that Sister White never went back on her promise to clear up the difficulties raised by Sadler and others, but he is unpersuasive. The evidence is clear. Mrs. White's second vision directly contradicted her earlier one. God first promised to help her answer all objections. Then when the Battle Creek brothers did exactly what she requested, God told her "Don't answer!" Mrs. White was typical of thousands of religious leaders down through the centuries who think God talks to them directly, and who invoke special communications from on high to justify their unwillingness to answer embarrassing questions.

Ten days later, on June 11, 1906, Sister White sent the following letter to Sadler and Dr. David Paulson:

Dear Brethren:

I have been working hard, and am weary; and yet I will not give up, for there is much to do. During the dedication of the Loma Linda Sanitarium, I spoke for a short time on the open platform on the lawn, while the wind was blowing. The exercises were very impressive. We also had an excellent meeting at the dedication of the Paradise Valley Sanitarium.

I am glad that these sanitarium properties have come into the possession of our brethren and sisters in the Southern California Conference. For years we have worked at a disadvantage; but now I am so thankful that in the providence of God many facilities have been placed within our reach, and we can encourage our brethren in Southern California to awake to their opportunities. Every one in that field should be grateful to God; for He has wrought for us in a remarkable manner.

The Sanitarium at Loma Linda is in need of larger quarters for their treatment-rooms. An addition for this purpose will be built this summer. The Paradise Valley Sanitarium has added a large wing to the main building, and is now provided with excellent treatment-rooms. The second story of the new part is finished for the accommodation of patients, but the third story is not yet finished. However, both institutions are in running order, and are making good use of the facilities they have.

Through circumstances that I could not well control, I have been suffering for some time from the weariness of constant anxiety. I am sensible of the fact that I am mortal, and that I must guard my physical, mental, and moral powers. The constant changing from place to place necessitated by travel, and the taking hold of public labor wherever I have gone, have been too much for me, in addition to the writings that I have been preparing day and night as the Lord has worked my mind by His Holy Spirit. And when I am meeting with evidences that these communications will be treated by some in accordance with the human judgment of those who shall receive them; when I realize that some are watching keenly for some words which have been traced by my pen and upon which they can place their human interpretations in order to sustain their positions and to justify a wrong course of action,—when I think of these things, it is not very encouraging to continue writing. Some of those who are certainly reproved, strive to make every word vindicate their own statements. The twistings and connivings and misrepresentations and misapplications of the Word, are marvelous. Persons are linked together in this work. What one does not think of, another mind supplies.

When the true converting power comes home to us as human agents, we see a power in God's plans, and embrace the evidence of the divine remedy for sin. "If we walk in the light, as He is in the light, we have fellowship one with another, and the blood of Jesus Christ His Son cleanseth us from all sin." I can rely wholly and unmistakably upon the sure Word of prophecy.

I am now carrying a very heavy burden for those who are lost in the mysteries of false science. I have had physical suffering of the heart; therefore I could not quickly answer the questions that you and Elder Sadler have presented to me. A severe cold has been upon me ever since the Loma Linda meeting. I assure you it is not because I do not respect you, Brethren Paulson and Sadler, that I do not answer your questions now. Pray for me, and I will pray for you; and as soon as I can, I will clear up, if possible, the misunderstandings regarding the work God has given me to do. Certainly a very great work is before us. I must now watch and pray and wait.

"And every man that hath this hope in him purifieth himself, even as He is pure."

Ellen G. White

One of the Battle Creek rebels, Dr. Charles Stewart, on May 8, 1907, sent Sister White (by way of her son) thirty typewritten pages raising serious questions about her integrity. He threatened to publish it if she did not reply in thirty days. She didn't. The letter was expanded to a pamplet of ninety pages and published in November, anonymously and undated, by "The Library Missionary Society, Post Office Box 239, Battle Creek." Titled *A Response to an Urgent Testimony from Mrs. Ellen G. White*, it came to be known as the "Blue Book." I have not seen a copy.

Several Urantians have said to me, "How is it possible that Sadler, a highly intelligent man, well acquainted with fraudulent and self-deceived mediums, could have come to believe that his brother-in-law was in genuine contact with celestial beings—and especially after having decided that Mrs. White was not always in touch with angels during *her* trances and dreams?" Indeed, Sadler believed in later years that Sister White's early visions were associated with epileptic seizures and would stop coming (as they did stop) when she passed menopause. Would not his disenchantment with Mrs. White have made it impossible for him to accept a new and different revelation channeled in a manner so similar to Mrs. White's revelations?

Here is my opinion. Sadler and his wife were devout Adventists until Sadler's early thirties when they were profoundly shaken by their awareness of Mrs. White's flawed testimonies. What was even worse, her refusal to admit her borrowings raised serious doubts about her honesty. I am convinced that this painful loss of a childhood faith left a huge void in the hearts of Sadler and Lena.

Like dedicated Communists who after learning of Stalin's crimes become Catholics, or like disenchanted Protestant fundamentalists who turn to Buddhism, Hinduism, or New Age concepts, I believe that Sadler, in his late thirties, sought desperately for a replacement of Mrs. White who would not disappoint him.

The Sadlers found this replacement in Wilfred, a relative they could not accuse of fraud. I believe that over a period of years they slowly became persuaded that Wilfred was the conduit of a new revelation superior to Adventism, though sharing a few basic Adventist doctrines. Just as James White, Sister White's husband, was indispensable in bringing his wife's revelations to humanity, so Sadler would be instrumental in bringing Wilfred's revelations to humanity.

I am convinced that in his older years Sadler thought of himself as chosen by God to carry this new epochal revelation to what he had always believed was a suffering, spiritually bankrupt world. Mrs. White's revelations were partly true and partly flawed. He, Sadler, would play a greater role in the world's religious history than Ellen White. So firm did this belief become, so dedicated and persuasive were the Sadlers in their hubris, that they managed to pass along this conviction to their son Bill, to their adopted daughter Christy, to hundreds of persons who moved in and out of the Forum, to the sons and daughters of Forumites, and to thousands of others who are today's Urantians.

In brief, I believe that Sadler, on a spiritual rebound from a lost love, came to think of himself as the prophet of a new and finer Christianity, a faith destined to cleanse the world and bring about a utopia of light and life.

14

Did Sadler Contribute to the Papers?
PART 1

There are many hints in the *UB* that a mortal, of whom Sadler is the most likely suspect, put into good English the early material channeled through Wilfred. We have mentioned before how we are told (*UB* 354) that the first 31 papers "were sponsored, formulated, and put into English" in 1934. Similar remarks about papers of the book's next two parts are made on pages 648 and 1319.

On page 1258 a remarkable passage appears:

> On many worlds the better adapted secondary midway creatures are able to attain varying degrees of contact with the Thought Adjusters of certain favorably constituted mortals through the skillful penetration of the minds of the latters' indwelling. (And it was by just such a fortuitous combination of cosmic adjustments that these revelations were materialized in the English language on Urantia.) Such potential contact mortals of the evolutionary worlds are mobilized in the numerous reserve corps, and it is, to a certain extent, through these small groups of forward-looking personalities that spiritual civilization is advanced and the Most Highs are able to rule in the kingdoms of men. The men and women of these reserve corps of destiny thus have various degrees of contact with their Adjusters through the intervening ministry of the midway creatures; but these same mortals are little known to their fellows except in those rare social emergencies and spiritual exigencies wherein these reserve personalities func-

tion for the prevention of the breakdown of evolutionary culture or the extinction of the light of living truth. On Urantia these reservists of destiny have seldom been emblazoned on the pages of human history.

Was there a "forward-looking" mortal, a member of the reserve corps of Urantia, who through his Thought Adjuster made contact with the secondary midwayers and materialized the *UB* papers in English? Clearly the person or persons who did this could not have included the sleeper because we are told by Sadler, in his appendix to *The Mind at Mischief*, that the sleeper had little interest in what he channeled, and in some cases the material was even contrary to his beliefs. This is reinforced by what the *UB* has to say about the sleeper on page 1208:

> The Adjuster of the human being through whom this communication is being made enjoys such a wide scope of activity chiefly because of this human's almost complete indifference to any outward manifestations of the Adjuster's inner presence; it is indeed fortunate that he remains consciously quite unconcerned about the entire procedure. He holds one of the highly experienced Adjusters of his day and generation, and yet his passive reaction to, and inactive concern toward, the phenomena associated with the presence in his mind of this versatile Adjuster is pronounced by the guardian of destiny to be a rare and fortuitous reaction. And all this constitutes a favorable co-ordination of influences, favorable both to the Adjuster in the higher sphere of action and to the human partner from the standpoints of health, efficiency, and tranquillity.

It is hard to believe that these statements apply to the "forward-looking personality." It seems to me that the forward-looking personality who put the papers into English was none other than Sadler himself.

I strongly suspect that Sadler is also referred to on page 1243 of the *UB* where it speaks of "a certain mortal [who] was recently admitted to the reserve corps of destiny." This particular man was so important to the fifth epochal revelation that "more than one hundred qualified seraphim sought the assignment" to be his pair of guardian angels. The two selected, we are told, were the "best adapted to guide this human being through his life journey."

Some of the terms in the first quoted passage need explaining. Midwayers are described at length in the *UB* on pages 862–67. The two main groups are called primary and secondary. Primary midwayers are closer to angels than to humans. Secondary midwayers are closer to humans than to angels. Both groups are midway between humans and angels, hence their name. Primary midwayers take orders from the Seraphim, and in turn give orders to secondary midwayers. Primary midwayers have difficulty contacting humans. Secondary midwayers, being almost human, have no such problem. They are in constant contact with us mortals, and can also interact with beasts and "material things." Through them contact was made with the "subject through whom these communications were transmitted."

Both orders of midwayers are nonmaterial and normally invisible to mortals. They neither eat nor sleep. They do not procreate. They come into being fully formed, rather than having evolved, although they grow "in wisdom and experience." Among them are "many great minds and mighty spirits." They "enter into the spirit of human work, rest, and play." They share our sense of humor and our worship. Secondary midwayers even have a kind of male/female distinction, often working in he/she pairs.

United Midwayers of Urantia, as their organization on our planet is called, have as their motto: "What the United Midwayers undertake, the United Midwayers do."

Originally 50,000 primary midwayers were assigned to Urantia; 40,119 joined the Caligastia secession, leaving 9,881 who remained loyal. The secondary midwayers on Urantia numbered 1,984 until 873 sided with the evil Caligastia. This left 1,111 secondary midwayers on our planet. They have been here for 35,000 years, "just outside the range of mortal vision."

Adding 9,881 to 1,111 gives, as the *UB* correctly states, 10,992 midwayers of both types on Urantia. They all have pledged not to leave the planet until released by higher authorities. Only one loyal midwayer, called "1-2-3 the first," has left. He lives now in Jerusem.

Many incidents in the New Testament, wrongly ascribed to angels and demons, were actually performed by loyal or disloyal midwayers. For example, loyal midwayers once released followers of Jesus from prison, and on another occasion delivered Peter from jail. Disloyal midwayers were responsible for New Testament accounts of demon possession. All these rebel midwayers have been held prisoners on another world since the Day of Pentecost. Since then they have been forbidden to enter into any human mind. Demon possession is therefore no longer possible. What today may be considered demon possession by fundamentalist Catholics and Protestants is no more than psychosis.

> Midwayers are the skillful ministers who compensate that gap between the material and spiritual affairs of Urantia which appeared upon the death of Adam and Eve. They are likewise your elder brethren, comrades in the long struggle to attain a settled status of light and life on Urantia.

The United Midwayers are a rebellion-tested corps, and they will faithfully enact their part in planetary evolution until this world attains the
goal of the ages, until that distant day when in fact peace does reign on
earth and in truth is there good will in the hearts of men.

Who belong to the reserve corps of destiny? The Chief of Seraphim
stationed on Urantia answers this question in Paper 114. They are the men
and women of each generation who are chosen by higher powers to assist
midwayers in their task of aiding evolving races. "As soon as men and
women appear on the stage of temporal action with sufficient mental
capacity, adequate moral status, and requisite spirituality, they are quickly
assigned to the appropriate celestial group of planetary personalities as
human liaisons, mortal assistants." These assistants are chosen because of
their "capacity for being secretly rehearsed for numerous possible emer-
gency missions," for their dedication to worthwhile causes, for their willingness to serve without recognition and rewards, and for the possession of
an advanced Thought Adjuster.

On Urantia, at the time the Chief of Seraphim wrote Paper 114, there
were twelve separate corps of destiny, with combined membership of 962
persons. The smallest corp had 41 members, the largest had 172. Among
the 962 were less than 20 "contact personalities." Secondary midwayers of
evolving worlds interact with contact personalities by "skillful penetration
of their minds." It was through such penetrations that the *UB*'s papers were
"materialized in the English language." This probably refers not to the
channelling by the sleeper, but to the reception, editing, and publication of
the channeled material by the "forward-looking" personalities in the
reserve corps of destiny. I have no doubts that Sadler, as the top member of
the reserve corps, believed his mind had been penetrated by midwayers
who authorized him not only to edit material coming through Wilfred, but
also to write portions of the *UB*.

When a member of the reserve corps dies, vital data from his or her
mind can be transferred to a younger successor by a liaison of two Thought
Adjusters. We are also told there is a group of a thousand mortals on
Urantia who make up an organization called the "cosmic reserve corps of
universe-conscious citizens." The Chief of Seraphim tantalizes us by saying he is forbidden "to reveal the real nature and function of this unique
group." Does it consist of select students of the *UB*?

It is surely clear that Sadler and other members of the contact commission, plus an unknown number of loyal Forumites, thought of themselves as belonging to the reserve corps of destiny. On page 1243 we learn

that the "destiny guardian of the human subject" used for the communication of Paper 113 is number 3, of group 17, of company 126, of battalion 4, of unit 384, of legion 6, of host 37, of the 182, 314th seraphic army of Nebadon. The assignment number of this destiny guardian is 3,641,852. This is also the number of the human contactee.

I asked Dr. Matrix, the noted numerologist who so cleverly analyzed Urantia's registry number (as explained in chapter 1), what he could make of the many numbers mentioned above. I will do my best to summarize the 30 pages Dr. Matrix faxed to me from his current home in Singapore.

Dr. Matrix began by noting that the seven numbers (3-17-126-4-384-6-37) add to 577, a prime. These seven numbers are followed by the six-digit number 182314 and the seven-digit number 3641852. Surely it cannot be a coincidence, Dr. Matrix reasoned, that 7, 6, and 7 count the number of letters in the names of Wilfred Custer Kellogg.

Consider, wrote Dr. Matrix, the following table:

1	2	3
4	5	6
8	A	B
C	D	E
F	G	H
I	J	K
L	M	N
O	P	Q
R	S	T
U	V	W
X	Y	Z

At the top of the table are the seven digits that appear in the two large numbers. For each letter in CUSTER and KELLOGG we have a choice of one of the two or three digits directly above it in the same column. You'll find that each of the thirteen letters in the two names has above it a digit that appears at the proper spot in the two numbers, with only one exception. The fifth digit of 182314 should be 3 or 6 instead of 1.

We know that mistakes occurred in some of the numbers cited in the first edition of the *UB*. On page 608 the number of Material Sons lost in the great Lucifer rebellion is given as 681,227. In the second edition this number was changed—I have no idea why—to 681,217. Was it to correct a printer's error? On page 486, "four thousand years" in the first edition becomes "forty thousand years" in the next printing. On page 477 "less than 1 / 2,000th" was altered to "more than 1/2,000th" in the second printing. On page 460 of the second edition we find that "sixty thousand" in the previous printing was changed to "forty thousand." "Secondary" became "tertiary" (413), and "Y" became "gamma" (474). Why were these changes made and who authorized them?

One would of course expect printer's errors to be inevitable in a book as massive as the *UB*, but such corrections (and there are more than a hundred) contradict the assertions, sometimes made by Urantians, that there was a miraculous absence of mistakes in the *UB*'s first printing.

We turn now to the sequence 3-17-126-4-384-6-37. Using the same key as before, the single digits 3-4-6 correlate with W, F, and E in WILFRED, but there seems to be no plausible way to correlate the other four letters. However, while this chapter was being written, Dr. Matrix faxed to me a truly amazing discovery. Assuming only one error in the seven numbers—6 should be 60—the letters of WILFRED can be obtained by applying the seven numbers, in a certain order, to the Bible's most famous, most quoted, best loved verse, John 3:16. The King James translation is as follows:

For God so loved the world that he gave his only begotten son that
whosoever believeth in him should not perish but have everlasting life.

The numbers are arranged 37-17-384-126-4-3-60. A count to the 37th letter ends at L. Seventeen more counts from L end on W. Continue 384 more steps (going back to the verse's beginning after you pass the end) and you reach E. A count of 126 arrives at F, 4 more at R, 3 more at D, and a final count of 60 goes to I. These are the seven letters of WILFRED!

The choice of John 3:16 for concealing the contactee's first name is appropriate because the verse has a special significance to both Seventh-day Adventists and Urantians. It clearly states that the unsaved will perish, not live forever. If the unsaved are to suffer forever in hell, surely their lives would be as everlasting as lives of the saved. The contrast with everlasting life is not everlasting torment, but everlasting death—a life cut off from existence "as though it had not been."

What should one make of all this? Dr. Matrix, the old scoundrel, is enormously skillful in juggling parameters so as to find amazing coincidences. We should not take them seriously. On the other hand, I firmly believe that 7, 6, and 7 *were* intended to count the letters of "Wilfred Custer Kellogg."

In view of Wilfred's pathological shyness it is unthinkable he would ever have allowed Sadler to identify him in the *UB* as the contactee for the new revelation. He could never have held up against the resulting publicity. We know he suffered throughout his adult life from stomach ulcers, a sign of stress and anxiety easy to understand considering the circumstances of his channeling. On the other hand, perhaps he did not wish to be forever unidentified as the contactee. It would be in keeping with his shy, secretive nature to provide, on page 1243 of the *UB*, the numbers 7, 6, and 7.

As for Dr. Matrix's technique of decoding those mysterious numbers, I suppose it is possible that Wilfred intended some of the correlations Dr. Matrix discovered, but carefully concealed them from other members of the Contact Commission. They would, therefore, be totally unaware of recording errors, and Wilfred would have been reluctant to call such mistakes to Sadler's attention. It is also possible that Sadler knew of the correlations, but that the Contact Commission decided to introduce a few errors to better conceal Wilfred's name.

Bill Sadler Jr. in his *Appendices to a Study of the Master Universe*, published posthumously in 1975, devotes pages 205–18 to the *UB*'s elaborate numerology, with special emphasis on 3 and 7. Dr. Matrix assured me that this section is much too trivial to be of interest. For example, in a section headed "interaction of 3 and 7," Bill missed completely the numerological significance of the number assigned to Michael (Jesus) on page 1513 of the *UB*. The number 611,121 is 3 times 7 times the prime number 29,101.

Dr. Matrix sent me other material on *UB* numerology which I have not given here. For example, he had a curious way of obtaining 666, the number of the Beast, from "533 Diversey Parkway," but I decided the technique was too far-fetched to include.

Among elderly Urantians who knew Sadler, several legends have taken shape about miraculous ways in which some *UB* documents came into Sadler's possession. Instead of being written or spoken by Wilfred, then typed by a secretary, it is claimed that Sadler once wrote down some questions and put them in his desk drawer. The next day, to his astonishment, the questions had been mysteriously replaced by answers. Sadler decided to make an experiment. He wrote another set of questions and put them in his safe deposit box at a Chicago bank. This was on Friday. Next Monday he opened the box. Again, the questions had vanished, replaced by handwritten answers. It is said that Sadler checked the handwriting against the scripts of those in the Contact Commission and the Forum. There were no matches.

Other anecdotes, even harder to believe, appear in Mark Kulieke's *Birth of a Revelation* (cited in chapter 7). These tales come, I am told, mainly from Meredith Sprunger and from a former Forum member, Carolyn Kendall. It is said that Sadler often put manuscripts in the bank's safety deposit box only to find them later edited by unknown hands. On one occasion, according to Sprunger, Sadler tried to tempt the revelators by putting ten-dollar bills between sheets. The original papers would vanish or be edited, but the bills always remained. As Kulieke adds, with no trace of humor, "The superhumans indicated they didn't have much use for money."

What is one to make of these miracle tales? There are four possible answers:

1. The unseen celestials sent material to Sadler by supernormal means. Sadler did not reveal this to everyone in the Forum because he knew it would be difficult for them to believe.

2. According to Kulieke, the bank's safety deposit box belonged to the Contact Commission. Now I never carry with me the key to my bank's deposit box, but keep it in the corner of a desk drawer. Surely everyone working at 533 would know where Sadler kept this key, particularly Wilfred who was Sadler's business manager. He handled Sadler's bank accounts and taxes, and probably was the person who made bank deposits and withdrawals. And I can't imagine Lena, Christy, and Bill Junior not knowing the whereabouts of this key.

Here is a plausible scenario. Someone in the Forum would feel indited by the midwayers to write a paper, but for one reason or another would not want Sadler to know who wrote it. The writer would give the manuscript to

Wilfred, or Bill, or Lena, or Christy, with a request for anonymity. Wilfred, Bill, Lena, or Christy would then put it in the Contact Commission's bank box without telling the doctor. Sadler would be genuinely mystified. This would allow him to write, as he did, that he himself did not fully understand how some of the papers were written and delivered.

Would it be reprehensible for, say, Christy to play such a trick on Sadler? Not necessarily. She may have justified the deception by reasoning that if she told Sadler how the document got there he would demand to know who gave it to her, and she would be obliged to tell. We know that Christy was capable of deception for what she thought were good reasons because of a letter that I reproduce in chapter 7—a letter denying that the appendix of *The Mind at Mischief* referred to either Ellen White or the *UB* transmitter.

3. Sadler made up these incidents, perhaps on the advice of what he believed was given him by midwayers, to conceal the fact that he and perhaps some of his relatives or friends, were writing certain papers and it would be unwise to reveal this to the Forum.

4. The miracle tales were myths conjured up by overzealous, imaginative Forum members to stress the supernatural aspects of what was going on. Today Sprunger, Kendall, and others are confusing false memories of having been told these myths by Sadler when actually they heard them attributed to Sadler by persons close to him.

I have in my possession a copy of a four-page, single-spaced document titled "How the Urantia Papers Came," written in the mid-1950s by one Webster Stafford, of San Francisco. It follows closely the account given in Harold Sherman's book, but contains additional anecdotes such as the following:

> Two years were consumed in questions and replies before the basic material started to come through. By this time a number of unusual phenomena—such [as]—that some of the answers or papers on the questions which were anwered in this two year period appeared in mysterious locations. For instance, sometimes the questions would be locked in a vault and the questions would mysteriously be removed during the night and a few days later the answers to these questions would appear on sheets of paper and in one instance, the answers appeared on the reverse or blank side of Western Union Telegraph blanks. However, it was interesting to note that the writing appeared right up to the point of the binding holding the sheets together in the pad to such an extent that it would be an impossibility for the human hand to write on a reverse side of a blank in a pad

without removing the pad from the binding. Then after considerable discussion between the "student visitor" and the observers or questioners seated during the periods of discussion the matter reached a climax in which the "student visitor" told the listeners that he had been instructed to tell them that he had received permission to give to them over a period of time a number of treatises or papers dealing with various subjects and that they would commence immediately delivering them such that they would be of benefit to all mankind.

Stafford goes on to say that the papers appeared regularly until 1941, to be followed by two to four years of revisions in which some of the papers were withdrawn. Many corrections were made and certain papers rewritten.

A small number of the individuals involved in the work were told that if they would appear at a specific location on the shore of Lake Michigan at a particular time that they would be permitted to see a seraphic departure. This they did and they saw passing through the sky a cigar-shaped conveyance lighted in which a number of Deities were supposed to be and were being transposed to another planet or universe.

Before he died Stafford gave a copy of this history to his friend Benjamin Adams, pastor of the Trinity Baptist Church in San Francisco. Reverend Adams submitted the document to Bill Sadler Jr. At the top of the document Adams wrote in longhand Bill's response: "Mr. William S. Sadler, Jr., declares that this account is largely fictional in nature. As his father is the Dr. 'S' of this narrative, we have no alternative but to accept his statement. The question still remains, however, as to how 'fictional' it is."

Obviously there is no way to know how fictional. Sadler never put these events in writing, nor am I aware of any early letters by Forumites that document such alleged supernormal occurrences.

When information is channeled during a trance, either through spoken or written words, it never emerges in a form as polished and consistent as the Urantia papers. Christy must have done some editing when she typed up the revelations, and there is little doubt that Sadler, perhaps others on the Contact Commission, edited the material in the light of suggestions by

Forum members. Such editing could then be authorized by reading the revised papers to the revelators by way of a sleeping Wilfred, or by personal contacts which Sadler and others felt they had with midwayers. The only question is: how much did Sadler and others add? Sadler could say truthfully that he did not write the papers, but that would not exclude the practice of substantial editing, cutting, and adding, then obtaining the approval of the midwayers for such changes.

Harold Sherman informs us, as I mentioned earlier, that he once tried to interest Christy in having a paper on ESP and other psychic powers included in the *UB*. Christy suggested to Sherman that if he would write such an article, she would submit it to the revelators for their consent to put in the *UB*. If this is true, and I have no reason to doubt Sherman, large portions of the *UB*, including entire papers, could have been written by Sadler or other mortals close to him, then authenticated by reading them to the sleeping Wilfred.

On page 1319 of the *UB* is this cryptic addendum:

> This paper, depicting the seven bestowals of Christ Michael, is the sixty-third of a series of presentations, sponsored by numerous personalities, narrating the history of Urantia down to the time of Michael's appearance on earth in the likeness of mortal flesh. These papers were authorized by a Nebadon commission of twelve acting under the direction of Mantutia Melchizedek. We indited these narratives and put them in the English language, by a technique authorized by our superiors, in the year CE 1935 of Urantia time.

"Indited" is a word used many times in the *UB*. It means "to write down," but we know from pages 84, 1618, 1848, and 1972, that in the *UB* it also means to be inspired to do this by a higher being. If Sadler wrote the above paragraph, he could be saying that he was inspired by a midwayer to write this particular paper.

Dr. Jacques Rhéaume, a former Catholic priest now living in Quebec, was for four years a good friend of Urantian Meredith Sprunger. He became convinced that Sadler wrote part of the *UB* under the belief he was indited to do so. This contention is defended in the more than 700 pages of Rhéaume's doctoral thesis, titled *Analyse d'un texte révélé: The Urantia Book* (Analysis of a Revealed Text: The Urantia Book.) It was written in French in 1983 for the University of Ottawa. In 1990 Dr. Rhéaume summarized his thesis in a paperback booklet, *Le Verbe s'est fait livre* (The Word Has Been Made Book), published in Quebec as Number 9 in a series of booklets on new religions. I agree completely with Rhéaume. I am convinced that Sadler was entirely capable of writing large portions of the *UB*, integrating them with the elaborate cosmology and mythology that had earlier been channeled by his sleeping brother-in-law.

My main reason for believing this is that too much material in the *UB* comes straight out of early books written by Sadler. Urantians who know about this rationalize it by saying that Sadler got his ideas from the revelators, then put them into his books. My experience has been that Urantians who make this claim have not yet obtained and read the books by Sadler in question.

Consider the strong emphasis in the *UB* on eugenics. Many *UB* pages advocate using eugenics to eliminate from Urantia a growing number of feeble-minded and other genetically inferior persons. As we have seen, Sadler's mentor, John Kellogg, was an ardent advocate of eugenics. Sadler himself wrote two books defending eugenics: *Racial Decadence: An Examination of the Causes of Racial Degeneration in the United States* (1922), and *The Truth About Heredity* (1927). His controversial opinions are repeated, sometimes almost word for word, in the *UB*.

Sadler's wife Lena shared her husband's enthusiasm for eugenics. Her paper "Is the Abnormal to Become Normal?" was first read before the Illinois Federation of Women's Clubs on May 19, 1932, and printed in the *Illinois Medical Journal* (September 1932). The same paper can also be found in *A Decade of Progress in Eugenics* (Williams & Wilkins, 1934), a collection of papers given at the Third International Congress of Eugenics held in New York in August 1932. Lena issues a stern warning against the increasing racial degeneration of America and recommends severe eugenic measures to stem the tide. The following paragraph is a sample of Mrs. Sadler's rhetoric:

> Here we are coddling, feeding, training, and protecting this viper of degeneracy in our midst, all the while laying the flattering unction to our souls that we are a *philanthropic*, charitable, and thoroughly Christianized people. We presume to protect the weak and lavish charity with a free hand upon these defectives, all the while seemingly ignorant and unmindful of the fact that ultimately this monster will grow to such hideous proportions that it will strike us down, that the future descendants of the army of the unfit will increase to such numbers that they will overwhelm the posterity of superior humans and eventually wipe out the civilization we bequeath our descendants; and all this will certainly come to pass if we do not heed the handwriting on the wall and do something

effectively to stay the march of racial degeneracy, for it is said that even now three-fourths of the next generation are being produced by the inferior one-fourth of this one.

A federally enforced sterilization law, Lena declares, "would result, in less than one hundred years, in eliminating at least 90 percent of crime, insanity, feeblemindedness, moronism, and abnormal sexuality, not to mention many other forms of defectiveness and degeneracy. Thus, within a century, our asylums, prisons, and state hospitals would be largely emptied of their present victims of human woe and misery. The indigent and aged paupers and the unfortunate degenerates of various types would disappear as a troublesome factor in civilized society."

On page 33 of *Racial Decadence*, Sadler used the same ten-percent figure for the proportion of our nation's "unfit" that should be sterilized. As for moral unfitness, Sadler firmly believed that "morality is hereditary" (page 131), and that "some races are more moral than others" (page 128).

If you are interested in refuting the crude eugenic views of the Sadlers, John Kellogg, and the *UB*, I urge you to read Allan Chase's 734-page work, *The Legacy of Malthus: The Spiritual Cost of the New Scientific Racism* (University of Illinois Press, 1980). On page 27 Chase calls Lena "an irascible Chicago surgeon." On pages 327–28 he accuses her of a form of infanticide. Not that she recommends murdering unfit babies, you understand, but in her shameful 1932 speech she actually opposed the practice of trying "to save every weak child that is born into the world" by giving free medical help to welfare mothers!

As late as 1936, when Sadler's massive *Theory and Practice of Psychiatry* was published, he was still recommending sterilization of inferior stock to prevent America's rapid racial deterioration:

> If we should thus conscript our degenerates—sanely classify and properly employ, incarcerate, or sterilize them—within a very few decades most of our charities, which are dealing largely with problems resulting from feeblemindedness, would go out of business; most of our jails and brothels would be empty; our courts would languish for want of cases; and fully two-thirds of our philanthropic and reformatory work having to do with poverty, vice, intemperance, delinquency, and crime would presently stop for want of the feebleminded grist which today keeps these mills of charity grinding.

When Sadler wrote *Racial Decadence* in 1922 the belief that America's genetic heritage was going downhill as a result of the rapid birthrate of blacks and the influx of inferior racial stocks from abroad was a popular doctrine, not only among eugenicists but also among journalists. The best-selling book of the period was Lothrop Stoddard's *The Rising Tide of Color Against White World Supremacy* (1920). The book was so influential and widely read that F. Scott Fitzgerald, in the first chapter of his masterpiece *The Great Gatsby* (1925), has Tom Buchanan make a thinly disguised reference to the book:

> "Civilization's going to pieces," broke out Tom violently. "I've gotten to be a terrible pessimist about things. Have you read 'The Rise of the Coloured Empires' by this man Goddard?"
>
> "Why, no," I answered, rather surprised by his tone.
>
> "Well, it's a fine book and everybody ought to read it. The idea is if we don't look out the white race will be—will be utterly submerged. It's all scientific stuff; it's been proved."
>
> "Tom's getting very profound," said Daisy with an expression of unthoughtful sadness. "He reads deep books with long words in them. What was that word we—"
>
> "Well, these books are all scientific," insisted Tom, glancing at her impatiently. "This fellow has worked out the whole thing. It's up to us who are the dominant race to watch out or these other races will have control of things."

I have not read Stoddard's best-seller. It would be interesting to determine how much Sadler cribbed from it. Note his use of "tide" in the following paragraph which closes the preface of *Racial Decadence:*

> And, therefore, while not considering these matters in too grave a light, but at the same time taking the mission which he has endeavored to fulfil in this and subsequent volumes quite seriously; it will be apparent that if but a little bit has been contributed to the clarification of these basic problems which confront the nation; if but a mite has been added to aid in solving the menacing difficulties discussed in this work; if but even a trifle has been added to the final turning of the tide of evil influences which jeopardize the white races in general and the American stock in particular, then will we have been repaid manifold for the research and other efforts entailed by the writing of this book.

Both "one hundred years" and "ten percent" turn up in the *UB* (818) in a paper describing the creation of a democratic socialist utopia on a planet incredibly similar to Urantia in its ethics and politics: "Efforts to prevent the breeding of criminals and defectives were begun over one hundred years ago and have already yielded gratifying results. There are no prisons and hospitals for the insane. For one reason, there are only about ten percent as many of these groups as are found on Urantia."

Which is more likely—that the Sadlers got these figures from the revelators, or that they worked their way into the *UB* because they were Sadler's opinions?

The *UB* (771) tells us that the birth rate of subnormal persons should be kept by the state just low enough to produce as many subnormals as needed for tasks that require an intelligence slightly about that of beasts. This, too, was Sadler's opinion.

In *Racial Decadence* (page 183) Sadler stresses the "inverse ratio" between the genetic health of persons, families, and peoples, and "the number of years they have been away from the soil."

This same inverse ratio is in the *UB* (768–770) where Melchizedek emphasizes what he calls the "land-man ratio" that underlies all civilizations. "Human society is controlled by a law which decrees that the population must vary directly in accordance with the land arts and inversely with a given standard of living." On page 886 the Chinese are praised for having a low "land-man ratio." On page 770 we are warned that the "worst traits of human nature" arise when population increases and the land yield is reduced.

I urge Urantians to read sections in the *UB* (see "Eugenics" in the *Concordex*) where eugenics is stoutly defended, then obtain and carefully read Sadler's *Racial Decadence*. Which is more plausible? That Sadler took his eugenics views from the revelators, or that Sadler put into the *UB* the long-held views of Kellogg and himself, then sought Melchizedek's approval?

Racist opinions, so characteristic of eugenics enthusiasts, are to be found both in Sadler's *Racial Decadence* and in the *UB*. On page 725 of the *UB* we learn that the black race is inferior to red Indians. On page 585 we are told it is good to have a eugenics program to eliminate inferior racial strains. The reason this is difficult to do on Urantia is that we lack judges competent to rule on the "biologic fitness or unfitness of the individuals in your world races." Again: "Notwithstanding this obstacle, it seems that you ought to be able to agree upon the biologic disfellowshiping of your more markedly unfit, defective, degenerate, and antisocial stocks." Disfellowshiping is an unusual word. Seventh-day Adventists use it as a synonym for excommunication.

On page 764 of the *UB* Australian natives and the Bushmen and Pygmies of Africa are called primitive races, "miserable remnants of the nonsocial peoples of ancient times." Their nature is backward, suspicious, antisocial. The Bushmen are again called an "inferior race" on page 1132. These statements reflect Sadler's opinion that such primitive cultures, as well as the African blacks, are genetically inferior to whites.

Should we feel remorse about a eugenics program to eliminate such low-grade races? Should we feel remorse about abolishing degenerate strains in our society? We should not, Sadler repeatedly says in *Racial Decadence*. Eugenics is a truly altruistic enterprise." Here is how the *UB* says the same thing on page 592:

> An idiot does not have much chance of survival in a primitive and warring tribal social organization. It is the false sentiment of your partially perfected civilizations that fosters, protects, and perpetuates the hopelessly defective strains of evolutionary human stocks.
>
> It is neither tenderness nor altruism to bestow futile sympathy upon degenerated human beings, unsalvable abnormal and inferior mortals. There exist on even the most normal of the evolutionary worlds sufficient differences between numerous social groups to provide for the full exercise of all those noble traits of altruistic sentiment and unselfish mortal ministry without perpetuating the socially unfit and the morally degenerate strains of evolving humanity. There is abundant opportunity for the exercise of tolerance and the function of altruism in behalf of those unfortunate and needy individuals who have not irretrievably lost their moral heritage and forever destroyed their spiritual birthright.

Which is more plausible: that Sadler was influenced by celestial beings to write *Racial Decadence*, or that his long-held views about the altruism of eliminating the unfit were put by Sadler into the *UB*?

Sadler vigorously opposed most racial intermarriage. "For obvious reasons," he wrote in *The Truth About Heredity* (page 275), "intermarriage between diverse races is to be deplored—particularly races of different color."

> These investigators conclude that intermarriage is extremely undesirable in the case of races who are so far separated in their traits and tendencies that intermarriage would result in the breaking down of inherent and valuable characteristics in both races, practically speaking, such marriages as would ignore the color line. Such intermarriages would tend to disrupt the long-continued association of certain mental and physical traits, which

have been long established and co-ordinated by heredity, and which have been confirmed by hundreds of generations of "natural selection." And of course, from the standpoint of eugenics, it is to be deplored when one of the races would be inferior as compared with the other, which happens to be the biologic fact as concerns the White and Negro races in this country. (page 272)

In *The Truth About Heredity* (page 187) Sadler said it this way:

The barrier of race has much to do with restricting natural selection, particularly in cases where the races are of different color, or in other ways greatly unequal, as in the case of the Negroes and the Whites.

Both Sadler and the *UB* (920) distinguish between racial interbreeding of superior stock, which can be beneficial, and racial interbreeding of a superior race with an inferior race, which can only be disastrous. Here are some passages from the *UB* (526, 719, 726, and 920, respectively):

But while the pure-line children of a planetary Garden of Eden can bestow themselves upon the superior members of the evolutionary races and thereby upstep the biologic level of mankind, it would not prove beneficial for the higher strains of Urantia mortals to mate with the lower races; such an unwise procedure would jeopardize all civilization on your world. Having failed to achieve race harmonization by the Adamic technique, you must now work out your planetary problem of race improvement by other and largely human methods of adaptation and control.

And thus it has ever been on Urantia. Civilizations of great promise have successively deteriorated and have finally been extinguished by the folly of allowing the superior freely to procreate with the inferior.

Stronger and better races are to be had from the interbreeding of diverse peoples when these different races are carriers of superior inheritance factors.

And the Urantia races would have benefited by such an early amalgamation provided such a conjoint people could have been subsequently effectively upstepped by a thoroughgoing admixture with the superior Adamic stock. The attempt to execute such an experiment on Urantia under present racial conditions would be highly disastrous.

Mixtures of the white and black races are not so desirable in their immediate results, neither are such mulatto offspring so objectionable as social and racial prejudice would seek to make them appear. Physically, such white-black hybrids are excellent specimens of humanity, notwithstanding their slight inferiority in some other respects.

What advice does the *UB* give on how subnormal persons are to be treated?

The normal man should be fostered; he is the backbone of civilization and the source of the mutant geniuses of the race. The subnormal man should be kept under society's control; no more should be produced than are required to administer the lower levels of industry, those tasks requiring intelligence above the animal level but making such low-grade demands as to prove veritable slavery and bondage for the higher types of mankind. (*UB* 771)

On page 812 we learn that on a nearby planet, where life is incredibly similar to life on Urantia but more advanced, habitual criminals and the incurably insane are put to death in gas chambers. Result? No prisons or hospitals for the insane. "Numerous crimes aside from murder, including betrayal of government trust, also carry the death penalty" (*UB* 818). These were Sadler's opinions. Did he get them from Melchizedek of Nebadon, or did Melchizedek pick them up from Sadler?

In both the *UB* (918–919) and in Sadler's two books about genetics we are told that marriages between cousins will improve a race if both persons are of "good stock." "If the heredity is good," Sadler writes, "there is no scientific objection." We have earlier remarked that Sadler could hardly have said otherwise in view of the fact that his wife's sister was married to her first cousin, Wilfred. Indeed, as we saw in that chapter, the *UB* has the same view about cousin marriages.

Sadler's ugly race views were earlier evident in his 1918 book *Long Heads and Round Heads, or What's the Matter with Germany?* According to Meussling's doctoral thesis on Sadler, he had first delivered a talk on this subject. The nation's Secretary of State was so impressed that he asked Sadler how long it would take to turn his speech into a book. Sadler said he could do it over a week-end. The book reads as if he did.

Dedicated to the nation's soldiers and sailors, the book is a passionate defense of our war against Germany. To explain what is wrong with the enemy, Sadler draws heavily on two books: Madison Grant's *The Passing of a Great Race*, and Henry Fairfield Osborn's *Men of the Old Stone Age*.

Dr. Sadler's racial views, as well as those of the *UB*, were heavily influenced by Grant, a New York attorney and blatant racist. His most influential books were *The Passing of a Great Race* (1916) and *The Conquest of a Continent* (1933). Both books had introductions by Osborn.

America, Grant claimed, was originally settled by a superior stock of Protestant Nordics—a stock rapidly being debased by interbreeding with inferior immigrant aliens. Unless we stem this "hybridization," America will go the way of ancient Rome. Blacks, Grant believed, were inferior to all other races. Their mental abilities, he wrote, "are in pretty direct proportion to the amount of white blood [a black] has." Even a mulatto with enough white blood to "pass," still has traits that "may insidiously go back to his black ancestry, and may be brought into the White race in this way."

How did Grant wish to solve the "Negro problem"? Our nation should enact strict laws against black-white marriages, and work hard to educate the Negro in birth control techniques that would slow down his rapid breeding.

As we shall see in chapter 16, the *UB* swarms with passages plagiarized from other books. Sadler himself liked to pilfer. Consider the following sentence by Grant: "The cross between a white man and a Negro is a Negro; the cross between a white man and a Hindu is a Hindu; and the cross between any of the three European races and a Jew is a Jew." (I quote from a chapter on racism in my 1952 book *Fads and Fallacies in the Name of Science* where I devote two pages to Grant.)

Here is how Sadler said the same thing in a passage from *Long Heads and Round Heads* that I will quote again later: "The cross between a white man and a negro is not a white man, but a negro. The cross between a white man and a Hindu is a Hindu; and a cross between any of the three more modern European races and a Jew is always a Jew." The copying is almost word for word!

Sadler finds Germany dominated by two main races:

1. The Nordics or Teutonics, who tend to have blonde hair, fair skin, and blue eyes. They also have long (dolichocephalic) heads. Nordics are highly intelligent. The world's greatest military leaders, statesmen, explorers, organizers, and inventors, Sadler is convinced, were all Nordics. He cites as examples: Cyrus, Alexander, Caesar, Charlemagne, and Napoleon. Among German leaders in 1918 he singles out the superior Nordic brain of General Von Ludendorff in his caption for the general's photograph.

2. The Alpines who tend to have round (brachycephalic) heads and dark eyes. Sadler reminds us that most mammals and all apes have dark

eyes. "It is, therefore, the opinion of most authorities that the primitive races of mankind had dark eyes."*

Most importantly, Alpines are a stupid, genetically inferior, brutish race. In the past they were mostly farmers. The book has a photograph of Germany's Field Marshall Von Hindenburg seen by Sadler as a quintessential Alpine. The caption calls him "force personified, dominant, brutal, devoid of idealism and with little or no imagination."

Ancient Rome's rulers were all Nordics, Sadler assures us, but Rome fell because of the decay that followed a rapid increase of inferior stock. Germany today is suffering a similar racial degeneration. Its superior Nordic stock began to decline after the shameful Thirty Years' War. Since then, Alpines, and other inferior strains, have become dominant. Although many military leaders are still Nordics, the majority of soldiers are stupid, round-headed, vicious Alpines. This explains "The brutal German joy of battle, the love of atrocity, and delight in suffering and torture."

Only about 10 percent of Germany is now Nordic, Sadler writes. Nordics still form the nation's upper class. "They are the same Germans as the chivalrous knights of old. They are of the kind-spirited people that gave us the Christmas tree with its tender sentiments and spiritual associations." Alas, round-headed Alpines now dominate the fatherland. They are a threat to everything we hold dear. The book closes with 25 reasons why America must win the war.

Our nation has not yet gone as far as Germany in racial degeneration, but Sadler fears it is slowly moving in the same direction. The original American colonies, he tells us, were largely Nordic, as were the early settlers of Canada. After the Civil War, waged by Nordics on both sides, there was a great influx from Europe of genetically inferior strains. Sadler quotes with approval the following lurid paragraphs from his mentor Madison Grant:

> The result is showing plainly in the rapid decline in the birth-rate of native Americans because the poorer classes of Colonial stock, where they still exist, will not bring children into the world to compete in the labor market with the Slovak, the Italian, the Syrian, and the Jew. The native American is too proud to mix socially with them and is gradually withdrawing from the scene, abandoning to these aliens the land which he conquered and developed. The man of the old stock is being crowded out of many

---

*Black and white photographs of Sadler show his eyes as gray. One Urantian who knew Sadler recalls his eyes as blue-gray, another thinks they were light green. In any case, they were not dark. Bill Sadler Jr.'s eyes were bright blue.

country districts by these foreigners, just as he is today being literally driven off the streets of New York City by the swarms of Polish Jews. These immigrants adopt the language of the native American; they wear his clothes; they steal his name; and they are beginning to take his women; but they seldom adopt his religion or understand his ideals, and while he is being elbowed out of his own home, the American looks calmly abroad and urges on others the suicidal ethics which are exterminating his own race.

Blacks present a special problem for the United States. Here is what Sadler has to say about them:

The doctrine that the negro slave of Civil War days was an unfortunate distant cousin of the white man, who had simply been deeply tanned because he had long lived under the tropical sun, and that his social and intellectual status was entirely the result of being denied the privileges of civilization and the blessings of Christianity, is still believed by many honest and well-meaning sentimentalists. This was the prevailing sentiment in Civil War days, and, mind you, I believe the Civil War was worth fighting either to save the Union or to free the black man. The black man deserved his freedom, but it has taken the white people of America almost half a century to wake up to the fact that more or less political freedom, a little education, good clothes, and ability to speak and write English and go to church has not been able to transform the negro into a white man or even into a black man with anything like equal powers and prerogatives of citizenship; and we are going to have similar experiences in this country with our Polish and Russian Jews and other Balkan immigrants. *The unfortunate thing about the "melting pot" is that it does not melt. Race is still the determining factor of civilization and citizenship.*

Our neighbor Mexico, too, is suffering from racial decline:

What the "melting pot" actually does, and what it threatens to do in this country, can better be seen by an ethnic study of Mexico and its people. Here the blood of the original Spanish conquerors (who, like all the world's explorers, were Nordics) has been absorbed by the inferior native Indian population, resulting in a race admixture which we now observe in the present-day inferior Mexican people; and from the days of Rome down to the present, these mongrel types have always represented retrograde movements in the civilization of the day.

It must be borne in mind that some of the more desirable specifications in the civilized races are of relative recent origin, and that when two greatly dissimilar races mix, the usual result is a quick gravitation downward to the more ancient, primitive, and lower type of man. The cross between a white man and a negro is not a white man, but a negro. The cross between a white man and a Hindu is a Hindu; and a cross between any of the three more modern European races and a Jew is always a Jew. In crossing the more recent blonde Nordic race with the older brunet Mediterranean race, it will be found that the older brunet type predominates. If the thoroughbred, blue-eyed Nordic man marries a thoroughbred, black-eyed Mediterranean woman, the children will all have either black or dark-colored eyes. There will be no blue-eyed offspring, and we must recognize that all the ministrations of a Christian civilization, and all the environment and education of democratic institutions, cannot now or ever will be able to alter these fundamental laws of human heredity.

It is worth mentioning in passing that Sadler's remarks about the Neanderthals and Cro-Magnon races, in *Long Heads and Round Heads*, closely parallel similar remarks in the *UB*. In both books the Neanderthals are called "great hunters." In both books we learn how they used reindeer for food and clothing, about their work with flint, their primitive religion, their final extinction by the Cro-Magnons, and the replacement of the superior Cro-Magnons by inferior breeds.

I am indebted to Douglas Hackleman for sending me copies of a fascinating exchange of letters between Dr. John Kellogg and Ales Hrdlicka, a distinguished anthropologist on the staff of the Smithsonian Institution. In a letter of April 1, 1918, Kellogg wrote: "I am sending you with this a little book entitled, 'Round Heads and Long Heads'. I think the author of this work has no scientific standing. I do not myself know enough of the subject to know whether there is any basis for his contention. If you can find time to just glance at the book and give me your opinion of it, I shall be very much obliged."

Dr. Hrdlicka replied (April 6):

Your favor of April first as well as the little book received, and I have read the latter from the beginning to the end. The author has made a very unfortunate step in invading the field of anthropology, of which evidently he is wholly ignorant, and of attaching himself to the wagon of Mr. Madison Grant with all his bias. The result is that whatever relates to the subject which is expressed by the title of the book is a mess of trash, and will seriously effect [sic] the rest of the little work which if published separately would have done some good. My first intention after reading the book was to write an appropriate review of it for our Journal: but it would have to be made so severe that it could only result in making an enemy which is better to be avoided. The anthropological part of the book is so bad that it will be condemned by all better instructed men anyway.

To this letter Dr. Kellogg responded (April 8):

I have yours of April 6.
    Your opinion of the book is what I thought it would be. It is, as you say, most unfortunate for a person to undertake to dogmatize in a field of which he is entirely ignorant.
    I wish you would reconsider your determination not to make a review of the book. It seems to me such literature ought to be condemned by competent authority. The author of the book has not any influence in circles that will do you or the *Journal of American Anthropology* any harm whatever. An authoritative criticism such as you would give would prevent commendatory notices by a considerable number of journals, the editors of which are as ignorant as the author of the book, and thus would prevent the extension of the vicious errors.

Which is more plausible? That Sadler's extreme opinions about heredity, race, and eugenics were derived from higher intelligences speaking through Wilfred or directly to Sadler by way of his Thought Adjuster and the Midwayers, or that these dreadful opinions somehow went from Sadler and his wife into the *UB*? There is no hint in Sadler's 1918 book that his views came from any other source than Grant and other writers of the time who were leaders of the eugenics movement.
    A careful reading of *Long Heads and Round Heads* will reveal many similarities with statements in the *UB*, not only in an overall stress on eugenics and racial degeneration, but also in many small details. We read on page 897 of the *UB* that the Adonites were round-headed and the Nordics were long-headed. Their descendants, we are told, are the two major races of Germany today. On page 898 we learn that the Cro-Magnon, or blue race, survives today among the Berbers, a Caucasian race in North Africa. On page 27 of *Long Heads* we find: "The Cro-Magnon type of head is almost identical with that of the present-day living Berbers."
    It has long been suspected, mainly because of the swarthy skin and facial characterstics of Ellen and her twin sister, that Mrs. White was part black. Although Adventist researchers have traced her family tree back for four generations, nothing has been published about the racial status of these ancestors. Almost all black Adventists take her Negroid blood for granted. It is known that she grew up in a poor section of Portland, Maine, known

as Moose Alley—an area largely populated by blacks. No photograph of Ellen's mother is known to exist, unless the Adventist church is keeping one under lock and key.

It is possible, I suppose, that antagonism between Sister White and Sadler may have played an unconscious role in Sadler's low opinion of black intelligence, or perhaps it was the other way around. Sadler strongly opposed black/white marriages. If Sister White's father was white and her mother black, and Sadler learned of this, it could have influenced his growing disenchantment with Adventism.

Whenever I call a Urantian's attention to the racist elements so plainly present in the *UB*, I am always reminded that the *UB* also says that all races are equally loved by the Gods and are part of the great brotherhood of man. I am not impressed by this argument. In the days of American slavery, when almost everyone in the south considered blacks mentally and morally inferior to whites, leading ministers were forever saying that of course God and Jesus love black men and women every bit as much as they love white people. However, because of their genetic inferiority, God intended the blacks to be slaves. The argument goes all the way back to Aristotle who defended Greek slavery on somewhat similar grounds.

When Sadler published *Modern Psychiatry* (1945)—the book is a condensed version of his earlier textbook *Theory and Practice of Psychiatry*, with very little change of wording—he seems to have abandoned most of his extreme views about race and eugenics. However, traces remain. On page 187, for example, repeating word for word a sentence in his earlier textbook, we find: "Like persons, races have their characteristic behavior, their attractive and repulsive traits." This follows a paragraph in which Sadler speaks of the unusually high rates of alcoholism and senility among the Irish, the tendency of Jews to become drug addicted and to suffer from manic depression and schizophrenia. Italians are, he says, "high in both schizophrenia and epilepsy," and blacks are high in "general paralysis and other disorders resulting from syphilis." More whites commit suicide than blacks, the English have a predisposition toward dementia praecox, and "the neuroses are more frequent among the Latin and Jewish peoples than in the northern European races." Sadler clearly regards all these predispositions as genetic.

Eugenics has been a topic of bitter controversy ever since British scientist Francis Galton suggested a century ago that the human race could be improved by selective breeding. The movement crested in the 1920s only to sink to a low after the discovery of how the Nazis had carried human breeding to horrific extremes in their efforts to eliminate Jews, Gypsies, and others they considered mentally or physically unfit. Stephen Jay Gould's *Mismeasure of Man* has become a classic attack on how easily genetics can be misused.

In recent years, as progress continues rapidly on mapping the human genome, eugenics is again fashionable. Many biologists now argue that feeblemindedness and even criminal behavior may be linked to genes. The prospect of improving humanity by selective breeding, as Kellogg and Sadler so enthusiastically recommended, continues to be controversial. There may be a consensus on negative eugenics for getting rid of hereditary diseases, both physical and mental, but intelligence is on a continuum, and there is little agreement on what behavioral traits, if gene linked, should be deemed undesirable.*

As for positive eugenics, the breeding of "superior" traits, there is even less consensus. Who is to decide what traits are superior? Do we want people to be taller, or whiter, or more heterosexual? Aldous Huxley's *Brave New World*, and H. G. Wells's *Island of Doctor Moreau*, may soon no longer be fantasies. The future is surely going to demand agonizing political decisions for which traditional religions and ethics offer no guidance.

---

*For an excellent overview giving pros and cons, see John Horgan's "Eugenics Revisited," in *Scientific American* (June 1993).

15

Did Sadler Contribute to the Papers?
PART II

Among all scientific claims set forth in the *UB*, the claim that most clearly reflects Sadler's own early opinions is the claim that evolution was non-Darwinian. As we said in a previous chapter, Darwinian evolution assumes that species evolved slowly, over thousands of years, by a steady accumulation of small changes. Darwin wrote, of course, before mutations were discovered. In modern evolutionary theory it is a gradual buildup of small changes in the DNA molecule that cause the slow formation of a new species.

The *UB*'s picture of evolution is quite different. Species are repeatedly described as arising "suddenly" from single mutations. Andon and Fonta, the first humans, were the result of just such a sudden genetic leap that distinguished them from their apelike parents.

In *The Truth About Heredity* (1927) Sadler devotes several chapters to evolutionary theory—chapters in which he defends a view proposed by the now forgotten Hugo de Vries (1848–1935), a Dutch botanist at the University of Amsterdam. De Vries spent years cultivating the evening primrose, so called because its yellow blossoms unfold in the evening. Some of the variations he produced were so different from their ancestors that he believed them to be new species. To these suddenly appearing "sports" he gave the name "mutations." In 1900 he published a collection of essays titled *Mutationstheorie*, or *Mutation Theory* in its English translation. After lecturing in America on his theory, he gathered a larger number of papers into a 1903 book later published in English as *Species and Varieties: Their Origin by Mutation.*

De Vries agreed with Darwin that natural selection, over enormous time periods, produced variations in a species, but never a brand new species. Such species, he argued, appeared at one bound, the result of a single mutation. Here are two quotations from *Mutation Theory*:

> The new species appears all at once; it originates from the parent species without any visible preparation, and without any obvious transition forms.

> New elementary species arise suddenly, without transitional forms.

De Vries's evidence for his theory was shaky, based as it was on observing a single plant species, but it had a considerable vogue around the world for more than 20 years, especially among botanists who hailed it as a major revision of Darwinism. This is how Sadler saw it in 1927 when he wrote *The Truth About Heredity.* "Mutation teaches that new types arise suddenly from the parent species," he wrote on page 212, "and not gradually as the result of a series of accumulated small variations." According to Sadler, de Vries's theory was "the greatest biologic advance since Darwin's day."

De Vries's theory was shortlived. The noted American zoologist Samuel Jackson wrote: "De Vries's *mutationstheorie* gained acceptance, especially in America, with a rapidity which was quite unjustified. It was regarded with extreme suspicion by most students of taxonomy and distribution." The primroses de Vries thought were new species were merely "sports," like a four-leaf clover. They did not arise from any change in the genes.

The notion that new species arise by sudden leaps was older than de Vries. As I mentioned earlier, the Catholic biologist St. George Mivart, a student of Thomas Huxley, advocated it in his 1871 book *The Genesis of Species.* Oswald Spengler, in volume 2, chapter 2, of his famous *Decline of the West* (1922), defended just such leaps. "The first proof that the basic forms of plants and animals did not evolve but were suddenly there," he said in a footnote, "was given by H. de Vries in his *Mutation Theory.*"

Erwin Schrödinger, one of the great architects of quantum mechanics, has high praise for de Vries in his famous series of lectures titled *What Is Life?* The lectures were published as a book in 1944. Schrödinger attributes the "jumps" of evolution to quantum jumps in genes; indeed, he calls de Vries's mutation theory the "quantum theory of biology," even though quantum mechanics was only two years old when de Vries first published his discovery.

Some more recent biologists have defended similar views, notably the geneticist Richard Goldschmidt, a German refugee from Hitler who became a professor at the University of California, in Berkeley, where he died in 1958. His controversial book *The Material Basis of Evolution* (1940; reprinted in 1982 with an introduction by Stephen Jay Gould) divided large mutations into two groups. Most of them produced "hopeless monsters" that quicklydied off because the changes were disastrous, but a small fraction of "hopeful monsters" became new species that survived. As Gould points out in an essay on Goldschmidt (in *The Panda's Thumb*), hopeful monsters were really not much different from their parents. Creationists like to caricature Goldschmidt's views by crediting him falsely with saying that a reptile's egg suddenly hatched into a bird with feathers. If changes were that abrupt, Gould asks, with whom would the hopeful monster mate?

De Vries's theory, and its reflection in the *UB*, is now totally discarded. It has nothing in common with Gould's "punctuated equilibrium" theory in which jumps take place over periods of thousands of years as a result of a sequence of small mutations. As I earlier remarked, these are "jumps" only in the sense that they are rapid relative to much longer periods of gradual change. But Sadler's enthusiasm for de Vries's flawed conjecture was unbounded. If you count the number of times he uses the words "sudden" and "suddenly" in his 1927 book, you'll find it almost equals the number of those words in the *UB*.

I suppose some Urantians will maintain that "suddenly," as used on the *UB*'s pages about evolution, should be taken as long periods of time in conformity with punctuated equilibrium. This is not possible. It obviously has the same meaning in the *UB* as it had for de Vries and Sadler. We are told, for example, that the first "true bird" made its "*sudden* appearance" 55 million years ago when it "sprang directly from the reptilian group" (*UB* 691). No reasonable interpretation of "sudden" is possible here because we know that birds took millions of years to evolve from reptiles. Much more likely is the intended meaning that the first true birds were hopeful monsters hatching from reptile eggs.

Reptiles themselves, we learn from the *UB* (686), appeared "*suddenly*" in "full-fledged form," which hardly suggests a slow transition over millennia. On many pages the *UB* is similarly specific. The first multicellular animals (*UB* 673) popped up "*suddenly* and without gradation ancestry." On page 691 we learn that "*Suddenly* and without previous gradation, the great family of flowering plants mutated." On page 693 we are told that the first placental animal "sprang directly and *suddenly*" from a reptilian ancestor. "The father of the placental mammals was a small, highly active, carnivorous, springing type of dinosaur." No chance for gradation here! The mutant jumps onto the stage in a single generation.

On page 701 we learn that 500,000 years ago the six colored races "mutated from the aboriginal human stock," and that this change occurred "*suddenly* and in one generation." And there is no denying that the *UB* describes the first true humans as abrupt mutants from apelike parents.

Which is more plausible? Did the revelators insert de Vries's false theory into the *UB*? If so, what purpose did this serve? Or did it slip into the *UB* by way of Sadler's enthusiasm for a theory popular at the time, and which seemed to allow for divine intervention in the process of evolution on Urantia?

The *UB* puts great stress on the benificent effects of humor and play, especially on pages 547 and 550. "Joyful mirth and the smile-equivalent," we are told, "are as universal as music." Humor and play are also essential aspects of life on higher morontia worlds. We cannot fully appreciate the advanced spiritual humor of those worlds, although it resembles the humor of our "higher types of humorists." Unlike so much crude humor on Urantia, it is never blasphemous, nor does it ever exploit the misfortunes of "the weak and erring."

Primitive races, the *UB* says, had no capacity for humor, nor is humor necessary among residents of Paradise. On levels in between, however, there is "increasing need for the mission of mirth and the ministry of merriment." Here on Urantia humor is often crude and inartistic, but "it does serve a valuable purpose both as a health insurance and as a liberator of emotional pressure, thus preventing injurious nervous tension and overserious self-contemplation." Humor and relaxing play are essential, not only on Urantia, but also on other worlds as we ascend toward Paradise. We will "enjoy the celestial equivalents" of our "earthly humor all the way up through" our "increasingly spiritual careers."

Sadler placed a similar stress, in all his mental health books, on the values of play and laughter. In *The Physiology of Faith and Fear*, published in 1912 but probably written before Wilfred began channeling, we find this paragraph (page 379):

> Laughter and light-heartedness seem to be a real value in the treatment of these melancholic subjects of chronic fear. They seem to serve the purpose of relieving the "attention spasm"; they get the mind off itself for a moment, and contribute greatly to one's ability to take up a new line of thought.

Worry and Nervousness (1914) has an entire chapter on play. "Good cheer, laughter, and light-heartedness seems to be of real value in the treatment of nervous states; they seem to relieve the attention spasm, they serve the purpose of getting your mind off yourself." (page 482).

In *The Mind at Mischief* (1929) the following paragraphs appear on page 61:

> 8. *Humor*—Humor is probably founded on the basic emotion of elation connected with the inherent instinct of self-assertion. We no doubt feel just a bit superior to everything that excites our humor, tho the element of surprise also may contribute to our laughter. There is also an element of rivalry in humor. We enjoy a joke just a little better when we have gotten the best of the other fellow. We laugh more heartily when the other fellow steps on a banana peel than we do when we pass through the same experience ourselves. There is an element of vanity in humor, and probably some pride, tho we must admit that of all human emotions, more particularly sentiments, this one of humor is the most difficult to define. I am not at all satisfied with any definition that has thus far been formulated. There is an undoubted temperamental bias to all our humor.
>
> Like play, humor is consistently the hand-maiden of joy. Seldom, if ever, does good humor culminate in sorrow. Humor is a sentiment peculiarly and exclusively human, and a "good story" can always be depended upon to promote good fellowship and develop the cheery side of human nature.

Here is a paragraph from *Piloting Modern Youth* (1931), written by Sadler and his wife:

> Many adolescents are prone to worry. They take the little happenings in their lives altogether too seriously. Sometimes this worry borders almost on despondency—at least temporarily; these overburdened youth are often all but melancholic. They worry about a great many physical con-

ditions—their appearance, facial blemishes, pimples, freckles, and so on. I think many of them worry because there is not enough variety in their lives; there is lack of interest because things are too monotonous. These overserious youth should be early encouraged to improve their sense of humor, to learn to tell funny stories. Humor is the saving grace of many a home, and a life preserver to tide over these serious young people to later years of increasing self-understanding and better appreciation of the values and relationships of human affairs.

Sadler's most ambitious work, *Theory and Practice of Psychiatry* (1936), has these passages:

> *Humor* is very difficult to define or comprehend. It seems to be in some way associated with the blunders of living. We take particular delight in the mistakes of others, especially of our would-be superiors. The crusader, the overambitious, the depressed, and the melancholic seldom enjoy humor. They are too much absorbed in what they are doing, thinking, or feeling. All nervous patients take themselves too seriously and, instead of enjoying a practical joke, are more likely to resent it as a personal insult.
>
> *By the cultivation of a sense of humor we enhance our social value;* we greatly enlarge our social opportunities, for most people show a preference for the society of their humorous fellows. It is the jocose individual who is most spontaneous, creative, happy, cheerful, broad-minded and tolerant. There is a refreshing and charming spontaneity about humor that makes such individuals unusually attractive.
>
> "A merry heart doeth good like a medicine." Good humor is a protection against taking oneself too seriously. The sense of humor is the best single criterion of the patient's psychopathology, and it also serves as a very reliable indicator of the degree of recovery of patients who are undergoing prolonged courses of treatment. No person who laughs at himself is very far from being passably normal.
>
> Nervous patients should be encouraged to tell funny stories. I make a practice of having many of my pupil-patients initiate each office consultation by narrating a humorous story. Great progress has been made when they learn how really to laugh at their fears, phobias, and compulsions.
>
> 7. A Sense of Humor.—Those who lack a sense of humor will make a sad mess of the ministry of mental hygiene. First, they will become so overburdened by the tribulations of their subjects that they will be in imminent danger of breaking down or blowing up. Second, they cannot help that

vast army of suffering mortals who take themselves and everything in life too seriously. Humor is contagious, but the melancholic patient is not going to catch it from a doctor who hasn't it.

Last but not least, see that a proper vein of *humor* runs throughout the rest cure. The patient should be swapping funny stories with his nurse or attendants. Encourage a rest-cure patient to indulge the "sense of the ridiculous." *Laughter is a mighty curative agent.* As a therapeutic procedure it may be somewhat crude and uncouth in its expression, nevertheless, there is efficacy in that little motto which we see hanging on the barber shop wall, "Smile, damn you, smile."

From *Modern Psychiatry* (1945):

VI. Humor—The antidote for taking one's self—even one's religion—too seriously.
     Humor is hard to define, but everybody knows what it is, and all of us know how to enjoy a good story when it is well told. People who have a well-developed sense of humor are not so likely to overwork and destroy their health. They are not likely to become social snobs. If you have a good sense of humor, you are not going to take your religion too seriously—you will not become overconscientious or fanatical. Humor and religion are both superanimal emotions.

The above paragraph is repeated, almost word for word, in *Mental Mischief and Emotional Conflicts* (1947). Sadler had a habit of constantly cribbing from his earlier books.
     Which is more credible: that Sadler got his notions about the importance of humor and play from the revelators, or did humor and play go from Sadler to the *UB*?

Free will is another attribute of human nature strongly emphasized in the *UB*. The emphasis is equally strong in the writings of Mrs. White, and one would expect it to be reflected in the opinions of Wilfred Kellogg and Dr. Sadler, both ex-Adventists. Here is how Sadler expressed it in his 1912 book *The Physiology of Faith and Fear* (page 470):

The Almighty, who gave existence to the human mind, never compels man to surrender or submit to anything against his own individual will, not even to the influence of the Divine Mind. God seems to possess such a respect for the will of man that He is more willing that man should do wrong (sin and have his own way), than do right (God's way) by coercion or compulsion.

Similar statements occur throughout Sadler's books. I will give only one more example, this from *Worry and Nervousness* (1914), page 289:

We believe that human beings are free moral agents, kings and queens in their own domains and that the Creator never intended that our minds should submit to be dominated by, be dictated to, or be controlled by any mind in the universe except that of man's Maker.

Another notion strongly defended in both the *UB* and in Sadler's early writings about religion is the distinction between faith and belief. "The acceptance of a teaching as true is not faith," says Melchizedek of Nebadon (*UB* 111), "that is mere belief." Compare this section, headed "Faith and Belief," with the way Sadler contrasts the two frames of mind on pages 315–16 of *The Physiology of Faith and Fear*. This book was written, in my opinion, more than eight months before Wilfred began channeling. The book's preface is dated January 1, 1912, so it must have been written much earlier.

"Faith means more than belief," Sadler writes. "To believe a thing is merely to accept it by our reason. . . . Faith calls for a complete and unconditional surrender of one's whole body, soul, and spirit, to the idea or thing which is believed in." Note that Sadler, like the *UB*, here distinguishes the body (including the brain), from a person's soul and spirit, distinctions retained from his Adventist past.

Let's turn now to economics and politics. One would assume, as all biologists do, that if intelligent life has evolved on other planets it would be wildly different from any life we know on earth. This view is even supported in the *UB* (667) where we are told by a Life Carrier that "Urantia life is unique, original with the planet. . . . There is no other world in all Satania, even in all Nebadon, that has a life existence just like that of Urantia."

Now consider Paper 72, to me one of the funniest papers in the *UB*. Supposedly transmitted by Melchizedek of Nebadon, it describes the political and social life on a planet "not far distant" from Urantia. We are not told the name or location of this planet. Yet its history and social organization so closely resemble that of Urantia that one suspects Melchizedek, having a weird sense of humor, of playing a gigantic hoax on *UB* readers.

Melchizedek's paper is confined to just one continent of our sister planet. The continent is about the size of Australia and supports a population of 140 million. Races are mixed, but they get along harmoniously. The average life span of a person is ninety years. Kings and rulers on the sister planet came and went until monarchy finally gave way to a unified, democratic, continent-wide nation. Its democracy is precisely the kind of government toward which Sadler hoped Urantia was moving.

There are three main divisions of government: executive, legislative, and judicial. The chief executive is elected every six years by universal suffrage. He (no mention is made of a possible she) is not eligible for reelection unless this is approved by at least 75 of the nation's 100 states. No third term is permitted.

The nation's legislature has three houses. Its judicial system consists of municipal and state courts, and a federal supreme court of twelve judges. Each judge must be older than 40 and younger than 75. Their decisions require a two-thirds vote. Voting rights among citizens begin at 20. Voting is compulsory. The right to marry without parental consent begins at 25. Children must leave home before they are 30. Although divorce is easy, there is only one-tenth the number of divorces there as here.

Education is compulsory. Persons of subnormal intelligence are segregated in colonies where sex for procreation is forbidden. Their work is confined to farming and animal husbandry. Everyone has to take a month's vacation every year. There are no churches, but people believe in God, and there is a "strange overlapping of religion and philosophy."

Capital and labor are antagonistic, but slowly learning how to cooperate. Slavery was abolished a hundred years ago. Wages and prices are not rigidly controlled, but there is a certain amount of government regulation. Workers have a five-day week, four of work, one of play. A working day is six hours. Citizens are increasingly enthusiastic about travel as a result of recent developments in new methods of transportation.

Two hundred years ago the profit motive dominated industry, but it is now giving way to more altruistic incentives. Public service is rapidly overcoming greed, and a public distrust is rising over both "idleness and unearned wealth."

"Self-respect-destroying charity" is being replaced by government entitlement programs. Every child is ensured an education, every adult is guaranteed a job, and medical care is provided for all the "infirm and aged." People retire at 65, though they can obtain state permission to continue working until they are 70. Federal funds for old-age pensions are taken from wages, from bequests by the wealthy, from compulsory labor, and from income from government-owned natural resources.

Imported goods are subject to protective tariffs. During peace, military service in four-year hitches is voluntary. The nation keeps a strong military establishment. There have been no civil wars since the continent developed a unified central government, but during the past two centuries the nation has waged nine "fierce defensive" battles, three of which were world wars. "When war is declared, the entire nation is mobilized."

The society and government of this nation, so incredibly like the United States, is superior to those of any Urantian nation. However, on the eleven other continents governments are "decidedly inferior to the more advanced nations of Urantia." So far, no "magisterial Son," such as Michael (Jesus) has come to the planet. Should one do so, "great things could quickly happen on this world."

I have touched only the highlights of a 13-page paper. It is impossible for me to conceive how an intelligent reader of the *UB* could seriously take this paper as describing actual life on another planet. It clearly is a statement of an earthling who would like to have his nation's social and political life carefully ordered. To suppose that a nation so similar to ours is flourishing on a planet not far away strains all credulity.

In 1942 Random House published Emory Reves's widely praised little book, *A Democratic Manifesto*. If you read this book carefully, you will find in the *UB* (1487–1491) a crisp, excellent summary of the arguments for a world state that are at the heart of Reves's book.

First, some statements from the *UB:*

War on Urantia will never end so long as nations cling to the illusive notions of unlimited national sovereignty.

Urantia will not enjoy lasting peace until the so-called sovereign nations intelligently and fully surrender their sovereign powers into the hands of the brotherhood of men—mankind government. Internationalism—Leagues of Nations—can never bring permanent peace to mankind. World-wide confederations of nations will effectively prevent minor wars and acceptably control the smaller nations, but they will not prevent world wars nor control the three, four, or five most powerful governments. In the face of real conflicts, one of these world powers will withdraw from the League and declare war. You cannot prevent nations going to war as long as they remain infected with the delusional virus of national sovereignty. Internationalism is a step in the right direction. An international police force will prevent many minor wars, but it will not be effective in preventing major wars, conflicts between the great military governments of earth.

Peace will not come to Urantia until every so-called sovereign nation surrenders its power to make war into the hands of a representative government of all mankind. Political sovereignty is innate with the peoples of the world. When all the peoples of Urantia create a world government, they have the right and the power to make such a government SOVEREIGN; and when such a representative or democratic world power controls the world's land, air, and naval forces, peace on earth and good will among men can prevail—but not until then.

These forty-eight states, having abandoned the twin sophistries of sovereignty and self-determination, enjoy interstate peace and tranquillity. So will the nations of Urantia begin to enjoy peace when they freely surrender their respective sovereignties into the hands of a global government—the sovereignty of the brotherhood of men. In this world state the small nations will be as powerful as the great, even as the small state of Rhode Island has its two senators in the American Congress just the same as the populous state of New York or the large state of Texas.

Now for some passages from Reves's book:

THE GOLDEN CALF to which the most devoted and mystic adoration of the masses goes in our days is: Sovereignty. No symbol carrying the pretension of a deity, which ever got hold of mankind, caused so much misery, hatred, starvation and mass execution as the notion "Sovereignty of the Nation."

Only if we are decided to enact international laws having the same characteristics as national laws, binding all nations, or at least a certain number of nations, can we lay the foundation for a peaceful development in international relations. Any conception of peace without mandatory international law is a hopeless dream. The criterion of any realistic interpretation of peace is its foundation on law.

The usual distinction between national law and international law, the former having coercive force, the latter without such coercive force, is a purely theoretical definition. It has no practical value whatsoever.

"International law," as we know it, is merely a system of norms, customs, rules, treaty obligations, without compulsive power. It is no law at all. It is a game. To call it "law" only makes the problems of international relationship even more confused.

The section in the *UB* that defends movement toward a world state is in Paper 134 of the book's Jesus section. We do not know when this section was written, but it was surely composed at a time when there was much tak about a world state as the only hope for permanent peace. In England, such prominent thinkers as H. G. Wells and Bertrand Russell had been preaching world government for decades. Wendell Willkie, the Republican nominee for president in 1940, wrote a book titled *One World*. Several American organizations were devoted to the ideal of world government, even planning a constitution and a flag for it.

Clyde Bedell, in his angry reply to the chapter about Urantianism in Harold Sherman's book, did not deny that there are striking parallels between the *UB*'s pleas for a global government and Reves's book. I could not, however, find any places where actual sentences or even phrases were copied. It is more a case of repeating the same arguments with occasional use of similar words. The *UB*, for example, speaks of war as a "symptom" of the disease of national sovereignty (*UB* 1491). Reves (page 134) also calls war a "symptom" of the struggle between sovereign nations.

Urantians are, of course, not in the least dismayed to find the revelators making use of published books—we cover this in our next chapter—but in the case of Reves's book, there is a distressing difficulty. The book was not published until 1942. Urantians believe the Jesus papers were written well before 1940. If the author of Paper 134 was heavily influenced by Reves's book, which seems so apparent, it would date the Jesus papers later than 1941.

We know that Sadler was impressed by Reves's book because in the foreword to *Prescription for Permanent Peace* (1944), written near the end of World War II, Sadler praises Reves's *Democratic Manifesto*. In a paragraph of acknowledgments he includes it among the books from which he quotes. The foreword also thanks "my long-time associate Wilfred C. Kellogg" for "having contributed many valuable suggestions."

The parallels between passages in Paper 134 and those in *Prescription for Permanent Peace* are actually much closer than the parallels with Reves's book. Indeed, Paper 134 reads as if Sadler is simply summarizing the themes of his 1944 book. Like Reves, Sadler pleads passionately for a world government as the only hope of preventing future wars. He repeatedly calls this a "Mankind Government." Note that this phrase is also in

Paper 134 (page 1489) in a paragraph I quoted earlier, as well as on pages 1490 and 1491.

Sadler's central themes are as follows. After winning the war America must abandon her schizoid inability to decide between isolationism and world leadership. If Uncle Sam fails to take the lead in working for a world government, "Uncle Ivan" will. (Curiously, Russia is repeatedly praised as a nation of democratic freedoms and good will!)

"The Soviet Union is now moving rapidly toward democracy," Sadler wrote on page 86, at a time when Stalin's ruthless dictatorship showed no signs of abating. "We anticipate no quarrel with Russia," he said on page 174, and predicted that after the Second World War ended, "Russia will continue to stand by our side in peace as in war" (176).

Mankind Government, Sadler writes, should have its own capital city, its own flag, seal, and anthem. It should run an international bank and a press for issuing international books, newspapers, and magazines. There should be a world language used by Mankind Government, such as basic English or maybe Esperanto. It would, of course, have an army to keep the peace. The United Nations are a step in the right direction, but much longer steps are needed. Other responsibilities of Mankind Government are relief for victims of fires, floods, famines, and earthquakes. It also must work actively toward improving "human stocks" and preventing racial degeneracy.

Here are two of many quotations from Sadler's book that are closely paraphrased in the *UB*'s Paper 134:

> Nationalism, or sovereignty, has really become a sort of pagan god to many peoples. While the forty-eight American states talk about "state sovereignty," they know it is only in a limited sense that they are sovereign, since these forty-eight states are subordinate in many matters to the Federal government. In this same way must the nations of this world ultimately unite and associate themselves in a global government.

> There can be no lasting peace so long as unlimited sovereignty, extreme nationalism, imperialism, and unrealistic ideas of self-determination continue to govern the foreign policies of nations. Some better basis for international relations must be instituted if there is to be an end to war.

As in his earlier 1918 book about Germany, Sadler continues to regard Germany as suffering from paranoia, egotism, envy, irrationalism, delusions of grandeur, Teutonic cruelty, and a complete lack of humor, but there are no references to the nation's long heads and round heads. Sadler also has grown beyond the crude racism in his earlier books. There are no disparaging remarks in *Prescription for Permanent Peace* about Jews and blacks, although Sadler has an annoying habit of always referring to the Japanese as Japs.

Which is more plausible? That Paper 134 was composed by celestial beings who had read Sadler's book and the books from which he borrowed, or that Sadler, perhaps with the help of Wilfred, wrote Paper 134?

Many of Sadler's "self-help" books were written in collaboration with his wife. There are passages in the *UB* so similar to advice given in popular books by the two Sadlers as to suggest that Lena may have had a hand in producing some of the Urantia papers. Consider, for example, this passage from *Piloting Modern Youth* (1931), by Sadler and Lena, in a chapter titled "A Chapter for Fathers":

> Too many American fathers are guilty of neglecting their families; they are altogether too much occupied with business. They work away from home at the office or factory. Too many come home only a few evenings a week, and then perhaps only to eat, dress, and take the family to the movie or some other form of entertainment. They play away from home at the club or at golf. Too little do they plan to be with the children at home or to play with them now and then on the family outings.

Compare this with the following paragraph from the *UB* (531):

> No ascending mortal can escape the experience of rearing children—their own or others—either on the material worlds or subsequently on the finaliter world or on Jerusem. Fathers must pass through this essential experience just as certainly as mothers. It is an unfortunate and mistaken notion of modern peoples on Urantia that child culture is largely the task of mothers. Children need fathers as well as mothers, and fathers need this parental experience as much as do mothers.

Which is more likely: that the above lines were written by a Brilliant Evening Star or by Sadler and/or his wife? We are told that the Brilliant Star merely "sponsored" the paper. Could this mean that the Star asked the Sadlers to write the paper, then authenticated it?

Computer programs have become common in recent years for determining whether two documents were written by the same or by different authors. The technique is usually based on the average frequency of such "marker" words as *and, the, but, which, that, however,* and so on. Attempts have been made to apply such checks to the *UB*. One effort, by Ken Glasziou and his son, in Maleny, Australia, concluded that at least five, possibly nine, persons had a hand in writing the *UB* papers. The results are summarized in "The Book," an article by the elder Glasziou in an international Urantian newsletter called *Six-O-Six* (May/June 1993), published in Frankston, Australia.

The evidence is unquestionable that Sadler edited and revised material coming through Wilfred or written by himself and others. This would give the *UB* its remarkable consistency. In addition to the statistical analysis by the Glaszious, another approach strikes me as equally fruitful, if not more so. It involves going through Sadler's many books to check unusua words and phrases, then determining how often those words and phrases occur in the *UB*. The results of my random search for seldom used words, and Leo Elliott's search for phrases of two or more words, have yielded astonishing results. A preliminary report on this ongoing project is given in Appendix E.

Many ideas about religious faith and prayer, in Sadler's very early books, parallel ideas expressed in the *UB*. Elliott called my attention to the following passage on page 476, from a chapter on "Prayer the Master Cure," in Sadler's *The Physiology of Faith and Fear* (1912). The identical paragraph is also in Sadler's *Worry and Nervousness* (1914, pages 491–92).

> True prayer is a sort of spiritual communion between man and his Maker, a sympathetic communication between the soul and its Saviour. We do not look upon prayer as a means of changing God's will. The Divine Mind does not need to be changed; He is ever beneficent and kindly disposed toward mankind. While prayer does not change God, it certainly does change the one who prays, and this change in the mind of the praying soul is sometimes immediate, profound, and often wholly inexplicable.

Here is how the author of a paper on prayer in the *UB* (998) said it:

> Remember, even if prayer does not change God, it very often effects great and lasting changes in the one who prays in faith and confident expectation. Prayer has been the ancestor of much peace of mind, cheerfulness, calmness, courage, self-mastery, and fair-mindedness in the men and women of the evolving races.

How do Urantian true believers react when confronted with so many ideas and so many seldom used words and phrases in the *UB* that are also found in Sadler's books? The most common rationalization is that Sadler picked up these ideas, words, and phrases from the supermortals! This is Meredith Sprunger's opinion. In a letter to me he said he himself in his writings frequently used words and phrases from the *UB*. Ken Glasziou told me, also in a letter, that I would have a good case for Sadler's editing of the Papers only if I could find similar words and phrases in books written by Sadler *before* the revelations began. Glasziou is among those who think the channeling began in 1906. Sadler's first two books, *The Science of Living* and *The Cause and Cure of Colds*, were published in 1910, so obviously there is no way to meet this challenge.

Now that information about the parallel words and phrases is getting around Urantian circles, another explanation is turning up. Here is how Urantian Dennis Shields justifies the parallels in a posting on the Urantial Internet (September 16, 1994):

> From what we know about the Book and the revelatory process the one person who needed to be sold on the revelation by the authors was WSS. We know that the authors admit to using human thought patterns exhaustively prior to resorting to revelation. Since they had access to human thought resources and they needed to have the lifelong involvement of WSS why couldn't they have tapped into his thought process or recorded thought (books) and used some of his phraseology in order to win the commitment from WSS that was required from some human in order to accomplish the process of recording this revelation in book form? . . . Maybe his own familiar phrases were used to hook Sadler on this project.

Other true believers have expressed similar notions. If the revelators, they argue, could copy material from many books, why couldn't they copy ideas, words, and phrases from Sadler's writings? Surely it is overwhelmingly more plausible that Sadler, in editing the papers, was unaware of how often his vocabulary and phrasing crept into the Fifth Epochal Revelation.

The most impressive part of the *UB* is the last section, almost a third of the book, that is a life of Christ. Hundreds of such biographies have been written, including one by Ellen White, but aside from fictionalized accounts, such as George Moore's *Brook Kerith*, no purported true biography of Jesus has provided so many details about events and teachings that appear nowhere in the four canonical gospels or in apocryphal gospels. Several Urantians have told me that reading this section of the *UB* was what converted them to the Urantian faith.

Similar emotions are often expressed by Seventh-day Adventists about

Mrs. White's life of Christ. Here is a remark by Robert Spangler that I came across in an unpublished paper by Douglas Hackleman:

> If I were to evaluate Ellen White on the basis of her looks and education—or her use of sources, failure to give credit, statements that seem to be out of harmony with present-day historical and/or scientific knowledge . . . I would cry out, I cannot believe! I will not believe!
>
> But I have had an experience with Ellen White's works. . . . I know what it means to see Jesus so vibrant, so real, so living in *The Desire of Ages* that tears of joy and thanksgiving stream down my cheeks. I know what it means to read the closing chapters of *The Great Controversy*, fall on my knees, and like Thomas of old grasp the feet of Jesus and cry out, "My Lord and my God!"

The *UB*'s Jesus section is indeed a well-written, impressive work. Either it is accurate in its history, coming directly from higher beings in position to know, or it is a work of fertile imagination by someone who knew the New Testament by heart and who was also steeped in knowledge of the times when Jesus lived.

I do not know who wrote the *UB*'s life of Jesus, though I suspect it was Sadler. No one knows the Bible more thoroughly than Adventist elders, and Sadler's knowledge of Scripture was awesome. It emerges in many of his books. Chapter 30, in one of his early books, *The Physiology of Faith and Fear* (1912), consists almost entirely of biblical quotations. *Worry and Nervousness* (1914) has three pages (452–54) of scriptural passages under the heading "Exceeding Great and Precious Promises." The same heading and the same passages appear 30 years later in *Modern Psychiatry* (765–67).

Piloting Modern Youth (1931) has a section headed "The Boyhood of Jesus." It opens: "I truly regret that we do not know more about the adolescence of Christ. It no doubt contained much that would be very helpful in guiding the youth of today." More significantly, Sadler puts into the mouth of young Jesus a statement within quotation marks that is not in the New Testament. He has Jesus say to his parents, after they have reproached him for leaving them to discuss religion with temple teachers: "What, don't you understand? I have a life mission to discharge. I have a service to perform for humanity, and even though I am but twelve years old, it is high time that I should be concerned with the business of getting started in my life-work."

Compare the above remarks, attributed to Jesus by Sadler, with what Jesus says to his mother on page 1384 of the *UB*. She had just rebuked him for vanishing for three days to spend time at the temple. Said Jesus: "Why is it that you have so long sought me? Would you not expect to find me in my Father's house since the time has come when I should be about my father's business?" (cf. Luke 2:49.)

Sadler must have been proud of his imaginary dialog because he repeats it word for word in a section on the boyhood of Jesus in *Adolescence Problems* (1948). Mrs. White liked to crib from others. Sadler loved to steal from himself. Hundreds of long paragraphs in his books are often repeated in later books with almost no changes. We have also seen how the *UB* contains material taken from Sadler's earlier books. In the next chapter we shall learn something even more amazing—that the *UB* itself is riddled with passages copied from human authors with never an indication they were not written by the revelators!

In *Piloting Modern Youth*, as well as in other books in which Sadler discussed religion, he emphasized (as does the *UB*) the evolutionary character of Christianity. "We should make sincere efforts to give our youth the truth about religious evolution, " he wrote, "fearlessly teaching comparative religion. The teachings of Jesus have nothing to lose by comparison with those of any and all the world's religious thinkers."

As an example of how portions of the Bible can be rephrased in modern terminology, he offers what he calls a "translation" of the 23rd Psalm in a way that would make it "intriguing and enlightening to the adolescent mind of the twentieth century." Here is Sadler's new version:

The Lord is my Divine Protector; I shall never know spiritual poverty.

The Lord helps me spiritually, as the low gear of my automobile helps me to climb hard hills.

The Lord renews my soul, as the calories and vitamins restore my strength and prevent disease.

The Lord preserves my spirit from harm, as vaccines prevent disease and antiseptics ward off contagion in times of dangerous epidemics. Thus I am enabled to enjoy peace of mind and health of body.

The Lord is my soul comforter and also my dynamo, charging my rundown batteries of mind and body, the better to resist my enemies, the microbes.

The Lord is the spiritual sunshine of my soul; the Lord is indeed the sunlight in my room bringing me the life and health of the ultraviolet rays.

Sadler continues:

What do modern city youth know about sheep and shepherds—except the poetic legends of literature and the flavor of lamb chops? Let us have the old versions in their poetic beauty as the traditional background for religion; but youth needs a new and practical paraphrase of the guidebook of morality—a twentieth-century translation of the incomparable teachings of the Hebrew prophets and of the Son of Man.

Let us have the beauty of the old and the practical help of the new. If our elders thrive on the old version, let them have it. If our youth can be helped by a new translation—an up-to-date restatement of old truths— then let us grant their right to satisfy such a soul longing.

Allow me to repeat here some opinions I have earlier expressed. I believe that Sadler, shaken by his discovery that Ellen White was at least part charlatan, came to believe that he himself was in direct contact with midwayers who were in turn in contact with still higher beings. I believe Sadler, especially after the death of his wife, became convinced that he was wiser, healthier, and better informed than Mrs. White; that he had been chosen by the Gods to be the prophet and founder of a new form of Christianity vastly superior to his abandoned Adventism.

As a youth and young man Sadler regarded Seventh-day Adventism as the remnant church, carrying a final message from God to a faithless generation destined to witness the Second Coming. About 1910 he came to see his church as misguided, perhaps even inspired in part by Satan. As the custodian of a new revelation, first coming mysteriously through his sleeping brother-in-law, he saw himself playing a role in history even greater than that of Mrs. White. I believe it was in this megalomaniac mood that Sadler, drawing on his vast knowledge of the Bible, confusing his own vivid imagination and superior writing skill with instructions from secondary midwayers, decided to outdo Sister White. He would create a life of Jesus that would swarm with details unknown even to Sister White and never before revealed!

In *The Truth About Spiritualism* (page 141), published in 1923, Sadler said this:

Every now and then someone arises who attempts to make other people believe in the things which they see or hear in their own minds. Self-styled "prophets" arise to convince us of the reality of their visions. Odd geniuses appear who tell us of the voices they hear, and if they seem fairly sane and socially conventional in every way, they are sometimes able to build up vast followings, to create cults and establish churches; whereas, if they are too bold in their imaginings, if they see a little too far or hear a little too much, they are promptly seized and quickly lodged safe within the confines of an insane asylum.

A few pages later Sadler repeats, in slightly altered sentences, the paragraphs I quoted earlier in chapter 6 (see pp. 102–103). He speaks of the "strange and unique religious movements" initiated by persons who go into nervous cataleptic trances and experience visions they believe come straight from God. He declares once more that these "prophets" are usually women. In most cases, he writes, their visions appear after adolescence and in no case that he has observed do the visions survive menopause.

There can be little doubt that Sadler had Sister White in mind when he wrote the above paragraphs. After his break with Adventism he became convinced that Mrs. White was a victim of partial cataleptic seizures. He correctly predicted that her visions would cease after menopause. It is one of the great and sad ironies of recent religious history that a man who could write the paragraphs quoted above would himself become the founder of a cult based on a revelation initially channeled through his sleeping brother-in-law!

Like Seventh-day Adventists, Urantians like to ignore as unimportant the *UB*'s frequent borrowings from human sources. That Mrs. White shamelessly plagiarized is beyond doubt. Nor can it be denied that she was aware of her plagiarisms, although not once did she or her husband James admit them. In his book *Life Sketches* James White wrote:

> Does unbelief suggest that what she writes in her personal testimonies has been learned from others? We inquire, What time has she had to learn all these facts? and who for a moment can regard her as a Christian woman, if she gives her ear to gossip, then writes it out as a vision from God? And where is the person of superior natural and acquired abilities who could listen to the description of one, two, or three thousand cases, all differing and then write them out without getting them confused, laying the whole work liable to a thousand contradictions? *If Mrs. W has gathered the facts from a human mind in a single case, she has in thousands of cases, and God has not shown her these things which she has written in these personal testimonies.*
>
> In her published works there are many things set forth which cannot be found in other books, and yet they are so clear and beautiful that the unprejudiced mind grasps them at once as truth. . . . If commentators and theological writers generally had seen these gems of thought which strike the mind so forcibly, and had they been brought out in print, all the ministers in the land could have read them. These men gather thoughts from books, and as Mrs. W. has written and spoken a hundred things, as truthful as they are beautiful and harmonious, *which cannot be found in the writings of others, they are new to the most intelligent readers and hearers.*

And if they are not to be found in print, and are not brought out in sermons from the pulpit, where did Mrs. W. find them? From what source has she received the new and rich thoughts which are to be found in her writings and oral addresses? *She could not have learned them from books, from the fact that they do not contain such thoughts.* And, certainly, she did not learn them from those ministers who had not thought of them. The case is a clear one. It evidently requires a hundred times the credulity to believe that Mrs. W. has learned these things of others, and has palmed them off as visions from God, than it does to believe that the Spirit of God has revealed them to her [italics added].

Substitute "*UB*" for "Mrs. White" in the above paragraphs, and the sentences could have been written by a dedicated Urantian.

Sooner or later, I am convinced, Urantians will have to face the fact that Sadler was one of the *UB*'s authors. It could not have been Wilfred, whose education was limited and who gave no evidence of writing skills. Initially, of course, basic material flowed through Wilfred while he was asleep, but as years went by Sadler, in my opinion, became convinced that the revelators had also chosen him to be the bearer of the great fifth epochal revelation.

Although Sadler lost his faith in Adventism, he never abandoned his faith in God and an afterlife, in the God-inspired teachings of Jesus, and in the enormous value of faith and prayer in treating the mentally ill. In *Theory and Practice of Psychiatry* (1936), pages 1114–15 are devoted to praising the teachings of Jesus which he says "may be quite divorced from His gospel of Salvation and His doctrine of the survival of the immortal soul." Still loyal to the "conditional immortality" of Adventist theology, Sadler (and the *UB*) reject the soul's innate immortality for an afterlife provided by the grace of God. A soul obviously cannot be immortal in essence if it can be annihilated!

The heart of what Jesus taught, Sadler writes in the book just cited, is simply expressed as "The Fatherhood of God and the Brotherhood of man." This linking of the two concepts, each demanding the other, runs like a refrain through the *UB*, especially in the Jesus section. The phrase, going back at least a century, was constantly invoked by the liberal, social-gospel Protestants of the nineteenth and twentieth centuries. Here is a typical use of the phrase by Shailer Mathews in *The Social Teachings of Jesus* (1905, page 62):

In a word, in the old social order Jesus saw the tyranny of selfishness and hatred; in the new, he sees a universal reign of love—the fatherhood of God and the brotherhood of men.

This expression, the fatherhood of God and brotherhood of men, is in many minds the substance of Christianity.

The *UB*'s Paper 99, "Social Problems of Religion," contains not a single thought that is not in Mathews' book. The heart of this work is the view that the ideal social order, the "Kingdom of Heaven" toward which Urantia is slowly evolving, is one "in which the relation of man to God is that of sons, and (therefore) to each other, that of brothers" (p. 54). Indeed, this has been the heart of liberal Protestantism for the past two or three centuries. Mathews quotes from a three-volume "liberal" life of Jesus by the German theologian Karl Theodor Keim (published in 1867, 1871, and 1872): "Briefly stated, the religious heaven of Jesus meant the Fatherliness of God for men, the sonship of men for God, and the infinite spiritual good of the kingdom of heaven is Fatherhood and Sonship."

Buell Gordon Gallagher, in his book *Color and Conscience* (1946, page 183) expressed it this way:

The idea of the universal brotherhood of all men is as profound as it is simple. We too easily assume that, because the idea is readily grasped, it is not profound; or, on an occasion when we glimpse some of the deeper meanings of the notion of brotherhood, we hastily avert our eyes lest we should be too shaken by the ethical insights of that moment. The demands upon personal and group conduct which the notion of brotherhood makes are fundamentally at variance with the demands made by racism. The belief in the Fatherhood of God and its necessary corollary, the brotherhood of man, is our greatest affirmative religious resource for attacking the caste system. Either God is the Father of all men or He is not. If we say he is not, we deny the Christian God and resort to some lesser pagan god of tribe or clan or race. That is what Hitler commanded his followers to do. If we accept the Fatherhood of God, we must accept the brotherhood of man.

One of the earliest uses of the phrase "Fatherhood of God and Brotherhood of Man" (according to the *Macmillan Book of Proverbs, Maxims, and Famous Phrases*, page 247) was by the famous Unitarian preacher and writer James Freeman Clarke (1810–1888). It is the first of "five points of Unitarianism" in his *Statement of Faith*. A friend of Emerson, Clarke was pastor of Unitarian churches in Louisville and Boston. For a few years he taught "natural religion" at Harvard.

Tryon Edwards, in *A Dictionary of Thoughts* (1899), has a section on "Brotherhood" that lists several quotations about the fatherhood of God and the brotherhood of man. (In the next chapter we shall see how this book was the source of the 28 aphorisms on pages 556–57 of the *UB*.) "There is no brotherhood of man without the fatherhood of God," wrote the Reverend Harry Martyn Field, a Presbyterian minister (born 1822) and author of many books. "The brotherhood of man is an integral part of Christianity no less than the Fatherhood of God." So said Reverend Lyman Abbott (1835–1922), a Congregationalist minister who, like Sadler, harmonized Christianity with biological evolution.

Charles Lemuel Thompson, pastor of New York's Madison Avenue Presbyterian Church from 1888, wrote: "The sixteenth century said, 'Responsibility to God.' The present nineteenth says, 'The brotherhood of man.'" Compiler Edwards even quotes himself: "Whoever in prayer can say 'Our Father,' acknowledges and should feel the brotherhood of the whole race of mankind."

There is no longer serious doubt that Wilfred was the sleeping conduit, yet he remains today a dim personality about whom little is known. Still living Forum members recall him as painfully shy—one who kept himself so much in the background during Sunday teas that everyone felt sorry for him. One Forum member described him as seemingly "frightened" by Forum gatherings. Christy is on record as saying that the channeler—of course she never identified him—had no education beyond the sixth grade. There is no evidence that Wilfred ever went beyond that grade, but like the channeler of *OAHSPE*, he obviously must have read widely, especially books on astronomy and general science. The compulsion throughout the *UB* to give precise large numbers surely reflects Wilfred's training as an accountant, a profession he practiced throughout his life. Having been raised an Adventist, it would not be surprising for him to share with Sadler a profound knowledge of the Bible.

Sadler, it should be remembered, was also an expert on world religions, about which he often lectured. His *Modern Psychiatry* has sections devoted to the world's leading faiths, as well as capsule summaries of the views of Plato, Aristotle, the Stoics, Epicureans, Cynics, and Skeptics. All six of these philosophers and schools are mentioned in the *UB* on pages 1335–38.

I believe that Sadler, unable to accept the split personalities of his brother-in-law, suffered in later years from a megalomania which neither he nor his admirers recognized. Like so many other charismatic leaders of religious cults, he saw himself selected by the Gods to be the founder and titular head of a new religion, superior not only to the one he lost, but to all other world faiths. It was a religion harmonious with science, free of many superstitions of traditional Christianity, destined to usher in, under the fatherhood of God, a world brotherhood, democratically organized—a brotherhood that would abolish war and establish on Urantia for the first time in its troubled history a world of love, peace, and justice.

According to the Winter 1992 issue of *The Fellowship Bulletin*, when the *UB* first came off the press many Forum members were enthusiastic beyond belief. They were convinced that in a very short time Urantianism would sweep the world. Dr. Sadler's son Bill predicted that in ten years at least 100,000 Urantia study groups would be flourishing.

At the first Executive Committee meeting in February 1955, someone proposed offering serial rights of the *UB* to *Life* magazine! This was sensibly voted down. Also voted down was a plan to advertise the *UB* in leading review journals, and to distribute it to major bookstores and libraries. As a compromise, unsolicited copies were mailed to such influential persons as Sholem Asche, Ralph Bunche, Arthur Compton, Norman Cousins, Aldous Huxley, Edward R. Murrow, Eleanor Roosevelt, and Edward Teller. As *The Bulletin* understates it, "Response was negligible."

As chairman of the Urantia Foundation's Education Committee, Dr. Sadler opened a school for training *UB* teachers. Seventy-one students enrolled. By 1960, seventeen were certified as "leaders," some of whom were later declared "Ordained Teachers." Note the word "ordained," strongly suggesting Sadler's hope to begin something resembling a church. Each year, *The Bulletin* continues, "fewer students enrolled—they were tough courses—and the growing emphasis upon science did not appeal to everyone. Eventually the school ran out of students and disbanded."

Since then the Foundation's plan has been not to promote the book, but to rely on slow growth—selling the *UB* by word of mouth, and through personal contacts. Will the cult eventually grow to be a great world religion, as Sadler and other founding members hoped, and as present believers still hope? Will today's leaders have the wisdom, as Mark Kulieke puts it in *Birth of a Revelation*, to "steer this latest revelation from the safe harbor out upon the high seas of evolutionary destiny"? Or is the Urantian movement doomed to fade like the Faithists of *Oahspe?*

16

Plagiarisms in *The Urantia Book*

On September 22, 1992, occurred one of the most startling disclosures in the history of the Urantia movement. That was the date on which Matthew Block, a young, devout, hopelessly naive Urantian who lives in Chicago, distributed an eye-opening four-page release titled "A Bibliographic Essay on Some Human Books Used in *The Urantia Book*." The release cited fifteen books which "were used in the inditement of some of the Urantia Papers. Each of these books contains sentences, paragraphs or even whole chapters whose phrasing and organization of thought or information are so closely paralleled in the Urantia Papers as to be unmistakable sources."

Some of these borrowings were known earlier, Block continues, but most were not known until he began finding them in the summer of 1992. He expects to uncover many more sources in the next few years. Rather than allow me to preempt his findings, he will not publish them fully until after my book comes out. Block is greatly enjoying his research and considers 1994 his most glorious year of discovery. He does not believe Sadler wrote a line of the *UB* or even edited the papers. Where parts of the *UB* echo material from Sadler's early books, Block is enormously impressed by how deftly the supermortals reinterpreted the borrowed ideas, as well as how cleverly they enhanced the passages copied from books by others.

As anyone who has read thus far knows, copying from other books, without giving credit to the original authors, was exactly the practice followed by Ellen White in writing the books she claimed were inspired by God and His angels. As I have earlier reported, many of her plagiarisms

327

were early recognized by Adventist leaders, but carefully concealed from the faithful. They were first made public in Elder D. M. Canright's 1919 biography of Mrs. White, but not extensively documented until ex-Adventist elder Walter T. Rea published *The White Lie* in 1982. Parallel passages from Mrs. White's works and copyrighted books by others are still being discovered.

Now that the extent of Mrs. White's plagiarisms are widely known, how do Adventists justify them? Few are willing to accept the conjecture that the copying was done by hired writers and editors, without Mrs. White's knowledge, because that would force them to admit she did not actually write her own books. They prefer to believe that Mrs. White, guided by the Holy Spirit, copied passages only when they expressed exactly the truths she wanted to convey! Yes, she stole passages by others, but the stealing was divinely guided. To put it bluntly, it was the Holy Spirit or angels who did the plagiarizing.

Walter Rea, and hundreds of other Seventh-day Adventists, were so appalled by the extent to which Mrs. White broke copyright laws that they sensibly decided her writings were of human origin. One might have expected Block to reach a similar conclusion about the Urantia Papers, but no—so powerful is the compulsion of true believers to rationalize embarrassing aspects of their faith that they are not in the least dismayed. One devout Urantian, with whom I have been in correspondence, exclaimed "Wonderful!" in a letter he sent after receiving Block's release. Block still has not the slightest doubt that the *UB*'s Papers were superhumanly indited. He reminds us that the *UB* itself (17 and 1343) states that the revelators did not hesitate to make use of existing human knowledge and ideas:

> Successive planetary revelations of divine truth invariably embrace the highest existing concepts of spiritual values as a part of the new and enhanced co-ordination of planetary knowledge. Accordingly, in making these presentations about God and his universe associates, we have selected as the basis of these papers more than one thousand human concepts representing the highest and most advanced planetary knowledge of spiritual values and universe meanings. Wherein these human concepts, assembled from the God-knowing mortals of the past and the present, are inadequate to portray the truth as we are directed to reveal it, we will unhesitatingly supplement them, for this purpose drawing upon our own superior knowledge of the reality and divinity of the Paradise Deities and their transcendent residential universe. (*UB*, 17)
>
> [*Acknowledgment:* In carrying out my commission to restate the teachings and retell the doings of Jesus of Nazareth, I have drawn freely

upon all sources of record and planetary information. My ruling motive has been to prepare a record which will not only be enlightening to the generation of men now living, but which may also be helpful to all future generations. From the vast store of information made available to me, I have chosen that which is best suited to the accomplishment of this purpose. As far as possible I have derived my information from purely human sources. Only when such sources failed, have I resorted to those records which are superhuman. When ideas and concepts of Jesus' life and teachings have been acceptably expressed by a human mind, I invariably gave preference to such apparently human thought patterns. Although I have sought to adjust the verbal expression the better to conform to our concept of the real meaning and the true import of the Master's life and teachings, as far as possible, I have adhered to the actual human concept and thought pattern in all my narratives. I well know that those concepts which have had origin in the human mind will prove more acceptable and helpful to all other human minds. When unable to find the necessary concepts in the human records or in human expressions, I have next resorted to the memory resources of my own order of earth creatures, the midwayers. And when that secondary source of information proved inadequate, I have unhesitatingly resorted to the superplanetary sources of information.

The memoranda which I have collected, and from which I have prepared this narrative of the life and teachings of Jesus—aside from the memory of the record of the Apostle Andrew—embrace thought gems and superior concepts of Jesus' teachings assembled from more than two thousand human beings who have lived on earth from the days of Jesus down to the time of the inditing of these revelations, more correctly restatements. The revelatory permission has been utilized only when the human record and human concepts failed to supply an adequate thought pattern. My revelatory commission forbade me to resort to extrahuman sources of either information or expression until such a time as I could testify that I had failed in my efforts to find the required conceptual expression in purely human sources.

While I, with the collaboration of my eleven associate fellow midwayers and under the supervision of the Melchizedek of record, have portrayed this narrative in accordance with my concept of its effective arrangement and in response to my choice of immediate expression, nevertheless, the majority of the ideas and even some of the effective expressions which I have thus utilized had their origin in the minds of the men of many races who have lived on earth during the intervening generations, right on down to those who are still alive at the time of this undertaking. In many ways I have served more as a collector and editor than as an original narrator. I have unhesitatingly appropriated those ideas and concepts,

preferably human, which would enable me to create the most effective por-
traiture of Jesus' life, and which would qualify me to restate his matchless
teachings in the most strikingly helpful and universally uplifting phrase-
ology. In behalf of the Brotherhood of the United Midwayers of Urantia, I
most gratefully acknowledge our indebtedness to all sources of record and
concept which have been hereinafter utilized in the further elaboration of
our restatement of Jesus' life on earth.] (*UB*, 1343)

It is worth noting that this policy of taking material from other writers
without acknowledging sources was precisely the policy Sadler himself
followed in many of his books. Here, for example, is a passage from the
foreword to his *Prescription for Permanent Peace* (1944) that sounds very
much as if it had been written by the authors of the *UB*:

> In writing a book of this sort one naturally gives expression to many ideas
> which have been absorbed from many sources. I have not been able to
> read such books as Brickner's *Is Germany Incurable*, MacIver's *Towards
> an Abiding Peace*, Lippmann's *United States Foreign Policy*, and Reves'
> *A Democratic Manifesto*, without being so favorably impressed that the
> ideas of these various writers find more or less expression in these pages.
>
> I regret that it is not possible for me to acknowledge the source of the
> many concepts presented here which I have gleaned from scores of
> authors, for not all of the ideas and sentiments herein contained were orig-
> inal with me. Far from it. These chapters embody my attempt during the
> past decade—more especially since Hitler invaded Poland—to "pick
> berries" off every available bush.

In his earlier book *The Physiology of Faith and Fear* (1912) Sadler
defended the practice this way:

> In the preparation of this volume, the author has made careful research in
> the literature touching on every phase of the many subjects considered.
> For this purpose he has had recourse not only to his own library, but to the
> various libraries of Chicago and the great Congressional Library at Wash-
> ington, D.C. In a work of this kind, designed for laymen, and where
> brevity is so essential, direct quotations have been avoided, although the
> leading authorities in physiology and psychology have been drawn upon
> for material in the preparation of this work and the various lectures which
> preceded it.

Mrs. White never acknowledged her hundreds of obvious plagiarisms.
Had she done so, she could not have justified them better than in the

manner of the two excerpts from the *UB* printed above, and the two passages by Sadler.

Block admits he was "quite surprised at the extent to which the revelators culled from books" unrelated to science, theology, and the life of Jesus. On the other hand, he is enormously impressed and pleased by how each book, from which the revelators borrowed, "was deftly and creatively used so as to seamlessly integrate human observation with revelatory supplementation or correction."

Rather than an embarrassment to Urantians, Block continues, knowing the books used by the revelators helps us to understand the Papers. He recommends that students of the *UB* should "openly acknowledge" the copying because it would "disarm debunkers of the Martin Gardner ilk who hold the notion that revelation always and necessarily means, to its gulled believers, complete superhuman inspiration."

Many Urantians have told me that one of the main reasons they believe the *UB* was written by superhumans is the fact that no one person or group of persons could possibly have acquired all the detailed historical and scientific knowledge needed to produce such a monumental, wide-ranging work. We now know, thanks to Block's amazing discoveries, that it wasn't necessary for the *UB* authors to have all that information in their heads. They just snatched it from human experts!

I have a dark suspicion that Block does not fully anticipate the effect of the bomb he has dropped on his brothers and sisters. It is one thing to make general use of material in published books without giving credit. It is quite another thing to copy sentences almost verbatim without quotation marks or any indication of a sentence's source. The latter is called plagiarism. It is against the law. Had *UB* copying of this sort been noticed in 1955, when the book first came off the press, publishers could have won cases against the Urantia Foundation for copyright infringements.

Consider, first, a page from philosopher Charles Hartshorne's *Man's Vision of God*, a book published in 1941 by the Chicago firm of Willett, Clark and Company. At that time Hartshorne was one of my teachers at the University of Chicago, and a well-known advocate of what has been called "process theology"—the view that God is in time and evolving along with the universe. On page 8 of this book Hartshorne lists seven possible meanings of "absolute perfection":

Absolute perfection in *all* respects.
Absolute perfection in *some* respects, relative
    perfection in all others.
Absolute perfection, relative perfection, and
    "imperfection" (neither absolute nor relative perfection),
    each in *some* respects.
Absolute perfection in *some* respects,
    imperfection in all others.
Absolute perfection in *no* respects, relative
    in all.
Absolute perfection in *no* respects, relative
    in some, imperfection in the others.
Absolute perfection in *no* respects,
    imperfection in all.

On page 3 of the *UB*, in its foreword, Block found the same seven meanings of perfection reprinted almost word for word:

1. Absolute perfection in all aspects.
2. Absolute perfection in some phases and relative perfection in all other aspects.
3. Absolute, relative, and imperfect aspects in varied association.
4. Absolute perfection in some respects, imperfection in all others.
5. Absolute perfection in no direction, relative perfection in all other manifestations.
6. Absolute perfection in no phase, relative in some, imperfect in others.
7. Absolute perfection in no attribute, imperfection in all.

Hartshorne assured me in a letter that his seven sentences were not published in any form prior to his 1941 book. Surely it is absurd to imagine, as one Urantian suggested to me, that the Orvonton Divine Counselor, who supposedly wrote the foreword before 1935 later "indited" Hartshorne to formulate the seven forms of perfection in words identical to those the celestial used in the *UB* six or seven years earlier!*

It is almost as hard to imagine that the Divine Counselor would read Hartshorne's book in 1941 or later, then copy down the seven types for his own use in the foreword. Is it not far more probable that Sadler or one of

---

*According to an old-timer in the Urantia movement, who asks to be nameless, the foreword was not written until 1946. He said in 1993, at a Urantian meeting in Hawaii, that Dr. Sadler and Bill Jr. wanted to write an introduction to the *UB*, partly for copyright reasons. The revelators rejected this notion, and responded with their own foreword. If this is true, it would explain how Hartshorne's seven definitions of perfection got into the foreword.

his associates, in writing the foreword, made free use of Hartshorne's book without thinking it necessary to mention Hartshorne? Hartshorne does not recall ever meeting Sadler, but he told me that he (Hartshorne) often spoke at the McCormick Theological Seminary where Sadler taught for many years. Regardless of who did the copying, it was certainly reprehensible, as well as against the law, not to give Hartshorne proper credit.

One of Bertrand Russell's best known essays is "A Free Man's Worship," first published in 1903 and since reprinted in numerous anthologies. Here are two of its most often quoted passages:

> Such, in outline, but even more purposeless, more void of meaning, is the world which Science presents for our belief. Amid such a world, if anywhere, our ideals henceforward must find a home. That Man is the product of causes which had no prevision of the end they were achieving; that his origin, his growth, his hopes and fears, his loves and his beliefs, are but the outcome of accidental collocations of atoms; that no fire, no heroism, no intensity of thought and feeling, can preserve an individual life beyond the grave; that all the labours of the ages, all the devotion, all the inspiration, all the noonday brightness of human genius, are destined to extinction in the vast death of the solar system, and that the whole temple of Man's achievement must inevitably be buried beneath the debris of a universe in ruins—all these things, if not quite beyond dispute, are yet so nearly certain, that no philosophy which rejects them can hope to stand. Only within the scaffolding of these truths, only on the firm foundation of unyielding despair, can the soul habitation henceforth be safely built.

> Brief and powerless is Man's life; on him and all his race the slow, sure doom falls pitiless and dark. Blind to good and evil, reckless of destruction, omnipotent matter rolls on its relentless way; for Man, condemned today to lose his dearest, tomorrow himself to pass through the gate of darkness, it remains only to cherish, ere yet the blow fall, the lofty thoughts that ennoble his little day; disdaining the coward terrors of the slave of Fate, to worship at the shrine that his own hands have built; undismayed by the empire of chance, to preserve a mind free from the wanton tyranny that rules his outward life; proudly defiant of the irresistible forces that tolerate, for a moment, his knowledge and his condemnation, to sustain alone, a weary but unyielding Atlas, the world that his own ideals have fashioned despite the trampling march of unconscious power.

Compare the above passages with the following paragraph from the *UB*'s preamble to Paper 102 (*UB* 1118):

> To the unbelieving materialist, man is simply an evolutionary accident. His hopes of survival are strung on a figment of mortal imagination; his fears, loves, longings, and beliefs are but the reaction of the incidental juxtaposition of certain lifeless atoms of matter. No display of energy nor expression of trust can carry him beyond the grave. The devotional labors and inspirational genius of the best of men are doomed to be extinguished by death, the long and lonely night of eternal oblivion and soul extinction. Nameless despair is man's only reward for living and toiling under the temporal sun of mortal existence. Each day of life slowly and surely tightens the grasp of a pitiless doom which a hostile and relentless universe of matter has decreed shall be the crowning insult to everything in human desire which is beautiful, noble, lofty, and good.

Can anyone doubt that the author of Paper 102 had Russell's essay before him when he wrote? Russell's "hopes and fears, his loves and his beliefs," become the revelator's "hopes . . . fears, loves, longings, and beliefs." Russell's "labors of the ages, all the devotion, all the inspiration," becomes "the devotional labors and inspirational genius." "Unyielding despair" turns into "nameless despair." Russell's "doom" that falls "pitiless" becomes "pitiless doom."

Block, who first identified this source, thinks it probable that Melchizedek of Nebadon, who is said to have written Paper 102, did not use Russell's entire essay as his source, but rather the quotations from it that appear in Rufus Jones's *The Inner Life* (1916). He thinks this because another book by Jones, *A Preface to Christian Faith in a New Age* (1932), provides material for the *UB*'s sections 5 to 10 of Paper 195. "Virtually every paragraph of section 10," Block writes, "is drawn consecutively from the last half of this book."

I turn now to Block's discovery of how James Henry Breasted's *The Dawn of Conscience* (1933) was used as a major source for the *UB*'s discussion of ancient Egypt's religious customs (sections 2 through 5 of Paper 25, and pages 1215–16 of Paper 111). Breasted was the University of Chicago's world-renowned Egyptologist. The proof that his book was the source goes far beyond the fact that its information is constantly summarized and rephrased. We know it was the source because of passages where Breasted's exact wording is repeated.

Here are some instances:

UB (1044)

The superstitions of these times are well illustrated by the general belief in the efficacy of spittle as a healing agent, an idea which had its origin in Egypt and spread therefrom to Arabia and Mesopotamia. In the legendary battle of Horus with Set the young god lost his eye, but after Set was vanquished, this eye was restored by the wise god Thoth, who spat upon the wound and healed it.

Breasted (102)

The battle of Horus with Set, which, as we recall, was a Solar incident, waged so fiercely that the young god lost his eye at the hands of his father's enemy. When Set was overthrown, and the eye was finally recovered by Thoth, this wise god spat upon the wound and healed it. This method of healing the eye, which is, of course, folk-medicine reflected in the myth, evidently gained wide popularity, passed into Asia, and seems to reappear in the New Testament narrative, in the incident which depicts Jesus doubtless deferring to recognised folk-custom in employing the same means to heal a blind man.

UB (1045)

The sloping entrance passage of the great pyramid pointed directly toward the Pole Star so that the soul of the king, when emerging from the tomb, could go straight to the stationary and established constellations of the fixed stars, the supposed abode of the kings.

When the oblique rays of the sun were observed penetrating earthward through an aperture in the clouds, it was believed that they betokened the letting down of a celestial stairway whereon the king and other righteous souls might ascend. "King Pepi has put down his radiance as a stairway under his feet whereon to ascend to his mother."

Breasted (73–74)

Much discussion has been caused by the fact that the sloping entrance passage of the Great Pyramid points directly towards the Pole Star. The hitherto unnoticed reason is obviously disclosed in the Pyramid Texts. When the king' soul emerged from this passage its direction carried it straight towards the circumpolar stars.

Breasted (78)

In the oblique rays of the sun also, shooting earthward through some opening in the clouds, they beheld a radiant stairway let down from the sky that the king might ascend. "King Pepi has put down this radiance as a stairway under his feet, whereon King Pepi ascended to this his mother, the living Uraeus that is on the head of Re."

UB (1046)

Amenemope taught that riches and fortune were the gift of God, and this concept thoroughly colored the later appearing Hebrew philosophy. This noble teacher believed that God-consciousness was the determining factor in all conduct; that every moment should be lived in the realization of the presence of, and responsibility to, God. The teachings of this sage were subsequently translated into Hebrew and became the sacred book of that people long before the Old Testament was reduced to writing. The chief preachment of this good man had to do with instructing his son in uprightness and honesty in governmental positions of trust, and these noble sentiments of long ago would do honor to any modern statesman.

Breasted (721–22)

Professor Lange of Copenhagen, who has contributed most to the understanding of this extraordinary treatise, in comparing Amenemope with his predecessors, says, "The religious views of Amenemope are much deeper and penetrate much more deeply into his entire world of thought [than his predecessors]. To the other teachers of wisdom piety is a virtue, the thought of death and eternity is a motive for virtuous conduct, it is God who gives riches and fortune. But for Amenemope the consciousness of God is the determining factor in his conception of life and his entire behaviour. "To his son, therefore, Amenemope constantly holds up this attitude towards life, that it is to be lived both in personal and official relations, in full realisation of momentary responsibility to God. This ultimate intensity of conscience and God-consciousness in the teachings of an Egyptian thinker in the Tenth Century B.C., before any of the Old Testament was written, is the more remarkable, because we now know that the Wisdom of Amenemope was translated into Hebrew, it was read by Hebrews, and an important part of it found its way into the Old Testament.

UB (1046)

This wise man of the Nile taught that "riches take themselves wings and fly away"—that all things earthly are evanescent. His great prayer was to be "saved from fear." He exhorted all to turn away from "the words of men" to "the acts of God." In substance he taught: Man proposes but God disposes. His teachings, translated into Hebrew, determined the philosophy of the Old Testament Book of Proverbs. Translated into Greek, they gave color to all subsequent Hellenic religious philosophy. The later Alexandrian philosopher, Philo, possessed a copy of the Book of Wisdom.

Breasted (328, 330)

In the wise conclusion that riches "make themselves wings" and fly away, Amenemope's graphic picture of the uncertainty and perishability of earthly good, we recognise a figure which has come down to us through the editor of the Hebrew Book of Proverbs, and in the life of the Western world has gained proverbial currency after three thousand years. Our sage regards dependence upon such fleeting human resources as futile; the only security is in God, pray to him and "thou art saved from fear." . . .

We thus have here in its oldest form the worldwide proverb, "Man proposes, God disposes." Such a widely distributed ancient Egyptian view of the relation of God and man suggests the whole question of the place of Egyptian moral evolution in the history not only of early man, but of Western civilization.

UB (1215–16)

The inhabitants of the Nile valley believed that each favored individual had bestowed upon him at birth, or soon thereafter, a protecting spirit which they called the ka. They taught that this guardian spirit remained with the mortal subject throughout life and passed before him into the future estate. On the walls of a temple at Luxor, where is depicted the birth of Amenhotep III, the little prince is pictured on the arm of the Nile god, and near him is another child, in appearance identical with the prince, which is a symbol of that entity which the Egyptians called the ka. This sculpture was completed in the fifteenth century before Christ.

The ka was thought to be a superior spirit genius which desired to guide the associated mortal soul into the better paths of temporal living but more especially to influence the fortunes of the human subject in the hereafter. When an Egyptian of this period died, it was expected that his ka would be waiting for him on the other side of the Great River. At first, only kings were supposed to have kas, but presently all righteous men were believed to possess them.

One Egyptian ruler, speaking of the ka within his heart, said: "I did not disregard its speech; I feared to transgress its guidance. I prospered thereby greatly; I was thus successful by reason of that which it caused me to do; I was distinguished by its guidance." Many believed that the ka was "an oracle from God in everybody." Many believed that they were to "spend eternity in gladness of heart in the favor of the God that is in you."

Breasted (49–50)

In beginning the new and untried life after death, the deceased was greatly aided by a protecting guardian spirit called the *ka*, which came into being with each person, followed him throughout life, and passed *before* him into the life hereafter. On the walls of the temple of Luxor, where the birth of Amenhotep III was depicted in sculptured scenes late in the Fifteenth Century before Christ, we find the little prince brought in on the arm of the Nile-god, accompanied apparently by another child. This second figure, identical in external appearance with that of the prince, is the being called by the Egyptians the *ka*. He was a kind of superior genius intended especially to guide the fortunes of the individual in *the hereafter*, where every Egyptian who died found his ka awaiting him. It is of importance to note that in all probability the ka was originally the exclusive possession of kings, each of whom thus lived under the protection of his individual guardian genius, and that by a process of slow development the privilege of possessing a ka became universal among all the people.

These are only a few of the passages in Breasted's book that are borrowed by the *UB*, often with phrases taken word for word. It is possible that such literal transcribing was unintentional. I know from my own experience that one can take extensive notes on a library book, or even a book one owns, under the impression that one is rephrasing the material in his own words. Months or years later, in referring to those notes, it is easy to forget that certain phrases had been copied verbatim.

Which is more plausible? That celestial beings did this kind of note taking, or that Sadler, or some other member of the Contact Commission or the Forum, believing himself or herself authorized by midwayers to write a certain Paper, consciously or unconsciously plagiarized?

I mentioned earlier Block's discovery of how the *UB* made use of Rufus Jones's *A Preface to Christian Faith in a New Age*. I was able to check this book, and although there is little word-for-word copying, occasionally words and phrases by Jones are repeated. Some examples:

UB (2084)

"The kingdom of God is within you" was probably the greatest pronouncement Jesus ever made. . . ."

Jones (130)

The great saying: "The Kingdom of God is in you," has been called by a modern Hindu the greatest revelation that any person has ever made.

UB (2085)

If the Christian church would only dare to espouse the Master's program, thousands of apparently indifferent youths would rush forward to enlist in such a spiritual undertaking, and they would not hesitate to go all the way through with this great adventure.

Jones (163–64)

If the Church is to recover its commanding place of influence in the life of the world to-day it must give a larger share of leadership to those who are young. The entire Church must be penetrated with a new spirit of adventure, and that spirit is peculiarly a characteristic of youth.

UB (2085)

The true church . . . is characterized by *unity*, not necessarily by uniformity. . . . [it] is destined to become a *living organism*.

Jones (143, 146)

There has been a curious and yet widespread tendency manifested to confuse unity with uniformity. They are totally different. . . .

The heart of Christianity would seem to be one that approached as closely as possible to a living, growing *organism*.

UB (2086)

There is great need [in modern education] for the teaching of moral discipline in the place of so much self-gratification.

Jones (194)

In speaking favorably, as has been done, of certain modern types of education, nothing should be said that would imply sympathy with any methods of education that neglect mental or moral *discipline*.

UB (2075)

As you view the world, remember that the black patches of evil which you see are shown against a white background of ultimate good. You do not view merely white patches of good which show up miserably against a black background of evil.

Jones (70)

The central faith of the chapter is . . . that in the ultimate nature of things the black squares are on a white background and not the white squares on a black one.

Many other phrases and ideas from Jones's book have found their way into the *UB*. "The world needs more firsthand religion" (*UB* 2083). "First-hand religion" is the title of Jones's third chapter. The *UB* (2083) tells how Christianity has "dared to lower its ideals." Jones (page 36) also bemoans the fact that Christianity has "lowered its ideals."

"The stream of modern Christianity drains many an ancient pagan swamp and many a barbarian morass; many olden cultural watersheds drain into this present-day cultural stream as well as the high Galilean tablelands which are supposed to be its exclusive source." So says the *UB* on page 2083. Compare this with Jones's *A Preface to Christian Faith in a New* Age (page 284):

"Christian civilization is, therefore, by no means a river with a single source. On the contrary, it drains swamps and morasses and remote watersheds as well as that high Galilean tableland from which the original stream emerged."

Jones writes on his first page that "disciples of a crucified carpenter . . . conquered the Roman Empire." The *UB* (2086) says: "disciples of a crucified carpenter. . . . conquered the Roman World."

If the reader can obtain a copy of Jones's book and read it carefully, then read Paper 195, it will be obvious that the *UB* paper is a skillful summary of Jones's basic themes. Which is more plausible? That a celestial being read Jones's book and summarized it, or that Sadler or one of his friends did the reading and summarizing?

On pages 556–57 of the *UB*, the Archangel of Nebadon lists 28 "statements of human philosophy" which he says are being used by instructors on the first mansion world to teach beginning students "the significance and meaning of mota." Mota is a term used in the *UB* for a higher form of logic and metaphysics.

Block's sensational discovery—how he ever happened to make it beats me!—was that almost all 28 statements are based on short quotations in an anthology titled *The New Dictionary of Thoughts: A Cyclopedia of Quotations*, compiled by Tryon Edwards. The book was titled *Jewels for the Household* when first published in 1852 as a work of 448 pages. It was enlarged to 664 pages in 1891 and retitled *Dictionary of Thoughts*. There were many later editions, revised and enlarged by others, culminating in 794 pages published as *The New Dictionary of Thoughts* by the Standard Book Company in 1957.

For some hard-to-fathom reason, most of the *UB*'s copying is from this anthology's first 33 pages. Below I will list on the left a statement as it appears in the dictionary (page numbers based on the 1957 edition), followed on the right by a similar statement in the *UB*. In most cases the copying is obvious. In others, only a basic thought is copied. In the latter case it is not always easy to locate the correlated quotation in a book of 794 pages. Block and I, working independently, agreed on the correlations given here. In two cases, statements numbered 6 and 23 in the *UB*, we were not able to find plausible parallel quotations. The author of the *UB* paper obviously had to use an edition of the anthology prior to 1957; it is possible that quotation sources for 6 and 23 were removed from the 1957 edition to which Block and I had access.

Edwards	*UB*
1. We should be on our guard against the temptation to argue directly from skill to capacity, and to assume when a man displays skill in some feat, his capacity is therefore considerable. (p. 1)	1. A display of specialized skill does not signify possession of spiritual capacity. Cleverness is not a substitute for true character.
2. The ablest men in all walks of modern life are men of faith. Most of them have much more faith than they themselves realize.	2. Few persons live up to the faith which they really have. Unreasoned fear is a master intellectual fraud practiced upon the evolving mortal soul.
3. A pint can't hold a quart–if it holds a pint it is doing all that can be expected of it. (p. 1)	3. Inherent capacities cannot be exceeded; a pint can never hold a quart. The spirit concept cannot be mechanically forced into the material memory mold.
4. Men are often capable of greater things then they perform.— They are sent into the world with bills of credit, and seldom draw to their full extent. (p. 1)	4. Few mortals ever dare to draw anything like the sum of personality credits established by the combined ministries of nature and grace. The majority of impoverished souls are truly rich, but they refuse to believe it.
5. Afflictions sent by providence melt the constancy of the noble minded, but confirm the obduracy of the vile, as the same furnace that liquefies the gold, hardens the clay. (p. 11)	5. Difficulties may challenge mediocrity and defeat the fearful, but they only stimulate the true children of the Most Highs.
6. ?	6. To enjoy privilege without abuse, to have liberty without license, to possess power and steadfastly refuse to use it for self-aggrandizement—these are the marks of high civilization.
7. What men call accident is the doing of God's providence. (p. 3)	7. Blind and unforeseen accidents do not occur in the cosmos. Neither do the celestial beings assist the lower being who refuses to act upon his light of truth.
8. Action may not always bring happiness; but there is no happiness without action. (p. 3)	8. Effort does not always produce joy, but there is no happiness without intelligent effort.
9. Only actions give to life its strength, as only moderation gives it its charm. (p. 3)	9. Action achieves strength; moderation eventuates in charm.
10. Every action of our lives touches on some chord that will vibrate in eternity. (p. 5) A right act strikes a chord that extends through the whole universe, touches all moral intelligence, visits every world, vibrates along its whole extent, and conveys its vibrations to the very bosom of God! (p. 4)	

Edwards	*UB*
11. I have never heard anything about the resolutions of the apostles, but a great deal about their acts. (p. 4)	10. Righteousness strikes the harmony chords of truth, and the melody vibrates throughout the cosmos, even to the recognition of the Infinite.
Actions are ours; their consequences belong to heaven. (p. 5)	11. The weak indulge in resolutions, but the strong act. Life is but a day's work—do it well. The act is ours; the consequences God's.
12. No man is more unhappy than the one who is never in adversity; the greatest affliction of life is never to be afflicted. (p. 6)	12. The greatest affliction of the cosmos is never to have been afflicted. Mortals only learn wisdom by experiencing tribulation.
13. Stars may be seen from the bottom of a deep well, when they cannot be discerned from the top of a mountain. So are many things learned in adversity which the prosperous man dreams not of. (p.6)	13. Stars are best discerned from the lonely isolation of experiential depths, not from the illuminated and ecstatic mountain tops.
14. Advice and reprehension require the utmost delicacy; painful truths should be delivered in the softest terms, and expressed no farther than is necessary to produce their due effect. A courteous man will mix what is conciliating with what is offensive; praise with censure; deference and respect with the authority of admonition, so far as can be done in consistence with probity and honor. The mind revolts against all censorian power which displays pride or pleasure in finding fault; but advice, divested of the harshness, and yet retaining the honest warmth of truth, is like honey put round the brim of a vessel full of wormwood.—Even this, however, is sometimes insufficient to conceal the bitterness of the draught.	14. Whet the appetites of your associates for truth; give advice only when it is asked for.
	15. Affectation is the ridiculous effort of the ignorant to appear wise, the attempt of the barren soul to appear rich.
	16. You cannot perceive spiritual truth until you feelingly experience it, and many truths are not really felt except in adversity.
	17. Ambition is dangerous until it is fully socialized. You have not truly acquired any virtue until your acts make you worthy of it.
	18. Impatience is a spirit poison; anger is like a stone hurled into a hornet's nest.
Give every man thine ear, but few thy voice; take each man's censure, but reserve thy judgment.	19. Anxiety must be abandoned. The disappointments hardest to bear are those which never come.
Giving advice is sometimes only showing our wisdom at the expense of another. (p. 9)	20. Only a poet can discern poetry in the commonplace prose of routine existence.

Edwards

15. All affectation is the vain and ridiculous attempt of poverty to appear rich. (p. 9)

16. Adversity is the trial of principle.—Without it a man hardly knows whether he is honest or not. (p. 6)

That which thou dost not understand when thou readest, thou shalt understand in the day of thy visitation; for many secrets of religion are not perceived till they be felt, and are not felt but in the day of calamity. (p. 11)

17. We should not be so taken up in the search for truth, as to neglect the needful duties of active life; for it is only action that gives a true value and commendation to virtue. (p. 4)

18. Anger is as a stone cast into a wasp's nest. (p. 24)

19. Let us be of good cheer, remembering that the misfortunes hardest to bear are those which never come. (p. 26)

20. You will find poetry nowhere unless you bring some with you. (pp. 28 and 488)

21. The highest problem of any art is to cause by appearance the illusion of a higher reality. (p. 31)

22. 'Tis not what man does which exalts him, but what man would do! (p. 33)

23. ?

24. The acts of this life are the destiny of the next. (p. 5)

Act well at the moment, and you have performed a good action for all eternity. (p. 4)

UB

21. The high mission of any art is, by its illusions, to foreshadow a higher universe reality, to crystallize the emotions of time into the thought of eternity.

22. The evolving soul is not made divine by what it does, but by what it strives to do.

23. Death added nothing to the intellectual possession or to the spiritual endowment, but it did add to the experiential status the consciousness of *survival.*

24. The destiny of eternity is determined moment by moment by the achievements of the day by day living. The acts of today are the destiny of tomorrow.

25. Greatness lies not so much in possessing strength as in making a wise and divine use of such strength.

26. Knowledge is possessed only by sharing; it is safeguarded by wisdom and socialized by love.

27. Progress demands development of individuality; mediocrity seeks perpetuation in standardization.

28. The argumentative defense of any proposition is inversely proportional to the truth contained.

Edwards

25. Greatness lies, not in being strong, but in the right use of strength.—*Bryant* (Page 249). [On page 251 the same statement is credited to Henry Ward Beecher.]

26. If you would thoroughly know anything, teach it to others.—*Tryon Edwards* (p. 333)

27. Individuality is either the mark of genius or the reverse. Mediocrity finds safety in standardization. (p. 302)

28. He who establishes his argument by noise and command, shows that his reason is weak. (p. 29)

Perhaps readers with access to Edwards' book can improve on the above parallels, and find sources in the book for the *UB*'s statements 6 and 23.

Why, in the names of the Most Highs, would instructors on the first mansion world consult an undistinguished Urantian anthology of quotations, then rephrase 28 of the book's dullest aphorisms, all on the anthology's first 33 pages, to use in teaching ethics to newly arrived Urantian personalities? Which is more plausible? That an archangel of Nebadon faithfully reported what higher beings on another planet are teaching former Urantians, or that Sadler or someone else owned an edition of *The Dictionary of Thoughts* and rephrased 28 quotations which he or she particularly liked but got tired of copying after going through the anthology's first 33 pages?

Two discourses by Jesus, outlining "true religion," are in the *UB* on pages 1728–1733. As Block was the first to discover, it seems as if Jesus had somehow peered into the future to read a 1904 book by Auguste Sabatier, a Protestant theologian at the University of Paris. The heart of what Jesus taught, says the *UB*, is that true religion is of the Spirit, based on human experience, not on the authority of past dogmas such as the religion of the Pharisees. The phrase "religion(s) of authority" is used by Jesus more than ten times in his two brief talks. From religions of authority, he said, one must progress to the freedoms of a "religion of the Spirit . . . wholly based on human experience."

Now this is precisely the central theme, including the same phrases, of Sabatier's work. Indeed, the title of his book is *Religions of Authority and the Religion of the Spirit*. His book attacks both Roman Catholic and Protestant religions of authority. Jesus could not, of course, have lambasted those faiths, but his attack on the authoritarianism of the scribes is essentially the same.

"Two systems of theology still confront one another" Sabatier writes in his preface, "the theology of authority and the theology of experience." He calls the latter "the religion of the Spirit." The gospel taught by Jesus, he writes (283), "implied the abrogation of religions of authority, and inaugurated as a fact the religion of the Spirit." The authority of the letter gave way to "holiness and love."

Sabatier (369ff.) distinguishes three stages of religious evolution. As Block recognized, they correspond to the "three manifestations of the religious urge" taught by Jesus on page 1728 of the *UB*. Sabatier's first stage is the uncivilized worship of nature in which persons fear "mysterious powers." The *UB* calls it a "fear" of "mysterious energies." The second stage is a civilized one governed by mind. Superstitions give way to moral laws and religious dogmas—the age of rational theology and church authority. The third stage, initiated by Jesus, is uncompelled faith in God the Father, coupled with the love of others. Sabatier calls this religion's "beautiful mission." Jesus in the *UB* calls it a "glimpse of the beauty of the infinite character of the Father in heaven—the religion of the spirit as demonstrated in human experience."

Need I point out that this debt to Sabatier's book casts grave doubts on the accuracy of the *UB*'s life of Jesus? This is not just copying by *UB* authors of prose material, but copying put into the mouth of Jesus!

The Life of Christ, by Ernest DeWitt Burton and Shailer Mathews (University of Chicago Press, 1901) was used by the author of the *UB*'s Jesus Papers in a puzzling manner. As Block discovered, only its chapter and section titles were copied: "The Man with the Withered Hand" (*UB* 1664), "The Widespread Fame of Jesus" (*UB* 1668), "More Parables By the Sea" (*UB* 1693), "The Crisis at Capernaum" (*UB* 1707), "The Woman Taken in Adultery" (*UB* 1792), and "The Discourse on Spiritual Freedom" (*UB* 1796).

Why the author of the Jesus Papers would steal only titles is hard to comprehend. Even more curious is the fact that he or she used only the book's first edition. In their revised edition of 1927 the authors dropped all the above headings except the one about the adulterous woman. Mathews writes in his preface: "The headings for sections have also been changed in the interest of a clearer analysis of the account of the work and words, the religious influence and ideals, of Jesus." For some reason, the *UB* author did not think it necessary to check the revised edition that would have provided such clarification. Could it be that he or she had access only to the 1901 edition?

We know that Sadler was familiar with Burton's writings because Burton's *Source Book for the Study of the Teachings of Jesus* (1928) is cited by Sadler in his list of references following the chapter on religious therapy in *Theory and Practice of Psychiatry*.

Two widely read books of the time, both by Walter E. Bundy, a professor of English Bible at DePauw University, had an enormous influence on the *UB*'s final Paper 196. The books were *The Religion of Jesus* (Bobbs-Merrill, 1928) and *Our Recovery of Jesus* (same firm, 1929). Block estimates that about 95 percent of the Paper's preamble and first two sections derive from those two books. "The last sections differ in tone and content," Block adds, "and may be original with the midwayers."

In the twenties the phrase "religious experience" was a popular one with writers on religion. Bundy must have used it more than a thousand times. William James titled his classic work on religion *The Varieties of Religious Experience*. William Ernest Hocking called his major book on religion *The Meaning of God in Human Experience* (1912). The phrase is used repeatedly in the Jesus Papers, especially in Paper 196.

Urantians like to quote from page 2091, "You may *preach* a religion *about* Jesus, but, perforce, you must *live* the religion *of* Jesus." On page 2090 the *UB* recommends that "religion about Jesus" be replaced by the "living religion of Jesus." On page 2089: "Jesus does not require his disciples to believe in him, but rather to believe *with* him." This distinction between religion about Jesus, and the religion of Jesus, is made over and over again in Bundy's two books. I will cite a few examples, keeping the italics of the original as I have done with *UB* quotes.

From *The Religion of Jesus:*

"[H]istorical Christianity has demanded first of all the sharing of *a faith about Jesus* rather than a sharing of *Jesus' own personal faith*." (253).

"Jesus did not demand that his followers believe *in* or *on* him, but that they believe *with* him" (264).

"Christianity from the moment of its birth was a *religion about Jesus* rather than *the religion of Jesus*" (277).

"*A religion about Jesus* may fit the pious patterns of the past. . . . but only *the religion of Jesus* can recommend and prove itself in the life and experience of modern men." (325).

"The hope of Christianity . . . is not a rigorous restriction of what may or may not be believed *about* Jesus, but is an unreserved release of all our powers to believe *with* him" (329).

"Jesus not only challenged his followers to believe *what* he believed, but also to believe *as* he believed" (264). The *UB*'s statement (2089) is extremely close in wording: "Jesus most touchingly challenged his followers, not only to believe what he believed, but also to believe as he believed."

"The common idea is that Jesus founded a religion—Christianity. But it is better history to say: *Jesus became a religion*" (277). The *UB* (2092) says it this way: "But the greatest mistake was made in that, while the human Jesus was recognized as having a religion, the divine Jesus (Christ) almost overnight became a religion." I see no improvement in the way the *UB* expands Bundy.

From Bundy's *Our Recovery of Jesus*:

"Christianity as *a religion about Jesus* has almost totally obscured Christian vision for *the religion of Jesus*" (2).

"Is a *religion about Jesus*, such as Christianity has always been, to furnish the body of our faith, or are we to turn to *the religion of Jesus?*" (7).

"He [Jesus] did not require that his disciples believe certain things *about* him, but that they believe *with* him. . . . It is not difficult to believe *in* Jesus, but to believe *with* him, to believe *what* and *as* he believed . . . is a religious task that lays hold on the deepest sources of human life" (10).

The *UB* (2092) has harsh words about Paul for having replaced the religion of Jesus with a religion *about* Jesus. This, too, is stressed by Bundy. In *Our Recovery of Jesus* he describes Paul's religion as a "different world," one "quite distinct from the religious experience of Jesus," and, "In the Christian experience of Paul the Christ of faith, not the Jesus of history, is the supreme religious authority" (32).

On page 2093 of the *UB* we read: "Jesus did not share Paul's pessimistic view of humankind . . . he viewed man positively, not negatively. He saw men as weak rather than wicked, more distraught than depraved."

Compare this with Bundy's words on pages 170–71 of *Our Recovery of Jesus*:

"He [Jesus] shared nothing of that Christian pessimism concerning humankind that has run like a strong stream from the thought of Paul down to the present. . . . Jesus' estimate of humankind is positive, not negative. . . . Jesus worked on the assumption that men are weak rather than wicked. . . . Jesus found men distracted and distraught rather than depraved and doomed."

Many other phrases in Paper 196 come straight from Bundy. The very first sentence of *The Religion of Jesus* is "Jesus was God's Galilea..." The *UB* (2088) calls Jesus "God's Galilean." Bundy writes (*Our Recovery of Jesus*, page 16): "He [Jesus] was one of them, a layman." The *UB* (2090–91): "The people heard him gladly because he was one of them, an unpretentious layman."

The author of Paper 196 (*UB* 2089) writes: "Jesus most teachingly challenged his followers, not only to believe *what* he believed, but also to believe *as* he believed. This is the full significance of his one supreme requirement, 'Follow me.'" Here is how Bundy says the same thing (*Our Recovery of Jesus*, page 10): "Jesus had no creed . . . no confession that he required of his disciples. The one great command of Jesus was, 'Follow me.'"

On page 2089 of the *UB* are two paragraphs about how Jesus' faith in God was like that of a child trusting his or her parents. The sentences are derived from a 20-page section of Bundy's *The Religion of Jesus*, a section headed "The Child Mind" (218ff). The *UB* also calls the mind of Jesus a "child mind." Bundy writes: "A final feature in the child mind is a singular lack of pretense" (226). The *UB* says: "There was no hesitating pretense in his [Jesus'] religious experience." Bundy stresses the child's sense of "wonder in the world," and how the "wonder-world" is part of all religious experience. The *UB* speaks of the child's response to the "wonder of the universe." Bundy stresses the child's "unreserved trust." The *UB* speaks of "the purity of a child's trust." Bundy stresses the child's "sense of security." The *UB* speaks of the child's "assurance of absolute personal security." Bundy emphasizes the child's "wholesome and sunny optimism." The *UB* speaks of the child's "trusting optimism."

Of all the books on his 1993 list, Block thinks that the one "most extensively used" by *UB* authors was E. Washburn Hopkins' *Origin and Evolution of*

Religion (Yale University Press, 1923). All of Paper 85, he correctly states, "is taken directly from the first eight chapters of the book, each section in the paper corresponding almost exactly to a chapter in the book." Material from Hopkins is also incorporated in Papers 86 through 90, and in Paper 92. "The preamble and section 1 of Paper 104," Block writes, "are taken directly from Hopkins' chapters on 'The Triad,' 'The Hindu Trinity,' 'The Buddhistic Trinity,' and 'The Christian Trinity.'" The *UB*'s constant stress on the fact that religions evolve is the central concept of Hopkins' book.

The extent of the *UB*'s debt to Hopkins is indeed astonishing. Not only are facts and ideas freely appropriated, but often the very phrasing is copied. Here are some sample instances:

"Man has worshipped everything on earth, including himself" (Hopkins, page 13). "At one time or another mortal man has worshipped everything on the face of the earth, including himself" (*UB* 944).

"At the present day the inhabitants of Kateri in South India worship a stone . . . and in Northern India. . . . Jacob after using a stone as a pillow annointed it and Rachel concealed stones in the tent" (Hopkins, pages 14–15). "Today the Kateri people of Southern India still worship a stone . . . and in Northern India. Jacob slept on a stone because he venerated it; he even annointed it. Rachel concealed a number of sacred stones in her tent" (*UB* 944).

"A group of five stones in India, thirty in Greece" (Hopkins, page 16). "A group of five stones was reverenced in India; in Greece it was a cluster of thirty" (*UB* 945).

"The ceremony of throwing a stone among the Romans involved the invocation of Jupiter. . . . Here may be mentioned the common practice in India of taking up a stone as a witness. If one wishes to hale an offender to court one seizes a stone and calls it an officer" (Hopkins, page 17). "The Romans always threw a stone in the air when invoking Jupiter. . . . In some regions a stone may be employed as a talisman of the law, and by its prestige an offender can be haled into court" (*UB* 945).

"Noses and ears were not perforated at first to carry rings, but the rings were carried to keep open the hole" (Hopkins, page 18). "Ears were not perforated to carry stones, but the stones were put in to keep the ear holes open" (*UB* 945).

"The Finns regard them [tree spirits] as gentle . . . while in Switzerland the wood-spirits are tricky" (Hopkins, page 25). "The Finns believed that most trees were occupied by kind spirits. The Swiss long mistrusted the trees, believing they contained tricky spirits" (*UB* 945).

"[I]n modern India and in Africa . . . the rainbow is a celestial snake" (Hopkins, page 51). "In both India and Africa the rainbow is thought to be a gigantic celestial snake" (*UB* 947).

"Fire-worship, which reached its highest point in ancient Persia . . . vestal virgins whose primary care was to tend the fire" (Hopkins, pages 49–50). "Fire reverence reached its height in Persia. . . . Vestal virgins were charged with the duty of watching sacred fires" (*UB* 947).

"Moon-worship . . . is probably older than sun-worship for it belongs more to the hunting stage than to the agricultural (Hopkins, page 55). "Moon worship preceded sun worship. Veneration of the moon was at its height during the hunting era, while sun worship became the chief religious ceremony of the subsequent agricultural ages" (*UB* 947).

"A savage . . . makes no very clear categories of beast, man, and god" (Hopkins, page 67). "The simple-minded savage makes no clear distinction between beasts, men, and gods" (*UB* 948).

The above are only a few of hundreds of parallels that can be found between Hopkins' pages and Paper 85, said to be "presented by a Brilliant Evening Star of Nebadon." It should be obvious to anyone that the Brilliant Evening Star was someone who had Hopkins' book before him or her, and simply summarized, often with identical words and phrases, the first eight chapters of Hopkins' work. There is scarcely a passage in Paper 85 that is not derived from Hopkins. If the Evening Star was truly a celestial being, surely he or she could have done better than just condense and reword the writings of a Yale University professor of Sanskrit and comparative philology! Would it not have been more honest if the not-so-Brilliant Evening Star had simply advised Urantians to buy and read Hopkins' book, rather than to take credit for an erudition he or she did not possess? Was it fair to Hopkins not to name him as the source?

As Block correctly perceives, Paper 85 is not the only one in the UB stolen from Hopkins. I will not weary the reader with too many parallels, but let the following almost randomly selected instances suffice.

"Now before sacrifice is thought of, the savage mourner indulges in mutilations . . . plucking of hair, cutting off of fingers, knocking out of teeth" (Hopkins, page 159). "The first sacrifices were such acts as plucking hair, cutting the flesh, mutilations, knocking out teeth, and cutting off fingers." (*UB* 977).

"Why Three should have become a 'holy number' has long been the subject of speculation. One modern theory suggests that, as man has three finger-joints . . . three became the base of order, hence holy" (Hopkins, page 291). "The ideas of triads arose from many suggestive relationships but chiefly because of the three joints of the fingers" (*UB* 1143). "Now it is true that we think in triads . . . yesterday, today, and tomorrow . . . sunrise, noon, sunset . . . father, mother, child" (Hopkins, page 291). "Man generally tends to think in triads: yesterday, today, and tomorrow; sunrise, noon, and sunset; father, mother, and child" (*UB* 1143).

"The Chinese ghost is placated by a threefold oblation of water. . . . the corpse clearly demands burial within three days" (Hopkins, page 293). "The dead are buried on the third day, and the ghost is placated by three ablutions of water" (*UB* 1143).

The discussion of fetishes in Paper 88 is taken largely from Hopkins. I will cite only a few of many examples. Hopkins writes (p. 119): "All those parts of the body which seem to have a life of their own . . . among these the nails and hair . . . are particularly apt to be taken as possessing soul-power." The *UB* (968): "Parts of the human body were looked upon as potential fetishes, particularly the hair and nails."

Hopkins (135): "More general is the ritual implying saliva-power. To spit thrice is to avert evil or a spirit. . . . To spit on a person is ordinarily to excercise soul-power against him. . . . in some African tribes the host spits on his departing guest as a compliment." *UB* (968): "Saliva was a potent fetish; devils could be driven out by spitting on a person. For an elder or superior to spit on one was the highest compliment."

In view of the *UB*'s heavy indebtedness to Hopkins it is not surprising that Sadler, at the close of his chapter "Religious Therapy," in *Theory and Practice of Psychiatry*, lists Hopkins' book as a major reference.

❧

On pages 1954–55 of the *UB* we are told that the inner peace Jesus gives to his followers is superior to the peace provided by stoicism and optimism. "A certain amount of both stoicism and optimism are serviceable in living a life on earth, but neither has aught to do with that superb peace which the Son of God bestows upon his brethren in the flesh." Block believes that this reflects pages 101–102 of George Palmer's *The Autobiography of a Philosopher* (1930).

Palmer was a Harvard professor of philosophy, best known for his books on ethics and for his translation of Homer's *Odyssey*. He was a devout Anglican, though liberal enough to abandon such doctrines as the Virgin Birth and to be repelled by such New Testament legends as that of

Jesus cursing a fig tree because it was barren. In his little volume of auto-biography Palmer distinguishes the peace of the Christian from "two inferior forms of hardihood"—stoicism, which "refuses to be crushed" by any disaster, and extreme optimism, which sees everything as happening for the best. However, there is no copying in the *UB* of actual sentences by Palmer.

We can be sure that Palmer's views were the source for the *UB*'s remarks about stoicism and optimism because Sadler himself credits Palmer as the source in his *Theory and Practice of Psychiatry*, written in the mid 1930s. Here is what Sadler has to say about Palmer on page 1115:

> Of all the well-known modern philosophers whose beliefs might very definitely be included in this category of Divine Sonship, the most oustanding is Professor George Herbert *Palmer*, long professor of philosophy at Harvard University. Professor Palmer very definitely emphasizes the consciousness of Divine Sonship as a central concept in his personal credo. He believes that morality consists in "the fullness of self-realization."
>
> After discarding Stoicism and optimism, Palmer was led to adopt as the theme song of his personal philosophy "the idea of the fatherhood of God," and he elaborated this concept until it came, in his system of belief, to embrace the following seven features:
>
> 1. Companionship—conscious membership in the universe family.
> 2. Cure of fear—the cessation of morbid dread.
> 3. The banishment of regret.
> 4. The removal of harshness and the feelings of slavery from the sense of duty.
> 5. The augmentation of the feeling of security.
> 6. The development of patience—deliverance from the tension of time.
> 7. Salvation from fatalism.
>
> Palmer's philosophy in its essence is summed up in his conclusion that in religion man faces God, while in morals he faces his fellows.

Which is more plausible: that a celestial midwayer studied Palmer, or that Sadler admired Palmer and introduced his distinction between Christian peace and the lesser peace of stoics and optimists into the *UB*?

There is not the slightest doubt that the "Mighty Messenger on duty in Nebadon," who wrote Paper 42 "by the request of Gabriel" (*UB* 484), carefully checked *The Architecture of the Universe* (1934). This book was written by William Francis Gray Swann, a physicist at the Franklin Institute. On pages 479–80 of the *UB*, in a section titled "Natural Philosophy," the Mighty Messenger speaks of a "renowned religious teacher" who maintained that seven was a fundamental number in nature because there are seven openings in the human head—eyes, nostrils, ears, and mouth. Had this man known chemistry, the *UB* continues, he would have based his belief on a firmer foundation: when the basic elements are "arranged in the order of their atomic weights," their properties fall into groups of seven.

Swann in a chapter titled "Progress of Natural Philosophy," tells how Francesco Sizzi, an eminent Roman Catholic contemporary of Galileo, argued that seven is fundamental in nature because of the head's seven openings. He could have done better, Swann writes, had he known that the properties of the chemical elements fall into groups of seven "when arranged in order of their atomic weights" (page 4).

As Block points out, "Many of his [Swann's] temperature, size, and distance estimates relating to intra-atomic and astronomic bodies are used in *The Urantia Book* as are several of his analogies and illustrations." Block cites this example:

> If the mass of matter should be magnified until that of an electron equaled one tenth of an ounce, then were size to be proportionately magnified, the volume of such an electron would become as large as that of the earth. If the volume of a proton eighteen hundred times as heavy as an electron should be magnified to the size of the head of a pin, then, in comparison, a pin's head would attain a diameter equal to that of the earth's orbit around the sun. (*UB* 477)

Here are the parallel sentences by Swann:

> The mass of the electron is so small that if you should magnify all masses so that the electron attains a mass of one tenth of an ounce, that one tenth of an ounce would, on the same scale of magnification, become as heavy as the earth.
>
> Then, we have the proton—the fundamental unit of positive charge— a thing 1800 times as heavy as the electron, but 1800 times smaller in size, so that if you should magnify it to the size of a pin's head, that pin's head would, on the same scale of magnification, attain a diameter equal to the diameter of the earth's orbit around the sun. (pages 44–45)

Note that the Mighty Messenger made a mighty mistake in copying from Swann. He says the magnified electron would have a *volume* equal to that of the earth when he should have said *mass*. It would be as massive as the earth, not the same size. On the other hand, Swann made a monumental error when he said the proton was 1800 times smaller than an electron in size—a mistake the *UB* does not repeat.

Preceding the paragraph quoted from the *UB* is this one:

> Each atom is a trifle over 1/100,000,000th of an inch in diameter, while an electron weighs a little less than 1/2,000th of the smallest atom, hydrogen. The positive proton, characteristic of the atomic nucleus, while it may be no larger than a negative electron, weighs from two to three thousand times more (*UB* 477).

Here the author wrote "less" in the second line when the word should have been "more." Someone corrected the mistake in the second printing of the *UB*, and in the last line changed "From two to three thousand" to "Almost two thousand."

Writing in a Urantia periodical on "Some Human Sources of *The Urantia Book*" (*The Spiritual Fellowship Journal*, Spring 1993, pages 9–13) Block quotes the following passage from Swann that deals with the arrangement of chemical elements in the periodic table:

> Starting from any one of them, and noting some property such as the melting point, for example, the property would change as we went along the row, but as we continued it would gradually come back to a condition very similar to that from which we started; and, as we continued our journey along the row, the same story would be repeated again and again. The eighth element was in many respects like the first, the ninth like the second, the tenth like the third, and so on. Such a state of affairs pointed not only to a varied internal structure, but also to a certain harmony in that variation suggestive of some organized plan in building the atom (page 64).

The Mighty Messenger paraphrases Swann (*UB* 480) as follows:

> Starting from any one element, after noting some one property, such a quality will change for six consecutive elements, but on reaching the eighth, it tends to reappear, that is, the eighth chemically active element resembles the first, the ninth the second, and so on. Such a fact of the physical world unmistakably points to the sevenfold constitution of ancestral energy and is indicative of the fundamental reality of the seven-

fold diversity of the creations of time and space. Man should also note that there are seven colors in the natural spectrum.

Today it is customary to speak of six colors in the rainbow—red, orange, yellow, green, blue, and violet—rather than wedge indigo between blue and purple. But the celestials, like Seventh-day Adventists, occultists, numerologists, and early Church Fathers, have (as we have seen) a special affinity for seven.

☙❧

All the source books on Block's list are out of print except for Breasted's. Secondhand copies are hard to find and costly, and often difficult to obtain on interlibrary loans. At the time I write, I have not yet seen copies of items 1, 2, 7, 8, 10, 15, 16, on the list of books below.

The list catches only the sources Block had uncovered by 1992. They appear in alphabetical order of the authors. After each title I note the portion of the *UB* which Block found to be the most heavily influenced by the source, in many cases with copying of exact wording.

1. W. G. Aston, *Shinto: The Way of the Gods* (1905). Paper 131. Block comments:

> Sentences from Aston's translation of the "Wa Rongo" collection of Shinto oracles, lightly rewritten or paraphrased, constitute the entire selection of Ganid's abstract of Shinto.

2. William Samuel Bishop, *The Theology of Personality* (1926). Foreword, Section 12; Paper 106, Section 8. Block writes:

> Although there appears to be no superhuman lifting of content here, Bishop uses the terms "trinity," "triunity," and—amazingly—"A Trinity of Trinities" in the exposition of his constructive theology. These terms are completely re-worked in *The Urantia Book*.

3. James Henry Breasted, *The Dawn of Conscience* (1933). Paper 95.

4. Walter E. Bundy, *The Religion of Jesus* (1928). Paper 196, preamble and Sections 1, 2.

5. Walter E. Bundy, *Our Recovery of Jesus* (1929). Paper 196, preamble and Sections 1, 2.

6. Ernest DeWitt Burton and Shailer Mathews, *The Life of Christ* (1927). Only the chapter and section titles of Part IV are taken from this book.

7. Paul Carus, *The Canon of Reason and Virtue: Being Lao-tze's Tao Teh King* (1913). Paper 94, Section 6, Paper 131, Section 8. "This translation of the *Tao te Ching,*" Block comments, "was used by the revelators in the reference to Taoism in Parts I, III, and IV."

8. E. V. Cowdry, editor, *Human Biology and Racial Warfare* (1930). Paper 51, Section 4; Paper 65, Section 2; Paper 82, Section 6. Writes Block: "The revelators use essays by Hrdlicka, Conklin and Davenport in their discussions of race differences, the dangers and benefits of race mixing, and the feasibility of a modest eugenics program."

9. Tryon Edwards, *The New Dictionary of Thought* (1957). Paper 48, Section 7.

10. Harry Emerson Fosdick, *The Hope of the World* (1933). Paper 131, Section 7. "Goodness is effective only when it is attractive" (*UB* 1874), Block says, "is the essence of Fosdick's sermon 'The Fine Art of Making Goodness Attractive'."

11. S. E. Frost Jr., editor, *The Sacred Writings of the World's Great Religions* (1943). Paper 131.

Block comments: "*The Urantia Book* appears to use the same translations of the Jain, Zoroastrian and Confucian writings as Frost, as well as the Aston Shinto translation. There is remarkable overlap in the passages selected in the two books." I differ from Block. There seems to me very little overlap, and I strongly suspect that the author of Paper 131 had another source for the quotations.

12. Charles Hartshorne, *Man's Vision of God* (1941). Foreword, Section 1.

13. E. Washburn Hopkins, *Origin and Evolution of Religion* (1923). Papers 85, 90, 92, 96, 104.

14. Rufus M. Jones, *The Inner Life* (1916). Paper 107.

15. Rufus M. Jones, *A Preface to Christian Faith in a New Age* (1932). Paper 195, Sections 5, 10. "Virtually every paragraph of Section 10, 'The Future'," writes Block "is drawn consecutively from the last half of this book."

16. Edmund Noble, *Purposive Evolution* (1926). Paper 42, Section 11; Paper 116, Section 7.

As Block points out, Noble's chapter 9 is titled "Cosmic Self-Maintenance: The Universe as Purposive." The phrase "cosmic self-maintenance" appears in the *UB* (482), twelfth line from bottom, with "purposive" following four lines later.

17. Henry Fairfield Osborn, *Man Rises to Parnassus* (1928). Paper 64,

Sections 2, 4; Paper 80, Sections 3, 8, 9. Block writes: "This book seems to be the prime source for the *UB*'s discussion of successive human races in Europe from the Foxhall peoples to the Neanderthals, the Cro-Magnons and the ancestors of the Nordics. The *UB* largely adheres to Osborn's geological, racial and cultural chronologies and to his characterizations of the cultures of these various peoples. Osborn's discussion of the Bretons is paralleled exactly on p. 899 of the *UB*."

Block has perhaps overstated the *UB*'s reliance on this book by Osborn, though there are spots in the *UB* which may be so indebted. For example, the *UB* says (899) that Bretons "still keep thunderstorms in the chimney as protection against lightning." Osborn says it more clearly: "In many of the chimneys of Brittany homes these ancient Celts still hang [charms] to ward off bolts of lightning" (page 158).

18. George Herbert Palmer, *The Autobiography of a Philosopher* (1930). Paper 81, Section 1.

19. Auguste Sabatier, *Religions of Authority and the Religion of the Spirit* (1904). Paper 155, Sections 5, 6.

20. W. F. G. Swann, *The Architecture of the Universe* (1934). Papers 41 and 42.

In the last of his 1992 releases Block estimated that writings published prior to 1936 "form the basis of about one-third of Parts I and II [of the *UB*], and at least two-thirds of Parts III and IV." He is overwhelmed by the "sheer brilliance" with which the revelators were able to combine copied material with fresh revelations they alone could provide.

Block is not in the least troubled by the fact that the *UB* authors violated United States copyright laws. On the contrary, he is delighted. Here is his comment on two passages from Swann's book:

> Notice the care and elegance with which the second passage is restated. While retaining the original sentence structures and using similar wordings, the superhuman presenter departs from the speculative tone of Swann's last clause, inserting a revealed statement of decisive significance in its place. Scores of other examples of this technique appear in the books listed below; their cumulative effect is truly astounding. Other patterns of referencing, equally ingenious, are also discernible; these will be brought forward in later essays.

Several pages could be devoted to similar quotations from Seventh-day Adventists struggling to justify Ellen White's copious pilfering. Here is a typical statement by Neal Wilson from his article "This I Believe about

Ellen G. White," quoted by Douglas Hackleman in an unpublished essay "Dissecting Ellen G. White Apologetics" (1983):

> Prophets, ancient or modern, selected their material well, Ellen White used authors of recognized quality . . . where they helped to fill out what she had been shown to be true, she wisely used them; when they gave evidence that they did not see the whole truth, she plainly stated the facts as they had been revealed to her by the Holy Spirit.

It is curious that the *UB*, which has no truck with reincarnation or with Hindu mysticism, would tell how Jesus toured Greece, Rome, and the Far East with two East Indian friends. There is a large occult literature claiming that Jesus once visited India. In 1908 the Yogi Publication Society of Chicago published Mystic Christianity, by Yogi Ramacharaka, the pen name of William Walker Atkinson (1862–1932). It is possible that this book may have had some influence on the *UB*'s Jesus papers.

Atkinson's little book denies the Virgin Birth (Joseph is assumed to be the real father of Jesus), but validates such miracles as the raising of Lazarus and changing water to wine. After Jesus' death, it was not his physical body in which he appeared to his followers, Atkinson maintains, but his spiritual "astral" body. A chapter on the youth of Jesus supports the view that in his twenties Jesus visited India, Egypt, and Persia:

> The occult legends inform us that He aroused great interest among the people of each land visited by Him, and that He also aroused the most bitter opposition among the priests, for He always opposed formalism and priestcraft, and sought to lead the people back to the Spirit of the Truth, and away from the ceremonies and forms which have always served to dim and becloud the Light of the Spirit. He taught always the Fatherhood of God and the Brotherhood of Man.

There are other parallels. On page 20 Atkinson identifies the Star of Bethlehem as the conjunction of Saturn and Jupiter "in the constellation of Pisces" in the year 7 BCE It would be interesting to know if Sadler knew Atkinson or if Atkinson ever attended the Forum.

It was on the Internet that I first learned from Stephen Finlan about the *UB*'s debt to *This Believing World*, a popular best-seller in 1926 by the London-born American journalist Lewis Browne. It is impossible to read the *UB*'s account without recognizing how Melchizedek of Nebadon copied from Browne's now forgotten book.

Browne writes (110):

"Mithras grew up to be the most strenuous champion of the sun-god in his war against the god of darkness, and the climax of his career was a life-and-death struggle with a mythical sacred bull. By finally slaying this bull . . . Mithras was exalted to the abode of the immortals, and there he dwelt as the divine protector of all the faithful on earth."

The *UB* (1082) phrases it this way:

"Mithras was conceived as the surviving champion of the sun-god in his struggle with the god of darkness. And in recognition of his slaying the mythical sacred bull, Mithras was made immortal, being exalted to the station of intercessor for the human race."

Note the parallel wording: "champion of the sun-god in his struggle [war] against the god of darkness." Melchizedek's only change is "war" to "struggle." "Exalted" and "sacred bull" are other copied words.

In the next paragraph Browne tells how the devotees of Mithras worshiped "three times a day" in "secret caves," and on December 25 hymns would be chanted, magic rites performed, and the flesh of sacrificial animals eaten and their blood drunk. This would unlock for them the seven gates, with seven keys. At the final judgment the wicked will be annihilated and the redeemed will live forever. These Mithra doctrines closely relate to earlier beliefs in the cult of Cybele. Now read what Melchizedek has to say about Mithra. It is a paraphrasing of what Browne tells us.

Urantians may argue that the revelator improved the wording of Browne's book, but this is far from evident. The simplest explanation is that some mortal who wrote Paper 98, thinking he was transmitting from Melchizedek, condensed and rephrased Browne to escape a clear violation of copyright laws, or else copied from old notes without realizing the similarities.

The *UB*'s brief discussion of Zoroastrianism (1050) is another instance of copying from Browne. Melchizedek emphasizes the influence of this religion on "three great religions"—Judaism, Christianity, and Mohammedanism. Exactly the same points are made by Browne at greater length on pages 216–19. On page 1051 the *UB* calls the Kaaba stone a "black stone fetish in a certain temple at Mecca." Browne (306) speaks of

"This fetish, a black rock enshrined in a small square temple called the Kaaba." Lewis Browne was no authority on comparative religion. One would have expected supermortals to crib from real experts.

One of Harold Sherman's letters to Harry Loose mentions a discovery by Forum members that a paper Sadler had received from the celestials contained a word-for-word copy of a passage in a book by Stuart Chase. Apparently either the passage or the entire paper was excluded from the *UB*. I have not been able to verify this. One old-time Urantian, who asks to be nameless, has confirmed the story but does not recall the book by Chase that was plagiarized.

Engraved on the wall of Gandhi's memorial in India are what the Mahatma called the Seven Sins of humanity:

1. Wealth without works.
2. Pleasure without conscience.
3. Knowledge without character.
4. Commerce without morality.
5. Science without humanity.
6. Worship without sacrifice.
7. Politics without principle.

On page 2086 of the *UB*, in a section on the future of Christianity, we find:

> Christianity suffers under a great handicap because it has become identified in the minds of all the world as a part of the social system, the industrial life, and the moral standards of Western civilization; and thus has Christianity unwittingly seemed to sponsor a society which staggers under the guilt of tolerating science without idealism, politics without principles, wealth without work, pleasure without restraint, knowledge without character, power without conscience, and industry without morality.

One would have thought that the supermortals would have had the decency to credit the seven sins to Gandhi. Perhaps Block can locate the book from which they copied.

In March 1994 I asked Meredith Sprunger, a leading *UB* defender, what he thought about *UB* copying from other sources. He responded in a letter by saying that if humans wrote the *UB* he would indeed be disturbed by plagiarisms. But if supermortals wrote the book, he would not be in the least disturbed. Indeed, he added, it would be "an excellent technique to assure relevant communication." He reminded me that the supermortals openly admitted in the *UB* that they made use of human sources.

Adventists, of course, now freely admit that Ellen White also made use of human sources, guided by angels and the Holy Spirit to select just the right passages to copy. I have done my best to persuade Sprunger to look into Adventist literature, but so far he has not been interested. In view of the many Adventist beliefs in the *UB* and the fact that the four main members of the Contact Commission were former Adventists, Sprunger's refusal to read Ellen White's books strikes me as dangerously close to the sin of willful ignorance.

Block is convinced that reading the source books has greatly deepened his understanding of the *UB*. For that reason he hopes other Urantians will do the same. It might even be worthwhile, he suggests, to republish some of the source books whose copyrights have expired.

Block intends to report on his ongoing investigations in mainline Urantian journals, and eventually to write a book about them. You can be sure that by the time my book is published he will have, in his untiring search, found numerous other sources, and that they will strengthen, not diminish, his belief that the *UB* could not possibly have been written by human authors!

This brings us face to face with an intriguing question which may never be answered. Who was or were responsible for the many plagiarisms? It is possible that Sadler, like his former guru Sister White, felt authorized by higher powers to copy material without giving credit, but I am inclined to think otherwise. Although Sadler undoubtedly edited all the Papers, it is hard to believe he would be guilty of such an illegal practice.

It seems far more likely that members of the Contact Commission and the Forum, convinced they were divinely "indited" to contribute to the *UB*, wrote many if not most of the Papers. Not being professional writers, they did not understand that the law obliges an author to cite sources when material is taken, almost word for word, from copyrighted books. They turned their work over to Sadler, perhaps surreptitiously by leaving manuscripts in his desk or even in his bank deposit box if they were able to obtain access to the key. This would account for several anecdotes and for Sadler's statement that he himself never fully understood how the Papers came to be written.

Sadler could not have been expected to be familiar with all the books from which material was stolen. However, by the time the *UB* went to press in 1955 he must have realized that such theft had occurred. This would explain paragraphs in the *UB* which give revelators their "out" by admitting they freely exploited the writings of others whenever they felt the ideas were appropriate.

In brief, Sadler did not write the *UB*. He merely edited and wrote portions of it. This would explain both the varying styles of the Papers, as well as the tendency of Sadler, as editor, to inject his own preferences for certain unusual words and phrases. To what extent the Papers by Forum members were "checked" by reading them to a sleeping Wilfred is another question we may never be able to answer. It seems plausible that as more and more Urantians came to imagine themselves under the influence of midwayers and thought adjusters, checking with Wilfred may have become unnecessary.

If we are to believe Harry Loose, Wilfred and his wife became increasingly frustrated and angered by the way Sadler had taken over the *UB*'s production, rendering Wilfred more and more irrelevant to the final product. I believe that Wilfred's secondary personalities initiated the early papers, especially those covering the *UB*'s fantastic cosmology and polytheism. But as the *UB* slowly grew in size, and Sadler and members of the Contact Commission and Forum came to feel "indited," the *UB* became the product of many hands—well meaning persons who simply did not realize they were violating the law when they stole from books published before 1955.

At the time I write (1994) Block says he has discovered scores of additional sources for material in the *UB*, but because he intends to write a book about them he is very secretive as to the authors and their book titles. He continues to be enthralled by how the supermortals cleverly improved on paragraphs they plagiarized. (Adventists say the same thing about Ellen White's borrowing.) It is likely to take many decades, as in the case of Mrs. White, before the full extent of *UB* copying is known. To repeat what I have said earlier, Urantians have long held that no single person or small group of persons could possess the wide-ranging knowledge needed for fabricating such a massive, complex work as the *UB*. They are right. Not only is the *UB* the work of many hands, but even the writers of its papers stole shamelessly from books available to them at the time.

In spite of the fact that the Foundation could have been sued in 1955 for violating book copyrights—and could even be sued today for stealing from books still under copyright—fundamentalist Urantians have found all sorts of strange ways to justify the pilfering. One Urantian has conjectured that the authors of the *UB* sought permission from human authors after they had ascended to a higher world! "They also could have obtained a level of 'permission' on a subconscious, superconscious, or even conscious level" from living authors! (I quote from an Internet posting.)

Another Urantian has written on the same network: "I find it quite easy to believe that the circumstances of Matthew Block's life were so contrived by seraphic influence and his curiosity so piqued by spirit leading that he was able to become the focus for this series of discoveries." In other words, the celestials did nothing "wrong" in copying, and Block is to be praised for discovering how skillfully they "enhanced" the pilfered passages.

17

Bitter Schisms

Throughout history, in all cultures, religious movements sooner or later develop irreconcilable internal disputes. Heretical Christian sects proliferated in the centuries following the death of Jesus. The Catholic Church split into Eastern and Western branches. The greatest schism was of course the Protestant Reformation. After that, Protestantism fractured into many large denominations and a myriad of smaller denominations and sects. Millions were killed in wars between rival factions. Tens of thousands were tortured and executed because of their heretical opinions. Far more Christians have been murdered by other Christians than were killed by Romans in the first few centuries of the faith. The history of other great world religions has been similar.

It has been similar also for small sects and cults. No sooner has a new religion arisen than members begin to disagree and split off to form rival movements. Consider the history of Seventh-day Adventism which has played such a major role in the formation of Urantianism. It had its origin in the great disappointment following the failure of farmer William Miller's prediction of 1844 as the year of Christ's second coming. The faithful split into several factions, of which the Seventh-day Adventists, under the leadership of Ellen White and her husband, James, became the most successful. Herbert Armstrong, the megalomaniacal founder of the Worldwide Church of God, began his absurd career in one of the small Adventist groups that survived the Millerite disappointment. It explains why so many Adventist doctrines are in Armstrong's idiotic theology. There have been other splinter Adventist movements, such as the Branch Davidians, which in turn divided into rival factions as we shall learn in the next chapter.

The Urantia movement started to undergo its own internal stresses in the 1970s when members began to challenge the Foundation's right to control, by virtue of its copyright, the publication and distribution of the *UB*. Under the stern, autocratic leadership of Martin Myers, the Foundation became almost as quick to take legal action to protect its interests as the Church of Scientology.

In 1977 the Foundation won its case against the Los Angeles group calling itself the Urantian School of Research. The defendants were William Burton King, Barbara King, and Doris George. They were sued for publishing a series of pamphlets and tracts containing material copied from the *UB*, and for using the name "Urantia" without permission.

In 1980 the Foundation won a similar lawsuit against Robert Burton for illegally copying and distributing portions of the *UB* to Congressmen in Washington, D.C., and for initiating a Spanish translation of the *UB*. The Foundation had delayed the case so long that Burton died before the court ruled against him.

That same year, fearful it might lose its tax exempt status, the Foundation petitioned the IRS for a ruling that when the Foundation sold copies of the *UB* to chain bookstores, the sales would be deemed sales to persons, not to stores. The IRS refused to so rule. The Foundation took their case to a U.S. Court of Appeals in 1982, but the court upheld the IRS ruling.

In 1982 the Foundation sued and eventually won a case against the First Urantia Society of Houston for using the three-circle trademark without permission. In 1988 the Foundation sued the Center for Urantia Book Synergy (CUBS), an independent organization in Santa Barbara, California, for using the name "Urantia." The Center issued a publication called *The Synergist* in which the word also appeared without permission. CUBS settled out of court after its funds were exhausted. (For CUBS' side of the battle, see *The Synergist*, Summer 1989, a 48-page special issue.) There were similar lawsuits against Arnold Zakow, against Don Petrie, and others.

Although the Foundation was not involved, an amusing court case involving one Ira Mullins deserves mention because the *UB* played a significant role. In 1972 Mullins was arrested in Mendocino County, California, for growing marijuana on his property. He and his wife operated what they called the Universal Life Church of Christ Light. Muffins was the "pastor." There was no church building. Members lived on the property in tepees.

According to the *California Reporter* (Vol. 123, pages 201–209), Mullins claimed that the use of marijuana, LSD, and Peyote, combined with reading the *UB*, had caused changes in his blood and brain, in turn inducing a transcendental state of "total and complete union with God and his Lord and Master, Jesus." Church members sat in a circle puffing marijuana as a "sacrament" while they meditated on the attributes of Christ, and "read selected passages from *The Urantia Book*." This was followed by discussion of the passages and how they applied to the daily lives of the worshipers. Mullins said he had held at least a thousand such ceremonies on his property.

Police were tipped off about these rituals by a cult member who had been living in one of the tepees. He was no longer welcome in the "church," Mrs. Mullins told the police, because of his excessive boozing. The court ruled against Mullins, and in 1975 an appeals court denied him a further hearing.

Mullins and his followers were not the first to combine *UB* studies with sacramental puffing of marijuana. In the late 1960s a group of Urantians in Hawaii, calling themselves members of The Religion of Jesus Church, became convinced that smoking hemp was a valuable sacrament. Dennis Shields, a loyal member of this curious "church" (its more than a hundred devotees are now scattered over the islands), defended its practice on the Internet (December 13, 1994). He said that smoking marijuana will bring Urantians "closer to God and God will be brought closer to those believers who choose to use hemp religiously."

The Urantia Movement came close to breaking apart in the early 1980s over claims made by Vern Bennom Grimsley, a young, energetic, handsome, charismatic Urantian leader who was a dynamic speaker and a skilled guitar strummer. In the early 1970s Vern started a Urantian outreach organization called the Family of God, originally headquartered at Berkeley, California, then later at nearby Clayton. It had the marvelous acronym of FOG. President Vern and his wife Nancy, and vice-president David Gray, promoted the movement by popular radio programs, handsomely printed brochures, and periodicals with such names as *The Spiritual Renaissance Herald*, *Update*, *The Family of God Journal*, *Family of God Diary*, and *In Touch*. FOG's purpose was to enlarge God's family by preaching the *UB*'s theme of the Fatherhood of God and the Brotherhood of Man.

Leaders of the Urantia Foundation, in Chicago, were initially supporters of FOG. Christy wrote an article titled "Our Challenge" for the first page of the first issue (Spring 1970) of *The Spiritual Renaissance Herald.* Her essay concluded:

> And may you all become valiant soldiers of the circles wholeheartedly enlisted in the solid ranks of those mortals who shall go forth in this coming battle for truth against error under the unfaltering leadership of the mighty seraphim of progress.

So taken was Christy by Vern's dedication to the cause and his evangelizing skills that she said the celestials had informed her that Vern was a member of the reserve corps of destiny. Martin Myers, who had been Vern's fraternity brother, was another enthusiastic FOG supporter. His foggy article, "The Question is the Father's: The Answer is Ours" graced the front page of the same periodical's second issue.

Then a funny thing happened to Vern.

He began to hear voices—voices he believed came from the same higher beings who wrote the *UB* papers. The voices warned against an impending third world war that would turn into a nuclear holocaust.

Easily swayed Urantians were so bowled over by Vern's predictions— some thought he was the new John the Baptist predicted by the *UB* (1866)—that they forked over millions of dollars to FOG, funds to be used to prepare the faithful for survival. A major contributor was said to be William Hales Jr. son of a founding trustee of the Urantia movement and father of John Hales, a currently prominent Urantian.

Christy was an early supporter of Vern's voices. So were Richard Keeler, David Kantor, Robert Slagle, David Elders, and other Urantian bigwigs still active in the movement. Bomb shelters were constructed. Caves were bought for hiding stockpiles of food. More than a million dollars in gold were stashed away. A few rifles and handguns were purchased to enforce security in the shelters. Hundreds of *Urantia Books* were stored in a cave in Parthenon, Arkansas, to preserve them from burning. A few foggy-brained Foggers actually sold their homes and businesses and quit their jobs to await the earth's doom.

Grimsley's grim warnings met with strong resistance among conservative Urantians. A massive typescript titled *The Vern Grimsley Message Evaluation* was released on June 17, 1984, to Urantian leaders. It was the work of Hoite C. Caston, now one of the Foundation's five trustees. Caston is a screen writer and director in Los Angeles. He and Martin Myers had been fraternity brothers and roommates at the University of Kansas. It was

Vern who introduced Hoite to the *UB* after he (Vern) learned about the book from Reverend Meredith Sprunger.

So damaging was Caston's report, which detailed all the reasons why Vern's channeling was spurious, that the Foundation kicked Grimsley out of the movement. Reverend Sprunger urged Vern to consider the possibility that he was hearing, not the voices of supermortals, but voices from his own unconscious. The urging fell on deaf ears.

Richard Keeler, who had managed FOG's investments, not only resigned from FOG. He changed his will in which he had, hard as it now is to conceive, willed all his wealth to FOG! As a philosophy major at the University of Kansas, he too had been a frat brother of Grimsley. Vern had introduced him to the *UB*. In a letter to Vern (November 20, 1983) Keeler said he "literally wept" when he resigned from FOG, calling it "one of the saddest moments of my life."

Vern and Nancy either separated or divorced, though I am told they are back together again. Former friends began to shun Vern as if, like Harold Sherman, he had become an unwitting agent of Caligastia. Grimsley and Nancy are said to be living in obscurity on a ranch in California where Vern is earning a living by managing a band. Although I am told he no longer is hearing voices, he still believes the voices he heard were genuine: the celestials *had* accurately warned him against an impending cataclysm—an event that was averted by historical changes even they did not foresee.

When I wrote to the University of Kansas alumni office, seeking Vern's current address, a card came back with the single-word message, "Lost." Two letters to him at an address I obtained from another source were never answered. My guess is that he remains a firm believer in the Fifth Epochal Revelation. It would be interesting to know what he thinks of the recent epidemic of Urantian channeling which we will introduce here and cover fully in the next chapter.

Many Urantian leaders who bought Grimsley's revelations either resigned their posts or were removed by the Foundation's trustees. Thomas Kendall, the Foundation's president, and his wife Carolyn, both Grimsley supporters, were voted out of office by the trustees. Martin Myers was voted the Foundation's new head. Richard Keeler became one of the board's five trustees.

David Elders was another pliant official who strongly defended Vern's voices. (We will have more to say about Elders in our final chapter). Although Dave has since changed his mind about Grimsley's channeling, he still thinks Caston's *Message Evaluation* was unduly harsh on Vern, unworthy of a Urantian who is supposed to love everybody.

❧

The Grimsley fiasco seems to have taught nothing to vast numbers of Urantian believers. In 1991 the movement entered a new and even more disruptive phase in which voices of celestials started to come through again, but now multiplied a hundredfold. I'm not sure just when this new channeling began, but the first major instance in the United States involved Jan Messenger, a woman active in a group of Urantians living in or near Woods Cross, Utah, a suburb of Salt Lake City. Like Grimsley, Jan is now receiving new revelations from the celestials. As early as 1989 her Thought Adjuster told her she had been chosen as a contactee for a second phase of the Fifth Epochal Revelation. Messages coming through her since early 1991 are available on thousands of typewritten pages.

The entities who began transmitting in Utah have such names as Ham, Abraham, Lazerik, Rayson, Norson, Horace, Will, and Melchizedek They have bestowed new names on members of the Woods Cross group. Jan is known as Rebecca. Thern Blackburn, the group's coordinator, is Joshua. All those in the group have been told they are now members of the reserve corps of destiny, leaders for bringing to Urantia the new revelations.

An embarrassing aspect of the Woods Cross channeling is that Duane L. Faw, a highly respected Urantian who produced *The Paramony*, is one of Jan Messenger's ardent supporters. As earlier mentioned, *The Paramony*, which Faw compiled and published on his own in 1986, lists 15,000 cross references that harmonize passages in the *UB* with passages in the Bible. It is a work of 389 pages, currently distributed by the Jesusonian Foundation, in Boulder, Colorado—a reference work owned and prized by most Urantians. Faw is a retired brigadier general of the Marines, a former appellate judge, and former professor of law at Pepperdine University.

General Faw had a tape made of Jan's channeling which he thought might heal the late movie star Michael Landon, then dying of cancer. Arrangements were actually made for delivering the tape to Landon, who died soon thereafter. The general is convinced that Adam and Eve are about to return to Urantia, as predicted in the *UB* (1025). He has offered to provide money for property on which to build a house for them!

Imagine how wonderful it would be to have Adam and Eve back on earth. They could appear on television talk shows to answer questions about exactly what went on in the Garden of Eden. They could clear up the mystery of where Cain got his wife by providing more details about what the *UB* relates only briefly on page 840, where we learn that Cain settled in the land of Nod, east of Eden, and married his distant cousin Ramona. They could display once and for all to creationists whether they do or do not have bellybuttons.

Meredith Justin Sprunger, as mentioned earlier, is a retired minister of the United Church of Christ. Born in 1915, and now living in Fort Wayne, Indiana, Reverend Sprunger has long been one of the Urantia movement's most dedicated defenders. For many years he was a psychological consultant in Indiana. He taught at Elmhurst College, and at the Indiana Institute for Technology where he headed the psychology department and for a time was the college's president. He is the founder and director of *The Christian Fellowship for Readers of the Urantia Book*, trustee of Boulder's Jesusonian Foundation, and editor of *The Spiritual Fellowship Journal*. As the author of numerous pamphlets and articles about the *UB*, he has been tireless in his efforts to introduce the Fifth Epochal Revelation to mainline Christian churches. So far these efforts have been spectacularly unsuccessful.

Sprunger is puzzled by Ham's claim that the "spiritual center" of the planet is Manitoba, Canada. This conflicts sharply, Sprunger writes, with the "Chicago contact information" that the spiritual center is "at the Grizzly Giant in the Mariposa Grove of Giant Sequoias in Yosemite National Park"! As we have seen, this is widely believed by old-timers in the Urantia movement, though whether or where this revelation is recorded I have not yet discovered.

Sprunger also criticizes Ham for identifying Norson as a teacher when the Chicago sleeper declared that Norson is the new "take charge planetary supervisor." This is the first I ever heard of Norson. His name does not appear in the *UB*. Evidently Sprunger is in possession of revelations which as far as I know have not been recorded or disseminated to the faithful.

I asked Sprunger in a letter if anything had ever appeared in print about Norson. He replied it had not, but that he had been told in private by Sadler, in the late 1960s, that Norson had taken over as the new spiritual superadvisor of Urantia. I assume Norson is a celestial, not an ascended mortal.

Sprunger's ability to harmonize his Christianity and respect for the gospels with the *UB*'s elaborate polytheism is a thing to marvel. He tells me in a letter that he is not bothered by the discoveries of plagiarisms in the *UB*. He refers me to the *UB* (1343) where the author of the Jesus papers says that more than 2,000 human sources were consulted in preparing the life of Jesus.

In 1993 Sprunger was twice interviewed at length by Urantian Larry

Mullins. A videotape of the two sessions, one in Boulder, the other in Quebec, was produced and distributed by the Invisible Fellowship of Urantia Book Believers, Box 19135, Boulder, Colorado 80308.

This tape must be heard to be believed. Springer comes through as a true believer—nothing will ever spring open Sprunger's mind—and enormously proud to have known Sadler personally. How well he knew Sadler is open to question. Sprunger was never a member of the Forum. He knew Sadler only by conversing with him on frequent visits to his home.

Sprunger says he was introduced to the *UB* by a Judge Hammerschmidt in 1955 shortly after the *UB* was printed.* He was greatly impressed by its life of Jesus because of the myriad details which "meshed perfectly" with the gospels. He found the *UB* profound, far-reaching, and self-validating.

Sadler never told Sprunger who the sleeper was, having taken a solemn vow not to reveal his name. "I guess it was a man," Sprunger added, a surprising remark in view of the *UB*'s clear statement that it was a man. Sprunger said he thinks the revelations stopped in 1952. Sadler told him, "They didn't even bother to say goodbye."

Lena was the first to believe. Sadler was skeptical for years, Sprunger tells us, but became convinced by the *UB*'s paper on the twelve apostles. In Sprunger's view, no human mind participated in any way in the production of the papers. Secondary midwayers took dictation from the contactee, wrote it down in longhand, and gave the papers to Sadler in mysterious ways. The handwriting did not match that of anyone in the Forum. The only role of humans, Sprunger insists, was to type the handwritten documents.

Sprunger repeats the myth that when Sadler put the original documents in his safe, with questions from the Forum, the papers would vanish only to reappear later in revised form. When Sadler once added ten dollar bills to a paper, the revelators took the paper but left the bills.

Sadler and others on the contact commission, which Sprunger guesses to have numbered six mortals, were allowed to converse directly with the celestials and even listen in on their meetings. "You should have heard the celebration among the midwayers." Sprunger says Sadler told him, "when the Jesus papers were finally approved."

In chapter 9 I called attention to a passage in *Oahspe* (Book of Es, chapter 20, pages 771–72) where we learn that angels communicated with

---

*Judge Louis Hammerschmidt, of South Bend, Indiana, was not a Forum member or a *UB* student. He had been given a copy of the book by William Furguson Harrah, a famous manufacturer and member of the Urantia Foundation's General Council. (See the entry on Harrah in *Who's Who in America*.) Hammerschmidt passed the book to Sprunger and asked him what he thought of it.

Lincoln and inspired him to free the slaves. I was dumbfounded to hear Sprunger say that Sadler told him Lincoln was a Urantian "reservist" whose Thought Adjuster was influenced by the celestials to write the Gettysburg address!

Sprunger was harsh on the Urantia Foundation's trustees for having lost their "sense of mission." Believers should increase their efforts to spread the Fifth Epochal Revelation around the world. It is only a matter of time, Sprunger believes, until mainline Christians accept the *UB*. The troublewith today's Christianity is that it has become "Christianized." By this Sprunger means it has become, as the *UB* so often repeats, a religion about Jesus rather than of Jesus.

Christians still think of Jesus as little more than a human incarnation of part of the trinity, Sprunger continues. Actually he was much more. He was the creator of our entire universe. Does Sprunger know that this is good Seventh-day Adventist doctrine? If so, he never says so. Nowhere in his interview does he mention Ellen White. He refers to Sadler as a former minister, but he could not bring himself to say he was a former Adventist minister.

Sprunger would like to see the Urantia movement develop real churches, complete with pastors, music, and hymns. He predicts that Jews will become ardent Urantians as soon as they recognize the mistake of their forefathers in rejecting Jesus. The United Midwayers, according to Sprunger, told Sadler they had "made war" on Communism. Sprunger really believes they were responsible for its recent downfall!

Sprunger refused to condemn the new channelers, but he added that to think they are adding anything new to the faith is "nonsense." Asked about the *UB*'s sexist language, Sprunger admitted it is indeed overly masculine, but this is not true of the book's ideas. The wording simply reflects how things were written at the time, such as using "man" as a generic term for humanity. Irene, Sprunger's wife, joined him briefly at the end of the second inverview. She chimed in to remind listeners that the *UB* speaks of a Mother Spirit among the Gods.

Although Sprunger denies he is a Urantian fundamentalist (he freely admits that the *UB* swarms with scientific blunders) he firmly believes it contains a genuine revelation from the higher-ups that is destined to revitalize Christianity and become the dominant religion of the world. Here is how he concludes a paper on "The Urantia Book and Christian Fundamentalism":

Every prophet in the history of the Old and New Testaments has met with unbelief and opposition. The priests of society have regularly stoned its prophets. Then their sons of another century build monuments to honor the prophets persecuted by their fathers. It is good to be cautious and critical; it is helpful to doubt and carefully evaluate. We need, however, to be open and objective enough to allow the spirit to lead us to larger truth. Jesus told his apostles that he would send the Spirit of Truth through which he would lead them to greater truths in the future. We must be sensitive to this Spirit of Truth. We need to learn to recognize truth in its many forms and varying appearances.

The URANTIA Book is such a new appearance of truth. You will find that The URANTIA Book will stand the test of critical examination. It is rooted solidly in the traditional spiritual truths of the Christian faith which have endured for centuries. Reading and studying The URANTIA Book will give you a deeper and larger vision of this saving faith and help you become a part of a spiritual renaissance which is dawning on our world.

In 1994 The Invisible Fellowship, in Boulder, published *The Urantia Book on Channeling and the "Teaching Mission,"* a 32-page report consisting mainly of *UB* quotations which contradict claims coming from the recent outburst of channeling. We will cover the Teaching Mission, a name for the current channeling, in the next chapter. The report is written by Larry and Joan Mullins, and Carol Hay, three editors of *Invisible Fellowship Magazine*. An appendix reprints, in slightly condensed form, a 1992 article by Sprunger on channeling, with "Further Comments" added by Sprunger in 1993. He is now much stronger in his opposition to the new channeling mania. This is how he put it:

> Although it is unintended, I can think of no more subtle way to disrupt unity in the Urantia movement and divert attention away from a dynamic outreach program to bring the Fifth Epochal Revelation to our world than the preoccupation with channeling and other psychic activities.

Why, in my opinion, is the Urantia movement destined to remain a minor cult? Surely one reason is the way it insults both secular humanists and Christians. It insults humanists and liberal Christians by its elaborate polytheism and its acceptance of so many New Testament miracles including the raising of Lazarus from the dead. It insults conservative Christians, Catholics and Protestants alike, by denying the Fall of Man and the Atonement, and by putting the *UB* far above the Bible as a source of religious truth. "The Urantia Book," Martin Myers has written, "is the most balanced, consistent and fair presentation of spiritual truth and universe fact ever available to the human race in book form." Urantians are not "Soldiers of the Cross." They are what Myers calls "Soldiers of the Circles." I quote from "Unity, Not Uniformity," a famous speech Myers delivered in 1973 at the First Western Urantia Conference—a speech reprinted in a 1990 *Special Report to the Readers of the Urantia Book.* My account of the Grimsley affair is taken mainly from this report.

Vern's warnings from the celestials, and the Woods Cross channeling, were only the beginnings of a mania that has since spread like wildfire through Urantian communities, threatening total disintegration of the movement. This is the lurid topic of our next chapter.

18

Joe Pope and the New Teachers

O n page 1866 of the *UB* is a prophecy about the coming to Urantia of another John the Baptist:

> Sooner or later another and greater John the Baptist is due to arise proclaiming "the kingdom of God is at hand"—meaning a return to the high spiritual concept of Jesus, who proclaimed that the kingdom is the will of his heavenly Father dominant and transcendent in the heart of the believer—and doing all this without in any way referring either to the visible church on earth or to the anticipated second coming of Christ. There must come a revival of the *actual* teachings of Jesus, such a restatement as will undo the work of his early followers who went about to create a sociophilosophical system of belief regarding the *fact* of Michael's sojourn on earth. In a short time the teaching of this story *about* Jesus nearly supplanted the preaching of Jesus' gospel of the kingdom. In this way a historical religion displaced that teaching in which Jesus had blended man's highest moral ideas and spiritual ideals with man's most sublime hope for the future—eternal life. And that was the gospel of the kingdom.

Joe Pope, a Urantian living in Vancouver, actually believes that this prophecy refers to him! As the Bible says, John the Baptist was the second Elijah. Pope (what an appropriate name!) is convinced he is Elijah the Third. He has made a series of audio tapes expounding his new revelation. You can obtain them (or could in 1994) by writing to him at 1868 E. Eleventh Avenue, Vancouver, BCE V5N 1Z1. Pope calls his tapes the "greatest inspired presentation ever granted a Urantia mortal throughout all past time." They are to be taken as a "companion revelation or appendix to the [*UB*] papers."

I have before me a form letter from Joe to his "Dear Urantia brothers and sisters," and a tract by Elijah III titled "Welcome to the New Earth." I will try to summarize, with frequent quotations, what this tract has to say.

Seven years of tribulation on Urantia began in 1990. A series of wars during this period will culminate in a worldwide nuclear holocaust. More than two billion persons, carefully selected by the higher powers, will be saved. The rest will die. Survivors will be transported by angels to a giant planet called Graceland. (Was Joe a childhood fan of Elvis Presley?) This transportation of the saved is what Protestant fundamentalists like to call the Rapture.

Those to be evacuated from a destroyed earth are even now being selected by invisible judges. The process began in 1987, but the final Resurrection on Judgment Day will not occur until the year 2021. It will take place on Urantia, but those who have been taken to Graceland will be able to watch the proceedings on a television screen. Wicked persons such as Hitler and Stalin will be annihilated. Satan was arrested in 1935. Caligastia was removed from Earth in 1954. They and other evil celestial beings will also be annihilated after Judgment Day. Salvation will depend entirely on a person's faith in God, regardless of his or her religious beliefs. "Jews, Moslems, Christians, Buddhists, Hindus, and so on," Joe writes, "can all count on salvation if their faith is sincere." Presumably atheists, no matter how good a life they led, will not escape obliteration.

Graceland was specially constructed by the gods. It is "an enormous sphere ten times the size of the earth." There are no oceans or mountains. It "abounds in celestial light and botanical grandeur. . . . Magnificent new cities stand unoccupied. Simple but comfortable homes have been made ready, along with free food, clothing, and other needs." Trees of Life provide medicinal needs. All food is vegetarian. Intelligent animals do the gardening, and talking fandors will carry passengers here and there. The economy of Graceland will be capitalistic, free of inflation and "paltry taxes."

Assuming you are among the raptured, an angel will put you to sleep, then dematerialize your body, "changing it to a state which can be flown through space. In this temporary state you will be taken to Graceland where your mortal body will be restored. This will take several days, but you will be unaware of the passing of time in your unconscious sleep." All good *UB* doctrine! For details on how the transportation process works, in case a catastrophe dooms an entire evolving planet, see the UB (582).

When you are reconstituted, all marks of aging will be erased and you will look as you did at age 25. I assume those under 25 will remain the same age. Your life span will be extended to 300 years. Infirmities will of course vanish. Childbearing will be painless. The blind will see, the deaf hear, the lame walk. Amputated limbs will be restored. Fillings and other artificial dental work will disappear, leaving perfect teeth. You will be able to see violet-hued lower orders of angels. You will receive telepathic powers which extend over a fifty-mile range. You will learn a new universal language that is now spoken on some four million inhabited worlds.

Among the saved will be 144,000 persons known as the Elect. These will be men and women who in the past, regardless of their religion, were tortured and murdered because of their faith. Their ranks will include Old Testament Prophets, five apostles of Jesus, Zoroaster, Mahatma Gandhi, Lincoln, and John Kennedy. How Joe figures the two assassinated presidents were killed because of their religious faith beats me.

Graceland is only a temporary abode for the raptured while the earth is rejuvenated and rebuilt by the gods. After about thirty years on Graceland, the same transport angels will carry the saved back to a New Earth. It will be a Utopia beyond all our dreams. Lord Machiventa, one of the "supernatural princes" who is billions of years old, will be sent to rule Urantia from his headquarters in Jerusalem. In his incarnated Urantia body he will have a dark complexion, and will be slightly less than six feet tall. Other supernal spirits, some barely visible, will also be sent to the New Earth. This group will include the 86 Trinity Teacher Sons now living in Paradise. Michael (Jesus) will some day visit the New Earth, as he has promised, but not even the angels (as we are told in Matthew 24:36) know when that will be.

Elijah III (Joe Pope) is the chosen messenger to warn us of all these great soon-coming events. In a letter to his Urantian siblings he writes:

> The day has come, even the hour! Proclaim to a world shaken by rebellion, default, war and suffering the Kingdom of God is at hand! . . . Let the word go forth . . . Avonal judges Urantia! Soon shall be ours the glorified advent of 86 Paradise personalities . . . the high Daynals of Trinity bestowal! Reveal to this distracted people their evolutionary transcendence . . . Graceland! They who have an ear, let them hear! . . . the sudden emergence of a wonderland culture that would have been now, had the Caligastia secession and Adamic default never darkened this globe.

I have not been able to learn much about Elijah Ill beyond the allegations that he was born in Canada, served in the Canadian military, has a degree in journalism, and for a short time was a television newsman in Philadelphia.

After a four-year silence Joe Pope surfaced again in February 1994 with another impassioned plea to his "Dear Urantian Brothers and Sisters." The letter was sent from his "Elijah Ministry," in Vancouver.

The final years of terrible tribulation, writes Joe, are "about to drop" like the "other shoe." With these awesome "events gradually closing in, I must raise sufficient funds to 'buy some free time' to complete preparations for the great undertaking I have been assigned."

Joe assures those who send him money that they will reap "real benefit" in the next world. As the "divine herald," appointed by Machiventa Melchizedek, Joe says he will plead with the Master to reward handsomely all those who support the Elijah Ministry in these "pre-kingdom days." Moreover, the ministry is registered in Canada as a religious charity, so those who send money can take tax deductions.

> Therefore I have written not to add to your financial burdens, but to declare with great joy that "opportunity knocks" with the promise of substantial return "benefits."
>
> If you prefer to wait for world hostilities to break out, thus rendering "obvious" the sphere's imminent deliverance, in order to convince yourself of the authenticity of my mission and message, you will earn only the "lesser reward for lesser faithfulness." For then it will be much easier for me to realize funds from a *public* and open worldwide appeal for the wherewithal to comfort and console God's chosen.
>
> Similarly, if you crumple up this letter and discard it out of disbelief or disinterest, you will be throwing away as well something of yourself, a matchless "value" truly in your best *self*-interest.
>
> Carted away with your trash will be your "future" memory of that glorious day when the Sovereign of a vast universe publicly, even cosmically, thanked you for supporting his herald when that support was so desperately needed on this confused and highly irregular globe. This incomparable "memory" you will dearly cherish for your entire eternal life. I urge you not to throw it away. This "opportunity," as most agondonter opportunities in time, knocks but once.

If Joe Pope and the Woods Cross channelers were the only Urantians now claiming direct contact with the supermortals, the Urantia movement might be slowly rolling along in its accustomed grooves. Alas, an awesome epidemic of channeling has taken place all over the nation, as well as in New Zealand, Canada, and Hawaii. There are rumors of its spread to France, Germany, and South America.

Although the messages coming through since 1991 occasionally contradict one another, there is a surprising amount of unity. The belief is that celestial "Teaching Messengers," many of them ascended mortals, are now preparing Urantia for a second phase of the Fifth Epochal Revelation. We are living in a "Correcting Time" that will precede the coming era of "life and light" predicted by the *UB* (598–600).

The seven stages of the life-and-light era are described on pages 627–29. During the first stage Urantia will be administered by three rulers: The Planetary Sovereign, the chief of the planetary corps of finaliters, and Adam and Eve. Adam and Eve will return to earth to serve as "unifiers of the dual leadership" of the other two rulers.

Eventually all inferior stocks will be eliminated and there will be one purified race, one language, and one religion (*UB* 624–26). Humans will live to be 500. Natural death will become less frequent as "Adusters increasingly fuse with their subjects," and many mortals are "translated from among the living" to higher worlds. Even in the first stage, Urantia will be the utopia described in the Bible's *Apocalypse* as the "new heaven and new earth."

The new teachers have revealed that Caligastia and his minions, having refused to repent, have all been annihilated "as though they had not been." No longer can they go about with their nefarious plans for undermining the Fifth Epochal Revelation. Spiritual circuits of communication, closed by the Lucifer rebellion while the *UB* was being transmitted, are now reconnected and open for the Fifth Revelation's second phase.

Machiventa Melchizedek, recently inaugurated as Urantia's Planetary Prince, has promised to return any day, in the flesh, to be followed by the Second Coming of Michael (Jesus) himself. It is hard to comprehend, but a group of gullible Urantians actually assembled at a motel in Naperville, Illinois, on April 24, 1993, to welcome Melchizedek's arrival. Needless to add, Melchizedek failed to appear.

The Urantians who expected Melchizedek to materialize in Naperville reacted to this disappointment in a way that mirrors, on a much smaller scale, of course, the Great Disappointment among Adventists in 1844 when Jesus failed to materialize as William Miller had predicted.

On August 6, 1993, Jeannie George, who made a special trip from Dallas to Naperville to welcome Melchizedek, mailed out a six-page document titled "When God Closes One Door, Another One Is Opened." This is exactly how the faithful Adventists who rallied around Ellen White and her husband reacted. They decided that Miller was correct on his date, but erred on the event. It was the day on which Jesus entered a heavenly Sanctuary and closed a door. God used Miller's false prophecy to test believers and to strengthen their faith for the open door ahead.

The prediction that Melchizedek would arrive in the flesh at Naperville had been proclaimed by Welmek, one of the supermortals. According to Welmek, Jesus himself had authorized the materialization. Why was it stopped? Because the Absolute, the Father, decided that in view of the sensationalizing of news about the Waco tragedy, it was not a propitious time for Melchizedek to be enfleshed. Not even Jesus knew of the Father's decision until the last moment!

However, according to Ms. George, it was a great occasion in Naperville. Those who met there were spiritually "energized" by a magical outpouring of love and peace. "I see this event," she writes, "as the starting point for the brotherhood of Man and the fatherhood of God materializing on our planet. . . . Allow some time to realize the doors that have been opened because of the work that was going on behind the scenes."

"In conclusion," she continues, "the event was planned in good faith that it would happen. No one has to blame anyone because it was delayed. The Father knows what is best for us all, and we thank him for this loving care and respect his all-knowingness. We received scores of blessings from the Naperville event. It is an event to remember. It really is the beginning of our planet starting to move forward under Michael's guidance."

An event? One can only marvel at the ability of believers to turn a non-event into a glorious happening!

The Teaching Mission, or TM as it is called, is spreading rapidly over the land. Thousands of Teachers are expected to arrive on Urantia, invisible of course, to speak through the mouths of new contactees. "I am a human from another planet who has fused with my Adjuster," declared Will, using a contactee in Tallahassee. "Humans are called upon to serve as Teachers in this effort established by Michael because it is thought that we have some natural sympathy for connections with humans on a planet such as yours."

The teachers have names as bizarre as those of the supermortals mentioned in the *UB*, and are now almost as numerous. The following list of more than 150 celestials, prepared in 1993, gives the names of the spiritual teachers then speaking through human "transmitters" in various Urantian groups around the country. It does not include Joe Pope or all the Woods Cross revelators. The list is growing so rapidly that it will be hopelessly out of date by the time this book is printed.

In January 1993 Patije Mills, a Urantian in Sarasota, Florida, was asked by Welmek, a celestial in touch with a group in Indianapolis, to prepare a list of known teaching groups, the principal contacts, and the names of the celestials being channeled. She recognized that the list was "partial, incomplete, and full of errors." I have copied from it the locations of the groups and the names of the celestials, but have omitted names of the transmitters and their addresses. To Mills's list I have added cities and celestials from a December 1994 list prepared by Allene Vick, of Bradenton, Floria.

Arizona, Sedona	Felicia
Arizona, Tucson	Seraphin
California, Arcadia	Astara and Adora
California, Malibu	Rayson
California, Los Osos	Hilson and Loriyana
California, Corona Del Mar	Signa and Bertran
California, Sabastopol	Jared
California, Santa Rosa	Jared
California, Bakersville	Andrea
California, Half Moon Bay	Oleana and Tarkas
California, Oakland	Althea
Colorado, Colorado Springs	Rizden
Colorado, Pueblo	Heironamas
Florida, Tallahassee	Will
Florida, Englewood	Oliver
Florida, Sarasota	Aflana, LorEl, VanEessa, VanEl
Hawaii, Kailua	Norsen, Aflana, and Sig-El
Idaho, Coeur D'Alene	Elyon and Aaron
Idaho, Pocatello	Daniel
Illinois, Naperville	Oren
Indiana, Indianapolis	Welmek
Indiana, DuBois	Amaden
Iowa, Burlington	Aranda
Kansas, Kansas City	Sara
Kansas, Lawrence	James
Maryland, Seabrook	Curtis and Iruka

Missouri, St. Louis	Josepha
Missouri, Kansas City	Ester and Thomas
New York, Buffalo	Andrea
Oklahoma, Norman	RonEl
Oklahoma, Tulsa	Welnora
Oregon, Corvallis	LinEl
Oregon, Newberg	Ambraisa
Oregon, Lebanon	Rokmar
Oregon, Portland	Norsen and Andronason
Oregon, Salem	Abigail
Pennsylvania, Pittsburgh	Andrew
Pennsylvania, New Blomfield	MaxEl
Pennsylvania, York	El Tanere
Tennessee, Nashville	Ham
Texas, Dallas	Anastacia and Ordon
Utah, Woods Cross	Ham
Washington, Spokane	Aaron
Wisconsin, Bailey's Harbor	Khar-El
Canada, Manitoba, Winnipeg	Horace
Columbia, Bogota	??
New Zealand	??

Ms. Mills follows the above list with a list of groups to whom teachers have been assigned and are awaiting contact:

Indiana, Evansville	Anna
Indiana, Bloomington	Raymon
New York, Rochester	Olando
North Carolina, Charlotte	Jonathen
New Mexico, Albuquerque	Tomas
Minnesota, Minneapolis	Rachim
Ohio, Cincinnati	Tarkas
Florida, Tampa	Ramsey

An anonymously prepared list was sent to me in early 1994. It contained the following names of celestials not on Ms. Mills list: Abicoralinia, Abilenia, Abithenia, Adolia, Afonta, Agmar, Ahmen, Amixia, Amstar,

Anastacia, Anasthia, Anelia, Aranda, Aronolac, Asterna, Ba-Kim, Bernatella, Bonizia, Camille, Castelon, Chanli, Chanti, Clois, Conanon, Corabena, Corali, Danalenia, Danezia, DrinEl, Elaine, Enizia, Esterna, Foehn, FramSon, Gabriel, GabrEl, GynsEl, Ham, HapsonEssa, Hapsonia, HarSon, Inessa, JaEI, JamEl, JanEl, Jinsetta, JoEl, Josphine, JuEI, Korsta, Kwinsetta, LamSON, LansmOn, LeNera, Lentzia, Liliania, Liliken, Lutzia, Machiventa, Malvatia, Malventia, Manotia, Mantutia, Maralena, Mekken, Merfilam, MordEL, Nexus, Nodken, Norsa, Nova, Odron, Olympia, Ophelia, OrabEL, Osario, Or-el, Parsa, ParstOn, Partalena, Paralina, Pharon, QuinsEtta, Raisalee, Ranasthea, Rinletta, RoiEL, Royce, Ruby, SamuEL, SamSon, Serenia, Singing Brook, Sygel, Timmin, Tosterra, TrtenTon, Tru-elee, Tutken, Tutzia, Valadatia, Valadontia, Vesheeda, Wenstor, Wynella, Zanbella, Zen, Zion, Zygel.

Because new teachers are coming through every week, it is impossible to give a definitive list. Perhaps by the time this book is published, a directory of some sort should be available, complete with addresses and phone numbers of the contactees, and a description of just who each celestial claims to be. So far they are a mixture of ascended mortals, midwayers, angels, Thought Adjusters, and higher superbeings.

It is not just Urantians who now think they are communicating with supermortals. As we learned in chapter 12, guardian angels are all over the land, in touch not so much with Catholics, evangelicals, and fundamentalists, who of course believe in angels, as they are with New Agers. Books on angels are proliferating, angel newsletters are appearing. There is a National Angel Collectors Club, and you can buy a deck of 52 angel cards with instructions on how to use them for contacting the celestials.

The book *Ask Your Angels* (Ballantine, 1992) claims to have been dictated by angels to its three authors. They recommend tuning into your body chakras (energy points) as helpful when you go into the stillness to talk to your guardian angel. Your angel can even channel through your fingers as you type. The authors recommend putting a lit candle, a crystal, or a fresh flower on the computer console before you boot up. You can tell when an angel is near because there often is a scent of flowers that comes from nowhere, and you may feel as if someone gently stroked your cheek or ruffled your hair!

It is not just Jesus, angels, and other supermortals who are now speaking through American transmitters but also the Virgin Mary. In October 1994 the media reported on two Catholic women, each channeling messages from Mary on the thirteenth of every month: Nancy Fowler, in Conyers, Georgia, and Rosa Lopez, in Hollywood, Florida.

On October 13 thousands of pilgrims stood in the rain for hours to hear Nancy's monthly message. "Our lady was radiant," said Mrs. Fowler. "She wore a white veil and dress and she was beautiful."

In Florida, the crowd to hear Rosa numbered some 23,500, with 45 police officers on hand, and an ambulance to aid pilgrims suffering heat exhaustion. Many reported seeing crosses and the face of Mary in the sky.

In the *Paradise Networker* (Summer 1994), a TM newsletter published by the Hawaiian Teaching Mission, transmitter Patije Mills describes the channeling process as follows:

> Many have asked how the TR "hears" the communications from the Unseen Helpers. I have tried many ways to demonstrate or describe the *process* but it is so often different for each new TR coming on line. Some of us "hear" but it is not usually like "hearing" and repeating a telephone conversation to a third party; some of us "see" either ticker-tape type or visualizations which can be interpreted with a meaning; some of us "smell"—perhaps the smell brings up a memory from our memory bank (subconscious) which means something to us which we can describe to others; some of us just begin thinking a few words very strongly that seem out of sequence from our other thoughts—a thought transference perhaps; and some of us "feel" a *knowingness* within; and some actually hear a quiet voice speaking to them!

One of the most enthusiastic promoters of the TM is Dr. Robert W. Slagle. His Ph.D. is in psychology, a topic he teaches at Sonoma State University, in Rohnart, California. He is also a licensed therapist. His book for children, *Tales of Joshua* (1980), retells the *UB*'s accounts of episodes in the childhood of Jesus. In 1994 it was reissued in a greatly expanded edition, its illustrations increased from 190 to more than 300, and with special boxes for children to use as a coloring book. This limited edition of 1,000 copies is available from the Family Relations Foundation, Box 462, Sebastopol, California 95473.

Slagle was a fervent Fogger who strongly supported Vern Grimsley's channeling and who seems to have learned absolutely nothing from FOG's ignominious collapse. At the opposite pole from Slagle is another ex-Fogger (he was in the fog for fifteen years), David Kantor, now an outspoken critic of the TM.

At a small gathering of Urantians in San Francisco (January 1993) both Slagle and Kantor were speakers. A gray-haired, bespectacled, softspoken man, Slagle began his speech by reading a message from Ham, the first of the U.S. celestial teachers. Ham spoke of the "correcting time" now expanding the UB revelation, of how Michael has made Machiventa Melchizedek the new Prince of Urantia, and how previously closed "circuits" of energy to Urantia are now being opened.

Slagle surprised me by saying that anyone was free to accept or reject any message from any unseen friend. He himself, he confessed, felt free to discard 80 percent or more of the TM communications "if they did not ring my bell." He denied that TM messages are being "channeled." He said he was impressed by the humor coming from the teachers.

Slagle was followed by a woman who teaches English to grade schoolers. She spoke passionately about how "dazzling" the teachers' spontaneous answers to questions are, and how "beautiful" their English phrasing is.

Kantor spoke next. He is a dark-haired young man, tall, good-looking, intelligent, and erudite. He gave nothing less than a history of Christianity from the time of Jesus to today, stressing the 2,000 years as a monumental preparation for the UB's Fifth Epochal Revelation. His main thrust was a quotation from Paul that ended his talk: "Study to shew thyself approved unto God, a workman that needeth not to be ashamed, rightly dividing the word of truth" (II Timothy 2:15.) In other words, don't just accept the UB's great "magnitude and power," but study history, science, and modern theology so you can embed the revelation in today's cultural context. He warned against the dangers of thinking you are in contact with supermortals. He recommended *The Meaning of Revelation*, by Richard Niebuhr (brother of Reinhold), who of course would have been mortified by the suggestion that the UB is a revelation from God.

Kantor had high praise for the discoveries of Matthew Block. He called them "wonderful" in revealing how skillfully the celestials had used human sources to root the UB in modern science and culture, thus greatly amplifying our understanding of the Fifth Epochal Revelation. On the Internet (December 9, 1993) he put it this way: "If you compare the source material with its re-expression in the UB, another level of revelation appears in that one can see how the material was slightly tweaked to precipitate a higher condensation of meaning in the mortal mind." As I have said earlier, this is precisely how Seventh-day Adventists justify Mrs. White's endless plagiarizing.

Kantor spoke briefly about the vast destructive force of Grimsley's voices; how severely FOG had damaged the hopes, ideals, careers, finances, and even the marriages of Urantians who took the voices seriously. More than three million dollars went down the foggy drain that could have been used to advance the *UB*'s genuine revelation. That Kantor believed the TMers were repeating Grimsley's delusions was implicit in his remarks.

In response to a question from the floor, Kantor spoke of how he had accepted FOG's prediction that the great war of destruction would occur on March 25, 1985, and how he had joined other Foggers in entering a bomb shelter the night before. What didn't happen the next day, he said, was "pretty interesting." This understatement produced loud laughter in the room.

During a question-answer period Sara L. Blackstock arose to say she had been a devoted Fogger who thought she was receiving messages from the supermortals. I learned from her posting on the Internet (July 5, 1993) that she began to get messages on January 2, 1985, and continued to receive them almost daily until March 25, the day the third world war was supposed to start. Indeed, both she and her husband Robert Blackstock—like Slagle he is a psychologist—were with others in the bunker. When nothing happened she became convinced, she told the audience, that her voices were *not* genuine messages from the unseen friends.

"How did you know that?" Slagle asked.

Because, she said, the third world war didn't happen.

"Did you pray it wouldn't?" Slagle asked.

"Yes."

"And it didn't," was Slagle's response.

The clear implication is that Sara's channeling, like Vern's, was genuine after all, but thanks to humanity's free will, and in response to prayers, the holocaust was mercifully averted!

A few Urantians have been perceptive enough to see how similar this failed event is to the experience of Jonah, in an Old Testament short story that always impressed me as the funniest book in the Bible. The writer Paul Goodman once described it as a typical Jewish joke.

Do you recall the plot? The Lord ordered Jonah to go to the "great city" of Nineveh and warn its people that the city would soon be destroyed for its wickedness. Jonah refused to do this. To punish Jonah for his disobedience, God caused him to be swallowed at sea by a huge fish. After three days in the fish's belly, Jonah prayed to God. Accepting Jonah's contrition, the Lord caused the fish to vomit Jonah out on dry land. Not wishing to suffer any more such indignities, Jonah went to Nineveh where he preached God's message of doom.

What happened? The people of Nineveh turned from their wicked ways, and God changed his mind. He did not destroy the city after all!

As one can easily understand, this "displeased Jonah exceedingly, and he was very angry." So depressed, in fact, that he asked God to take away his life.

The Lord agreed that Jonah had a right to be angry. However, he insisted he had done right to spare Nineveh because it contained more than 120,000 poor souls who could not tell their right hand from their left. Besides, did not the city also have "much cattle"?

The Jonah analogy fails in this respect. There is no evidence that either Grimsley or Slagle are angry with the supermortals for allowing FOG's prophecy to be falsified. One can only be amazed by their powers of self-deception.

In 1993 Slagle distributed a remarkable 23-page document titled *Welcome to Change*. It is a passionate, deeply felt defense of what TMers call the second phase of the Fifth Epochal Revelation, the correcting time, now under Michael's supervision. The mission is worldwide. Closed circuits have been opened, and thousands of teachers, not just from our universe but some from superuniverses, are in contact with anyone who goes into the stillness and sincerely seeks such contact. Many of the teachers are ascended humans.

Slagle writes that at first he was skeptical of the TM, but after hearing tapes of messages, from Ham and others, and experiencing personal contact with a teacher, he became convinced that the new channeling fulfills the *UB*'s prediction on page 2082: "Urantia is now quivering on the very brink of one of its most amazing and enthralling epochs of social readjustment, moral quickening, and spiritual enlightenment."

Slagle buys it all. He even buys *The Course in Miracles*, said to have been dictated to a human by none other than Michael himself. Slagle's favorite word, used scores of times in *Welcome to Change*, is "experiential." It is through his personal experience, guided by his thought adjuster and the Spirit of Truth, that he found conversing through a transmitter with unseen friends to be an "awesome" experience. It rang his "truth bell." He felt a "new buoyancy." In the stillness he himself finally made direct contact with celestials, though so far he says he has been able only to transmit a few words.

Slagle expresses the great joy he felt when he first learned that Lucifer, Caligastia, and other rebels had refused to repent and were mercifully obliterated by the Father. "My soul soars as I realize the tortuous hand of the wicked Prince is gone." He quotes supermortal Will: "Our Father wept with the news of this decision." Caligastia, Slagle assures us, has not been on Urantia since 1985.

Slagle is a typical fundamentalist. Yes, he admits the *UB* contains a few errors, but they are trivial and negligible. He believes that Adam and Eve were eight to ten feet tall and rode on the backs of fandors. He also grants occasional mistakes now coming from the teachers, but he finds amazing truth and unity in what they are saying.

David Kantor, the most outspoken Urantian to oppose the TM, had many interesting things to say in 1993 on the Urantial Internet. He was raised, he said, a Christian fundamentalist. Reading Teilhard de Chardin was his first "stepping stone" for climbing out of primitive Biblicism. For a while he flirted with Zen and other eastern faiths. He still admires the writings of Paramahansa Yogananda and Rabindranath Tagore. Then came his discovery of the *UB*, and he has been a believer ever since. He is not a Urantian fundamentalist, but he sees the *UB* as containing the "best model of reality" he has yet encountered.

It was Christy who persuaded David to offer his services to Grimsley, and for 15 years he worked for Vern, accepting his voices as genuine. His emotional commitments and experiences in FOG, and the "social close-ness" he felt with other Foggers, were so overwhelming, he wrote, that even today he struggles vainly for words to explain them.

The same is true, he continues, of the emotions that crushed him after March 25, 1985 passed, and he had to adjust his mind to the awful realization that he and his fellow Foggers had been had. He still finds it painful to talk about FOG's sudden crash and how he felt himself "peering into the abyss of total insanity." So powerful were these emotions that he believed that not until he entered the mansion worlds would he be able to comprehend fully what had happened.

The Foggers were so absorbed in their shared delusions that Vern would throw away without reading any letter from a Urantian skeptical of his voices. David confesses that he himself "did not want ever to hear from anyone who didn't believe our messages because my own hold on them was so tenuous that I relied on that hold for my entire social identity and psychological well being." He sees the same type of "closed, subjective isolation of self" developing in the TM movement. The TM virus, he added, is spreading rapidly and doing untold damage to the Fifth Epochal Revelation. He is aware that it is precisely this elation of belonging to a semi-secret core of true believers that can lead to the excesses of Jonestown and Waco.

During the FOG days, David reveals, Vern's marriage was "plagued with violence," and he was developing an alcohol dependency, both carefully concealed from his followers. When messages from the unseen friends began coming through other Foggers, Vern was greatly annoyed by this erosion of his authority. After the crash of March 25, Kantor says he became involved in legal actions to prevent Vern from ever repeating his folly with other Urantians.

For weeks after the great disappointment of March 25, David discloses, Foggers were telephoning him to argue that Vern's voices were authentic, but that history had taken an unforeseen turn and spared Urantia a nuclear holocaust. Those who phoned with these rationalizations, Kantor adds, are the same persons now supporting the Teaching Mission.

Although Kantor has only harsh words about Grimsley's paranoia and hunger for power, he speaks glowingly of Vern's oratory, and his "beautiful and lofty ideals." His talks "were among the most spiritually moving sermons I have every heard." But Vern too closely resembled, Dave writes, the Wizard of Oz, using clever "magic tricks" to deceive his disciples.

> Didn't you ever notice that Vern never participated in social events in which he was not in control? Did you ever see him attend workshops at a conference and participate like anyone else? Did you ever see him even sit around in a discussion group and participate like one of us? He was always either in the limelight and in control, or not there lest he be discovered. Don't you think that David Koresh was an inspiration to his people? How about Jim Jones, or any of the televangelists who carefully craft their personas as tools for political and personal gain?
>
> After March 25, 1985, all the FOGers got together and issued a public apology and statement, which we all signed, with the exception of Vern. He refused to even attend a single one of the many post-mortem meetings we held to try and understand what had happened to us.

Kantor suspects that Christy may have used Vern to prevent Berkeley Elliott, in Oklahoma City, from building a power base to rival the Chicago Brotherhood!

Today Kantor and his wife Rebecca—she once worked, by the way, as Christy's secretary—are deep in the study of modern Christian theology. Kantor is enormously impressed by recent biblical scholarship and the works of both Catholic and Protestant thinkers. I have mentioned his admiration for Richard Niebuhr. Others he lists on the internet as mentors include Gerd Thiessen, Sally McFague, Ian Barbour, Mary Gerhardt, and

Avery Dulles. He is convinced that Christian theologians are now attempting to unify science, philosophy, and religion in precisely the way recommended by the *UB*. He sees himself as struggling to steer between two dangerous "zones of intoxication"—he overly emotional and the overly intellectual.

I see Kantor as rapidly broadening his religious perspective. I would not be surprised if in a few years he follows his friend Leo Elliott in making a clean break with the Urantia cult.

So far not much has been channeled that is out of harmony with the *UB* or contains anything essentially new or significant. Most of the communications from on high have the same banal quality as messages that came through the great direct-voice mediums and automatic writers of the past. The term "channeling" clearly applies to the transmission of messages from entities on a higher plane of existence, but those in the Teaching Mission, like all Urantians, are reluctant to use the term because it suggests a kinship with New Age channeling and reincarnation. They prefer to call their contactees "Transmitter-Receivers" or TRs.

Anyone can become a TR. Considerable literature is now being published here and there on how to "go into the stillness" and pray for the light. In no time you will be contacted by a Teacher! Aflana, who speaks to more than one TM group, announced in 1992 that the celestials were working on a technique by which they soon could be dimly seen by their transmitters! Newsletters are popping up all over the place to report the latest Teaching Mission events.

One of the least puerile of the Teaching Mission newsletters is *Spirit Quest*, published in Ohio by Jim Cleveland. He lives not in Cleveland but in Cincinnati where a group is channeling Tarkas and Bakim. Issue six (July 1994) is a plea for Urantians to stop squabbling about the Teaching Mission and try to love one another. "It's the experience itself that authenticates the Teaching Mission," he writes, "same as reading the Urantia Book substantiates that revelation. . . . You know what you know. And you can tell the critics that they just had to be there—and they can, simply by going into the stillness with an open mind and heart."

Responding to a question, Tarkas informed the Cleveland group that the Lucifer rebellion has indeed been finally adjudicated and "rebel spirits now pose no problem to TM participants who are 'washed in the Father's love.'"

Cleveland continues to publish his doggerel. Here is the final stanza of his song "All Are Blessed":

In the Heaven up there, we'll stay the path
To the Father's brilliant light
Where all that's good that we do share
Lie precious in His sight.
It's a tough life here; it's a trial sometimes
Faith comes when you know the score
That the life down here is just a part
And the Heavens hold so much more.

The May 1994 issue of *Spirit Quest* quotes from a long essay by Eric Johnson, of Denver, defending the authenticity of Vern Grimsley's voices. There really was a danger then, he writes, that World War III would erupt from a Soviet first strike.

> Vern was serving the role of Jonah, sent to warn the city of Nineveh. He warned, we prayed, the danger passed, and God was pleased. But we were unforgiving toward Vern, and ourselves if we were his followers. Little did we know that the well-stocked camps and caves were a fallback position in case the whole thing did blow up. And it almost did. Thank God it didn't, but that doesn't mean that Vern's information was wrong nor that the process was bogus.

Eric (he is 19) bemoans the Foundation's lackluster efforts to evangelize the world. He hopes the Teaching Mission will revitalize the Fifth Epochal Revelation. Study groups are urged to follow the lessons in *A Course in Miracles* and to practice "touchy-feely" exercises that promote love for one another.

Cleveland published a song he has written titled "Backseat Children." It opens with this forgettable stanza:

If we'll just get along, the trip will pass
by joyfull and serene
And we will share our time in wonderment
And watch the passing scene
With the Father's road map well in hand
Our guidance from Supreme
We can make the world a better place
Each day our spirits sing.

An energetic group of Urantians in West Sedona, Arizona, called the Aquarian Concepts Community, is sending out literature announcing that Machiventa Melchizedek himself has informed them that in December 1989 the Creator Son of our local universe appointed him Planetary Prince. West Sedona has been chosen for his headquarters. He and his assistants are, of course, invisible because they inhabit a higher dimension.

The May/June 1993 issue of this group's periodical, *The Salvington Circuit*, features a four-page message from Melchizedek. He says he is calling forth "the cosmic and Urantian reservists to bring about and usher in the first stage of light and life on Urantia within the jurisdiction and overcontrol of the Bright and Morning Star of Salvington as mandated by Christ Michael," and "transmitted through the Material Complement, Gabriel of Sedona." Caligastia is not dead, as other TMers maintain, but doing his best to discredit the Sedona group. Donations for their great work can be sent to their Planetary Center of Light, POB 3946, West Sedona, AZ 86340.

The Sedona group, taking instructions from a celestial called Paladin, maintains that the original *UB* papers contained information supporting both reincarnation and astrology. Because Sadler personally did not believe in either, he began a "systematic degradation of these papers" by removing all references to astrology and reincarnation. This New Age group claims that the *UB* contains only the first tenth of the Fifth Epochal Revelation. The other nine-tenths are now being supplied by their celestial contacts.

In the early 1980s a Urantian in Toronto who calls himself Edward began to go into trances and is now channeling a variety of angels. You can read all about this in Timothy Wyllie's crazy book, *Dolphins, ETs, and Angels*. It was first published in 1984, but is currently available in a 1992 paperback from Bear and Company, a Santa Fe, New Mexico, publisher of occult literature.

Wyllie is a British architect who for fifteen years was a leader of The Church of the Final Judgment, founded in England by Robert De Grimson. (It is now called The Foundation Faith in God.) Members in long black robes went about teaching that Jesus and Satan would reconcile, humanity was on its way to destruction, after which Jesus would return to earth and Satan would carry out Christ's judgments.

Wyllie buys everything on the New Age scene: out-of-body travel, ESP, psychic healing, aliens in UFOs, and so on. On page 32 he tells how you can make a cloud disappear by focusing "warm energy" on it. He found he could communicate telepathically with dolphins. A dolphin in Clearwater Bay, Florida, introduced Wyllie to the *UB*'s angels. "You know enough about us now," the dolphin said (page 218), "but you know very little about them!"

The *UB* hit Wyllie like a ton of bricks. He is convinced that the Fifth Epochal Revelation is ongoing, energy circuits have been opened, and the angels are contacting Urantians everywhere to usher in the great age of "Light and Life." I don't know what is going on now in Toronto, but in 1982 Edward was channeling Shelena, Shandron, Durandior, Talantia, Beatea, and Joy. A friend of Wyllie actually saw Caligastia peeking through his second-floor bedroom window. "It was not . . . a pretty sight." When the friend embraced the shade, the archfiend vanished, leaving the friend feeling "a tangible wave of forgiveness and love whirl through the Universe" (page 141). The book closes with a message from Michael produced by Edward "in a flood of automatic writing."

It looks as if New Agers are starting to discover the *UB*. What does Shirley MacLaine think of it, I wonder?

Will the epidemic of new channeling—Joe Pope, the Woods Cross group, the Sedona group, and the increasing number of participants in the Teaching Mission—eventually fade away as completely as Grimsley's voices? Or will it sound a death knell for the Urantia movement? Already it is splintering Urantia study groups into two bitterly warring camps— those who accept the new teachers and those who don't. The conflict is especially bitter in the Los Angeles area where Duane Faw leads the TMers and Lyn Lear leads the opposition. It is no surprise that the Urantia Foundation, threatened with further disintegration, has disowned the entire TM as spurious, possibly even initiated by a still active Caligastia. True believers in an inspired Bible rarely look kindly on new revelations intended to supersede it.

Can you imagine Mormons taking seriously a new revelation dictated by a church member who claimed to be in contact with the angel Moroni? Or Moslems accepting a new revelation from Gabriel that updated the Koran? It is, of course, why mainline Christians have no interest in the Book of Mormon, the Koran, the writings of Ellen White, the Bible of the Reverend Sun Moon, or the Urantia Book. It is why those of Jewish faith are not inspired by the New Testament. For religious movements centered around a holy and divinely inspired book, one Bible is enough!

The claims of so many Urantians that they are in direct contact with the revelators and are now receiving messages for the faithful are similar to claims that have periodically dogged the Adventists. Long before Ellen White died there were women in the church who had visions that for a brief time rivaled those of Mrs. White, but which she effectively silenced by reporting that God told her these rival visions were spurious. The two most prominent cases involved Anna Garmive, of Petosky, Michigan, and Anna Phillips Rice, of Ogden, Utah. Other Adventist women had similar visions after Mrs. White's death.

D. M. Canright, in his biography of Ellen White, wrote (170–71):

> An editorial in the *Advent Review*, Aug. 19, 1915, says: "In our personal experience we recall at least a dozen during the last two or three decades who have claimed they had the prophetic gift. Two or three of these have drifted into the wildest phantasies. Others frankly acknowledged later in their experience that they had been mistaken, and settled down to a quiet experience. Others are, perhaps, still nursing their fancy."
>
> By this it will be seen that there have been among Seventh-day Adventists right along numerous persons who *fancied* they had the gift of prophecy. The editor correctly attributes all these to their *fancy*. These had no Elder White to encourage and back them up. So their visions finally ceased, as Mrs. White's in all probability would have done under similar circumstances.

By far the funniest of all self-declared successors to Mrs. White was Mrs. Margaret W. Rowen, of Los Angeles. As Adventist Richard Schwarz tells her demented story in his history of the church, *Light Bearers to the Remnant*, a year after Ellen White died in 1915 Mrs. Rowen announced that God had chosen her to carry on the work. She was then about 40 and had been an Adventist for four years.

Mrs. Rowen's visions exactly counterfeited Mrs. White's. Her body became rigid, her eyes open and unblinking. No signs of breathing. She opened and closed her trances with shouts of "Glory! Glory! Glory!" Her breakaway church, called Reformed Seventh-day Adventist, published a journal titled *The Advocate*. She forged a document signed by Ellen White that declared her (Rowen) the remnant church's new leader and actually managed to sneak it into the White Estate files at Elmshaven. When it was proved a forgery, Mrs. Rowen accused church officials of fabricating it to discredit her. She was disfellowshipped by her Los Angeles church in 1919.

After the Great Disappointment of 1844, when Jesus failed to appear on the date William Miller had predicted, there were a few feeble attempts by individuals to set new dates, but the Seventh-day Adventists, after being formally organized as a church, have been careful never again to predict a specific date. In 1923 Mrs. Rowen made the mistake of announcing the time of the Second Coming as February 6, 1925. When nothing happened, she said she had forgotten how long it would take Jesus to make the journey to earth after starting from heaven on February 6!

Mrs. Rowen's most ardent disciple was a simple-minded physician named B. E. Fullmer. Enmity slowly festered between them. In 1926 he confessed it was he who had slipped the false E. G. White document into the White files. When he discovered that Mrs. Rowen was pilfering tithe money for personal use, he broke completely with her. Mrs. Rowen's anger knew no bounds. On February 27, 1927, Fullmer was knocked unconscious by a blow on his head with a piece of pipe. Neighbors called police. They found Mrs. Rowen and two aides beside the unconscious Fullmer, with a shovel for burying the body. Fullmer recovered. The three pleaded guilty to "assault with a deadly weapon," and were sentenced to San Quentin Penitentiary. Mrs. Rowen was paroled after a year in prison. She shifted her headquarters to Florida, where she and "Rowenism" faded into welcome obscurity.

The latest example of a former Adventist who imagined himself in direct contact with God and the angels was Vernon Howell, who called himself David Koresh and ran the Branch Davidian cult near Waco, Texas. The cult's lineage goes back to an Adventist splinter group led by Benjamin L. Roden (1905–1978). Roden claimed to be the successor of Victor Tasho Houteff (1885–1955). An immigrant from Bulgaria, Houteff convinced himself that Adventists had become corrupt and lukewarm, and that God had chosen him to reform the movement. In 1935, after his Los Angeles church expelled him, he led a small band of followers to Lake Waco, in Texas, where he established the Mount Carmel Center.

Houteff's eschatology was called The Shepherd's Rod after the title of Houteff's first book, *The Shepherd's Rod*, a 255-page work which he published himself in 1930. (Volume 2 of this work appeared in 1932.) The "rod" refers to the rod of Moses who led the first exodus from Egypt. Houteff saw himself as leading a second exodus of the remnant faithful out of the "Egypt" (worldliness) of a degenerating mother church. He interpreted "Hear ye the rod" (Micah 6:9) to mean that Moses' rod figuratively spoke—the only talking rod in history!

In 1942 Houteff named his group the Davidian Seventh-day Adventists. He taught that the remnant faithful, numbering at least 144,000 (Revelation 7:4; 14:1 and 3) would soon gather in Palestine where they would establish the Kingdom of David in preparation for the return of Jesus. This event would be the opening of the fifth seal (Revelation 6:9), about which Koresh claimed he was writing a treatise.

After Houteff died in 1955, the year the *UB* was published, his widow, Marcella, took over the sect. Mt. Carmel Center then had about 125 residents. She sold the Lake Waco property and moved the headquarters fifteen miles northeast to Elk, Texas, just outside Waco, renaming it "New Mt. Carmel." It was there she made a mistake as stupid as Mrs. Rowen's—a mistake strongly opposed by many Davidians. She announced that on April 22, 1959, God would remove all the Jews and Arabs from Palestine so that the Kingdom of David could be established there.

When this date passed and nothing happened, most of her followers left the area, embarrassed and disillusioned. Some went back to Seventh-day Adventism, others joined mainline churches, still others went nowhere. In December 1961 Marcella apologized for her blunder and tried unsuccessfully to dissolve the sect. She is still living, at age 75 as I write, but she has gone underground and her whereabouts are unknown. I have been told that she is living in California, having changed her last name to Eakin.

A few of Mrs. Houteff's followers hung on in the New Mount Carmel Center under the leadership of Benjamin Roden, a businessman from Odessa, Texas. They renamed themselves the Branch Seventh-day Adventists. After Roden died in 1978, his wife Lois took over. When she died in 1986, control of the cult passed to her son George.

In 1982 a young guitar-strumming, long-haired Texan named Vernon Wayne Howell, born in 1959 in Houston to an unmarried teen-age mother, arrived in Waco. He had just been booted out of the Seventh-day Adventist church in Tyler, Texas, at age 21, for sleeping with a 15-year-old daughter of a church elder. By then he had become a devout Rodenite.

For a while Howell tried without success to establish a branch of the Davidians in Los Angeles. Back in Waco, he and the much older Lois Roden became lovers. Her son George charged Howell with raping his mother, and the two men were soon locked in a power struggle for control of the colony. There was a gun fight in 1987. Roden was shot but not killed. A hung jury lead to Howell's acquittal on the charge of attempted murder. According to Ivan Solotaroff's article "The Last Revelation from Waco," in *Esquire* (July 1993), George was declared insane in 1990 after killing a man he claimed Howell had sent to kill *him*. Roden was sent to the Vernon (Texas) state mental hospital where he remains today.

In 1990 Howell, now the cult's top banana, changed his name to Koresh, Hebrew for Cyrus, and named his cult the Branch Davidians. Apparently he was unaware that an earlier Florida cult called Koreshanity had been led by Cyrus Teed who also called himself Koresh. The Koreshans believed that our earth is a hollow sphere, and we live on its inside! You can read all about Koreshanity in my *Fads and Fallacies in the Name of Science*, and in chapter 2 of my *On the Wild Side*.

On February 28, 1993, a hundred or so federal agents stormed the Waco cult's headquarters to arrest Koresh for stockpiling illegal weapons. Four agents and several Branch Davidians were killed in the brief gun battle. A joke made the rounds: the letters of WACO stand for "We Ain't Coming Out." On April 19, after federal agents battered holes in the wall of the compound and filled its rooms with nonlethal tear gas, Koresh is believed to have ordered the place burned to the ground. Eighty-seven of the faithful did indeed stay inside. It was the most horrifying case of mass murder-suicide since Jim Jones poisoned hundreds of his followers. Koresh's skeleton had a bullet hole through the forehead.

Small groups of loyal Davidians carry on Houteff's doctrines in other U.S. cities, Canada, England, West Africa, South America, and the Philippines. They disagree among themselves as much as they disagree with Seventh-day Adventists. The largest group is in Exeter, Missouri. It originated in 1961 among a group of former Waco Davidians, led by Martin J. Bingham (1905–1988) who had strongly opposed Mrs. Houteff's crazy prophecies. They first organized in California as Davidian Seventh-day Adventists, and were headquartered in Riverside, California, until 1970 when they moved to property purchased in Exeter. Their Universal Publishing Association, Bashan Hill, Exeter, issues many periodicals and distributes literature promoting Houteff's views and prophecies.

The Exeter Davidians have no connection with the Waco cult, whose leader they believe was insane. Like all Davidians they see themselves as true Seventh-day Adventists who are still loyal to the teachings of Sister White. We are not "offshoots" of Seventh-day Adventism, Houteff declared in a 1949 sermon, but "upshoots." To this day the Davidians remain dedicated to the teachings of Houteff—doctrines which they believe their mother church abandoned more than a century ago.

In 1993 who should turn up in Waco but George Roden's former wife Amo Bishop Roden. According to *Time* (January 17, 1994) she is living in a metal shack on the cult's property where she sells videotapes claiming the fire was started by flame throwers on FBI tanks.

As for the claims of the new Teaching Mission channelers on the Urantian scene, it is impossible to guess how many of the faithful are now taking these revelations seriously. A soft approach toward the current epidemic was taken by Urantian Stephen Ian McIntosh in his article "Channelers Expose Urantia Book Fundamentalism," in *Urantian Sojourn* (Spring/Summer 1992). Although McIntosh is critical of the new channeling, he refuses to repudiate it totally. He cautions Urantians to be open-minded, to wait and see how things develop. "At this point," he writes, "a final judgment about these channeled communications would be premature. . . . I am ambivalent. I do not dismiss them with hostility."

Moreover, McIntosh thinks that although the *UB* is "holy scripture," and "the most powerful and important book the planet has ever known, it is by no means a perfect and final work." In other words, Urantian fundamentalists should not dismiss the new channeling merely because it may conflict at some points with what the *UB* says. "Fear-based paranoid speculation seems to be a specialty among some associated with *The Urantia Book*, but hopefully, the majority of level-headed readers will not manifest hostility toward this new development until actual events call for such a reaction."

The Urantia Foundation vigorously rejects the Teaching Mission. Its *Urantia News* (November 1993) warned against the outburst of what it calls New Age "channeling." The *UB* is quoted as cautioning readers not to mistake the "uprush of the memories of the unconscious levels of the human mind" for divine revelation (*UB* 1099). Quoting from the same page: "Under no circumstances should the trancelike state of visionary consciousness be cultivated as a religious experience." And from page 2089 a passage is quoted about how Jesus never indulged in seeing visions or hearing voices.

Ironically, to anyone not a Seventh-day Adventist or a Urantian, both Adventism and the *UB* had their origin in precisely this kind of channeling. Ellen White based her doctrines on visions and dreams. The *UB* rests on voices first channeled by Wilfred, then later heard by Dr. Sadler and others close to him.

The latest issue I have seen of the *T/R News Network* (vol. 2, no. 7, August 1994) is filled with excerpts from messages recently sent by the celestials through TM transmitters. These messages all seem to agree that the following events will take place very soon:

1. The return to earth of Adam and Eve. According to Norsen, "They even await now in great joy at the opportunity our gracious Son and the Father and the Most Highs and the Ancients of Days have given them."

2. The return to earth in visible form of Machiventa Melchizedek, now Urantia's Planetary Prince. Said Lleewena: "We are making preparations for his arrival upon Urantia. He did, indeed, briefly visit you at Naperville last April, however for reasons unknown he did not remain long. The return visit is currently being scheduled for sometime in November/December of this [1994] year. His exact destination is not yet released to us."

3. Soon after Machiventa Melchizedek's arrival, Michael himself will again incarnate on Urantia in visible human form.

4. The celestials will construct on Urantia twelve "universities" for teaching and ushering in the era of light and life. Their actual construction, according to Daranadek, must await the delivery of "manite," a material made of morontia, to be used for building the "upper levels of your schools." This is the first anyone ever heard of manite.

5. The Tree of Life that once flourished in Eden will be replanted on earth. It will be needed, says Norsen, to provide sustenance for the material bodies of the Melchizedeks when they materialize here.

In September 1994 I received in the mail an unsolicited packet of 50 brochures sent by Beryl McCandless from a Pittsburgh Teaching Mission Group. Beryl's letter has a dove of peace at the top and a rainbow printed across the page. On the brochure is a message transmitted through Beryl by Gabriel "in accord with the direction of beloved brother Michael." Contributions to the Teaching Mission are solicited. The letter concludes with "Love, Light and Joy!"

Gabriel's message is so typical of the trivialities coming through TM transmitters, that I print below its last four paragraphs:

It does not take recitations, preparations, degrees, specialization or permission to come to me. My children of earth, all it takes is an earnest, humble heart that is simple and sincere. I ALWAYS listen! You shall know by the peace that fills you that I have heard and lovingly blessed you.

I speak to ALL, especially those who feel they are not worthy. Worth is but a word used in judgment, not in love. I AM LOVE. You were fashioned in love. Where I AM there is LOVE.

Children, to know me is to know yourself. How glorious is this revelation! When you love me you begin to love yourself. In loving yourself you begin to love your neighbor as yourself! This wonderful perfect circle is continuous without end!

LOVE is all. I AM LOVE. I am all there is. You are a part of this all. YOU. You are loved. I am God the Father Almighty who loves you!

In the summer of 1994 believers in the Teaching Mission got together in Spokane, Washington, for their first annual conference. Robert Slagle was the keynote speaker. More than a hundred Urantians attended, many driving to Spokane all the way from Florida. Some notion of their enthusiasm for the new "correcting time" can be gained from a description of the conference on the internet, written by Fred Harris of Tallahassee. The "joy and excitement," he wrote, ". . . turned into a hugfest." Slagle, Byron Belitsos, and others gave inspirational speeches. Lilly Frazier sang solos. Rick Giles and Hal Bynum picked guitars. Jeannie George delivered a standup comedy act.

"In the end," Harris continued, "we hugged and hugged. . . . The Love that Jim McCallon mistakenly says came from my eyes was nothing more than a reflection of the love that was being poured out. . . ." The Teachers came through their channels with "encouragement and confirmed that much was in the process to assist the world in the healing powers it needs. We were all asked to seek the stillness daily and to provide service and joyful countenance to those we chance to meet on our paths."

The conference closed with everyone singing what Harris calls the "now famous hug song." I suppose it is some sort of progress in the Urantia movement when believers hug each other more than they hug the *UB*.

19

The Great Rebellion

Another grave threat to Urantian unity, as serious as the events detailed in the two previous chapters, is a recent rebellion by rank and file Urantians against the Urantia Foundation at 533 Diversey Pkwy., Chicago. The rebellion was led by David Elders, president of the Urantia Brotherhood, and his vice president, Mrs. Marilynn Kulieke, a cousin by marriage of Mark Kulieke, whom we met earlier.

The bitter dispute erupted in 1990. At the controversy's center is the Foundation's insistence that it has sole control over the copyright and sales of the *UB*, and sole control over the use of the Urantia trademark, three azure-blue concentric circles on a white background (*UB* 606). Moreover, for decades the Foundation trustees have followed a policy of holding back promotion of the *UB* in accord with what they claim are strict orders from the revelators. "Slow growth," the words often capitalized, is the strategy that Martin Myers, until recently the Foundation's head, insists he was told by the celestials to follow. In a 1973 lecture titled "Unity, Not Uniformity," he said: "Over-rapid growth would be suicidal. The book is being given to those who are ready for it long before its world-wide mission."

So far the Urantia movement has made no effort to establish churches or ordain ministers, although from 1956 to about 1969 Sadler ran a Urantia Brotherhood School whose classes met weekly at 533 Diversey. Helen Carlson, whom we encountered in chapter 7, was the school's registrar. It awarded the title of "certified leader" to students who passed six major courses, and the title of "ordained teacher" to students who passed twelve courses. The word "ordained" surely indicates, as I have earlier suggested, that Sadler had some sort of organized church in mind. At any rate, the idea of a formal church never materialized, and most records of the Brotherhood School were long ago destroyed.

Since then the Foundation has stressed the slow spread of the faith through local study groups consisting of ten or more members, and their personal contacts with outsiders. There are no sacred rituals at meetings of these study groups. Helen Carlson has testified that Forum meetings usually closed with a benediction. There is no Urantian marriage service, although there is a published funeral service. In recent years a growing number of believers, notably Rev. Meredith Sprunger, have expressed hope for transforming the movement into a full-fledged church with ordained ministers, rituals, and Urantian hymns.

For reasons that escape me, the *UB* seems to have aroused more excitement among French-speaking people than in the United States. In 1961 a three-volume French translation by Jacques Weiss was published in Paris with the title *La Cosmogonie d'Urantia*. It quickly sold out. (Weiss, incidentally, is an occultist who firmly believes in reincarnation.) The Urantia Foundation took Weiss to court for not having obtained permission to translate. The Foundation later issued its own translation in 1982 with the new title of *Le Livre d'Urantia*. It has since attracted a large following in France and in French-speaking Quebec.

As might be expected, the *UB*'s popularity in France and Quebec has generated several French books that attack the movement. I know of four: *L'Évangile de l'an 2000* (1974), by L. Gagnon, a Catholic priest; *Le mythe de l'Urantia* (1981), by Ms. L. Michaud, of Scarborough College, University of Toronto; *A Propos de The Urantia Book et de la Bible* (1982), by G. Giroux; and *Le Verbe s'est fait livre* (1990), by Jacques Rhéaume, a professor of theology at Laval University, Quebec. Rhéaume's doctoral thesis on the *UB*, written for the University of Ottawa, is also in French. All four books attack the *UB* for its radical departures from Christian orthodoxy. Michaud argues that the *UB* was inspired by Satan, a view held also by many Seventh-day Adventists who are aware of the *UB*.

Unofficial translations of the *UB* have appeared in Spain, Finland, and Estonia. As I said earlier, official translations into Russian and Dutch are said to be in progress. In 1993 authorized Finnish and Spanish translations were published, as well as the *UB*'s eleventh edition in English, and exhaustive English and Finnish concordances. In Spain a writer named J. J. Benitez has for years been plagiarizing the *UB* by incorporating vast chunks of it into four fantasy novels with another underway. The Foundation seems powerless to do anything about it.

The Urantia Brotherhood was established in 1955 by 36 Forum members to serve as the Foundation's right arm, especially in handling *UB* sales and distribution. In 1989, when the Foundation denied the Brotherhood the right to sell the *UB*, or to use the name "Urantia" or the three-circle logo, the Brotherhood decided to secede. Since 1955 it had been headquartered at 533 Diversey, in the same building occupied by the Foundation—the building where the Sadlers lived and operated their medical practice.

After breaking away, the Brotherhood changed its name to the Fifth Epochal Fellowship (FEF) and in 1989 moved a few blocks south of Diversey to 529 Wrightwood Avenue, in the Lincoln Park area. Its former periodicals, *Urantia Brotherhood Bulletin* and *The Urantian* continue under the new names of *The Fifth Epochal Fellowship Bulletin* and the *Journal of the Fifth Epochal Fellowship*.

At the time I write, 18 of the 21 *UB* societies, including FUSLA (First Urantia Society of Los Angeles), have voted to leave the Foundation and affiliate with the Fifth Epochal Fellowship. Three of the Foundation's five trustees, Gloriann Harris (she also worked as office manager and accountant), Frank Sgraglino, and Helena Sprague, resigned in 1989 to be replaced by friends of Martin Myers. One of the new trustees is Mrs. Patricia Sadler Mundelius, of Danville, California, the daughter of Bill Sadler Jr.

Lyn Davis Lear, the wife of television mogul Norman Lear, is an active member of the Fifth Epochal Fellowship. She serves on its Council with a term lasting until the year 2000. A few years ago when Norman asked her what she most wanted for her birthday (or maybe it was for a wedding anniversary), she is rumored to have said the best present he could give her would be to read the *UB*. I do not know if Norman has since done this. If so, I cannot imagine him taking the *UB* as an authentic revelation from celestials.

To replace the lost Brotherhood, the Foundation created a Urantia Brotherhood Association. Myers, a graduate of the University of Kansas Law School, resigned his post as vice president of a Chicago bank and trust company to devote full time to running the Foundation. Born in Kansas in 1941, the son of a medical doctor, Myers was introduced to the *UB* by his Sigma Chi fraternity brother Vern Grimsley. (Grimsley's FOG apostasy was covered in chapter 17.) Myers is on record as saying that opening the *UB* was one of the happiest moments of his life.

In 1992 the new trustees voted unanimously to expel Myers from the ruling board. Now living in Evanston, Illinois, he is in the process of suing the trustees for "wrongful discharge." One of the trustees, K. Richard Keeler, has started legal action against Myers and his wife, Diane, seeking an injunction to prevent them from publishing a libelous document about

Keeler's brush with the law for the alleged abuse of a young girl. Keeler is demanding a return of all copies of the document.

As of August 1994 the Foundation's five trustees were Patricia Mundelius (president), Richard Keeler (acting executive director), Thomas C. Burns, Hoite C. Caston, and Philip A. Rolnick. Keeler is said to be the main financial contributor to the Foundation. Born in Bartlesville, Oklahoma, he inherited a multimillion-dollar fortune from his father, an official of the Phillips Petroleum Company.

The rebellion against the Foundation reached an explosive point in 1991 when the Foundation initiated legal action against Kristen Maaherra. Maaherra is a Finnish name meaning "Lord of the Land." Married and with four children by a previous marriage to a man no longer living, Maaherra resides in Jamestown, Colorado, a town about ten miles northwest of Boulder, with her present husband, Eric Schaveland. She has been a devout Urantian for more than 20 years. The Foundation's wrath against her was aroused when she prepared an index to the *UB*, put it on a computer disk, and distributed free copies of the disk, as well as printouts, to friends. True to its former compulsions, the Foundation promptly sued Maaherra for violating their 1955 copyright on the *UB*, which they had renewed in 1983.

The Foundation also claims that Maaherra violated their registration of the three-circle logo by putting it on her disk. Maaherra contends that this symbol is as much public domain as the Christian cross, the Jewish Star of David, or the Buddhist yin-yang bisected circle. Why, she wants to know, is she forbidden to put the circles on her mailbox or wear them as a lapel pin? Incredibly, the Foundation also ordered her not to wear her wedding ring because it displays the three circles!

It is amusing to note that the currently popular *Course in Miracles*, which purports to have been dictated to Helen Schuctman by none other than Jesus himself, is also copyrighted. The Foundation for Inner Peace, holder of the copyright, is as quick to forbid unauthorized copying from the book as is the Urantia Foundation. Helen never doubted it was Jesus who guided her hands while she typed the *Course in Miracles*, nor is this doubted by Kenneth and Gloria Wapnick, who helped edit the *Course* and are its leading drumbeaters. As the Wapnicks say in their newsletter, *The Lighthouse* (September 1993), portions dictated by Jesus were removed from the *Course* "as directed by Jesus himself," just as the supermortals directed Sadler to remove some channeled material from the published *UB*. Copyright restrictions on the *Course* are covered in the March 1993 issue of *The Lighthouse*.

Exactly how was *The Course in Miracles* copyrighted? Details are given by the Wapnicks, and by Judith Skutch Whiston and Robert Skutch (Judith's former husband), in *The Lighthouse* for December 1992. The four listened to the "Voice of the Holy Spirit" before making any decisions about publishing the *Course*, but they were unprepared for Jesus' explicit instructions to Helen that the *Course* be copyrighted. This first struck the four as "out of character" when applied to a work written by Jesus; nevertheless "we of course listened to Jesus and proceeded to contact the Copyright Office. . . . We were informed that a copyright could not be granted to a non-physical author such as Jesus, nor to 'Anonymous.'" On the other hand, they could not put Helen's name on the *Course* because Jesus had forbidden her to associate her name with it. They compromised. The copyright was registered as "Anonymous" followed by Helen's name in parentheses.

Maaherra and her attorney Joe Lewis, of Washington, D.C., contend that the *UB* is as much public domain as the Bible. They argue that the Foundation's copyright and its renewal are both illegal. To be copyrighted in the United States a work must have a human author or authors who are specified. The celestial authors of the *UB*, Maaherra insists, obviously are not human. It is worth noting that Harold Sherman, in his famous chapter about the *UB* in *How to Know What to Believe*, anticipated just such a lawsuit. "It is possible," he wrote (page 94), "that the copyright [on the *UB*] is not valid because it is not copyrighted in any individual's name. This point may have to be decided, one day, in a court of law."

The Foundation has countered by claiming that the Urantia movement is not a religion because it has no churches or ministers, and that the *UB* is not a Bible but essentially a "philosophical" work "partly written" by human authors. They are able to say this because Bill Sadler Jr. is known to have written the *UB*'s table of contents! On these flimsy claims the Foundation has called the *UB* a "work for hire." They have likened it to Moses receiving from God the Ten Commandments. God is the true "author" of the commandments, but because Moses wrote them down on stone tablets, he would be eligible to copyright them as the "author."

Such arguments strike breakaway members of the Foundation as nothing more than a greedy ploy intended only to preserve the Foundation's iron grip on *UB* sales. In 1959, by the way, the IRS gave the Foundation tax-exempt status on the grounds that it "operates exclusively for religious and charitable purposes." So much for the Foundation's claim that the Urantia movement is in no way a "religion."

Maaherra's quixotic battle against the Foundation is strongly supported by a satirical magazine called *Urantian Sojourn*, published by an angry group in Boulder calling itself the Scattered Brotherhood. The magazine's title reflects our brief sojourn on earth as we prepare for our endless journey through the stars to Paradise. Its pages feature vitriolic attacks, dramatized by cartoons and caricatures of Myers and other former Foundation trustees. They are called wimps, tyrants, liars, charlatans, unbalanced rage-aholics, deceitful, prestige-grubbing secular sociopaths, godless, contemptible, nefarious, mad, maniacal, corrupt, brutal, nasty, and persons who enjoy stomping on other people's heads. These are only some of the epithets I circled on the pages of *Sojourn*'s first four issues. I eagerly await the fifth.

The Foundation has sued Maaherra for $50,000 in damages plus court costs. If she publishes a Braille edition of the *UB*, as she plans, the Foundation has vowed to sue again. So far, the only benefactors of this battle have been lawyers. Julio Edwards, a disinterested member of the Boulder group, has likened the situation to two farmers in dispute over who owns a cow. One pulls the cow's head, the other pulls the tail. While this tug of war goes on, a lawyer comes along and milks the cow. Needless to add, each side of this bitter conflict accuses the other of being under the influence of Caligastia. The invective going back and forth between the warring sides is incessant. It seems oddly out of place for members of a cult that professes to follow the teachings of Jesus about loving one's enemies.

Mark Kulieke, writing in the July 1993 issue of the Urantian journal *Pervaded Space*, has an article lambasting the Foundation for what he deems an unjustified increase in the price of the *UB* from $34 to the "outrageous price of $48."

> With the price increase, demand will fall once again. Your policies are keeping truth-seekers from finding the soul-satisfying truths contained in *The Urantia Book*. This was a colossal blunder in 1979 and will be again in 1993. With a price increase will go most remaining shreds of support you still enjoy. This is as it should be. I personally regard you as the single greatest obstacle to the welfare of the fifth epochal revelation and will do all in my power to bring your control to a permanent end. You are unfaithful stewards and your day of reckoning will ultimately come.

When it became increasingly clear to the Foundation that it might well lose its *UB* copyright, it began to do all it could to prevent its lawsuit from reaching court. For four years it has adopted a "scorched-earth" tactic, using every delaying maneuver possible to force Maaherra to run out of funds. Enormous sums are of course being spent by the Foundation on legal fees, money obtained from the faithful, to battle this brave and persistent woman. Why the trustees should have been so upset by her index is beyond me. The first edition of the *UB*, in 1955, stated that an "exhaustive index" would soon be published. It was not until 1994, almost 40 years later, that the Foundation finally published its *Concordance* to the *UB*, a massive work now selling for $65.

In 1991 Bernard C. Dietz, head of the U.S. Copyright Office's renewal section, gave a deposition concerning the copyright status of the *UB*. He said his office constantly is sent material purporting to have been written by God, by angels, or by a variety of nonhumans. After the moon landing it received many works said to have been written by extraterrestrials. Musical compositions came from Martians. One person submitted the writings of Invisible Mouse. Asked for a photograph of the author, the applicant submitted a blank page.

To summarize this hilarious deposition, Dietz agreed that Moses provides the best analog. Had Moses said he was the true author of the Ten Commandments he would have been granted a copyright. But if he said he was only the "scribe," the copyright would have been witheld unless he identified a human author eligible for copyright protection in the United States.

In brief, the *UB* can hold a legitimate copyright only if it can identify humans as actual authors. The Foundation has refused to do more than say that the following persons acted as scribes: Dr. Sadler, his son Bill, members of the Forum, members of the Foundation, and the sleeper whose name they will not disclose. All five trustees of the Foundation have testified to their belief that the authors of all the *UB*'s papers are supermortals.

In 1994, responding to a series of questions posed by Maaherra, the trustees made plain that the *UB* papers are a collaboration of work by celestials, Forum members, and the "contact personality" whom we identified earlier as Sadler. Here is how the trustees expressed it:

> The URANTIA Foundation admits and states that it did not write the text of those portions of The URANTIA Book that are denoted as the Foreword and the Papers which are numbered 1–196 and which are printed at pages 1–2097 of The URANTIA Book. However, the URANTIA Foundation states that its predecessor, a group of individuals called the Contact Commission, some of whom were among the original members of the Board of Trustees of the URANTIA Foundation, did actively participate

in the origination of some of the text of the Urantia Papers by their working closely with both the human "contact personality," and by their asking questions and providing feedback to the various personalities who provided the text of the above denoted portions of The URANTIA Book and who are identified as the sources of that material in The URANTIA Book itself.

In April 1994 the Foundation responded to Maaherra's "Request for Admission" with a lengthy set of answers. The trustees admitted that the *UB* drew frequently from books by humans, but they vigorously denied that any human wrote a single line in any of the papers. All the papers were typed by Christy to give to the printers, but she made no changes in the text. No human added "any style, arrangement, manner of expression, or any subject matter of his or her own."

The trustees concede that questions about the papers were raised in Forum meetings and taken to the sleeper to be revised according to what the celestials said through him. The papers in their published form are the final versions authorized by the unseen friends. "While writing any of the original manuscript of any of the portions of the *UB*," the trustees stated, ". . . the human person or persons did not add any subject matter . . . and reduced to written form only that which was transmitted to such persons by the source of the text."

Note that this wording does not preclude the possibility that humans may have considered themselves indited by midwayers to write portions of the *UB*. If, for instance, Sadler believed he was in contact with a midwayer and inspired to alter or write portions of the papers, or even an entire paper, this would not be regarded as Sadler acting as a "human." Because the actual words would come from a midwayer, Sadler would be only the scribe serving as the conduit.

In November 1994 the Foundation, through its attorneys, issued 86 pages of supplementary answers to Maaherra's questions. It is a curious document, enormously repetitious in citing the same quotations over and over again from two documents which most Urantians had not known existed. One is a *History of the Urantia Movement*, written by Sadler at an unspecified date, and a similar history prepared by Christy, also undated by the attorneys.

The Foundation's answers added little not previously known aside from revealing the existence of the two histories. Sadler's quoted passages fail to make clear whether the sleeper and the "contact personality" were the same or different persons. Sadler refers to the contact personality in an oblique way which easily could be taken as a reference to himself. Later on he refers to the "sleeping subject," a term he had not used earlier.

The Foundation assured their attorneys they were "unable to identify" the sleeping subject. They assume he was also the contact personality, an assumption that could be right, but I suspect is not. The trustees call the sleeper a "patient" of Sadler's. They deny knowing when the sleeper began his spoken and written channeling, but are sure it was not prior to 1904. They base this on Sadler's contention that 20 years passed from the start of the channeling to the arrival of handwritten papers in 1925. The 1904 date is, of course, sharply contradicted by Sadler's claim in the appendix of *The Mind at Mischief* that the revelation began in 1911. As I have said before, it is hard to believe Sadler could have been off by six or seven years. I have previously given my reasons for thinking the channeling did not come to Sadler's attention until the summer of 1912, although Wilfred may have been channeling before then.

The most revealing quotation from Sadler's history is his statement (repeated five times in the document prepared by the Foundation's attorneys) that "The Midwayers were very real to us—we frequently talked with them during our various 'contacts.'" This makes clear that Sadler and other members of the contact commission believed they were engaging in direct dialog with the supermortals in the same way that so many Urantians today believe they are in dialog with their unseen friends of the Teaching Mission. There is no longer the slightest doubt that Sadler, after his wife died, believed himself "indited" to edit the papers, perhaps even write some of them, under the impression he was under instruction from the celestials. Although I do not question Sadler's honesty and sincerity, I am convinced that he fell victim in his declining years to delusions of self-importance and grandeur of the sort that occasionally descend upon the elderly.

The trustees deny knowing why the sleeper was Sadler's patient. This puzzles me because Harold Sherman, in his account of the origin of the papers as told to him by Sadler, informs us that Sadler treated the sleeper as a patient as soon as he became aware that the man was talking and writing in his sleep. For years Sadler remained skeptical of the authenticity of the sleeper's messages, but looked upon him in the same way he continued to look upon Sister White, as a voice channeler and automatic writer to whom he was unable to attribute either fraud or unconscious self-deception. In his history, Sadler repeats what he said in *The Mind at Mischief* about the "one or two cases" he had encountered of such unexplainable phenomena.

When Sadler says 20 years elapsed between the initial channeling and the appearance of the first paper, he may be referring to the finalizing of the papers and their preparation for printing in the *UB*. On page 1319 of the *UB* we read: "We indited these narratives and put them in the English language, by a technique authorized by our superiors, in the year CE 1935 of Urantia Time."

Sadler's "20 years" of contact experience may refer to 20 years from the first channeling in 1911 or 1912 to 1931 or 1932 when the papers began to appear in written form, and which he finished editing a few years before 1935. Remember, the Forum merely responded by asking questions about material recorded in shorthand and typed by Christy. The actual papers appeared later. When Sadler speaks of the "first paper" coming through before 1925 he may not mean a final written paper, but only the channeled material on which the first paper was based.

Sadler's statement that 20 years elapsed from the start of his "pre-education" and the arrival of the first paper about 1925 seems to date the initial channeling of the sleeper as 1905. Is there a way to reconcile this with Sadler's repeated assertion in *The Mind at Mischief* that the channeling did not begin until 1911, and which I think was Sadler's memory lapse for a true date of 1912?

Yes, there is a way if we assume that Sadler is the contact personality as distinct from the sleeper. He writes in his history of the "early years" that the unseen friends were "engaged in a thoroughgoing testing of the contact personality, rehearsing the technique of communication, selecting the contact commissioners—in fact, in a general way setting the stage for the subsequent initiation of the presentation of the Urantia Papers."

We know that in 1906, when Sadler wrote his lengthy letter to Mrs. White, he was starting to have doubts about her visions. From 1906 until 1912 Sadler was surely going through a period of intense confusion about his Adventist faith. He became receptive to such Adventist heresies as evolution, the denial of the Virgin Birth, and other non-Adventist beliefs adopted by his former associate Dr. Kellogg. When Sadler wrote his history of the Urantia movement, he may have looked upon this transition period as one during which the unseen friends were testing him and preparing him for the reception of Wilfred's channeling when it began in 1912. This is, of course, only my best guess. It may well be that Wilfred was also the contact personality, and there is some other plausible explanation for the large discrepancy between Sadler's "20 years" and his 1911 date.

The Foundation's claim that the Urantia movement is not a religion is of course nonsense. Here are some statements from a lecture by Bill Sadler Jr.:

I think there is a possibility . . . of developing from this blue book a religion the like of which this world has never yet seen. . . . The Urantia Papers present, I think, the most sane religion that's ever been offered to the human race. . . . Pull theology and cosmology out of this—this complicated book is the simplest religion ever presented to man. . . . think the Urantia Brotherhood, the *Urantia Book*, the Urantia movement, represent the best effort of all superhuman beings concerned to get an international religion started, a mankind religion.

It's a tall order, but Urantians are as convinced of its truth as Mary Baker Eddy and her followers, or the Mormons, or the Muslims, or the Moonies, or orthodox Christians and Jews are convinced that *their* religion is destined eventually to sweep the world. Some fundamentalists, and sects such as the Adventists and Jehovah's Witnesses, are less optimistic. They see themselves as a "remnant church," upholding God's truth in the face of mounting opposition by the rest of humanity until the Second Coming of Jesus does away with the unsaved and brings an end to a history controlled by Satan.

In January 1993 Kristen Maaherra wrote: "By suing me, the Foundation has swallowed a poison pill. If they admit the superhuman authorship of the Papers in court, they lose the copyright. If they say they hired a human to write the Papers, they lose their credibility with the readers—not to mention the Ancients of Days."

In 1994 Urantian Chris Hansen published a soft-cover reprinting, two columns per page, of the *UB*'s Jesus Papers. He calls the book *God's Bible*. You can buy it for $9.95 plus $3.00 for shipping, from God's Bible, POB 327, Navsink, New Jersey 07752. If the Foundation wins its case against Maaherra, they will undoubtedly sue Hansen for an obvious violation of their copyright.

The Urantia movement is a striking example of how intelligent persons can be drawn into a cult and become committed to a set of beliefs that seem preposterous to outsiders. When I was researching my old book *Fads and Fallacies in the Name of Science* (1952), I came across a Florida cult called Koreshanity. (I mentioned it briefly in the previous chapter.) Members were convinced that the earth is hollow and we live on the inside of the shell. One believer described his conversion by saying that when he studied the cult's literature and listened to sermons by its guru, his mind suddenly snapped. "I was inside!"

He meant of course that he suddenly believed he was actually on the interior surface of a hollow earth. His remark has always struck me as a marvelous metaphor for quick conversions to a religious faith. Persons reach a point in life when they suddenly find themselves accepting the doctrines of a community of believers who share a common set of beliefs and whose friendships reinforce one another's convictions. The mind snaps. They find themselves "inside."

Kristen Maaherra has put her faith crisply. "Either the Urantia Papers are the fifth epochal revelation to the planet, or they are not. Either the Papers were authored by divine beings, or they weren't." Those like Kristen who choose to accept the first of these alternatives are soon overwhelmed by the emotion of belonging to a community of God's chosen people who are in possession of a great secret Truth unknown to outsiders. It is a powerful emotion, almost impossible to abandon, typical of how members feel in small, offbeat religious cults. They are inside, and the rest of humanity, poor souls, are all outside.

There is a joke about a Urantian who received a phone call from one of the seraphim.

"What did she say?" the man's wife asked.

"She told me she had good news and bad news. The good news is that God has become so annoyed over the multiplicity of religions on Urantia that he has ordered Michael and his angels to take drastic steps to eliminate this confusion. They are planning to abolish all religions except one."

"How wonderful!" exclaimed the wife. "We've been hoping that would happen ever since the fifth epochal revelation was given to us. What's the bad news?"

"The bad news," her husband replied, "is that the phone call came from Salt Lake City."

You can vary the joke by substituting Israel, Mecca, or Rome.

Mind-sets of true believers are almost impossible to alter by arguments. To them it is always the skeptic whose mind seems set in concrete, unable to accept the Great Truth that to them is so obvious. It is inconceivable, to give some examples, that Gilbert Chesterton, who converted to Roman Catholicism late in life, would ever have given up his new-found faith. It is impossible to imagine that Sir Arthur Conan Doyle, raised a Catholic but a convert to Spiritualism, would ever have admitted that mediums do not exude ectoplasm from their noses or that fairies do not frolic in Irish glens. It is inconceivable that Billy Graham, as he nears the end of his long career, would be moved by arguments that God is not cruel enough to torment unbelievers forever in hell fire, or that Jesus did not walk on water or rise bodily from the tomb. It is inconceivable that Shirley MacLaine will ever write a book debunking reincarnation and all the other occult junk that befuddles her brain.

No convert is so dedicated to a new religion as one who abandons a childhood faith. Sadler is a good example. He was brought up a Seventh-day Adventist, and it took him many years to become disenchanted with Ellen White and her church. Somehow he managed to break away. The tragic and comic aspects of his life, aspects that make his complex personality so fascinating, are that he replaced his faith in Sister White with an even stranger faith. Skeptical at first, something in his brain snapped and he found himself inside.

Although Sister White's plagiarisms played a role in his break with Adventism, so committed was Sadler to his new faith that he edited and published a massive new Bible which swarms with passages copied from copyrighted books! As Harry Loose wrote to Harold Sherman, after Lena's death something happened to Sadler's personality. From a hard-nosed skeptic of channeling, he became as gullible as Shirley MacLaine about the channeling of his own brother-in-law. It is because of this astonishing switch of an intelligent, gifted man, from one cult to another, that I found his story sufficiently riveting to devote considerable time to writing a big book about him. My dear wife, I must add, thinks that writing this book was a total waste of my energies.

I also must confess that I wrote this book because I found Urantianism to be almost as funny as Mormonism, Christian Science, and Sun-Moonism. I find Martin Myers, the deposed leader of the movement, as comic as Jimmy Swaggart, Oral Roberts, and Tammy Faye Bakker.

Let me close with a marvelous expression of the mind-set of a true believer:

> To me truth is precious. I love it. I embrace it at every opportunity. I do not stop to inquire, Is it popular? ere I embrace it. I inquire only, Is it truth? If my judgment is convinced my conscience approves and my will enforces my acceptance. I want truth for truth's sake, and not for the applaud [sic] or approval of men. I would not reject truth because it is unpopular, nor accept error because it is popular. I should rather be right and stand alone than to run with the multitude and be wrong.
>
> The holding of the views herein set forth has already won for me the scorn and contempt and ridicule of some of my fellowmen. I am looked upon as being odd, strange, peculiar; as being a little weakminded; as having a broken wheel or a slipping cog in my mental machinery. But truth is truth and though all the world reject it and turn against me, I will cling to truth still.
>
> I am deeply grateful to Mrs. A. C. Caldwell, Tieton, Washington, and

all others who indorse my views and who have contributed so generously their financial support.

I shall be pleased to receive any fair, kindly, courteous criticism of these views from any of my readers. But please read the little volume through before you condemn it or its author.

Yours for Enduring Truth,

C.S.D.

Who wrote those stirring words? They are from the preface to *A Reparation: Universal Gravitation a Universal Fake*, a third revised edition (1931), by Charles Sylvester DeFord. It is a book proving that Urantia is as flat as a pancake.

Note added as the book goes to press

On February 10, 1995, Warren K. Urbom, United States Senior District Judge in Arizona, awarded Kristen Maaherra a Summary Judgment declaring that the *UB*'s copyright renewal is invalid. The book is now in public domain. It is not yet known if the Urantia Foundation intends to appeal. Also undecided is whether the Foundation's trademark on their logo of three concentric circles remains valid.

"Thank you, Jesus!" Maaherra exclaimed in a report she mailed to friends on February 11. "God's gift to all his children on the planet belongs to us all."

Appendix A

Books by William Sadler Sr.

The following bibliography of books and pamphlets by Sadler and his wife, Lena, is as accurate as I can make it. The items are in chronological order. Many of the books had later editions, often revised and expanded, sometimes with a change of publisher and title. In a few cases Lena's name was added as coauthor on a later edition.

1901   *Someone Cares for Your Soul.* Oakland, California: Pacific Press, a Seventh-day Adventist house. This is an eight-page tract to hand to the unsaved. It is one of a series in what was called the Apples of God Library. I list it here because it is the earliest known printed item by Sadler aside from his contributions to periodicals.

1909   *Soul-Winning Texts, or Bible Helps for Personal Work.* Another religious tract. It was printed by the Central Bible Supply Company, Chicago.

1910   *The Science of Living, or the Art of Keeping Well.* Chicago, McClurg, 420 pp. Revised edition, 476 pp.

1910   *The Cause and Cure of Colds.* Chicago: McClurg, 147 pp. Revised and expanded in 1930. In 1938 it was further expanded to 253 pp., with Lena added as coauthor.

1912   *The Physiology of Faith and Fear, or, the Mind in Health and Disease.* Chicago: McClurg, 580 pp. Expanded to 602 pp. in 1925.

1914   *Worry and Nervousness, or the Science of Self-Mastery.* Chicago: McClurg, 135 pp. Expanded to 605 pp. in 1923.

1916   *The Chicago Therapeutic Institute: The Reliance Baths.* Chicago: Winship. Pamphlet?

1917   *Measuring Men*. Chicago: Winship. Pamphlet?

1918   *Long Heads and Round Heads, or, What's the Matter with Germany?* Chicago: McClurg, 151 pp.

1922   *Race Decadence: An Examination of the Causes of Racial Degeneracy in the United States*. Chicago: McClurg, 421 pp.

1923   *The Truth About Spiritualism*. Chicago: McClurg, 211 pp.

1923   *What a Salesman Should Know About His Health: A Straight Talk to Salesmen About Keeping Fit*. Chicago: Darnell, 125 pp.

1924   *Personality and Health*. Chicago: American, 128 pp. Reissued in 1930 (Chicago: Rockwell, 128 pp.) with the title *The Business Woman: Her Personality and Health*.

1925   *Constipation: How to Cure Yourself*. Chicago: McClurg, 296 pp. Reissued by Health Press in 1930.

1925   *Americanitis: Blood Pressure and Nerves*. New York: Macmillan, 176 pp.

1925   *The Elements of Pep: A Talk on Health and Efficiency*. Chicago: American, 142 pp. Reissued (Chicago: Rockwell, 142 pp.) as *The Road to Attainment: The Elements of Pep*.

1926   *How You Can Keep Happy*. Chicago: American, 292 pp. Reissued by the same publisher in 1930 as *The Quest for Happiness: How You Can Keep Happy*, with Lena as coauthor.

1927   *The Truth about Heredity: A Concise Explanation of Heredity Written for the Layman*. Chicago: McClurg, 512 pp.

1928   *The Truth about Mind Cure*. Chicago: McClurg, 206 pp.

1929   *The Mind at Mischief: Tricks and Deceptions of the Subconscious and How to Cope with Them*. New York: Funk and Wagnalls, 400 pp.

1930   *The Boy and His Body*. Torch, 59 pp.

1936   *Psychiatric Educational Work*. A 1936 lecture. I do not know the publisher.

1936   *Theory and Practice of Psychiatry*. St. Louis: Mosby, 1231 pp.

1938   *The Mastery of Worry and Nervousness*. Chicago: American, 258 pp. Reprinted 1943 by Wilcox and Follett, 282 pp.

1944   *Prescription for Permanent Peace*. Chicago: Wilcox and Follett, 202 pp.

1945   *Modern Psychiatry*. St. Louis: Mosby, 896 pp. Reissued as *Practice of Psychiatry*, 1953.

1947   *Mental Mischief and Emotional Conflicts: Psychiatry and Psychology in Plain English*. St. Louis: Mosby, 396 pp.

1948   *Adolescence Problems: A Handbook for Physicians, Parents, and Teachers.* St. Louis: Mosby, 466 pp.

1948   *A Doctor Talks to Teen-agers.* St. Louis: Mosby, 379 pp.

1952   *Courtship and Love.* New York: Macmillan, 209 pp.

1990   *The Evolution of the Soul.* Posthumous printing of a 1941 lecture. Jesusonian Foundation, 35 pp.

Books With Lena Sadler as Coauthor or by Lena Alone

1916   *The Mother and Her Child.* Chicago: McClurg, 456 pp.

1920   *How to Reduce and How to Gain.* Chicago: McClurg, 271 pp. Reissued in 1938 (Chicago: American, 293 pp.) under the title *Diet and Food Values with Key to Weight Control.*

1925   *How to Feed the Baby.* Chicago: McClurg, 300 pp. Her entry in *Who's Who in America* lists this book as by Lena alone, but at the front of Sadler's *Mind at Mischief* it is listed by Sadler alone. Perhaps both names are on the title page.

1925   *The Essentials of Healthful Living.* New York: Macmillan, 481 pp. Is this a reissue of Sadler's *The Science of Living?*

1930   *The Woman and the Home.* Chicago: Heath, 407 pp.

1931   *Piloting Modern Youth.* New York: Funk and Wagnalls, 370 pp.

1937   *Psychiatric Nursing.* Anna B. Kellogg, Wilfred's wife, is on the title page as a third author. St. Louis: Mosby, 433 pp.

1938   *Living a Sane Sex Life.* Chicago: American, 344 pp.

1938   *The Sex Life Before and After Marriage.* Chicago: American. Pages? Is this the above book with a different title?

1938   *The Truth about Mental Healing.* Chicago: American, 223 pp. Is this a reissue of Sadler's *The Truth about Mind Cure?*

1938   *The Cause and Cure of Headaches, Backaches, and Constipation.* Chicago: American, 298 pp.

1940   *Growing Out of Babyhood: Problems of the Preschool Child.* New York: Funk and Wagnalls, 350 pp.

Appendix B

Books by Harold Sherman

FICTION:

1926   *Fight 'em, Big Three.* Appleton
        Mayfield's Fighting Five. Appleton
        One Minute to Play Grosset.
1927   *Touchdown!* Grosset
        Beyond the Dog's Nose. Appleton
        Cameron MacBain, Backwoodsman, with Hawthorne Daniel.
        Appleton
        Get 'em, Mayfield. Appleton
1928   *Hit by Pitcher.* Grosset
        Block That Kick! Grosset
        Bases Full! Grosset. *Safe!* Grosset
1929   *Over the Line.* Goldsmith
        Don Rader, Trailblazer. Grosset
        Flashing Steel. Grosset
        Hit and Run! Grosset
1930   *Hold That Line!* Grosset
        Flying Heels and Other Hockey Stories. Grosset
        Ding Palmer, Air Detective. Grosset
        Batter Up! Grosset
        Number Forty-Four, and Other Football Stories. Grosset
        Shoot That Ball! and Other Basketball Stories. Grosset.
1931   *The Land of Monsters.* Grosset
        It's a Pass! Goldsmith
        Slashing Sticks and Other Hockey Stories. Grosset
        Strike Him Out! Goldsmith. *Goal to Go!* Grosset.

1932   *Interference and Other Football Stories.* Goldsmith
        Down the Ice, and Other Winter Sports Stories. Goldsmith
        Double Play! and Other Baseball Stories. Grosset
        Crashing Through! Grosset
        Under the Basket, and Other Basketball Stories. Goldsmith
        The Tennis Terror, and Other Tennis Stories. Goldsmith
        Let Freedom Ring! N. H. White Jr.
1933   *Tahara Among African Tribes.* Goldsmith
        Tahara: Boy King of the Desert. Goldsmith
        Tahara: Boy Mystic of India. Goldsmith
        Tahara in the Land of Yucatan. Goldsmith
        Captain of the Eleven. Goldsmith
1934   *The Fun Loving Gang; in Wrong Right.* Goldsmith
1935   *The Fun Loving Gang—Always Up to Something.* Goldsmith
1936   *The Winning Point.* Saalfield
1946   *The Green Man: A Visitor from Space.* Century
1948   *Call of the Land: A Novel of High Adventure in 4-H Club Work.*
        Donahue
1979   *The Green Man and His Return.* Amherst

Nonfiction:

1935   *Your Key to Happiness.* Kinsey
1942   *Thoughts Through Space,* with Hubert Wilkins. Creative Age
1944   *Your Key to Married Happiness.* Putnam
1945   *Your Key to Youth Problems.* Putnam
1948   *Your Key to Romance.* Pegasus
1949   *You Live After Death.* Creative Age
1950   *You Can Stop Drinking.* Creative Age
1953   *Know Your Own Mind.* G. & R. Anthony
1954   *The New TNT.* Prentice-Hall
1956   *Adventures in Thinking.* Master
1957   *TNT, the Power within You,* with Claude Bristol. Prentice-Hall
1958   *How to Turn Failure into Success.* Prentice-Hall
        How to Use the Power of Prayer. C. & R. Anthony
1964   *How to Make ESP Work for You.* DeVorss
1965   *How to Solve Mysteries of Your Mind and Soul.* DeVorss
1966   *The New TNT.* Prentice-Hall

1967	*Wonder Healers of the Philippines.* DeVorss
1969	*Your Mysterious Powers of ESP.* World
1970	*How to Foresee and Control Your Future.* Fawcett
1971	*How to Take Yourself Apart and Put Yourself Back Together Again.* Fawcett
	Know Your Own Mind. Fawcett
1972	*The Harold Sherman ESP Manual.* Human Development Associates
	Your Power to Heal, with Ambrose and Olga Worrall. Harper
1974	*You Can Communicate with the Unseen World.* Fawcett
1976	*How to Know What to Believe.* Fawcett
1978	*How to Picture What You Want.* Fawcett
1981	*The Dead Are Alive!* Amherst

PLAYS AND MOVIES

1933	*Her Supporting Cast* (play)
1935	*The Little Black Book* (play)
1942	*The Adventures of Mark Twain* (Warner Brothers movie)

I have not listed record albums and cassette tapes. Many of Sherman's non-fiction books were later reprinted by other houses.

Appendix C

Sherman's Letter to Sadler

Harold Sherman's strenuous effort to add to the *UB* a paper defending psychic phenomena and communication with the dead was colorfully expressed in a registered letter he sent to Sadler. The letter appears in Sherman's chapter on the *UB* in *How to Know What to Believe.* "Dr. Norton" is Sherman's name for Sadler, and the *UB*'s title is altered to *The New Revelation Book.* Here is the letter in full:

Dear Dr. Norton:

Some several months after we came here and had carefully read the New Revelation papers, I questioned you concerning the glaring absence of any paper on "psychic phenomena"—such as humans have verifiably experienced on earth in times past and are experiencing now. And yet the book deals authoritatively with many phases of spiritual phenomena beyond the grasp, sensing, and actual understanding of average man.

Eventual readers of this great document in public form are going to be expected to accept the existence of all these higher phenomena on faith. But, since man is an experiential being, and we must consider him on the basis of his present development and enlightenment, he is going to be sorely perplexed at finding no mention or explanation of "psychic experiences" which he KNOWS he has had—which give him evidence that TELEPATHY, under certain conditions, is a fact; that there are such things as ASTRAL visitations on occasion; and that the so-called DEAD *are* permitted to return on certain missions and under certain circumstances. I am not talking spiritualism when I make this latter statement.

You decided, personally, long years ago on your own admission to me, that there were no genuine phenomena except that of the nature you had encountered with the "instrument" and the other "sleeping contacts" reported to you.

Millions of humans now living and still to be born will challenge this attitude as reflected in the pages of *The New Revelation Book*, for too many "psychic experiences" are occurring right along to which they can testify. And no scientist can laugh these experiences off or explain them away.

It is a great error and will arouse great controversy, confusion, and dissension for *The New Revelation Book* to indicate positively that no one can communicate with the dead and that the dead, under no circumstances, can or do return to this earth. This is a deliberate wrong statement—an untruth—and cannot have been made by higher intelligences, for they KNOW better. With *The New Revelation Book* containing such false inferences, many humans who have had genuine experiences are not going to know what sections of the book to believe or disbelieve, and they are apt to end up by doubting it all.

I submitted a series of questions covering the entire subject to "psychic phenomena" months ago. Were they carefully gone over by you and the other "contact commissioners" and presented for consideration and possible answering in the former regular manner, or were they pigeon-holed arbitrarily by you because you have a set human conviction that none of the "psychic phenomena" are actually existent?

Have you, by your attitude, altered or excluded any material or truths which should be in this *New Revelation Book*?

You know, in your own mind and heart, the steps you have taken which have not been authorized by higher intelligences. You will have to answer for each one of these steps . . . but there is still time for you to clear up *much*.

It should hardly be necessary for me to remind you that, if any material intended for *The New Revelation Book* has been withheld or wrongly interpreted or purposely misunderstood or altered for personal or biased reasons, or because of a "closed mind" attitude—you will be held responsible as trusted custodian for centuries yet to come.

My only interest, as always, is in the purity, unadulterated genuineness, and complete authenticity of *The New Revelation Book*. I shall know, and others will know, if when it is published, any of the papers have been tampered with for any human reason whatsoever.

Sincerely,
(signed) Harold Sherman

Appendix D

The Story of Joseph of Arimathaea

The following apocryphal document was translated from the Greek by
Montague Rhodes James. I quote from the book he edited, *The Apocryphal
New Testament* (Oxford, 1924):

> I. 1. I, Joseph of Arimathaea, who begged the body of the Lord Jesus
> from Pilate, was imprisoned by the Jews on that account. These are the
> people who provoked their lawgiver Moses, and failing to recognize their
> God crucified his Son.
>
> Seven days before the passion of Christ, two condemned robbers
> were sent from Jericho to Pilate, whose crimes were these.
>
> 2. The first, Gestas, used to strip and murder wayfarers, hang up
> women by the feet and cut off their breasts, drink the blood of babes: he
> knew not God nor obeyed any law, but was violent from the beginning.
>
> The other, Demas, was a Galilaean who kept an inn; he despoiled the
> rich but did good to the poor, even burying them, like Tobit. He had com-
> mitted robberies on the Jews, for he stole (plundered) the law itself at
> Jerusalem, and stripped the daughter of Caiaphas, who was a priestess of
> the sanctuary, and he took away even the mystic deposit of Solomon
> which had been deposited in the (holy) place.
>
> 3. Jesus also was taken at even on the third day before the passover.
> Caiaphas and the multitude of the Jews had no passover but were in great
> grief because of the robbery of the sanctuary by the thief. And they sent for
> Judas Iscariot who was brother's son to Caiaphas, and had been persuaded
> by the Jews to become a disciple of Jesus, not to follow his teachings, but
> to betray him. They paid him a didrachm of gold daily; and as one of Jesus'
> disciples, called John, says, he had been two years with Jesus.
>
> 4. On the third day before Jesus was taken, Judas said to the Jews: Let

us assemble a council and say that it was not the robber who took away the law, but Jesus. Nicodemus, who had the keys of the sanctuary, said No: For he was a truthful man. But Sarra, Caiaphas' daughter, cried out that Jesus said in public, 'I can destroy the temple' (&c.). All the Jews said: We believe you. For they held her as a prophetess. So Jesus was taken.

II. 1. On the morrow, being Wednesday, at the ninth hour, they brought him into Caiaphas' hall, and Annas and Caiaphas asked him: Why didst though take away the law? He was silent. Why wouldst thou destroy the temple of Solomon? He was silent.

2. In the evening the multitude sought the daughter of Caiaphas, to burn her with fire, because the law was stolen and they could not keep the passover. But she said: Wait a little, my children, and let us destroy Jesus, and the law will be found and the feast kept. Then Annas and Caiaphas privily gave gold to Judas and said: Say as you said before, that it was Jesus who stole the law. Judas agreed, but said: The people must not know that you have told me this: and you must let Jesus go, and I will persuade them. So they fraudulently let Jesus go.

3. At dawn of the Thursday Judas went into the sanctuary and said to all the people: What will ye give me if I deliver to you the destroyer of the law and robber of the prophets? They said: Thirty silver pieces of gold(!). But they did not know that it was Jesus of whom he spoke, for many thought him to be the Son of God. And Judas received the thirty pieces.

4. At the fourth and fifth hours he went out and found Jesus walking in the street. Towards evening he obtained a guard of soldiers. As they went, Judas said: Whomsoever I shall kiss, take him: he it is that stole the law and the prophets. He came to Jesus and kissed him, saying: Hail, Rabbi. They took Jesus to Caiaphas and examined him. 'Why didst thou do this?' but he answered nothing. Nicodemus and I left the seat of the pestilent, and would not consent to perish in the council of sinners.

III. 1. They did many evil things to Jesus that night, and on the dawn of Friday delivered him to Pilate. He was condemned and crucified with the two robbers, Gestas on the left, Demas on the right.

2. He on the left cried out to Jesus: See what evils I have wrought on the earth; and had I known thou wert the king, I would have killed thee too. Why callest thou thyself Son of God and canst not help thyself in the hour of need? or how canst thou succour any other that prayeth? if thou be the Christ, come down from the cross that I may believe thee. But now I behold thee, not as a man but as a wild beast caught and perishing along with me. And much else he spake against Jesus, blaspheming and gnashing his teeth upon him: for he was caught in the snare of the devil.

3. But Demas, on the right, seeing the divine grace of Jesus, began to cry out thus: I know thee, Jesus Christ, that thou art the Son of God. I see thee, Christ, worshipped by ten thousand times ten thousand angels; for-

give my sins that I have committed: make not the stars to enter into judgement with me, or the moon, when thou judgest all the world: for in the night did I work my evil plans: stir not up the sun that now is darkened for thy sake to tell the evil of my heart: for I can give thee no gift for remission of sins. Already death cometh on me for my sins, but pardon belongeth unto thee: save me, Lord of all things, from thy terrible judgement: give not power unto the enemy to swallow me up and be inheritor of my soul, as of his that hangeth on the left; for I see how the devil taketh his soul rejoicing, and his flesh vanisheth away. Neither command me to depart into the lot of the Jews, for I see Moses and the patriarchs weeping sore, and the devil exulting over them. Therefore before my spirit departeth, command O Lord that my sins be blotted out, and remember me the sinner in thy kingdom when thou sittest on the great throne of the Most High and shalt judge the twelve tribes of Israel: for thou hast prepared great punishment for thy world for thy sake.

4. And when the thief had so said, Jesus saith unto him: Verily, verily, I say unto thee, Demas, that to-day thou shalt be with me in paradise: but the sons of the kingdom, the children of Abraham, Isaac, and Jacob, and Moses shall be cast out into the outer darkness: there shall be weeping and gnashing of teeth. But thou only shalt dwell in paradise until my second coming, when I shall judge them that have not confessed my name. And he said to the thief: Go and say unto the cherubim and the powers that turn about the flaming sword, that keep the garden since Adam the first-created was in paradise and transgressed and kept not my commandments and I cast him out thence—but none of the former men shall see paradise until I come the second time to judge the quick and dead—And he wrote thus: Jesus Christ the Son of God that came down from the heights of heaven, that proceeded out of the bosom of the invisible Father without separation, and came down into the world to be incarnate and to be nailed to the cross, that I might save Adam whom I formed: unto my powers the archangels, that keep the doors of paradise, the servants of my Father: I will and command that he that is crucified with me [enter in,] receive remission of his sins for my sake, and being clothed with an incorruptible body enter in to paradise, and that he dwell there where no man *else* is ever able to dwell.

And when this was said, Jesus gave up the ghost on Friday at the ninth hour. And there was darkness over all the land and a great earthquake, so that the sanctuary fell, and the pinnacle of the temple.

IV. 1. And I, Joseph, begged the body and laid it in my new tomb. The body of Demas was not found: that of Gestas was in appearance like that of a dragon.

The Jews imprisoned me on the evening of the sabbath.

2. When it was evening on the first day of the week, at the fifth hour of the night, Jesus came to me with the thief on the right hand. There was

great light; the house was raised up by the four corners and I went forth: and I perceived Jesus first, and then the thief bringing a letter to him, and as we journeyed to Galilee there was a very great light, and a sweet fragrance came from the thief.

3. Jesus sat down in a certain place and read as follows: The cherubim and the six-winged that are commanded by thy Godhead to keep the garden of paradise make known to thee this by the hand of the robber that by thy dispensation was crucified with thee. When we saw the mark of the nails on the robber that was crucified with thee and the light of the letters of thy Godhead, the fire was quenched, being unable to bear the light of the mark, and we were in great fear and crouched down. For we heard that the maker of heaven and earth and all creation had come to dwell in the lower parts of the earth for the sake of Adam the first-created. For we beheld the spotless cross, with the robber flashing with light and shining with seven times the light of the sun, and trembling came on us, when we heard the crashing of them beneath the earth, and with a great voice the ministers of Hades said with us: Holy, Holy, Holy, is he that was in the highest in the beginning: and the powers sent up a cry, *saying*, Lord, thou hast been manifested in heaven and upon earth, giving joy unto the worlds (ages) and saving thine own creation from death.

V. 1. And as I went with Jesus and the robber to Galilee, the form of Jesus was changed and he became wholly light, and angels ministered to him and he conversed with them. I stayed with him three days, and none of the disciples were there.

2. In the midst of the days of unleavened bread his disciple John came, and the robber disappeared. John asked who it was, but Jesus did not answer. John said: Lord, I know that thou hast loved me from the beginning: why dost thou not reveal this man to me? Jesus said: seekest thou to know hidden things? art thou wholly without understanding? perceivest thou not the fragrance of paradise filling the place? knowest thou not who it was? The thief that was on the cross is become heir of paradise: verily, verily, I say unto you, that it is his alone until the great day come. John said: Make me worthy to see him.

3. Then suddenly the thief appeared and John fell to the earth: for he was now like a king in great might, clad with the cross. And a voice of a multitude was heard: Thou art come into the place of paradise prepared for thee: we are appointed to serve thee by him that sent thee until the great day. After that both the thief and I, Joseph, vanished, and I was found in my own house, and I saw Jesus no more.

All this I saw and have written, that all might believe on Jesus and no longer serve Moses' law, but believe in the signs and wonders of Christ, and believing obtain eternal life and be found in the kingdom of heaven.

For His is glory, might, praise, and majesty, world without end. Amen.

Appendix E

Unusual Words and Phrases That Sadler and The Urantia Book Have in Common

WORDS IN COMMON

In searching for unusual words that Sadler's books and the *UB* have in common, I made use of the indispensable word index prepared by Kristen Maaherra and her friends. My list obviously is far from complete. It would be instructive if someone with more time and energy than I would search all of Sadler's books for unusual words, then check their frequencies in the *UB* as compared with their frequencies in books not by Sadler. I would be pleased to hear from readers of any unusual words I have missed in my hasty, random searching.

I began my research by going through the introduction to Sadler's longest work, *Theory and Practice of Psychiatry*, and circling the following words: *salubrious* (page 2), *multitudinous* (8), *conjoint* (40), *augmentation* (42), and *sojourn* (4).

Salubrious is in the *UB* four times, *augmentation* 11 times plus some hundred variants, and *sojourn* more than 200 times. *Augmentation* is also used by Sadler in *Mental Mischief* (364), *Modern Psychiatry* (629), and in many other places. *Sojourn* is another word Sadler liked to use (e.g., *The Mastery of Worry and Nervousness*, 227 and 255; *The Physiology of Faith and Fear*, 520; and *Adolescence Problems*, 116, where he speaks of man's "earthly sojourn"). *Multitudinous* is in the *UB* five times, and *conjoint* more than a hundred times!

A quick scanning of the last chapter of *Theory and Practice* located *engraft* (1116), and on page 1118, *ennobling*, *cognizant*, and *connote*. In the *UB engraft* is on page 573, *ennobling* appears 15 times with 22 variants, *cognizant* 24 times, and *connote* seven times.

431

In the last chapter of Sadler's *Mental Mischief* (1947) I circled the words *ministrations* (page 368) and *propensities* (page 370) as unusual. *Ministrations* appears over and over again in Sadler's books (e.g., *Modern Psychiatry*, 629, 680). *Ministration*, in singular and plural forms, is in the *UB* more than 40 times. *Propensity*, also singular and plural, is in the *UB* 14 times. On page 990, the *UB* calls religion a *prophylactic* that serves as "a technique for disease prevention." In *Mental Mischief* (309) Sadler speaks of the "prophylactic value of religion" in curing "human disease."

Sadler was fond of the word *factualize*. In variant forms it is in the *UB* in 14 places. *Impartation* is another of Sadler's favorite words. It's in the *UB* seven times. *Supermaterial* is not in any dictionary, but Sadler uses it many times in *Modern Psychiatry* (e.g., 25 and 756), and *Theory and Practice* (e.g., 234). This word is in the *UB* more than 35 times. I earlier called attention to *disfellowshipping* in the *UB*, a term commonly used by Seventh-day Adventists for excommunication.

Socialization is another unusual word that was one of Sadler's favorites. Chapter 57 of *Modern Psychiatry*, titled "Socialization," uses the word throughout. In the *UB* it appears more than twenty times, especially on pages 493–95—pages that read very much as if Sadler wrote them. He also liked the word *multifarious* (e.g., *Theory and Practice of Psychiatry*, vii, 430, and *Modern Psychiatry*, 245). It is in the *UB* four times. On page 431 of *Theory and Practice*, and 246 of *Modern Psychiatry* is the word *multiform*. The *UB* uses this word twice.

Preachment is another word Sadler liked (e.g., *Theory and Practice*, 1084; *Modern Psychiatry*, 769). It is in the *UB*, in singular and plural form, at least eight times. *Habiliments* is so strange a word that I have never encountered it except on page 1088 of *Theory and Practice*, and on page 772 of *Modern Psychiatry*. Indeed, I had to look it up in a dictionary to find out just what it means. Yet here it is in the *UB* on five different pages. Sadler speaks of the "habiliments of space." The *UB* (1182) mentions the "habiliments of time." I hope no Urantian is going to suggest that Sadler acquired his taste for this bizarre word by reading what the revelators wrote!

How often in reading have you encountered the word *consanguineous?* Sadler used the word many times; in *The Truth About Heredity* (187, 268, and 270), in *Theory and Practice of Psychiatry* (152), and elsewhere. The word is in the *UB* on four different pages. On page 1488 you'll even find *superconsanguineous.*

Contrastive is still another uncommon word to be found in both Sadler's books and the *UB*. Sadler has it on pages 74 and 678 of *Modern Psychiatry*, pages 77, 250, 452, and 1003 of *Theory and Practice of Psy-*

chiatry, and pages 246 and 254 of *The Mastery of Worry of Nervousness*. The word is used by *UB* authors on six different pages.

Ideational is in *Modern Psychiatry* (260), *Theory and Practice of Psychiatry* (234, 456), and *Adolescence Problems* (100). The *UB* uses it six times. *Individuation(s)* is in *Theory and Practice* (33, 36) and in the *UB* three times. *Organismal* is in *Theory and Practice* (46, 47, 220, 281), in *Modern Psychiatry* (47, 48), and in the *UB* three times. *Reactional* is in *Theory and Practice* (275, 345), and in the *UB* once. *Adaptive* is in *Adolescence Problems* (69) and six times in the *UB*. *Preponderance* is in both *Modern Psychiatry* (195) and the *UB*. *Physiologic* is in *Modern Psychiatry* (185) and in the *UB* thrice.

Enthroned and *dethroned* were words Sadler liked (e.g., the former in *The Physiology of Faith and Fear*, 444, the latter in *The Theory and Practice of Psychiatry*, 217). *Enthrone* is in the *UB* once, *enthronement* five times. *Dethroned* is in the *UB* three times.

Authors of the *UB* liked to push several words together to make one word, and this also was a habit of Sadler. For example, *hereinafter* is in the *UB* twice. I haven't yet found this word in one of Sadler's books, but *hereinbefore* appears in *Theory and Practice of Psychiatry* (216).

Sadler's *The Mastery of Worry and Nervousness*, first published in 1938, bristles with uncommon words that also appear in the *UB*. Here are some of them:

Enshrouds (82). The *UB* uses *enshroud* once, *enshrouded* five times, *enshrouding* three times, *enshroudment* twice, and *enshrouds* twice.

Manifold (3, 7). (Sadler also uses it in the preface to *Race Decadence*, viii.) The *UB* uses it at least 78 times!

Unremembered is a somewhat pedantic way to say forgotten. Sadler has it twice on page 46, and the *UB* has it thrice on page 451.

Interassociation (136) is in the *UB* at least 25 times, *interassociated* appears ten times, and *interassociate* once. Sadler used *interassociation* frequently in later books (e.g., *Modern Psychiatry*, page 696).

Veritable (137) is in the *UB* 19 times.

Commensurate (144) is in the *UB* five times.

Ebullition (284) is in the *UB* on page 303. Sadler also uses this curious word in *The Truth About Spiritualism*, 110, 144, 182, and 210.

Disgorgement (252). It's in the *UB* twice.

Both Sadler and the *UB*'s authors were unduly fond of long unhyphenated words starting with "over." The index of Sadler's *Theory and Practice of Psychiatry* lists *overanxious*, *overindulgence*, and *overspecialization*. Each of these words is in the *UB*. The index of *The Mind at Mischief* shows a frequent use of *overconscientiousness*. This, too, is in the *UB*. *Overcontrol*, often used by Sadler (e.g., *Prescription for Permanent Peace*, 127) appears more than 40 times in the *UB*. *Overload* is on page 186 of *Modern Psychiatry*, and in the *UB* three times. *Overtaxation* is in the same Sadler book (67), as well as in the *UB*. *Overawing*, a most unusual word, is in *Modern Psychiatry* (151), in the *UB* twice, with *overawe* also twice, and *overawed* five times. *Overmuch* is a somewhat cumbersome way of saying "too much." Sadler uses it occasionally (e.g., *Piloting Modern Youth*, 95). It's in the *UB* at least a dozen times. *Overburdened* and *overserious* are *UB* words used by Sadler (e.g., *Piloting Modern Youth*, 51).

These "over" words abound in the *UB*, but it is difficult to find them in Sadler's books because so few are in the indices. It might be worthwhile if some industrious soul would go through Sadler's writings looking for "over" words that are also in the *UB*.

Focalized is an unusual substitute for "focused." The Sadlers speak of "focalized emotion" on page 333 of *Piloting Modern Youth*. *Focalized* is in the *UB* ten times, *focalize* and *focalizes* are there six times. Sadler speaks of *focalization* in many places (e.g., *Theory and Practice of Psychiatry*, 967). *Focalization(s)* is in the *UB* 14 times, and *focalizer(s)* twice. Sadler also was fond of *focal* (e.g., *Modern Psychiatry*, 196). So is the *UB* where it appears more than 16 times.

Forms of the verb *eventuate* are seldom used by writers. Sadler was fond of them (e.g., *Modern Psychiatry*, 670) and so is the *UB*. *Eventuate* is used 14 times, *eventuated* at least 19 times, *eventuating* seven times, *eventuation* at least 12 times, and *eventuates* ten times. *Chronicity* is seldom encountered outside of Sadler's books (e.g., *Modern Psychiatry*, pages 674 and 787), but it is in the *UB* three times.

I have never come upon *commingled* except in books by Sadler (e.g., *Modern Psychiatry*, 517, and *Adolescence Problems*, 91). The word is in the *UB* no less than 11 times. Which is more likely?—that Sadler acquired a liking for this word by reading papers written by celestials, or that the word often came to mind while he was editing the papers?

Misadaptation is another word I never encountered until I found it on pages 674 and 660 of Sadler's *Modern Psychiatry*, page 260 of *Theory and Practice of Psychiatry*, and page 245 of *The Mastery of Worry and Nervousness*. A check of the *UB*'s index shows it in the *UB*, in singular and plural forms, at least ten times.

How often have you seen *confusional*? Sadler uses it in *Modern Psychiatry* (669), and so do the supermortals on pages 738 and 1206. How about *ununified*? Sadler was fond of the word (e.g., *Modern Psychiatry*, 60, and *Theory and Practice of Psychiatry*, 1121). You'll find it in the *UB* on pages 507 and 1480. *Notwithstanding* was another favorite Sadler word (e.g., *Adolescence Problems*, 35, 223, 226; *Piloting Modern Youth*, 49). It's in the *UB* at least 150 times! In *Adolescence Problems* (369) Sadler uses *upstepped.* The *UB* uses it 13 times, and *upstepping* nine times.

Modern Psychiatry (215) has the uncommon word *predilections.* The *UB* uses it on three pages, and the noun's singular form twice. *Similitude* is in *Modern Psychiatry* (732) and in the *UB* seven times. *Changeableness*, instead of the simpler *changeability,* is in *Theory and Practice of Psychiatry* (825) and in the *UB* once. *Negativistic,* instead of negative, is in the same Sadler book (825) and thrice in the *UB.*

How often have you encountered the strange word *constitutive*? Sadler liked to use it (e.g., *Theory and Practice of Psychiatry*, 826, 827). The *UB* uses it no less than 16 times!

Enfeebled is a word Sadler often used (e.g., *Theory and Practice of Psychiatry,* 260, 890, 892, and *Modern Psychiatry,* 516). The *UB* uses it twice (713, 1607). *Reassociation* is in *Theory and Practice of Psychiatry* (1043), *Modern Psychiatry* (718), and in the *UB* (341). Sadler speaks of *segmental* phenomena (*Theory and Practice of Psychiatry*, 54). The *UB* uses *segmental* twice, and *segmentalized* twice.

Betokens is an old-fashioned word that Sadler liked (e.g., *Piloting Modern Youth,* 109, and *Theory and Practice of Psychiatry,* 1111). The *UB* authors also liked the word, using it no less than six times. *Betoken* appears twice, *betokened* five times, and *betokening* once.

Vainglorious is not often encountered. Sadler uses it on page 1112 of his *Theory and Practice of Psychiatry.* The *UB* has it four times, *vaingloriously* and *vaingloriousness* each once.

To say that X is *denominated* Y is a rather cumbersome, pompous way of saying A is called or named Y. I'll wager the reader has never come upon *denominated* used in this way. Sadler so uses it in *Modern Psychiatry* (186) and *Theory and Practice of Psychiatry* (141). The word is similarly used in the *UB* no less than 25 times!

Directionizes is an awkward substitute for "directs." Sadler uses it occasionally (*Theory and Practice of Psychiatry,* 39, and *Modern Psychiatry,* 830). I've never come across the word elsewhere except in the *UB* where *directionize* is used at least ten times, *directionization* nine times, *directionized* four times, *directionizers* once, and *directionizing* once. Did Sadler pick up this strange word—I can't even find it in my *Webster's New Collegiate Dictionary*—from the revelators, or did he add it to the Papers when he edited them?

Centripetal is a word almost exclusively used by physicists. Sadler uses it in a curious way (*Theory and Practice of Psychiatry*, 79, and *Modern Psychiatry*, 75) to refer to a mental attitude. So does the *UB* on page 760. On the same two pages of the Sadler books just cited, is the word *benumbent*. The *UB* twice uses the word *benumbing*.

Both Sadler and the *UB* authors were fond of using words that start with *super*. I've never seen *superanimal* except on page 79 of *Modern Psychiatry* and page 65 of *Mental Mischief and Emotional Conflicts* and on five pages of the *UB*. I earlier cited Sadler's use of *supermaterial*. On page 63 of *Modern Psychiatry* there is a line containing both *superintellectual* and *superemotional*. Both words, similarly unhyphenated, are in the *UB*. *Superconsciousness* is in Sadler's *Physiology of Faith and Fear* on pages 66, 68, 76. The *UB* uses it six times. If I had the time and patience I would go through Sadler's books to list all his "supers" that prefix another word without a hyphen. In the index of the *UB* there are more than a hundred such words.

Encompass is another uncommon word that Sadler liked to use (e.g., *Modern Psychiatry*, 648). The *UB* uses it at least 25 times. *Encompassed* appears 11 times, *encompasser* once, *encompasses* 18 times, *encompassing* 13 times, and *encompassment* twice.

Sadler is the only writer I know who occasionally calls a person who believes in religion a *religionist*. (See pages 1009 and 1086 of *Theory and Practice*, and pages 684 and 770 of *Modern Psychiatry*.) The word is in the *UB* at least 27 times; *religionists* is there at least 28 times.

Antidote is a common noun. How often have you seen it used as a verb? Sadler speaks of a helplessness not *antidoted* by a materialist philosophy (*Adolescence Problems*, 400). The *UB* (1616) speaks of a feeling of insecurity *antidoted* by faith in God.

Instead of "look at" or "examine" Sadler liked to say *scrutinize* (e.g., *Theory and Practice*, 1125, and *Modern Psychiatry*, 780). The word is in the *UB* three times, *scrutinized* is there three times, and *scrutinizing* once.

Each word in the title of Sadler's 1944 book *Prescription for Permanent Peace* begins with P. Just for fun, I browsed through its pages and circled unusual words starting with P: *Propensities* (7), *proclivity* (7), *preponderant* (158), *preponderance* (196), *paramount* (114), *personification* (122), and *perforce* (101). The *UB* writers also liked these words. *Propensities* is there six times and *propensity* is there eight times. *Proclivity* is in the *UB* three times, *proclivities* four times. *Preponderant* and *preponderance* are each there once. *Paramount* is in the *UB* nine times, and *personi-*

fication at least 14 times. I have seldom encountered *perforce* except in a Sadler book. He uses it in many other books (e.g., *Theory and Practice of Psychiatry*, 1082, and *Piloting Modern Youth*, 239). This peculiar word is in the *UB* no less than a dozen times!

In passing I noticed a few other big words in *Prescription for Permanent Peace* that were also used in the *UB*. *Hegemony*, for instance (on pages 185 and 200), is used twice in the *UB*, and *machinations* (190) is used seven times.

Sadler closes his preface to *The Mind at Mischief* by thanking Dr. Meyer Solomon "for his many helpful suggestions, which have added to the *repleteness* of this volume." I have never encountered "repleteness" in any other book, yet it is used in the *UB* no less than nine times. In the same volume you'll find *lodgment* (page 6) and *vicissitudes* (204). Sadler used both words many times in other books. *Lodgment* appears 11 times in the *UB* and *vicissitudes* at least 24 times!

Creedal is far from a common word. Sadler uses it in *Theory and Practice of Psychiatry* (252), and the *UB* on five different pages.

Sadler oftentimes liked to compress *oftentimes* by spelling it *ofttimes* (e.g., *The Physiology of Faith and Fear*, 34, and *Theory and Practice of Psychiatry*, 257, 259, 262, 273, 564). This is how it is spelled in the *UB* on pages 276, 547, and 976.

In Sadler's two books on heredity and eugenics, two of his favorite words are *betterment* and *uplift*, each used so often that there is no point in citing the scores of pages on which they appear. *Betterment* is in the *UB* eight times. *Uplift* appears 21 times, *uplifted* seven times, *uplifter(s)* 20 times, *uplifting* twice, *upliftment* once, and *uplifts* once. *Fecundity* is another unusual word scattered throughout Sadler's writings on eugenics. It's in the *UB* at least three times.

On page 501 of *The Physiology of Faith and Fear*, Sadler speaks of "superstitious *vagaries*." In the *UB* we find "mythologic *vagaries*" on page 1140, and "intellectual *vagaries*" on page 1493. In the same book (280), Sadler uses the words *upbuilding* and *rebuilding* in a single sentence. *Rebuilding* is in the *UB* once, *upbuilding* seven times.

Veritable is not a common word. Sadler used it at least three times in his 1912 book *The Physiology of Faith and Fear* (217, 345, 348). The *UB* has it no less than 18 times. Sadler (348) speaks of a "*veritable* bondage." On page 771 of the *UB* "a Melchizedek sometimes stationed on Urantia" speaks of "*veritable* slavery and bondage."

I have never come upon *aforetime* except in Sadler's *Physiology of*

Faith and Fear (e.g., 189). The word is not even in *Webster's Collegiate Dictionary*. Yet the *UB* uses it five times. *Inasmuch* was another word Sadler liked (e.g., ibid., 99). The *UB* uses it 36 times!

Espoused is another uncommon word often used by Sadler (e.g., *Long Heads and Round Heads*, 56). It appears ten times in the *UB*, *espouse* five times, and *espousal* once. On page 73 of *Prescription for Permanent Peace* Sadler uses the word *presage*. In singular, plural, and past-tense form this word appears eight times in the *UB*.

Supernal is a word Sadler liked. In *Theory and Practice of Psychiatry* (1081) he speaks of "*supernal* goals." The *UB* uses the word more than 75 times, and on page 141 you'll even find "*supernal* goals." On page 346: "the supreme *goals* of their *supernal* careers." Did Sadler pick up the phrase "supernal goals" from the supermortals, or did it enter the *UB* through Sadler's heavy editing?

In his preface to *Theory and Practice of Psychiatry* Sadler uses the words *vested*, *aspire*, and *furtherance*. *Vested* is in the *UB* nine times, *aspire* 15 times, and *furtherance* at least 16 times. *Diminution* is on page 42 of the same Sadler book, and in the *UB* eight times. *Differential*, page 40, is in the *UB* no less than 49 times! Sadler speaks of a "differential attitude." The *UB* (150) refers to a "differential spiritual attitude." On page 38 of the same volume Sadler writes of a "frontal attack." "Frontal attack" can be found in the *UB* on page 1551, in the paper on the twelve apostles—the paper Sadler said persuaded him that the life of Jesus was written by no human being.

Phrases in Common

Leo Elliott, a former Urantian, knows the *UB* much better than I. He has found hundreds of phrases, of two or more words, that Sadler used in his books and which also appear in the *UB*. Here are some from *The Physiology of Faith and Fear* (1912), followed by references in the *UB*.

Poured out (9, *UB* 25 times); *citadel of the mind* (50, *UB* 1229); *channels of thought* (18, 69, *UB* 1039); *unreasoning fear* (45, *UB* 556); *brought to bear* (55, 57, 76. *UB* three times); *architect of eternal destiny* (57, 62, *UB* 1134); *depleted energies* (60, *UB* 548); [character] *is the grand sum of sensations* (60, *UB* [self] *is more than the sum of one's sensations*, 1479); *spontaneous association of ideas* (75, *UB* 709); *noble aspirations* (97, *UB* 1480); *many an ancient* (107, *UB* 777, 2083); *ill humor* (79, *UB* 1989);

temple sleep (81, 91, 101, *UB* 991); *white and black magicians . . . good and bad demons* (81, *UB white and black magic . . . good and bad spirits* 774); *cults and isms* (90, *UB isms and cults* 1098); *dead level* (474, *UB* 1207).

Some more. *Expenditure of vital energy* (115, *UB* 778); *paralyzed by fear* (118, *UB* 1745); *pale with fright* (124, *UB* 1846); *dominated by fear* (129, *UB* 1243, 1437); *fellow feeling* (108, *UB* 946); *every phase* (113, *UB* 13 instances); *under the influence* (114, *UB* seven times); *bordering on* (114, *UB* 13 times); *never fails* (114, *UB* seven instances); *salutary influence* (137, *UB* 597); *in every way favorable* (149, *UB* 743); *implicit faith* (164, *UB* 739, 2029).

And still more! *Marvelous transformation* (176, *UB* 593); *ductless glands* (182–83, *UB* 737); *within certain limits* (186, *UB* 115, 538, 581); *should be remembered that* (186, *UB* 13 times); *pause to consider* (187, *UB* nine times); *victims of fear* (187–88, *UB* 1836); *desirable state* (188, *UB* 927); *stream of humanity* (189, *UB* 1098); *partakes of the nature of* (200,*UB* 468, 536); *to set in operation various influences* (202, *UB, to set in operation those influences,* 658); *effectually removed* (203, *UB* 1529).

Largely dependent on (221, *UB* 338, 1013, 1043); *Modern civilized races* (221, *UB* 956); *bondage of fear* (323, *UB* seven times); *liberty of faith* (321, *UB* 1564); *fight the good fight of faith* (324, *UB* 1766); *temporal sojourn on earth* (324, *UB* 69); *less fortunate fellows* (330, *UB* 927).

Of their own choosing (318, *UB* three times); *moral mandates* (318, *UB* 43, 1087); *absolutely no limit* (318, *UB* 50, 276); *it is interesting to note* (324, *UB* 1189); *saving power* (328, *UB* 1107); *merry heart* (329, *UB* 1445, 1674); *shackles of fear* (261, *UB* 1302); *gems of truth* (261, *UB* 1102); *notwithstanding all this* (262, *UB* 846); *formative period* (265, 279, *UB* 888); *is equivalent to the* (269, *UB* seven times); *by precept and example* (280, *UB* 1840, 1094); *mightily influenced* (296, *UB* 1104); *it must be borne in mind* (284, *UB* 767).

The world is filled with (342, 344, *UB* 1098, 1766); *Take ourselves less seriously* (346, *UB* 549); *purely instinctive* (350, *UB* 909); *The uncertainties and vicissitudes of life* (351, *UB, the uncertainties of life and the vicissitudes of existence,* 51); *in constant fear of* (159, *UB* 950); *spirit of infirmity* (360, *UB* three times); *prisoners of despair* (360, *UB* 2035); *intelligent men and women* (361, *UB* 1048, 1198); *sons and daughters of God* (361, *UB* four times); *especially is this true* (365, *UB* five times); *practice of the presence of God* (381, *UB* 1133); *morbid introspection* (395, 406, *UB* 1561); *a monotonous or tedious mode of life, chronic worry, a disposition to magnify small difficulties* . . . (388, *UB* 1611: *There is always danger that monotony of human contact will greatly multiply perplexities and magnify difficulties*).

Chanced to visit (428, *UB* 1797, 1873); *favorably to influence* (438, *UB* 970, 1256); *stands need of* (469, *UB* 914, 2082); *blind and unreasoning* (471, 496, *UB* 1102); *more or less mysterious* (477, *UB* 115, 739, 1105); *the province of prayer* (476, *UB* 995, 999); *put forth every effort* (483, *UB* 1765); *we are forced to recognize* (484, *UB* 364); *incessant struggle* (487, *UB* four times); *safety valve* (491, *UB* 549, 929); *fettered with fear* (493, *UB* 1192,1437).

The *UB*'s discussions of primitive humans and today's racial types closely parallel statements in Sadler's 1918 book *Long Heads and Round Heads*. Leo Elliott has found dozens of phrases that occur in this book as well as in the *UB*. Here are just a few: *so-called Heidelberg race* (9, *UB* 719); *moral and intellectual suicide* (47–48, *UB*, intellectual and moral suicide, 2079); *it must be borne in mind* (66, *UB* 767); *this is just as true of* (68, *UB* three times); *spontaneity of action* (76, *UB* 448); *we are forced to recognize* (115, *UB* 364); *spiritually insolvent* (156, *UB* 1229).

Here is a partial list of phrases Elliott found in Sadler's *The Truth About Spiritualism* (1923) that also turn up in the *UB*.

Slumber season (48, *UB* 1208); *simply will not* (11, *UB* 2083); *night season* (48, 129, *UB* 503, 592, 954, 1703); *nefarious scheme* (58, *UB* 607, 1567); *certain unstable types of human beings* (161, *UB* 1714); *age after age* (180, *UB* 586, 1247, 1919); *spiritual forces of the realm* (187, *UB* 1836); *universal mind* (150, 192, *UB* 11 times).

In *The Mind at Mischief* (533) Sadler recalls a patient who taught himself geology so well that "He can pick up a stone any time and tell you its origin, history, and destiny." In the *UB* (1339) we read: "By the times of Jesus the Jews had arrived at a settled concept of their *origin, history, and destiny.*" And on page 215: ". . . three phases of universe reality: *origin, history, and destiny.*"

The revelators, in a much-quoted passage (*UB* 1109), explain why they are forbidden to report on "unearned or premature knowledge." On page 38 of *The Truth About Spiritualism* Sadler speaks of seeking "unearned knowledge" from fortune tellers and mediums.

On page 323 of *Piloting Modern Youth*, by Sadler and his wife, he refers to Jesus as "the lad of Nazareth." The phrase appears in the *UB* five times.

Of more than a hundred parallel phrases that Leo Elliott discovered in the *UB* and in Sadler's *Race Decadence* (1922) here is a small sample: *of the next and future generations* (8, *UB* 941); *fully cognizant* (83, *UB* seven times!); *the weak and feeble* (90, *UB* 1474); *it should not be inferred that* (205, *UB* 710, 733); *we are forced to recognize that* (260, *UB* 364); *clearly distinguishable* (276, *UB* 455); *usually designated as* (276, *UB* 699); *blind and unreasoning* (368, *UB* 1102); *failure to establish* (370, *UB* 859).

Sadler's *The Mind At Mischief*, his all-time best seller, swarms with phrases that betray his heavy editing of the *UB* papers. Here is a small sample of what Leo Elliott has discovered:

Intellectual vagaries (VII, *UB* 1493); *It must . . . be borne in mind* (3, *UB* 767; *borne in mind* appears five times); *brought face to face with* (3, *UB* 300; *face to face* appears 35 times); *Under certain conditions* (5, *UB* eight times); *It is entirely possible* (6, *UB* 22, 756, 1178, 1182); *The heart is deceitful above all things and desperately wicked* (this quotation from Jeremiah is on page 7, and is quoted in the *UB* twice [1609, 1630]); *certain unstable types of human beings* (9, *UB* 1714); *under the immediate supervision* (10, *UB* 257, 292, 415, 1987); *spontaneous association of ideas* (14, *UB* 402, 709); *to bear in mind* (15, *UB* 855, 1329); *more or less complete control* (16, *UB* 470); *sorry plight* (24, *UB* 839, 840, 975, 1348, 1810, 1834); *creative imagination* (22, *UB* 13 times).

Really and truly (29, *UB* six times); *How does it come that* (30, *UB* 1792); *uncontrolled, unstable* (31, *UB*, *imperfect choice, uncontrolled . . . and unstable* 1301); *in a certain sense* (31, *UB* 12 times); *to be wondered that* (33, *UB* 795, 977); *developed to the point where* (39, *UB* 566, 675, 841).

Fatal to human happiness (43, *UB*, *fatal to happiness* 1220); *modern civilized peoples* (43, *UB* 1922); *must not overlook the fact that* (51, 53, *UB* 901); *further augmented by* (52, *UB* 423, 1251); *the satisfaction of living* (53, *UB* 1799).

Numerous passages in the *UB*, found by Elliott, condense a longer passage in *The Mind at Mischief* in much the same way that it condenses passages from books by other authors. Here for example are two sentences from page 47 of *The Mind at Mischief*:

No other primary emotion is capable of such beneficent use or such monstrous abuse. No other primitive instinct can contribute so much to human happiness when properly exercised; and likewise no other innate emotion can cause such suffering and sorrow when overindulged or otherwise perverted.

Compare this with the following sentence from the *UB* (914)

No human emotion or impulse, when unbridled and overindulged, can produce so much harm and sorrow as this powerful sex urge.

Real or fancied (59, *UB* 945, 995); *which betokens the exercise of* (60, *UB* 1183); *it is entirely possible* (67, *UB* 22, 756, 1178, 1182); *species of self-deception* (70, *UB* 614, 982); *nothing more nor less than* (71, *UB* 958, 967, 969, 983, 1005, 1590); *within the confines of* (74, *UB* seven times).

And further parallels between *UB* style and *The Mind at Mischief*: *nothing more nor less than* (182, 242, *UB* six times); *in this connection* (183, *UB* 11 times); *I had to look up a lot of texts for this woman, such as* "*A merry heart doeth good like a medicine,*" (182, *UB* see 1445 and 1674); *a conscience void of offense* (184, *UB* 1736); *inherent weaknesses* (190, *UB* 2082); *avenue of escape* (196, *UB* four times); *majority of those who* (197, *UB* 294, 1501, 1633); *far in advance of* (201, *UB* five times); *one thing is certain* (208, *UB* seven times); *moral coward* (211, *UB* 1987, 1996, 1113, 1769); *should be made clear* (218, *UB* six times); *transient episode* (220, *UB* 501); *not for one moment be entertained* (222, *UB* 2010); *every now and then* (229, *UB* six times); *all down through the ages* (231, *UB* seven times); *new and strange* (234, *UB* five times); *overlook the fact that* (248, *UB* 734, 901, 1608, 2063); *spontaneous association of ideas* (249, *UB* 402, 709); *not the slightest doubt that* (253, *UB* 1239, 2010).

I have not listed passages in which ideas expressed in *The Mind at Mischief* turn up with slightly different phrasing in the *UB*. For example, Leo Elliott found this in Sadler's book: "Probably the only reason that women appear to have more intuition than men is that they are less trained in logical reasoning," 249. Here is how the *UB* puts it on page 938: "Women seem to have more intuition than men, but they also appear to be somewhat less logical." Did Sadler pick this up from the celestials, or did the Chief of Seraphim stationed on Urantia pick it up from Sadler? Or did Sadler and Lena write Paper 84, feeling indited by the Chief of Seraphim?

The arena wherein (77, *UB* 139, 160, 853, 1318); *thousands upon thousands* (77, 78, *UB* 16 times); *should be borne in mind* (78, *UB* 828, 1158, 1324, 1858); *conflict arises out of the fact that* (78, *UB* 486); *routine drudgery* (78, *UB* 774); *spontaneous association of ideas* (93, *UB* 709); *freely and frankly* (111, 116, *UB* 941); *must not overlook the fact that* (113, *UB* 901); *understood, more or less fully* (113, *UB, more or less fully understood*, 1769); *nothing more nor less than* (116, *UB* six times); *perfect integration* (116, *UB* 738); *it is not strange* (116, *UB* 16 times!).

Still more parallel phrases between *The Mind at Mischief* and the *UB*, selected from further researches by Leo Elliott:

Unfailingly exhibit (119, *UB* 1299); *In accordance with the* (119, *UB* 105 times!); *it behooves us to* (120, *UB* 1532, 1744); *blind and unreasonable* (121, *UB*, *blind and unreasoning*, 1102); *We are forced to recognize that* (122, *UB* 364); *confronted with the necessity of* (122, *UB* eight times!); *bondage of fear* (132, *UB* seven times); *mobilized in his mind* (135, *UB*, *mobilize in his mind* 402); *vague and indefinite* (146, *UB* 488, 713, 1022); *it must be remembered that* (149, *UB* 840, 1070); *compelled to admit* (152, *UB* 1853); *We are forced to recognize* (152, *UB* 364); *had their origin in* (155, *UB* seven times); *utterly beyond* (159, *UB* nine times!); *[Jesus] the author and finisher of our faith* (*UB*, *Jesus, the author and finisher of our faith*, 2091); *real education . . . an outgrowth of mingling . . . with your fellow men* (176, *UB*, *real education . . . obtained by mingling with his fellow men*, 1363); *origin, history, and destiny* (176, *UB* 215, 1339); *Roaming the universe* (359, *UB* 1178); *it is entirely true that* (364, *UB* 1946); *but the vestibule* (361, *UB* 1225).

Exceedingly difficult (261, *UB* 21 times); *of time and space* (271, *UB* 197 times); *The absurdity and grotesqueness of our dreams . . .* (291, *UB*, *The absurdities of dreamlife . . . your grotesque dreams*, 1208); *disposed to accept* (294, *UB* 831, 1812); *inclined to believe* (302, *UB* 56, 1844, 1919, 2027, 2031); *wicked conspiracy between* (315, 324, *UB* 991); *inordinately perplexed* (322, *UB* 1611); *all down through the ages* (351, *UB* seven times); *earnest souls* (352, *UB* 976); *well-nigh universal* (356, *UB* 982).

Elliott has so far investigated only five of Sadler's books, and I have listed only a very small portion of the parallel phrases he has found. One can expect thousands more as Elliott's search or similar searches by others continue.

Piloting Modern Youth, written by Sadler and his wife, contains many phrases that turn up in the *UB*. Here is only one example, found by Leo Elliott who is just starting research on this book. On page 3 the Sadlers write: "And thus does the adolescent find himself in the midst of. . . ." The *UB* (1684): "Thus did the Master find himself in the midst of. . . ." By the time my book is published, Leo may have an extensive list of other parallels.

Readers who desire a fuller listing of Elliott's references can contact him at Route 1, Box 48, Charlottesville, Virginia 22903, or by email at 76440.1416@Compuserve.com.

Appendix F

Acknowledgments

Among former Urantians to whom I am indebted for help in writing this book, I owe my greatest debt to Martha Sherman. Mrs. Sherman graciously allowed my wife and me to visit her in Arkansas and chat about the five years she and her husband, Harold, were members of the Urantia Forum. In addition she has allowed her daughter Marcia access to her husband's voluminous "diary"—notes, letters, and other documents that are a priceless source of information about the early years of the Urantia movement. Marcia has been tireless in searching through this material and copying for me items of special interest. My debt to her is as great as it is to her mother. I cannot thank "M and M," as they sign their letters, enough for their assistance and friendship.

Iola Martin, a Seventh-day Adventist who for a time was fascinated by the *UB*, I wish to thank for being the friend by correspondence and telephone who first disclosed to me that Wilfred Kellogg was the *UB*'s original contactee. She has also helped in many ways to introduce me to Adventist sources of information about Dr. Sadler and his relationship with Dr. Kellogg and Ellen White.

A letter from Julio Edwards to the *Skeptical Inquirer* was my first introduction to the *UB*. He has since given generously of his time and knowledge in correcting errors and offering advice for improving this book's early drafts. Julio thinks my tone should be less harsh and combative. Perhaps he is right. I am inclined to assume that no true believers in a cult ever alter their faith as a result of rational arguments, and I like to quote H. L. Mencken's remark that one horse laugh is worth a thousand syllogisms. I would be much surprised if any Urantian abandoned his or her faith as a result of reading this book, though I would of course be pleased.

Leo Elliott has become a friend who has given invaluable aid in supplying information I would not otherwise have acquired, especially his discovery of hundreds of phrases which the *Urantia Book* and Sadler's early books have in common.

Among Urantians still within the fold who have had the courage and willingness to dialog with me, some even to visit, I owe special thanks to Richard Bain, Kristen Maaherra, Ernest Moyer, Matt Neibaur, Ken Raveill, Buddy Roogow, and Meredith Sprunger.

Jacques Rhéaume deserves thanks for giving me copies of his booklet *La Verbe s'est fair livre* (The word has been made book), attacking the Urantia movement, and for providing a copy of his massive Ph.D. thesis (also in French) about the movement.

Richard Schwarz, an Adventist historian, shared with me on a visit his impressions of Dr. Sadler, whom he interviewed prior to writing his admirable biography of Dr. John Kellogg.

Ronald Numbers' splendid biography of Mrs. White was an essential source of information about her and her relations with Kellogg and Sadler. I thank him also for lending me from his library rare copies of books by Dr. Sadler.

Many dedicated Urantians refused to reply to letters of inquiry, or to assist in any way once they realized I was writing a book that would not support their beliefs. Among this group I particularly wish *not* to thank Mark Kulieke, Vonne Meussling, Florine Sadler, John Seres, Scott Forsythe, Patricia Mundelius, Berkeley Elliott, Matthew Block, Vern Grimsley, Dan Massey, Barrie Bedell, and Martin Myers. However, knowing well their mind sets, I cannot fault them for their attitude.

Martin Gardner

Postscript

More than a decade has gone by since this book was first published, and much has happened within the Urantia movement during those years. Among the many new books about the movement, I reluctantly limit my comments to the following eight.

Ernest Moyer, a dedicated Urantian, in 2000 published *Birth of a Divine Revelation*. His bitter attacks on me and on this book come close to libel. Moyer is convinced that Wilfred Kellogg could not possibly be the sleeping "instrument," though he offers no evidence for a different candidate. Much of his history is taken from my book. For example, he prints in full a long letter that Sadler sent to Ellen White—a letter I had a hard time tracking down. I assume he still believes that UFOs are spacecraft piloted by the higher-ups and that Urantianism is destined to be the world's great new religion prior to the return of Jesus.[1]

Five marvelous paperbacks, issued by Square Circles Publishing, in Glendale California, have the general title of *The Sherman Diaries*. All five are compiled and skillfully edited by Saskia Praamsma and Matthew Block.

For anyone interested in the *UB*, skeptic or true believer, *The Sherman Diaries* are essential reading. Photographs on the front covers—four of Harold Sherman and his wife, Martha, and one of the building at 533 Diversey Parkway—are almost worth the books' prices. Inside the covers are rare photos of prominent Urantians.

Volume 1 is for me the most interesting because of its many letters to and from Harry Loose, and its glimpses of Wilfred Kellogg running like a frightened rabbit to avoid contacts with Sherman. The fourth volume, covering the years 1944 and 1945, reveals a raft of new plagiarized discoveries by the indomitable Block. (See pages 38, 51, 102, 142, 190, 213, 225, and 263.)

Loose's letters show him to be a man of monstrous ego. Throughout his strange friendship with Sherman, he plays the role of a guru possessing vast wisdom and psychic powers, a man secretly involved with the *UB*'s origin, a man with esoteric knowledge that he can only partially pass on to Sherman. Loose also comes through in his correspondence as capable of outright lying, especially about the "bifurcation" that allowed him to make astral body visits to a mythical Catholic priest in South America. He obviously deceived Sherman about his out-of-body visit to Sherman's Hollywood apartment while he (Loose) was asleep miles away. In spite of his deep devotion to the *UB*, on page 157 he has high praise for Christian Science!

On page xiii of volume 1 the Kelloggs are quoted as saying that Loose was never present while the "instrument" was channeling. There is not the slightest evidence that Loose knew the sleeper's identity. Amusingly, the Kelloggs say they witnessed every channeling episode. Some Urantians take this to prove that Wilfred was not the channeler. But if he was, then of course he and his wife would be there when the channeler spoke in his sleep! There are great photos in volume 1 of Sherman and Martha, and their two beautiful daughters, Marcia and Mary. There are rare photos of Loose and even rarer pictures of Wilfred.

Volume 5 of *The Sherman Diaries* was published in 2008. It covers the years from 1946 to the publication of the *UB* in 1955. In spite of what Harold liked to call the "blow up," he and Martha continued to attend the forum to hear papers read aloud, usually by Bill Sadler but occasionally by Wilfred Kellogg. Bill read them with such fervor and emotion that it often brought him to tears.

The papers covered in volume 5 are from the *UB*'s section on the life of Jesus. Sherman found them markedly inferior to the earlier papers. Adjectives he used to describe them include fictitious, unnatural, hackneyed, uninspired, distasteful, offensive, inconsistent, and "peppered with clichés and timeworn phrases," they are a poorly written "hodgepodge" and "rotten to the core." Sherman became convinced that Sadler himself revised the Jesus papers, perhaps even wrote portions of them. He constantly lashes Sadler for burning the original manuscripts, making it impossible for future scholars to learn how radically they were altered.

Throughout the diaries Sadler is portrayed as a self-centered, egotistical tyrant, quick to anger and ruthless in his control over forum members. Most of them, Sherman tells us, were former or present mental patients of Sadler, fearful of crossing him in any way. He thinks Sadler deliberately delayed publication of the *UB* so he could maintain dominance over forum members.

Volume 5 also covers Sherman's prolific output of popular novels, including science fiction novels such as *The Green Man* and *The Green Man Returns*, his many nonfiction uplift books, his plays, and his constant lecturing on such topics as how to stop smoking, the key to happiness, life after death, mysteries of the mind, and so on. The diaries record his firm belief that Earth is being observed by aliens in UFOs from other planets. Dr. Joseph B. Rhine and Harold's good friend Norman Vincent Peale weave in and out of the book, as well as Ray Palmer, the small hunchback who edited *Amazing Stories* and other pulp periodicals.

I was favorably impressed by two of Sherman's strong convictions, He opposed the notion, which runs through the Jesus papers, that entrance into heaven depends on a person's beliefs, not his or her deeds. As Martha writes (page 184), "Harold has made the point that no God with infinite justice would ever have so narrowed opportunities for survival of lowly human creatures as to have required that they *believe* to be saved."

Sherman also had little respect for the doctrine of reincarnation. Here is how he put it in a letter on page 399:

I am convinced, as are you, that reincarnation is a myth; that other influences from higher realms cause humans to feel they are remembering a past life. I think, on occasion, that obsessions have taken place, where a discarnate entity has taken over the consciousness of an individual, causing people to think this personality really reincarnated. I have observed, however, that many humans are unthinkably accepting reincarnation. I cannot conceive of God, the Great Intelligence, punishing man by causing him to be born blind because he may have put out the eyes of a fellow human some hundreds of years ago . . . *without* giving this man a *memory*, so he could know *why* he was being punished. What is to be gained by punishment without a knowledge of *why* we are being penalized? If the father whips his child without telling the child why he is getting a beating, what good does it do the child? Certainly God is more intelligent that this. And there are too many dimensions beyond this life for man to continue his evolution—God does not need to cause his creatures, however lowly they may be, to return to the world they have left if survival is a fact, as I now believe it is.

Volume 5 ends with details about a project almost impossible to believe, yet a project that Sherman took with utmost seriousness. He had become a friend of a man named Wilbur Stafford. Stafford had convinced himself and Sherman that the *UB* was in essential harmony with three earlier major revelations: the writings of Swedenborg, a book by the "Seer of Poughkeepsie," and OAHSPE!

Swedenborg was a Swedish medium who during trances conversed with Jesus, angels, devils, Moses, Saint Paul, Martin Luther, John Calvin, and assorted kings and queens of the past. In *The Earth and the Universe*, Swedenborg described the inhabitants of Mercury, Venus, Mars, Jupiter, Saturn, and the Moon. Here is how I summarized these visions in chapter 33, "Psychic Astronomy," of my book *The New Age*:

> Mercurians see the Sun as huge, but their climate is moderate. The women are small, beautiful, and wear linen caps. The men dress in tight-fitting blue raiment. They have good memories and a vast knowledge of astronomy. Their oxen and cows are like ours, only smaller. Venusians are divided into two races, one "mild and humans," the other a race of cruel, stupid giants. Martians speak in "sonorous" tones, live on fruit, and wear clothes made from the bark of trees. The lower parts of their faces have a black skin color.
>
> Jovians are kind and gentle, living on fertile lands where there are many wild horses. Although grouped into nations, warfare is unknown. Those in warm climates go naked except for loincloths. Their tents and low wooden houses have sides decorated with stars on blue backgrounds. When they eat they sit on the leaves of fig trees with their legs crossed. Curiously, they do not walk erect but "creep along" by using their hands.
>
> Saturnians are "upright, modest" people who live on fruits and seeds. Their planet's rings appear in the sky as "white as snow." Moon people are about the size of our seven-year-olds. Their voices, which sound like "thunder," are produced by expelling air from their abdomens. </>

The Seer of Poughkeepsie was a Spiritualist medium named Andrew Jackson Davis. His most popular book was titled *Principles of Nature: Divine Revelations and a Voice of Mankind*. My copy was a twelfth printing that ran to 756 pages. Sir Arthur Conan Doyle described this book as "one of the most profound and original books of philosophy ever produced." Here is how I wrote about it in the *New Age* chapter:

> Many familiar ploys of later psychic charlatans were pioneered by Davis. He earned large sums of money by clairvoyantly peering into people's bodies, diagnosing their ailments, and prescribing strange remedies. He performed what magicians call "eyeless vision"—having his eyes covered and reading documents handed to him. Doyle, who devotes a chapter to the Poughkeepsie Seer in his *History of Spiritualism*, was impressed by Davis's prophesies of horseless carriages, airplanes, typewriters, and the growth of spiritualism. Doyle makes much of the fact that Davis was uneducated and read almost nothing, though there is ample evidence that he

was a voracious reader of books on philosophy, science, and religion. He founded and edited magazines, spewed forth a steady stream of articles, tracts, and pamphlets, lectured widely, and was more admired by his contemporaries than any psychic today. When he died in 1910, at the age of 84, he was running a small bookshop in Boston and his popularity was on the wane.

Davis's visions disclosed that all our planets are inhabited except Uranus, Neptune, and an unnamed ninth planet that occultists later identified as Pluto. The closer a planet is to the sun, the younger its age and the more gross and imperfect its inhabitants. Davis probably got this notion from Swedenborg, though it is also defended by Kant in a 1755 work on cosmology—"a view to be praised for its terrestrial modesty," comments Bertrand Russell in his *History of Western Philosophy*, "but not supported by any scientific grounds." Kant believed, as did Swedenborg, that there are other galaxies like our Milky Way, with planets that also teem with life.

Mercurians, Davis declared, have a "powerful retentive memory," but their ferocious animal nature generates perpetual warfare. "At this moment," he continues, "one of those destructive battles is about being consummated." Bodies of the Mercurians are completely covered with hair, giving them an appearance that "would be to us no more pleasing than that of an orangutan." Two barren deserts, covering almost all of the planet's surface, are surrounded by boiling water. Severe winds blowing over the hot water cause great destruction.

Most of Venus, Davis reveals, is covered with water, and its atmosphere is "nearly like that which encompasses the earth." Astronomers then knew little about the rotation of Venus. Davis gives it a period of 23 1/2 hours. It is now known to be 243 days, but let's not waste time on dull errors. Venusians on one side of the planet are kind, but their reasoning powers are weak. On the other side of Venus the inhabitants are giant savages—Davis here follows Swedenborg—who practice torture and cannibalism, sometimes devouring their own children.

Seven pages are devoted to the Martians—small humanoids with blue eyes and yellow faces. Davis confirms Swedenborg's revelation that the lower parts of their faces are dark in color. They are kind folk with high morals, who communicate by facial expressions. "When one conceives a thought . . . he casts his beaming eyes upon the eyes of another; and his sentiments instantly become known."

Of the asteroids that circle the Sun between the orbits of Earth and Mars, Davis writes only about the four then known: Ceres, Pallas, Juno, and Vesta. All bear only plant life, "although an era is now approaching that will call into existence a class of zoophytes." Eventually the four will coalesce into a single planet.

Davis's vision of Jupiter closely parallels Swedenborg's. The Jovians are larger and more beautiful than we are, and much more intelligent. "They do not walk erect, but assume an inclined position, frequently using their hands and arms in walking." Their upper lips are unusually prominent. The giant planet is free of diseases, but the Jovian life span is only about 30 years. Their nations are united in peaceful brotherhood.

The geography of Saturn is "very beautiful," Davis writes, "it being divided into two-thirds water and one-third earth." Its inhabitants represent the highest stage of development in our solar system—even more intelligent, beautiful, and good than the Jovians. Their heads are "very high and long," with brains composed of cortical glands, "each of which attracts and repels, performing systolic and diastolic motions" like those of our heart. I spare the reader Davis's dull description of the lower forms of Saturn's animal life.

On OAHSPE, a book even crazier than the works of Swedenborg and Davis, see chapter 9 of the book you hold.

Back to Sherman. Stafford persuaded him that a book about the great revelations of Swedenborg and Davis, and OAHSPE, and possibly other major revelations, all shown to mesh with the revelations of the *UB*, would quickly become a sensational best seller. The two men, Sherman and Stafford, would be the book's authors, and the royalties would be split fifty-fifty. Sherman was enthusiastic about the project. Alas, this monumental volume never materialized because Stafford died after a stroke. Volume 5 of *The Sherman Diaries* includes a moving letter Sherman sent to Stafford's widow telling her what a great man her husband was.

J. T. Manning's *Source Authors of the Urantia Book* (Square Circles, 2003) is a 535-page book on *UB* plagiarism. I assume Manning is a true believer because he doesn't consider these many passages to be purloined. His book contains biographies of all the source authors as well as their photographs and opinions. There is no mention of Sherman or Loose or Wilfred, or my book, though Manning has dozens of favorable quotes from Moyer's eccentric history.

Now for a curious little mystery. Although the name of philosopher Charles Hartshorne, the University of Chicago's famous pantheist, is cited eleven times in Manning's book, no chapter in the book is devoted to him. This is in spite of the fact that on page 3 of the *UB* there is a long passage on seven ways to define "absolute perfection." The passage is taken almost word for word from Hartshorne's 1941 book, *Man's Vision of God.* (See pages 331–33 of my book for details.) It is a flagrant, shameful plagiarism that could have been the basis for legal action if Hartshorne had known about it and wanted to sue for copyright violation. Why Manning omitted this whopping theft from his book beats me!

Saskia Praamsma, coeditor of *The Sherman Diaries*, is a recent convert to Urantianism. In 2001 Square Circles issued her book *How I Found the Urantia Book and How It Changed My Life*. The volume is a compilation of 324 testimonies by persons who became converts.

Two testimonies are of special interest. Saskia tells how as a child she was raised by an agnostic mother who quarreled constantly with her father, a Jehovah's Witness. Her brother introduced her to the *UB*. After a failed marriage and several frustrating relationships, she began reading the *UB*. "Pieces of the jigsaw puzzle," she writes, "began to fit together into a detailed tapestry." It was "the happiest day of my life." She "wept tears of joy and relief."

> On that day I turned my life around 180 degrees. All my attitudes and values were changed in one fell swoop. I read the book for three months straight, barely coming up for air. I learned where I came from, where I was going, and why I was here. What I had believed to be important was meaningless, and that's why happiness had eluded me. I discovered that there is no happiness apart from God. The stress and tension dropped away, the furrows in my brow relaxed, and I still hadn't read a word about Jesus—that came much later. In fact, I resisted reading about him until I had exhausted all the other papers. But when I finally did, I was ready to accept him and his teachings wholeheartedly. Since that day I have had peace of mind—the peace which passes all understanding.

Matthew Block's testimony is equally impressive. He tells how as a youth his mother's beliefs in psychic phenomena—she was fascinated by pyramid power—were passed on to him. At twelve he rejected his childhood Judaism, while retaining a firm belief in a personal God. Working as a "boy Friday" for an unnamed Philadelphia psychic, he attended a metaphysical class with his mother. The speaker displayed a *UB* and allowed Block to glance through it. At first the text repelled him. Later he bought a copy, and the more he read, the more he found it inspiring.

> The book seemed to glow as it rested on my desk. But it took several months to integrate the book into my life and thoughts. The pull of astrology and psychic phenomena was still strong; I kept thinking of Jesus as a Leo and had trouble squaring Edgar Cayce's account of Jesus with the Urantia Book's. Nevertheless the Urantia philosophy beamed its way

through the occult haze, and I gradually stopped thinking in terms of astrology and reincarnation.

In 1977, I decided to return to school, choosing a university in Chicago to be near the Urantia headquarters. Thus began a twenty-plus-year association with the Urantia movement, during which I worked as a volunteer and, later, a paid employee of Urantia Brotherhood (now called the Urantia Book Fellowship). Since 1992 I've been doing research into the sources of the Urantia Book, an endeavor that has immeasurably enriched my understanding of the whole Urantia Book phenomenon. But that's another story.

Now for a big surprise. I wonder how many Urantians today know that Block, since he wrote the above words, has become totally disenchanted with the *UB*. Like Saskia, he has turned 180 degrees, but in the opposite direction. The more plagiarisms he uncovered (the list is now in the hundreds), the more he became convinced that the *UB* is a fraud perpetrated by Sadler. He is writing a book about his latest research and his startling conclusions.

Block is now convinced that the *UB* is entirely the work of humans, especially the work of Sadler. Of course Sadler believed he had been chosen by the higher-ups to edit the material coming from the sleeping channeler and others, even to write some of the papers himself. Block's coming book is sure to be another bombshell.[2]

In surfing through Praamsma's anthology, I was struck by how many converts were raised Roman Catholics, conservative Protestants, or orthodox Jews. Consider the typical case of Lyn Davis Lear, the wife of Norman Lear. She writes of being brought up in a fundamentalist Presbyterian family. Early in life she began to question fundamentalist doctrines, especially the horrendous belief that poor children in India are destined for hell because they lack a faith in Jesus.

One day, at a shopping mall bookstore, Lyn found on a shelf a copy of the *UB*. "I read the front and back flaps and started to cry. I just knew this book had the answers I had been searching for. . . . Discovering *The Urantia Book* and its teachings has, without a doubt, been the single most important event in my life." Most Urantians in Saskia's book were introduced to the *UB* by a friend or a relative. Mrs. Lear is a rare exception.

Dick Bain, whose flawed commentary on *UB* science is discussed in my chapters 10 and 11, also contributed a testimonial to Praamsma's book. He writes movingly of how Meredith Sprunger introduced him to the *UB*. "I have since found some flaws in the science content [of the *UB*]," he writes, "but the spiritual teachings transcend that of any book on philosophy that I have encountered."

Sprunger also provided a testimonial. Now retired, he continues to promote the *UB* in any way he can. He writes about reading the Jesus papers "with tears streaming down my face."

Other Urantians mentioned in my book are in Praamsma's anthology: Philip Calabrese, Byron Belitsos, Larry Mullins, Fred Harris, to cite a few. Michael Pitzel, who constructed a model of the ultimaton (see my book, page 182), tells how the *UB* pages "seemed to glow" when he began reading them. At the time he was chief chef and manager of a vegetarian restaurant called A Small Planet, near the campus of Michigan State University where he was studying topology.

Several recent scientific discoveries relate to *UB* predictions. Urantians were jubiliant in 2002 when a globe almost as large as Pluto was found circling the sun in an orbit beyond Pluto's. Urantians were even more excited when a larger and heavier body, Eris, was spotted still more distant from the sun. Does not the *UB* speak (pages 656–58) of two undiscovered planets beyond Pluto?

Not so fast! In the next three years, astronomer Michael Brown, who discovered the first two "planets," found three more. Eris is a trifle larger than Pluto and has its own tiny moon. All five, astronomers have since concluded, should not be called planets. They are large asteroids that have wandered inward from the Kuiper belt, a dense cloudy region containing millions of icy balls of varying sizes. Of course, it is all a matter of semantics. Even Pluto, to the dismay of many astronomers, has been demoted from a planet to a large Kuiper asteroid. In brief, the solar system lost a planet and gained five big asteroids.

On page 214, I mention the laboratory creation of short-lived elements with 102 through 111 electrons. This contradicts the *UB*'s assertion that no elements exist with more than 100 electrons. In recent years, elements with 112 through 118 electrons have been created.

On page 187, I erred in saying that the *UB*'s number for the Andromeda galaxy is 876,927. It is 876,926. This was called to my attention by correspondent Bruce Williams. He also mentioned the curious fact that the *UB* gives this same figure for the number of suns in the first dispersion. Williams also mentioned that on the *UB*'s page 687 it says that seventy-five-foot-long dinosaurs "have never been equaled in bulk by any living creature." The celestial author forgot about blue whales.

I hope no reader took seriously pages 281–83 on which my imaginary numerologist, Dr. Irving Joshua Matrix (note the 666 embedded in his name), did his best to decode the three mysterious numbers that the *UB* assigns to the "instrument." I remain convinced, however, that it is no coincidence that the seven numbers 3–17–126–4–384–6–37 correlate with the seven letters of *Wilfred*, that the six digits 182314 correlate with the six letters of *Custer*, and that the seven letters of *Kellogg* correlate with the digits 3641852. This seems to me too accurate a triplet of correlations to be coincidental.

The best coding procedure I have been able to come up with since my book was written springs from an observation that all six letters of *Custer* appear in the phrase *Christ Jesus*. If we rearrange the digits 182314 to 123418, we can apply the following procedure.

The 1 of 123418 gives us *C*, the first letter of *Christ Jesus*. Go forward two letters to *R*, then three letters to *T*, four letters to *U*, one letter to *S*, and finally (back to *C*), and eight letters to *E*. This hits all six letters of *Custer*. Probably sheer coincidence.

Perhaps some clever reader can find more convincing ways to decipher the three mysterious numbers. Maybe the seven numbers in the first sequence refer in some way to words in a document or a book? Or did whoever wrote the *UB*'s paper have nothing more in mind than correlating numbers with the letters in Wilfred's three names?

Because I have made only a flimsy effort to keep up with trends in the Urantia movement (my name understandably vanished from all mailing lists), I asked Julio Edwards, a Colorado student of the cult, to answer a few questions. From him I learned that the current trustees are Gerd Jameson, Richard Keeler, Seppo Kanerva, George Michelson, and Mo Siegel. Jay Peregrine is executive director.

General Duane Faw is still active in the Teaching Mission, though its bizarre development is rapidly declining. No one seems to know what has happened to former trustee Martin Myers.

I'm told that Joe Pope has moved on to higher worlds. Friend and former Urantian Leo Elliot has also passed away. Gabriel of Sedona continues to run his sad little group in Arizona. Vern Grimsley, I am told, is still a true believer. Appeals concerning the copyright status of the *UB* have been exhausted, and its papers, thanks to a lawsuit by Harry McMullin, are now public domain.

I haven't the foggiest notion of whether the Urantia cult is growing or if its followers are slowly evaporating as older "soldiers of the circles" die off. Religions, even lowly cults, take a long time expiring. The great gods of ancient Greece survived the Roman Empire, and Zoroasterism still flourishes in Bombay!

J. T. Manning, I'm told by Matthew Block, is the pseudonym of a young financial analyst who once worked for a firm in New York City. He used the alias on his book because his wife doesn't approve of his fixation on the *UB*.

Helen Carlson, sister-in-law of Sadler's son Bill, died in 1996 at the age of ninety-two. Robert Slagle is leading a *UB* study group. Barrie Bedell also teaches a study group. Mark Kulieke contributed an article on the origin and history of the Urantia Brotherhood to the *Spiritual Fellowship Journal* (vol. 15, Spring–Summer, 2006). The same issue contained an article by Dick Bain in which he does his best to reconcile the two seemingly different celestial regions called Orvonton, and Meredith Sprunger wrote on "The Call to Ministry." The Urantia Brotherhood, by the way, has changed its name to the Urantia Book Fellowship.

Norm DuVal, a retired postman, is a Urantian fundamentalist. He denies that there are any errors, historic or scientific, in the *UB*. There are only trivial printer's errors. In 1995 he perpetrated on the Internet a twenty-three-page hatchet job on my book. It is saturated with ad hominem insults and distortions of what I actually wrote.

An example of such a distortion is DuVal's claim that I, like Matthew's gospel, call the star of Bethlehem a star. Yes, but I made clear that the so-called star might have been what the *UB* claims—a conjunction of Jupiter and Saturn. I never said the star was a star. Indeed, I said just the opposite.

DuVal bashes me for emphasizing the absence in the *UB* of any reference to the big bang. He has a simple justification for this absence. The big bang is not mentioned in the *UB* because it never happened! Today's cosmologists who think it did are all wrong.

Why have geologists never found a fossil of a fandor? Because, DuVal tells us, fossils of birds are extremely rare. Fandor fossils are likely to turn up any day. The giant birds must have existed because the *UB* says they did, and the *UB* is never wrong.

Instead of writing a detailed rebuttal to DuVal's passionate attack, I will turn the other cheek and credit DuVal with a few hits. On page 23 of my book's first printing, I refer to "Eadoman tribes." No such tribes exist, DuVal says correctly. Had he checked the book's second printing, he would have found a correction of this printer's mistake to "Badoman tribes."

Another obvious printer's error occurs on page 199 of my book's first printing. The date of a supernova explosion is given as 1054 BCE when it should have been AD. Again, had DuVal checked the book's second printing, he would have seen this corrected. Indeed, there are dozens of similar typographic mistakes in the flawed first printing that DuVal failed to notice.

On page 30 I made a serious error. I referred to the Holy Spirit and what the *UB* calls the Spirit of Truth as one and the same. The *UB* distinguishes the two. The Holy Spirit is part of the Universe Mother Spirit. The Spirit of Truth is an entity that entered the minds of early Christians on the day of Pentecost. I was misled by the fact that all orthodox Christians, Catholic and Protestant, accept the account in the book of Acts of how the Holy Ghost provided the gifts of Pentecost.

DuVal blundered on page 4 of his diatribe when he said that Sadler was booted out of the Adventist church. Sadler left the church, but he was never disfellowshipped.

I made much of the fact that conservative Christians firmly believe in the doctrines of Christ's blood atonement and the Virgin Birth. Why are both doctrines denied in the *UB*? Because, DuVal pontificates, they simply are "not true."

I spare the reader further comments. Liberal Urantians, such as Meredith Sprunger, do not hesitate to admit that there are many errors, especially science errors, in the *UB*. They cite the *UB*'s words about how the science of the papers is subject to corrections and how the higher-ups felt constrained not to go beyond the science of the day. But Urantian fundamentalists see the *UB* as flawless in every respect except for minor typographical mistakes, a few of which were corrected in later printings. Nothing will shake DuVal's belief that fandors were real giant birds, that the big bang has to be a myth because the *UB* ignores it, and that the *UB*'s wild cosmology, with its weird extraterrestrial creatures and its endless hierarchy of gods and mansion worlds, is all described in the *UB* with impeccable accuracy.

Most of the Bible's great miracles, according to the *UB*, never took place. Only a few of the lesser ones, such as the turning of water into wine, were true suspensions of the laws of physics! Surely such hard-shell fundamentalism, as unshakable as the fundamentalism of Jerry Falwell or Jimmy Swaggert, is destined to fade as Urantianism slowly grows into a saner, more mature sect.

Do a Google's search on "Matthew Block" for Ernest Moyer's vitriolic attack on Block for (1) having abandoned his former acceptance of the *UB* as a product of higher intelligences, and (2) for his belief that Sadler wrote most of the *UB*, borrowing shamelessly from books by others, not only for the *UB*, but also for many of his own books.

Block, Moyer concludes, lacks "spiritual rebirth" and is "in peril of serious mind disruption and consequent psychosis." A Google search will also reveal a brief biographical sketch of Moyer, complete with color photographs. The sketch makes clear, in Moyer's own recent words, that he still believes Earth is being monitored by higher beings in UFOs and that there will soon be a "nuclear holocaust," followed by a utopia in which the world will be converted to peace and to the *UB*'s religious faith.

On page 128 I said that Sherman's notes and diaries were sealed until 2000. In that year the seal was indeed broken. Until then the strongest evidence that Wilfred Kellogg was the sleeper was the chapter on the *UB* in Sherman's paperback *How to Know What to Believe*. The chapter reveals that the sleeper and his wife lived in an apartment below the Sadlers in a building owned by Sadler in La Grange, Illinois. We know that in 1912, the most probable year for the start of the channeling, a newly married Wilfred and Anna occupied an apartment below the Sadlers in La Grange. No person known to have lived there at the time, except Wilfred, could possibly have been the sleeper. Let's hope that volume 6 of *The Sherman Diaries* will lead to solving the dark mystery of the sleeper's identity.

NOTES

1. See Moyer's 2000 booklet *Our Celestial Visitors*, published by himself. A blurb describes the book as "a report on Ernest Moyer's investigations into our celestial visitors program of genetic and spiritual rehabilitation for this world."

2. Block's forthcoming book will contain overwhelming evidence that Sadler, in his own books, borrowed heavily from other writers without giving credit. An example is Sadler's *The Sex Life Before and After Marriage*. It was first published in 1938 with his wife, Lena, listed as coauthor, then reissued five years later under the new title of *Living a Sane Sex Life*, with Sadler as the only author.

Sadler's book is saturated with passages that are obvious rewordings taken from Havelock Ellis's 1933 classic, *Psychology of Sex*. I find it amusing that Sadler followed a practice of plagiarism similar to that of Ellen G. White, the prophetess and a cofounder of Seventh-day Adventism, the sect of which Sadler was a former minister.

Name Index

The following index does not include the names of biblical persons or supermortals. Page ranges with passim indicate the person was discussed repeatedly but not continuously.

Abbot, Lyman, 325
Abegg, Arthur, 95
Adamic, Louis, 138
Adams, Benjamin, 286
Addams, Jane, 136, 149
Adler, Alfred, 37
Adler, Mortimer J., 23n, 251–52
Aird, Marion Paul, 191
Alfvén, Hannes, 183
Amadon, George Washington, 76, 77n, 98, 255
Ambrose, Saint, 248
Anderson, Kermit, 218
Andrews, Samuel J., 208–209, 217
Aquinas, Thomas, 192, 193n, 250
Arens, William, 218
Aristotle, 26, 91, 300, 325
Armstrong, Herbert, 234, 247, 248, 365
Asche, Sholem, 326
Aston, W. G., 356, 357
Atkinson, William Walker, 359
Augustine, Saint, 207, 253
Ayer, James, Jr., 85

Baade, Walker, 199
Bain, Martha Frances. *See* Sherman, Martha Frances Dam
Bain, Richard, 185, 197, 210, 211n, 214, 222
Baker, Dorinda, 86
Baker, Robin, 201, 202
Bakker, Tammy Faye, 415

Bald, Rosalia Thora Nana, 43
Barbour, Ian, 391
Bates, Joseph, 84
Baum, Lyman Frank, 23
Baumgartner, Elsie, 43, 151
Bedell, Barrie, 446, 457
Bedell, Clyde Orvis, 130, 131, 132, 133–34, 157, 158, 179–80, 314
Bedell, Florence Evans, 179
Belitsos, Byron, 182, 402
Belk, Henry, 141–42, 153
Benitez, J. J., 404
Bethe, Hans, 206
Biggs, David, 129
Bingham, Martin J., 399
Bishop, Troy, 194
Bishop, William Samuel, 356
Blackburn, Thern, 370
Blackstock, Robert, 388
Blackstock, Sara L., 388
Blake, William, 191
Block, Matthew, 182, 327–34 passim, 335n, 339, 341, 345–47 passim, 349–58 passim
Bohr, Niels, 213
Bolton, Frances Eugenia "Fanny," 79, 80, 81, 82n
Bordeau, A. C., 77n
Boscovitch, R. J., 212
Bouchard, Charles, 58
Brahe, Tycho, 200
Breasted, James Henry, 334n, 335, 336, 337, 338, 356

Browne, Lewis, 360, 361
Bucklin, Russell, 157
Bunche, Ralphe, 326
Bundy, Walter E., 347, 348, 349, 356
Burkhart, Raymond A. (Mrs.), 147
Burns, Norman T., 238
Burns, Thomas C., 406
Burton, Ernest DeWitt, 346, 347, 356
Burton, Robert, 129, 366
Burton, Ruth, 129
Butler, Clara, 95
Bynum, Hal, 402

Calabrese, Philip, 182, 193, 194
Canright, Dudley Marvin, 75–76, 78,
    82, 328, 396
Carlos, John, 145, 146–47
Carlson, Helen, 117, 185, 403, 404
Caston, Hoite C., 368–69, 406
Caus, Paul, 357
Caylett, Susan, 52n
Chamberlin, Thomas, 168, 187, 188
Chardin, Teilhard de, 390
Charlesworth, James H., 249
Chase, Allan, 289
Chase, Stuart, 130, 153, 361
Chesterton, Gilbert K., 39, 414
Christensen, Emma Louise "Christy,"
    43–45, 63, 116–21 passim, 125,
    129, 132–33, 150, 151, 156, 160,
    220, 275, 284–87 passim, 368,
    390, 391, 410, 412
Christensen, Nels, 43
Clark, David H., 207
Clarke, James Freeman, 324
Cleveland, Jim, 392, 393
Clough, Mary, 79
Coles, Larkin B., 75, 78
Compton, Arthur Holly, 326
Cousins, Norman, 326
Cousins, William A., 145–46
Covert, William, 35, 262
Cowdry, E. V., 357

Daly, Reginald, 198
Dammon, Israel, 85–86

Dante, 192
Darwin, Charles, 195–96, 303–304
Darwin, George, 203
Davidson, Gustav, 192
Davis, Alexander Jackson, 450–52
Davis, Ella, 82
Davis, Josephine, 143
Davis, Marian, 79, 81, 82, 82n
Deane, Ben. See Karle, Dent
DeFord, Charles Sylvester, 416
De Grimson, Robert, 394
De Vries, Hugo, 303–305
DeYoung, James, 207
Dietz, Bernard C., 409
Dietz, Robert, 199
Doré, Gustave, 191
Doyle, Arthur Conan, 177, 414, 450
Drake, Benjamin, 210
Dulles, Avery, 392
Dully, D., 95
Durant, Will, 68, 95
du Toit, Alexander, 199
Dyson, Albert H., 151

East, Edward Murray, 257
Eaton, Ella E., 53
Eddington, Arthur Stanley, 188, 188n
Eddy, Mary Baker, 10, 94, 413
Edison, Thomas A., 53, 224
Edwards, Julio, 408, 445–46
Edwards, Thomas, 238
Edwards, Tryon, 324, 325, 341–45,
    357
Elders, David, 368, 369, 403
Elijah III. See Pope, Joe
Elliott, Berkeley, 391, 446
Elliott, Leo, 137, 317, 392, 438,
    440–42 passim, 443, 445
Epiphanius, 248
Eremita, Marcus, 248
Evans, Florence. See Bedell, Florence
    Evans
Evans, I. H., 262

Faw, Duane L., 180, 370, 395, 456
Fermi, Enrico, 213

Field, Henry Martyn, 325
Finlan, Stephen, 360
Fisher, Osmond, 198
Fitzgerald, F. Scott, 290
Fletcher, Horace, 64n, 64–65
Forsythe, Scott, 446
Fosdick, Harry Emerson, 357
Fotheringham, D. R., 217
Fowler, Lorenzo, 52
Fowler, Nancy, 385–86
Frazier, Lilly, 402
Freeman, Eileen Elias, 252
Freud, Sigmund, 37
Friedlander, Michael, 198
Friedman, Polly, 121
Froom, LeRoy Edwin, 235, 238
Frost, S. E., Jr., 357
Fullmer, B. E., 397

Gagnon, L., 404
Gallagher, Buell Gordon, 324
Galt, Robert H., 119
Galton, Francis, 67, 300
Gamow, George, 210
Gandhi, Mahatma, 361, 379
Garmive, Anna, 396
Geller, Uri, 148, 154
Gentry, Robert, 232
George, Doris, 366
George, Jeannie, 381, 382, 402
Gerhardt, Mary, 391
Gibbs, Nancy, 251–52
Giles, Rick, 402
Gill, Leone, 40
Ginsburgh, Irwin, 186
Giroux, G., 404
Givens, Frances, 114
Glass, David, 181
Glasziou, Ken, 185, 215–16, 317–18
Godwin, Malcolm, 193
Goldschmidt, Richard, 305
Goodman, Paul, 388
Gould, Stephen Jay, 195, 301, 305
Graham, Billy, 39, 251, 414
Grant, Madison, 294–95, 296, 298, 299

Gray, David, 367
Gray, William, 136, 138
Gregg, Alice Elizabeth, 82
Gregory, William, 214
Grimsley, Nancy, 367, 369
Grimsley, Vernon Bennom, 44, 367, 368–70, 375, 386–95 passim, 405, 446, 456
Gusler, Rachel, 150

Hackleman, Douglas, 87n, 298, 319, 359
Hales, Carrie, 154
Hales, G. Willard, 153, 154, 154n, 157
Hales, John, 154, 368
Hales, Mary Lou, 154
Hales, William, Jr., 368
Hammerschmidt, Louis, 372, 372n
Hanish, Ottoman Zar-Adusht, 138
Hansen, Chris, 413
Harrah, William Furguson, 372n
Harris, Fred, 402, 455
Harris, Gloriann, 405
Hartmann, William C., 138, 249n
Hartshorne, Charles, 331–33, 332n, 357, 452, 453
Hay, Carol, 374
Haynes, Carlyle B., 181, 244
Hermas, 192
Herrick, Paul, 221–22
Hesse, Dorothy, 147
Hilton, James, 207
Hocking, William Ernest, 347
Hodder, Delbert H., 86n
Holmes, Arthur, 198
Hook, Milton Raymond, 98
Hopkins, E. Washburn, 249–352, 357
Horgan, John, 301n
Horn, Merrit, 194
Houteff, Marcella, 398
Houteff, Victor Tasho, 397–98, 399
Howard, Virginia, 161
Howard-Browne, Rodney, 85n
Howell, Vern "Koresh," 397, 398–99
Howland, Andrew M., 174, 175, 176
Hoyle, Fred, 186

Hrdlicka, Ales, 298
Hruska, Charles, 52n
Humbolt, Alexander von, 198
Hunter, Charles, 85
Hunter, Frances, 85
Huxley, Aldous, 301, 326
Huxley, Thomas, 196, 304

Ideler, Christian Ludwig, 207
Irenaeus, 217

Jackson, La Toya, 162n
Jackson, Samuel, 304
James, Montague Rhodes, 242, 427
James, William, 9, 32, 347
Jeans, James, 187–90 passim, 199,
    203–206 passim, 210
Jesus, 379
Johnson, Eric, 393
Jones, Alonzo T., 76, 257
Jones, Donald F., 257
Jones, Jim, 391, 399
Jones, Rufus, 334, 339–41, 357
Joyce, James, 171

Kagan, Melvin, 130
Kant, Immanuel, 32, 451
Kantor, David, 368, 386–92 passim
Kantor, Rebecca, 391
Karle, Dent, 120, 151, 157
Keeler, Richard, 368, 369, 405, 406,
    456
Keim, Charles Theodor, 324
Kellogg, Anna Bell, 37–39 passim, 98,
    99, 114–15, 119, 150, 156, 419
Kellogg, Charles Leonides Sobeski, 97
Kellogg, Edward, 97
Kellogg, Emma, 99
Kellogg, Emma Ruth, 37, 100
Kellogg, John Harvey, 35–39 passim,
    48–49, 51–74 passim, 98–99, 107,
    142, 163, 175, 235, 254–61
    passim, 268, 271, 288–91 passim,
    298–301 passim, 412, 445–46
Kellogg, John Phillips, 98
Kellogg, John Preston, 51, 99

Kellogg, Joseph, 99
Kellogg, Lena Celestia. See Sadler,
    Lena Celestia (Kellogg)
Kellogg, Merritt Gardner, 52, 53
Kellogg, Moses Eastman, 95, 97–98
Kellogg, Nathaniel, 99
Kellogg, Ray Stanley, 97, 98
Kellogg, Ray Stanley, Jr., 98
Kellogg, Ruth, 150
Kellogg, Smith Moses, 36, 37, 99
Kellogg, Wilfred Custer, 34, 37, 39,
    51, 66, 93, 97–111 passim, 122,
    129–30, 150, 156, 178, 227, 255,
    281, 283, 309, 314, 445, 447–48,
    459
Kellogg, William Keith, 36, 66, 67, 82,
    97, 101, 254
Kemble, Howard, 52n
Kendall, Carolyn, 115, 121, 122, 284,
    285
Kennedy, John F., 379
Kepler, Johann, 207, 208
King, Barbara, 366
King, William Burton, 366
Knight, J. Zebra, 9
Kobiella, Bernard J., 149
Kolvoord, John, 98
Köppen, Wladimir, 198
"Koresh." See Teed, Cyrus "Koresh"
Koresh, David. See Howell, Vern
    "Koresh"
Kress, David, 78
Kulieke, Alvin L., 118, 181
Kulieke, Barbara. See Newsom,
    Barbara
Kulieke, Marilynn, 403
Kulieke, Mark, 118–24 passim, 154,
    284, 326, 403, 408, 446, 457
Kulieke, Warren H., 118
Küng, Hans, 94

Landon, Michael, 252, 370
Lane, Arbuthnot, 58
Larson, Bob, 254n
Lear, Lyn Davis, 405, 454
Lear, Norman, 405

Leibniz, Gottfried Wilhelm, 212
Lerner, Eric J., 183
Lewis, Joe, 407
Lincoln, Abraham, 168, 373, 379
Locke, John, 23n
Lohman, Kenneth, 201
Longfellow, William Wadsworth, 240,
    246
Loose, Harry Jacob, 101, 116, 121,
    132, 135–60 passim, 361, 363,
    415, 447–48, 452
Lopez, Rosa, 385
Lucas, Norma, 101
Lynch, David, 135
Lynch, Marcia Sherman. See Sherman,
    Marcia

Maaherra, Kristen, 406–10, 413, 414,
    416, 431, 446
MacCulloch, John Arnott, 219
MacLaine, Shirley, 9, 176, 395, 414–15
Marrs, Tex, 254n
Marshall, Roy K., 208–209, 216
Martin, Lola, 445
Marvin, U. B., 198
Massey, Dan, 178, 182, 446
Mathews, Shailer, 323, 346, 356
Matrix, Irving Joshua, 13, 13n, 14,
    173, 281, 282, 283
McCallon, Jim, 402
McCandless, Beryl, 401
McCarron, Walter, 42
McCullough, David, 52n
McFague, Sally, 391
McIntosh, Stephen Ian, 400
Mencken, H. L., 5, 445
Messenger, Jan, 370
Metcalf, Richard, 52n
Metchnikoff, Elie, 58
Meussling, G. Vonne, 38–39, 294, 446
Michaud, L., 404
Middendorf, E. von, 201
Miller, Gerrit, 215
Miller, Russell, 198
Miller, William, 84, 245, 365, 381,
    382, 397

Mills, Patije, 32, 383, 384, 386
Minkowski, Rudolf, 199
Mitchell, Edgar, 143
Mivart, St. George, 195–96, 304
Mohammed, 10, 14n, 246
Moon, Sun, 10, 395, 415
Moore, George, 318
Mosley, John, 209
Moulton, Forest Ray, 168, 187, 188
Moyer, Ernest, 446, 447, 452, 458,
    459, 459n
Mullins, Ira, 366–67
Mullins, Joan, 374
Mullins, Larry, 372, 374, 455
Mundelius, Manfred K., 40
Mundelius, Patricia Helen, 40, 405,
    406, 446
Murphy, Gardner, 142
Murrow, Edward R., 326
Myers, Diane, 405
Myers, Martin, 366, 368, 369, 375,
    403, 405, 408, 415, 446, 456

Naeye, Robert, 189
Neibaur, Matt, 185, 210, 215, 216, 446
Newbrough, John Ballou, 10, 162–64,
    169, 170, 173–78 passim
Newbrough, Justine, 174
Newman, Horatio Hackett, 217n
Newsom, Barbara, 121, 181
Nichol, Francis D., 78, 272
Niebuhr, Richard, 387, 391
Noble, Edmund, 357
Numbers, Ronald, 52n, 75, 80, 446

Oblensky, Dmitri, 245
O'Regan, Brendan, 154
Osborn, Henry Fairfield, 294–95, 357,
    358
Ostling, Richard, 85n
Oursler, Fulton, Jr., 252
Overton, Richard, 238
Owen, R. S., 95

Paine, Thomas, 168
Palmer, George Herbert, 352–53, 358

Palmer, Ray, 162n, 164, 169, 449
Paul, Deo, 95
Pauli, Wolfgang, 213
Paulson, David, 258, 260, 272, 273
Peale, Norman Vincent, 142, 449
Pearson, Denver, 223
Peirce, Charles, 32
Petrie, Don, 366
Phillips, John, 98
Picard, Jerry, 100
Piper, Leona, 9, 120, 127, 227, 228
Pitzel, Michael, 182, 455
Plato, 26, 325
Pope, Joe, 377–402 passim, 456
Post, Charles William, 67
Price, George McCready, 94, 181, 215
Pritchard, Charles, 208
Puharich, Andrija, 148
Puthoff, Harold, 143

Ramacharaka, Yogi, 359
Rapp, George, 247
Raveill, Ken, 446
Rawson, Albert Bigelow, 217
Rea, Walter T., 76, 76n, 78, 328
Reed, Lucas, 231
Reves, Emory, 133, 312, 313, 314, 330
Rhéaume, Jacques, 287, 404, 446
Rhine, Joseph Banks, 236, 449
Rice, Anna Phillips, 396
Roberts, Oral, 415
Roberts, Richard, 85n
Robertson, John, 244
Robertson, Pat, 85n
Robinson, Fred, 178
Roden, Amo Bishop, 399
Roden, Benjamin L., 397, 398
Roden, George, 398
Roden, Lois, 398
Roebling, John, 52n
Rolnick, Philip A., 406
Roogow, Buddy, 42, 101, 446
Roosevelt, Eleanor, 326
Ross, Mark, 220
Rowen, Margaret W., 396–97, 398
Rowley, Marion, 131

Russakov, Sharon, 42
Russell, Bertrand, 314, 333–34, 451

Sabatier, Auguste, 345, 346, 358
Sadler, Charles, 40
Sadler, Emma Louise Christensen. See
    Christensen, Emma Louise
    "Christy"
Sadler, Florine, 41, 43, 446
Sadler, Judith, 40
Sadler, Lena Celestia (Kellogg), 36–40
    passim, 93, 98, 100, 114–15, 119,
    130, 150–51, 228, 271, 274, 299,
    307–308, 316, 419
Sadler, Mary, 35
Sadler, Samuel Cavins, 35
Sadler, William, III, 40, 42, 134
Sadler, William Samuel, 24, 34, 35–50
    passim, 51, 57, 62–68 passim,
    73–76 passim, 86–87, 93–160
    passim, 162, 173, 181, 184–88
    passim, 198–201 passim, 204,
    208, 212, 213–29 passim, 233–44
    passim, 250, 255–76 passim,
    277–301 passim, 303–26 passim,
    327, 330–38 passim, 341, 345,
    347, 352–53, 359–73 passim, 394,
    400–415 passim, 417–20, 421,
    427–30 passim, 431–43 passim,
    445–48, 454–59 passim, 459n
Sadler, William Samuel, Jr., 37–45
    passim, 117, 118, 130, 132,
    149–51 passim, 154, 180, 283,
    286, 296, 332n, 407, 409, 412,
    457
Sadler, Willis, 40
Salamis, Bishop of. See Epiphanius
Salyer, Bert M., Jr., 41, 129, 130, 131
Schaveland, Eric, 406
Schrödinger, Erwin, 304
Schuctman, Helen, 406
Schwarz, Richard W., 53, 63, 65, 84,
    86, 93, 107, 396, 446
Seres, Florine, 41, 43
Seres, John J., 41, 446
Sgaraglino, Frank, 405

Sherman, Harold Morrow, 101, 111,
113–34 passim, 135–60 passim,
171, 178–79, 285–87 passim, 314,
361, 369, 407, 411, 415, 421–23,
425–26, 447–49, 452–53, 459
Sherman, Marcia, 132, 135–36, 144,
149, 445, 448
Sherman, Martha Frances Dam, 100,
128, 135, 139–51 passim, 154–57
passim, 171, 178, 445
Sherman, Mary Alcinda, 142, 149, 448
Shields, Dennis, 318, 367
Sider-Pelligrini, Antonio, 198
Sinnott, Roger, 207
Skutch, Robert, 407
Slagle, Robert, 368, 386–87, 388, 389,
390, 402, 457
Smith, Joseph, 10, 249
Solomon, Meyer, 119, 437
Solotaroff, Ivan, 398
Spangler, Robert, 319
Spengler, Oswald, 304
Sprague, Helen, 27, 405
Sprunger, Irene, 373
Sprunger, Meredith Justin, 44, 222,
223, 284–87 passim, 317, 362,
369–74 passim, 373n, 404, 446,
455–58 passim
Stafford, Webster, 285, 286
Standish, E. Myles, 189
Stewart, Charles E., 75, 258, 274
Stewart, Jimmy, 252
Stoddard, Lothrop, 290
Stoes, K. D., 174, 175
Swaggart, Jimmy, 85, 415
Swann, Ingo, 143, 154
Swann, William Francis Gray, 354,
355, 358
Sweet, Frances Van de Water, 162

Tagore, Rabindranath, 390
Targ, Russell, 143
Taylor, Geoffrey, 186
Taylor, George W., 98
Tecumseh, 209
Teed, Cyrus "Koresh," 399, 413

Teller, Edward, 326
Tenney, George C., 94, 98
Tenskwatawa, 209–10
Thiessen, Gerd, 391
Thompson, Charles Lemuel, 325
Tillich, Paul, 94
Tower, E. B., 86
Trail, Russell Thatcher, 52
Turnbull, John, 162
Turnbull, Rachel, 162

Unamuno, Miguel de, 32
Urbom, Warren K., 39

Van Bond, Edward, 99, 115
Vandeman, George, 231
Velikovsky, Immanuel, 185, 209
Vick, Allene, 383
Vico, G. B., 212
Victorius, 216

Waddle, Ray, 85n
Walker, Barbara G., 131
Walsh, William, 246
Wapnick, Gloria, 406–407
Wapnick, Kenneth, 406–407
Washburn, J. S., 262
Washington, Booker T., 176
Waterson, David, 215
Wegener, Alfred Lothar, 198–99
Weiner, J. S., 215
Weiss, Harry, 52n
Weiss, Jacques, 404
Wells, Herbert George, 301, 314
Whiston, Judith Skutch, 407
White, Arthur L., 82
White, Ellen Gould, 35–37, 48–49,
51–58 passim, 52n, 63, 66, 66n,
71–74, 75–82 passim, 83–93
passim, 86n, 105–10 passim, 127,
129, 154, 178–83 passim, 191,
204, 207, 222, 227–45 passim,
251–55 passim, 257–75 passim,
285–300 passim, 309, 318–23
passim, 327–30 passim, 358–65
passim, 373, 387–400 passim,

411–15 passim, 422, 445–47,
459n
White, James, 51, 83–86 passim, 274,
322, 365
White, James Edson, 89, 98, 245
White, William C., 89, 261–62
Whorton, James, 61
Whyte, Lancelot, 212
Wieleler, Karl Georg, 207
Wiers, Walter, 162, 172
Wilcox, Ella Wheeler, 176
Wiley, Elnora W., 207
Wilkins, Hubert, 132, 142, 422
Willkie, Wendell Lewis, 314
Willmer, Sarah Mildred, 39–40, 99,
114, 115

Wilson, Neal, 358
Wilson, Sara Isabelle, 35
Winebrenner, N., 95
Wisenbacker, Michael B., 182
Wright, Frank, 185
Wyllie, Timothy, 394–95

Yeagley, H. L., 201
Yogananda, Paramahansa, 390
Yukawa, Hidekai, 213

Zakow, Arnold, 366
Zoroaster, 379